NEW PRODUCTS MANAGEMENT

THE IRWIN SERIES IN MARKETING

F   I   F   T   H   E   D   I   T   I   O   N

NEW PRODUCTS MANAGEMENT

C. Merle Crawford
The University of Michigan

Boston, Massachusetts   Burr Ridge, Illinois   Dubuque, Iowa
Madison, Wisconsin   New York, New York   San Francisco, California   St. Louis, Missouri

Irwin/McGraw-Hill

A Division of The **McGraw·Hill** *Companies*

Irwin Book Team

Publisher: *Rob Zwettler*
Sponsoring editor: *Nina McGuffin*
Editorial coordinator: *Andrea Hlavacek*
Marketing manager: *Colleen J. Suljic*
Project supervisor: *Susan Trentacosti*
Production supervisor: *Bob Lange*
Senior designer: *Heidi J. Baughman*
Assistant manager, desktop services: *Jon Christopher*
Compositor: *Douglas & Gayle, Ltd.*
Typeface: *10.5/12 Times Roman*
Printer: *R. R. Donnelley & Sons Company*

Library of Congress Cataloging-in-Publication Data

Crawford, C. Merle (Charles Merle), 1924–
    New products management / C. Merle Crawford. -- 5th ed.
        p.   cm.
    Includes index.
    ISBN 0-256-18778-9
    1. New products—Management.   I. Title.
HF5415.153.C72   1996
658.5'75--dc20   96–11275

Printed in the United States of America
    4 5 6 7 8 9 0 DOC 3 2 1 0 9 8

The ideas in this book have percolated over my entire business lifetime, and they have been tested in years of college classes. However, they have also been enlarged, adapted, and tested in use with some 5,000 executives, both here at the University of Michigan and in the offices and training facilities of many firms here and abroad. To them I dedicate this fifth edition. Thanks for your help.

New products have always been of interest to both academics and to practitioners, but organized, college-level instruction on the subject of new products management traces to the 1950s. But by the 1990s a new products management discipline has evolved. The Product Development and Management Association has flowered to over 2,000 members in some 30 countries around the world, over 300 colleges have courses on the subject of new products, and the field's journal, the *Journal of Product Innovation Management*, is now successfully into its 13th year of publication. The job of new products manager or director is becoming much more common and is offering much earlier entry than 10 years ago; we also see the emergence of higher level positions for careers to build to. The association has raised the issue of certification, is now very much an international operation, and has been able to do what many others have not—that is, merge the thinking and activity of professors and practitioners.

How This Book Views the Field of New Products Management.

Such exploding growth means that we still take a variety of approaches to the teaching of the new products subject—management, marketing science, technical, creative, design, and so on. This book provides the management approach, with a marketing slant. In every organization (industry, retailing, government, churches, etc.) there is a person or group of persons who, knowingly or unknowingly, are charged with getting new goods and services (both are products) onto the market. More and more today those people are new products managers or project managers or team leaders. They lead a truly multifunctional group of people, with the perspective of a general manager, operating as a company within a company. They must deal with the *total task*—strategy, organization, concept generation, evaluation, technical development, marketing, and so on. They are not finished with their work until the new product has achieved the goals assigned to the team—this usually means some form of sales or profit, and it certainly means the task is not finished when the new product is put onto the shipping dock.

Consequently, we now try to avoid a common functional bias—it is rare today to hear that "R&D runs our new products activity" or that "marketing tells everyone what to do." When a functional specialist takes over a new products team, that person must learn the general manager viewpoint, regardless where he or she reports in the firm.

Furthermore, this book calls on all of the contributing disciplines, stresses recent research findings, and strives for a level of sophistication equal to that of the best practitioners in this field. Instructors wishing to emphasize any of the specialty viewpoints within the general field of new products management will want to supplement the book with specialized material.

On the other hand, this book is not a research report on *typical* industry practice. It goes well beyond that and includes experimental work conducted by the more advanced practitioners and conceptual developments by academics.

Some Basic Beliefs That Guided the Writing

People who have used the first four editions of this book know my unique viewpoints on the subject. But for newcomers, and of course all students are newcomers, here are some of them.

1. Product innovation is one single operation in an organization. It has parts (strategy, teams, plans, etc.) but they are all just parts. Any operation that runs as separate pieces misses the strength of the whole.

2. The field is still new enough that it lacks a systematic language. This makes it very difficult for students, who are accustomed to studying subjects where a term means something, and only that something. I wish this were so in new products. What should we do—slip and slide around over the many terms and their variations? I believe we should not, and proposed a set of terms in the third edition of this book that seemed to fit and deserve consideration. The Glossary was accepted, so it has been expanded and strengthened in this edition. The terms are used consistently throughout the book, and I urge students to accept them. Some of the new terms proposed will survive, and others will die a quiet death, losing out to different and better terms that become widely accepted. The Glossary is found in Appendix E and I encourage use of it.

3. Ideas learned without application are only temporary residents in your mind. To become yours, a concept must be applied, in little ways or in big ones. Thus, the book is peppered with applications, short cases, and other opportunities for using the concepts studied. Projects are encouraged in the Instructor's Manual. There are even more examples from the business world, and up-to-date references on all important topics.

4. As much as I would like them, and have diligently tried to find them, I believe there are no standard sets of procedure for makers of consumer

packaged goods or of consumer durables, industrial goods, services, etc. There are no recipes.

Like a marketing plan and a production plan, there is a best plan for any particular situation. A manager must look at the situation and then compile a set of tools and other operations appropriate to that situation. All large firms use scores of different approaches, not one.

5. This leads to a favorite "ouch" of mine—the *halo* effect. The halo effect hurts the field of new products more than anything else—more than competition, more than government, more than tight budgets. The halo effect shows in the statement "It must be a good thing for us to do—3M does it, GE does it, or Hewlett-Packard does it." Those are excellent companies, but one reason they're good is they spend lots of time and money studying, learning from others. They have huge training programs in product innovation and bring in every expert who appears on the scene with what looks like a good new products management idea. They assume everything they do is wrong and can be improved. You should too. This book does. Citations of their actions are given as examples, not recommendations. These well-known firms have many divisions, and hundreds of new products under development at any one time. Managers there don't even know what each other is doing, nor do they care, in the prescriptive sense. Each group aims to optimize its situation, so they look around, see what others in comparable situations are doing (inside and outside their firm), and pick and choose to fit them. To the extent there are generalizations (e.g., there should be some form of strategy), these will stand out as you work your way through the course. But what strategy to choose—and exactly how one should determine it—becomes situational.

6. An example of this lies in the next belief—should new products strategy rest on the base of technology or market? This choice has been argued for many years. But the argument is usually specious, moot. Most firms seek to optimize both, a sort of dual-drive strategy. Of course, true to the previous point, firms will build on one or the other if the situation seems to fit—for instance, DuPont's platform program to find applications for the superstrength fabric Kevlar, or auto components firms who rely on OEM (original equipment manufacturer) engineering to spell out exactly what they want. And yet, DuPont works to advance that technology, and the components firms are evolving their own engineering operations!

So, the great variety in approaches used by businesspeople is not a testimony to ignorance, but to thinking. On a majority of the issues facing us today, intelligent people can come down with different views. Don't misunderstand, one view is not necessarily better than the other, but it is made better by its defense, not by who said it or who used it.

Decisions are the same—they are not necessarily right or wrong at the time they are made. Instead, the manager who makes a decision has to *work hard to make that decision turn out right*. The quality of the work is more important than the quality of the decision. An example of this phenomenon is the sadness we feel when a manager says, "We're looking for the really great idea." Managers of product innovation *make* ideas great, they don't *come* that way.

7. Lastly, I have tried to implement more clearly the view that *two* things are being developed—the product and the marketing plan. Two development processes are going on in tandem. Marketing strategy begins at the very start and runs alongside the technical work and beyond it. This means that the chapters on marketing have to first recap all that has happened before the time for actually writing out a marketing plan.

Changes in the Fifth Edition

This is an aside to teachers—past and potential adopters of *New Products Management*. First, much work on the fourth edition focused on the multifunctional process that has evolved so strongly in product innovation. We have always been multifunctional (marketing, finance, manufacturing, etc.), but now cooperation has turned into collaboration, committees into teams, and teams into small companies within big companies. You will find this multifunctional aspect appearing throughout the book, especially in "Technical Development" (Part IV). Allied with this has been an effort to tie topics horizontally—the product innovation charter is not covered in Chapter 4 and then forgotten—later chapters show how it used. The same for evaluation—-the topic shows up first in Chapter 2 and concludes only after a successful launch in Chapter 22.

Second, since the first edition, there has been the issue of whether the material should be grouped by topic (e.g., ideation, evaluation, marketing) or by actual operating sequence in the firm. The fourth edition took up the operational view, and this fifth edition extends it. After concept generation comes Part III on "Pretechnical Evaluation," followed by Part IV on "Technical Development." Product use testing is now in Part IV, as a part of the technical development activity. That's where business does it, and it learns best that way. Market testing now follows development of marketing plans, because that is where it occurs in real life. The organizational topics stay early in the technical development phase, where they were moved in the fourth edition. Financial analysis has moved up from Chapter 19 to Chapter 11, as requested by many users.

Another influence of cross-functionalization of the field has been a threat to functional courses. New products management is, more often than not, a marketing course. But the marketing people in business are finding themselves deeply involved in technical matters, in manufacturing process problems, in dealing with vendors, in arranging meetings between their engineers and customers, and many other such activities. Functional battles between technical, manufacturing, and marketing people are indefensible, whether on new products or on the established business.

This means that the book now considers nonmarketing views as they naturally come up. We don't pigeonhole engineers to Chapter Y, or industrial designers to Chapter Z.

Third, special effort has been made to pull the pieces together because, after all, that is the way we run new product operations these days. Teams deal with *all* of the issues—manufacturing people help plan marketing strategy, and a scientist will participate in process development. The A-T-A-R model precedes technical development.

Fourth, several new chapters have been added. A new Chapter 2 explains the key concepts driving product innovation today. These concepts (e.g., continuous stakeholder involvement, pretechnical product and marketing plan requirements, and a triple stream process) operate throughout the course, not just in one section of the book. Second, the product protocol has gained such industry support (deliverables, requirements, call it what you wish) that it required a separate chapter (Chapter 12). Third, to cover the full analytical process in marketing strategy, a third marketing chapter was required (Chapter 19). Some reductions came in eliminating the "Future" chapter and in consolidating the public policy discussion into one chapter.

Fifth, effort has continued (and intensified) to make the book relevant to its users. Since a text revision is actually a new product, I have tried to make it even more customer-oriented. The publisher invested twice as much money in the review process. Product examples, cases, and applications stress products that students buy and use.

New terms are included, as used in business, even though some of them will turn out to be buzz words—*fuzzy front end, continuous learning*, and *platforms*. One part of the "Future" chapter was retained in a new Appendix F—that was the set of 48 guidelines that can be used to appraise any organization's new products program.

And, though not yet in cyberspace, where some future edition must certainly come forth, this edition introduces several interaction activities—where a challenge in a chapter has its answers at the end. Another user-driven change was to use bold font on all special terms as they first appear.

Sixth, the cases have been strengthened. Five are new, three were rewritten and lengthened, and several others received experience-based tweaking.

Seventh, the index was made much more detailed, and special effort has been made to consider the special needs of the business-to-business world, service developers, high-tech firms, designers, and those with a more global viewpoint. Such topics are interspersed at many points.

Eighth, there was a strong effort to improve graphics. Many list figures have been replaced, and there is a much stronger Power Point presence.

It was a major revision, and I sincerely hope it meets your needs. A new Instructor's Manual, reflecting the changes in this edition, is available through the Irwin representative.

To the Practitioner

Because this book takes a managerial focus and is updated extensively, it is useful to the practicing new product manager. It has been used in many executive education programs. Great pains have been taken to present the "best practice" of industry and offer footnote references to business literature.

The Applications

From the first edition, the ends of chapters do not have a list of questions. Rather, I have culled from many conversations with students questions and comments they received from business managers on their fly-backs. These comments are all built into a conversation with the president of a conglomerate corporation. Explanation of how to use them is given at the end of Chapter 1.

Merle Crawford

A C K N O W L E D G M E N T S

Many persons help write a book of this type, and it is impossible to thank them all. Great aid came from the staff of the Document Retrieval Department of the Michigan Business School Kresqe Library.

From business, hundreds have helped—on field trips and during executive seminars. Scores of former students have given generously of their ideas, by telephone calls, campus visits, and the many things they have sent me. Academic colleagues continue making probably the greatest direct contribution, by reacting to previous editions. Thanks also to the especially thoughtful and constructive reviewers recruited by Richard D. Irwin:

Dr. Barry Bayus
University of North Carolina–Chapel Hill

Professor Donald Hughes
DePaul University

Dr. Terry Bristol
Oklahoma State University

Professor Donald Saunders
University of South Alabama

Dr. Peter Gillett
University of Central Florida

Dr. Eusang Yoon
University of Massachusetts–Lowell

Merle Crawford

C O N T E N T S   I N   B R I E F

C O N T E N T S

xvii

3   The New Products Process   40

PART IV

TECHNICAL DEVELOPMENT

13   Development Structure   245

14   Development Team Management   261

PART V

MARKETING

17 The Task of Strategic Launch Planning   322

18 Strategic Action Dimensions   339

New Products Management

I   OVERVIEW AND PREPARATION

This book is divided into parts. They are (I) Overview and Preparation, (II) Concept Generation, (III) Pretechnical Evaluation, (IV) Technical Development, and (V) Marketing. They follow the general flow of the new products process, though we will see later that the stages are not sequential, compartmentalized steps or phases. They are almost fluid, and overlap with each other.

The first chapter in Part I is the customary introduction. It attempts to answer the questions most often asked about such a course. The second chapter covers the basic requirements or key essentials of this unique field. The third chapter covers the new product process as a whole, and the fourth chapter deals with the strategic planning that lies at the very base of new products work. It guides a new products group or team, just as corporate or SBU strategy guides the unit as a whole.

For your use there is a complete glossary of new product terms in Appendix E.

1   THE MENU

When someone mentions new products, we often think about technology—virtual realities, fiber optics, Pentium chips, gene splicing, and the like. Other times, we think about far simpler items—caffeine-free colas, new movies, new musical groups, fast foods, and new flavors of frozen yogurt. Both views are correct—new products run the gamut from the cutting edge of technology to the nth version of the ball point pen.

You have opted to study how these things come about. It would be nice to say they come from an orderly process, managed by experienced persons well-versed in product innovation. But, they may not. Years ago, Art Fry became famous for an idea that became Post-it notes, when his hymnal page-marking slips kept falling out. He had a rough time persuading others at 3M that the idea was worth marketing, even though it soon became the second largest volume supply item in the office supply industry!

If you come from a background in a more established discipline (e.g., engineering, finance, or marketing), you may be confused about the uncertainty you meet in this book. If so, welcome to the land of creative exploration. In this field, we create new things but often are not sure just what they will be, what they will cost, exactly who will want them, how we will distribute and sell them, and how some regulator in a government office somewhere will react to them.

We do know a lot about how new products should be developed, but the ideal conditions discussed in a textbook are rarely matched in practice.[1] Managers face the world as it is, not as they would like it to be—budget crises,

---

[1] A recent study showed that even a long-established industry, with leading firms that have new product reputations, can go wrong. For example, only 43 percent did a detailed market study, and only 54 percent did any type of trial sell. See R. G. Cooper and E. J. Kleinschmidt, "Major New Products: What Distinguishes the Winners in the Chemical Industry?" *The Journal of Product Innovation Management,* March 1993, pp. 90–111.

downsizing, competitive surprises, even personal problems such as illnesses. We have to be very flexible, and creative.

Some people call this activity **product innovation management,** some call it **product planning,** and some (from a very biased perspective) call it **research & development (R&D)** or **marketing.** In this book, it is called the most descriptive term we have: **new products management.**

This opening chapter is entitled "The Menu" because it is built around a series of questions that students of the subject often ask.

Why Is This an Important Field of Study?

First of all, it's *big business.* Over a hundred billion dollars are spent yearly on the technical phase alone. Over 10,000 new products are marketed every year in the United States alone, though no serious effort has ever been taken to find an exact total. Hundreds of thousands of people make their living producing and marketing new products.

But, let's go behind those numbers—the real reason for this course is that *new products hold the answer to most organizations' biggest problems.* Competitors do the most damage when (1) there is so little product differentiation that price cutting takes everyone's margins away or (2) when they have a desirable new item that we don't. Profits fall when we cannot ask for, and get, a good margin over our costs, when total sales fall because customers no longer prefer our product over the products of others, when new competition enters our markets with lower prices or superior features, when regulators pressure us not to market a proposed new product or alter one already out there, when customer service has to carry all the load instead of being a strong partner to the product itself, when our best technical employees begin drifting away to competition, when there are not enough monies to permit manufacturing innovations that enhance product quality, and when our product development programs seem to take forever to come up with something that is exciting to customers.

A successful new product does more good for an organization than anything else that can happen. The very reason for an organization is the benefit or value its operations provide to others, and for which they pay. And in a competitive world this means that what we offer must be better than what someone else offers, at least part of the time. This is true in all organizations, including hospitals, churches, colleges, and even political parties. Look at the winners in those arenas and ask yourself which ones are popular and growing. In a recent article, "How to Escape a Price War," *Fortune* gave product innovation as the primary answer, and who doesn't want to escape a price war?[2]

In a firm with a string of great new products, you don't hear many complaints about having to cut overhead, reduce staff, sell off pieces of the corporate whole,

---

[2]Andrew E. Serwer, "How to Escape a Price War," *Fortune,* June 13, 1994, pp. 82–88.

prepare for trial on price conspiracy charges, buy back stock while it is cheap, or get used to the style of a new CEO. A cartoon once showed two obviously unsuccessful street musicians, and the tambourine player complained: "You say it's a market research problem...I say you're a lousy fiddle player."

Business firms expect, and get, a *high percentage of their sales and profits from new products.* For example, in a study by the Product Development and Management Association, business managers said, on average, that "33.2% of this year's sales will come from internally developed products introduced within the past 5 years."[3] For the next five years they were expecting 45.6 percent from new ones.

Another reason for studying about new products is that *the new products process is exceedingly difficult.* Most of the decisions are made with far less information than desired. Hundreds of individuals are involved in the creation of a single product. Almost all are from individual departments (sales, engineering, manufacturing) where they may have their own agenda. We will soon see that the complexity of multifunctional operations and decisions is a characteristic of product innovation. And new products do fail, though at a much lower rate than the 80–90 percent you may have heard.[4] (See Figure 1–1.) Generalizations don't mean much, and from firm to firm the failure rate varies widely. Some well managed firms now shoot for a maximum of 10 percent failure. Others, like large food firms, may be happy to hold failure to 60 percent. The failure rate in Japan is lower than that in the United Kingdom. Unfortunately, each "study" uses different definitions and information gathering methods. One study asked marketers the percentage of their upcoming new products that they *expected* to fail!

It's a Great Life.   Perhaps the best reason for studying this field is that *it is fun and exciting;* so many new things (see Figure 1–2), competitors trying to

FIGURE 1–1

New Product Failure Rates

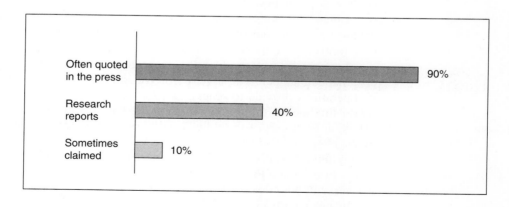

Often quoted in the press   90%

Research reports   40%

Sometimes claimed   10%

[3]Albert L. Page, "Assessing New Product Development Practices and Performance: Establishing Crucial Norms," *Journal of Product Innovation and Management,* September 1993, pp. 273–90.

[4]C. Merle Crawford, "New Product Failure Rates: A Reprise," *Research Management,* July–August 1987, pp. 20–24.

FIGURE 1–2   The Excitement of Recent Winners

Apple Power Book	IBM Tape Library Dataserver	Sara Lee Wonderbra
Gillette Sensor razor	NCR 7880 Workstation	Mighty Morphin Power Rangers
Reebok Pump sneaker	Internet	Baby Think It Over
Motorola MicroTac cellular phone	General Motors Visa card	Black and Decker Snake Light
	The Club	Christian Dior's Svelt
Chrysler LH cars	No-Wrinkle Dockers	Myst computer game
IBM ThinkPad notebook	Bell Ident-A-Call	*The Lion King*
Hewlett-Packard printers	Lotus Notes	Arizona iced tea
Thermos Thermal Electric Grill	Chrysler minivans	Compaq Presario 425
Bioject's Biojector	*The Bridges of Madison County*	Apple's Newton messagepad
Xerox Liveboard	Barney	Nabisco Snackwells

---

outguess each other, battlefield promotions when things are going well, huge successes where small clusters of people can honestly claim they made hundreds of millions of dollars for their firms. It's rewarding and stimulating to see an object come into being for the first time, to see a critical consumer or industrial need squarely met, to see a new service performed for the first time, to be invited to a corporate dinner where the CEO shakes the hands of persons awarded patents during the past year, to have distributors fighting for shipments of your new product, to see your brand make its television debut.... New products managers can't be rewarded commensurate with their dollar contributions, for various reasons (except in entertainment fields), but winners get promoted. They often have a personal imprint on bigger pieces of the corporate charter, and the rewards of general managers. And the pride of meaningful accomplishment.

Of course, there is risk—personal risk and corporate risk. But we are not uncomfortable with that. In fact, we spend a lot of our time seeking out opportunities where we can gladly assume some risk in order to achieve the very qualities this life is honored for. Nothing ventured, nothing gained.

How Does This Field Relate to Other Courses We Take?

The answer depends on what the instructor decides to do. New products management can be taught from many different perspectives—technical, marketing, legal, and so on. It can emphasize the strategic dimension, or the creative task, or the market research tools of concept evaluation, or the marketing planning and commercialization aspects, or the whole ball of wax.

It is usually taught as a marketing course and picks up on the product tool of the marketing mix. Most introductory marketing texts have a chapter or two on products, touching on some of the key sections of this book.

But even if taught from a marketing perspective, the definitions are changing. This is a **multifunctional** world—your school probably has been creating courses that cross departments or schools. Functional **"chimneys"** or **"silos"** are harder to defend in colleges too. What we used to call marketing decisions are now team or project decisions—so are decisions on manufacturing and technical matters. A new products manager may be in a marketing department, but the viewpoint must be that of a generalist. In Chapter 13 we will see the impact of this on organization structures.

So, this book approaches new products from a general manager viewpoint, with special attention to the tasks traditionally associated with the marketing department. But, marketing people cannot hide from the responsibility to think broadly, to be ready to play a role on a new products team, to deal with any and all decisions that will determine the new product's outcome. Thus, we will deal with team structure and management, financial analysis, concurrent engineering, product liability, and much more.

In any event, new products require the expertise of all areas—finance, manufacturing, legal, human resources, strategy, marketing, and so on. New products managers are general managers, *without* line authority. It's the same with ongoing product managers in consumer-driven companies, who also are general managers for their products, without formal authority over those they must get to work together.

Don't We Study about New Products in Other Courses, Too?

Yes, but there are two dramatic differences. First, as just stated, we will study *all aspects of new products at one time*—not just their marketing, financing, or manufacturing. But second, and maybe more important, we will work from the view of one who *manages* the overall process. Someone has to put it all together and keep it together. That person may be called by many different titles, but **new products manager** is becoming more common. And that person usually comes from either marketing or technical departments.

What Does That Mean to Us, as Students?

For starters, you should *begin shaking off any particular functional viewpoint* you may have. New products managers may come from marketing, and they will often return there. But for now, they are *new products people,* working with all functions, being biased to none. And biased against none, too. A marketing "type" may not appreciate the thoroughness of a research scientist. And that scientist may not appreciate the marketer's enthusiasm, which sometimes leads to what the scientist thinks are rash and unwarranted conclusions. Now is a good time to begin thinking like a general manager. The scientist must also.

Secondly, this course of study calls for a *strong creative contribution*. Not only do we create new product concepts; in many firms, that's easy. The tough creativity is *how best to develop and market them*—devising a concept-testing method that works, screening a totally new idea the firm has never faced, and figuring out how to integrate engineers into a trade show booth effectively, how to position a product that creates its own new category, how to produce it on present equipment, how to name it in a way that communicates yet doesn't confuse, and on and on. No answers are found in the back of this book. We never will know whether any one decision was right, just whether the total package of decisions worked out.

Being creative means we *travel on unmarked roads.* Most of our decisions are made on grossly inadequate facts. Not that we don't know what facts we need or how to get good estimates of them—we usually do. But there's never enough time or money. And what seems to be a fact in January may not be a fact come June, when we actually introduce the new item.

So, we do several things that make lots of people nervous. One, we use **heuristics**—little rules of thumb that firms have found work for them: "On items such as this, about 30 percent of the people who hear of a new brand try it" or "When the product engineer from R&D disagrees with the process engineer from manufacturing, it's better to go with manufacturing." Heuristics sometimes leave us holding an empty bag, but without them, projects just won't move forward fast enough.

Another technique is to use *simple intuition*—hunch, gut feel. This explains why most managers want new products people to have spent time in ongoing operations before moving on to new products work.

Another way to soften the problem is to *select people to rely on.* Look not to how a recommendation is defended, but to who is making it. This builds close team relationships similar to those often found in sports, politics, or a surgery—other areas where tough decisions have to be made under impossible conditions.

This suggests another key difference between this course and many of your others. We are *dealing with people under intense pressure.* Take, for example, the group of about 15 people sent by IBM from Armonk to Boca Raton during the dawn of the personal computer era, 1980. They were given one year to create and market a new product, which eventually became known as the IBM PC. Literally billions of dollars were at stake—the difference between becoming a major player in a new market or missing the boat completely. Virtually every day, someone on that team had to make a decision that could close the show. When studying how strategy shapes decisions that guide teams throughout a project, or how more firms today telescope their market testing into simultaneous regional rollouts, remember that pressure.[5]

For better or worse, pressures have mounted in the middle 1990s as managements have adopted **value** as their key guideline—new products now must have quality *and* be low in price. Value is a tough taskmaster. Fortunately, we know how to design for it, and how to measure it.

You may also be taking a course that deals with innovation in manufacturing (often called operations in service firms), and you may wonder how **process** innovation differs from **product** innovation. The answer is that they are a team.

---

[5]Two books tell the story of pressure: Tracy Kidder, *The Soul of a New Machine* (New York: Avon, 1981), the story of a new minicomputer at Data General, and G. Pascal Zachary, *Show Stopper* (New York: Free Press, 1994), the story of the Windows NT operating system.

FIGURE 1–3   **Not All New Products Are Planned—But Their Managers
Knew Them When They Saw Them**

A Raytheon engineer working on experimental radar noticed that a chocolate bar in his shirt pocket
melted. He then "cooked" some popcorn. The firm developed the first commercial microwave oven.
A chemist at G. D. Searle licked his finger to turn a page of a book and got a sweet taste. Remembering
that he had spilled some experimental fluid, he checked it out and produced aspartame (NutraSweet).
A 3M researcher dropped a beaker of industrial compound and later noticed that where her sneakers
had been spashed, they stayed clean. ScotchGard fabric protector resulted.
A DuPont chemist was bothered by an experimental refrigerant that didn't dissolve in conventional
solvents or react to extreme temperatures. So, the firm took the time to identify what later became
Teflon.
Another scientist couldn't get plastic to mix evenly when cast into automobile parts. Disgusted, he
threw a steel wool scouring pad into one batch as he quit for the night. Later, he noticed that the
steel fibers conducted the heat out of the liquid quickly, letting it cool more evenly and stay mixed
better. Bendix made many things from the new material, including brake linings.
Others? Gore-Tex, dynamite, puffed wheat, Dextro-Maltose, LSD, penicillin, Dramamine, X rays,
pulsars, and many more. In each case, a prepared mind.

Sources: DuPont and Bendix cases, *The Innovators* (New York: Dow Jones, 1968); Raytheon, Searle, and 3M cases,
Kenneth Labrich, "The Innovators," *Fortune,* June 6, 1988, p. 56.

A new product may call for a new manufacturing or distribution process, and
every new product benefits from an innovative process. A new process may assist
a current product by improving its quality, features, or cost. That in turn may
lead to a new product, as a line extension. The two are partners, and this book
will refer to process often.

The last difference worth noting here is in *application.* Sometimes the new
product process is almost accidental; we call it **serendipity,** which means accidents happening to the prepared mind, as shown in Figure 1–3. But such events
are not really accidents. At least 28 scientists had observed mold killing off their
bacteria colonies before Alexander Fleming pursued the phenomenon into the
discovery of penicillin.[6] So, we must practice. You cannot learn how to develop
a new product concept by reading about attribute analysis or gap analysis. You
must *do* them. The same goes for product use testing, positioning, contingency
planning, and many more. Application opportunities appear at the end of every
chapter, plus small cases that give you a chance to think about the chapter's
material in a market setting.

Ok, So What Is a New Product?

Figure 1–4 lists the types of items included in the definition of new product.
This list is from the developer's view, and may include things you would exclude.

---

[6]For more on serendipity, see Martin F. Rosenman, "Serendipity and Scientific Discovery,"
Journal of Creative Behavior, Second Quarter 1988, pp. 132–38.

FIGURE 1–4   What Is a New Product?

Commonly accepted categories:
1. *New-to-the-world products:* Products that are inventions; e.g., Polaroid camera, the first car, rayon, the laser printer, in-line skates.
2. *New category entries:* Products that take a firm into a category new to it. Products are not new to the world; e.g., P&G's first shampoo, Hallmark gift items, AT&T's Universal Card.
3. *Additions to product lines:* Products that are line extensions, flankers, etc., in the firm's current markets; e.g., Tide Liquid detergent, Bud Light, Apple's Mac IIsi.
4. *Product improvements:* Current products made better; virtually every product on the market today has been improved, often many times.
5. *Repositionings:* Products that are retargeted for a new use or application; the classic case is Arm & Hammer baking soda, which was repositioned several times as drain deodorant, refrigerator deodorant, etc.

Variations not commonly accepted as new products: New to a country, new channel of distribution, packaging improvements, and different resource or method of manufacture.

For example, can we have a new item just by **repositioning** an old one (telling customers it is something else)? Arm & Hammer did, several times, by coming up with a new refrigerator deodorant, a new carpet freshener, a new drain deodorant, and more, all in the same package of baking soda. Even with the same brand name. These may be considered just new uses, but the firm's process of discovery and development are the same. And a new use (particularly in industrial firms) may occur in a completely separate division. DuPont, for example, uses basic fibers in many different ways, from technical to consumer. Financial firms use their common databases for different markets. Similarly, brand names have long been used as platforms for launching line extensions. The familiarity of leading brands, such as those shown in Figure 1–5, indicates how easy this is.

The **new category** listing in Figure 1–4 raises the issue of the imitation product, a strictly me-too. If a firm introduces a brand of light beer that is new to them but is identical to those already on the market, is it a new product? Yes, it is new to the firm, and it requires the new products process. It is a new product, managerially.

As an aside, people often get the idea that to imitate is bad and to innovate is good. This idea is incorrect. The best strategy for any situation is the one that maximizes attainment of company goals, in that situation. Imitators may get rich while far-out inventors go to bankruptcy court. Though it has been presumed that the first firm into a new market gets a solid head start, recent research shows that true innovators actually don't do very well—smart followers tend to take over.[7]

That the other types of new products (**new to the world, additions to the line,** and **improvements**) are included in Figure 1–4 is no surprise. Generally

---

[7]See Peter N. Golder and Gerald J. Tellis, "Pioneer Advantage: Marketing Logic or Marketing Legend?" *Journal of Marketing Research,* May 1993, pp. 158–70.

FIGURE 1–5   **Classic Brand Names**

Long-time brands, many dating to the 1800s:

Budweiser	Bell	Hamilton	Sears
Ivory	Wrigley	Grape Nuts	Colgate
Coca-Cola	Kleenex	Post	Hershey
Maxwell House	L. L. Bean	Gorham	Goodrich
Kodak	Ford	Domino	Upjohn
General Electric	Fruit of the Loom	Lipton	Gillette
Oreo	Steinway	JCPenney	

Which of these have the most value today as launch pads for new products?

speaking, the farther down the list, the less expensive and difficult they are to make. In Chapter 4 we will look at the strategic dimension of these different new product options.

Does This Book Cover Such Things as New Services, New Business Products, and New International Products?

Professionals in all fields often use terms differently than the public uses them. We do too, and a clear example is the term **product.** The public often talks about products and services. Many new products professionals (not all, by any means) talk about **goods and services,** both of which are products. The reason is simple: almost anything marketed today has a tangible component and an intangible component. Fax machines are tangible, but they yield a service, which is intangible. Automobiles must be serviced, both before and after the sale. Does one get an intangible hair cut, or a tangible head of cut hair? Insurance companies provide a carefully written policy as a tangible component to their intangible service. In fact, some service marketers believe it is important to force a tangible component, something for the user to see and hold.

Some people go further and say there are *only* services. Everything we buy does something for us (whether food, machine, or sermon), and if we keep this in mind we can see the importance of involving the end user in the development process. So, the simplest approach is to talk about new products, whether goods or services. Banks, for example, commonly organize their marketing and service innovation around "product" managers.

Some people say services are different because their creation involves the user; but, many industrial goods are developed in partnerships with users. Others point out that services cannot be inventoried and thus do not have a distribution system. But the means of creating those services can be inventoried and must be distributed (e.g., window-washing franchises or motel beds).

The distinction between **business-to-business products** and **consumer products** is equally vague. A spectrum from, say, a nuclear power installation on one end to a package of chewing gum on the other end has no middle dividing point. Individuals may buy computers for use in their homes, whether they are insurance agents or parents interested in helping their children. So, is the computer a business product or a consumer product? Businesses buy printer paper, as do homemakers, and often from the same store. How about a retirement plan offered by a bank? What are new types of public protest signs designed and produced by a local printing firm? Does it really matter?

Sometimes the distinction is based on who buys the product: business products by *groups of people* and consumer products *by individuals.* But, individuals buy industrial goods worth billions of dollars, often by computerized purchase-order systems based on inventory-level trigger points. And, most consumers buy houses, cars, $10,000 trips, and college educations as groups.

On the **global** front, it doesn't really matter whether a new product is being developed for customers nearby or around the world. The farther away the end users are and the more they differ in customs and preferences, the more difficult the innovation task will be. But the explosion in Yugoslavia reminded us that there is little homogeneity *within* many nations.

So, the key lies in doing what is appropriate for the situation, much as a carpenter's choice of materials and tools depends on the job. A particular saw or piece of sandpaper has no merit in the generic sense, but it may be perfect for a particular piece of work, whether a church door, factory door, or a doll house door. The same applies to the new products process, in which we package up different programs from the same assortment of tools. The point is, the methods used for different types of product innovation differ. But that difference is of little interest to the manager. The manager's task is to choose a unique set of methods appropriate to the case at hand. Much as we would like them, there are no generic packages such as a "tool kit for business product innovators" or "tool kit for service developers."

Incidentally, the same thinking applies to so-called high-tech products and to nonprofit organizations as well. Many religious, art, musical, and social service organizations send people to the same executive new product programs attended by managers from Kimberly-Clark and Techtronics.

On What Basic Ideas or Concepts Is This Field of Activity Built?

Several basic ideas have already been mentioned (e.g., the role of creativity and the vexing problem of risk and reward). However, the *complexity of operations and decisions is the most dramatic hallmark of product innovation.* New products managers must be orchestrators. There has never been a simple new products operation. Scores, or even hundreds, of individuals are involved; for many of them, a new product just means more work. One new products manager said, "We've got fine people working at this company, so my job is to see that no ball hits the ground." He meant it is easy for slipups to occur, even when capable people are doing the work.

Figure 1–6

*Resistance to
Innovation of
All Types*

Why do people resist change?

The desire to hold onto something worthwhile—maybe social status or a job.

The desire to avoid making a major expenditure. Change costs money!

The desire to perpetuate a lifestyle or a comfortable way of doing things.

The inherent tendency of a group to force conformity on all its members.

Stereotypes:
  The *Ritualist* likes innovation but won't work for it.
  The *Retreatist*, or passive cynic, wants no change, but won't work actively against it.
  The *Neanderthal*, or active cynic, resists innovations and works hard against them.

Another hallmark of this field is the regrettable fact that *product innovation (like all innovation) must be pushed.* Innovation is an unnatural human event. As individuals and as organizations, we build roadblocks against it. So, new products managers have to spend a major share of their enengy just opening doors to change. By the way, fear of change, and thus resistance to it, is called **kainotophobia,** a word as complicated as is the phenomenon it describes. See Figure 1–6 for some types of resistance to innovation. Chrysler in 1991 was having trouble making enough cars to meet the demand for its new fold-down child's seat, but Ron Zarowitz had spent two years getting management interested, and four more years pushing against internal resistance, even though he was a manager able to get attention.[8]

---

[8]Brian Dumaine, "Closing the Innovation Gap," *Fortune,* December 2, 1991, pp. 56–62.

FIGURE 1–7

*The Conflicting
Masters of
New Products
Management*

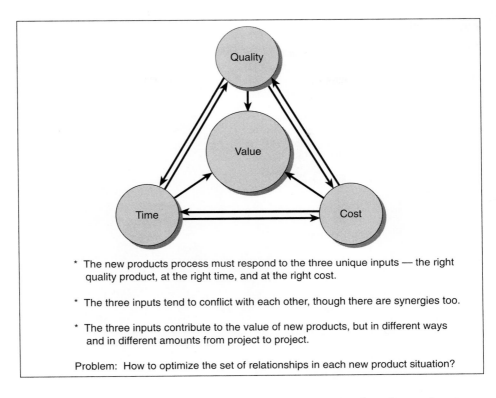

* The new products process must respond to the three unique inputs — the right quality product, at the right time, and at the right cost.

* The three inputs tend to conflict with each other, though there are synergies too.

* The three inputs contribute to the value of new products, but in different ways and in different amounts from project to project.

Problem: How to optimize the set of relationships in each new product situation?

Yet another hallmark is *the conflicting set of masters that the product innovation function must serve.* This dilemma is shown in Figure 1–7. Especially today, new product managers are ordered to serve up products that have valuable attributes (meet the end user's needs), but that are also of high manufacturing and design quality (stimulated recently by the Baldrige Award), are of low (competitive) cost, and are on the market in very little time. These mandates can sometimes work in tandem (e.g., some firms have found they can make things better when they make them fast, and others claim by increasing the design quality they can lower the real, net cost of production); but they can also conflict. A new product manager has to be able to spot the synergies, and to work toward balancing the conflicts.

Besides these general hallmarks, there are specific ones—very basic and demanding. Because they serve as the backbone of this field, we will look at them in Chapter 2. Though some of the terms may be strange to you now, a peek at what's coming is given in Figure 1–8.

Don't Most Real Innovations Come from Small Firms and Inventors?

Many do, and many don't. No one has ever figured out the actual numbers, and no one ever will because of the problem of definitions. Certainly there is much

FIGURE 1–8

*The Management
Task Has Changed!*

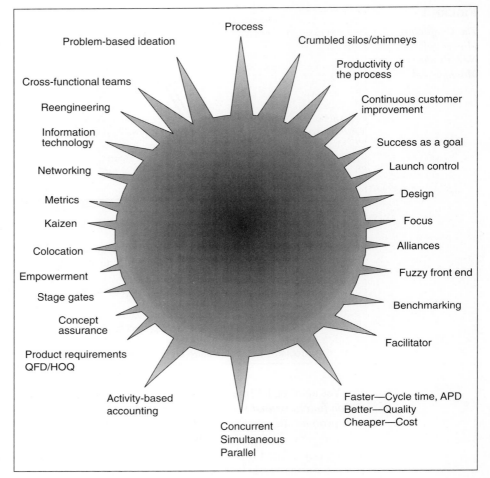

new-to-the-world type of innovation in small firms and even in garages. Such work is difficult and usually disappointing; it is comparable to wildcatting for oil, where one can get rich but usually loses the investment. Such product innovation work is better located in situations where the investors are willing to take great risks, as small-firm owners are. For better or worse, the owners of larger firms often are not, so we find the ballpoint pen was not invented by a pen firm, paperback books did not come from the leading publishers, overnight package delivery did not come from transportation firms, and the jet engine did not come from any of the motor industries. Yet many big firms support massive investments in technical research, from which come many new-to-the-world products; firms such as Merck, DuPont, and Corning come to mind. Technology is a key player today, in all sizes and types of organizations. (See Figure 1–9 for what one technical group feels are its top contributions.)

FIGURE 1–9   Thirty Products That Changed Our Lives

1. Personal computer	2. Microwave oven	3. Photocopier
4. Pocket calculator	5. Fax machine	6. Birth control pill
7. Home VCR	8. Communication satellite	9. Bar coding
10. Integrated circuit	11. Automatic teller	12. Answering machine
13. Velcro fastener	14. Touch-Tone telephone	15. Laser surgery
16. Apollo lunar spacecraft	17. Computer disk drive	18. Organ transplanting
19. Fiber-optic systems	20. Disposable diaper	21. MS-DOS
22. Magnetic resonance imaging	23. Gene-splicing technique	24. Microsurgery
25. Camcorder	26. Space shuttle	27. Home smoke alarm
28. CAT scan	29. Liquid crystal display	30. CAD/CAM

Source: A survey of technology people by *R&D Magazine,* reported by Carl Vogel, "Thirty Products That Changed Our Lives," *R&D Magazine,* September 28, 1992, pp. 42–46.

There is room for both large and small firms, and in fact both use the same concepts. Specifically, both inventors need to be working on a genuine problem, find a solution to that problem, and communicate the solution to those needing it. The garage inventor will use focus groups ("I talked to three people I got together in a trade show booth") and market test rollouts ("First I sold some to one company, then used their success to convince another company, and so on"); but you may not recognize the methods right off the bat.

Is New Products Management an Art or a Science?

I believe very strongly that new products management is a combination of art and science. Art, of course, is essentially based on intuition, experience, hunch, or gut feel. Therefore, when managers lack the experience or information to make a reasoned decision, they must go with what they feel is right. In other situations, managers simply reject analytical offerings and go with a hunch. Many times, managers are under the gun and make whatever decision keeps the project moving. I have heard executives say that a particular project was "something never done before, so there's no book on this one."

Yet, the pressure on new products people is sometimes unkind. Managers may yield to it, and deny themselves the chance to do what would make a much better product. For example, three tests are critical in product innovation: the **concept test** (to determine if the intended user really needs the proposed item), the **product use test** (to see if the item actually developed meets that need), and the **market test** (to see if we have an effective marketing plan). These three tests are the most difficult to rationalize under day-to-day pressures. They are often skipped, or done poorly.

Another example concerns marketing science—the many new techniques (e.g., trade-off/conjoint analysis, financial sensitivity testing, and sales forecasting via mathematical models) developed by marketing academics. These methods are not academic playthings. Today they are operational in some of the best firms in the world, yet they are not used nearly as much as they should be.

This book tries to compromise these views, always looking at various options as the manager would look at them. There are no criticisms of art; the intuitive greats in this field are cited for their success. More analytical methods are right there, too, for those with the time, money, and inclination to use them.

Can Innovation Really Be Taught?

Yes it can, and we know this both from experience in running executive seminars and college courses, and from field research. There is the art dimension (discussed above) and we know that great artists and entertainers often work mainly from instinct. But every innovative act that must meet commercial goals can benefit from the proven methods of new products management.[9]

Does This Field of Activity Have a Unique Vocabulary?

Yes, it does, for two reasons. One, it is an *expanding field,* taking on new tasks and performing them in new ways. Second, it is a *melting pot field,* bringing in the language of scientists, lawyers, advertisers, accountants, marketing planners, corporate strategists, organizational behaviorists, and many more. Because many of these people talk about the same event but use different phrases to describe it, communication problems occur. The solution is to forge a common acceptance of terms and to urge acceptance of one term for each new concept or activity as it arises. We are doing this, and rapidly, and there is proof in the glossary given in Appendix E.

But your study of new products management will be complicated by the unresolved problems. For example, there is continuing confusion over the terms **invention** and **innovation.** Use of these terms by the general public varies all over the lot, but to managers invention refers to the dimension of uniqueness—the form, formulation, function of something. It is usually patentable. Innovation refers to the overall process whereby an invention is transformed into a commercial product that can be sold profitably. The invention may take but a few moments, whereas the innovation may take years (though, oddly, the reverse can be true, as with a pharmaceutical chemical innovation). We have far more inventions than we do innovations.[10]

---

[9]See Jan A. Buijs, "Innovation Can Be Taught," *Research Policy,* 1987, pp. 303–14. In this Netherlands research study, consultants taught managers in 155 small and medium-sized industrial firms.

[10]For a discussion of these terms, plus many more that cause us problems, see Tudor Rickards, "Innovation and Creativity: Woods, Trees, and Pathways," *R&D Management,* April 1991, pp. 97–108.

New products managers should understand Net Present Value, dual ladders, intrapreneurship, positioning, strict liability, and other traditional terminology of this field. But they also need to know about the newer concepts—product innovation charter, protocol, and launch control plan. People who have not studied with this book may not understand such terms. And, the problem becomes much worse from a global perspective. Take, for example, the term **design.** In U.S. new product work, design means essentially industrial design or engineering (premanufacturing) design; in Europe, however, design means the entire technical creation function from initial specs to the shipping dock. To some design people, it means the entire product innovation function.

For another problem, look at **new products management,** meaning management of the entire process from early strategic thinking through launch to final success in the market place, and **new products development,** meaning the middle portion of the process, from the idea to the shipping dock. In other words, from when you have an idea that seems to have merit to when you prove you can manufacture it. The conflict will not go away soon.

The new products field has no definitional authority, as the accounting and legal professions have. The American Marketing Association recently issued a new set of definitions, and that helps. But for now, we just have to slog along, the best we can. The glossary in Appendix E is based on the product terms written by this book's author for the American Marketing Association definitions book, plus scores of "nonmarketing" terms. All are consistent with how they are used in this book.

Does the Field of New Products Offer Careers?

It does indeed, though not many are entry positions for people right out of college. Generally, managements want new products people to know the industry involved (to permit the customer focus mentioned earlier) and the firm's various operations (that multidimensional, orchestration task also mentioned). So, most new products managers get assigned to new products work from a position in a functional department. For example, a scientist finds working with marketing and manufacturing people interesting, a cost accountant begins costing out new products, a market researcher specializes in benefit segmentation, a salesperson earns a reputation for good new product concepts, a manufacturing engineer takes a liking to designing new systems, or a management development specialist finds personal satisfaction in training people to accept change. Each of these people is a candidate for full-time work on new products.

Of course, if a new graduate already has had the necessary job experience, direct assignment to new product work is likely, especially an engineer coming out of a business degree program.

The specific jobs in this field are three. First is **functional representative on a team,** sometimes full-time, more often part-time. An example is a marketing researcher or a production planner. These people may be representatives on many teams or on just a few. They are often project managers in training, but many functional people want to stay in their functions. The second job is **project manager** or **team leader.** This role, sometimes called "little president," is leader of a team of people representing the functions that will be required. The third position is **new products process manager,** responsible for helping project managers develop, and use, good new product processes. The job is necessary where new product activity is heavy.

Given All of This, What Will We Be Doing in This Book?

Chapter 3 shows the road map—the entire product innovation system. It begins somewhere back in the organization's strategic planning; for example, Henry Ford wanted the lowest priced Model T possible, Dan Gerber wanted better products for babies, and the Bell companies want customers to buy time on their wires and glass fibers. These goals help drive the new products program.

The end point of a new program is when the new product achieves its objectives. Now, many students think the program is done when the new product is marketed; so do many businesspeople, and they talk about turning a new product over to the "regular" people. But, the project is done *only* when the new product has sold enough, made enough profit, established a strong toehold in a new market, effectively thwarted a particular competitor—whatever the goal was at the time the new product project was initiated. And (this is a recent change of viewpoint) no one who worked on that new product should be permitted to "finish early." They shouldn't sign off until the goal has been reached.

A new products mile relay race is a four-person mile, not four people running quarter miles. When a customer buys a new item and says it arrived in bad shape, someone from manufacturing and/or distribution had better be on hand to take care of that problem. In firms that still think of product innovation as a linear process (a relay race), the salesperson has to deal with customer problems alone; the support people are busy on other projects. But this happens less frequently in the better-managed new products operations.

After the overview of the process in Chapter 3, we will take up the task step-by-step. First is **strategy,** for the overall product innovation program and for each project or team assignment. Second, we look at **concept generation,** how we come up with new concepts. Third, we move into the **pretechnical** (early evaluation) stage. We try to decide just how good those concepts are, both now and later as they evolve through the technical development stage where concepts are fleshed out. Fourth is **technical development** and **marketing,** the big pair of simultaneous activities in which cost estimates become budgets, manufacturing processes become factories, and sales plans become sales calls. Though they go on side-by-side, in true cross-functional format, they work best here in sequence.

Then, knowing the entire process, we can look at *public policy issues*—how we handle the products that some members of society think we shouldn't have—from internal combustion engine cars to 60 sizes of potato chips in non-biodegradable packages.

At the end of each chapter are four "Applications." These are questions or statements made by the president of a firm where you are interviewing for a job. (Most of them actually came from job interviews students had after studying this field.) They are conversational questions, but from a top manager who wants answers, not evasions. If you read an application and have no idea what the president is talking about, glance back through the chapter for clues.

Last, if your course is built around some form of practice (individual or team projects and other such assignments), each chapter may offer some challenge for that. If not, try to come up with your own new product concept during your study of Chapters 5 through 7, and then work that idea down through the course. You can do your own concept testing, your own strategic market planning, and so on.

Does All This Actually Work?

The Product Development and Management Association now sponsors a Corporate Innovator of the Year award. This award is not for a great new product, but rather for a sustained program of new product success over at least five years. And award winners must tell attendees at the association's annual conference how they did it. In most of these cases, one could take their systems right from the tools in this book. Winners range from Merck to New Pig, from American Cardiovascular Systems to Nabisco, from Keithley Instruments to NordicTrack, and from Marriott to Bausch & Lomb. Frank Svet, speaking for winner Harris Broadcasting, said the firm had actually done so well on new products that their Japanese competitor withdrew from the market. The Nabisco story is given in the case for Chapter 3.

The chairman of Monsanto (not yet an award winner) once said his firm's approach was to find a problem, arrange people, solve the problem, provide resources for implementing the solution, and promote and diffuse. The task for you is learn how to take these seemingly simple steps and build a full system of actions that will bring them to life.

The opportunity for people who do the job right must be huge, given such nonwinners as LaChoy's Fresh and Lite line of egg rolls (what was it, a deodorant or a beer?) and a BIC perfume bottled in a lighter-fluid-shaped container. But we can't be too confident—do you remember one author's first book, small, thin, and selling for around $15 (violating all the rules) titled *The Bridges of Madison County* (over four years on *The New York Times* bestseller list)? Things like this do happen, particularly in the worlds of art, entertainment, and taste.

Summary

This chapter has introduced you to the general field of new products management. You learned how the activity is (or should be) found in all organizations, not just business. You learned how this course of study relates to others, what a new product actually is, and that services and business products are covered, not just cake mixes, videos, and cars. You got a feeling for where the field stands today, the hallmarks of our activity, our problems with vocabulary, and possible careers.

Applications

At the end of each chapter are four questions that arose at one time or another in a job interview. The candidate was a student who took a course in new products management, and the interviewer was a high-ranking person in the firm (here portrayed as the president). The questions came up naturally during discussion, and they are tough. Often, the executive didn't intend them to be answered so much as talked about. Occasionally, the executive just made a comment and then paused for the applicant's reaction. Each question or comment relates to something in the chapter.

Imagine you are the person being interviewed. You do not have the option of ducking the question or saying "I really don't know." If, in fact, you really don't know, then glance back over the reading to see what you missed. It's also a good idea to exchange answers with another student taking the course, given that most of the applications involve opinions or interpretations, not recitation of facts.

1. "I'm a great believer in serendipity. We've gotten several big winners that way. I've always wondered, though, how to manage an operation to get more of it. Any ideas?"

2. "When you were talking a while ago about taking risks, I wondered just whose money you were talking about. A fellow I know out in California insists that all new product team members invest their own money (with his) in their projects. Fifty thousand dollars is not unusual. In that system I'll bet you would be seeking to *avoid* risks, not trying to *find* them."

3. "Funny thing, though, it sure does frustrate me when I hear a division general manager's strategy is to imitate other firms. Now, I know some firms might reasonably use imitation, but none of my divisions should. Should they?"

4. "I would like to be sure as many of our people as possible support innovation, but I know some people in the firm just can't react positively to proposed innovation, no matter how much we need it. Tell me, how do you think I should go about spotting the worst offenders, and what should I do with them when I find out who they are?"

2   KEY CONCEPTS

Setting

In Chapter 3 we will undertake a trip through the processes used to develop and market new goods and services. The rest of the text will elaborate on each of the parts in that process. Therefore, you will benefit from looking, in Chapter 2, at a set of concepts you will be meeting over and over again in the various parts of the process.

Why and How Did These Key Concepts Come About?

New products management, as management tasks go, is quite new. Organizations have been developing new products for as long as there have been organizations, but serious study of those efforts first appeared around 1975. It picked up steam through the 1980s and is still growing.

We have learned a lot—we now talk about "best practices" and "success factors." What these are, unfortunately, sometimes depends on what was found in the latest study. Over the next 10 years this should settle out, but you will be studying the field while we are not yet all that certain.[1]

---

[1] From the scores of studies, one has analyzed the results of 47 others: Mitzi M. Montoya-Weiss and Roger Calatone, "Determinants of New Product Performance: A Review and Meta-Analysis," *Journal of Product Innovation Management*, November 1994, pp. 397–417. A later study covered financial services; see Robert G. Cooper et al., "What Distinguishes the Top Performing New Products in Financial Services," *Journal of Product Innovation Management*, September 1994, pp. 281–99. And another study focused on the success of new product marketing in China; see Mark E. Perry and X. Michael Song, "Identifying New Product Success in China," *Journal of Product Innovation Management*, January 1994, pp. 15–30.

Some concepts are now widely accepted, and others seem to be gaining in use. Some have come up quite recently, but appear so logical to practitioners that we can forecast their eventual research validation.

In this chapter, you will read about the full set—proven and yet unproven. They are the underpinnings for almost all that follows. Here is one: Almost everyone now believes that a *new product activity should have frequent, or almost continuous, involvement of the intended end user, from the beginning of the project through to its successful culmination in sales or profits.* This target group is defined in the *strategic stage*, new product concepts for the end user are developed in the *concept generation stage*, the end user's approval of the concept is obtained in the *pretechnical screening stage*, the end user's needs and activities serve as the base for the *technical work that gives form to the concept*, and for the *testing of it*. The *marketing plan* is built directly on end user attitudes, beliefs, and practices, and its effectiveness is confirmed by them.

Unfortunately, there is one danger to presenting these concepts here in Chapter 2—some are difficult to explain at this overview point. But, not explaining them now causes worse problems. At an appropriate place, later, you will hear full explanations and rationale for each concept, but for now if there is something unclear, you can refer to the index, and read ahead.

Figure 2–1 shows the full list of concepts that will now be discussed.

Higher Level Strategy

Except in small organizations new products work is done by people scattered all over the organization chart. There are exceptions, of course, when strong-minded executives interested in new products personally lead projects; for example, a Sony CEO personally managed the Walkman project, and Edwin Land, owner of Polaroid Corporation, personally created what became the first instant camera and other items in that firm.

But, new product processes usually begin as corporate or strategic business unit (SBU) *strategies.* Almost every organization has some overall guiding strategy today, spelling out its sphere of activity (the electronics business), its long-term goals or purposes (diversify out of reliance on furniture), and guidelines as to how they will achieve those goals (we will innovate, but not be pioneers). The guidelines may be general (high ethical standards consistent with law), or very specific (advances will be achieved via acquisition in locations outside the home country). These strategy statements are sometimes called mission statements.

As such, they set the framework for almost all product activity. At Polaroid as long as Land was the leader, everyone knew that new product projects would be "almost impossible." At GE, new products people knew that Welch demanded an entry be directed to being #1 or #2 in its market. At Ford, years ago, everyone worked on new "black cars."

FIGURE 2–1

The Key Concepts for Managing a New Products Program

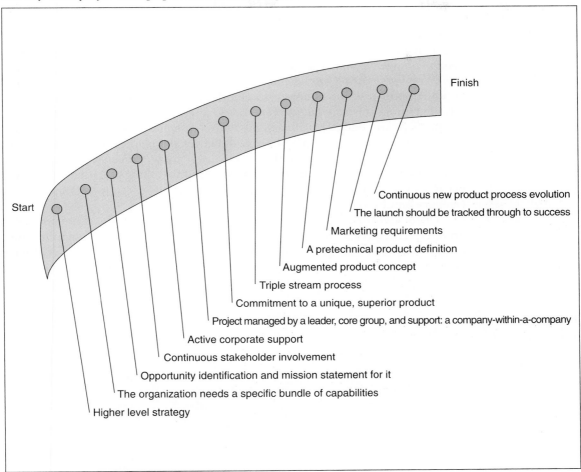

Today it's more complicated than this, but evidence shows corporate strategy is necessary, and should do three specific things for new products operations. First, *it should offer product strategies for segments of the operation.* There should be a clear mandate to every strategic business unit, showing what (if any) new product directions are expected. The SBU can be given narrow market focus (e.g., Germany) or product line focus (e.g., machine tools) or technology focus (e.g., fiber optics in telecommunications). At some time, every new product project will require corporate or SBU support, and there should be no doubts about whether a project can expect it.

Second, *corporate strategy should accept a risk/gain project portfolio view.* Managers sometimes become so enamored of a particular new product activity that they order more and more of it. Land, for example, followed his "almost impossible" idea to its logical conclusion—his instant moving picture product (called Polavision) failed, and he lost control of his own firm. Managers today reject single-form new product strategies. They recognize that current products need (1) improvements and almost trivial modifications to stay viable, (2) near line extensions (often called flankers) to offer buyers a choice, and (3) new entries based on new technologies. (See Figure 2–2.) These projects are quite different, and each may be good or bad. One may have very little risk and little direct return; another may risk the entire enterprise but, if successful, save it from bankruptcy. Some may be scheduled for the near future and others the far out future. Since we often talk about the new product *pipeline*, managements now refer to **pipeline rationalization**, meaning two things: (1) the right number of projects for our resources and (2) the right blend of projects by product category and by risk/gain.

Third, *corporate strategy should require a technology base on every product.* The advantage that a new product offers the market should come from a technical strength of the firm, and there should be technology-driven projects—creations where a technical accomplishment permits a new product for which there was not, up to that point, any expressed desire from the marketplace.

FIGURE 2–2

*Four Versions of
New Products
Risk/Gain Portfolio*

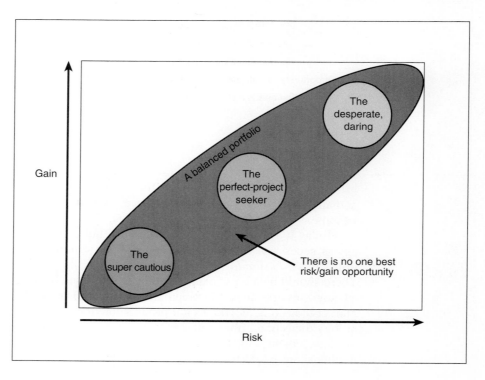

The Organization Needs a Bundle of Specific Capabilities

Recent research has shown that successful projects are associated with quality performance (proficiency) by one or more key players in the new products operation. A firm's key players will vary some, depending on strategy, but we usually see the same bunch. First on most lists is *technology*, as mentioned in the previous section. But technology does not mean just in research labs. A technology is a system or set of people and things that permit work. A soft drink bottling system is a technology. Avon's small-order-handling system is a technology. Cincinnati Milicron's engineering design capability is a technology.

In a virtual tie with technology is a bundle of skills in *marketing*. The needs and desires of the marketplace are an essential input to product innovation. And the end product must be presented to the end user in a way that stimulates trial and adoption. Just as some marketing firms have lacked technical skills, some technical firms have lacked marketing skills.

A new member of the triad is *operations/manufacturing*—maybe a factory, a laboratory, a set of carpet cleaning franchisees, an actuarial department in an insurance company, or even the legislature in a government. It is where the good or service is prepared or offered. It could be the classroom where this subject is discussed tomorrow. No matter how well designed or marketed, if the organization cannot deliver on the promised product, success cannot be assured. In the best firms today, manufacturing capability begins its development at the very start of the project, and may even be decided in the strategy if that is where the technology strength is located.

There are some other capabilities needed today, though the list is industry-dependent. Two skills are moving up the list—*human resource management* (HRM) and *information technology* (IT). They both relate to how new product projects are being managed today. HRM people are apparently critical in building the inventory of potential team leaders, and in training those selected for this most difficult task. IT people hold the answer to **colocation**, the physical grouping of teams that contribute so much to a new product project. Their answer: **digital colocation**, or the virtual colocated team. On a slightly broader plain, IT also permits effective networking, something we will see actually makes the "company within a company" that new products projects become.

Opportunity Identification and Mission Statement for It

Planned product innovation requires that there be an opportunity on which to focus action. Corporate or SBU leaders need *some situation where the potential end users have activities, attitudes, and needs that match in some key way with the skills and resources of the firm.* Opportunities can be sought in two different ways. One, reactively, they can be selected from among those that just show up—suggestions by various managers, a sudden competitive move, a proposal from a director, and the like. Two, they can be sought deliberately, with criteria beforehand, in an *active* search. The latter take more time and effort, and they require that someone has thought about the firm and what its key resources are. They also require the "someone" who does the searching, an opportunity identification (OI) specialist who knows what and how to search. Active searching finds the best opportunities and will leave fewer good ones for competitors. Incidentally, one key place we seek opportunities is in competitor vulnerabilities.

An opportunity usually comprises a combination of some market group or activity and some company strength, usually a technology. *This focus permits each project (each company-within-a-company) to have its own mission (strategy) statement.* The content varies from firm to firm, but the common elements will be discussed in Chapter 4 as a **product innovation charter**.

Continuous Stakeholder Involvement

If we are to develop a new product that meets the goals for it (sales, profits, whatever), it must be acceptable to the end user. Therefore, we now believe that a new product process should have **end user involvement**. But, the buying/using decision is often a complex one, where advisors, resellers (and even vendors) play roles, so we use the term **stakeholder**. And, because it rather defeats the purpose if we work for a year on an item only to hear the stakeholders say they don't like it, we now feel *we should involve stakeholders from the very beginning, and often. And not just surveyed once or twice; we need continuous stakeholder involvement.*

But why involve them at all? Don't steel firms know what car makers need? Don't pharmaceutical companies know what consumers want in headache relief? Don't business software companies know what sales managers need in the form of electronic field sales operations reporting? The answer used to be yes; today it is clearly no. Producer creativity and technologies have gone far beyond end user capabilities. Even physicians are almost incapable of judging new pharmaceutical products today.

Stakeholders can best contribute if they have the chance to do so at various points in the process. This won't be very often if a limited view is taken of what comprises that process. Look at Figure 2–3, and note four different perspectives we sometimes encounter. The A view, on the left, is often the view of technical people, and it is the one that sees new product development as running from idea to shipping dock. But, a more common view now is D, where the process begins with strategic decisions and only ends when the purposes of the project have been fulfilled.

Those purposes almost always involve more than "launch a product"—perhaps the firm wants sales, profits, market share, launching pads for other items, competitive thwarting, and more. These purposes cannot be achieved in the first

FIGURE 2–3

*What Does the New
Product Process
Cover?*

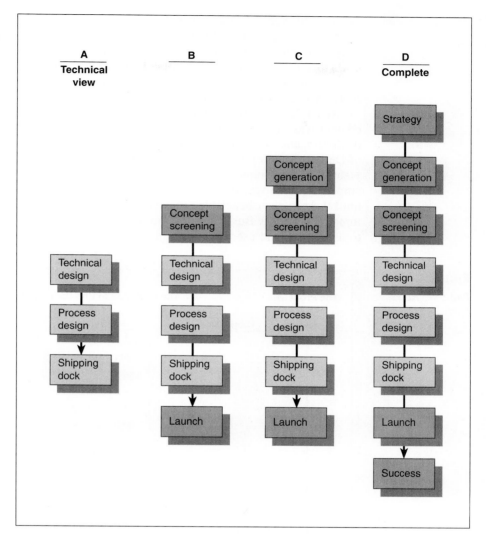

weeks, and therefore the team's responsibility is not discharged at time of launch. We can only wonder what would happen if the NASA launch crew went on vacation the day after launch! Yet, some firms still release team members back to their departments, or to new projects, upon launch.[2]

---

[2]Saturn managers were still conducting customer clinics in 1993, two years after launch of the product, 39 in that year alone.

The difference to the stakeholder shows in Figure 2–4. The earliest view of stakeholder input (especially that of the end user) was when there was a failure and the firm wanted to know why. Over time, inputs were gradually sought on matters just above that role, up to "contribute need/problem." Recently, this list is expanding even more, leading to the column of input roles on the right hand side of the figure. You can see why we talk about *continuous* involvement, or at least *iterative*.[3]

When Xerox developed its massive document-publishing system, Docu-Tech, contact was made with target users at least five times from early investigation of their needs in this area through to post-sale satisfaction. The chairman/CEO of Dell Computer described less of a procedure but more of a philosophy, but it yields the same inputs. Dell sells direct, views service as its ultimate weapon, empowers employees to fix problems on the spot, won't market a new product until there is clear benefit to the customer, and insists that all employees be customer advocates.[4] Business literature also has numerous studies listing methods to use in this end user involvement.[5]

FIGURE 2–4

End User Roles, Early Days to Now

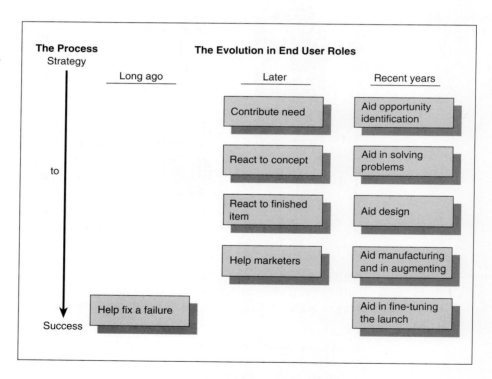

The Process
Strategy

The Evolution in End User Roles

Long ago	Later	Recent years
	Contribute need	Aid opportunity identification
	React to concept	Aid in solving problems
	React to finished item	Aid design
	Help marketers	Aid manufacturing and in augmenting
Help fix a failure		Aid in fine-tuning the launch

to

Success

---

[3]See Kate Bertrand, "Betting the Ranch on a New Product," *Business Marketing*, July 1991, pp. 29–34.

[4]Michael S. Dell, "Making the Right Choices for the New Consumer," *Planning Review*, September/October 1993, pp. 20–22.

[5]For example, see Allan J. Magrath and Kenneth G. Hardy, "Building Customer Partnerships," *Business Horizons*, January/February 1994, pp. 24–28.

Some new products people say that concept generation and early technical work best proceed without much customer input, because customers don't really have very much to say, particularly when we are seeking a new-to-the-world product. In rare cases this is true, but only to the point where the concept begins to take product form—that's when the end users should be involved. (Service developers are often forced into this because of the customer's unique involvement as a **coproducer**.)[6] In most cases, stakeholders have a great deal more to tell us than we give them credit for. For example, it is only in recent years that manufacturing people (inside the firm!) have been involved from the beginning—technical developers used to think they had nothing to contribute either. If firms discount manufacturing, it is easy to discount a user far off somewhere.

Lastly, some managers say OK to end users, but refuse to entertain involvement by resellers, vendors, consultants to end users, banks, and others. Again, there are situations where each of these may be inappropriate, but can you imagine Merck developing a new hypotensive agent without working with internists and cardiologists, who, actually, are but advisors to patients? Or a defense contractor not wanting to deal with Army ordinance specialists on weapons that will be used by artillery crews out on some hill?

Active Corporate Support

In previous key concepts, there was assurance that the firm had ample resources for product innovation activity, and that each opportunity had to find a resource fit. Now, however, we turn to the specific new product project, and to those things upper managements must give the project if it is to optimize its chances.

First is *resource availability*.[7] A firm may have an outstanding metals laboratory, but it may be so tied up in long-term basic work that projects can't use it. Or, the "charge" for its use may exceed budgets in the various divisions or SBUs. The same with resource centers like manufacturing process engineering. On many projects there will be need for strategic alliances with organizations outside the firm—vendors, end users, competitors, resellers—these almost always require upper management involvement and support. At the start of any new

---

[6]Some technical developers like this idea for their items too, and talk about coconstructing and coinventing. Firdaus E. Udwadia and K. Ravi Kumar, "Impact of Customer Coconstruction in Product/Service Markets," *Technological Forecasting and Social Change*, November 1991, pp. 261–72.

[7]A recent Product Development and Management Association study showed that "insufficient resources is the most frequently mentioned obstacle to successful product development." See Albert L. Page, "Assess New Product Development Practices and Performance: Establishing Crucial Norms," *Journal of Product Innovation Management*, September 1993, pp. 273–90.

product project there should be review of the team's specific resource needs and arrangements made for them. This includes review of financial resources, too, often more restricted than new products people anticipate.[8]

Second is the matter of *policy exceptions*. On-going operations usually do well under a rather clear and concise set of policies—policies covering budget variances, personnel transfer, job descriptions, geographic locations, manufacturing standards, capital investment return percentages, and more. Many of these are inappropriate on new product projects. Some projects must violate so many policies that managements pack the team up and send them across town or far away. Other times managements forget their needs, and stick to policies that crimp team leaders.

Third is *management style*. CEOs display highly varied postures toward their new product teams. Some smother the teams with attention (decisions, that is) and destroy any hope that team members will take ownership and give their own maximum attention. Other CEOs do the opposite—they get so busy with today's problems that they forget new products. Both are wrong. A requirement of team success seems to be that upper managements learn just what types of support each team needs (they vary greatly), and give it. A difficulty is that many team leaders are inexperienced and cannot tell managements their needs. Another difficulty is that management style essentially creates a culture, and we lack definitive evidence on the role of culture.

Project Activity Managed by a Leader, Core Group, and Support: A Company Within the Company

Throughout this book you will hear of teams—team this and team that. But not all new work is done by teams, as you probably visualize them. Much of it—for example, product improvements—is done by the regular organization, perhaps a product manager, or a sales manager, or a marketing committee, or even an executive committee. Various people in the firm operate as a group, but don't see themselves as a team, and we will see in Chapter 13 that there are group "options."

But we do know that however constituted or named, there should be clear designation of a core subgroup of people who will take the lead in each project. And they should accept this. Most often, today, they are called a team, and we will do so in this book. The core team should have a leader, and it should have a larger group of people who support the project from time to time. (See Figure 2–5.)

---

[8]Technology-based firms face this problem often, as R&D results can be unpredictable. For success factors (actually failure factors) in such firms, see Michael S. Rosenberg and Bruce McK. Thompson, "Rooting Out the Causes of Inefficient Product Creation," *PRISM*, Second Quarter, 1993, pp. 97–112. A good example of intraindustry alliance is Kodak, Fuji, Canon, Nikon, and Minolta cooperating in the development of a major new film. See Wendy Bounds, "Photography Companies Smile over 'Smart Film,'" *The Wall Street Journal*, July 25 1992, p. A2.

FIGURE 2–5

The Team: Leader,
Core, Support

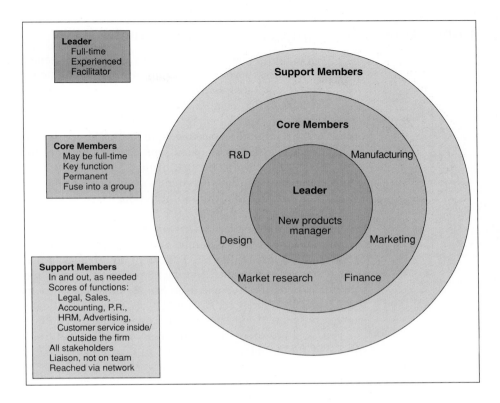

This, then, is the key concept: *New product project work is performed by a leader,*
a core-multifunctional team, and a resource group. The leader can come from anywhere but should be experienced in new product work; the core team usually has
one or more technical people, a manufacturing person, a marketing and/or marketing research person, and one or two others depending on the situation. The
resource group may be from legal, human resources, information technology,
finance, advertising agency, strategic alliance partner, sales, end user, or scores
more places.

The team leader is usually "dedicated," that is, assigned full-time to the project. Core team members may be dedicated but are usually not. Resource people
(e.g., the company attorney) work with many teams.

A new product team is almost never free to act as an independent company
(though there have been subsidiaries created, sometimes to isolate potential legal
liabilities from the parent organization). But we now know there must be some
degree of unity here, there must be some acceptance by the core team of its
responsibility, they must "buy in," or take some "ownership." *In return, and*
consistent with how much they buy in, they must be **empowered**.

Commitment to a Unique, Superior Product

It is not enough to have good strategy, good management preparation, and a good organization. These will *permit* good new products management, but too often it just doesn't happen. Why? If there is one reason above all others, if there is one concept in this chapter that should be the last one violated, it is the *commitment to producing a unique, superior product*. Obviously, if things are well organized, if there are capable people doing the work, and if a good process is used (see the next key concept) it *probably* will happen. But research shows that more products are lost to this factor than any other. It's easy—look at Pillsbury (where people know dough products) and how they lost Oven Lovin' Cookie Dough. Consumers didn't think the product was worth the price differential on it. Their new product program for this item called for national launch without product use testing or market testing.[9]

Note the two words—unique and superior. That means no me-too (ho-hum, tired) products, unless there is important uniqueness in the *augmentation* circle, such as service or warranty. But the more critical term is superior, and that means superior in benefit to the end user. Some phrases used by managers on this point are: "meets customer needs better," "solves problems customers have with competitive products," and "has better value-in-use."[10]

Products are thought to fail when end users lack the problem the product solves, or the product doesn't solve it, or the marketing (communication) fails to get the message across. These are all measurable, in advance, by three key tests in the recommended process. We can learn, for sure, whether our new item is unique, and whether it offers a superior solution to a problem the end user has. Note, however: Whether we know the product is superior is not as important as whether the customer knows. Superior products can fail if communication fails, even when the item is a piece of medical equipment.[11]

Like all of the concepts in this chapter, this requirement of product quality is important on both goods and services.[12]

Triple Stream Process

The most difficult of the key concepts may be this one, concerning process. There will always be a process by which each new product is created and marketed—even if totally accidental or purchased from some other firm.

---

[9]Kathleen Deveny, "Failure of Its Oven Lovin' Cookie Dough Shows Pillsbury Pitfalls of New Products," *The Wall Street Journal,* June 17, 1993, p. B1.

[10]See Stratford Sherman, "How to Prosper in the Value Decade," *Fortune,* November 30, 1992.

[11]John H. Friar, "Competitive Advantage through Product Performance Innovation in a Competitive Market," *Journal of Product Innovation Management,* January 1995, pp. 33–42.

[12]Christopher J. Easingwood and Christopher D. Storey, "Marketplace Success Factors for New Products," *Journal of Services Marketing,* no. 1 (1993), pp. 41–54.

But usually there is a *deliberate set of activities* that are supposed to lead to a successful new product launch, and such activities are usually listed as a ladder or series of stages, as shown earlier in Figure 2–4.

This is not enough, because *we actually are developing three things, not just the new product itself*. Look at Figure 2–6. Simultaneously with the *product's* creation, there is creation of the marketing plan and an acceptable evaluation—three parallel streams. In all three streams, the key stage is the last, but it takes them all to get there.

FIGURE 2–6

The Triple Stream Process

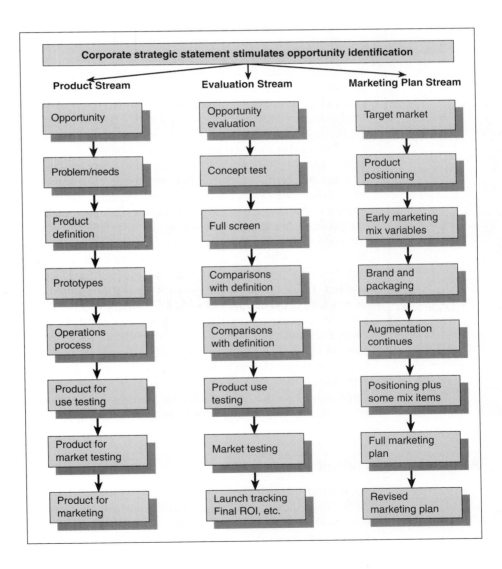

The **marketing plan** may seem to appear out of nowhere. Some new product process charts have a box labeled Marketing Plan, with no prior actions on it. But you know from several of the key concepts discussed in this chapter that parts of the marketing plan came at the very beginning. An opportunity usually relates to a particular group of people or firms. We **target** on them, study them, ask them about their problems, etc. And develop a product to help them on those problems.

Even more, early in the pretechnical phase, we talk to end users about our idea, seeking to learn if they really do have the problem we thought they did, and then we ask them whether our new product concept will help solve it. This is **new product positioning**, a key element in marketing strategy. Further, as taught in marketing courses, marketing strategy calls for a **marketing mix**, and we made sure in the strategic planning that our firm had the resources (sales force, advertising skills, whatever) that marketing might ultimately need. Managers from the various sales and marketing departments have been involved in the project, some from the very beginning. And along the way down the product stream, there were decisions on packaging and branding (whether a computer chip or a new Arctic cruise). Lastly, from the very beginning we have been studying how much might we have to spend marketing the new item. The only marketing decisions made near the end concern operating details.

The **evaluation stream** is usually thought of as a net present value calculation, plus any other key accomplishments expected from the new product. But, like the marketing plan, this has been under construction from the very beginning, where we evaluated the size and nature of the opportunity. The evaluation stream is deceptive—we evaluate various things at different steps down through the process, but they are all surrogates or predictors of the eventual outcome. If we want to develop that new arctic cruise mentioned a moment ago, pointing to those people who have a particular fascination with arctic regions, we ask such questions as, just how many such people are there? do they travel a lot? what do they think of our idea? what do they think when we have the full cruise description worked out? how many of them received the selling brochure and made immediate orders? how many showed up at the pier? how high did cruise costs eventually go? down to the ultimate, did we make our $137,000 and 42 percent target ROI on the cruise? All of the earlier questions spoke to something in that final calculation, just as every *technical step* along the way spoke to some attribute of the eventual product, and every *marketing step* spoke to some line or paragraph in the final marketing plan. No one goes merrily along, hoping to be pleasantly surprised when the project is finished!

Augmented Product Concept

As mentioned in Chapter 1, Figure 2–7 shows how we view a new product. At its core there is end user benefit, the real purpose for which this product was created. It varies from market segment to market segment, and from time to time. In the middle circle is the "thing," almost always partly tangible and partly intangible. It is what the customer buys in order to get the core benefit. In the outer ring are the **augmented attributes** of every new product—service, know-how, and image.

The point is, *customers and end users buy fully augmented products*, and their core benefit may partly come from the augmentations. New products managers cannot focus only on the formal product. What engineering and manufacturing deliver to the shipping dock will acquire its augmented wrapping before it is sold. Sometimes the augmentation comes first. A management may say: We have an outstanding brand name, but how can we best capitalize on that by marketing new products? The key augmentation took place prior to any tangibility whatsoever.

A Pretechnical Product Definition

In Chapter 9 we will deal with one of the newer key concepts, one on which there is still some disagreement and some further clarification needed. Prior to undertaking the major body of technical work, there should be agreement on *just what benefits the new item is to bring to what end users*. Some people call these benefits their critical utility factors (CUFs).

FIGURE 2–7

The Augmented Product Concept

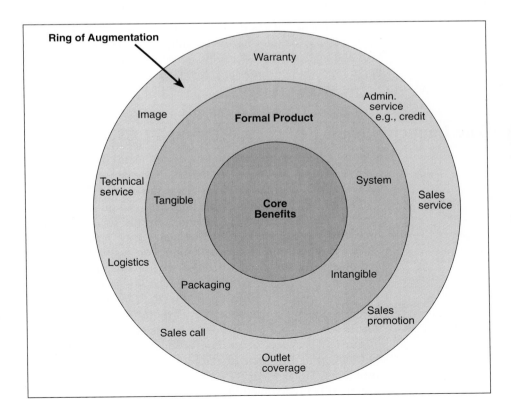

The product needs to be defined. This definition gives clear direction to people in the technical development stage, yet, by speaking in benefits, it leaves specific form and features to their best creative minds. They know when they are finished, which helps keep the project on schedule. To get the list of benefits there almost has to have been contact with the end user and all involved end user advisors. The definition is then used in assessing technical output—product testers have the criteria in hand. Comparative testing against competitive products is usually required. In sum, a clear **product definition** sharpens up all of the work to follow technical development, including marketing planning.

Marketing Requirements

Just as there are technical requirements in the product definition, there should be requirements for the marketing plan. Not just sales or profits—those are the end result of *all* the actions taken in the project. Rather, *just exactly what are the required incremental contributions of the marketing plan?* These are usually associated with some checklist or marketing paradigm. The paradigm used in this book is that of A-T-A-R: Marketing must generate **awareness** of the item and its offer, its positioning statement, and its key attributes; persuade the end user to make a decision to **try** the product; have the product **available** where the end user can get it conveniently; and assure that the trial usage is successful and leads to **repeat usage**, in other applications and over time. A marketing plan must demonstrate how it will do these things.

The Launch Should Be Tracked through to Success

Upon launch, marketing (and the entire team) has the task of following progress in the marketplace, to assure that all of the necessary results do come about. This is action in the NASA mode of "Houston control." No team can take a new product to market with all possible problems out of the way—there may still be end user misunderstanding, a key end user advisor may let us down, a competitor may make a surprise move, the product itself may prove to have a defect, a regulator may order a halt in the launch, and so on.

But, the *team can indeed have anticipated most of these problems, and have worked out at least a tentative reaction for each one.* For the very critical ones, there is a stand-by program ready for instant deployment. (See Figure 2–8.) In some launches there may be nothing particularly to worry about; adding a turnip flavor to the frozen yogurt line is not a major risk. Nor will there be many surprises on a new biogenetic product which was in field trials for six years before permission came to market it. Firms differ in their strategy toward launch problems. Some favor a "let's get it right the first time" approach and others prefer to launch something, get a jump on the competition, and then work out

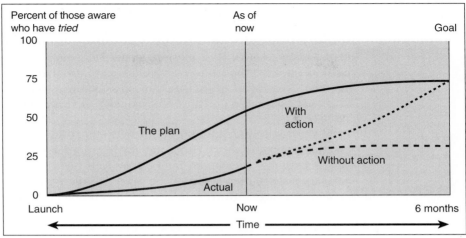

FIGURE 2–8

Concept of Launch Tracking to Success, with Remedial Action

the wrinkles as they show up. No matter, it is the task of the team to *manage* whichever type of launch is chosen.

Continuous New Product Process Evolution

Managements today are beginning to feel that their new product processes (like other processes) are good, but always improvable and not long lasting. They are evolving toward something more permanent, perhaps, but that does not matter—their desire is to apply the Japanese principle of **Kaizen**, making continuous improvements, no matter how good it seems to be today. Bull Worldwide Information Services draws its reengineering bull's-eye with the end user in the center.

They want **organization learning**, not just individual learning, so they search constantly for better ways of doing every step in the new product process. And they now layer performance with careful metrics (numerical measures) to find out where improvements can be made. Some managements talk about **development process improvement (DPI)** as an ongoing way of life. The conduct of one-time, after-the-fact post mortems is much less popular today.

Summary

Throughout the practice of new products management today run several key ideas, or concepts. Each is experienced-based, and in most cases research-confirmed. They are powerful, and almost guarantee that programs which embody them will be successful. Not every new product will be successful, of course; there's no way (and no desire) to take all of the risk out of this field. But there is no longer an excuse for the common errors of the past.

There are many other good ideas and good techniques, but they are less critical or they relate only to one particular phase of the process. They can, and will, be introduced as we make our way through the book. But the key ideas in this Chapter 2 you will be meeting again and again. I strongly urge you not to refuse them, even though in practice there are many arguments to skip one now and then. Almost all of the key concepts require extra time and extra money, disadvantages that loom large in these days of reengineering, budget slashing, and speed.

How can we defend taking time and money for them? Simple. Scores of research reports, on large firms and small, from Korea to Ontario to Israel, on high-technology products to foods, very well done and not so well done, and with very little conflict among them, say to use these concepts. Consultants report the same message—firms with new product problems almost without exception are violating one (usually more) of the key ideas.

The key concepts are no panacea, of course. They must be applied with managerial savvy, and there are exceptions. As they appear later in the book, you will get better acquainted with them, and, hopefully, more comfortable with them. If it is in your nature to resist rules, take solace in the successes of the great individualists who have peopled this field—many have succeeded by relying on an intuitive conviction. Like with product inventors, however, most of them have more scars than dollars in the bank.

Applications

This section continues the interview under way between a graduating student (you) seeking a job in the new products field and the president of a large conglomerate corporation. A full explanation came at the end of Chapter 1, but the main idea is to think carefully about the executive's questions or comments. In most cases they have no correct answer but in one way or another involve something from the chapter just finished.

1. "Perhaps that professor who wrote your book feels new products fail because there is no need for them or because they fail to meet peoples' needs, but in my experience the cause is pure and simple incompetence on the part of individual managers. I could eliminate failures completely if I could just eliminate incompetence. I'll bet you agree."

2. "I get a kick out of this term *stakeholder*. Whenever business speakers want to impress someone, they use terms like *mission*, *strategic alliance*, and *stakeholder*. That could include the grounds crew out there in front of this building. They have a stake in the business, but I don't want them muddling around in our new products operation. I *do* want the right stakeholders, because I agree with the idea, so maybe you could tell me *which* stakeholders should be invited to participate?"

3. "You've got me confused on one thing. First we need an opportunity, and then we need company skills to match the opportunity, right? Then we need a strategy to exploit the opportunity. But, you then said I need to have a strategy to guide me in looking for good opportunities. I was lost at that point, but then you added that the skills we have are a key input to strategy. A process like that will keep staffers in their jobs for years, like dogs chasing their tails! "

4. "You really struck home with me on that matter of dedication—putting a team leader on a project full time, and maybe doing the same for some of the core team people. I have never seen anything make a project move like having full-time people on it. So, I tried a while back to prepare a financial model that would help me determine when I could afford to use full dedication and when I would have to have leaders take two or even three teams at a time. I was having trouble with it, then got distracted. Could you help me work through that?"

3 THE NEW PRODUCTS PROCESS

Setting

Chapter 1 gave a feeling for today's new products situation, and Chapter 2 described the 13 key concepts that drive us in our work. Now would be a good time to start talking about just how we do it, but the various activities aren't going to make much sense unless you and the book are looking at the same picture. So, we will start with the overall process—that combination of steps/activities/decisions/goals and the like, that, if performed well, will churn out the new products the organization needs.

First, we need a word about our special viewpoint in this chapter, after which there will be a short story (saga) to help show the overall picture and identify several key activities. This will lead into the full process and its managerial aspects.

"It Doesn't Work That Way"

Businesspeople often look at designs of the overall new product process and say, "It doesn't work that way in our firm." As you read in Chapter 1, a carpenter doesn't use all the tools in the toolbox when building any particular door. Any manager using this generic system must cut and fit it to the situation at hand. If the president says, "No concept testing on this item," then no concept testing—but that doesn't make it right.

The Highlighter Saga

The following story introduces the new products process.

Betty Wall had been covering a sales territory in Omni Manufacturing Company's college market for three years, selling, among other office supplies, a line of highlighting products. They were the usual collection of colors, widths, sizes, and shapes. This was an important market for Betty's firm, and Omni shared the lead with Trion, Inc. But Betty knew the market was mature, the life cycle far past the dynamic growth stage with no real excitement for several years. Moreover, she had heard from the purchasing agent at Kinsville College that Trion was developing a new concept in highlighters. Apparently, it involved a clear liquid that reacted with ink to give each letter a broader, deeper, and more shiny appearance. Trion was having trouble with the concept, but Betty was worried about her commissions from the Omni line.

So, she called David Raymond, the newly appointed product manager for office supplies, and told him her story and her fears. David asked the market research department to make a quick scan of the highlighter situation—sales, shares, profits, rumors of innovation, and so on. Sure enough, the market was very mature; competitors and customers were complacent. Market research also uncovered the Trion test product, which sounded impressive.

David then discussed the situation with the vice president of marketing, who agreed there was a significant threat to the cash flow from office supplies. When Omni's president confirmed that highlighters were important to the firm's future, David was asked to come up with a solution to the combined problem of maturity and competitive innovation.

Fortunately, some brainstorming within the product management group, combined with astute thinking on the part of two technical people, led to the concept of a *solid* highlighter. No one was sure it would work (pulling liquid from the air). But, the basic idea seemed sound, several focus group sessions with office workers and students were positive, technical people reaffirmed it should be feasible, a scan of its fit with the rest of the firm (safety, production facilities, and so on) scored highly, and preliminary financial analysis gave it an OK.

David, as product manager, was given leadership on the project. He put together a team of four people to run the operation, ordered more market research, listed the desired consumer benefits of the new product according to the research to date, and laid out a time schedule that would get this new product to the market before Trion got there with theirs. Technical people went to work on the solid-material concept, and David began thinking about the best marketing strategy for the product. On one of his visits across to the lab, Phyllis Chaterji, the technical member of the team, showed him the first prototype, finished just the evening before. David arranged to show it to some potential customers. They liked the idea very much. So, Phyllis continued her work, final specifications were written, some semifinished product was produced for David to place in offices and dorms to see if it worked in practice, and manufacturing went on to plan the facilities change and a new process.

With this information, David was able to make a financial analysis, with preliminary product cost estimates and a marketing budget. Management approved, and the product was headed for market. Further product field testing was undertaken to get users' full reactions, the product's formulation was fine-tuned, manufacturing locked in on a process and bought the equipment, and marketing fleshed out the marketing plans with an advertising agency and help from the sales department.

When everything looked good, David got approval to start production on the final product and introduce it to markets along the Middle Atlantic coast (Trion's strongest area) and Quebec province. He and a market research analyst practically lived in those areas for almost a month. They knew customers might misunderstand how the product was to be used, so they were ready to run off some expensive in-store displays that gave better instructions. As it turned out, the displays were needed; the problem was overcome, sales took off, and the product was rolled out to the rest of the United States, Canadian, and selected European markets. Fortunately for Omni, too, because Trion was ready with its product at about the same time. Suddenly, a very mature market was exciting again.

What Happened in That Saga?

We just read a whole year's activity in a few minutes. The story, of course, was unreal, but the situation was typical. The story began with an ongoing operation that faced a problem. The problem was studied, and the solution was checked against ongoing new product strategy and then approved for action. Various developmental and evaluative steps followed, along with gradual development of the marketing plan. Launch was on a limited basis, and the manager had anticipated a problem that he was able to handle quickly and successfully. By the time you finish this book, you may have some criticisms of David Raymond's decisions and actions.

This situation is typical in that the new products process does not usually begin with an idea. It is folklore that someone, somewhere, wakes up in the middle of the night with a great insight. It can happen, but successful new product programs are not built on such slender hopes. If an idea walks in through the door, fine, but the process usually begins with what amounts to strategy—the mature market and the competitive activity were threats to Omni. With management's concurrence, action got under way.

Note, too, that development does not take place behind the closed doors of a research lab—there are many interim tests of fit and progress. And, marketing doesn't start when the product is finished—it often starts before ideation, as it did here.

Last, the process is not over when the new product is launched. It ends when the new product is *successful*, usually after some in-flight corrections (such as with the special instore display piece).

Let's now look at the full process, including many steps and options that didn't appear in the highlighter story. Incidentally, the new product concept in that story may have seemed crazy, or dumb, or impossible. Most great ideas look pretty bad when they first appear, but we have good methods for sorting them out.

The New Products Process

Figure 3–1 shows the way the new products process is usually presented, and all too often carried in the minds of managers. There are five sequential phases (in a linear fashion); when one is finished, another begins, and so on to launch. If you think about the highlighter saga, above, you can identify those phases.

But, such neat, linear sequencing is just not typical. Figure 3–2 gives what is the reality. That figure shows the five phases, as in Figure 3–1, but there is a huge difference. The activity is not **sequential**, but **overlapping**.

FIGURE 3–1

The Product Innovation Process

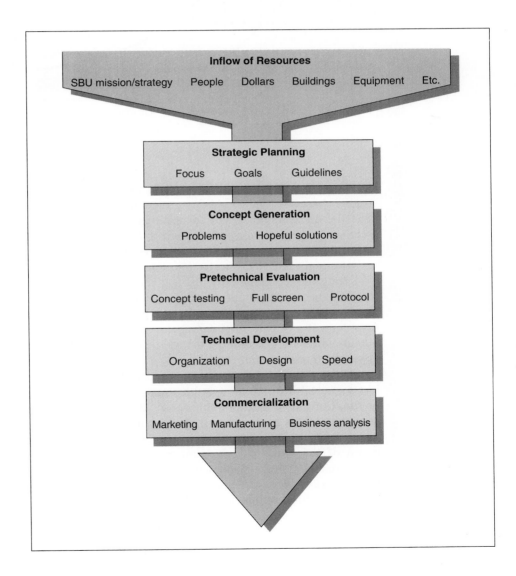

FIGURE 3–2

*The Production
Innovation
Process, in Actual
Practice:
The Impact of
Simultaneous
Operations for
Speed*

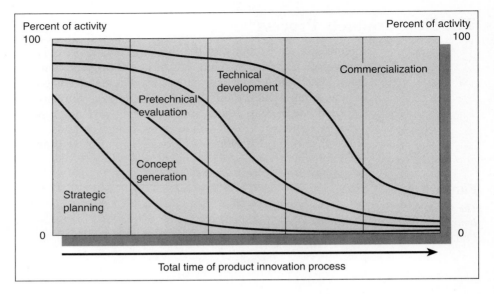

For example, in the very beginning of a project most attention should be on the strategic aspect—how would this project jibe with our mission statement, do we have the basic interests and capabilities for the work being considered, what would we expect to gain from it, and so on. But, thought is already going to the technical, by technical people. Marketers are already sensing how the proposed activity might aid other products in the line.

Neat staging or phasing with clear checkpoints has other drawbacks. For one, it tempts one firm to adopt the process of another firm, only to find that it doesn't fit. Too, phasing causes queues, where projects are piling up in line for the big review meetings. One chief engineer, following such a review meeting, released 500 drawings for one product in a single day. The glut resembled a rodent going down the throat of a large snake.

There is something else significant in Figure 3–2. Although it uses terms like technical development and commercialization, don't think that this refers to functions or departments. Technical people *lead* the technical development, but others participate, some very actively, including marketing research and sales people. Commercialization sounds like a marketing activity, but much of the marketing is done back during earlier phases, *and* during commercialization the manufacturing people are busy setting up production capability. Legal people are clearing brand names, lab people are running tests on early production output, and so on. Emphatically, this is no hand-off-a-baton relay race.

All of which makes it tough for us to label the work being done. Department labels imply territory, or turf, and those are rejected today. Activity labels, such as those in Figure 3–2, mislead, but they do make one point: Today's product development is a **multifunctional program**, where all functions work together to accomplish the required tasks. The tasks have no set time and no set performer. But, the key ones must be done, if the project is to have the greatest chance for success.

Now let's take a longer look at each of those general phases.

Strategic Planning

Three main streams of activity feed strategic planning. They are (with an example for each):

Ongoing marketing: The annual marketing plan for a CD ROM line calls for a line extension to meet encroachment of a new competitor selling primarily on price.

Ongoing corporate planning: Top management adopts a strategy that says either "own" a market (meaning get either a first- or second-place share), or exit it. This will require new product activity in all desirable markets where the firm holds a minor position. 3M recently shifted technical resources from basic research toward nitty-gritty product development, with profound impact on most new product processes.[1]

Special opportunity analysis: An inventory is taken of the firm's operations (manufacturing and other) skills. It turns up several that have been overlooked or just not appreciated—any one of them might serve as the base for a new program.

From these come opportunities (pleasant or unpleasant) for new product activity. They sort into four categories, again with examples:

Underutilized resources—a bottling operation, for example, or a strong franchise with dealers.

New resources—particularly technical discoveries (e.g., DuPont's discovery of Kevlar triggered analyses that still haven't stopped).

External mandate—something outside the firm dictates or strongly suggests a new line of innovation (recall the highlighter).

Internal mandate—managements make the suggestion. Most common is the growth gap, where someone extends a sales or profit line to the point where it wants the line to be in, say, five years. They then extend the sales line of current products to see a gap that almost always exists between the two lines. That gap is the **product innovation** (and/or **acquisition) gap.**

---

[1]Kevin Kelly, "The Drought Is Over at 3M," *Business Week*, November 7, 1994, pp. 140–41.

The process of creatively recognizing opportunities is called **opportunity identification**. Next, these suggestions must be carefully and thoroughly described, then analyzed to confirm that an opportunity does, indeed, exist. Recall that one of the first things David Raymond did was order a scan of the highlighter market. And, of course, no firm wants to exploit *all* opportunities; some are better than others. Some may not fit with company skills, some are too risky, some require more money than the firm has. So, most firms have **ongoing**, or **standing, strategies** about product innovation, against which the opportunities must be checked. For example, Waterford had a strategy that no new product would jeopardize the firm's great image. Cincinnati Milicron's strategy demanded any new product be highly innovative, not a me-too. So, each opportunity must find a strategy, either standing or specially written for it.

Opportunity identification and the other parts of strategic planning for new products are covered in Chapter 4.

Concept Generation

In some cases, merely identifying an opportunity pretty well spells out what is wanted (e.g., an opportunity to add a small size of toothpaste for travelers). Most times, however, it's not so clear, and the ideation process will be demanding.

The most fruitful ideation involves identifying problems and suggesting solutions to them. For example, if the strategic planning activity focused on "people moving their families over long distances" as an opportunity, the first ideation step is to study those people, and find what problems they have. This problem-finding-and-solving activity has become quite sophisticated; it is no longer the caricature of a group sitting around a table, pouring out ideas.

In the meantime, unsolicited ideas are coming in over the phone and in the mail from customers, erstwhile customers, employees (especially sales, technical, and operations), and every other source imaginable. These ideas are reviewed briefly by whoever receives them to see if they are even relevant to the firm and its strategies. They are then put with the ideas that came from problem-solving activities.

Concept generation (problem solving, as well as some other types of ideation) is covered in Chapters 5 through 7.

Pretechnical Evaluation

Sometimes called screening, pretechnical evaluation is the stage when the ideas that came from the concept generation activity are evaluated. First, they get a very cursory entry screen, because the flow of new product concepts is huge—into the thousands in many firms. You no doubt gave the highlighter idea such an immediate screen, liking it or disliking it.

But what happens next is the first formal type of evaluation. Depending on the idea, this may be end user screening or technical screening, or both. The work may be extensive and difficult, or it may take no more than a few telephone calls. In the highlighter saga, technical people actually proposed a solution to the competitive problem, and then there was a concept test to see what potential consumers thought about it.

Ultimately, these views all come together in what is often called *the* screen, that is, the final screen. It uses a scoring model of some type and results in a decision to either undertake development or quit. If the decision is to go ahead, the people involved should write out a statement of what is wanted in the new product. Firms using quality function deployment (a method of project management and control) see this as the first list of customer needs; a more common generic term is **product description** or **product definition**. In this book it will be called **product protocol**. Protocol means agreement, and it is important that there be agreement between the various groups *before* extensive technical work gets under way. The protocol should, to the extent possible, indicate *benefits* the new item is to yield, not the features the new item is to have.

Pretechnical evaluation is very difficult, because we have very little hard information at that point. In fact, the first three stages (strategic planning, concept generation, and, especially, pretechnical evaluation) constitute what is popularly called the **fuzzy front end** (of the new product process). This doesn't mean our *minds* are fuzzy; it means the *product concept* is. By the end of the project, most fuzz will have been removed, but for now, we move with more daring than the data allow. The various pretechnical evaluation actions are covered in Chapters 8–11.

Technical Development

This is the phase during which the item acquires finite form—a tangible good or a specific sequence of resources and activities that will perform an intangible service. Its form varies all over the map, but we often find the following pieces.

Resource Preparation. Often overlooked by new products managers is a step called *resource preparation*. For product improvements and some line extensions, this is OK, because a firm is already up and going in a mode that fits products that are close to home. The culture is right, market data are good, and ongoing managers are ready to do the work. But, a particular innovation charter may leave familiar territory, forcing problems of fit. If a firm wants **discontinuous products** (i.e, products quite different from those now available), then the team may need special training, new reward systems, revisions in the firm's usual project review system, and special permissions. Without adequate preparation of the ball field, a firm doesn't get much home field advantage.

The Major Body of Effort. Next comes what all of the previous steps have been leading up to—the actual technical development of, not one thing, but three: the item or service itself, the marketing plan for it, and the evaluation at various stages. It almost always involves the triple stream character mentioned in Chapter 2 as a key factor. The product (or better, the concept) stream involves bench work (goods) or systems design (services), prototypes, product specifications, and so on. It culminates in a product that the developers hope is finished—produced, tested, and costed out.

While that work is going in, marketing planners are active in their stream. There will be market scans, to keep up with changes out there, and the gradual development of what will eventually be a marketing program. The marketing activity is completely interlaced with technical activity, because we need to fix marketing decisions as soon as possible. So, as the product takes early technical form, package design starts up, brand name deliberations begin, and tentative marketing budgets appear. A technical disappointment down the line may junk the early package design, name, or whatever. But we have to pay that price; we can't wait for each step to be conclusive before going to the next one.

The third of the three steams also runs through the technical development stage. We evaluate whatever we have at various points—an early prototype, for example, or the results of an end user product test. By the time this stage winds down some, however, we want to be assured that the new product actually does solve those problems we began with.

Comprehensive Business Analysis. If the product is real and customers like it, some firms like to wrap it all up in a comprehensive business analysis (with a business plan) and move into commercialization. But because the phases merge and overlap so, any financial analysis at this juncture is more speculation than reality. The full technical development phase is covered in Chapters 12–15.

Commercialization

Traditionally, the term **commercialization** has described that time or that decision where the firm decides to market a product. We associate this decision with building factories or authorizing agencies to proceed with multimillion-dollar advertising campaigns.

It's a bit more subtle than that now. The commercialization decision is more attitude than anything else. A firm can always pull out, even during a test market, so commercialization should not mean the Go in a Go/NoGo decision. It tends to come just prior to some very expensive step; so, on consumer products, the decision is sometimes made just days before TV contracts are signed. In the pharmaceutical business, in which 8 to 10 years of technical work are required, the commitment to market is really made prior to undertaking the years of technical work; the results of such a program must, by law, meet medical needs and work effectively and safely. Little is left to decide. Other firms, especially on non-capital-intensive product improvements, just slide along the development trail until they are in the market. They see no dramatic commercialization point at all.

The commercialization phase, for some products, is life in a pressure cooker. Everything is rush, everything is critical. Manufacturing has been in the technical development picture from early on, but now it is in scale-up mode. And the marketing program, which first began taking shape during strategic planning, now is getting the hundreds of tactical details required for launch. The critical step—if a company takes it—is the market test, the first time the marketing program and the product dance together. This step is pure dress rehearsal, and managers hope any problems discovered are fixable between dress rehearsal and opening night. If they aren't, the opening has to be delayed; General Foods and Procter & Gamble have in a few cases kept products in market test for years.

This final preparation phase is sometimes accompanied by too much managerial change, variations in overall priorities and funding, unmet technical goals, and personal failures on little things that grind the project to a halt. We will talk a bit later about the type of management needed during this stage.

Another key activity during the commercialization phase is planning for launch control. Everyone knows that when space shuttles leave the launch pad, a plan of control has been carefully prepared. "Houston Control" runs it, seeking to spot every glitch that comes up during launch and hoping it was anticipated so that a solution is on board, ready to use.

New products managers do the same thing, some formally and some very informally.

Launch

When everything says go, the launch takes place. But, remember that most new products are improvements or minor line extensions. They may attract almost no attention. Other new products (say, a major cancer breakthrough or a potential AIDS cure) are so important they get top TV news coverage. We will see later that the launch period involves several clearly identifiable substages, ending when the new product moves into its own orbit of continued growth.

The commercialization phase, including launch, is covered in Chapters 16 through 20.

The Concept Life Cycle

You may have noticed by now that the new products process essentially turns an opportunity (the real start) into a profit flow (the real finish). It begins with something that is not a product (the opportunity) and ends up with another thing that is not a product (the profit). The product comes from a situation and turns into an end.

What we have, then, is an **evolving product,** or better, an evolving concept that, at the end, may become a product. We see this as the **concept life cycle.** (See Figure 3–3.) Here are those stages, like individual frames in a movie film:

Opportunity concept—a company skill or resource, or a customer problem. (For demonstration, let's assume that skim milk drinkers don't like the watered look of their favorite beverage.)

Idea concept—the first appearance of an idea—"maybe we could change the color…"

Stated concept—a form or a technology, plus a clear statement of benefit. See Chapter 5. (Our firm's patented method of breaking down protein globules might make the liquid more cloudy; emphasis on the might, at this time.)

Tested concept—it has passed an end user concept test; need is confirmed. (Consumers say they would very much like to have such a milk product, and the method of getting it sounds fine.)

Full screened concept—it passes the test of fit with company situation.

Protocol concept—a statement (product definition) of the intended market user, the problem perceived, the benefits that a less watery skim milk would have to have, plus any mandatory features. (Our new product must taste as good or better than current skim milk and it must yield exactly the same nutritional values.)

Prototype concept—a tentative physical product or system procedure, including features and benefits. (A small supply of a full-bodied skim milk, ready to consume, though not yet produced in quantity.)

Batch concept—first full test of fit with manufacturing; it can be made. Specifications are written, exactly what the product is to be, including features, characteristics, and standards. (Skim milk ingredients: Vitamin A source, fat, fiber, and so on.)

Process concept—the full manufacturing process is complete.

Pilot concept—a supply of the new product, produced in quantity from a pilot production line, enough for field testing with end users.

Marketed concept—output of the scale-up process from pilot—milk product that is actually marketed, either for a market test or for full scale launch.

Successful concept (new product)—it meets the goals set for it at the start of the project. (New, Full Body Skim has achieved 24 percent of the market, is very profitable, and already competitors are negotiating licenses on our technology.)

FIGURE 3–3

The Life Cycle of a Concept

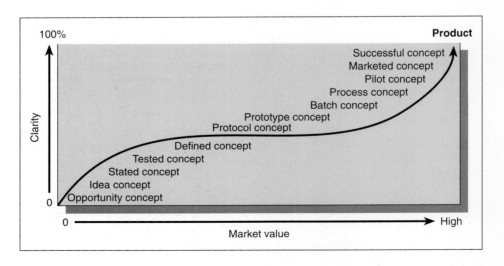

Some firms have as many as three production models or prototypes. So, the idea that a new product suddenly "emerges" from R&D—like a chicken from an egg—is simply incorrect.

Differences by Type and Level of Organization

The Anheuser-Busch, Strohs, and Coors brewing companies seem to have quite different new product strategies. Their new product activities and results also differ. But the strategy of Coors is not the same at all times, as when nonalcoholic beers came along, for example. Strohs, being smaller, for a long time had a more defensive strategy (and thus a very fast, lower-risk development process) while the leader in technology spent far more time early in the process making sure that the required qualities of the product were not lost. (A few, such as Schlitz, failed to do this.) Some large firms, with strong product lines, will do a quick development on a me-too product just to keep distributors happy.[2]

Too, within a single firm at one time, product decisions are being made at different levels—specifically, at top corporate level, at strategic business unit level, and at product platform level (e.g., the LH line of cars at Chrysler and Dockers at Levi Strauss).

Processes also vary in complexity, the grandparent of all perhaps being the "new health care plan" that floundered after so many months of strategy, ideation, technical developments, and so on, early in the Clinton administration. The steps that any new product management group uses will be a function of pressures like these, resources of the moment, education and experience, and much more. By no means have we achieved widespread adoption of the best methods. (See Figure 3–4.)

The Requirements of a Good New Product Process

Experience has given us a good feel for what makes a good process, and the requirements will now be shown. (Though, we must not be too serious; Figure 3–5 shows what one veteran new products writer claimed made for success, and he wasn't entirely tongue in cheek.) And keep in mind that every process is hard to define, in practice, although new product benchmarking has proven successful to some firms.[3]

---

[2]For information along these lines, see the research sources given in Chapter 1 for Figure 1–11. Two other studies that addressed the matter of what steps are taken and what ones are skipped are Robert G. Cooper, "New Products: The Factors that Drive Success," *International Marketing Review*, no. 1 (1994), pp. 60–76 (where comparisons are made between industrial products in general and chemical products in particular), and Larry Dwyer and Robert Mellor, "New Product Process Activities and Project Outcomes," *R&D Management*, January 1991, pp. 31–41.

[3]Certain firms are well-known for processes that warrant benchmarking: Beckman Instruments, Calcomp, Cincinnati Milacron, DEC, Hewlett-Packard, 3M, Motorola, and NCR are leaders. See Otis Port, "Beg, Borrow—and Benchmark," *Business Week*, November 30, 1992, pp. 74–75.

FIGURE 3–4   **Rates of Use of Selected New Product Process Steps**

	Percent of Firms Using		
Step	*PDMA Members**	*Canada†*	*Australia, England, and Belgium‡*
1. Detailed market study	Not reported	25%	57%
2. Concept searching	90%	NR	NR
3. Concept screening	76	92	96
4. Concept testing	80	NR	NR
5. Business analysis	89	63	76
6. Product development (technical)	99	89	93
7. Customer field (use) testing	NR	66	78
8. Market testing	NR	23	34
9. Use testing or market testing	87	NR	NR
10. Trial production setup	NR	49	70
11. Separate marketing plan	NR	68	NR

*Product Development and Management Association, in Albert L. Page, "Assessing New Product Development Practices and Performance: Establishing Crucial Norms," *Journal of Product Innovation Management*, Septermber 1993, pp. 273–90.

†Robert G. Cooper and Elko J. Kleinschmidt, "An Investigation into the New Product Process: Steps, Deficiencies, Impact," *Journal of Product Innovation Management*, June 1986, pp. 71–85.

‡Larry Dwyer and Robert Mellor, "New Product Process Activities and Project Outcomes," *R&D Management*, January 1991, pp. 31–41.

FIGURE 3–5   **20 Clues to New Product Success**

1. Has the product been in development for a year?
2. Does your company now make a similar product?
3. Does your company now sell to a related customer market?
4. Is research and development at least one-third of the product budget?
5. Will the product be test marketed for at least six months?
6. Does the person in charge have a private secretary?
7. Will the ad budget be at least 5% of anticipated sales?
8. Will a recognized brand name be on the product?
9. Would the company take a loss on it for the first year?
10. Does the company "need" the product more than it "wants" it?
11. Have three samples of advertising copy been prepared?
12. Is the product really new, as opposed to improved?
13. Can the decision to buy it be made by only one person?
14. Is the product to be made in fewer than five versions?
15. Will the product not need service and repair?
16. Does the development team have a working code name?
17. Will the company president (or division general manager) see the project leader without an appointment?
18. Did the project leader make a go of the last two projects?
19. Will the product be on the market for more than 10 years?
20. Would the project leader quit and take the item along if the company said it wouldn't back it?

Note: According to the developer of this list (New Product Development, a newsletter firm in Point Pleasant, New Jersey), 11 to 14 yes answers indicates probable success, 8 to 10 yes answers indicates a coin toss, and below 8 says to forget it.

Source: Reprinted by permission of *The Wall Street Journal*, © Dow Jones & Company, Inc., Septermber 24, 1981. All rights reserved.

Visitors who ask to see a firm's new products process won't see much. Whatever the firm is doing is so intertwined with the ongoing operation that the new product dimensions are vague. In small firms, for example, where much innovation originates, the ongoing and the new are essentially the same. All players on one team are players on the other. Even in large firms, where many people specialize full time on new products, most of the players work both games.

Furthermore, the process is fluid, changing. Iterations may be needed, as when a failure at one stage forces the play to return to an earlier stage. If a concept fails its screening test with intended consumers, it heads back to the ideation stage or even farther back to the opportunity identification stage. And if a competitor makes a surprise entry, the project may take a risky skip of several stages right into production. Believe it or not, a key task of a new products managers is to keep other players on the team up to date on just where the project is.

People also don't think alike. One school of thought holds that the product innovation process begins with ideation. They believe opportunity identification and other early parts of the process that precede ideation are part of ongoing planning, done by corporate staff analysts. The danger of this view is that the new products activity may be constrained. A management staff group may say to the new products staff, "Let's develop a new solid form of our highlighter," rather than, "The market has matured, our share has stabilized; we need *something* that reactivates the market." Another danger is that one function (such as technical or marketing) may work alone too long, closing off options the other group could bring to the ball game. Some firms unintentionally motivate their technical staffs to keep their ideations secret until they are well along, because that is the only way technical people can be sure to get their names on any patent that issues!

As mentioned in Chapter 2, another view holds that the new products process ends with launch. Some even hold that it ends if the new products team turns the new product over to the established group to market. Most people today disagree. Regardless of who markets the product, the innovation team should continue playing the game. Dow has several experienced salespeople brought in to join the R&D staff temporarily and handle the initial launch and selling effort. If the product succeeds, then they turn it over. Consumer firms' product or brand managers manage the innovation project from the beginning, so there is no need to turn anything over to anybody.

The Process Should Meet the Conditions of the 13 Key Concepts Given in Chapter 2

When a process is failing to produce, we usually find that one or more (often several) of the key concepts have been lost. For example, in the early 1980s Xerox overhauled its new products process and, for the first time, put manufacturing people on teams with technical and marketing people. Prior to that time, manufacturing people were presented with a fully designed new copier and told to figure out how to manufacture it! Full multifunctionality is often a blind spot, and other functions have now also earned early involvement—legal (product liability), design (ergonomics), finance (risk analysis), packaging (sometimes the essence of the innovation), and vendors (upstream coupling). The name of the game is teamwork.

Another of the 13 key concepts forces managers to be aware that they are developing *three* things, not just one. Making the middle stream of activity (evaluation) mandatory automatically forces the team to deal with the three primary causes of new product failure: need, meeting need, and marketing. (Figure 3–6 shows how these are derived.)

FIGURE 3–6

Why Do New Products Fail?

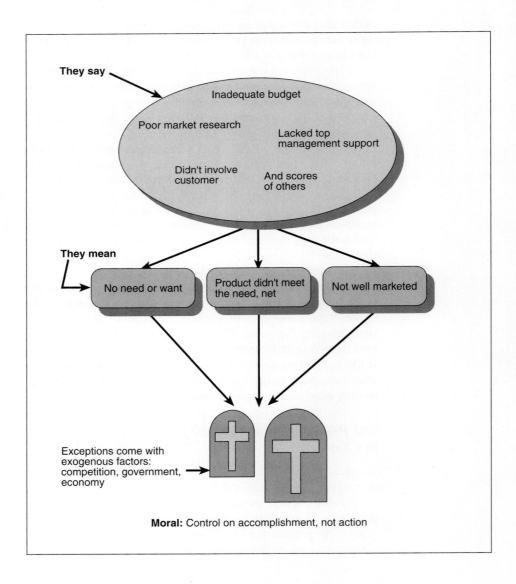

The last of the 13 key concepts, called continuous new product process development, means that we have to measure the productivity of the process we are using. Measuring performance requires preset management guidelines, usually called **metrics**, so now those who develop new processes must spell out exactly what that process is to produce, when, how much, etc. No more of this "developing the process on the run," unless, of course, an emergency demands it.

The Process Should Provide Some Structure of Checkpoints Along Its Way

Called many things over the years, these checkpoints are now most often called **stage gates**—points where a stage of activity (e.g., pretechnical evaluation) ends and the process managers measure whether the project has reached the goals for that stage. For example, before technical development begins full force, we like to have assurance from the intended end user (and that person's or firm's network of advisors) that what we intend to develop will indeed meet needs they have. This is a key concept, and some form of concept testing determines it. The team, its leader, and the management group to whom that leader is responsible can be assured that the pretechnical evaluation stage is finished successfully.[4]

The stage gate should not be a toll gate, where everyone stops while some authority on high is appealed to, makes some ruling, and then allows work to resume. Some new products people work with absolute metrics at the gates—for example, producing a sales and cost forecast that shows an internal rate of return of at least 45 percent. This may give control, but it is poor management of the new product process. Instead, the team should be able to state at the start what *conclusion* they want to be able to reach at each stage. And these are about the same for all firms.

Let's take a couple of examples. The first stage in most processes is strategic planning—opportunity identification and evaluation, combined with a statement how that opportunity will be used. The end point is a strategy, and in this book (Chapter 4) is called a **product innovation charter**. Another key stage is usually that of technical development, the end (gate) of which is having the product in some form that will permit the intended end user to say, "Yes, that is what I wanted; thanks." It may be a prototype, or a finished product that we have already been producing on a production line. It may actually be just a promise—in a case where product can be produced only after an expensive facility has been erected. This happens with many new chemicals. In such a case we can't have product in hand, so we seek some *other* assurance, some other means of becoming satisfied that if we go ahead, we will end up with what meets customer needs.

---

[4]Detailed information on stage-gate use is, of course, often confidential. There has been one published study; see Paul O'Connor, "Implementing a Stage-Gate Process: A Multi-Company Perspective," *Journal of Product Innovation Management*, June 1994, pp. 183–200.

FIGURE 3–7

*Information-Based
Stages, Not Things
or "Management
Approvals"*

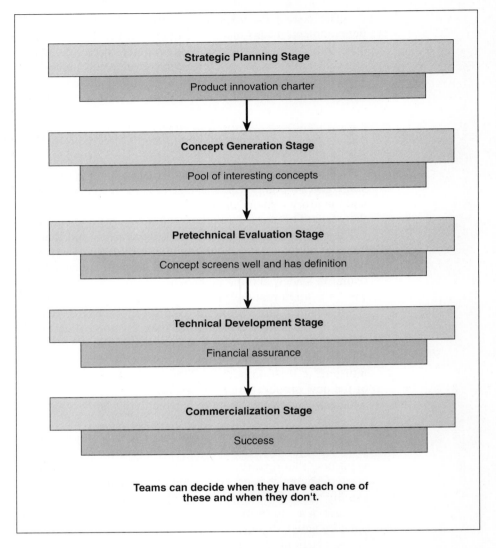

FIGURE 3–7

Information-Based Stages, Not Things or "Management Approvals"

Some people have called stage gates **info-gates**. (See Figure 3–7.) Some call them **accomplishments**, or, popular today, **deliverables**.[5] We ask a team to produce certain things in a stage, to deliver a set of conditions or set of things or set of knowledge. If they deliver these, they are ready to move ahead. The

---

[5]For more on deliverables (also a good overall source on the new product process, particularly the technical portion of it), see Milton D. Rosenau, Jr. and John J. Moran, *Managing the Development of New Products* (New York: Van Nostrand Reinhold, 1993).

deliverables may be tangible: "A sales forecast of $3,000,000." But they may have to be judgmental: "We're confident we can produce *x* millions of the units by September." That may sound tangible, but the important part of the statement is, "We're confident." Incidentally, the latter one combines a time dimension, very important in most processes today.

The precise definition of a stage is not important—we no longer work hectically for 6 months, then stop for several weeks while the board gathers to review what we have done and wave us on. They may go through that ceremony, but we don't wait—we overlap into the next stage long before the last bit of the previous stage is finished. The process is thus almost fluid. (See Figure 3–8.)

The other aspect of stage gates concerns who makes the decision that one has been reached, or passed. Historically, the approver was always management, usually high management. Today, in some firms, the decider is actually the team—this means **empowered teams**, teams who have been structured with capable people, with a good statement of their goals (charter) and with any special rules being understood by all. Though risky to top managements, critical situations can demand empowerment, and the team actually measures its own progress against the same types of gates used in other situations. Obviously, the team should know which situation is which.[6]

The Process Should Allow the Team and Its Support Group Substantial Degrees of Freedom

Empowerment can loosen up the stage gates, but there are many other ways teams can be hobbled. Remember that a new products team is a **horizontal form of management**. Creating new products takes us across all functions, thus risking conflict with all of the **chimneys** or **silos**—the functions, such as marketing and manufacturing. Each of the functions (and not just the big ones) has its own rules or methods of operation, sometimes called paradigms. Each is apt to be headed by a **power player.**

The finance department may have a policy saying that "all major expenditure requests going before the board of directors must be accompanied by environmental impact statements." This can ruin a new product project, because we're not finished. We cannot measure environmental effects with the certainty that impact statements require.

There can be hundreds of these roadblocks. The new product process must be designed in a way to deal with them—perhaps spelling out particular conflicts that can be waived, perhaps by putting a key functional person on the team to learn more about why the new product requires some exceptions, perhaps by delaying

---

[6]The person most responsible for the term *stage gate* recently cautioned managers against adopting rigid processes that cannot react to changing conditions. See Robert G. Cooper, "Third Generation New Product Process," *Journal of Product Innovation Management*, January 1994, pp. 3–14.

FIGURE 3–8

*Various Ways of
Running a Project*

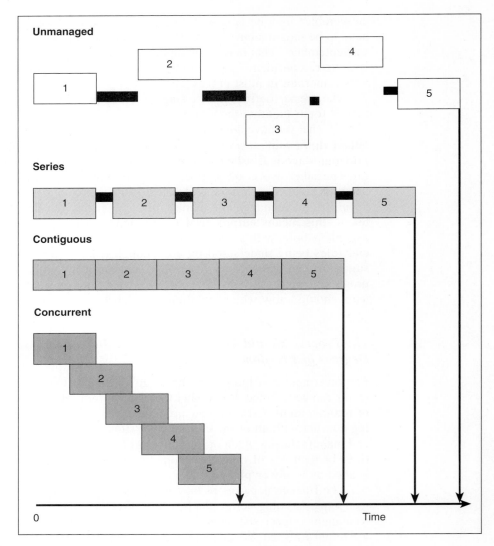

the time when certain functional obligations will be met, and so on. And each exception must usually be negotiated with the chimney involved. In Chapter 12 we will see that the core team (major players, continuously active) are selected with an eye to their being influence agents back in their departments at critical times.

The New Product Process Must Be Flexible to Changing Conditions

We have talked about the need to have new product processes designed to fit their situations, not be packaged systems from some book or even from another firm. What happens when such a situation changes (as it always will, and often)? The process must have some flexibility or, as some say, be **contingent**. There is comfort in fixed process steps, but not for new products people—only danger and frustration lie in that direction.

The New Product Process Must Deal with Especially Critical Points in the Development

When the first Saturn automobiles were introduced, the management team laid plans to deal with what they called **moments of truth**. For example, their market research had shown that potential car buyers were especially affected by what they ran into the first time they went to a dealership to look at a new car. The impressions at that point were burned into their minds, and influenced everything they saw or heard later. So, Saturn arranged a special reception for visitors to the showrooms—host sales people that were paid a salary, refreshment counters with hot coffee, products clearly on display and open to full examination, and information sheets that answered common questions.

The critical points in a new product's development vary greatly and can only be found by examination. One technology-based firm developed a wastewater treatment system that could be hooked up to toilets in rural service stations located on land that "perked" poorly (that could not support field tile systems). The device returned water approved for drinking. But, the firm failed to note that professional sanitary engineers must evaluate all such systems before local public health bodies will approve them for installation. A moment of truth was missed, and the marketing was put on hold for over a year.

Developers should cite each moment of truth as early as possible, and the process designed to handle it.

The New Product Process Should Integrate the Team with the Rest of the Firm and Rest of the World

Almost no team can produce a new product by itself. It uses a huge complex of other functions within the firm and an equally complex group of organizations outside the firm. Full network diagrams flow off the edge of papers they are written on. And each of those groups is working right along on things that interest it. Few of them really need what the new product offers. For example, resellers yawn when manufacturers rave about a new product that just shifts consumption from one brand to another, leaving nothing but cost and trouble to the reseller. Ditto for service organizations, new advisor groups (e.g., architects or physicians), recycling systems, and vendors to, or customers of, firms a new product is designed for. A new product process needs to incorporate all of these players, smoothly and cooperatively, with good communication.

The New Product Process Should Permit a Smooth Launch

Many new products people (voluntarily or by management edict) consider it their task to *prepare* a new product for marketing by the established departments of the firm. Such a *baton transfer* often spawns a dropped baton. Glitches occur because of lack of involvement (ownership), lack of understanding of new product needs, lack of time to do the work, conflict between the new item and items the launch people are already working hard on, and so forth. If the new product must be handed over, so be it, but the process can be tweaked to ease the problem, and preparations can be made for expected glitches.

The New Product Process Should Provide for Organization Learning

It is much easier to create improved new product processes if the firm learns all it can from every project. This usually means finding what was and wasn't done and what happened during the process and afterwards. Some developers are in such a hurry that they don't compile the records (or hold the sessions) needed for organization learning.[7]

Implications for Aspiring New Products Managers

The preceding discussion suggests various attitudes, training, and experience guidelines for people who would like to become managers in the new products process. Here are several:

1. Be multifunctional, not functionally parochial. Have experience in more than one function (marketing, manufacturing, etc.). The broader, the better.
2. Be risk takers, willing to do whatever is necessary to bring a product to market, including facing the wrath of management.
3. Be general manager types—more interested in managing than in doing. Scientists and sales managers can lead new products teams, but they must cease being scientists and sales managers.
4. Be a combination of optimist and realist, aggressor and team player, leader and follower. New products managers are required to play all the roles.

---

[7]Organization learning is important to the process evolution referred to in Chapter 2. This continuing overhaul has been called reengineering in recent years, but at the moment that term appears less desirable. For an example of how it has been done (at Hallmark), see Robert S. Buday, "Reengineering One Firm's Product Development and Another's Service Delivery," *Planning Review,* March/April 1993, pp. 14ff. For some of the theory, see Daryl McKee, "An Organization Learning Approach to Product Innovation," *Journal of Product Innovation Management*, September 1992, pp. 232–45.

5. Have a strong creative bent to achieve better product characteristics and to carve out new ways of doing things.

6. Be comfortable in environments where chaos and confusion seem to reign. Be able to work with depressives, euphorics, and those with no emotion at all.

Fortunately, such managers do exist—and in increasing numbers. I hope you become one of them.

Summary

In this chapter, we studied essentially one thing: the system of phases and activities used in the process of developing and marketing new products. We looked at a simplistic version of this process in a hypothetical situation with highlighter pens. We then went through the process, phase by phase, talking about each one. In that explanation, we noted actions taken or not taken by the people in the office supplies firm.

Following that discussion, we looked at the requirements of a new product process—the criteria by which we judge them.

We now turn to Chapter 4, and the first of the major stages in the process—the strategic planning function. This will include the various forms of strategy to guide the evaluation of available opportunities and the specific products they yield. That will prepare us to begin the study of concept generation.

Applications

More questions from that interview with a company president:

1. "I've got to make a speech down in Dallas next month. It's part of a conference SMU is having on the general topic of opportunity identification. They want me to explain why OI is sometimes more important than brainstorming and other techniques of concept generation. Seems to me it isn't. What do you think?"

2. "You were telling me a moment ago about a three-pronged development process for new products (technical, marketing, and evaluation). Well, I disagree. We develop a new product first; we have to. When we know what the product will be, *then* we can estimate its costs, prepare advertising for it, and so on. We simply couldn't do all of these things at one time."

3. "Several years ago I was General Manager of our high-technology metals division in Italy. We were developing some fabulous applications of space-age technologies in products throughout Europe and parts of Asia—both in government labs and with private firms. Some of our metals were half

glass and no one really knew all they could do. Now, I tell you this because you said your book argued some against tight controls by upper managements at the stage-ending points. No way. On some projects, yes, I would let them go a long way, but on others I wanted approval rights frequently! I never had time to figure it out, but I often wondered why I let some of the projects go and kept tight rein on others. Suppose it related to government restrictions? Or maybe I just trusted some people more than others."

4. "One of the scientists working in our German office furniture subsidiary told me the other day that he actually has to be involved in developing at least six different products for every one we market. He said they were "precursors," I think it was, of the final product. He even said he didn't know what product we would ultimately end up marketing. What in the world did he mean by all that?"

CASE: NABISCO SNACKWELL'S[8]

As of 1993 Nabisco put intense emphasis on new products and had 30 percent of sales from them. In the previous five years they had had five $100 million products. They stressed that the following story of SnackWell's (first year sales of almost $200 million) was typical of their firm, but the process might not be for other firms because all innovators are not alike. Nabisco's way was the result of an overhaul made when they realized they were suffering the "silo" problem and others. People were not talking to each other. In their new process, they sought new segments, not confined to foods, and not confined to traditional food channels. For example, one new product effort involved selling individual-size packages of snacks in video stores and movie theaters.

Their process had three key requirements: (1) the item had to fill a real gap, (2) the item had to be on a key trend, and (3) the whole project had to be executed flawlessly. Doing only one or two just did not work in the food business. Gaps were discovered in two ways. First was a sophisticated gap analysis method of studying markets, probably built around the methodologies in Chapters 6–7. Second was a method of attribute analysis that sought ways a cookie could be created especially for a user, for an occasion, or just physically different. For SnackWell's, the gap was a user gap—cookies for *adults*. Kids had theirs, but adults did not have cookies with the attributes *they* wanted—namely, "great taste, fat-free, better for you."

The second requirement, on a key trend, was satisfied easily—there was very strong growth in adult population, and adults clearly wanted wellness.

The third key, flawless execution, was achieved as follows. Nabisco believed in ideation and creativity. Ideas came from employees generally, from gap analysis (above), and from their special environment in the technical development departments. They encouraged blue

---

[8]In 1993, the Product Development and Management Association gave Nabisco their Outstanding Innovator Award for having a sustained program of new product creation and marketing. Two members of that firm told this Nabisco story to the annual International Conference of that association in San Diego.

sky ideation, they provided a "skunkworks" environment by allowing time off to further personal concepts, staffers could present their ideas to management at annual May Fairs, and they ran brainstorming sessions where development people were joined by marketing, finance, operations, and R&D.

New product concepts that looked good (as SnackWell's did) were given a feasibility check (could they retool for it, did it interfere with production, etc.). Then it went into quantitative testing—first screened against the firm's market research database to see if the numbers generally looked OK (that trend issue), and then into simulated test marketing (STM) with volumetric financial scenarios. The STMs sought consumers' reactions to the concept and used sales waves of actual product so that they could get consumers' reactions to the taste-and-measure reuse. At this point, if consumers liked it, they were ready to reconfirm the company's ability to produce and market such a product.

Next came the marketing phase and technical development phase. Marketing tasks included branding. They wanted a direct, memorable name that communicated something positive about the product. In this case, the apostrophe in SnackWell's communicated a homemade sound—like grandma's. Television commercials were developed for social settings where the key points were stressed—here were cookies that had no fat (or very low fat) but yet tasted great and were "better for you." The settings were also full of fun. Later a different campaign was built around the shortage of product (with factory people running to hide from customers) showing how what happens *after* launch can change plans. In this case, a problem became a sales booster.

Next came a major public relations effort: press kit, recipe suggestions, a nutrition booklet, and other items. Then Sunday coupons, inserts, cash register coupons, samples, and other material.

In the meantime, the technical development work was under way, and the whole thing was on a cross-functional basis, with teams representing all of the key player groups. They tested various technologies, checked production sites, and insisted on cost feasibility.

The commercialization phase (which followed evaluation and technical feasibilities) called for several things. First, advertising and packaging graphics were developed (the green package color associated with health), the product formula was settled, final product specifications were written, they made an acceptance run in production, cost feasibility was checked again, and they were ready for the implementation phase. Implementation involved actual production, shipment of samples to the sales force, shipment of product to the trade, and running of commercials.

Senior management was involved early in this project, as soon as the product concept was shaped, and again at select points down the line. At Nabisco they tried hard to get top management's contributions early, not near the end when most of the plan has been implemented.

The presenters insisted that there was no one thing that made them successful, but there were three keys: a gap, an on-trend product to fill that gap, and a technical and marketing development process that gave flawless execution.

How does this process compare with what you just read in Chapter 3? In spite of their obvious success, would you question anything they did? Also, did you spot any of the key concepts from Chapter 2 in this case?

4 STRATEGIC PLANNING FOR NEW PRODUCTS

The Product Innovation Charter

Setting

Chapter 3 discussed the process of creating and marketing new products, from strategy to postlaunch tracking and evaluation. Chapter 4 offers the first step in that process. Strategy is the base for new products management and serves as a loose harness for the integration of all the people and resources used in generating new products. We will look first at what a team needs in its strategy statement and then at where its inputs originate—that is, in corporate strategy, in platform strategy, and in influences from many other sources. We will then take a more complete look at the team strategy, what we will call a product innovation charter—its drivers, it goals and objectives, and its "rules of the road." That will be followed by examination of how we go about finding good opportunities on which the charters are built.

Why Have Strategic Planning?

Let's look in on a team of people developing a small, portable computer printer. One member is thinking of using a new *battery*-based technology, while another team member is concentrating on potential customers who happen to work in environments where *wall plugs* are available! Marketing research people plan to *pretest* the product extensively, while manufacturing engineers assume time is critical and are *designing finished production capability* from the beginning! A vendor picked to supply the tractor mechanism has to check with the team leader almost every day because the team has not decided exactly what functions the printer will serve or the target user! And the team is being guided by requests from the sales department, which is currently calling on *smaller* firms although, in fact, the biggest potential is thought to be in *large* firms and governments! This team has not developed strategy.

Team guidance, just as corporate or strategic business unit (SBU) guidance, comes partly in the form of strategy. Its purpose is *to focus and integrate team effort and to permit delegation.* Bausch & Lomb almost lost its market position in the 1980s when its managers concentrated for too long on improving old products and thus almost missed new products like extended-wear contact lenses. Being forced to review their strategy, they found many more opportunities and are now successfully capitalizing on them (e.g., disposable contact lenses).

What Form Does a New Product Team's Strategy Take?

The people who lead a new product project function as a *company within a company.* They may be loosely tied together in a committee, or they may be fully dedicated (full time) managers sent off somewhere in a **skunkworks**, to address a difficult assignment. They represent all of the necessary functions. They are led by a group leader, team manager, or a project manager. This leader is a general manager, managing a set of functions. For these people, a new products strategy does several things.

It charts the group's direction—where it *must* go, and where it must *not* go. What technologies it will capitalize on, and what markets it will serve.

It tells the group its goals and objectives—why it exists, what its role is, what its purpose is.

It tells the group how it will play the game—what the rules are, what activities someone thinks important enough to require, how innovative it will be, what the special quality, time, and cost constraints are, and a host of miscellaneous things.

For this, we will use the name *product innovation charter* (PIC), because it is for products, not processes and other activities, it is for innovation (even a me-too is an innovation for the firm that markets one), and it is a charter (defined as a document that gives the conditions under which an organization will operate). It allows delegation, permits financing, and calls for personnel assignments, all within the agreed-to focus. As one manager put it, "The charter tells us what we must do, what we cannot do, and, by subtraction, what we may do, if we wish." For new product teams, plowing off into unknown waters, such a charter is invaluable.

The PIC will be covered more later, but an example of one is in Figure 4–1. For now we should look at what leads up to it. What are the inputs? For this, please look at Figure 4–2; it will guide us as we go through the following discussion.

Some Inputs Come from Corporate Strategy

Corporate leaders make many strategy statements, but three types interest us in new products. First is the *nature of the game*, the "business we are in," the focus

---

FIGURE 4–1   Contents of a Product Innovation Charter, and Its Application to a Firm in the Computer Industry

---

Production Innovation Charter

Background: Key ideas from the situation analysis; special forces such as managerial dicta; reasons for preparing a new PIC at this time.

Focus: At least one clear technology dimension and one clear market dimension. They match and have good potential.

Goals-Objectives: What the project will accomplish, either short-term as objectives or longer term as goals. Evaluation measurements.

Guidelines: Any "rules of the road," requirements imposed by the situation or by upper management. Innovativeness, order of market entry, time/quality/cost, miscellaneous.

A sample PIC for an intangible, in the business-to-business world, written from inquiry. It combines the background in with the market portion of the focus.

Focus	A major growth opportunity for a new field service is the smaller office that over the past three years has bought one of the new computer systems designed for such offices. Because they are found in every conceivable location and because they purchase computer equipment with the intention that it last a long time, they offer a unique service problem. This opportunity will be addressed using (1) our systems analysis skills and (2) our field service capabilities.
Goals-Objectives	The goals of this activity are (1) to overcome all reasonable objections about service levels by this group and (2) to increase our net operating revenues from the sale of these new services by at least $18 million per year.
Guidelines	These goals will be achieved by creating unique service approaches that are based on current field service resources, hopefully protected from quick competitive emulation, without extensive development expenditures either inside the firm or outside, and with an absolute minimum of development time.

---

of the firm's activities. It defines the ball field, cites core competencies, marks off the out-of-bounds. Second is *what the organization intends to accomplish there*, its goals and objectives. Third is *the guidelines or rules of the road*, basic activities which will achieve those goals and objectives. Such top-level strategies, sometimes called **mission statements**, are usually applied across the firm's entire operations, but our interest is in how they affect the new products operation.[1]

Figure 4–2 gives a picture of the flow from top corporate strategic thinking down to where a PIC can be written. How these reach new product teams is shown in Figure 4–3. You will see three levels of strategy—the **corporate level**, a **platform level** (which besides platforms shows marketing planning, technical planning and several others), and a **new product project level** (where the charters are). They differ only in the breadth of their application, since they all concern

---

[1] Some CEOs use corporate strategies more aggressively than others; see Rita Koselka, "It's My Favorite Statistic," *Forbes*, September 12, 1994, pp. 162–76. Because a PIC is a mission statement for a project, it might be helpful to see what *Fortune* editors thought about two recent books on mission statements. See Alan Farnham, "Brushing Up Your Vision Thing," *Fortune*, May 1, 1995, p. 129.

FIGURE 4–2

The Flow That Produces Product Innovation Charters

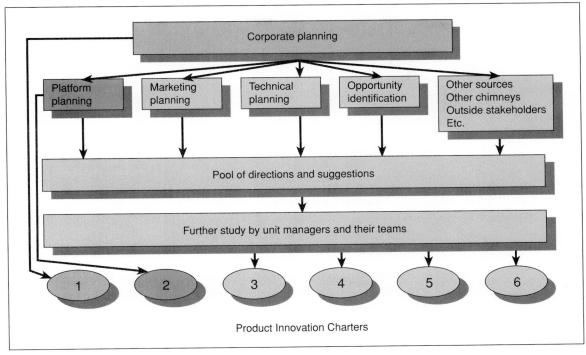

the same three categories of focus, goals, and activities. Corporate strategies apply to platforms and directly to projects that are not a part of platforms (note the heavy line going directly from corporate level to a PIC); platform strategies apply to those projects created under them (some so directly that they in effect bypass the thinking of the project team). So, a new products team has some strategy from corporate, some from platforms, some from other parts of the firm, and some developed by the team itself.

Platforms require some explanation. They are of several types, all of them for situations where several projects are close together and share some strategic needs. In the automobile business, Chrysler has its LH **car platform**, from which the Concorde and Intreped came. The General Motors Saturn did not come from a platform, but it has become one as it grows and adds other items (the station wagon is apparently to be the first). A platform of interest to sneaker wearers is Nike's focus on ground/melted sneaker soles—after several years of trying to find product/markets (dog beds, medicine balls), they have found success in basketball courts, and they are cutting their annual $300,000 landfill costs to boot.

Perhaps the most used are **brand** platforms. Brands may be billion dollar assets, so many brand platforms are personally driven by CEOs. For example, when Robert

FIGURE 4–3

*The Role of
Platforms in
Project PICs*

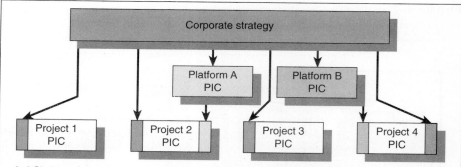

Ital Clothing Company has a corporate value strategy—new lines will provide obvious value to customers. But, Platform A is a higher-priced line of clothing, and Platform B is for industrial and commercial uniforms. Both have value, their form of it, as a value assignment from corporate. The projects are four separate new lines of clothing, and all four will meet the value strategy, but Project 2 must deal with a special Platform A strategy of "highly innovative" while Project 4 must deal with a special Platform B strategy of "attractive styling but durable."

Siegel took over management of Stride Rite, he identified Top Siders and Keds as brands he would build the firm around. He changed the firm from a *product* maker to a *brand* maker, and said, "They want mules, we'll sell mules."[2] Brands can serve as the launching pad for scores of products, all having in common the brand and any strategies applying to that brand. Chrysler recently saw value in its Plymouth nameplate, and rescued it as the platform for a stream of new products aimed at the younger generations. Owners of leading brands work to keep them that way, as platforms, and no one works harder or more successfully than Gillette.[3] Kodak built a new platform when it marketed the FunSaver camera, from which came derivatives Weekender, a flash format, FunSaver II, Portrait, Weekender II, and other versions, all perhaps planned from the beginning.

Another common platform is the category—product-type category or customer category. Most marketing effort today is conducted at category group levels—one overall plan for cake mixes, for do-it-yourself tools, or for finance courses in a college. For example, DuPont has special finishes platforms for doing business with the automobile industry, the marine industry, and the furniture industry, among others. Any strategic change in one of those areas influences all new products developed under that umbrella. Oddly, though Intel has its chips (486, Pentium) as *corporate* strategic platforms, they are not *new product* platforms because each is a product, not a group of products. Customers such as Gateway will have a chip as a new product platform, however.

---

[2]Zina Moukheiber, "They Want Mules, We'll Sell Mules," *Forbes,* September 12, 1994, pp. 42–44.

[3]Patricia Sellers, "Brands: It's Thrive or Die," *Fortune,* August 23, 1993, pp. 52–56.

One type of customer platform plays a major role in the globalization of business. A firm may have a corporate strategy that is global, then a regional platform (South America), a country platform (Chile), and then projects within the Chilean operation.

A **strategic business unit** is a platform; so is a **trade channel grouping** (e.g., Kraft's institutional foods operation). And then there are variations within almost every firm. Marriott, for example, has, among other things, a very serious corporatewide strategy of customer satisfaction, a platform strategy of value for its Courtyard, and a prestige platform for its giant new resorts (each big enough to have its own team). A resort built and operated under the Courtyard platform would be different from a resort built and operated by the prestige platform, and different from a new, experimental resort being developed for application on the moon. (If there were one, it would certainly be so important it would be directly under corporate control, and not inhibited by restrictions common to any one of the platforms.)

New Product Strategy Inputs from Special Analyses and Other Sources

Opportunity Identification

Throughout the firm, in the course of doing their jobs, people are discovering new opportunities—a salesperson learns that a customer is moving into a new market, a scientist finds unexpected activity in a compound, a finance VP notes a fall in the prime rate, a director urges that we look more carefully at what the Environmental Protection Agency is doing. Many firms have persons working full time at this, in departments called Opportunity Identification. They essentially audit the firm and any environment relevant to it. Of course, some firms disagree: Burlington Northern's position is, "We all have our fans out there, but just like football coaches, we don't consult the fans on our strategies."[4]

Underutilized Resource.   It may be that the organization has not sufficiently exploited past technological breakthroughs. Perhaps R&D leadership decides its people have not built the ideal strategic alliances with marketing divisions, or, more common today, with particular customer groups.

New Resource.   Managers in Division A have been encouraged to develop products that utilize the strong market position (or, say, telecommunications resources) of newly acquired Division B.

---

[4]Daniel Machalaba, "New Paint Job Stokes Controversy over a Warbonnet's True Colors," *The Wall Street Journal*, September 18, 1995, p. B1.

External Mandate.   Regulators impose new restrictions on use of petroleum-based synthetics, and the CEO wants all divisions to seek new products that capitalize, actively, on these regulations.

Internal Mandate.   New corporate leadership orders a companywide design program to clean up a hodgepodge of packages and brands. Or, common today, an SBU commits to a total quality management program and orders an upgrading of all product lines. Toshiba said they wanted to be king of the MS-DOS laptop market, and thus automatically rejected all suggestions about developing a laptop for other operating systems.[5]

Management's Druthers

Other inputs arise from what appear as management fads or whims, but actually in most cases represent common reactions to market conditions. For example, at this time we see an obsession with the **triad of quality, speed, and cost**. New products (actually, all new corporate programs) must enhance the quality of offerings to the customer, must emerge from development in an absolute minimum of time, and must have a cost structure that permits a lower price. Another thrust right now is on **value**, a consequence of the triad just mentioned. Still another input comes from the in-house competition encouraged by firms such as Johnson & Johnson when they fragmentize their unit structures.[6]

And, of course, in the human world there are always the special requests from CEOs, COOs, and directors. Sometimes called **government jobs** by new products people, these projects are resisted mainly for their untimely intrusions, not their quality. The Sony Walkman was such a government job, and it was resisted so strongly by both technical and marketing people that the chairman personally took over as its project manager. The CEO of Calvin Klein Cosmetics had a rule that there would be "no rules"—he thinks it permitted the first (and very successful) unisex scent.

Noncorporate Strategic Planning

Although the major thrust of strategic planning comes from the top down (see discussion of corporate and platform strategies earlier), much of it also comes from the heads of the functions (**silos** or **chimneys**) in the firm—marketing, technical, manufacturing, and finance, and from the planning of suppliers, distributors, and others. Like it or not, such groups frequently have the power to affect new product work. Specifically, paper manufacturing is done on such huge and expensive machines that such firms often have strategies with a statement:

---

[5]John E. Rehfeld, "What Working for a Japanese Company Taught Me," *Harvard Business Review*, November–December, 1990, pp. 167–76.

[6]Donald M. McCloskey, "Noble Survivors," *Across the Board*, January 1994, pp. 25–30.

All new items, if paper-related, must be manufacturable on our current lines. Financial conditions may warrant restrictions such as "no new products that require more than $3,000,000 capital investments." Suppliers of materials (e.g., chemicals or metals) often require (usually smaller) firms to buy and use what they make. Distributors today are gaining such strength that even the largest manufacturers must deal with their logistics, information technology, and market segmentation restrictions.

But the greatest functional inputs come from marketing, where ongoing planning uses a range of techniques designed to give sharper market focus and new positionings. For example, look at Figure 4–4. It shows a variation on the traditional product-market matrix. The cells show variations in innovativeness risk as a firm brings in new product types or technologies (operating mode change) or markets products that require change in how people buy or use them. A simple flavor change (product improvement) would probably involve no risk at all, but substituting a computer line for face-to-face dealings in the field of medicine (diversification for a computer services firm) would involve great risk to the producer of the service. Marketing managements want to have balanced-risk portfolios, and yet want to take advantage of new technologies and new markets; their decisions are major inputs to new product strategy.

FIGURE 4–4

Degree of Innovativeness as a Matter of Strategic Risk

Risk		Change in operations or marketing mode		
		None	Some	Great
Change in use/ user mode	None	None	Low	Medium
	Some	Low	Medium	High
	Great	Medium	High	Dangerous

Application: This matrix has gone by several names: Product/Market, Technology/Application, and Market-Newness/Firm-Newness. In all cases, the issue is the risk of innovativeness. Risk on the user side is just as much a concern to us as risk within the firm. Every new product can be positioned on this chart somewhere, and that position is important if it is accepted as a project. Selecting one section to be preferred over the others is a matter of strategy.

A second analytical device is the traditional **"dogs and cows" matrix**, where the various "pieces" of a business are plotted in a matrix with dimensions on current share of market and market growth. (Variations on what was a Boston Consulting Group creation have gone by "General Electric" and other names.) Obviously, the desirable category is a high share in a high-growth market. Unfortunately, few analyses disclose big opportunity in the other cells: A big share in a growing market is a **star**, a big share in a level or declining market is a **cash cow**, a small share in a growing market is a **question mark**, and a small share in a level or declining market is a **dog**. Requests for new product work often take such form as:

- We need continuing, modest improvements in Product X to lengthen the time it can be kept as a cash cow.
- We need immediate, major improvements in Product Y if we are to keep its position at the top of its rapidly growing market.

Miscellaneous Sources

In contrast to the top-down and the horizontal (functional) approaches, some inputs can start at the lower level of activity and influence upwards, as when a new product is so successful it drives corporate strategy to change. For example, an *ethical* pharmaceutical firm once "unintentionally" marketed a very successful new *proprietary* food product, with the result that a new division was created (to isolate the consumer advertising activity from the rest of the firm) and new strategies created to optimize its opportunity.

Sometimes, a slow and gradual restructuring of business practice can influence new product strategies almost without anyone realizing it. For example, the 1980s and 1990s have seen a gradual movement in service products to add **tangibilization** and for tangible products (goods) to add (or emphasize) services. McDonald's features its arches, Prudential has long had its rock, banks create a physical setting that suggests security, and Federal Express gains tangibility from its employees and the computers they hold in their hands. Every one of these is a product improvement, the change coming in the augmentation to the basic offering (see Chapter 2 for the augmentation concept).[7]

A Closer Look at the PIC

Strategy statements take almost as many forms as there are firms preparing them, but they tend to build around the structure given in Figure 4–1. They can be for an *entire firm* (if very small or very narrowly conceived) or for a *standing platform* of activity within a larger firm (e.g., the Black & Decker brand of tools)

---

[7]Allan C. Reddy, Bruce D. Buskirk, and Ajit Kaicker, "Tangibilizing the Intangibles: Some Strategies for Services Marketing," *Journal of Services Marketing*, no. 3 (1993), pp. 13–17.

or for a *specific project* (such as Hewlett-Packard's 4L laser printer). A PIC generally speaks to an opportunity (the focus), not to the specific product or products the group is yet to create—there may be one, or several. Oscar Mayer embarked on the development of *a* "big weiner" only to find later they needed Big&Juicy in six different flavors for U.S. regions. Of course, when products are very complex (the Saturn automobile, an air express service for the Asian market, or a nation's new health plan), one product is all the team can handle.

The PIC should be in writing, but for various reasons it often is not, and it should be given to all participants, but again it often is not. This is unfortunate, because a secret strategy that exists only in the minds of a few leaders will not do much for a team of 30 people.

Section 1 of the PIC: Background

This section of the PIC answers the question, "Why did we develop this strategy, anyway?" To the extent necessary, it recaps the analysis behind it.

Section 2 of the PIC: The Arena (Area of Focus)

In today's competitive marketplaces, it takes focus to unlock the necessary power of innovation. Just as a laser can take a harmless light and convert it into a deadly ray, so can a commitment to, say, the delivered-pizza business or to the xerographic process convert limited resources into a strong competitive thrust. As one developer said, "We like to play on fields that tilt in our direction."

Core competencies are a place to start. Marketers focus down by targeting and segmentation. Technical people, all too often fenced in by time, limited facilities, and money, don't relish yet another focus mechanism.

But the idea of an arena is growing—managed, of course, in a way that is constructive, not harmful. Focus is achieved almost entirely by use of four types of strengths or leverage capabilities: technology (Xerox's xerographic technology or Scott's paper mills), product experience (Strohs chose to focus on the "beer business"), customer franchise (Stanley Tool's hold on the woodworker), and end use experience (Chase Manhattan's international division). We used to have lots of these "one-legged" (or one-dimensional) strategies, but today competition makes such a risk more than managements can defend. Edwin Land relied totally on the polarization technology for many years, until he tripped on something his salespeople could not sell—Polavision instant movies.

Similarly, market-oriented firms (especially consumer packaged goods firms in food, drug, and toiletry categories) used to just survey consumers, find they wanted green biddies more than yellow ones, and tell the lab people to create them. This too worked pretty well, as long as there were significant unmet needs and competitors who reacted slowly.

Today, either approach is too big a gamble. Consumer giants Frito-Lay and P&G have major laboratory research facilities, and technology-driven

FIGURE 4–5

Power/Potential
Dual Drive Matrix

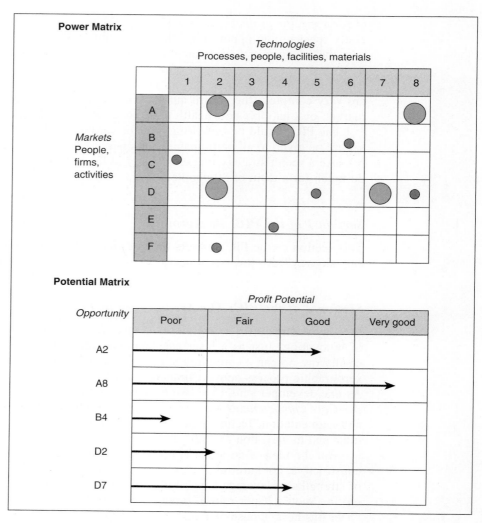

Hewlett-Packard has announced that it wants a strong market commitment behind every new product program. Whereas we used to talk about a technology-driven firm *or* a market-driven firm, we now talk about **dual-driven** firms. The balanced strategy of dual drive is clearly the winner in recent research.[8] Some managers want this broadened to **business drive**, meaning *all* of the functions of the firm. See Figure 4–5.

---

[8]Robert G. Cooper, "New Product Strategies: What Distinguishes the Top Performers?" *Journal of Product Innovation Management*, September 1984, pp. 151–64.

Technology Drivers.   The most common technological strengths are in the *laboratories*. Corning used to say it would develop those products—and only those products—that exploited the firm's fabulous glass technology. Today's global competition makes it tougher for Corning (and others) to hold a superior position in a technology defined so broadly.

Many times, a firm finds it has a valuable ***non**laboratory* technology. Avon has an efficient small-order-handling technology. Other operations technologies include soft-drink distributed bottling systems and White Consolidated's efficient appliance production lines. The Deloitte & Touche consulting division built new services around its capabilities of analysis and interpretation of financial information.

Even harder to see are the technologies in **marketing**. For example, some packaged-goods firms view their product management departments as technologies. Other examples include physical distribution systems, customer technical service, or creative advertising departments.

We also know that **product specialization** can offer bodies of knowledge that are capable of doing work, if they are focused and strengthened. A rapidly growing Korean manufacturer says, "I want to be the Toyota of furniture"—whatever the material or wherever the global location.[9]

Market Drivers.   The other half of the dual-drive strategy also comes from two sources: **customer group** and **end use**. The best new product ideas are based on customer problems, and these problems serve as the heart of the concept generation process described in Chapters 5–7.

The Hoover Company once had a strategy of developing new vacuums for "people who already had one"—the two-vacuum home concept. Other firms have relied on demographic dimensions for focus, for example, Toro's "young couples," and Olivetti's "banks and law offices." As examples of more abstract dimensions, Hallmark concentrates on "people who care enough," and Helena Rubenstein once targeted "real women." Welch-Allyn, maker of high-tech medical devices used in doctors' offices and hospitals, says, not jokingly, if you have a cavity we want to see it, and if you don't have a cavity but need one we will make it. The latter part of that statement refers to their device for aiding in noninvasive gall bladder removal.

Firms producing services find customer-focus comfortable, since many of their operations involve the customer as an actual *co-producer* of the service. This has led many firms to involve the customer as an integrated partner in the new product development process.

Occasionally, a firm can concentrate on one single customer; for example, an auto-parts firm may build new items for Ford or for General Motors. But, when Cullinet focused successfully on its customer base and made lots of money,

---

[9]Wee Sang-sik, as quoted in an article by that name in *Forbes*, May 16, 1988, p. 92.

IBM focused on Cullinet's *non*customers and ended up blindsiding their competitor with a new language (SQL).[10] A variation on the single-customer focus is **mass customization**—where we offer a customers a product of their individual choice. Marriott's Courtyard has made this successful in the motel business, but a new example is the Dow Jones *Personal Journal* "newspaper." The customer selects favorite columns, news topics, stocks and mutual funds to follow, and so forth, and the personal paper is delivered *continuously* via computer.

The second way of focusing on the market side is on a particular **end use** or **activity**, say sports or skiing. General Instrument Corporation's new products program concentrated exclusively on wagering. User (previous paragraph) and end use (here) may sound alike, but they are not. For example, focusing on skiers or skiing would both provide new equipment, but skiing would also lead to new lodges, new slopes, new travel packages, and services for lodge owners (who may not even be skiers). Carborundum focused for a long time on metal removal (an outgrowth of its line of grinding wheels), wherever that removal took place. Even though users differed greatly, their metal removing had a lot in common.

A variation on customers as market drivers is the distributor that a manufacturer wants to have a better franchise with. Hallmark's line of small gift items was originally developed to help their card shop franchisees make more money. Anheuser-Busch's Eagle snacks was developed to hold distributor attention and interest.

Combinations: Dual-Drive.   Now, putting one *technical* driver together with a *market* driver yields a clear and precise arena focus. The major new products program of University Microfilms was oriented to the *technology of microfilming* and the *market activity of education*. Microfilm readers for libraries were just one new line. UMI's early use of this strategy would have rejected photocopiers for schools or microfilm readers for law offices.

The Signode Corporation set up a series of seven new product venture operations and asked each group to select one company technology and one market opportunity that matched that company strength. The first team chose *plastics extrusion* (from Signode's primary business of strapping materials) and *food manufacturing*. This team's first new products were plastic trays for packaged foods headed into microwave ovens.

Section 3 of the PIC: Goals and Objectives

Anyone working on product innovation ought to know the purpose, because work can change in so many ways if the purpose changes. The PIC uses the standard definition that goals are longer-range, general directions of movement, whereas objectives are short-term, specific measures of accomplishment. Thus, a PIC may aim for market dominance (as a goal) and 25 percent market share the first year (as an objective).

---

[10]Esther Dyson, "Don't Listen Too Hard," *Forbes*, May 16, 1988, p. 112.

Both goals and objectives are of three types: (1) profit, expressed in one or more of the many ways profit can be stated; (2) growth, usually controlled, though occasionally a charter is used defensively to help the firm hold or retard a declining trend; and (3) market status, usually increased market share. General Foods, for example, insisted that new product teams entering new markets plan to dominate them. But the American Regitel Corporation, marketers of point-of-sale machines, aimed to be Number 3 in its markets, even though the parent firm wanted to be Number 1 as a general policy. There has been lots of criticism of market share as a new product goal, but a recent analysis of available data shows it is still a viable objective.[11]

Miscellaneous goals have also been used. They are not trivial to the firms using them. For example, Kimberly-Clark may or may not achieve its goal of getting Kleenex into every room in the home. And the firm that tried to "avoid acquisition," didn't.

Section 4 of the PIC: Special Guidelines

To this point, we have filled out three sections of the PIC form. But research shows that almost every new product strategy has a fourth section—some guidelines, or "rules of the road." They may be managerially imposed, or consensus thinking of team members.

Degree of Innovativeness.   How innovative does a management want a particular group to be? The options range from first-to-market (whether a new nylon stocking or a Frisbee) to strict imitation.

First-to-market is a risky strategy. It goes by several other names, including **pioneering**. There are three ways to get it, the first of which is by **state-of-the art breakthrough**. Pharmaceutical firms use that route most of the time. Other products that came from such programs include bubble memory, the pacemaker, compact discs, and television. But most first-to-market products do not extend the state of the art. They tweak technology in a new way, sometimes called **leveraged creativity**. The third category is **applications engineering**, where the technology may not be changed at all, but the use is totally new. Loctite has done this scores of times, for example, by using glue to replace metal fasteners in electronics and automotive products.

Far more common than pioneering is the strategy of **adaptation**. Being adaptive means taking one's own or a competitive product and improving it in some way. The improvement may be technical (a high-density floppy disk versus a double-density one, or the Excel's improvement on Lotus 1-2-3) or nontechnical (new flavors of soda). It gets to be very popular as a recession strategy.

---

[11]Mark J. Chussil, "Does Market Share Really Matter?" *Planning Review*, September–October 1991, pp. 31–37.

Some adapters seek almost trivial change, anything that can be used in advertising. Others follow what is called "second but best"; the improvement is to be major, and the follower intends to take over the market, if possible. General Electric followed this strategy for many years prior to 1980. Harris Corporation, on the other hand, entered markets where others had pioneered and used its great technical know-how to create a niche with a slightly improved product. The firm's chairman said Harris tried to be strong in technology and to enter a product in a timely manner. Sometimes a firm begins a line by being first-to-market, and then follows with increasingly less innovative line extensions, even imitations of leapfrogging competitors.[12]

Adaptation alone is risky. The pioneer often obtains a permanent advantage; if other things are equal, the first product in a new market gains an average market share of around 30 percent. But the second firm can take over the market and win the category if its adaptation is clearly superior.[13] In fact, some firms flat out say it is best to come in later, with an adaptation version that becomes accepted as the standard for that category.

Michael Porter helped clarify the type of adaptation needed in successful competitive strategy when he listed the three key criteria: (1) the firm must be capable of delivering the adaptation, (2) it must be difficult for a competitor to copy, and (3) it must be one for which the customer is willing to pay a sufficient premium in the price.[14]

The third level of innovativeness is **imitation**, or **emulation**. In a classic event late in 1979, *Advertising Age* quoted S. W. Lapham, the new products director of Sterling Drug's subsidiary Lehn & Fink: "Replicate, don't innovate." Imitation was a surefire way to succeed.[15] Lapham cited several products that had been successfully copied—Jell-O Pudding followed My-T-Fine, Country Time lemonade mix followed Wyler's, and Stayfree feminine napkins followed Kotex. After recommending that any imitator be careful to sufficiently research the right entry to copy, Lapham described how his firm copied Airwick's Carpet Fresh. Love My Carpet was "developed" and marketed in less than six months. He said: "Trying to innovate as the only way to success is one of the greatest myths of new products ever invented. I have to believe it was created by a marketing research company." A few weeks later, another *Advertising Age* article announced that Lehn & Fink was being sued by Airwick for infringing on the Carpet Fresh patents.[16] Imitation has its risks, too!

---

[12]For more information about this idea, see Steven C. Wheelwright and W. Earl Sasser, Jr., "The New Product Development Map," *Harvard Business Review*, May–June 1989, pp. 112–25.

[13]Peter N. Golder and Gerard J. Tellis, "Pioneering Advantage: Marketing Logic or Marketing Legend," *Journal of Marketing Research*, May 1993, pp. 158–70.

[14]As interpreted by Byron Sharp in "Competitive Marketing Strategy: Porter Revisited," *Marketing Intelligence and Planning*, no. 1 (1991), pp. 4–30.

[15]"Different Strokes," *Advertising Age*, December 17, 1979, p. 4.

[16]"Lehn & Fink Philosophy Draws Suit by Airwick," *Advertising Age*, February 11, 1980, p. 71.

Cooper Tire & Rubber (on tires) and White Consolidated (on white appliances) are well known for deliberately waiting to see winners emerge.

Timing.   The next category of guidelines variation—timing—has four options: first, quick second, slower, and late. The decision to be **first** is pioneering, just discussed. A **quick second** tries to capture a good second-share position, perhaps making no significant improvement, or just enough to promote. The strategy is very demanding, because such a firm has to make the decision to enter the market before the innovator is successful or has even come to market. Waiting risks letting the second spot go to aggressive competitors. Striving for a **slower** entry is safer in the sense that a firm knows the outcome of the pioneer's efforts and has time to make a more meaningful adaptation. But, the good market opportunities may be taken by quick seconds. The last timing alternative, **late** entry, is usually a price entry keyed to manufacturing skills.

Miscellaneous.   The field of guidelines is loaded with special situations. One popular guideline relates to brand franchise. A brand is like a charged battery, easy to hook up a new line to. Jell-O-*this* and Jell-O-*that*. **Brand equity** describes the *value* of an established brand. Market research can measure the value of any brand for any particular market (e.g., Duracel, if put onto a different type of battery). The measurements actually tell the amount of "free" promotion and integrity the brand equity yields to a new item that uses it.

Pierre Cardin once said: "I have the most important name in the world. I give my name only to the best products."[17] He knew that brand-franchise strategy is not without its dangers. A bad product can damage a good name. Or conversely, the new product can be so successful it takes over the main brand (think of Miller Lite and the formerly famous Miller High Life).

In contrast to a strong brand, some firms have a *weak* marketing arm. For example, a large mining machinery firm told its product innovators to come up with products that *did not* require strong marketing; the firm didn't have it and didn't want to invest in getting it. A pharmaceutical firm said, "It must be *patentable*." A small computer firm said all new products must be *parts of systems*, while an even smaller computer firm said, "Nothing that must be part of a system"! A food firm said, "Don't put anything in a can that Frito-Lay can put in a bag." And on and on.

Moving around in a market or product line can be dangerous. An example: Honda was very successful using a four-wheel steering system because it put the innovation into a two-door coupe with a sporty image, whereas Mazda failed when putting it on a five-door hatchback that was positioned for safety and durability.[18] On complex products, integrity must be specifically stated as a strategy and sought continuously.

---

[17]Richard C. Morais, "What Is Perfume but Water and a Bit of Essence?" *Forbes*, May 2, 1988, pp. 90–95.

[18]Kim B. Clark and Takahiro Fujimoto, "The Power of Product Integrity," *Harvard Business Review*, November–December 1990, pp. 107–18.

Most firms use many different strategies at the same time. For example, a few years back, Texas Instruments was concurrently using R&D as its strength in MOM memories, manufacturing as its base for low-priced watches, and consumer studies for its line of games. Last, but not least, many CEOs lay inviolable conditions; for instance, Rupert Murdoch said (of his Twentieth Century Fox) that "we're not making huge, expensive bets on movies," and for 1993 budgeted only one film over $30 million.[19]

Finding the Right Opportunities for Focused Arenas

Auditing a firm's strengths and weaknesses is not easy. Critiquing other people, while always touchy, is doubly so here because the people (marketing or technical) being audited are so often the very people touting their own favorite strategic directions. A report on the PICs of movie producers disclosed that (1) Warner Bros. was spending lavishly on its top stars, depending on them to make successful movies; (2) Paramount Pictures took star courting a step further by luring top directors and producers as well and giving them lucrative contracts; and (3) Walt Disney Studios, on the other hand, elevated the story over the stars and "made its mark by conceiving a genre of slapstick, class-warfare comedies."[20] Each strategy can be traced to a strength of the company involved.

Potentially fruitful options in technologies or market places may seem hard to find, but we are surrounded by them. Figure 4–6 shows a partial list. Every one has been the basis for a team's new product assignment at least once. In fact, one of the most valuable creative skills in product innovation is the ability to look at a building, an operation, a person, or a department and visualize how it could be used in a new way. This skill can be developed—and should be practiced.

Evaluating Opportunities

Proposed opportunities must be evaluated, and a form for this is given in Figure 4–7. But there will always be other factors peculiar to the firm involved. For example, DuPont looks to see if the technology will be a *necessity* in the application and if the firm has previously demonstrated special *expertise* in it. Dow asks, "Can we *own that market?*" Other firms ensure the presence of someone high enough in the firm to help the technology weather annual budget revisions.[21]

---

[19]Nancy J. Perry, "The Future Is Glued to the Tube," *Fortune*, September 21, 1992, pp. 99–100.

[20]Christopher Knowlton, "Lessons from Hollywood Hit Men," *Fortune*, August 29, 1988, pp. 78–82.

[21]W. David Gibson, "A Maze for Management: Choosing the Right Technology," *Chemical Week*, May 7, 1986, pp. 74–78. For bests on people, not technologies, see Nicholas Kandel, Jean-Pierre Remy, Christian Stein, and Thomas Durrand, "Who's Who in Technology: Identifying Technological Competence Within the Firm," *R&D Management*, July 1991, pp. 215–28.

FIGURE 4–6   Market and Technology Opportunities

Market Opportunities	*Technology Opportunities*
User (category)	Product type
User (for our product)	Specific product
Customer (buyer)	Primary packaging
Influencer	Secondary packaging
Potential user	Design process
Nonuser	Production process
Demographic set	Distribution process
Psychographic set	Packaging process
Geographic set	Patent
Retailer	Science
Wholesaler	Material
Agent	Individual
Use	Management system
Application	Informatin system
Activity	Analytical skill
Franchise	Expert system
Location	Project control
Competitor	Quality attainment
Regulator	Project design

Issues That Arise in the Process of Creating Charters

Do we have to develop our own PIC, or are there standard ones to choose from?
The PIC should reflect the situation for which it is written. But there are useful concepts; for example, one set of options is: Prospectors (new business), Analyzers (new ways of doing current business), Defenders (moving early to protect a business), and Reactors (move after competitors do). But these are more aids to situation analysis than replacements for it.[22] Hewlett-Packard set out to beat the Japanese in printers, and cut a strategy from whole cloth—patents, cost cutting, price cutting, and the like.[23]

Now that a new products manager has written a PIC, is that it?   Hardly. Upper managements must approve them. Moreover, projects must usually share resources (R&D, process development, market research, and so on), so they must

---

[22]R. E. Miles and C. C. Snow, *Organizational Strategy, Structure and Process* (New York: McGraw Hill, 1978). Comments on this and similar analytical devices can be found in Michael H. Morris and Leyland F. Pitt, "The Contemporary Use of Strategy, Strategic Planning, and Planning Tools By Marketers: A Cross-National Comparison," *European Journal of Marketing*, no. 9 (1993), pp. 36–57.

[23]Stephan Krieder Yoder, "How H–P Used Tactics of the Japanese to Beat Them at Their Game," *The Wall Street Journal*, September 8, 1994, p. A1.

FIGURE 4–7   **Evaluation Forms for Market and Technology Opportunities**

Factors for Judging a Market Opportunity	*Score 1–5 Points*		*Factors for Judging a Technology Opportunity*
How large is the demand in this area? Is it, for us, a major source of new business or a minor one?	_____	_____	How unique is this technology? Are we the only ones who have it?
What is the current degree of felt need or unrest in this area? Do potential customers agree?	_____	_____	What is the value of things it does or permits us to do?
How well will our new product solve the customer's problem?	_____	_____	In what stage of the technology life cycle is this technology? (The earlier the better.)
How unique, relative to compttition, will our product be?	_____	_____	How controllable is it? Do we have it tied up with a patent, with licensing, as a trade secret?
How easy will it be for us to explain and demonstrate our new products?	_____	_____	Can we extand the technology by further work?
What is the life-cycle stage of the marketplace activity involved with this opportunity?	_____	_____	Is it going to be inexpensive for us to use, or will it take major investments?
Is there a ready technology that would match this opportunity?	_____	_____	Is it going to take a long time to use?
Is this market free of any entrenched competitors?	_____	_____	Will it take us into new, risky ball games?
Do we have a trade channel that fits this opportunity?	_____	_____	Are products of this technology marketable by us alone?
Is this opportunity easy for us to study?	_____	_____	Are products of this technology manufacturable by us alone?
Will this market opportunity stir controversy within the firm?	_____	_____	Will this technology receive the support of company people who must support it?
Total Score	_____	_____	(Over 35 in each column = Good.)

be coordinated. And they must fit together as a product innovation portfolio, in the usual financial sense.[24] When Nabisco won an Outstanding Corporate Innovator Award from the Product Development and Management Association in 1993, the company extolled its good strategies, but emphasized that a full set of solid management techniques made the strategies successful.

---

[24]Some of this is found in Timothy M. Devinney and David W. Stewart, "Rethinking the Product Portfolio: A Generalized Investment Model," *Management Science*, September 1988, pp. 1080–1095.

Are there differences in all this when the firm has a global perspective?
Only in amount, not kind. The more countries in which a firm operates, the more
options and opportunities it has. Some firms talk about "global" products.[25]

How does the idea of "strategic window" come into this process?   The concept of strategic windows does apply to new product strategic planning, because
being first or second has such large rewards. Yet, being too early has also cost
many firms dearly, so a fast window fly-by should not dominate common sense.

Where does licensing or acquisition fit in?   Acquirable technologies or market strengths are certainly fair game for inclusion in strategies. Upjohn originally acquired from Europe the U.S. rights to a product they named Motrin, and
just before the patent ran out they sublicensed the technology to two other manufacturers for what became Nuprin and Advil. Speculation is that they will do
the same thing on their hair-restorer Rogaine.

You haven't mentioned fads, yet millions of dollars are made this way.   Yes,
it seems to happen every day, but very few firms have a strategy of capitalizing
on fads. And few fad-based innovators succeed enough to have a strategy.

Do these new product strategic techniques apply to nonprofit organizations?
Indeed. A study of the best-run nonprofits contained comments about
problem analysis, unified sense of direction, incentives, fewer high-risk projects
when resources are limited, acquisition versus internal development, adapting
operations to a strong culture, orienting to the customer, and building coalitions.[26]

**Is strategic new product planning all good, or are there legitimate criticisms
of the approach discussed in this chapter?**   A cartoon often shown around
this field has a senior executive standing beside a person sitting at a drawing
board. The executive says: "Panelli, we've completed our market analysis. Design
something domestic and electrical."[27] Technical people, in particular, often object
to PICs. They sometimes ask whether Thomas Edison could have worked for
GE, the firm he founded. The answer is to have planned—as well as unplanned—
innovation. Many firms now have programs specifically designed to aid the boot-
legger or moonlighter. One 3M scientist received an Oscar from the Hollywood
film industry for his method of increasing the reflectiveness of movie screens,
but he had to develop the process at night and on weekends because his (strate-
gically driven) superior had to deny him time for it.[28]

---

[25]In the late 1980s, a Gillette scent expert was told to find his first "intentionally global"
fragrance. Barbara Carton, "Thank Carl Klumpp for the Swell Smell of Right Guard," *The Wall
Street Journal*, May 11, 1995, p. A1.

[26]John A. Byrne, "Profiting from the Non-Profits," *Business Week*, March 26, 1990, pp. 66–78.

[27]This cartoon is by "Nelson," but its origin is undocumented.

[28]The fabulously successful new product system used at 3M has been described many times, but
a good presentation is in "Masters of Innovation," *Business Week*, April 10, 1989, pp. 58–63.

Summary

Chapter 4 has dealt with the most important and difficult step in the entire new products process: developing a sound strategy to guide the subset of people and resources charged with getting new products. Strategy turns such a group into a miniature firm, a microcosm of the whole.

We first looked at what such strategic guidance might be—a format here called a product innovation charter. We then studied the sources of ideas and mandates that yield the charter and how the charter's three action sections can vary. The chapter ended by looking at some important issues that often arise when discussing new product strategy.

We can now begin the study of concept generation—the subject of three chapters in Part II.

Applications

More questions from the interview with the president:

1. "I'm afraid I don't follow your reasoning very well when it comes to this matter of innovativeness—being a pioneer, an adapter, quick second, and so on. Seems you've always got to come up with something new, or it simply won't sell. I believe we agreed on that earlier when we discussed the concept that winners market unique, superior products. Further, if you've got something new, why in the world would you ever want to be less than first to market with it? You'll lose your uniqueness that way. Sounds like you've taken a simple practice and made it complex."

2. "I didn't like what you said a minute ago about that internal mandate. I take it you were referring to top management. Well, the implication is that you new products people study markets and technical skills, make rational decisions, and come up with sound strategy, while presidents just shoot from the hip with a 'Do this' or 'Do that.' Is that what you really mean?"

3. "Somewhere along the line, R&D gets the short end of the stick. Now, I know about the arguments for strategy, but I really do feel that R&D deserves a better shake than to simply be told to do this or that. Some of our top people are in R&D—our electronics division has a couple of the world's best fax technicians. If I were doing it, I think I would have R&D prepare the first draft of a PIC, at least their areas of a PIC, and then have other areas like manufacturing add to it. When all of the interior departments have their sights properly set, I would ask marketing to reconcile the PIC with the marketplace. Otherwise, we'd have the tail wagging the dog when it comes to the new products function."

4. "We're a large corporation, with many businesses. So I can't really get a handle on this platform idea. Good concept, maybe, but not very operational. Several years ago, I spelled out seven cardinal guidelines for

all new product work in the firm. I suppose each group executive VP's platform would add some to that, and then each division management group would have its platform. If you carry that down to operating units, and marketing groups, there might be 25 drivers laid on any poor new products group before it even did its own thinking! Is this what you think really happens?"

CASE: MICROSOFT WINDOWS 95

On Thursday August 24, 1995, the greatest marketing event ever (or so thought observers at the time) took place. Not just in the United States, but around the world. Thousands of articles had been written about Windows 95, but on that day over 500 reporters descended on Redmond, Washington, to hear the country's richest man announce it, though over 2,000 beta test sites had been using it for up to two years. A PR extravaganza of the first order, the events of the day included perhaps a hundred million dollars of advertising, tall balloons, the Empire State Building swathed by color spotlights, dancers and music groups from Broadway to New Zealand, and long lines of people waiting at 11:59 P.M. on the 23rd to get an early package—including many who didn't particularly need the product at that time but wanted to be in on one of the truly all-time great hypes.

Meanwhile, back at the ranch, industry observers were thinking along other lines. They saw the announcements, but they speculated on what lay behind them. Microsoft (and Bill Gates) had done a lot of things the past few years, and word had leaked out about several more big ones coming over the next couple years. Windows 95, almost certain to be a dominant new industry standard, was part of a huge wave of activity in the general area of computer-based communications. Internal data processing and spreadsheets were important on PCs, but industry profits were thought to ride on networking, communicating *between* PCs and *between* PCs *and computers in other items such as printers and telephones.*

Many observers said Microsoft was not actually marketing an operating system (95), but another link in a larger system that would ultimately serve a market composed of managers of server computers and networks that run corporations. For example, in 1995 Merrill Lynch was buying 25,000 PCs and 600 servers to network their entire system of 600 regional offices and 12,000 brokers. Union Carbide announced plans to replace a mélange of servers and networked desktops (including 15 different e-mail systems) with 70 servers and Windows 95 on every desktop.

These people needed communication of all types. Microsoft was already marketing its Windows NT, a networking system. Another new product, combining Windows NT, Windows 95, and other tools, was scheduled for entry in 1996. Another item would be in team computing, using groupware, where IBM held sway at the time with Lotus Notes. Gates had admitted talking with Ted Turner and people at NBC relative to news services. To some, Microsoft seemed to be trying to serve the needs of all nontechnical people who wanted to use the information superhighway. Ease of use was a common phrase.

One observer voiced the opinion that Windows 95 would turn out to be Bill Gates's Trojan horse, particularly with its Miscrosoft Network (MSN) built in. Punch one button and

---

Source: This case is prepared from many public information sources.

be in the Internet. No need to rely on traditional access firms such as CompuServe or the hundreds of smaller firms around the world. No need to use the products of what threatened to be the toughest competitor Gates ever faced, Netscape Communications. Netscape was trying to develop any and all software used in the Internet, especially that used to stroll down the Web. Miscrosoft was said to be about ready to market Blackbird, software for "enriching" the Web sites.

Gates's actions made almost everyone in the industry an enemy. The Windows 95 launch had focused on managers at America Online and associates, Novell networking, IBM (again), Oracle, and on and on. Still, Microsoft had stubbed its toes in some ways. The firm had been years behind schedule on some products, and had failed outright on Microsoft At Work and others. Perhaps even more dangerous, industry had always feared being dependent on one supplier—already there was concern that Microsoft should not be allowed to push competition out. The Justice Department had protested the marketing of Windows 95 because of the Internet access program (MSN) in it, but they did not move to stop the launch.

Question: Given what you know about the computer world plus the information above, try to write out what the Windows 95 product innovation charter might have said. Follow the format of Figure 4–1. Include in the background section of that charter what higher level strategic plans may have been in place to help guide it.

The Concept Generation Process

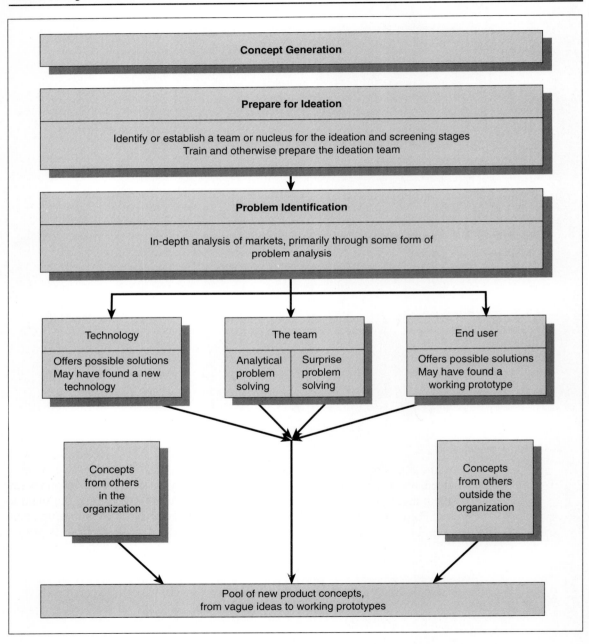

II   CONCEPT GENERATION

Chapter 3 showed the overall new products process, which provides for strategic planning first. The rationale is that one should seek new products that are best for the particular firm. Ideation goes on constantly. Many employees of every organization come up with new product possibilities, and in no way will the act of creativity ever be constrained into a diagram. That's part of the fun of it! But, there are common patterns, and we manage to those patterns.

Look at the figure on the opposite page. Starting at the top, we see Prepare for Ideation. People inside, and outside, the firm don't hold up ideating until we "prepare," of course, but managed creativity is much more successful if we assign much of the task to people with strong creative capabilities. Then, early on, we want to focus on problems and needs. So, by one means or another, we try to identify and clarify one or more specific problems that creativity can be focused on. Most of what follows does just that, but there still is a lot of freelance ideation going on.

Activity takes place in five areas, shown on the figure. On the left, most firms have a technology operation (R&D, engineering, whatever) in which completely new technologies (e.g., Kevlar, OCR) are being sought. Technical people are also on hand to help solve problems identified earlier. On the right side, end users (indeed, all stakeholders in the marketplace) also do freelance ideation, and some of them actually design their own products, produce prototypes, and put them to work. For example, a dentist or an X-ray technician may well conjure up some device this way. They, too, stand ready to help us solve problems we identify.

In the meantime, in the middle of the diagram, the in-house team members working on this project do their own problem solving. And, they engage in other activities (see Chapter 7) which produce "surprise" products. These, of course, are not problem-driven, so they must find out if someone has a problem that fits the "solution."

While all of this goes on, people everywhere are telling us about their ideas—employees throughout the organization, their families, complete strangers...everybody, it seems. They come in on the left and right sides of the figure, lower down. The consequence is a pool of ideas—we will call them concepts—and filling this pool is the subject of Chapters 5–7.

One caveat: Ideation is a huge topic, and there are hundreds of methods. The best are here, and a set of others often used is in Appendix B. What works on a pizza would not work on a fiber optic sensor. And nothing in the world of creativity lends itself very well to research, so what most firms do is what satisfies them.

5   CONCEPT GENERATION: PREPARATION AND ALTERNATIVES

Setting

This chapter takes us through four topics. First, to managers, comes the task of preparing the firm for ideation. This means getting the right people and putting them in the correct environment. Second, a creative person needs to know what is being searched for—that is, what is a concept and how is it typically found and identified? Third, you will explore a specific system of active (not reactive) concept generation, including approaches that seem to work. One part of that system—using employees and nonemployees in a search for ready-made ideas—will be discussed in this chapter, and the others will follow in Chapter 7.

Preparation

Many people think of product innovation beginning with a new product idea. But Chapter 4 showed it's far better to select a playing field and some rules (have a strategy) before starting the game.

The Product Innovation Charter

Think about these items from a hypothetical charter (Chapter 4) in a firm making bathtubs:

- Our new product concepts should be useful to older persons, and others with physical handicaps.
- New products coming from these concepts must make use of the firm's strong design capabilities, as well as copper metal.

Assuming the PIC work was well done, any person trying to come up with new bathtub ideas for this firm had better know the game plan, or many ideas created will simply be wrong. Strategy helps.

Finding the Right People

Organizations known for their innovative product programs are also known for being staffed with highly creative people. Deciding which people will be creative is not easy. Research has shown that cognitive abilities are essential, and one summary of the data cited intelligence, knowledge, and thinking style.[1] The intelligence is essentially IQ, especially for scientific fields, but non-IQ street smarts are felt to be equally important outside the highly technical areas. Knowledge means the breadth of background in the relevant field (the charter focused arena). Thinking style puts stress on the individual's ability to integrate, reorganize, or restructure existing understandings.

Being creative, to us, means getting ideas with a high degree of usefulness. Mental patients frequently have ideas, but they are not very useful in the new product sense. Conversely, the inventor of the Frisbee had a great idea, but it was apparently his only invention. We want people who are "quality prolific."

Research reports suggest two different types of creative people: those with artistic creativity and those with scientific creativity. But new product creatives (inventors, really) need both, as depicted in Figure 5–1. Engineers without the touch of the artist and artists without scientific strength are probably less successful in new products ideation.

The field of industrial design is so clearly a merger of art and engineering that controversy exists over which school in a university should house it. The inventor is not inconsistent if sensitive *and* analytical, intuitive *and* observant, impulse-sensitive *and* persevering.

Some great creative talent has been labeled eccentric. One historical review showed the following:

FIGURE 5–1

The Three Forms of Human Creativity

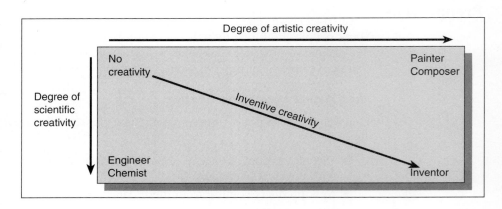

---

[1]Firdaus E. Udwadia, "Creativity and Innovation in Organizations," *Technological Forecasting and Social Change*, 1990, pp. 65–80.

Schiller kept rotten apples in his desk; Shelley and Rousseau remained bareheaded in the sunshine; Bossuet worked in a cold room with his head wrapped in furs; Milton, Descartes, Leibniz, and Rossini lay stretched out; Tycho Brahe and Leibniz secluded themselves for very long periods; Thoreau built his hermitage, Proust worked in a cork-lined room, Carlyle in a noise-proof chamber, and Balzac wore a monkish working garb; Grety and Schiller immersed their feet in ice-cold water; Guido Reni could paint and de Musset could write poetry only when dressed in magnificent style; Mozart, following exercise; Lamennais, in a room of shadowy darkness; and D'Annunzio, Farnol, and Frost, only at night.[2]

Most creative persons are not eccentric, but they do announce themselves by leaving a lifetime trail of creative accomplishments. They are creative as children and never become uncreative. This is the bottom line for us, since people being considered for new product team assignments can be evaluated on their past. People without a lifetime trail usually blame unfamiliar environments, overpowering bosses, limited opportunities, and the like.

Management's Role in Making Creative People More Productive

Creative people can benefit from training, though their personal capabilities serve as barriers to making them Einsteins. Figure 5–2 shows that we can enhance creativity, to a point. One study showed that 32 percent of firms were doing creativity training, using particularly (1) in-house courses, (2) the Center for Creative Leadership in Greensboro, North Carolina, and (3) the Center for Studies in Creativity at State University of New York at Buffalo. Many smaller companies have good reputations as suppliers of this training. As an executive at DuPont said: "We are in a race with a lot of competitors, here and abroad. If we

FIGURE 5–2

Creative Performance as a Two-Factor Consequence

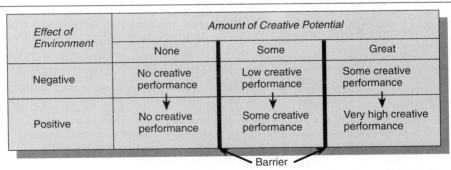

Comment: The environment (including management) can markedly increase an individual's creative performance, but only within the limits of the individual's basic creative potential.

---

[2]H. B. Levey, "A Theory Concerning Free Creation in the Inventive Arts," *Psychiatry*, no. 3 (1940), pp. 280–91.

are going to outperform them, we will have to think and act more creatively than they do."[3]

Such training programs run the gamut from introductory classes in traditional brainstorming to elaborate sessions that include games and horseplay. Some of the busiest creativity trainers use some of the wildest techniques, including variously colored hats and "guided fantasies." Obvious, but often overlooked, is training in the company's products, its markets, competition, technologies used, and so forth.

Newly born ideas are extremely fragile, quite the opposite of the strong and almost unstoppable concepts that are 80 percent of the way through the process. By then, many ideas have picked up one or more powerful "owners." So, if we give idea generators a hard time, show no appreciation for their ideas, offer no particular encouragement, they simply let the ideas slide by, vowing to "not waste my 'genius babies' on those clods." Or, they just don't seem to find the time to work them into more useful and acceptable shape.

John Cleese, of Monty Python fame, is now a training consultant. He jokes, "No more mistakes and you're through!" This sparks a sense of excitement in creative people, and there's nothing like excitement to get the innovative juices going.

Managements therefore have two packages of activity, one designed to encourage the creative function, and the other to remove roadblocks that thwart it.

Activities to Encourage Creativity

Today's managers recognize that innovators are apt to be different and need special treatment. *Accommodative* is the word. Innovators can't be allowed to violate rules at will, but it's good to recognize individuality, be tolerant of some aberrations, and be supportive under stress. Former Apple CEO John Sculley said: "I would worry if there weren't always a little bit of anarchy in the organization. It's like arsenic: A little is medicinal, but a lot can kill you."[4]

Too, managements should allow innovators freedom to associate with others in similar positions. This freedom extends to all functional areas and to outside the firm as well—no locked cells. Management should also permit innovators to help select projects for development, though this is often difficult. Job assignments should be challenging. Creative people don't lack confidence and, in fact, often consider their present assignments a waste of time. This means they will determine whether an assignment is worthy—no one can tell them.

Some firms deliberately create competitive teams and have them race to a deadline. Bell & Howell's management once faked the news of an impending competitive breakthrough to speed up a scientific group. Even without direct

---

[3]Ray Wise, "The Boom in Creativity Training," *Across the Board*, June 1991, pp. 38–42.

[4]"Sculley's Lessons from Inside Apple," *Fortune*, September 14, 1987, p. 117. This article speaks directly to the matter of managing creative people productively.

competition, people are more creative when they are actually asked to be—that is, told to seek novel solutions to problems.[5]

Another technique is "free time." It runs as high as 20 percent in some firms. The 3M Company is a major follower of this technique (with Post-it notes being one beneficiary). Flextime is a similar tool, but for creatives it means letting employees take work home or stay in their work places and work all night if they want.

Surprisingly perhaps, transferring creative personnel also helps. Creative people have a "need for novelty" and want to change situations occasionally.

Then, of course, we see a wide range of unique techniques developed by individual firms, especially those known for their creative achievements. Texas Instruments (TI), for example, had a program called IDEA (identify, develop, expose, and action). Sixty IDEA representatives throughout TI could dole out funds (without higher approval) for projects proposed by personnel who did not have enough influence to get funds through normal channels. Speak & Spell and Magic Wand were two notable results of such funds.

The 3M Company has a long history of innovation, so it is not surprising that a chairman once said: "We do expect mistakes as a normal part of running a business, but we expect our mistakes to have originality."[6] 3M is also known for its tolerance of tinkerers, an example being:

> Another young lab worker was experimenting with tiny glass beads, more a novelty than a product. He was told to get back to his regular work. And he did. But, fortunately, because he was a bachelor, he could return to his lab and his pet bead project after normal working hours. This he did, and many nights he burned the midnight candle. Today those tiny beads are on reflective road bridges and bridge safety signs all over the world. And, no longer a bachelor, he eventually took his wife to an Academy Awards presentation where he received an Oscar for a bead-based front screen projection system for moviemakers.[7]

A former president of Medtronic was once asked to fire an engineer who had been working at home, on his own time, on a project that had been refused funding. He didn't fire him, and eventually that product brought Medtronic over one billion dollars of earnings![8]

In general, creative operations should be in areas conducive to exchange of ideas, office arrangements should make people comfortable, and distractions should be held to a minimum.[9]

---

[5]Christina E. Shalley, "Effects of Productivity Goals, Creativity Goals, and Personal Discretion on Individual Creativity," *Journal of Applied Psychology*, April 1991, pp. 179–85.

[6]L. W. Lehr, "The Role of Top Management," *Research Management*, November 1979, pp. 23–25.

[7]Ibid., p. 24.

[8]Dale Olseth, at 1995 International Conference of the Product Development and Management Association.

[9]Many firms today achieve a good environment in California research centers. In one of them, IBMer Ted Selker had an idea: It took about one second for the hand to move from a keyboard to a mouse, and one second to return; the human thumb and forefinger have the greatest sensory and motor control. Ten years later, IBM marketed the ThinkPad, with Selker's fingertip device on it. Selker shows an amazing fit with the stereotype of inventor scientist. See Laurie Hays, "Abstractionist Practically Reinvents the Keyboard," *The Wall Street Journal*, March 6, 1995, p. B1.

A good summary of practice in some firms with reputations for creativity used these terms: Accommodate, stimulate, recognize, and reward, but also direct, protect, and be creative yourself.[10] The conclusion of that article was: "The chief rewards for most creatives remain exactly as H. L. Mencken described them more than 60 years ago: Freedom, opportunity, and the incomparable delights of self-expression."

Special Rewards

There is no question about the value of recognizing creative achievement. But, creative people are usually unimpressed by *group* rewards. They believe group contributions are never equal, especially if the group is company employees, for many of whom creatives have great disdain. This is unfair; large portions of successful creativity are now set in groups, and we know more now about how to make group judgments work. But creatives do like personal accolades—preferably immediately. The famous Thomas Watson of IBM commonly carried spare cash in his pockets so he could reward persons with good ideas when he heard them.

Some firms are more controversial—they give idea creators a piece of the action. For example, a chemical company manager said, "We are going to make you rich…10 percent of everything that comes in the door."[11] The practice is more common in Europe than in the United States, but no one seems to feel it will grow.

Campbell Soup has Presidential Awards for Excellence. Many firms have annual dinners to recognize employees who obtained patents during the year. In one of the most dramatic reward systems, Toyota and Honda have their champions follow the new product out the door and take over its on-going management.[12]

The Removal of Roadblocks

Figure 5–3 shows a compilation of "killer phrases" that can do so much to stop creativity. They are easy to use and occur regularly in conversation. They are often well-intentioned, and they may be accurate statements of status quo. But they are extremely discouraging to fragile ideas, and only conscious effort by managers can help scare them away.

Some organizations use a technique called itemized response. All client trainees must practice it personally. When an idea comes up, listeners must first cite all of its advantages. Then they can address the negatives, but only in a positive mode. The recommended language for bringing up a negative is as follows:

---

[10]Alan Farnham, "How to Nurture Creative Sparks," *Fortune*, January 10, 1993, pp. 94–100.

[11]Michael G. Duerr, *The Commercial Development of New Products* (New York: The Conference Board, 1986), p. 14. Unfortunately, Duerr tells of other cases where the threat of job loss was used effectively to motivate creative people.

[12]This idea, and many more like it, are discussed in Russell Mitchell, "Masters of Innovation," *Business Week*, April 10, 1989, pp. 58–62.

FIGURE 5–3   Killer Phrases: Roadblocks to Creativity in the Generation of New Product Concepts

"It simply won't work."
"Are you sure of that?"
"You can't be serious."
"It's against our policy."
"Let's shelve it for the time being."
"That won't work in our market."
"Let's think about that some more."
"I agree, but..."
"We've done it the other way for a long time."
"Where are you going to get the money for that?"
"We just can't do that."
"Who thought of that?"
"It's probably too big for us."
"I believe we tried that once before."

We don't usually do things that way."
"It seems like a gimmick to me."
"It's good, but impractical."
"That sounds awfully complicated."
"Production won't accept that."
"People will think we're crazy."
"Engineering can't do that."
"You could never sell that downstairs."
"But who is going to drive that idea?"
"OK, but let's slow down a bit."
"I'm afraid there's precedent in this."
"We have too many projects now."
"We'll need more background on that."

"OK. Now—let's see what would be the best way to overcome such-and-such a problem." Note that this constructive comment assumes the problem can be overcome, and the listener offers to help. Creative Realities, Inc., another creativity firm, uses modified versions of the same approach.

A classic review of history, *Failure of Success*, had a section presenting the most famous rejections of all time, one of which was by a journal editor to rocket pioneer Robert Goddard: "The speculation...is interesting, but the impossibility of ever doing it is so certain that it is not practically useful."[13] This shouldn't surprise us, given the conviction of many people that "managing creatives" is an oxymoron.

The Concept

Given creative and exciting people, just what is it we want them to produce? What is this thing called concept? How does it differ from a new product? When does it come about? (You may want to review the section entitled "The Concept Life Cycle" in Chapter 3.)

Let's start with the end point, the successful marketing of a new product, and back up. A new product only really comes into being when it is *successful*—that is, when it meets the goals/objectives assigned to the project in the PIC.

When launched, it is still in tentative form, because changes are quite apt to be necessary to make it successful. Therefore we say it is still a concept, an idea that is not fulfilled.

---

[13]Alfred J. Marrow, ed., *The Failure of Success* (New York: AMACOM, 1972), pp. 76–93. This section was subheaded "Rejection" and offered many examples.

Back before technical work was finished, the product was even more of a concept. To understand this, and see how it relates to the ideation process, we have to look at the three inputs required by the creation process.

- **Form.** This is the physical thing created, or in the case of a service, it is the sequence of steps by which the service is created. Thus, with a new steel alloy, form is the actual bar or rod of material. On a new mobile phone service it includes the hardware, software, people, procedures, etc., by which calls are made and received.

- **Technology.** This is the source by which the form was attained. Thus, for the steel alloy it included, among others, the steel and other chemicals used for the alloy, the science of metallurgy, product forming machines, cutting machines, and more. Technology is defined in product innovation as the power to do work, as you will recall from Chapter 4. In most cases there is one clear technology that is at the base of the innovation, the one that served as the technical dimension of the focus arena. Sometimes there are two.

- **Benefit.** The product has value only as it provides some benefit to the customer that the customer sees a need or desire for.

We put these together this way: *Technology permits us to develop a form that provides the benefit.* If any of those three is missing, there cannot be product innovation, unless one buys a product ready-made and resells it without change. Even then, there would be some change in the service dimension—where it is sold, how it is serviced, etc. Even clone makers add value, if nothing more than price; we even hear computer buffs say something like: "XYZ makes better clones than PDQ does!"

Oddly, the innovation process can start with any one of the three dimensions, and can vary in what happens second (see Figure 5–4). Here are the primary ways:

Customer has a NEED, which a firm finds out about. It calls on its TECHNOLOGY to produce a FORM that is then sold to the customer.

A firm has a TECHNOLOGY that it matches with a given market group, and then finds out a NEED that group has, which is then met by a particular FORM of product.

A firm envisions a FORM of product, which is then created by use of a TECHNOLOGY and then given to customers to see if it has any BENEFIT.

Any of the three can start the process, and in each case either of the other two can come second. Now, you may say, so what is the difference? The difference is too often that between success and failure. Putting benefit last is very risky, since it comprises a solution trying to find a problem. Du Pont for example spent many years finding applications where Kevlar could yield a profitable benefit.

Therefore, we like to put benefit first. Incidentally, even technology–driven scientists actually put benefit first in most cases because they have some idea of need that is leading them in their efforts. For example, a pharmaceutical

FIGURE 5–4

The New Product Concept

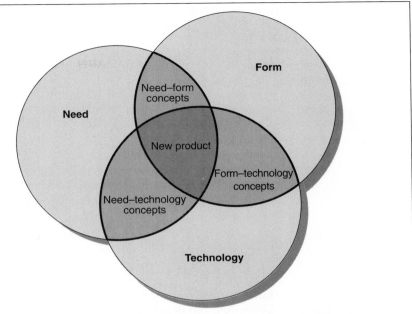

Concept: "A far better way of meeting the learning needs of computer users is to utilize modem-based online systems to let them see training videos on the leading software packages." (This has a well-known need/benefit and stipulates the several technologies that will be used; but exactly how this service will function is still to be worked out.)

Another way of stating this concept would be: "XYZ Corporation has a national telecommunications network in place, and also owns a chain of video rental stores. Surely there is some way we can use these capabilities to help meet the training needs of home-based computer users." Again, this offers the market need and the technologies; it still lacks method/process, which is the service product's equivalent of form. (Note how close a new product concept can come to sounding like the focus/arena of a Product Innovation Charter.)

Here are two statements that may *sound* like new product concepts, but clearly aren't:

"Let's create a new way of solving the in-home training/educational needs of personal computer users." (Need, but no form and no technology. Just a wish, like a cure for cancer.)

"I think we ought to develop a line of instructional videos." No specific market need/benefit, and no form—just a technology.

chemist seeking a new compound for lowering blood pressure knows how widespread that problem is. Given benefit, preferences vary. Some people like to visualize what type of finished product could meet the need, and then design that form. Others like to give technical people the basic benefit(s) and let them use their available technologies without restraint on form.

This book follows the latter approach. Granting that in practice, all versions exist, and no one would throw out a good idea just because it came up in the "wrong" way, the fact remains that we are speaking about management. If one wants to design the best way to go about product innovation, then, in general, the best way is to have first the benefit, then the technology, and then the finished form.

Thus, for example, the whole of Chapter 6 will deal with how we go to customers and find out what their problems are. In Chapter 10 we will talk about a form of product description (called a protocol) that is written out prior to undertaking technical development; the description is primarily benefits. Features (form) are put into it only if they seem absolutely essential (e.g., required by law).

Let's put this all into a simple case, and maybe the issues will become clearer.

The Soft Bubble Gum Example

Many years ago, bubble gum was sold in small chunks, rolls, or sheets. The material was quite hard and difficult to soften to where bubbles could be blown. Let's imagine we worked at a bubble gum company in those years. Imagine also three different people walked into the new products office one week, at different times, each with an "idea" for a new product. Each was unaware the others were coming in.

One person said: "Our most recent customer satisfaction report disclosed that consumers would like a bubble gum that doesn't take five minutes to soften up. No bubble gum offers this *benefit*." The second person was a product manager who said, "I was thinking last week about the features of bubble gums and noted that all of them are hard; maybe ours could be made softer, and flexible" (*form*). The third person was a scientist who had just returned from a technical forum and said, "I heard discussion of a new chemical mixing process that keeps foods from drying out; maybe it would be useful in our business" (*technology*).

Each of these people had a germ of an idea, but as a concept each suggestion wasn't really very useful. The first person had something on a par with a cancer cure—benefit, but no way to supply it. The product manager had no idea whether consumers would like flexible gum or how it might be made. The scientist didn't know what the technology would do to traditional bubble gum or whether consumers wanted a change.

A new product concept would result if the first person met up with either the second or the third. If the second, they would ask the lab for a technology that would produce the sought form and benefit. If the third, they would undertake lab work to find the exact form of the new technology (e.g., how soft).

What might best sum up the point that a concept is evolving from its creation until it metamorphoses into a new product, is the saying of one manager: "Don't waste your time trying to find a *great* new product idea; it's our job to take a rather ordinary idea and *make it* into a successful new product."

The Concept Statement

Ideas, concepts, new products, etc., are all words in common use. But, as in all disciplines, we have to clarify them for understanding. Medical books draw sharp distinction between common cold, sinusitis, upper respiratory infection, and so on, even though as patients, we don't care.

Figure 5–4 showed that any two of the three (form, benefit, technology) can come together to make a concept, a potential product. All three together produce a new product that may or may not be successful. Often, there is little difference. For example, inventors frequently call on companies with a prototype in hand. This is a concept that is virtually finished—it has form, based on a technology, and you can be sure the inventor knows a benefit it provides. Of course, firms know from experience that the inventor usually overstates the benefit, the technology will have drawbacks that make it impractical to use in a plant, and the form is very tentative, based primarily on tools and space in a crude workshop.

At the other extreme the very first thought about a new product may be so incomplete that nothing can be done with it as is. For example, the scientist returning from the technical forum had only capability—nothing that had value to anyone in the bubble gum firm.

Once a concept appears, with two of the three dimensions (technology, form, benefit), we have to screen it before undertaking development. That part of the process comes in Chapter 9, and it requires what we call a **product concept statement**. Technical people and intended customers must tell us the concept is worthy of development. Their review of the concept statement allows this *if* the concept tells them what they need to know to make that judgment. A concept statement will usually do this if it has two of the three basic essentials (technology, form, benefit).

If you were asked, "How would you like zero calorie ice cream?" you could not really answer. You probably already find yourself thinking, what will it taste like, what is it made of, what's the catch? To do concept testing, we need a concept statement that meets these information needs. It would be a waste of time to ask taxi company owners whether they would like a cab with a 10-cents-per-mile operating cost. They might say sure, but that answer would change quickly if told we planned to use Caterpillar tractor technology.

Sometimes the technology will tell us something useful about the concept: a flashlight that burns 10 times as bright because it uses arc-welding technology. Or, a light based on fiber optics technology that comes wound on a wooden spool of the size used for thread. Or, a flashlight that uses a pyramidal reflector rather than a conical one. Each of these statements offers more or less information and permits you to get better or worse reactions.

A concept, then, is *a verbal and/or prototype expression that tells what is going to be changed and how the customer stands to gain (and lose)*. Early on, the information is quite incomplete, but when marketed, the concept is (hopefully) complete. Anything that doesn't communicate gain and loss to the intended buyer is still just an idea that needs work.

An interesting demonstration of the three-facet concept source came when Eddy Goldfarb, a famous toy inventor, was asked how he did it. He replied, "Notice what things your child plays with, and try to spot what's lacking." He also said he likes to look for new processes and materials and "for holes—you know, a lack of a certain item on the market." These statements cite benefit, technology, and form, in that order.[14]

The importance of these three dimensions varies by industry. In most industries, one of the three often needs no attention because of general knowledge within the industry. Pharmaceutical new products people do not have to check out the desirability of stopping body fluid buildup or of eliminating cancer. Furthermore, pharmaceutical expertise is available to manufacture virtually any new drug, so technology is the only unknown—companies spend billions on that.

On the other hand, the leading food companies presume the kitchens and factory can put together anything the customer wants, so benefit (ascertained through taste tests, for example) becomes the prime variable.

In the automobile industry, car manufacturers so dominate the new products process that components suppliers are told what benefit is wanted and then work with either technology or form for its innovation.

In these three different industry situations, discussion with new products people quickly indicates the critical avenue of innovation for their firm or industry. And the distinctions are not moot—they provide the direction for the idea stimulation process.

Still, it takes all three. If a project aborts, it may be the fault of the department with the "easy" task. For example, a television manufacturer's marketing research may show that consumers want a television set that will increase in volume as room noise picks up and decrease in volume as room noise subsides. This research engenders the idea for the new product, so the process would be demand-induced. But, in reality, the technical side of the business has the toughest task.

The reverse of this came when a small Michigan firm attempted to find markets for a new development in reticulated vitreous carbon. The situation was clearly one where technology provided the breakthrough; but, again ironically, the pressure was on marketing to find applications to yield adequate volume for a profit. It couldn't, and the firm folded.

Two Basic Approaches

Now, given some agreement on language, we can go back to the original question: How should we go about generating new product concepts? The diagram given in the figure at the start of Part II showed five routes—technology, end user, team, other insiders, and other outsiders. Two of these involve receiving product ideas created by others, and three of them involve a managed process run by the team. This distinction is the one that makes managerial difference, and it is the one we will use in this book. Like getting a new garment, we can

---

[14]Fran Carpentier, "Can You Invent a Toy?" *Parade*, December 1981, pp. 14–15.

buy one ready-made or make it ourselves. Here we will discuss the ready-made source, and in Chapters 6 and 7, doing it ourselves.[15]

Of course, most firms use both ready-made and tailored. But in each industry it is common knowledge as to which has a better batting average. For example, food manufacturers usually will not even read new product suggestions sent in by consumers. They have more than enough concepts of their own, consumer suggestions are very repetitive or old ideas, and even just glancing at hundreds of thousands of ideas every year would be almost impossible.

Yet, in some other industries (e.g., toys and tools) inventors thrive. There are even inventors' fairs, where inventors are invited to display their creations. And some manufacturers have employee and customer idea contests. Even in the food industry, one firm (Pillsbury) has found it profitable to run an annual Bake-Off Contest to capture thousands of new recipes for their possible use. Some inventors become famous, such as Andrew Toti, now almost 80, a classic eccentric with *hundreds* of patents, and still active.[16]

One thing we know for sure: concept generation should be an active not reactive process. No Maytag repairmen, please!

Gathering Concepts Already Created

Experience in the field of product innovation has it that 40 to 50 percent of new product ideas are ready-made, coming at least partially from employees, suppliers, end users and other stakeholders, and published information. (See Figure 5–5.)

Many organizations have evolved ways (seminars, visits to customers' plants, etc.) to more systematically involve user groups because these groups have been so productive. ARCO actually ran full-page *Wall Street Journal* ads that reproduced good suggestions sent in by the public and encouraged more.

Appendix A lists and discusses the most common sources of ideas already created. They are many, diverse, and of varying quality. However, one of those sources deserves special attention—the customer, consumer, user. People who use a product often have ideas for improving it, but unfortunately, their ideas are usually rather obvious. Black & Decker reportedly received over a thousand suggestions for a new product that would be a Dust-Buster type bug catcher.

Even if new, most consumer users' concepts are for product improvements, not significant line extensions or new-to-the-world products. But, in some industries, the end user plays quite a different role. For example, manufacturers of scientific instruments and plant process equipment report the

---

[15]In the discussion of creativity methods that follows through Chapters 5, 6, and 7, plus the methods in Appendix B, we cannot possibly cover all methods that have been suggested. For those who want more, see Trevor Sowrey, *The Generation of Ideas for New Products* (London: Kogan Press, 1987).

[16]Michael Ryan, "Don't Throw Out That Good Idea," *Parade*, June 11, 1995, pp. 12–13.

FIGURE 5–5

*Sources of
Ready-Made New
Product Concepts*

*The Best Sources
Have Bold Box Lines*

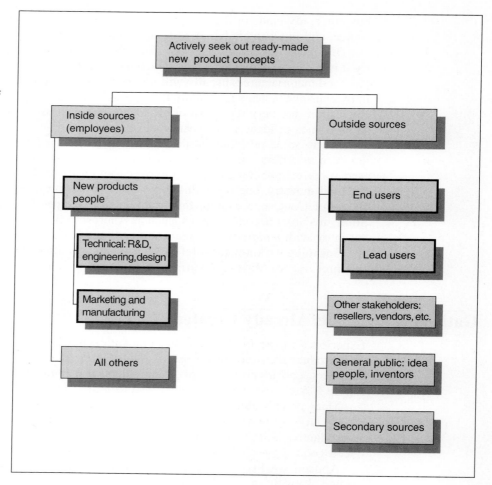

majority of their successful new products came originally from customers. (In contrast, manufacturers of engineering polymers and of chemical additives for plastics report no projects coming from customers.)

The most useful development in user-oriented ideation involves identifying the **lead** (meaning out-in-front) users associated with a significant current trend (e.g., fiber optics in telecommunications).[17] These firms (or individuals) are at

---

[17]The best summary of findings and recommendations in this area can be found in writings of the person who essentially invented the approach: see Eric von Hippel, *The Sources of Innovation* (New York: Oxford University Press, 1988). A later version is Cornelius Herstatt and Eric von Hippel, "From Experience: Developing New Product Concepts via the Lead User Method: A Case Study in a 'Low-Tech' Field," *Journal of Product Innovation Management*, September 1992, pp. 213–21.

the leading edge of the trend, have the best understanding of the problems faced, and expect to gain significantly from solutions to those problems. Although usually fairly easy to identify, they may also be outlanders, or not established members of that trade. And, if they are really leaders, they may think they have already solved their problems. But in an evolving trend, their solutions will not hold up; product developers can work with them to anticipate their next problem. Lead users are especially helpful in giving new product ideas because their work is of the problem-find-solve type, a method stressed in the next chapter.

One way to determine whether a particular industry can benefit from working directly with users to gather concepts is to ask whether customers are tinkerers. For example, dentists are; so are medical technicians and farmers. In some of these industries, the participants not only have good ideas, but have prototypes as well, and may even have undertaken a form of manufacturing by making prototypes for their friends.

In time, we will probably see less emphasis placed on going to end users for new product ideas because we are now involving end users so effectively on our new product teams. (See Chapter 13.) This brings their needs and problems directly onto the table. But there will always be firms where they don't wait to be asked—they go right ahead and prototype up their ideas. A new example of this today is the information technology field, especially computers and telecommunications, where end users have become quite sophisticated.

The use of the public at large, rather than end users, came out lately when NordicTrack won the Outstanding Innovator Award from the Product Development and Management Association. In the company presentation to the conference, the new products manager gave complete credit to its complement of freelance inventors; the firm does no systematic ideation itself (no R&D), because it gets such a good flow of good ideas from inventors, which, incidentally, it cultivates much as internal creatives are cultivated.

Not as dramatic, but as a demonstration that good ideas can come from almost anywhere, is the case of Nicholas Graham, founder of the Joe Boxer Corporation. His rock singer career failed to pay the rent so he turned to bold-patterned neckties. These sold well, and a Macy buyer suggested the patterns might look great on boxer shorts. He made them, they sold well too (both for male and female, apparently), and he quickly became a millionaire.[18]

New products managers also do not forget employees outside the mainstream of technical or marketing new product work. In fact, collecting these ideas is thought to be so desirable that a new method has been developed for it, and case studies are now beginning to appear.[19]

---

[18]Randall Lane, "The Boxer Rebellion," *Forbes*, September 12, 1994, pp. 74–78.

[19]The method, called Organization Sweep, is discussed in Chris Miller, "Panning for Gold," *Visions*, published by the Product Development and Management Association, July 1994, pp. 6–9. The case history is Jeff D. Felberg and David A. DeMarco, "From Experience: New Idea Enhancement at Amoco Chemical: An Early Report from a New System," *Journal of Product Innovation Management*, December 1992, pp. 278–86.

Summary

Chapter 5 has introduced concept generation for new products. First we noted that management has the task of preparing an organization for concept generation. This includes applying the strategic guidance of a product innovation charter, finding and training creative people, and then creating an environment for them to work in where they can be motivated to produce.

Next came a look at the concept itself, what it is, what it isn't, and how it comes into existence. The concept is built around ideas of technology, form, and benefit, and is tested by whether it can communicate to an intended buyer what the proposed product is all about and whether it appears useful.

After noting that there are two broad categories of approaches to getting good new concepts, we explored the one that involves looking for ready-made concepts. Many firms use this approach heavily, and all should make at least some use of it. There are legal problems here, of course, and the chapter concluded by outlining the steps to follow in handling ideas that come from nonemployees.

This prepares us to look at the most difficult, but by far the best, method for creating new product concepts: problem-based ideation. This is the subject of Chapter 6.

Applications

More questions from that interview with a company president:

1. "You mentioned this guy Nicholas Graham, the one who introduced those boxer shorts with loud and colorful designs. I didn't know what was going on at the time, but I was flying Virgin Air to London one night and a couple people from that firm stood up, and began passing out yellow boxer shorts decorated with eyes and smiles. They invited everyone to put them on and then parade up and down the aisle singing songs. Belive it or not, many did. Now, I found out later that the Britisher who owns Virgin also owns Joe Boxer. So when you told me about that great idea coming from a Macy buyer, I had to laugh. Seems to me that the admittedly great boxer shorts were more a promotional success than a creative one. With marketing people like those at Joe Boxer, who needs great new product concepts?"

2. "I found it very interesting that your professor wants the new product project to end only when it achieves the success expected of it. As the person giving them the money for that project, I sure agree. But, that means the marketing people are sort of carrying the ball for the technical people. You know, technical made it and the sales force sells it. If the sales and marketing people fail to do their jobs, the technical people go down the drain with them. That doesn't sound right, somehow."

3. "In-house inventors are tough to deal with. Right now we have this Ph.D. in physics, a really great person, bright as they come, and terribly creative. Has had no less than 11 ideas go to market since she joined the firm four years ago. But she feels we don't reward her properly, even though she is on a good salary, shares an annual bonus with all the other persons in research, and even got a special bonus of $5,000 last year. Frankly, I think she will leave us if I don't find some way to let her have an equity position in some of her ideas. What do you think of her argument, and how might I arrange something if I wanted to?"

4. "We have a small operation in Spain, running a computer repair, resale, and rental operation, for businesses, not residential. They are supposedly trying to be creative and innovative, but so far as I can tell they haven't had a good new service idea for four years. I've got my eye on a good consultant to go in there and review their environment, their motivating systems, and so on, but first I want to know if they have creative people. How could I find that out?"

CASE: THE KIDS WISE UP

Here are some sad tales from 1989:

Educational toy chain Enchanted Village carried chemistry sets, computers, and the like—and went out of business after five years.

Video Technology, Inc., marketed a new educational video system called Socrates. But after lackluster sales, the firm turned to noneducational toys to increase its business.

Chemistry and biology sets in 1988 were down 27 percent from 1987.

The *Master Scientist* and *Monster Lab* series was discontinued by Mattel early in 1989. *Talking Toby*, a 10-pound plastic robot that Coleco created to play word games with eight-year-olds, was withdrawn from the market after a year.

What was going on? Some people thought the educational toy market had hit its peak and was a typical mature market. A stock market analyst said calling a toy educational was the kiss of death. The term *edutainment* was dead. Enthusiastic parents who liked to flash cards in front of crib children had apparently slacked off or gone to other devices. The result was the demise of specialty retailers like Enchanted Village.

Marketing research showed that about two-thirds of educational toy sales were from electronic toys and building sets. Staple lines (such as puzzles, word games, and flash cards) made up the rest.

Some of the reasons were thought to be known: some educators had been less than enthusiastic, the developers had sometimes created confusion about exactly what their products were, and child development experts sometimes told parents to just let their children play.

Source: Based partly on Joseph Periera, "Educational Toys Receive a Failing Grade as Kids Wise Up to Their Parents' Game," *The Wall Street Journal,* April 11, 1989, p. B1.

Worst of all, perhaps, the basic idea—parents should use toys to con their children into more school when they thought they were playing—hadn't worked. The kids caught on fast. And, of course, many of these edutainment toys were not entertaining. Toby, for example, was a one-trick robot.

Not all educational toy producers were willing to throw in the towel. Video Technology was focusing its attention on preschoolers, and others were trying toys that actually were more fun, like educational characters such as Big Bird and Cookie Monster. The founder of Enchanted Village was about to open a new chain of mom-and-pop stores in academically oriented neighborhoods.

Some toy makers felt the problem was that they hit a really good idea only rarely; when they did, sales were fine, and even the 1988 market share of 5 percent yielded sales of around $750 million for all educational toys. So, one issue seemed to be how they should go about getting new product concepts.

They knew they got hundreds of ideas each year, with no end of inventors in garages and basements around the world. Maybe these ideas should have been studied more carefully. Too, they knew their own staffs had literally thousands of ideas, generated from spending their time making and selling the current lines.

But these approaches had always been available, and as one said, "Look where we are!" One toy developer said she wanted to get into a new dimension of creativity—something that would produce toys that were genuinely fun, so much fun that kids would want to play with them as such. Yet these toys would be almost secretly educational. But how to do that, she didn't know. She did know that she couldn't survey kids and ask them what problems they had. And she had great faith in her own creative skills, if she could just think of a new way to give them a new boost of power. An environment, a technical stimulus, some motivational device, a thought-jogger, what? Supposedly, creative people could come up with new things, including methods of creativity.

6   CONCEPT GENERATION: PROBLEM-BASED IDEATION

Setting

Chapter 6 will be devoted to what is the most productive concept generating system that we know—the problem-based approach of finding and solving customers' problems.[1] It seems obvious, and easy. Ask customers what their problems are and have a scientist put together the solution! But, it's not that simple.

Just getting customers involved is often difficult. Learning their toughest problems is more difficult, partly because they often don't know their problems very well. Many departments of a firm may be involved, not just the technical ones. You might want to glance back at the diagram on the page starting Part II, which shows how problem-based ideation fits in with other gathering of new product concepts.

The Overall System of Internal Concept Generation

Every ideation situation is different and varies by the urgency, the skills of the firm and its customers, the product, the resources available, and so on. But, one general approach, that of problem-based ideation, works best, and can be modified to fit virtually every situation. The steps are diagrammed in Figure 6–1.

The flow, essentially, is from study of the situation, to use of various techniques of problem identification, to screening of the resulting problems, and to development of concept statements that will then go into the evaluation

---

[1]Regardless of today's popular emphasis on creativity, Doug Carlston, CEO of Broderbund, insists he does best building software (even for children) squarely on needs. See Andrew Kupfer, "Identify a Need, Turn a Profit," *Fortune,* November 30, 1992, pp. 78–79.

FIGURE 6–1

*Problem-Based
Concept
Generation*

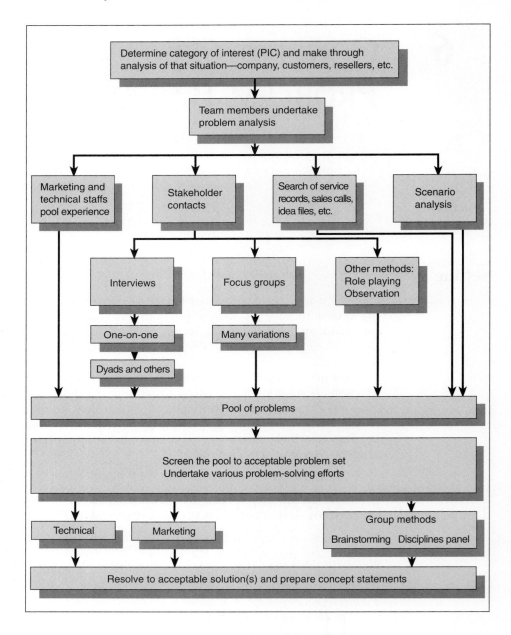

phase. The whole system is based on close involvement with parties who have information to help us, primarily stakeholders, the biggest part of which are end users.[2]

Recall from Chapter 3 that the leading cause of new product failure is the absence of a perceived need by the intended end user. If our development process begins with a problem/need the end user has and agrees is important, then we have answered the toughest question. Fortunately, organizations today are getting close to their stakeholders. (See Chapter 2.) But stakeholder integration is especially tough on high-security new product matters. So we figure out how to do it, just as customer satisfaction managers have. New ways appear almost daily. For example, Martin-Marietta has what the Japanese call an antenna shop in Reston, Virginia, where 33 high-power work stations sit in readiness for customers to visit, try out the firm's latest software developments, talk with company people about their problems on software, and actually take short steps toward developing new software there in the facility.

Gathering the Problems

Figure 6–1 showed four sources for needs and problems of stakeholders. Two of these involve direct access within the firm, a third calls for problem analysis, and the fourth for scenario analysis.

Internal Records

The most common source of needs and problems comes from an organization's routine contacts with customers and others in the marketplace. Daily or weekly sales call reports, findings from customer or technical service departments, and tips from resellers are examples.[3] Sales files are peppered with customer (and reseller) suggestions and criticisms. Warranty files will show where problems are. Customer satisfaction studies are useful, as are the files of the groups working on total quality management.

Industrial and household consumers sometimes misunderstand products and erroneously project into their use of products what they are *seeking*. A complaint file thus becomes a psychological projective technique. One approach to handling user complaints is the hot line or toll-free number. It helps defuse

[2]Chapter 2 described the term *stakeholder* as the full set of end users and all persons who influence the behavior of the end users—advisors, financiers, consultants, architects, physicians, even many resellers. In some markets, such as that for medical equipment, the nonusers may be more influential than users are. See Wim G. Biemans, "User and Third-Party Involvement in Developing Medical Equipment Innovations," *Technovation,* April 1991, pp. 163–81.

[3]Research regularly documents the role of sales/customer contacts. For application among high-tech firms, see Teresa Pavia, "The Early Stages of New Product Development in Entrepreneurial High-Tech Firms," *Journal of Product Innovation Management,* March 1991, pp. 18–31.

criticism and can lead to new products. And at least one firm's R&D employees actually work at customer sites to hear their problems firsthand. Hallmark and American Greetings have carried market contacts to a new level by mall-installations of kiosks where consumers can actually create their own new cards. American calls it Creatacard and learns from what the customers create.

Unfortunately, long-standing problems can become "part of the wallpaper" and thus forgotten. The routine market contacts should be heavily supplemented with the technique of problem analysis.

Direct Inputs from Technical and Marketing Departments

Understanding about end users and other stakeholders also lies in the minds of marketing and technical people. Most of them have spent time with customers and end users, sometimes many years of it. Team representatives from these two functions should canvass their colleagues, seeking out every piece of evidence on problems. They have to take the initiative on this, because most of these people are busy; it's strictly "you call me."

It's good to remember too that technical people may be found anywhere in the business, not just in R&D or engineering—especially in manufacturing, technical service, and regulatory affairs. Sales people may not be considered in marketing, and thus are sometimes overlooked.

The only real problems with using in-house people to report on customer problems are (1) each suggestion is usually someone's perception of what the customer problem is, and (2) there is usually a solution given with each suggestion. In fact, sometimes we have to ask what new product customers are asking for and then ask why; the why is what we want to know at this time.

These problems, including the time and difficulty of actually gathering memories, lead us to depend more on active search for stakeholder problems. That is, making direct contact with all relevant stakeholders, asking them what their problems and needs are. And, although all of the above market contacts and searches around the firm help us compile useful problems, the methods of direct user contact are what we usually mean when we say problem analysis.

Problem Analysis

It seems that every history of an industry, a business firm, or a famous businessperson cites some key time when a new good or service capitalized on a problem that others didn't sense or appreciate. But, **problem analysis** is much more than a simple compilation of user problems. Although the term *problem inventory* is sometimes used to describe this category of techniques, taking the inventory is only the beginning—analysis is the key.

As an advertising agency executive once said: If you ask people what they want in a new house and also ask them what are their problems with their current house, you will get distinctly different subject matter on each list. If you then observe their subsequent behavior, it becomes clear their problem list is a far better predictor than the want list.

Users verbalize their wants in terms of current products, whereas problems are not product specific. Thus, if you ask what a person needs or wants from a shampoo, the answers will be clean hair, manageable hair, and so on—replies reflecting recent promotions of product benefits. But if you ask, "What problems do you have with your hair?" the answers may range into areas (e.g., style or color) unrelated to shampoo. See Figure 6–2 for an example of what we are looking for in problem analysis.

The General Procedure

There are several variations in problem analysis. But the general approach is the following:

Step One: Determine the appropriate **product or activity category** for exploration. This has already been done if the product innovation charter has a use, user, or product category dimension in the focus statement.

Step Two: Identify a group of **heavy product users** or activity participants within that category. Heavy users are apt to have a better understanding of the

---

FIGURE 6–2   Problem Analysis Applied to the Telephone

Here are 22 telephone problems that came up in a consumer study. See if you can generalize to a smaller number of problems. Then select the one big problem that sounds most productive for telephone new products people.

Keeping the unit clean.
It keeps falling to the floor.
Getting entangled with the cord.
Finding it in the dark.
Getting privacy in the house.
Who "out there" can hear me?
Staying away from message phones.
Getting past message phones.
Difficult in looking up numbers.
Dealing with the busy signal.
Hard to hold, if arthritic.
Can't just move the phone from room to room, building to building.
Peddlers and pollsters.
My arm and ear get tired.
Bell ringing conflict: too loud but sometimes I can't hear it.
It is a very disruptive instrument.
I can't see facial and body language.
Getting flustered making emergency calls.
People who call wrong number in the middle of the night.
Fear of what a ringing may be for.
"If you want Sales, punch 1," etc.
Knowing when to call people, the best time.

problems, and they represent the bulk of the sales potential in most markets. A variation is to study nonusers to see if a solvable problem is keeping them out of the market.

Step Three: Gather from these heavy users or participants a **set of problems** associated with the category. Study the entire system of product use or activity. This is the inventory phase mentioned earlier, but far more is involved than just asking respondents to list their problems. A good method of doing this is asking respondents to rate (1) the benefits they want from a set of products and (2) the benefits they are *getting*. The differences indicate problems. Complaints are common, and often taken as requests for new products. But they are apt to be just the result of omniscient proximity, meaning that users face a minor problem frequently so it is the first one mentioned. Some firms have had success observing consumers or business firms actually use products in a given category—for example, observing skiers as they shoot down a hill, or office workers handling a mailing operation. More on this in a minute.

Step Four: Sort and **rank the problems** according to their severity or importance. Various methods can be used for this, but a common one is shown in Figure 6–3. It utilizes (1) the extent of the problem and (2) the frequency of its occurrence. This "bothersomeness" index is then adjusted by users' awareness of currently available solutions to the problem. This step identifies problems that are important to the user and for which the user sees no current solutions.

Georgena Terry made a special study of women's bicycle needs and came up with a line of bikes that have shorter tubes to permit reaching the handlebars more easily, smaller brake levers and toe clips, and wider seats. An interesting feature of her bikes is a smaller front wheel, which gives better stability.[4]

Another unmet need that had existed for years was the noisy candy wrapper in the theater. Gene Shalit, then of NBC's "Today Show," complained one

---

FIGURE 6–3   The Bothersomeness Technique of Scoring Problems

The following is an abbreviated list of pet owners' problems found by manufacturers of pet products.

	A Problem Occurs Frequently	B Problem Is Bothersome	C $A \times B$
Need constant feeding	98%	21%	.21
Get fleas	78	53	.41
Shed hairs	70	46	.32
Make noise	66	25	.17
Have unwanted babies	44	48	.21

Source: Burton H. Marcus and Edward M. Tauber, *Marketing Analysis and Decision Making* (Boston: Little, Brown, 1979), p. 225.

---

[4]Mary Guterson, "A Bicycle Built for Women," *Venture*, April 1987, p. 15.

morning about crackling candy bar wrappers. An expressway-commuting executive from Hercules, Inc., overheard his comment and asked the laboratory for a "silent candy wrapper." Polypropylene provided the answer, though not without tricky effort on heating, waterproofing, and airproofing.

Another problem that had been obvious for years was only recently solved—making scissors that have vertical squeezing action and horizontal blade action. The leverage makes weak hands effective working units. Still another problem was found where people would have bet there were none—in the consumption of yogurt. When asked, people said they always wished for something to chew on! General Mills answer: *Yoplait Crunch 'N Yogurt*—over $50 million the first year, just sitting out there waiting for someone to ask!

Another classic occurred when Nike let Reebok storm past them in the women's market for athletic shoes—Reebok simply went out and talked to women about their athletics—and found them with leg and knee injuries sustained while doing aerobics. Out came a special line of shoes. Nike started pouncing on every consumer need—by 1994 they had 799 shoe models!

Problem analysis is especially appropriate for firms in a global operation. For example, bathroom fixture makers completely missed Japanese women's special need for an oversize sink. Because the Japanese typically bathe in the evening, and young women like to wash their hair in the morning, a larger sink sold well.

Methodologies to Use

The generalized structure of problem analysis still contains the question of how to gather the list of consumer problems. Many methods have been used, but the task is difficult. The consumer/user often does not perceive problems well enough to verbalize them. And, if the problems are known, the user may not agree to verbalize them (for many reasons, including being embarrassed). Much of the sophistication in newer technologies was developed specifically to deal with these problems, and will be discussed in Chapter 7.

Experts.   We have already mentioned going to the experts—using them as surrogates for end users, based on their experience in the category under study. Such experts can be found in the sales force, among retail and wholesale distribution personnel, and in professionals who support an industry—architects, doctors, accountants, and the staffs of government bureaus and trade associations. Zoo experts first publicized the problem of elephant keepers being killed when trying to cut the big animals' toenails. Today an Elephant Hugger grabs an elephant, rolls it over on its side and holds it there, while the keeper cuts away. The inventor is now working on a giraffe-restraining device.[5]

---

[5]Laura E. Keeton, "Marketers Debate the Best Way to Trim an Elephant's Toenails," *The Wall Street Journal*, February 25, 1995, p. B1.

Published Sources.   Also as mentioned earlier, published sources are frequently useful—industry studies, the firm's own past studies on allied subjects, government reports, investigations by social critics, scientific studies in universities, and so on.

Stakeholder Contacts.   The third, and most productive, is to ask household or business/industry consumers directly. The most common method of doing this, by far, is direct, one-on-one interviewing. Sometimes this is a full-scale, very formal, and scientific survey. Other times the discussion is with lead users, an idea-generating method discussed in Chapter 5; lead users often are the first to sense a problem, and some go on to respond to it themselves. Still other times, it may be no more than conversations with some key customer friends at a trade show, because a problem statement may come from only one person and yet be very significant for us. Because many end users don't think all that much about the products they use, and often just accept them as parts of living, even very informal discussions with individuals can reopen thinking, and bring to mind things forgotten.

A second technique for stakeholder inquiry, and a popular one, is the **focus group.** The focus group is designed to yield the exploratory and depth-probing type of discussion required and it *can be* easy and inexpensive to set up and use. If done wrong, it only *appears* that way. Granted, in this case we are not seeking facts or conclusions, just genuine problems, and the focus group method works well by stimulating people to speak out about things they are reluctant on when in one-on-one interview situations. It's much easier to talk about one's problems when others in the group have already admitted they have problems too.

But, even in a single focus group, the costs are deceptive. Such sessions can cost from $3,000 to $10,000 in normal usage. Even at $3,000, a two-hour meeting of 10 people will yield about 10 minutes of talk per participant. Since the cost is $300 per participant, that's talk at the rate of $30 per minute, or $1,800 an hour! It had better be very good indeed.

Although the focus group technique is common, the outcome is not always, or even usually, successful. The focus group is a **qualitative** research technique. Unlike the traditional survey, it depends on in-depth discussions rather than the power of numbers. A problem analysis focus group should be asked:

- What is the real problem here—that is, what if the product category did not exist?

- What are the current attitudes and behaviors of the focus group members toward the product category?

- What product attributes and benefits do the members of the focus group want?

- What are their dissatisfactions, problems, and unfilled needs?

- What changes occurring in their lifestyles are relevant to the product category?[6]

Other suggestions for helping guarantee the usefulness of focus group findings are to invite scientists and top executives to the sessions, and to avoid what some people call **prayer groups:** managers sit behind the mirror and pray for the comments wanted rather than really listening to what users are saying. Be sure the focus groups are large enough for the interactions and synergy that make them successful, and don't expect focus group members to like your products, or care about the activity being studied, or be consistent, or hold back from hurting your feelings.[7] Today we are hearing of cyberspace focus groups or digital focus groups, mini-focus groups (2–4 people), and other modifications.

Yet another method of gathering problems directly from stakeholders is that of **observing them.** It often uses the technology of work simplification. One firm studied the maintenance and cleaning of hospital floors by setting up a special motion study laboratory where hospital personnel were brought in to clean floors under observation by company personnel. Observation may also be quite simple—as when Ziba Design noticed people holding to the crosspiece of a window washing squeegee, rather than to the handle. So the firm designed a new squeegee without a handle, just a round holder for the rubber strip.[8]

Another stakeholder contact method is **role playing**. Though role playing has long been used in psychology to enhance creativity, there is little evidence of its successful use in generating ideas for new products. Presumably, it would be valuable in instances where product users are unable to visualize or verbalize their reactions. It should also be valuable where consumers are emotionally unable or unwilling to express their views—for example, in areas of personal hygiene.

Unfortunately, though users are the best place to begin the ideation, and problem analysis is widely used in one form or another, most firms still do not have organized systems to exploit this source. Considering that Levi Strauss got the idea for steel-riveted jeans from a Nevada user in 1873, one must wonder why not.[9]

---

[6]"When Using Qualitative Research to Generate New Product Ideas, Ask These Five Questions," *Marketing News,* May 14, 1982, p. 15.

[7]Judith Langer, "Personal Encounters with Buyers the Key to Successful New Products," *New Product Development* [newsletter], February 1988, p. 5. For good advice on the running of new product focus groups, see Edward F. McQuarrie and Shelby H. McIntyre, "Focus Groups and the Development of New Products by Technologically Driven Companies," *Journal of Product Innovation Management,* March 1986, pp. 40–47. A comprehensive source on all aspects of the subject is Jane Farley Templeton, *Focus Groups* (Chicago: Probus Publishing, 1987).

[8]Industrial designers are increasingly involving the end user. Three case histories (two of them services) are discussed in Susan Ciccantelli and Jason Magidson, "From Experience: Customer Idealized Design: Involving Customers in the Product Development Process," *Journal of Product Innovation Management,* September 1993, pp. 341–47.

[9]Two general sources that are helpful on the matter of working with customers are P. Ranganath Nayak, Albert C. Chen, and James F. Reider, "Listening to Customers," *Prism,* Second Quarter 1993, pp. 43–57; and Karl T. Ulrich and Steven D. Eppinger, *Product Design and Development* (New York: McGraw-Hill, 1995).

Scenario Analysis

So far, we have talked about going to technical and marketing people within the firm for ideas on customer problems, about searching the many files and record-keeping places where customer concerns can be found, and about problem analysis. The fourth general method shown in Figure 6–1, **scenario analysis**, comes into play because the ideal problem for us to find is one the end user *will* have, but does not at this time. A future problem is a good problem because most problems we find in interviews and focus groups have already been told to competitors and anyone else who will listen. Providers of the goods and services have been working on them for many years, for example, flimsy music stands and steam on bathroom mirrors. We have time to solve a *future* problem and have that solution ready to market when the time comes.

Unfortunately, end users usually don't know what their future problems will be. And they often don't really care, not right now. So they are not much help in interviews. This is where scenario analysis becomes valuable. Here's how it works.

If we were to describe apartment life 20 years from now, we would probably see lots of windows and sunlight coming in. If a furniture manufacturer were doing this scenario analysis, an analyst could immediately see problems and possible solutions: those apartment dwellers will need (1) new types of upholstery that are more resistant to the sun and (2) new types of chairs that will let them continue such activities as conversing and eating but also let them gain exposure to all that sunlight.

The Whirlpool Corporation has had a continuing task force painting a picture of what life will be like in the kitchen and laundry room when the United States hits a predicted water shortage crisis. This tells them what problems we *will be* having, and they will be ready with a line of appliances that will wash with very little (or actually no new) water.

The scenario analysis procedure is evident: first, paint a scenario; second, study it for problems and needs; third, evaluate those problems and begin trying to solve the most important ones. Painting a scenario does not yield a new product concept directly; it is only a source of problems, which still must be solved.

Scenarios take several different forms. First, we distinguish between (1) **extending** the present to see what it will look like in the future and (2) **leaping** into the future to pick a period that is then described. Both use current trends to some extent, of course, but the leap method is not constrained by these trends. For example (all hypothetical, including the numbers) an extend study might be: Currently, homeowners are converting from individual housing to condominium housing at an annual rate of 0.9 percent. If this keeps up for 20 years, there will be 7 million condominium units in use, which will present a need for 250,000 "visitors'" motel units in major condominium areas to house visitors who cannot stay in the smaller units with their hosts. The thinking of the "utopian" school is sometimes used.

By contrast, a leap study might be: Describe life in the year 2010 in a major urban area of Germany contrasted with life in a similar setting in France.

Leap studies can be **static** or **dynamic.** In dynamic leap studies, the focus is on what changes must be made between now and then if the leap scenario is to come about—the interim time period is the meaningful focus. In static leaps, there is no concern about how we get there. Figure 6–4 shows a dynamic leap period in which the auto dealer service problem no longer exists. The time between now and then is broken down to yield the technical breakthroughs needed soon to reach that ideal condition. The leap scenario needn't be high probability; it can be just a goal or anywhere in between. For example, a bicycle manufacturer might imagine a city built entirely on pillars, steel-mesh roadways, people wearing virtually no clothing at all, in air-conditioned hothouse environments, and so on. What implications would these conditions have for new bicycles?

Some current trends are better than others, when you are building scenarios. They are called **seed trends**. Using seed trends involves extending whatever current trends have meaning to the firm doing the analysis. But, the secret is to pick the trends with major lateral impact, and business media offer lots of

FIGURE 6–4

The Relevance Tree Form of Dynamic Leap Scenario

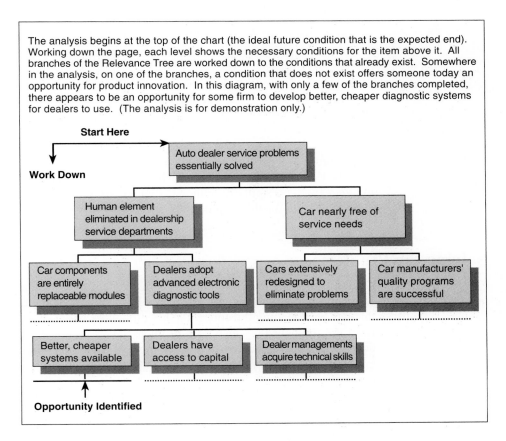

The analysis begins at the top of the chart (the ideal future condition that is the expected end). Working down the page, each level shows the necessary conditions for the item above it. All branches of the Relevance Tree are worked down to the conditions that already exist. Somewhere in the analysis, on one of the branches, a condition that does not exist offers someone today an opportunity for product innovation. In this diagram, with only a few of the branches completed, there appears to be an opportunity for some firm to develop better, cheaper diagnostic systems for dealers to use. (The analysis is for demonstration only.)

FIGURE 6–5   Seed Trends as an Extend Scenario

What Was In for 1995	*What Was Out for 1995*
Ice rinks, figure skating	*Mortal Kombat*
Tim Allen	Jerry Seinfeld
Ginseng	Rap
Wonder Bras	Jogging
Selective diets	Restrictive diets
Assisted suicides	Life support
South Bronx	Orange County
The Far Right	Liberalism
Tax cuts	Health care reform
Large screen TVs	Government
Jobs	Unemployment compensation
Huge stores	Small stores
Window ledge receivers	Sixty-channel TV
50%–70% sales	Buying at list price
Charter schools	Derivatives
Long hours	CBS
Business class	Mario Cuomo
Windows 95	Hillary Rodham Clinton
Nevada-Idaho	California
Digital colocation	The dollar in yen
Overtime	Hong Kong
World Wide Web	Replacement sports
Family Club Meds	Far-out fashion

Source: Gathered from many different sources, especially print media.

help. Figure 6–5 gives you a chance to see how perceptive various experts were in early 1995 when they predicted what would be "in" and "out" during the coming year (and, presumably, somewhat later). Would these predictions have made good scenarios for developing new goods and services?[10]

Solving the Problems

Once an important user problem has been identified, we can begin solving it. Most problem solving is probably done by members of the new products group that has been leading the concept generation work so far. They do it instinctively, from the moment they hear of a problem. There is no way we can quantify or describe the methods they use, since most of them are intuitive.

---

[10]For more on using scenarios, especially how to separate temporary fads from meaningful trends, see Harold S. Becker, "Developing and Using Scenarios—Assisting Business Decisions," *The Journal of Business and Industrial Marketing*, Winter/Spring 1989, pp. 61–69.

However, many problems are sent into the technical areas for a more systematic attempt at solution. Here science and intuition rule, side by side. Some firms have it as a strategy that problem solutions must come from R&D or engineering, with the solution itself being found in the application of some specific technology. A bus line wants travel problems solved by busses, and a bank probably wants problems solved by borrowing money. Besides technical people, the creative talents of marketing people are often used as well.

Group Creativity

New products people use individual problem-solving effort, but many think that group effort can do more. The secret of group creativity is that two heads are better than one. Some scientists protest loudly that this is not true, that the synergism of groups is very much overplayed. Generally, individuals can handle really new ideas and find radical solutions to problems better than groups can. Some feel that one reason small firms are more innovative than large firms is that they do not often use group creativity.

Students understand the values of individual and group thinking; you know pretty well when it is better to work on an assignment alone, and when with a group. You also know the problems of managing a group discussion.

The essence of today's group efforts to solve problems first appeared in 1938. Advertising executive Alex Osborn wrote a book about a technique he called **brainstorming.** All of the group ideation techniques developed since that time are spin-offs of his process and embody one idea: One person presents a thought, another person reacts to it, another person reacts to the reaction, and so on. This presenting/reacting sequence gives group creativity its meaning, and the various techniques developed simply alter how ideas are presented or how reactions take place.

Brainstorming

Osborn's approach, still taught and used today, includes two basic principles and four rules of conduct. Because the term has worked its way so deeply into our language, it is widely abused. It is good for new products people to recognize bad brainstorming when they see it, because bad brainstorming just won't work. The two principles are:

Deferral of Judgment.   This requires participants to be free to express any idea that comes to mind without having to worry about criticism from others in the group. The judicial mind weighs evidence, but it discourages the free flowing of ideas.

Quantity Breeds Quality.   According to associationist psychology, our thoughts are structured hierarchically; the most dominant are the habitual thoughts with which we are most comfortable. To have really new ideas we must break through these conventional ideas, and Osborn felt that achieving a large number of ideas requires breaking from the habitual.[11]

These two principles led to the following four rules for conducting a brainstorming session:

- All criticism is ruled out; even chuckles and raised eyebrows are banned.
- Freewheeling is welcomed—the wilder the better, with no inhibitions whatsoever. Divergent or lateral thinking should be forced by the leader.
- Quantity is wanted, so nothing is permitted to slow the session down (such as taking time to record an idea clearly or completely).
- Combination and improvement are achieved when each person's suggestion is carried to another stage of development or application by the next person.

These rules, in their pure form, are impossible to follow. Leaders often interrupt the process itself by trying to follow them. Also, since brainstorming was invented as a method of problem solving, participants should have experience in the general field with which the problem is concerned—product experience, in our case. They should be told the precise problem being attacked. They should be a diverse group but able to communicate (they can be co-workers or strangers).

The biggest change in the practice of problem solving over the past 20 years is to use brainstorming combined with other tools of creativity. We still try to avoid the **bazooka effect** (state an idea only to have someone shoot it down), but also to avoid the scores of easel sheets with hundreds of "ideas" scribbled on them. As one group creative says, the easel sheets are "full of spaghetti—a lot of bright ideas that are full of flaws...brainstorming is, too often, just permission to dump everything that has been in your head."[12]

Instead, the group deliberations are exploratory, evaluative in a constructive way, hours long (versus the 20-minute brainstorming session), and built toward a few specific solutions that appear operational.

There have been many attempts to stick with the basic idea of brainstorming, but to tweak it in some way to overcome the problems. Some of the more common techniques, such as the Phillips 66 Groups and reverse brainstorming, are described in Appendix B.

Disciplines Panel

Some new products people believe creativity groups should actually work on a problem, not just talk about it, particularly in situations calling for significant

---

[11]Alex Osborn, *Applied Imagination,* 3rd ed. (New York: Charles Scribner's Sons, 1963).

[12]Personal quote form Mark Sebell, co-founder of Creative Realities, a creativity training firm in Boston.

FIGURE 6–6

The Disciplines Panel for Group Ideation

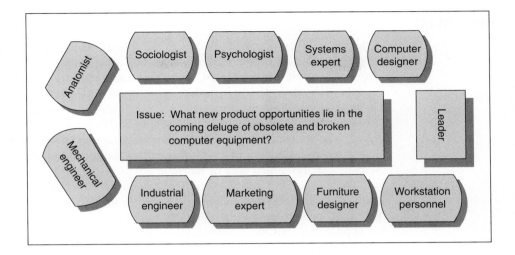

Anatomist

Sociologist

Psychologist

Systems expert

Computer designer

Mechanical engineer

Issue: What new product opportunities lie in the coming deluge of obsolete and broken computer equipment?

Leader

Industrial engineer

Marketing expert

Furniture designer

Workstation personnel

innovation, not line extensions. Their approach is to assemble experts from all relevant disciplines and have them discuss the problem as a panel. There may be just one meeting of the panel, but usually there are several lengthy meetings (see Figure 6–6).

A panel on new methods of packaging fresh vegetables might include representatives from home economics, physics, nutrition, medicine, ecology, canning technology, marketing, plastics, chemistry, biology, industrial engineering, agriculture, botany, and agronomy. Sometimes the panel consists of both company personnel and outside expert personnel. An example of a combined effort was when executives from Atlas Copco Roc Tec, a mining-equipment firm, met with a group of experts to solve this problem: How to dig ore and feed it onto a conveyor belt in one operation. Among the people on the panel was an entomologist who described how a praying mantis functions, from which came a large tractor with shovels on each side that dug the ore and shoveled it onto a belt that ran down the middle of the machine. Another example came from the shampoo industry, where a consumer need (to put on hair conditioner that actually sought out split ends and go to work there) was expressed, only to be met by a statement from an R&D person present that the then current products all did that! That surprising comment led to a very successful new product which made the claim that others had overlooked.

Whirlpool had always heard that different countries in Europe wanted their own types of washing machines. Disagreeing, the firm set up a few platforms, made machines with very little differences, and designed and manufactured them very well. Such "global" thinking led them into market dominance—consumers were willing to change when they were given a good alternative!

Summary

Chapter 6 began our study of the many specific techniques developed by concept creators to aid them in their work. The most common approach is based on the paradigm of "find problem, solve problem," requiring participation by many people in the firm, plus stakeholders and others outside the firm. Then we looked at the many techniques developed to spot problems. These included (1) inputs from technical and marketing departments, (2) search of internal records from sales calls, product complaints, customer satisfaction studies, and more, (3) problem analysis as a way of involving end users and other stakeholders, and (4) scenario analysis as a way of learning about future problems.

Once problems are discovered, efforts at solution can begin; most efforts are individual thinking and analysis, whether in the office or in the lab. One major group of techniques use the label of group creativity; it includes a great variety of approaches, but most are variations of brainstorming.

Next we will turn to some methods called analytical attributes, created over the years to aid marketing managers in seeking improvements while they are waiting for the approach of problem-find-solve to bear fruit. This is the approach where we start with form, then see if there is a need, and if so, then develop the necessary technology.

Applications

More questions from that interview with the company president.

1. "I recently met the president of a Florida university who had previously researched the new products operation in Silicon Valley firms. He wasn't impressed. Said that sales reps told over and over about getting suggestions and tips from their customers and sending them in on daily call reports, but nothing ever happened. Apparently, upper level sales and marketing executives only rarely have much customer contact, yet don't capitalize on the contacts of sales people. You have any ideas on how I might go about being sure this condition doesn't exist in our various divisions?"

2. "I personally love to watch for a trend and predict some new product from it. For example, just to see how good you are at creative thinking, here are some trends I noted recently in the press. Can you think of two possible products suggested by each?

    a. Lofty goals are giving way to very personal wants; there is less social globalism; the focus is inward; support for many social programs such as environmentalism is clearly on the wane.

    b. There has been great growth in bulk foods, items in barrels that we dish up ourselves, while at the same time an overwhelming trend to eating out (cutting in-home meal preparation).

    c. AT&T tells us that the very idea of long-distance calling will soon disappear. All calls will be charged by distance and time, even within a city. They will be even cheaper than now, and in fact many of them will go via computer networking in digital form.

    d. Life is more and more focused around celebrities—sports, TV, politics, etc. Population has grown so big that people can only relate to famous faces and names. Everything they do is interesting and attracts intense involvement by many millions of people."

3. "I believe in problem analysis—that's at the heart of things. But I sure don't like those focus groups. I sat in on a couple last year, and all the people did was chat. And the chatting never seemed to lead to anything. After the second one was over, I quizzed the moderator, and she agreed that there had been a lot of rambling. She kept talking about the gems of knowledge we found—common threads, I believe she said. Now, honestly, isn't that pure bunk? However, she did say she thought focus groups would be especially useful in Eastern Europe, where businesses have so many needs, and we have to be sure to cull down to the most critical ones. I wonder, suppose our Swiss trucking division could use focus groups to help them develop new services for Eastern European businesses?"

4. "You know a lot about rental of formal wear, like tuxedos and formal gowns, I imagine. Can you take me through a problem analysis, using the formal wear rental market as an example? Several of our divisions are involved in retail business, and I'm curious to see what problems you come up with that we haven't solved yet."

CASE: THE AMERICAN HEALTH CARE SYSTEM

There are several very important long-term trends operating within the American health care system. This summary cannot do them complete justice, but taken together they paint a clear picture of a system in a state of disequilibrium. For organizations attempting to serve the medical needs in such a milieu, forecasting is very difficult.

    1. Costs. However expressed, the American health system is growing more costly by the minute. Operating in the general area of a trillion dollars a year, annual increases have recently been in two digits. There is no clear topping out point yet, though some systems of doctor selection are having a good effect. The system, unlike Canada's, has no automatic, built in cost-capping mechanisms.

    2. Scientific complexity. Each day seems to bring new ways of alleviating pain and suffering. But each improvement also brings higher costs, and often limited availability. Some improvements appear to be clearly beyond our ability to deliver them on a large scale.

Source: Though set in the United States, this case will fit most of the developed societies of the world today; it was compiled from many public information sources.

3. Fairness. The American system appears to at least partly ration health care service on the basis of wealth, and at least partly on the basis of whether one's job provides health benefits. This leaves millions of people without protection.

4. Politics. Given our current inability to provide comprehensive health coverage to everyone (in the context of cost and scientific advances just above), politicians are frustrated as to the directions in which we should go. This generates harmful friction in the nation's system of government. Though not a society that condones revolutions, the United States seems to be on the verge of potentially devastating social unrest.

5. Productivity. There is ample evidence that the health care system is woefully wasteful and managerially backward. We use many medical techniques that apparently contribute little to health, we are slow to adopt useful innovations, and in general operate the health system without proven techniques of motivation and reward. There are many islands of success in this country (e.g., the Kaiser Permanente health plan) that are not being copied. There is abundant overcapacity, in spite of a recent wave of mergers and acquisitions. There is no central computer base that compiles success/failure statistics on medical procedures and treatments.

6. The "market system." Although more market oriented than the systems in use in other advanced societies, our system in fact is not a free one. We so inhibit it that its inherent advantages are lost. For example, the market system currently in use has struggled through several years of cost cutting, but opportunities to continue to do so are probably getting fewer.

7. Lack of restraint. At the present time, many doctors and hospitals are paid for the services they render, whatever their cost. The traditional fee-for-service system lacks internal systems of control except where physicians and hospitals have agreed to fixed charges, and in these, critics claim the quality of service delivered has fallen.

8. Population. The society to be served continues to grow, and seems destined to go on this way for at least a long time.

There are many other problems, most as subsets of the big categories just listed. And there are many players—patients, nonpatients, providers (hospitals, physicians, nurses, and more), payers (insurance companies, employers, governments, and more), and critics and commentators (politicians, economists, educators, editors, and more).

The setting cries out for some type of scenario analysis, particularly for an organization such as a for-profit hospital. Your client is a modest chain of eight such units, located primarily in Alabama and Georgia. The issue, of course, is what new services (products) should the management of those hospitals be developing? Those services would be offered to the employer/insurer community (medical procedures are beyond us in this case). And they would be designed to help solve the problems those people face at the time they are marketed.

The above list of problems could be used, but they are problems of the moment. They are being attacked from all fronts. Your task is to make a leap scenario—try to visualize the health system that will be in place five years from now, given the political situation, recent governmental programs, and other changes going on at the time you are doing your analysis. Be specific in listing at least one major problem the employer/insurer group will be facing. Don't just say "high costs." Try to find a problem they don't have now, but which you feel they will have five years out. They perhaps don't even know they will have this problem, or if they do, they are not thinking about it at this time.

Then, working in a group with several other students, try to find at least one way in which product innovation in these hospitals could help solve that problem. Think too about the problems you had as you worked this assignment; would managers in the hospital have them if they used the scenario leap method?

7 ANALYTICAL ATTRIBUTE APPROACHES

Setting

In Chapter 6, we studied an approach to concept generation that involves identifying users' problems, and finding solutions to them. The problem-based approach is the best because product concepts found by the problem/solution route are most likely to have value for the user.

However, as part of the problem-solving phase and also independently from the problem approach, techniques from another approach are also being used. Everyone involved with the creation and sale of goods and services can make use of these techniques, including some who don't even know they are doing formal concept generation. What these techniques do is create views of a product different from the usual ones—they can seem almost magic, but are quite deliberate. They can appear to be strictly fortuitous, or lucky, when they work, and they have indeed worked—many times, as with adding a third stocking to a package, quick-drying inks, and VCRs combined with TVs. But actually they are quite deliberate and purposeful, allowing discovery—serendipitous findings that come to people who know what they are looking for.

What, and Why, Are Analytical Attribute Techniques?

The key here is getting that different view of current products. As an example of how far-out they can appear to be: Light a candle, sit close to it, and hold near the flame the product you are studying, stare directly at and through both the flame and the product, describe what you see in that vision. Actually, most of these techniques are quite reasonable, and with clear logic in them.

Analytical attribute techniques capitalize on the concept that any future change in a product must involve one or more of its current attributes. Therefore, if we were to study those attributes, changing each one in all the ways it could be changed, we would eventually discover every change that could ever

127

come about in that product! Others capitalize on relating one attribute with another attribute, or to something else in the environment—forcing these relationships, whether normal and logical or strange and unanticipated. They all can work, as you will see. And they have been used in all product categories from polymer processing technologies at Kodak to the LH car line at Chrysler to eyeglasses and cereal flakes.

Analytical attribute techniques are felt to be more useful in Western culture than in Eastern. Western (particularly European and North American) thought goes heavily toward rearranging things, while Eastern (Asian) thought tends to start work anew.[1] Commodity-type products are a major focus, because slight rearrangements can differentiate one item from its competitors, thus making it able to carry a higher price.

What is a product attribute? Figure 7–1 shows the set of them. A product is really nothing but attributes, and any product (good or service) can be described by citing its attributes.[2]

FIGURE 7–1   **A Typology of Attributes**

A. **Product attributes (for our purposes) are of three types:**
   Features   Functions   Benefits

Features can be many things:

Dimensions	Esthetic characteristics	Components
Source ingredients	Manufacturing process	Materials
Services	Performance	Price
Structures	Trademarks	And many more

Benefits can be many things:

| Uses | Sensory enjoyments | Economic gains |
| Savings (time, effort) | Nonmaterial well-being | And many more |

Benefits are either direct (e.g., clean teeth) or indirect (e.g., romance following from clean teeth).

Functions are how products work (e.g., a pen that *sprays* ink onto the paper). They are unlimited in variety, but are not used nearly as often as benefits and features.

B. **Analytical attribute approaches use different attributes:**
   Dimensional analysis uses features
   Checklists use all attributes
   Trade-off analysis also uses determinant attributes
   Several methods in Appendix B use functions and benefits

---

[1]Jacquelyn Wonder and Jeffrey Blake, "Creativity East and West: Intuition versus Logic," *Journal of Creative Behavior*, Third Quarter 1992, pp. 172–85.

[2]Attribute measurement and assessment are not the exact science their terminology suggests. For a rather distressing but enlightening report, see James Jaccard, David Brinberg, and Lee J. Ackerman, "Assessing Attribute Importance: A Comparison of Six Methods," *Journal of Consumer Research*, March 1986, pp. 463–68.

Attributes are of three types: features, functions, and benefits; benefits can be broken down in an almost endless variety—uses, users, used with, used where, etc. Concept generation is a creative task, so great liberty has been taken with definitions in its activity. The classification system used in this book is an attempt, and no more than that, to arrange them for study.

A spoon is a small shallow bowl (*feature*) with a handle (another *feature*) on it. The bowl enables the spoon to *function* as a holder and carrier of liquids. The *benefits* include economy and neatness of consuming liquid materials. Of course, the spoon has many other features (including shape, material, reflection, and pattern). And many other functions (it can pry, poke, project, and so on, as junior high school cafeteria managers know all too well). And many other benefits (such as pride of ownership, status, or table orderliness).

Theoretically, the three basic types of attributes occur in sequence. A feature permits a certain function, which in turn leads to a benefit. A shampoo may contain certain proteins (feature) that coat the hair during shampooing (function), which leads to more shine on the hair (benefit).

The analytical attribute techniques covered here are: dimensional analysis, checklists, gap analysis, trade-off analysis, relationships analysis, and analogy. Many more are given in Appendix B.

Dimensional Analysis

Misnamed, dimensional analysis uses any and all features, not just measurements (such as spatial—length, width, etc.). The task involves listing *all* of the features of a product type. Product concept creativity is triggered by the mere listing of every such feature, because we instinctively think about how that feature could be changed. Rarely is anything worthwhile found in dimensional analysis until the list is long. It takes a lot of work to push beyond the ordinary, and to see dimensions that others don't see.

Some of the most interesting features are those a product doesn't *seem* to have. For example, the spoon discussed above also has aroma, sound, resilience, bendability, and so on. Granted, the aroma may be hard to detect, the sound (at the moment) may be zero, and the resilience may be only when pushed by a vice. But each feature offers something to change. How about spoons that play musical notes as children move them to the mouth? How about spoon handles that can be squeezed to play notes? How about spoons that smell like roses?

Listing hundreds of features is not uncommon. Figure 7–2 shows a shorter list, but perhaps it suggests what must be done. Successful users claim that just citing a unique dimension sparks ideation, and that the technique has to be used to be believed.

FIGURE 7–2   Dimensional Attributes of a Flashlight

Using dimensional analysis, here are 80 dimensions. There were almost 200 in the analyst's original list. A change in any one of them may make a new flashlight.

Overall unit:
Weight
Rust resistance
Balance
Gripability
Shock resistance
Shear force
Heat tolerance
Insulation material
Automatic flasher
Manual flasher
Distance visible
Length
Hangability
Stain resistance
Cold tolerance
Flexibility
Insulation color
Translucence
Focus of beam
Closure type
Lining material
Buoyancy
Flammability
Malleability
Compressibility
Reflectiveness
Surface area/color
Closure security
Material of case
Color

Number body seams
Water resistance
Diameter
Washability
Weight of metal
Explosiveness
Smell of unit
Number of tags
Snagability
Sealant material

Lens:
Material
Opacity
Color
Strength
Texture

Springs:
Number
Material
Length
Strength
Style

Switches:
Number
Pressure
Noise
Type
Location

Bulb:
Number
Shape
Size
Gas type
Thread strength
Length of stem
Filament shape
Thread size
Filament material
Shatter point
Thread depth
Amperage

Batteries:
Number
Size
Terminal type
Direction
Rechargeability

Reflector:
Depth
Diameter
Shape
Durability
Surface
Color
Temperature limit

Checklists

From early forms of dimensional analysis evolved one of today's most widely used idea-generating techniques—the checklist. The most widely publicized checklist was given by the originator of brainstorming:

Can it be adapted?   Can something be substituted?

Can it be modified?   Can it be magnified?

Can it be reversed?   Can it be minified?

Can it be combined with anything?   Can it be rearranged in some way?

FIGURE 7–3   Checklist of Idea Stimulators for Industrial Products

---

Can we change the physical, thermal, electrical, chemical, and mechanical properties of this material?

Are there new electrical, electronic, optical, hydraulic, mechanical, or magnetic ways of doing this?

Find new analogs for parallel problems.

Is this function really necessary?

Can we construct a new model of this?

Can we change the form of power to make it work better?

Can standard components be substituted?

What if the order of the process were changed?

How might it be made more compact?

What if it were heat-treated, hardened, alloyed, cured, frozen, plated?

Who else could use this operation or its output?

Has every step been computerized as much as possible?

These eight questions are powerful; they do lead to useful ideation. If you want more, Appendix C has the ultimate in checklists; it contains 112 questions, in many categories, with *examples for each*.

Business and industrial goods analysts use such features as source of energy, materials, ease of operation, subassemblies, and substitutable components. (See Figure 7–3 for an abbreviated list of such industrial checklist questions.)

Checklists produce a multitude of potential new product concepts, most of them worthless. Much time and effort can be spent culling the list. The technique is frequently used as an aid in *problem solving*. Some people make up a matrix, putting product types or brands down the left side, and the checklist factors across the top. This helps find individual product deficiencies that can be capitalized on for particular market segments.

Gap Analysis

Gap analysis is a statistical technique with immense power under certain circumstances. Its *maps of the market* are used to determine how various products are perceived by how they are positioned on the market map. On a geographical map, New York City is much closer to Pittsburgh than it is to Los Angeles. But on a *nearness-to-the-sea* map, New York City would be right next to Los Angeles. On any map the items plotted tend to cluster here and there, with open space between them. These open spaces are gaps, and a map that shows gaps is, not surprisingly, called a **gap map**.

Several levels of sophistication will be cited, because many firms prefer to use the technique in a simple form, while others have achieved their greatest success with the more complex versions.

Gap maps are made in three ways: (1) A manager uses *known data* to plot products on a map to make a **determinant gap map**, (2) a manager uses customer *attribute ratings* (AR) to get data from users for an **AR perceptual gap map**; and (3) a manager uses *overall similarities* (OS) to get data from users for an **OS perceptual gap map**.

Thus, determinant maps use *our* factors and *our* scores, AR perceptual maps use *our* attributes and *customers'* scores, and OS perceptual maps use *customers'* attributes and *customers'* scores.

Determinant Gap Maps

Figure 7–4 shows a map of snacks prepared by a new products manager seeking to enter the snack market. The map consisted of two dimensions (he personally thought crunchiness and nutritional value were important in snacks). Scales ran from low to high on both factors. Each brand then in the market was scored by the manager on each of the two factors.

This may appear rather arbitrary and dangerous. But remember, concept generation takes place *after* strategy (the PIC) has targeted a market or user group to focus on. Either the firm had experience in this market (a strength) or the market was researched.

FIGURE 7–4

Gap Map for Snack Products

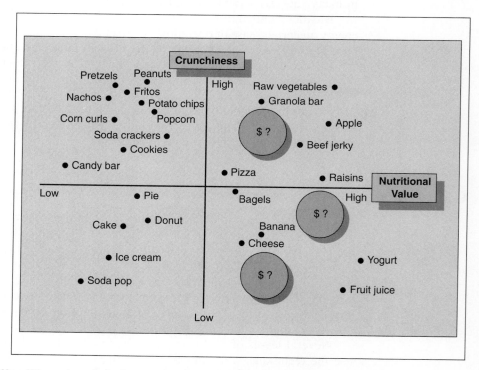

Note: This map is purely for demonstration, not research-based.

Each brand was then entered on the diagram (Figure 7–4) according to its scores. The result was a map of the brands, each in relationship to all others, on these two factors. Many maps could have been prepared, each with a different pair of attributes. They can also be three-dimensional.

Attributes used in gap analysis should normally be **differentiating** and **important**. Consumers differentiate snacks on their crunchiness and on their nutritional value, and these attributes are important in buying snacks. Snacks also have different shape esthetics, but these are not often used to differentiate one from another. Even if they were, most people would probably not think them important.

Attributes that both differentiate and are important are called **determinant attributes**, because they help determine what snacks are bought. Some of the determinant attributes in an industrial study (of siding) were appearance/status, maintenance/weathering, application/economy, and dent resistance.[3]

The reason it is important to use determinant attributes in making the maps is that our purpose in this method is to find a spot on the map where a gap offers potential as a new item, one that people might find different and interesting.

For example, on the snacks map in Figure 7–4 the circles with $? marks inside them are gaps, and thus new product candidates. Note that the large number of snacks makes our gaps few and small—for example, the gap of semi-high crunchy and semi-high nutritional is close to the granola bar, the apple, beef jerky, and soda crackers.

Students disagree with some of the placements on that snack map. But they also disagree when the positions come from customer research (see perceptual gap maps, below). We all do. Experienced managers using solid market knowledge can get pretty close, usually close enough to permit identification of any large gaps where there are no products currently.

Although determinant gap maps are speedy and cost efficient, the method misses customer perceptions that, though inaccurate, may nevertheless be the ones driving their decisions. To handle this problem, we have perceptual gap maps.

AR Perceptual Gap Maps

Unlike the previous method, attribute ratings (AR) perceptual gap mapping asks market participants (buyers and users of the products) to tell what attributes they believe products have. For example, product users may think candy bars are high in nutrition—doubtful, but if this were so, then any map putting candy bars low in nutrition is incorrect for seeking perceptual gaps. Determinant maps are based on real reality, and perceptual maps on marketplace reality. They both have a place in our work.

---

[3]Steven A. Sinclair and Edward C. Stalling, "Perceptual Mapping: A Tool for Industrial Marketing: A Case Study," *Journal of Business and Industrial Marketing*, Winter/Spring 1990, pp. 55–66.

Usual methods of market research are used to gather people's perceptions, including focus groups and individual interviewing. The procedure (with many variations in practice) first asks consumers what attributes are *important* in their purchases of products in the subject category. These are put in a list, and factor analysis (or multiple discriminant analysis) is used to sort down to important ones.

These, or other, users then score each product on each of the final factors (the determinant attributes). From these data, AR perceptual gap maps are drawn. They look like the snack map in Figure 7–4, and the search for gaps proceeds as before. If the research was accurate, any gaps found are more likely to interest the users.[4]

OS Perceptual Gap Maps (with Similarities Data)

AR perceptual maps early on suffered a criticism that led to a variation preferred by some product innovators. The problem was that users sometimes make purchase decisions using attributes they cannot identify. These "phantom" attributes don't show up on the lists, are not included as map dimensions, and by their absence distort the analysis. Too, some users have difficulty scoring attributes, even when they are aware of them, because of various aspects of focus group settings, privacy, and so on.

Du Pont offered an early example of the phantom problem. The company sold filler material for pillows and wanted to find the best type and form of filler to enhance its sales to pillow manufacturers. But Du Pont market analysts found that consumers could not clearly describe the attributes of pillows and could not communicate the attributes they wanted in pillows.

So, the firm created many different types of pillows and then gave them to consumers three at a time, along with the question, "Which two are most similar, or which one is least like the other two?" Du Pont's research was much more complex than this question implies, but, in essence, the firm was now able to use a computer algorithm to convert the "similarities" data into a map showing closeness of products, *regardless of which attributes created that closeness.*

Figure 7–5 shows a similarities map of European cheeses. Note there are no dimensions; people were not asked to score the cheeses on different attributes, but only how similar each was to others. Analysts studied the map carefully, did some regression analysis, using known attributes of these cheeses, and hypothesized that the vertical dimension was popularity. They felt that a horizontal dimension might be mildness/pungency. A third dimension was found to run from northwest to southeast on the map, as products seemed to line up with

---

[4]For more information on the use of factor analysis in new products, see Uwe Hentschel, "On the Search for New Products," *European Journal of Marketing*, no. 5 (1976), pp. 203–17; and for full development of the mathematics, see Edgar E. Pessemier, *Product Management*, 2nd ed. (New York: John Wiley & Sons, 1981).

Figure 7–5

Nonmetric Perceptual Map of the U.K. Cheese Market (without dimensions)

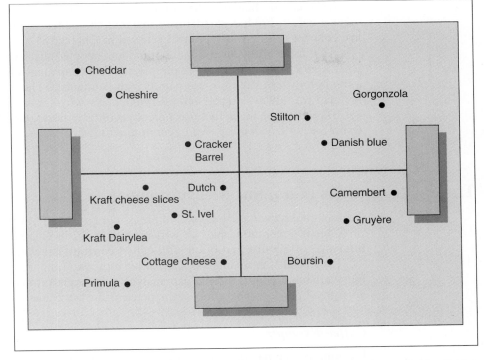

Source: Gordon Douglas, Philip Kemp, and Jeremy Cook, *Systematic New Product Development* (London: Halsted Press, 1978), p. 74.

native cheeses on the upper left and foreign cheeses on the lower right. Again, a reader familiar with the U.K. cheese market at that time might disagree.

Comments on Gap Analysis

All gap mapping is controversial, but perceptual maps especially so. The input data come entirely from responses to questions about how brands differ. Nuances and shadings are necessarily ignored, as are interrelationships and synergisms. Creations requiring a conceptual leap are missed. In the early 1800s, for example, gap analysis might have led to breeding faster horses or to wagons with larger wheels, but it probably would not have suggested the automobile.

The most damaging aspect is that gap analysis discovers *gaps*, not *demand*. Gaps often exist for good reasons (e.g., fish-aroma air freshener). New products people still have to go to the marketplace to see if the gaps they discovered represent things people *want*. This has led to **preference maps**, which are three-dimensional diagrams from the technology of computer-aided design, where dimensions matching those on a gap map are the *x* and *z* axes, but the *y* axis shows preference levels. The result resembles a blanket laid down over objects of various sizes; high levels show where preferences lie, and low levels of preference lie between the humps of high preference. New products people hope a gap in product availability matches the peaks in preference, and often use concept testing to find out (discussed in Chapter 8).[5]

And, as in all of ideation, new products people must avoid being bound by what is now "impossible." For example, for years gap maps on analgesics showed a big hole where strength was paired with gentleness. The strong/gentle part of the map was always empty, and everyone knew why—an over-the-counter analgesic could not be made that was potent yet didn't irritate the stomach. Of course, Extra-Strength Tylenol proved everyone wrong.[6]

Trade-Off Analysis (Conjoint Measurement)

The next analytical attribute technique is more a tool of concept evaluation than of concept generation, and we will meet it again in Chapter 9. It is **trade-off analysis** (originally, and often still, called **conjoint measurement**).

Recall that after finding the *determinant attributes* (important attributes on which the available products differ), gap analysis plots them on maps. Trade-off analysis instead puts *all* (not pairs) of the determinant attributes together in new *sets*.

Coffee Example

Presume coffee has three determinant attributes: *flavor*, *strength*, and *intensity of aroma*. If we could find five different flavors, three different strengths, and four different aroma intensity levels, these attributes could be put together in 60 different combinations. Consumers could then be asked their preference (although 60 possible new products are too many for one consumer to handle). One favorite would emerge from this array, and unless that particular combination was already on the market, we would have our new product.

Given that a serious study of this type may turn up 10 determinant attributes (not 3), and that each attribute may have 5 to 8 possible measurements (e.g., flavors), the number of possibilities gets completely out of hand.

Enter trade-off analysis. By using fractional factorial design, researchers can array, say, 10 proposed new products including the full *range* (though not every step) of attribute variations. But with only 10 products most consumers won't be able to find the exact combination they want. So they must choose the combination that most closely meets their desires by trading off attributes wanted

---

[5]Further information on using preference data in conjunction with gap maps can be found in Samuel Rabino and Howard R. Moscowitz, "Detecting Buyer Preferences to Guide Product Development and Advertising," *Journal of Product Innovation Management*, September 1984, pp. 140–50.

[6]A managerial discussion of perceptual mapping can be found in Robert J. Dolan, *Managing the New Product Process* (Reading, MA: Addison-Wesley, 1993).

FIGURE 7–6

Coffee Attribute Utility Curves

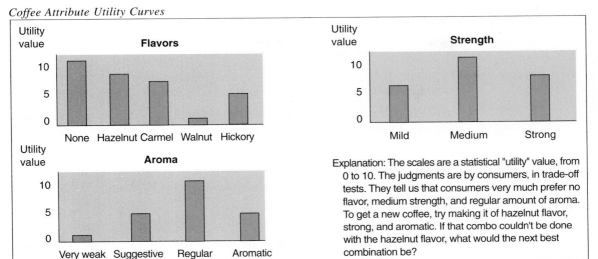

Explanation: The scales are a statistical "utility" value, from 0 to 10. The judgments are by consumers, in trade-off tests. They tell us that consumers very much prefer no flavor, medium strength, and regular amount of aroma. To get a new coffee, try making it of hazelnut flavor, strong, and aromatic. If that combo couldn't be done with the hazelnut flavor, what would the next best combination be?

most against those wanted less. We all do this when our favorite brand of something is not in the store and we have to find a close substitute. See Figure 7–6 for the way factor utility scores are sometimes presented.

What happens next demonstrates the real power of trade-off analysis. A computer program calculates a utility function for each of the 10 attributes. The analyst can then order up the one new product (perhaps never thought of before) that optimizes the 10 variables—so much of this, so much of that, and so on. If that product already exists in the market, the next best product can be derived. Trade-off analysis does actually generate new products. Some people have called the method product optimization because of how it works.

Appliance Example

The Sunbeam Corporation wanted to expand its kitchen mixing appliances sales in various countries around the world. But what variations did each country want? The company identified three types of attributes—silhouette, features, and benefits. The determinant attributes for each appliance were identified, and the range for each selected. For instance, silhouettes had about 10 combinations— low versus high, strong versus stylized, and so on.

Cards representing new products that combined specific silhouettes, features, and benefits were prepared. Consumers in the various countries were asked to sort the cards by preference from top to bottom. If a person wanted a low, strong silhouette, a large number of variable speeds, a very quiet motor, and the ability to use on semiliquids, one card may have had the right silhouette, speed, and noise but couldn't be used on liquids. Another could be used on liquids and had the right silhouette and noise but had only three speeds. To choose one, the consumer would have to trade off speed variety against use on liquids. With hundreds of consumers doing this, a good picture for each attribute can be obtained and the optimization process begun.[7]

Service Example

Another example concerned not a consumer good, but an industrial service—information retrieval for sale to financial institutions.[8] Twelve attributes were considered important, and each was given a range for the test. Here are 3 of the 12:

Nature of output	Speed of delivery	Output format
Citation only	Within hours	Photocopy
With documentation	Within days	Microform
With interpretation		

The research procedure was the same one that Sunbeam used. The research firm put together a set of cards representing many different versions of the proposed service and covering all characteristics of the 12 attributes. Financial firms were approached, rankings of the cards were made, utility functions were determined, and the ideal service was calculated and returned to the financial institutions for evaluation.

It is said that some cooks do much the same with recipes. After looking at preparations currently being made, their different ingredients, amounts included, etc., they in effect use trade-off analysis. They try to find the ideal combination of ingredients, cooking, serving, and the like. Then they make some up, and find people to try it on.

Because business buyers tend to make a more rational analysis of product features, trade-off analysis is becoming increasingly valuable for industrial product innovation. Applications (though not necessarily successful) include snowmobiles, health care systems, aircraft, lift trucks, and computer software.[9] The process of involving study of sensory reactions to physical stimuli is also called psychophysical measurement; psychophysics is a long-time tool of experimental psychology.

---

[7]The Sunbeam example is described in Albert L. Page and Harold F. Rosenbaum, "Redesigning Product Lines with Conjoint Analysis: How Sunbeam Does It," *Journal of Product Innovation Management*, June 1987, pp. 120–37.

[8]The financial information example is discussed in detail in Yoram Wind, John F. Grashof, and Joel D. Goldhor, "Market-Based Guidelines for Design of Industrial Products," *Journal of Marketing*, July 1978, pp. 27–37.

[9]See Dick R. Wittink and Philippe Cattin, "Commercial Use of Conjoint Analysis: An Update," *Journal of Marketing*, July 1989, pp. 91–96; and Dick R. Wittink, Marco Vriens, and Wm Burhenne, "Commercial Use of Conjoint Analysis in Europe: Results and Critical Reflections," *International Journal of Research in Marketing*, January 1994, pp. 41–52. Good explanations of the complex aspects can be found in Robert J. Dolan, *Managing the New Product Development Process* (Reading, MA: Addison-Wesley 1993), note 4.

Recent Modification

A troublesome aspect of trade-off analysis shows when studying products that naturally have a large number of determinant attributes. Services tend to produce this problem more than goods do—for example, property insurance. Analysts had to restructure a traditional form of conjoint measurement called SIMALTO by adding *cost* and *savings* to each of the attribute trade-off utilities as shown in Figure 7–6. They then gave consumers budgets to spend on their choices, and thus captured a lot of variables in a *willingness to pay*. They kept the power of the original set of trade-off attributes without having to use the data-losing method of conjoint calculations.[10]

Another method of dealing with the complexities of many product situations is use of what is called **discrete choices**, which also is a method for dealing with very complex situations.[11] Yet another method of reducing complexity is to mail respondents floppies on which are product feature attributes. The trick is to sort down quickly to just the very important features. This reduces the number of choice combinations. The whole thing, including making up the choice sets (like the cards) and taking votes on them, is done in the disk and is mailed back in the same form.

Relationships Analysis

Several of the concept-generating methods we have been looking at *compare* things: perceptual maps compare attributes, and group creativity is stimulated by reasoning from a known to an unknown, for example. But the comparisons are incidental to a larger issue in those methods. We will now look at two analytical attribute techniques that go right to the point—forcing things together for examination. These two techniques are the **two-dimensional matrix** and the **morphological matrix**.

About the Dimensions Used in Relationships Analysis

Recall that Figure 7–1 said attributes are **features** (such as length), **functions** (such as coating hair with protein), and **benefits** (such as economy and health). But other aspects of products are not always included as attributes in definitions— for example, different places of use, occupations of users, or other items the product is used with. **Relationships analysis** techniques use them too. We seek any and all dimensions that help, and there is no fixed set of these. Hopefully, the examples shown in this chapter will suggest the view you should take in creating the matrixes.

---

[10]Peter D. Morton and Crispian Tarrant, "A New Dimension to Financial Product Innovation Research," *Marketing and Research Today,* August 1994, pp. 173–79.

[11]Steven Struhl, "Discrete Choice Modeling: Understanding a 'Better Conjoint than Conjoint,'" *Quirk's Marketing Research Review*, June/July 1994, pp. 12–15ff.

FIGURE 7–7 Two-Dimensional Matrix Used for New Insurance Products

	Person/Animal Insured									
Event Insured Against	*New-borns*	*Geniuses*	*Troubled Kids*	*Rich Uncles*	*Dogs/ Cats*	*Tropical Birds*	*Salt Water Fish*	*New Job-holders*	*Newly-weds*	*New Parents*
Injury from fire	1	2	3	4	5	6	7	8	9	10
Getting lost	11	12	13	14	15	16	17	18	19	20
Normal death	21	22	23	24	25	26	27	28	29	30
Being insulted	31	32	33	34	35	36	37	38	39	40
Being kidnapped	41	42	43	44	45	46	47	48	49	50

Examples of new product concepts: An insurance policy that protects new parents if they get lost (20), or that protects newlyweds from the risks of being kidnapped while on their honeymoon (49), or that protects geniuses from the damage of being insulted (32). Fortuitous scan methods mostly produce nonsense, but like the others, the two-dimensional matrix often produces a surprise that, upon careful thought, makes sense.

Two-Dimensional Matrix

The simplest format for studying relationships is seen in Figure 7–7, which shows two attribute sets for insurance. Only partial lists of two dimensions (event insured against and person/animal insured) are used, but just these two provide 50 cells to consider. Notice that only by forcing relationships could we *expect* to come up with a special policy that protects new parents if they happen to misplace their new child, or that protects newlyweds from the costs of overcelebrating their honeymoon. In the case of the insurance example, to analyze the results we would just start with #1, think about it, then to #2, and so forth.

In contrast to most of the methods studied to this point, relationships analysis goes direct to a new product idea—for instance, aerosol ice cream. The number of two-dimensional matrixes that can be prepared is almost unlimited. Keep looking at different ones until you're satisfied with the list of new possibilities found, or are convinced that the technique "just isn't for me."

Morphological or Multidimensional Matrix

The next method, **morphological matrix**, simultaneously combines more than two dimensions. The matrix can include many dimensions, and the technique originated many years ago when a scientist was trying to further development on what became the jet engine.[12]

[12]The scientist used 11 parameters (dimensions), each of which had between two and four alternatives; that set yielded 36,864 combinations (possible engines). Incidentally, that matrix also yielded two combinations that became the German V-1 and V-2 rockets in World War II. See Fritz Zwicky, *Discovery, Invention, Research: Through the Morphological Approach* (New York: Macmillan, 1969).

A classic example shown in Figure 7–8 covers household cleaning products. Consumers were surveyed and asked to provide the following information about their recent use of such items:

1. The cleaning instruments used.
2. The basic ingredients in the cleaners used.
3. The objects cleaned.
4. The type of package or container the products came in.
5. The substances removed with the cleaners.
6. The textures or forms of the cleaners.

Figure 7–8 shows the six categories and the items reported within each category. The new products manager's task was to link up combinations of those items. One common technique is to have a computer print out all possible combinations, which are then scanned for interesting sets. Other analysts just use a simple mechanical method of reading the rows across; the top row says, how

FIGURE 7–8   Relationships Analysis: Morphological Technique—Dimensions Relevant to a Household Cleaner

Dimension 1: Cleaning Instrument	Dimension 2: Ingredients	Dimension 3: Objects to Be Cleaned			Dimension 4: Package	Dimension 5: Substance to Be Removed	Dimension 6: Texture
Broom	Alcohol	A/C filters	Glass	Screens	Aerosol	Blood	Cream
Brush	Ammonia	Air	Glasses (eye)	Shoes	Bag	Body odors	Crystals
Damp mop	Deodorizing agents	Aluminum	Grill	Skis	Bottle	Bugs	Gaseous
Dry cleaning	Disinfectant	Boats	Jewels/jewelry	Stainless steel	Box	Burns	Gel
Dry mop	Pine oil	Brooms	Leather	Stoves	Can	Dirt	Liquid
Hose	Scenting agents	Brushes/combs	Linoleum	Synthetics	Easy-carry	Dust	Powder
None		Cabinets	Mops	Tiles	Easy-pour	Food	Solid
Rag		Carpet	Motorcycles	Toilets	Jar	Germs	Wax
Sponge		Cars	Ovens	Tools	Spray	Glue	
Steel wool		Cement	Paint brushes	Toothbrushes	See-through	Grass stains	
Vacuum		China/crystal	Pans	Toys	Tube	Grease	
Wet mop		Clothes	Pets	Upholstery	Unbreakable	Mildew	
		Corfam	Pictures/	Vinyl	Unspillable	Mud	
		Curtains/draperies	paintings	Walls	Odors		
		Diapers/pails	Pillows/	Water	Oil		
		Dog houses	mattresses	Windows	Paint		
		Fences	Plastic	Wood	Rust		
		Floors	Pool	Wool	Spots		
			Refrigerators		Streaks		

Interpretation: Using only the top item from each of the six dimensions, we could get a cream substance packaged in an aerosol package, to be applied to a broom, whereby the alcohol in the cream would clean blood from shoes. This is only one of many thousands of combinations the morphological approach would generate from the above lists.

Source: Charles L. Alvord and Joseph Barry Mason, "Generating New Product Ideas," *Journal of Advertising Research*, December 1975, p. 29.

about a cream substance, in an aerosol package, to be applied to a broom, whereby the alcohol in the cream would clean blood from shoes? The second row asks about a bag of ammonia crystals to be applied with a brush so that body odors can be removed from skis! After going through the rows, the analyst systematically alters one item in each row with one from another, and so on. All analytical attribute techniques produce noise from which good ideas must be picked; but what at first appears to be noise may simply be a great new idea no one would have thought of easily without the matrix.

In any event, the structure shown in Figure 7–8 should be followed. Creation of the columns was discussed at the beginning of this section of the chapter. The number of items in each column is either (1) the entire set, as in the survey above, or (2) a selection representing the full array. For example, a study of play wagons might have a column headed number of wheels, and the rows would be two, three, four, five, and six; but the height column might just have rows of 6 inches, 8 inches, and 12 inches (low, medium, and high).[13]

Analogy

We can often get a better idea of something by looking at it through something else—an analogy. Analogy is so powerful and popular that it is used heavily as part of the problem-solving step in problem-based methods (Chapter 6).

A good example of analogy was the study of airplane feeding systems by a manufacturer of kitchen furniture and other devices. Preparing, serving, and consuming meals in a plane is clearly analogous to doing so in the home, and the firm created several good ideas for new processes (and furniture) in the home kitchen.

An analogue for bicycles might be driving a car—both incorporate steering, moving, slowing, curving, and so on. But the auto carries more passengers, has four wheels for stability, variable power, built-in communications, on-board service diagnosis and remedial action, and the like. Each difference suggests another new type of bicycle; some of these types are already available. The bicycle could also be compared to the airplane, to skating, to the submarine, to swimming, and at the extreme (for illustration) to a mouse in a maze.

The secret, of course, is finding a usable analogous situation, which is often difficult. The analogy should meet four criteria:

1. The analogy should be vivid and have a definite life of its own.
2. It should be full of concrete images.
3. It should be a happening—a process of change or activity.
4. It should be a well-known activity and easy to visualize and describe.

---

[13]For a report of several applications of this technique, see Simon Majaro, "Morphological Analysis," *Marketing Intelligence and Planning*, no. 2 (1988), pp. 4–11.

Airplane feeding systems and driving a car qualify easily. And, perhaps to their surprise, an analogy of the machine gun ammunition belt helped seed company developers think of a roll of biodegradable tape studded with carefully placed seeds to be laid along a furrow.

Analogy is used in several of the specialized techniques in Appendix B.

Summary

We have now finished a review of several analytical attribute techniques. The techniques varied from the very simple yet challenging dimensional analysis to intermediate methods such as morphological matrix to complex methods such as gap analysis and trade-off analysis. But even the most complex are available in somewhat simplified versions, and can be used by a manager as a result of reading this chapter, with or without help from a skilled marketing research department or advertising agency.

The essence of attribute analysis, in every case, is to force us to look at products differently—to bring out new perspectives. We normally have fixed ways of perceiving products, based on our sometimes longtime use of them, so forcing us out of those ruts is difficult.

Anyone reading this in preparation for a specific ideation activity is encouraged to scan the list of over 40 other techniques in Appendix B.

The problem-based approach is, of course, recommended in all cases. The analytical attribute methods are supplementary, and any particular situation may respond to one or more of them. Some trial and error is recommended; keep early trial simple until a successful output is achieved. Some new products managers say any one technique will bring perspectives that the others don't. This is particularly true when user perspectives are sought.

We are now finished with concept generation and, hopefully, have several good concepts ready for serious review and evaluation before undertaking costly technical development. We meet evaluation in Part III, Chapters 8–12, entitled "Pretechnical Evaluation."

Applications

More questions from that interview with the company president.

1. "I guess I really like checklists best—they're easy for me to understand and use. I've never seen this one by Small that you mentioned—wow, four pages of ways. Is all that really necessary? Couldn't just as good a job be done with, say, one page? And incidentally, I must confess I'm slightly confused by the terminology. Tell me, what is the difference again between the checklists I like and what you call dimensional analysis?"

2. "As you can probably tell by now, I am an engineer by training and have always enjoyed playing around with one form of analytical attributes. We

call it attribute extension, where we forecast the future changes in any important attribute of a product. You know, like the amount of Random Access Memory in a PC. I recently asked our cable TV division to take five dimensions of a cable TV service and extend each out as far as they can see it going and tell me what ideas they get from it. I mentioned number of channels and types of payment as examples. Could you do something like this for me now . . . that is, take five dimensions of cable TV service and extend them? It would help me get ready for their presentation Thursday."

3. "Another method you say you studied is of great interest to me, for reasons I'll not go into. It's gap analysis, especially the idea of maps. Several of our best divisions produce and sell services. Is the gap map method applicable to services? Could you please take, say, the college education "market" and draw up a product map for it? I understand it can be done by a manager at a desk, although, of course, it wouldn't be nearly as accurate as if we had all the technical data, and so on. But could you try?"

4. "Several of our divisions work in the women's clothing markets. As you know, they are all specialized these days, this segment or that segment. Getting hard to come up with a new segment, one that has some size and would be responsive. So, when you were talking about morphological matrix, which I liked, I thought about women's attire. One way to innovate would be to come up with new settings, or occasions, situations where we could devise a whole outfit. Sort of like wedding, or race track, or picnic, though we know of them and have clothing for them, of course. Sort of a *package* of apparel and accessories But, there must be many we don't think of now. Would that morphological matrix method work on that?"

CASE: RUBBERMAID INC.

Rubbermaid has consistently received awards as a well-managed company. It made the *Fortune* magazine list for three consecutive years in the early 90s. It posts growth rates of 15 percent, even in tough times, with important contributions from new products. About 200 new items are introduced each year. Some are line extensions, and others enter, or even create, entirely new markets.

The firm's success is based partly on creating and producing high quality, functional, plastic products for the housewares, the office, the industrial, and the farm markets in addition to specialty products such as toys, educational and recreational products, and furniture. In recent years items have ranged from a spatula to a cooler used on a golf course and from a child's 15-pound minicar to lawn furniture. Category brands include Little Tikes, Gott, Blue-Ice, and Sunshine.

Source: This case was prepared from many public information sources.

The firm makes almost a half–million different items, boasts a 90 percent success rate on new products, and obtains at least 30 percent of its sales each year from products less than five years old.

The firm's new product strategy is to meet the needs of the consumer. The new product rate is high, and diversification is desired. It is market-driven, not technology-driven, although in recent years the firm has identified such technologies as recycling new plastic parts from old tires for which it is seeking market opportunities. This practice of seeking opportunities for specific technologies will increase as a fall-out of the firm's current use of speeded-up product development.

For idea generation, Rubbermaid depends on finding customer problems that can be built into the strategic planning process. These problems are sought in several ways, principally by using focus groups. The company also uses comments and complaints from customers, an example of which came when then-CEO Stanley C. Gault heard a Manhattan doorman complaining as he swept dirt into a Rubbermaid dustpan. Inquiry determined that the door-man wanted a thinner lip on the pan, so less dirt would remain on the walk. He got it.

Each complaint is documented by marketing people, and executives are encouraged to read the complaints. One complaint by customers in small households who found the tradi-tional rack-and-mat too bulky to store, led to a compact, one-piece dish drainer. The Little Tikes toy division actually molds a toll-free number into each toy to encourage complaints and comments. They have to watch the legal ramifications, of course, and may require idea submitters to sign a waiver giving up their rights to their ideas.

The firm generally finds its problems by using problem analysis in focus groups and solves them internally. They occasionally use scenario analysis to spot a problem. But sce-nario analysis is much less useful than problem analysis, because the lead times are so short; their new product cycles make them concentrate mainly on already existing problems. The organization is kept conducive to newly created ideas by promoting cross-functional asso-ciation between workers. Problem-find-solve is encouraged at all levels.

Some other new items have been:

- Bouncer drinkware was created for people who fear using glassware around their swimming pools.
- A lazy susan condiment tray and other patio furniture products came from studies of lifestyle changes.
- People working at home told of problems that led to a line of home office accessories, including an "auto-office," a portable device that straps onto a car seat and holds pens and other office articles.

The firm also runs a day care program, where researchers observe children having prob-lems with toys and test their new toys.

Generally, Rubbermaid does not make much use of attribute listing and other fortuitous scan methods of ideation, including the various mapping approaches. It does find that product life-cycle models can be useful, and it closely tracks competitive new product introductions.

However, Rubbermaid is always looking for new ways by which it can come up with good new product concepts. They know from experience, for example, that they will find new ways for using problem-find-solve techniques. And perhaps the fortuitous scan meth-ods can be of greater use than what is now perceived.

The Pretechnical Evaluation Stage

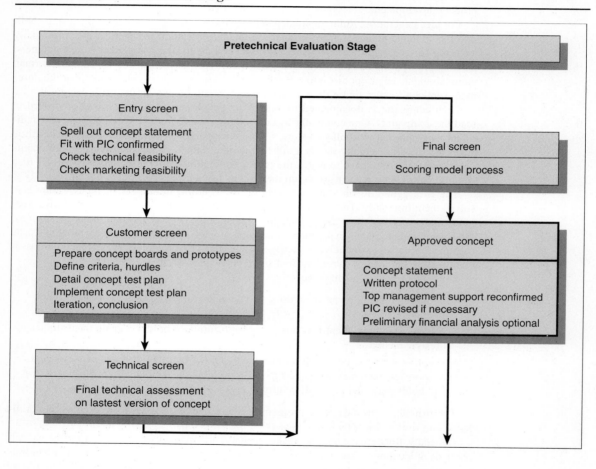

III   PRETECHNICAL EVALUATION

Part II completed our study of the various methods of generating new product concepts. The next task is to undertake evaluation of these concepts. Evaluation takes place at many different times and in different ways, by different people, for different reasons. Therefore, a *system* of evaluations is needed, an idea that will be explained in Chapter 8.

Then, beginning in Chapter 9, we will look at the different phases in that system. (See the accompanying figure.) Concept testing is the first major tool and will be discussed there. Chapter 10 covers the activity generally called a *full screen,* a step where the concept is judged by how well it fits the company and its marketing strengths. Chapter 10 also covers some work needed before the concept can be turned over to the technical departments for development, a subject that we will face in Part IV.

The evaluation tools discussed in Chapters 9 and 10 are those that precede technical development. Once prototypes or service configurations begin to appear, evaluation begins again, first in the form of product use testing and later in market testing, and more. These are covered in later chapters. All of these efforts at evaluation are themselves major topics, so our discussions must be selective. Unfortunately, industry uses many of the tools in different ways, so they tend to blend together at the edges. When, for example, does a prototype concept test become a product use test?

Likewise, industry often combines two or even three of the tools. For example, in some industries it is very easy to prepare prototypes so some of these firms like to do an early customer survey that is partly market analysis, partly concept test, and partly prototype test, particularly when the idea first emerged in prototype form.

Finally, industry developers have been all too willing to invent terminology. Therefore, we have had to do some standardizing of terms, and some of the decisions won't be acceptable to all people. Appendix E contains a glossary of terms as used in this text.

8   THE CONCEPT EVALUATION SYSTEM

Setting

Before looking into the various specific techniques used to evaluate new product concepts, we need something to give us an overview. Something that will show why there are so many evaluation techniques, none of which are used all the time. Chapter 8 offers this view, and shows several key analytical concepts that help us decide which techniques to use in any particular situation: The triple streams, the cumulative expenditures curve, and the A-T-A-R model. We will even cover potholes and surrogates, among other ideas.

You will recall from Chapter 3 that new products fail because (1) there was no basic need for the item, as seen by intended users, (2) the new product did not meet its need, net, considering all disadvantages, and (3) the new product idea was not properly communicated (marketed) to the intended user. In sum, they didn't need it, it didn't work, they didn't get the message. Keep these in mind as you see how an evaluation system is constructed.

What's Going On in the New Products Process

New products actually build up the way rivers do. Great rivers are systems with tributaries that have tributaries. Goods that appear complex are just collections of metal shapes, packaging material, fluids, prices, and so on. A good analogy is the production of automobiles, with a main assembly line supported by scores of subsidiary assembly lines scattered around the world, each of which makes a part that goes into another part that ultimately goes onto a car in that final assembly line.

If you can imagine the quality control people in auto parts plants evaluating each part before releasing it to the next step, you have the idea of a new product evaluation system. The new product appears first as an idea, a concept in words or pictures, and we evaluate that first. As workers turn the concept into a formed piece of metal, or software, or a new factory site preparation service, that good or service is then evaluated. When a market planner puts together a marketing plan, its parts are evaluated separately (just as minor car parts are) and then evaluated again in total, after it is added to the product.

The fact that we evaluate the product and its marketing plan as separate and divisible pieces is what lets us telescope the development process into shorter periods of time. There was an era when we went through a new product's development step by step, nothing "ahead of its time." But today we may be working on a package before we actually have finished product, we may be filming part of a commercial before the trademark has been approved and finalized.

This sometimes causes some backtracking, but the cost of that is less than the costs of a delayed introduction. It does require, however, that we have thought through carefully the item's overall development needs—and, which of those needs are crucial, and which not crucial. Any evaluation system *must* cover the crucial ones.

Purposes of Evaluation

Although the overall purpose of evaluation is to guide us to profitable new products, each individual evaluation step has a specific purpose, keyed primarily to what happens next. For example, the very first evaluation *precedes* the product concept. (See Figure 8–1, which shows where evaluation takes place relative to

FIGURE 8–1

Evaluation Takes Place in Every Phase

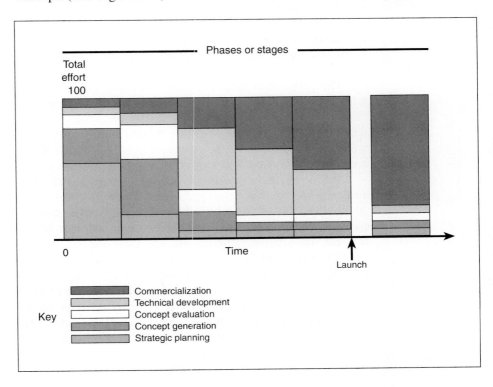

other activities.) The first judgment or assessment is made on an **opportunity.** Someone decided the firm had a strong technology, or an excellent market opportunity, or a serious competitive threat—whatever. As discussed in Chapter 4 on strategy, a judgment was made that if the firm tried to develop a new product in a given area, it would probably succeed.

This early evaluation step (direction) is shown at the top of Figure 8–2. Where should we look? What should we try to exploit? What should we fight against? The tool is opportunity identification and evaluation, also discussed in Chapter 4. This tool keeps us out of developments where we stand a poor chance of winning; in other words, it makes sure we play the game on our home field. This direction is provided in the product innovation charter.

After ideas begin to appear in the idea generation phase (next row under ''Evaluation Task,'' in Figure 8–2), the purpose changes: to avoid the big loser or the sure loser. We want to cull them out and spend no added time and money on them. We're sometimes wrong, of course, but usually we're right, and this step is essential if we are to focus limited resources on the worthwhile concepts.

The initial review segment of activities also tries to spot the potential big winners. Most good concepts are just that—good. A few show hope of becoming great, and we want to recognize them as soon as possible. These get added effort, usually in the form of a very complete concept testing and development program.

That activity leads us to the third level, deciding whether to send the concept into full-scale technical development. This decision, if the amounts to be spent make it an important decision, will benefit from a very thorough scoring model application where we answer the question: Should we try to develop it?

The decision to enter the technical phase introduces the part of the process where the parallel or simultaneous activities are done (referred to earlier). All through this phase we are continually asking, have we got what we want? Is this part ready? Is that system subset cleared for use? Does the software not only work, but produce what the customer needs? A protocol check tells whether we are ready to develop a product for serious field-testing.

Technical development is naturally iterative: one new discovery leads to another, directions are changed, specific attempts fail, and we have to back up. At Hollingsworth & Vose, an industrial specialty paper company, gaskets are tested five times in this stage—in-house lab test, customer lab test, customer engine test, car manufacturer engine test, and fleet test.

Sooner or later the technical efforts yield a product that evaluators say meets the request. Attention then turns to getting the item commercialized, leading to the issue of whether the firm has proven itself able to make, and market, the item on a commercial scale. It is usually resolved by some form of market testing.

Later on, of course, the developers (and others in the firm too, unfortunately) will be asking the "in retrospect" question: should we have done all this? The purpose is not to find a guilty party for a product that bombed but, rather, to study the evaluation process to prevent a repetition.

FIGURE 8–2

The Evaluation System

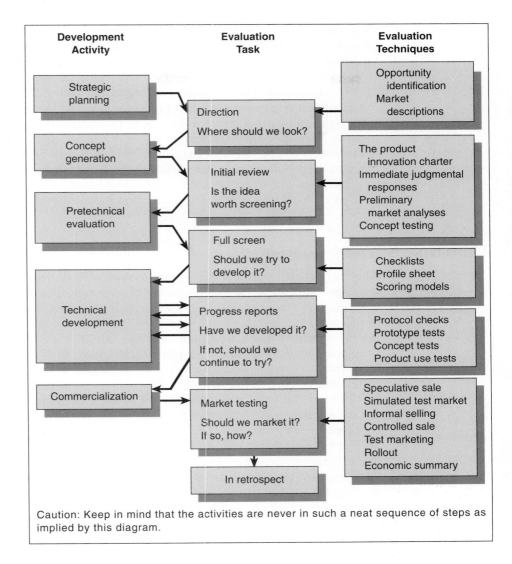

Development Activity	Evaluation Task	Evaluation Techniques
Strategic planning	Direction — Where should we look?	Opportunity identification — Market descriptions
Concept generation	Initial review — Is the idea worth screening?	The product innovation charter — Immediate judgmental responses — Preliminary market analyses — Concept testing
Pretechnical evaluation	Full screen — Should we try to develop it?	Checklists — Profile sheet — Scoring models
Technical development	Progress reports — Have we developed it? — If not, should we continue to try?	Protocol checks — Prototype tests — Concept tests — Product use tests
Commercialization	Market testing — Should we market it? If so, how?	Speculative sale — Simulated test market — Informal selling — Controlled sale — Test marketing — Rollout — Economic summary
	In retrospect	

Caution: Keep in mind that the activities are never in such a neat sequence of steps as implied by this diagram.

Balanced Product Innovation Portfolio

The evaluation system keeps the new product operation efficient, and we will talk more about this in a minute. Keep in mind, however, that any one product being evaluated is not alone. Most organizations have several products under development, sometimes scores or even hundreds of them. Managements would like to think that every project will yield a big profit. They won't, so we think in terms of a **portfolio** of new product projects.

Different firms put together different portfolios. The stable, healthy firm usually has a mix of projects from low-risk, short-term ones to high-risk, longer-term ones. The portfolio of a conservative firm avoids the high-risk projects. A firm in trouble seeks only higher-risk projects of a short-term nature. Of course, a firm that hasn't heard of product innovation portfolio strategy will have no focus and will accept anything that comes along and looks good.

An evaluation system can be developed for each of those project types. For example, the firm that needs new product help fast will tend to skip early checkpoints, and will narrow down to just one or two alternative formats during technical development. They will tend to put in one major check late in the process, not to warn it to stop (that risk has already been accepted) but rather to make sure the marketing plan communicates and that the distribution system is in place.

Unfortunately, some firms take pride in one evaluation system, and force it to fit all evaluation situations. Overevaluation and underevaluation usually result.

The Triple Streams Concept

Another way of looking at the overall evaluation task during the new product development process was shown as a key driving concept in Chapter 2. (See Figure 2–6.) It emphasized that *three* main streams of activity take place during most of this process. Though we call it new product development, we are also preparing the product's **marketing plan** and the **evaluation** of both the product and the plan, together. The marketing plan actually starts first, if the management is using product innovation charters. The arena/focus section of a PIC identifies a market use or user, which in time will become the marketing plan's target market. This, of course, is months before the product itself appears.

An evaluation system (down the middle of Figure 2–6) has to integrate and coordinate the two outside streams of activity. Every effort is made to avoid a product that marketing can't sell. And, of course, marketing can't sell "from an empty basket," demonstrated by the—perhaps apocryphal—story about an Alberto Culver shampoo. Television commercials were finished and at the networks ready for showing before the chemist could find an appropriate formulation! If that is the way they often operated, the evaluation system would have to be built accordingly.

The Cumulative Expenditures Curve

As mentioned earlier, the new product evaluation system flows with the development of the product. What evaluation occurs at any one point (how serious, how costly) depends greatly on what happens next. Figure 8–3 shows a key input to the design of any evaluation system: in the middle of that figure, a gradually upward-sloping curve represents the accumulation of costs or expenditures on a typical new product project from its beginning to its full launch.

This **cumulative expenditures curve**, taken from various studies over the years, is just an average. It need not reflect any one firm, but it is typical of many durable consumer goods, nontechnical business-to-business products, and

FIGURE 8–3

Cumulative
Expenditures—All-
Industry Average
Compared to
Occasional
Patterns

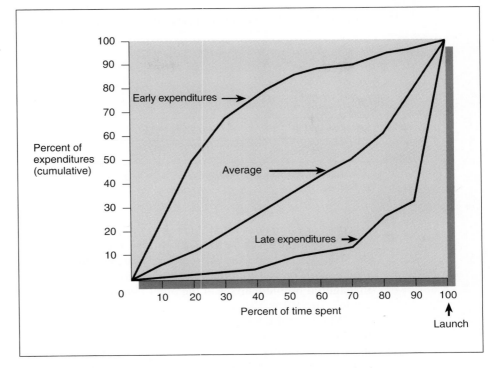

many services. Shown with the average curve are two others. The early expenditures curve is representative of product development in technical fields, such as pharmaceuticals, optics, and computers. R&D is the big part of the cost package, and marketing costs are relatively small. The lower curve in the figure shows the opposite type of firm, say, a consumer packaged goods company. Here the technical expenditures may be small, but a huge TV advertising program is needed at introduction.

These are generalizations, and individual exceptions do occur, such as when Procter & Gamble spends years developing a fat substitute called Olestra or Upjohn marketed a line of generic drugs. The point is, whoever develops a concept evaluation system needs to know what situation it is for. No evaluation decision is independent of considerations on what will be done next, how much will be spent, or what points of no return are passing. An old Chinese proverb says, "Spend your energy sharpening the edge of the knife, not polishing the blade."

The Risk/Payoff Matrix

Figure 8–4 applies these ideas in a **risk/payoff matrix.** At any single point in the evaluation process, the new products manager faces the four situations shown. Given that the product concept being evaluated has two broad ultimate outcomes

FIGURE 8–4   **Matrix of Risk/Payoff at Each Evaluation**

Decision is to: → ↓ *If the product were marketed*	*A* *Stop the project now*	*B* *Continue to next evaluation*
A. It would fail	AA	BA
B. It would succeed	AB	BB

Comment: Cells AA and BB are "correct" decisions. Cells BA and AB are errors, but they have different cost and probability dimensions.

(success or failure) and that there are two decision options at the time (move on or kill the project), there are four cells in the matrix.

The AA cell and the BB cell are fine; we drop a concept that would ultimately fail, or we continue on a concept that would ultimately succeed. The managerial problem arises in the other two cells. AB is an error: a winner is discarded. But BA is also an error: a loser is continued to the next evaluation point.

Which error does the manager most want to avoid? The answer depends on the dollars. First, throwing out a winner is very costly, because the ultimate profits from a winning product are bound to be much greater than all of the development costs combined, let alone those in just the next step. So error AB is many multiples of BA.

Except, of course, for opportunity costs. What other project is standing by waiting for funding? When good candidates wait in the wings, the losses of dropping a winner are much less because the money diverted will likely go to another winner.

The point is, a manager must think of these matters when deciding what evaluation to do. If the net costs of the next step in any situation are low, then a decision will probably be made to go ahead, perhaps with very little information. For example, when IBM had just one year to develop and market the original PC computer, it felt the losses from delay greatly exceeded the gains from concept tests, lengthy field use tests, market tests, and so on. The company didn't do any. On the other hand, General Foods kept Brim coffee in market tests for several years, because it wanted to make sure the market plans were correct before undertaking the very expensive national launch.

A good example of what the risk matrix can lead to came when Pillsbury announced that it had, in one year:

1. Failed with Appleeasy because it had, at the last minute, cut the amount of apples in reaction to increasing apple prices.
2. Failed with vegetable yogurt because people simply didn't like the idea.

3. Failed with presweetened baked beans because people liked to sweeten their own.

4. Succeeded with Totino's Crisp Crust Frozen Pizza.

Sales of the frozen pizza were over $60 million the first year, while none of the losers cost the company as much as $1 million. There were some morale problems in this case because no developers like to have a new product fail. And the R&D people were very much aware that the losers were internal developments whereas the frozen pizza came mainly from an acquisition. But no one can fault the overall financial outcome from this "package" of four decisions.

The Decay Curve

The risk matrix decisions lead to the idea of a **decay curve,** as shown in Figure 8–5. That figure depicts the percentage of any firm's new product concepts that survive through the development period, from the 100 percent starting out before concept testing to the 2 percent (estimated from various studies) going to market. The discarded 98 percent dropped off at various times during the process, and when they drop off is primarily determined by the analysis of the risk matrix.

Decay curve C is roughly the shape of one decay curve from a leading company in the paper industry that wanted to kill off all possible losers early and spend time developing only those proposals worthy of marketing. This was their strategy, and their evaluation system implemented it faithfully. In the 1990s, managers have put a high priority on this type of cleaning out of bad ideas—

FIGURE 8–5

Mortality of New Product Ideas— The Decay Curve

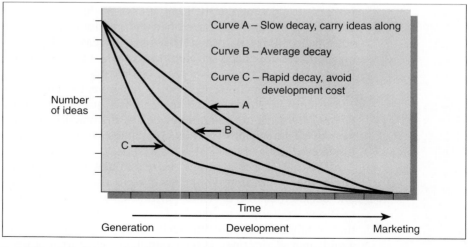

Source: Hypothetical representation based on empirical data in various sources, including *New Products Management for the 1980s* (Chicago: Booz Allen & Hamilton, 1982), p. 14.

freeing up the pipeline, they call it. Decay curve A represents one for a service firm that had very low development costs and wanted to drop a project only when there was solid evidence against it. The paper company spent time making careful financial analyses even before technical work began; the service firm started up a project and just let it keep going until the contrary evidence built up.

Thus, the decay curve is partly a plan and partly a result. The two should be synchronized. Its value as a managerial concept lies in helping the manager see the need for thinking through the stream of development costs and the risk/payoff matrix (above) for each new product concept as it starts its journey through development. When it is working, you will hear statements such as, "On that chip, let's make sure the customer will want it if we can make it; no sense in spending all that money only to find there's no buyer for it." And, in the building next door, "Don't worry about Ed's doubts at this time; we can reposition the fertilizer spreader at the last minute if we have to, even change several of the key attributes if we want. Let's just get going, now!"

Planning the Evaluation System

The previous considerations help set the tone for management decisions on an appropriate evaluation system for any particular new product concept. There are four other relevant, but less demanding, concepts that help us decide whether to concept test, how long to run a field use test, whether to roll out or go national immediately, and how thorough a financial analysis to demand.

Everything Is Tentative

It's easy to imagine that building a new product is like building a house—first the foundation, then the frame, then the first floor, and so on. Unfortunately, product aspects are rarely locked in that way. Occasionally they are, as when a technical process dominates development, or when a semifinished product is acquired from someone else, or when legal or industry requirements exist.

We usually assume everything is tentative, even up through marketing. Form can usually be changed, and so can costs, packaging, positioning, and service contracts. So can the marketing date and the reactions of government regulators. So can customer attitudes, as companies with long development times have discovered.

This means two long-held beliefs in new product work are actually untrue. One is that everything should be keyed to a single **Go/No Go decision.** Granted, one decision can be decisive—at times, for example, when a firm must invest millions of dollars in one large facility or when a firm acquires a license that commits it to major financial outlays. But, many firms are finding ways to avoid such commitments, for example, by having another supplier produce the product for a while before making a facilities commitment, or by negotiating a tentative license, or by asking probable customers to join a consortium to ensure the volume needed to build the facility.

The other untrue truism is that financial analysis should be done as early as possible to avoid wasting money on poor projects. This philosophy leads firms to make complex financial analyses shortly after early concept testing, although the numbers are inadequate. The paper products firm whose decay rate was presented in Figure 8–5 (curve C) rejected hundreds of ideas before realizing that early financial analysis was killing off ideas that would have looked great after further development. The financial analysis is best built up piece by piece, just like the product itself. We will see later how this works.

Still another tentative matter is the marketing date. Marketing actually begins very early in the development process—for example, when purchasing agents are asked in a concept test whether they think their firm would be interested in a new item. Rollouts (discussed in Chapter 21) are now so common it is hard to tell when all-out marketing begins. General Electric once invested in a small, $20 million facility for a new heat-resistant plastic for circuit boards. After IBM and some other customers approved the product, GE announced it would build a full-scale, $50 million plant. Dr. Roland W. Schmitt, chief of research in the lab where the product was invented, put it this way: "Marketing people are wrong as often as technical people. It is important to approach markets as well as science in an experimental fashion."[1]

Often no one pulls a switch and marketing instantly begins. We more often sneak up on it, which clearly affects the evaluation system.

What results in some cases is a sort of a **rolling evaluation.** The project is being assessed continuously, figures are penciled in, premature closure is avoided, and participants avoid mind-sets of good and bad.

Potholes

One critical skill of product developers is the ability to anticipate major difficulties, the potholes of product innovation. In automobile travel, **potholes** are always a problem, but they only become costly when we fail to see them coming in time to slow down or steer around them. The same thinking applies to new products: we should carefully scan for the really damaging problems (the "deep holes") and keep them in mind when we decide what evaluating we will do.

For example, when Campbell Soup Company undertakes the development of a new canned soup, odds are in its favor. But experience has shown two points in the process when it may fail, and if it does, the product won't sell. The first is *manufacturing cost*—not quality, that's one of the company's key strengths. But there is always a question about whether the chosen ingredients can be put together to meet market-driven cost targets. The second is whether consumers

---

[1]Stratford P. Sherman, "Eight Big Masters of Innovation," *Fortune*, October 15, 1984, p. 80.

think it *tastes good*. So the company's evaluation system is set never to overlook these two points.

A flour miller once said his biggest pothole was a quick entry by a price-cutter, because that industry had virtually no patent protection or other barriers to competitive entry. He planned on it in every case, and didn't go ahead without an answer. A software developer said his biggest pothole was customer unwillingness to take the time to learn to use complex new products. He had several worthwhile products in the graveyard to prove it.

In fact, if a manager thinks through the matter of potholes carefully (scans the road ahead) there are more benefits than just to the evaluation system.

The People Dimension

Product developers also have to remember they are dealing with people, and people cause problems. For example, although R&D workers are quite enthusiastic early in the life of a new product, the idea may have little support outside of R&D; it is fragile and easy to kill. Late in the development cycle, more people have bought in on the concept and are supportive because they have played a role in getting it to where it is. Consequently, the now-strong proposal is tough to stop.

This means that an evaluation system should contain early testing that is supportive. In fact, concept *testing* is sometimes called concept *development,* to reinforce the idea of helping the item, not just killing it off. Later in the cycle, hurdles should usually be tough and demanding, not easily waved aside. One firm designated its market research director as a "manager of screens"; his task was to impose absolute screens, such as "A new food product, in home placement testing, must achieve a 70 percent preference against its respective category leaders." If less than 70 percent of the testers preferred the new item, it was stopped, period. This sounds severe and arbitrary, but it shows how difficult it sometimes is to kill off marginal products late in development.

Another people problem relates to personal risk. All new product work has a strong element of risk—risk to jobs, promotions, bonuses, and so on. Consequently, some people shy away from new product assignments. We're always under the gun from someone—an ambitious boss, a dedicated regulator, an aggressive competitor, a power-hungry distributor, an early critic who was overruled within the company, and more. A good evaluation system, built on a thorough understanding of the road the new item will follow as it winds its way through development, protects developers from these pressures. The system should be supportive of people, and offer the reassurance (if warranted) that players need.

Surrogates

The timing of factual information does not often match our need for it. For example, we want to know customer reactions early on, even before we develop the product, if possible. But we can't really know their reactions until we make some of the product and give it to them to try out. So, we look for **surrogates**, or pieces of information that can substitute for what we want to learn but can't.

Here are four questions to which we badly need answers and four other questions that can be answered earlier (thus giving *clues* to the real answer):

Real Question	**Surrogate (Substitute) Question**
Will they prefer it?	Did they keep the prototype product we gave them at the end of the concept test?
Will cost be competitive?	Does it match our manufacturing skills?
Will competition leap in?	What did they do last time?
Will it sell?	Did it do well in field testing?

Note, each response has little value except to help answer a critical question that cannot be answered directly.

Surrogates often change at different times in the evaluation process. For example, let's go back to one of the questions just above: Will cost be competitive? At different times during the project, the surrogate used might be:

Time 1: Does it match our skills?

Time 2: Are the skills obtainable?

Time 3: What troubles are we having in making a prototype?

Time 4: How does the prototype look?

Time 5: Does the manufacturing process look efficient?

Time 6: How did the early production costs turn out?

Time 7: Do we now see any ways we can cut the cost?

Time 8: What is the cost?

Time 9: What is the competitive cost?

Only when we know our final cost and the competition's cost can we answer the original question. But the surrogates helped tell us whether we were headed for trouble.

The A-T-A-R Model

The last tool that we use for designing an evaluation system for each new project as it comes along is based on how we forecast sales and profit on a new item. The calculation is much like a pro forma income statement, an *array* of figures allowing us to see what the profits will look like based on where we are at any one time in the development.

The basic formula, shown in Figure 8–6, is based on what is known in the marketing field as the **A-T-A-R concept** (awareness-trial-availability-repeat). This is taken from what is called **diffusion of innovation**, explained this way: for a person or a firm to become a regular buyer/user of an innovation, there must first be awareness that it exists, then there must be a decision to try that innovation,

FIGURE 8–6   A-T-A-R Model

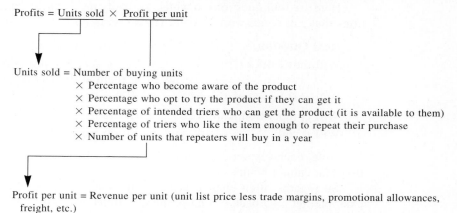

Profits = Units sold × Profit per unit

Units sold = Number of buying units
        × Percentage who become aware of the product
        × Percentage who opt to try the product if they can get it
        × Percentage of intended triers who can get the product (it is available to them)
        × Percentage of triers who like the item enough to repeat their purchase
        × Number of units that repeaters will buy in a year

Profit per unit = Revenue per unit (unit list price less trade margins, promotional allowances,
    freight, etc.)
                – Costs per unit (usually cost of goods sold plus direct marketing costs)

Therefore:

Profits = Buying units × Percent aware × Percent trial × Percent availability × Percent repeat ×
    Annual units bought × (Revenue per unit – Costs per unit)

then the person must find the item available to them, and finally there must be the type of happiness with it that leads to adoption, or repeat usage.[2]

We want to use the formula to calculate all the way to profit, so we expand it to include target market size (potential adopters), units purchased by each adopter, and the economics of the operation. But at the heart of the calculation is A-T-A-R.

Let's take a simple example to explain how it works. Assume we have developed a new device to replace the security bars owners attach to steering wheels in expensive sports cars. It is built on an electronic principle of metal adherance. To use the paradigm for a final sales forecast, we need the following (hypothetical) data:

Number of owners of such sports cars: 3 million.

Percentage of target owners who we think we can make aware of our new device the first year on the market: 40 percent.

Percentage of "aware" owners who will decide to try the device during the first year and set out to find it: 20 percent.

Percentage of customary auto parts and mass retailers whom we can convince to stop the new device during the market introduction period (to keep it simple for this demonstration, assume that potential buyers are

---

[2]The basic A-T-A-R sequence has been broken down further into many microsteps. One example of this extension is John H. Antil, "New Product or Service Adoption: When Does It Happen?" *Journal of Consumer Marketing,* Spring 1988, pp. 5–16. Too, some people use this model in abbreviated form, stopping at unit sales. They calculate market share and make conclusions on that.

busy and probably will not seek beyond one store if they cannot find it there): 40 percent.

Percentage of the actual triers who will like the product and buy one for a second car: 50 percent.

Number of devices a typical user will buy in the first year of ownership: 1½.

Dollar revenue at the factory, per device, after trade margins and promotion discounts: $25.

Unit cost of a device, at the intended volume: $12.50.

The profit contribution forecast, based on the A-T-A-R model, would be 3 million $\times$ .40 $\times$ .20 $\times$ .40 $\times$ .50 $\times$ 1.5 $\times$ ($25 - $12.50) = $1,800,000.

What we did was prepare a mathematical formula and ran it through one set of data. Since the development was about finished when the calculation was made, the forecast was fairly solid. But, the formula could have been used at the very beginning as well. Only a few figures (e.g., number of potential adopters) are known at the start, but estimates can be plugged into the other spots, and the whole thing set up for use down the line.

As with the other parts of this chapter, the A-T-A-R model gives us guidance on evaluation system design. You can immediately see the importance of awareness, trial, and so on. That means tests will have to be run where customers are checked out for their interest in trying, their reactions after trying (how likely would they be to try again?), and whatever else contributes to the formula.

There is nothing magic in the formula; it simply states the critical factors, and shows their relationship to each other and to the sales and profit forecasts.

Two things are important about this model's sales and profit forecasts for the security device:

1. *Each factor is subject to estimation*, and in every development phase we are trying to sharpen our ability to make the estimates. For example, we may be trying to check the introductory promotion's awareness-building capability. Or just how much price discounting we must do to motivate a first purchase of the device. Or how much trust the buyer places in the unit after it is installed. We may be worried about how we're going to get enough distribution to make the product available when car owners seek it.

2. *An inadequate profit forecast can be improved only by changing one of the factors*. For example, if the forecast of $1,800,000 profit contribution is insufficient, we look at each factor in the model and see which ones might be changed and at what cost. Perhaps we could increase the retail margin by 5 percent and get another 20 percent of stores to stock it. On the other hand, perhaps an increase in advertising would produce more awareness. Qualitative changes (such as a new advertising theme) can be made in addition to the quantitative. The proposed changes are then run through the formula again, which yields

another set of results, some more changes, and so on. Sometimes the issue raised is so fundamental that it is more efficient to cycle back to an earlier phase in the development. The fact that the model is set up in spreadsheet format makes for easy simulations and what-if tests.

A-T-A-R is a term that came from consumer products marketing. Industry has traditionally used slightly different language, so a natural question is, "Does the model apply to all types of new products, including industrial ones, and services too?" The answer is absolutely, though each term may be defined slightly differently in different settings.

See Figure 8–7 for the definitions of terms that vary. A consumer **buying unit** may be a person or a home. For office furniture, it will perhaps be a facility manager; for industrial products, it will generally be a purchasing or engineering person (part of a team); and for a consumer bank loan, it will once again be a person or a family. Product developers know what these definitions should be; the target users were selected partly because we know them well.

Without a precise definition there can be no worthwhile measurement. In each case, something about the term tells you how to define it. For **awareness,** we want to know if the buying unit has been sufficiently informed to stimulate further investigation and consideration of trial. If it has only heard the product's name, it probably won't.

For **trial,** you may already be wondering how a potential buyer could "try" the security device that must be installed in a car, that is, try it in risk situations, waiting for a thief to challenge it. The answer is that we get as close to the perfect answer as we can, and that sometimes calls for ingenuity. Otis Elevator Company, for example, is not selling cake mixes—they simply take prospective buyers to a site where the elevator under consideration is already installed. The trial is not perfect, but it is close enough for real customer learning. Sometimes firms use **vicarious trial** where a person or firm who *did* try something shares results with someone who can't try it. But trial there should be, and Chrysler

---

FIGURE 8–7   Definitions Used in A-T-A-R Model

Buying unit means purchase point; may be each person or department who participates in the decision.

Aware means someone in the buying unit hears about the existence of a new product with some characteristic that differentiates it; subject to variation between industries and even between developers.

Available means the percentage chance that if a buyer wants to try the product, the effort to find it will be successful; often "percent of stores that stock it." Direct sellers have 100 percent availability.

Trial is variously defined; may be use of a sample in an industrial setting where such use has a cost associated with it; in most situations, means an actual purchase and at least some consumption.

Repeat is also varied; on packaged goods, means to buy at least one (or two or three) more times; on durables, may mean be happy and/or make at least one recommendation to others.

---

once wanted a new item tried so badly that they paid people $50 if they would take a demonstration ride (and later show proof of purchase of a new car within a month). It can be done.

In a trial, we want two things to happen:

1. The buying unit went to some expense to get the trial supply—if there was no cost, then we can't be sure there was evaluation of the product message and interest created. Anyone can taste some sausage in a supermarket, but that doesn't mean the taste was a true trial.

2. The buying unit used the new item enough to have a basis for deciding whether it is any good.

For **availability**, we want to know whether the buyer can easily get the new product if a decision is made to try it. This factor is more standard, and for consumer products is usually the percent of those outlets where our target buyers shop where the firm has stocking of the new item. (The percentage may be weighted by the sales volumes of the stores sampled.) If the firm sells direct, there is always availability (unless the factory has extended back orders). Business-to-business often uses distributors of some type, usually under some franchise or semifranchise agreement, again pretty much assuring availability. But many small firms cannot be sure of availability, and spend much of their marketing money on trying to get it.

Repeat is easy for consumer packaged goods (usually, a repeat purchase), but it really means the trial was successful—the buying unit was pleased. For one-time purchases (industrial or consumer), we have to decide what statistic will tell us that. Some people use the direct one: "Were you satisfied?" Sometimes, an indirect one—such as, "Have you had occasion to recommend the product to others?"—is better. In the case of the car security device, buying one for another car would be a good measurement. In any case, a firm should arrive at some acceptable definition and stick with it, thus building up experience to measure against.

Where Do We Get the Figures for the A-T-A-R Model?

Figure 8–8 shows where we customarily get the data for the A-T-A-R model and, thus, how the model ties the entire evaluation process together. You are not yet acquainted with the various tests, but they will be tied into the A-T-A-R model as they come up. Though various evaluation events can help on several of the key factors, we are usually most interested in the one event that makes the biggest contribution—noted as "best" in the figure. And, we should know which these are prior to starting the evaluation. That way, we spend our limited funds first on the best steps and then on others if funds are available. Too, if we have to skip a step (for example, the concept test), we immediately know we are leaving open the question of whether users are likely to try the item when it becomes available. If we are going to do product use testing, then it should be set up in a way that lets us go through a concept test in the process of getting people to sign up for the use testing. It's later than we wanted, but better now than not at all.

FIGURE 8–8   Items in the A-T-A-R Model Have Multiple Sources: A Rolling Evaluation

| A-T-A-R Item | Various Sources of Estimates for It | | | | |
	Basic Market Research	Concept Test	Product Use Test	Component Testing	Market Test
Market units	Best	Helpful	Helpful		Helpful
Awareness*		Helpful	Helpful	Best	Helpful
Trial		Best	Helpful		Helpful
Availability†	Helpful				Best
Repeat (adoption)			Best		Helpful
Consumption	Helpful	Helpful	Helpful		Best
Price per unit	Helpful	Helpful	Helpful	Helpful	Best
Cost per unit‡				Helpful	Best

Key: Best = The best source for that item.
     Helpful = Some knowledge gained.

---

*Awareness is often gauged by the agency that develops the advertising.

†Availability is usually estimated by sales management, and doubts about the figure are key to selection among market testing methods.

‡The cost component in profit contribution is internally estimated, usually prior to actual start-up. But, valid figures can come only after some significant production.

Regarding Sales Forecasting in General

What we have been doing, of course, is making sales forecasts—predicting just how many of an item or new service we will sell. We need forecasts so badly that they are a basic input into every stage of the evaluation process—from opportunity to retrospect. (After the whole thing is over, some critics will be making their "forecasts" of what might have been!) Forecast importance has led to many techniques and devices, far more than can be covered here. Many of them are not relevant to new products, and many of them are just elaborate techniques of guessing. As one wit said, forecasting is difficult, especially forecasting the future. And no business situation has more unknowns than a new product.

Most sales forecasting techniques have a paradigm of some kind—a model of the situation. For example, one of the most common is analogy—forecasting a new item compared to a prior new item. Another is to use market share—forecast the percentage of customers who will switch and multiply that percentage times total market sales. But A-T-A-R brings the paradigm right down to a specific new product—it calls for numbers that usually can be researched, and it uses them in a managerial way. We will see in Chapters 17–19 how it lies at the very base of the marketing program—what else is there for the marketing effort to do than achieve awareness, trial, availability, and repeat use?[3]

---

[3]One of our top sales forecasting experts recently addressed the new product situation, particularly the issues surrounding the many techniques. See Robert J. Thomas, "Issues in New Product Forecasting," *Journal of Product Innovation Management,* September 1994, pp. 347–53.

Summary

Each step in a proposed new product evaluation must be done well, of course. But deciding what evaluations to do, and when to do them, is also critical—maybe even more so.

So, we think in terms of an evaluation *system* for new products. The system's distinct purposes are more involved than a simplistic, "Will it sell?" primarily because we usually don't know if it will sell until late in the process, if even then. Instead, the system provides pieces of information that assist the project in its journey toward the market. And the triple steams diagram showed that we actually are developing a marketing plan and a financial statement right alongside the product itself.

So, this chapter looked at the factors that aid in designing an evaluation system. First came the cumulative expenditures curve, the risk/payoff matrix, and the decay curve. Then we looked at several descriptors of most situations, the primary one being that almost everything about a process situation is tentative. The product itself is still evolving, at least until it sells successfully, the actual date of marketing is increasingly unclear as firms adopt limited marketing approaches, evaluation actually begins with the innovation charter well before ideation, and a product is an assemblage of many parts, each requiring its own evaluation. There are potholes to be considered.

Because we can't ask people whether they will buy a product whose actual characteristics are still unknown, we must adopt surrogate questions. These are questions consumers probably can answer, and from these questions we can surmise what we want to know. For example, early in the process we use concept tests because a verbal concept statement is all we have.

The net result is a new products manager who knows the purposes of evaluation, the descriptors of the situation, and the specific decisions to be made, and who is aware of the surrounding pressures and can thus select the specific evaluation tools for a particular system. The system should be unique because no two situations are alike.

Lastly, we looked at the A-T-A-R model, which tells us some of the critical steps, and how our information about them can be used to forecast sales and profits, and to design an evaluation system accordingly.

What are the specific tools, what can each do, and what are their weaknesses? The ones we use prior to entering technical development are covered in the next two chapters. Others come later.

Applications

More questions from that interview with the company president.

1. "During a recent management meeting, two of my division managers (both in the U.K., incidentally) got into quite a tussle over the programs they use to evaluate new product ideas. One of them said he felt evaluation was

very important; he wanted to do it quite completely, and he certainly didn't want anyone working to further the development of an item unless the prospects for it looked highly promising. The other manager objected to this, saying she wanted products to move rapidly down the pike, saving the serious evaluation for the time when she had the data to make it meaningful. Both persons seemed to have a point, so I just let it ride. What do you think I should have said?"

2. "Recently I was reading an article about Xerox, and its president was saying how he wanted to drive new product costs down earlier, freeze the specs earlier, eliminate duplication of effort, and get new products into customer hands earlier in order to learn more about performance and costs. Using the idea of an evaluation system, can you tell me what you would say to that president about what he wants to do?"

3. "I don't know what your profs would say, but it often seems to me that we might be just as well off if we didn't do any evaluation on new products. Just produce the ones we're convinced will sell the best and really support those. Let's face it—we never have reliable data anyway, and everyone is always changing minds or opinions. Never knew so many people could say I told you so."

4. "Tell you another funny thing about evaluation—seems as though the folks involved in it never use the facts or data that they should and instead use some sort of surrogate data. I don't see why you have to beat around the bush. Why not just gather the real facts in the first place and not use those substitutes?"

CASE: CONCEPT DEVELOPMENT CORPORATION

Late in 1990, three bridge-playing friends in a southern college town decided to start their own firm. One, Bob Stark, worked for General Motors as a planning manager in a local assembly operation. The second, Betsy Morningside, was a speech and theater professor at the college. The third, Myron Hite, was a CPA who worked for one of the Big Eight accounting firms.

All three were exceptionally creative and especially enjoyed their bridge sessions because they had a chance to brag about their new creations and to hear the creations of the others. It was all for fun until one evening it struck them that it was time to stop the fun and start making some money from their many ideas. So, they quit their jobs, pooled their savings, rented a small, three-room office, hired a couple of people, coined the name Concept Development Corporation, and started serious work.

A professor from the college was asked to "make a contribution to local entrepreneurship" by setting up a system to evaluate their ideas. They fully realized they were better at thinking up things than evaluating them. They also were aware of their deficiencies: little staff, little money, little experience in making things like the ones they created, and little time before their meager savings disappeared completely.

Source: This is a real situation, slightly camouflaged.

They began with two product areas. One was toys, broadly defined as things children played with, especially toys used for educational activities. The other area was writing services, something they had not intended to work on but which arose as temporary spin-offs from the abilities of one of the two people they hired. These services primarily involved designing and writing instruction sheets for area firms (training manuals, copy for package inserts, instruction signs—anywhere words were used to instruct people in doing things). The individual had some background in instructions, and was experienced in writing and layout work. So they decided to sell his services too.

Their strategy was to develop unique toys that required little up-front expenditures (e.g., dies and packaging equipment). They were all three too creative to settle for imitation. Most toys would have some game or competitive aspect, be educational, and involve paper, color, numbers, and the like. They figured "most of the stuff would be for children under 12." And, of course, they needed products that would catch on fast and sell well.

The writing services would be partly reactive in that they would do whatever clients asked them to do. But, being creative, they also planned to create innovative services—new ways of meeting industry and business needs. For example, they wanted to offer a special test/training service: after developing a training manual or instruction sheet, they would have some employees for whom the piece was developed come to a special room where they would read the material, apply it in some fashion, be tested on it, and so on. What they delivered to the client would be proven to work. They had many such ideas.

The professor went back to the college and decided to let a new products class assist in the assignment. The students were asked to think about the new firm's situation, the general evaluation system in Figure 8–2, and the various purposes and special circumstances discussed in Chapter 8 and then come up with one general guideline statement of evaluation policy for the toy ideas and another for the new services. They hadn't yet studied specific techniques (such as concept testing), but they could clearly indicate which of the six major stages in Figure 8–2 were the most critical, where the toughest decisions would be, and so on. The professor was especially interested in what the students felt were the differences between the evaluation of toys and the evaluation of services.

9 CHARTER AND PRESCREENING

Setting

This chapter is the first of two spelling out the various tools for evaluating new products (goods and services) *prior* to undertaking technical development. Chapter 9 will cover the product innovation charter and market analysis activities, which occur before the idea appears, and the initial reaction and the concept testing, which occur immediately after the idea appears.

The Importance of Up-Front Evaluations

In recent years there has been a big increase in activity at the pretechnical stage of the process. There still is not nearly enough, but the practice is spreading for four reasons. Three come from the triad of quality, time, and cost, discussed in Chapter 1, and the fourth from marketing.

The biggest cause of new product failure is that the intended buyer did not see a need for the item—no purpose, no benefits worth the price. It is in concept testing, a key part of this chapter, where we get our first confirmation that this will be a *quality* product. We save *time* by gathering information and making decisions that help assure the product will move through development fast, and with a minimum of looping back to correct some problem. Spending time here saves time overall.[1] We lower cost in several ways, one coming when we avoid the rising cumulative expenditures curve you just met in Chapter 8—with

---

[1] Several studies show this; see, for example, Albert L. Page and John S. Stovall, "Importance of the Early Stages in the New Product Process," in *Bridging the Gap from Concept to Commercialization* (Indianapolis, IN: Product Development and Management Association, 1994); Robert G. Cooper and Elko J. Kleinschmidt, "Determinants of Timeliness in Product Development," *Journal of Product Innovation Management*, November 1994, pp. 381–95; and Mitzi M. Montoya-Weiss and Roger Cantalone, "Determinants of New Product Performance: A Review and Meta-Analysis," *Journal of Product Innovation and Management*, November 1994, pp. 397–417.

the cost curve ever rising, the best time to get off a loser is at the bottom of the curve. Another cost cutter is the elimination of the many losers naturally picked up in an aggressive concept generation program. It's difficult to cut at this point, but we have to, so we want to do it in the correct way. Last, information gathered here helps us make cost forecasts—just how close are we going to be to competition on the proposed item, and how draconian must our efficiencies be.

Quality, time, and cost—there is no better reason for taking action at this point. But highly relevant is that this is also the stage where we set the basic marketing strategy on firm ground. We confirm the target market (the user whose needs we are trying to find and solve) and settle on a product positioning statement (just how the new item will be better than others already out there). The positioning statement guides all the rest of the marketing activities.

So, we will look at what happens here, what firms are doing, and how one sets about doing what seems to be the very best approach—concept testing.

The Product Innnovation Charter

The earliest evaluation a firm makes is *of itself and its situation*. That evaluation yields a priori conclusions about new product proposals. The firm reaches these conclusions while making basic strategic decisions, as discussed in Chapter 4 on the product innovation charter. These decisions decree what types of new products fit best. For example:

Smith & Wesson wanted items to sell to law enforcement agencies.

Remington sought new uses for powdered metal technology.

Nabisco sought technological breakthroughs in snack foods.

The dimensions covered by a charter are shown in Figure 9–1. Of all possible new product concepts, the firm decides to reject (*in advance and without knowing the concepts*) those requiring technologies the firm does not have, those sold to customers about whom the firm has no close knowledge, those which demand too much (or too little) innovativeness, and those violating any other guideline in the PIC. These directions exclude most new product ideas. A few years ago the business press told us that all low-quality gift items had already been negatively evaluated by Hallmark management, and all items not related to oil wells had been prerejected by Rucker.

The charter given to new products management thus eliminates more product ideas than all the other evaluations combined, and by coming at the beginning of the new products system, it precludes the unfortunate practice of having unwanted proposals eat up valuable development funds before they are detected.

Market Analysis

The second evaluation that precedes appearance of the concept is an in-depth study of the market area that the product innovation charter has selected for

FIGURE 9–1

*The Exclusion
Power of a
Product
Innovation
Charter*

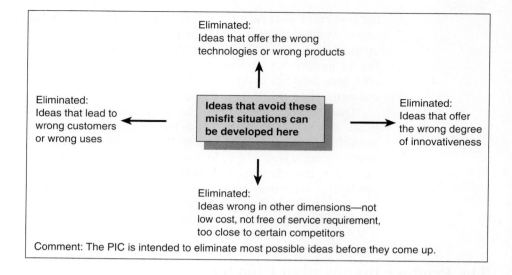

Eliminated:
Ideas that offer the wrong
technologies or wrong products

Eliminated:
Ideas that lead to
wrong customers
or wrong uses

**Ideas that avoid these
misfit situations can
be developed here**

Eliminated:
Ideas that offer
the wrong degree
of innovativeness

Eliminated:
Ideas wrong in other dimensions—not
low cost, not free of service requirement,
too close to certain competitors

Comment: The PIC is intended to eliminate most possible ideas before they come up.

focus. The study takes place immediately after the PIC is approved, and the depth of the study depends on how well the firm already knows the market selected. Ongoing ideation in support of present product lines takes place within a standing type of PIC, and no special study is necessary (assuming current product managers do their jobs correctly).

In the Rucker Company example above, new products people knew the oil industry well, but they didn't know everything about it. Moreover, their new products would probably be developed for specific new uses within that industry, about which the firm perhaps knew very little. But, in most cases, the PIC-designated market is not thoroughly understood and the market analysis is helpful.

Initial Reaction

Concept generation follows the market analysis just discussed. Concepts begin flowing in, usually very fast, and opinions on them are formed instantly. But most firms have evolved some special technique to handle this deluge more systematically, and, for want of an established term, we call it **initial reaction**.

At Oster, each idea that came from the marketing or administration departments went to the sales vice president first, and each idea from the technical departments or production went to the engineering vice president first. If one of these vice presidents approved the idea, it was sent to the other. If both approved, the idea went to a committee and the system became more formal. The two people making the initial reaction primarily used their experience of many years in the small-appliance industry.

Quick and inexpensive initial reactions must resist the "bazooka effect" (where suggestions are quickly blasted out) so several provisos apply:

1. *The idea source does not usually participate in the initial reaction.* A person who has an idea may want to explain it and argue for it, but this person should probably not have a vote in the decision to advance the idea or drop it.

2. *Two or more persons are involved in any rejection decision*, based on the "fragility of new ideas" concept discussed in Chapter 8. The rejection percentage is much higher here than at any other stage, but involving two or more persons dilutes the biases of a single person. The Oster system did not have this safeguard because either vice president could kill the suggestion.

3. *The initial reaction, though quick, is based on more than a pure intuitive sense.* The evaluators are trained and experienced, records are kept and reviewed, and objective aids are sought.

One of several techniques used in this initial reaction is the product innovation charter. Knowing whether a firm wants to be first or last, high risk or low risk, internally or externally developing, and stay in shoes or add handbags leads to quick and decisive action.

Most firms also make use of heuristics (rules of thumb) for this rough screening. For example, managers look at the scale required (is it in our league?), the competitor we would have to face, state of the art the idea would require, and the fit with our manufacturing and marketing operations.

Some managers prefer to use a small-scale informal survey at this initial reaction point, particularly when some aspect of the proposal extends beyond the evaluator's experience. But such surveys should be held to the level of telephone checks with professional colleagues.

Concept Testing and Development

Years ago, when Alan Ladd, Jr., reigned as top judge of new movie scripts at Twentieth Century-Fox Film Corporation, he revealed that his product proposal evaluation system ended about as soon as it began. He would just read a script and decide whether to make the movie. He and his small staff knew their markets well, had a guiding product innovation charter, and combined their knowledge and the charter with personal judgment to reach decisions. They did not use concept testing, full screening, or product use testing. Ladd said: "It's based on my intuition and experience. There's no way to put it on a chart or graph or formulate it."[2]

---

[2]Earl C. Gottschalk, "How Fox's Movie Boss Decides that a Script Is a Powerful Winner," *The Wall Street Journal*, May 17, 1979, p. 1. Many years later, he was still doing the fast reaction, and had some major successes—e.g., winners *Star Wars*, *Nine to Five*, and *Thelma & Louise*. But he had also worked at several different studios, and had marketed some misses—*The Right Stuff*, *Quigley Down Under*, and *Not Without My Daughter*. See Ronald Grover, "Can Alan Ladd Jr. Make Leo the Lion Roar?" *Business Week*, August 12, 1991, pp. 65–66.

Perhaps. Some agree with Mr. Ladd, but most do not. Most major firms make frequent use of **concept testing**. It is a mandatory part of the process for makers of consumer packaged goods. And use is growing in industrial firms, which actually invented it. Business-to-business firms have always spent much time talking with users about their needs and problems, what suggestions they have, what they think about various ideas, and so on. They just never called it concept testing.

But first, let's deal with some concerns about this activity—there are times when it doesn't help. When the prime benefit is a **personal sense**, such as the aroma of a perfume or the taste of a new food, concept testing usually fails. The concept cannot be communicated short of actually having some product there to demonstrate. A type of kids' gum popular in the early 90s (sour gums called Cry Baby and Warhead) tasted so bad that even product use testing showed they hated it. But, when available, they became masochistic to the tune of almost $100 million a year.

Second, concepts embodying new art and entertainment are tough to test. Whistler could not have concept-tested his idea for a painting of his mother, nor could the inventor of the Ferris wheel have surveyed people to ask what they thought of it. The thrill simply had to be experienced personally. The same for Arnold Schwartzenegger's movie *Junior*. It tested poorly and sold well.

Third, when the concept embodies some **new technology** that users cannot visualize, it is also a weak tool. Kodak realized this when it tried to concept-test its new disc camera. So did Alberto-Culver when it first tested the concept of hair mousse. Women accustomed to sprays could not imagine putting "stuff like that" on their hair. Only after the company developed the product and set up training classes in salons did women agree to try the mousse. Another example was when physicians rejected the concept of a heart pump—they could not know the full attributes (and thus the risks) of such a product before work was completed. Ditto on pump baseball gloves, which kids thought would be great until they put them on and found too snug a fit.

Fourth, there are times when firms mismanage concept testing and then blame the tool for misleading them. Coca-Cola asked their customers to taste-test New Coke and got favorable replies. But they then took that taste testing to mean customers would buy the product when it got a new name. This is actually the same problem as the heart pump—customers were asked to predict their behavior without knowing all the facts. They can't, but will if asked, and will deceive developers who aren't careful. Another mismanagement was when several fast food chains asked customers if they wanted diet burgers. Not only was it an unknown taste situation (above) but people are notoriously inclined to predict "worthy" behavior and then do something else.

Fifth, consumers sometimes simply do not know what problems they have. We discussed this in the chapter on problem-based ideation. Steelcase, for example, found they could not use concept testing on special furniture for use by teams. The team members had no feeling for what they didn't have, so Steelcase observed them in action and came up with a winner: furniture that lets them do some of their work collaboratively and some privately. The microwave oven was a similar example—we didn't know what to do with it even after it hit the market, and certainly could not have responded helpfully to researchers asking us what we thought about the concept.[3]

Oddly, in spite of evidence to the contrary, some new products people have doubts about concept testing on business and industrial products and on services. Regarding the former, if one sticks to situations where the customer has the ability to make judgments, those judgments are worth gathering. However, major technological breakthroughs don't qualify for that, and we just have to take the risk. On services, there is no question that people can tell us what they see is useful if they can see it (but watch for the intangibles cited above). They can. But because there is usually little technical development on services, there is less *need* to do concept testing. If it is simple to go from concept to full service description (a form of prototype), then the services firm can proceed to what is called **prototype concept testing**. Such testing is, of course, much more reliable, with a prototype to talk around.

Concept testing is useful in most cases, and right now the burden of argument lies with the person who wants to skip it. Unfortunately, however, we will hear about such firms as Suga Test Instruments Company of Tokyo, which marketed its $1.3 million artificial snow machine, for a long time. Designed for utilities, car manufacturers, battery makers, outdoor clothing makers, and others, the snow machine met with almost zero adoption. True, it made more and better snow than any other machine, and it did the work inside a five-story building. But every target market already had methods for product testing and did not need the new machine. No one had bothered to ask them.[4]

A similar case came up when CalFare Corporation (without concept testing) developed shopping carts with a "special 5th Wheel" that locked into place if the cart was taken from the premises (and run over a rough surface). The cart would then only go in circles. But, most stores said no thanks. They feared negative publicity that would scare customers away. A competitor said it often happened that the cart went awry and started circling around the dairy department. The developers were caught off guard by the very negative reactions they got.[5]

What Is a New Product Concept?

Webster's says a concept is an idea or an abstract notion. Businesspeople use the term *concept* for the product promise, the customer proposition, and the real reason why people should buy. It is a stated relationship between product features (form or technology) and consumer benefits—a claim of proposed satisfactions.

---

[3]Some of these examples are discussed in Justin Martin, "Ignore Your Customer," *Fortune*, May 1, 1995, pp. 121–28.

[4]Marc Beauschamp, "Cold Shoulder," *Business Week*, October 6, 1986, p. 168.

[5]David Jefferson, "Building a Better Mousetrap Doesn't Ensure Success," *The Wall Street Journal*, November 18, 1991, p. B2.

This promise is open to four interpretations:

1. The *producer's* perception of the *features* of the new product.
2. The *consumer's* perception of the *features* of the new product.
3. The *producer's* estimate of the *benefits* delivered by that set of features.
4. The *consumer's* estimate of the *benefits* delivered by that set of features.

These are only forecasts, or guesses, at this time—not reality, even with a prototype in hand. They rest on expectations.

Thus, a **complete new product concept** is a statement about anticipated product features that will yield selected benefits relative to other products or problem solutions already available. An example is "A new electric razor whose screen is so thin it can cut closer than any other electric razor on the market."

Sometimes a part of the concept can be assumed; for example, saying "a copier that has twice the speed of current models" assumes the benefits of speed can go without saying.

The Purposes of Concept Testing

Recall that concept testing is part of the prescreening process, preparing a management team to do the full screening of the idea just before beginning serious technical work. We are looking for information to help the screeners use scoring models and write out product protocols, which we cover in Chapter 10.

Therefore, the *first* purpose of a concept test is to identify the very poor concept so it can be eliminated. If music lovers, for example, cannot conceive of a compact disc that will last forever and thus reject it out of hand, the concept is probably a poor one.

If the concept passes the first hurdle, a *second* purpose is to estimate (even crudely) the sales or trial rate that the product would enjoy—a sense of market share or a general range of revenue dollars. Some people believe this buying prediction is worthless. Others claim a clear, positive correlation between intention and purchase. One longtime practicing market researcher claimed to have confidential data showing correlations of 0.60 and well above.[6]

The buying intention question appears in almost every concept test. The most common format for purchase intentions is the classic five-point question: How likely would you be to buy a product like this, if we made it?

1. Definitely would buy.
2. Probably would buy.

---

[6]Personal communication with Anthony Bushman, later Professor of Marketing, San Francisco State University.

3. Might or might not buy.
4. Probably would not buy.
5. Definitely would not buy.

The number of people who definitely would buy or probably would buy are usually combined and used as an indicator of group reaction. This is called the **top-two-boxes** figure, from the fact that the questionnaire has boxes to check. Incidentally, Nabisco says "try" not "buy," because buyers really are still quite tentative at this point.

Whether this many people will actually purchase the item is not important. Researchers have usually calibrated their figures, so they know, for example, that if the top two boxes total 60 percent, the real figure will be, say, 25 percent. They do this from past experience, discounting what people tend to say in interview situations. Direct marketers can do the best calibration, because they will later be selling the tested item to market groups they surveyed; they can tell exactly how actual behavior matches stated intentions. The data banks of the Bases Group, the largest supplier of concept tests, permit a client company to calibrate all of its concept test questions, by product type. For a price, Bases translates a client's raw intentions data into probable intentions.[7]

Incidentally, sometimes experience calibrates the probable intention *higher* than the respondents answer during testing. On complex products, people often use caution at concept testing time but end up buying the product when they have a chance to see the final item and hear all about it. (Recall the heart pump.)

The *third* purpose of concept testing is to help develop the idea, not just test it. Concepts rarely emerge from a test the way they went in. Moreover, a concept statement is not enough to guide R&D. Scientists need to know what attributes (especially benefits) will permit the new product to fulfill the concept statement. Because the attributes frequently oppose or conflict with each other, many trade-offs must be made. When better to make them than when talking with people for whom the product is being developed? Some firms use the same analytical device discussed in Chapter 7 for concept generation—trade-off (or conjoint) analysis.

Concept Testing Research Procedure

There is no such thing as a standard concept test, in practice. There probably are no two experienced market researchers who use the same steps, but there is

---

[7]Other concept testing suppliers listed recently in a publication from the Leo Burnett advertising agency were: Conway/Milliken, Custom Research, Elrick & Lavidge, FRC Research, Information Resources, Longman-Moran Analytics, Market Decisions, Moskowitz Jacobs, NFO Research, Total Research, and The Vanderveer Group. Most of these have international operations.

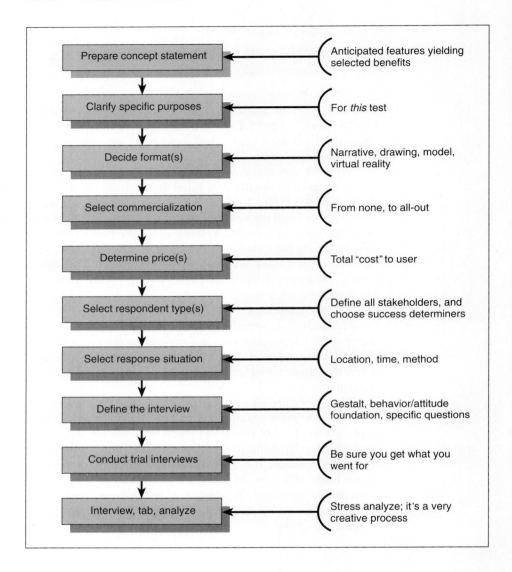

a general pattern. (See Figure 9–2.) Even a general pattern, however, wouldn't include the "antenna shops" used by Martin-Marietta for their software line. (See Chapter 6.)[8]

_____

[8]For more on this general approach, see Antonio S. Lauglaug, "Technical-Market Research—Get Customers to Collaborate in Developing Products," *Long Range Planning*, April 1993, pp. 78–82.

Prepare Concept Statement

A concept statement states a difference and how that difference benefits the customer or end user: "This new refrigerator is built with modular parts; consequently, the consumer can arrange the parts to best fit a given kitchen location, and then rearrange them to fit another location."

If you think this sounds somewhat like a positioning statement, you are correct. And if the interviews are with a logical target group of potential buyers, the principal parts of a marketing strategy are in place—target market and product positioning. This is consistent with the statement in Chapter 8 that the product and its marketing plan are developed simultaneously, in the triple streams of activity.

Practitioners urge that any concept statement should make the new item's difference absolutely clear, claim determinant attributes (those that make a difference in buying decisions), offer a chord of familiarity by relating in some way to things familiar to the customer, and be completely credible and realistic. And short, as short as possible, although there have been concept statements of 3–5 pages that worked very well in complex technical situations.[9]

This information is usually presented to potential buyers in one of four formats:

1. Narrative (verbal).
2. Drawing, diagram, sketch.
3. Model or prototype.
4. Virtual reality.

Figure 9–3 shows an example of the narrative format. Some people prefer a very brief presentation, giving only the minimum of attributes and letting the respondent offer additional ones. Others prefer a full description, approaching what a diagram or prototype would provide. In the pure narrative, the concept is totally intangible, though there are ways to provide some measurement when doing concept tests of services.[10]

Figure 9–4 demonstrates the use of a drawing. Drawings and diagrams usually must be supplemented by a narrative statement of the concept.

Prototypes, or models, are a more expensive form of concept statement, because many decisions have to be made about the new product to get it into a

---

[9]Robert E. Davis calls these testable concepts in "From Experience: The Role of Market Research in the Development of New Consumer Products," *Journal of Product Innovation Management,* September 1993, pp. 309–17. Regarding clarity, Anheuser-Busch said consumers had difficulty understanding Bud Dry, even when it was marketed. Perhaps the reason lies in what an executive said it was: "A cold-filtered draft beer—not pasteurized—with no aftertaste, basically a full-alcohol, light beer, a cleaner beer."

[10]An example of how services can be somewhat quantified is shown in a study of retail service by A. Parasuraman, Valerie Ziethaml, and Leonard L. Berry, *Servqual: A Multiple-Item Scale for Measuring Customer Perceptions of Service Quality* (Cambridge, MA: Marketing Science Institute, 1986).

FIGURE 9–3   **Mail Concept Test Format—Plain Verbal Description of the Product (Good or Service) and Its Major Benefits**

A major soft-drink manufacturer would like to get your reaction to an idea for a new diet soft drink. Please read the description below before answering the questions.

> *New Diet Soft Drink*
>
> Here is a tasty, sparkling beverage that quenches thirst, refreshes, and makes the mouth tingle with a delightful flavor blend of orange, mint, and lime.
>
> It helps adults (and kids too) control weight by reducing the craving for sweets and between-meal snacks. And, best of all, it contains absolutely no calories.
>
> Comes in 12-ounce cans or bottles and costs 60¢ each.

1. How different, if at all, do you think this diet soft drink would be from other available products now on the market that might be compared with it?

   ☐ Very different
   ☐ Somewhat different
   ☐ Slightly different
   ☐ Not at all different

2. Assuming you tried the product described above and like it, about how often do you think you would buy it?

	Check one
More than once a week	☐
About once a week	☐
About twice a month	☐
About once a month	☐
Less often	☐
Would never buy it	☐

Source: NFO Research, Inc., Toledo, Ohio.

---

prototype. Whoever builds an early prototype makes lots of decisions about the item that probably should be kept open at this early date. Prototypes are useful only in special situations, as, for example, with simple-to-prepare food products or, at the other extreme, with concepts so complex that the buyer cannot react without more knowledge than a simple narrative would give. A firm in Canada was trying to get reactions to the concept of a traveling medical examining unit that would be driven to various corporation offices where examinations would be given. The answer was to build a small model of the unit, showing layout, equipment, and so on.[11]

The fourth type of concept format, where it can be used, captures the advantages of the prototype without most of the disadvantages. Steelcase, the office

---

[11]Robert G. Cooper, *Winning at New Products* (Reading, MA: Addison-Wesley Publishing, 1986), p. 59.

FIGURE 9–4

Mail Concept Test—Sketch

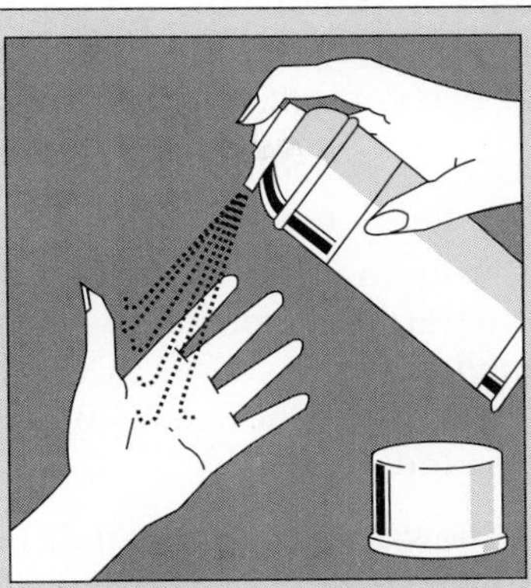

Aerosol Hand Cleanser
A large-size can of hand cleanser concentrate that completely eliminates those lingering unpleasant odors that come from handling fish, onions, garlic, furniture polish, etc. Not a covering odor! Just press the button and spray directly on the hands, rub for a few seconds, and rinse off under the faucet. 24-ounce aerosol can will last for months and can be easily stored. Costs $2.25.

1. How interested would you be in buying the product described above if it were available at your supermarket?

Check one

I would definitely buy ☐
I would probably buy ☐
I might or might not buy ☐
I would probably not buy ☐
I would definitely not buy ☐

Source: NFO Research, Inc., Toledo, Ohio.

supply firm, has a software system that allows them to "build" three-dimensional images of office concepts. The interviewee can actually walk around rooms, seeing things from any angle. This virtual-reality approach permitted them to win a big contract for the Olympic Village at the 1996 Atlanta Olympics—the games management could not only see but also modify on the spot every room in the layout.[12]

The real question is, "What does it take to communicate to the buyer what we have in mind?" From that point on, it is a question of the cost of better displays versus the need for that information in making forecasts of buying intentions. For office furniture, most buyers want lots of details, but for turnip-flavored yogurt, one sentence would probably work.[13]

[12]The information was presented by William Miller at the Product Development and Management Association Conference, Southfield, Michigan, January 1995. Further information on the use of personal computers in concept testing can be found in William M. Bulkeley, "More Market Researchers Swear by PCs," *The Wall Street Journal*, March 15, 1993, p. B1.

[13]Don't laugh. Green Giant Vegetable Yogurt in four "flavors" (cucumber, beet, tomato, and garden salad) scored well on concept tests (87 percent top two boxes). But the firm couldn't deliver what the concept seemed to promise to consumers—crunchy, etc. Sales failure.

Commercialized Concept Statements. A special variation, regardless of format, concerns whether to make the statement in **commercialized** (promotional) mode. Compare these two concept statements:

> Light Peanut Butter, a low-calorie version of natural peanut butter that can provide a tasty addition to most diets.
>
> A marvelous new way to chase the blahs from your diet has been discovered by General Mills scientists—a low-calorie version of ever-popular peanut butter. As tasty as ever and produced by a natural process, our new Light Peanut Butter will fit most weight-control diets in use today.

Those statements show little *substantial* difference, yet they will draw different reactions. Commercialized formats produce "more realistic" evaluations (that is, greater acceptance), but they risk the bias of good or poor advertising copywriting. Proponents say noncommercialized statements won't provoke typical market reactions in this commercial world. Critics answer, why evaluate the advertising when all we want at this time is reaction to the concept?

Neither form is *better* than the other, and many managers simply go for a compromise—a gentle sell that puts advantages in language stakeholders are used to.

Offering of Competitive Information. Customers of all types know much less about their current products and other options than we would like. A new concept may well offer a benefit that the customer doesn't realize is new. One solution is to provide a full data sheet about each competitive product. The issue was researched (on dog food), and results showed no significant difference, though most of the data did bend slightly in favor of the new product when there was full information.[14] And many new product managers don't like to overload the concept statement; it diffuses the message and confuses the customer.

Price. Another issue turns on whether to put a price in the concept statement. The examples in Figures 9–3 and 9–4 both mention price. The Bases Group insists on price in its concept tests. Some people object, saying reaction to the concept is wanted, not to its price. Yet price is part of the product (actually, a product attribute in the customer's eyes) and buyers can't be expected to tell purchase intentions without knowing price. An exception occurs for those complex concepts (e.g., the medical examinations van, above) requiring many decisions before the cost is known.

---

[14]James B. Miller, Norman T. Bruvold, and Jerome B. Kernan, "Does Competitive-Set Information Affect the Results of Concept Tests?" *Journal of Advertising Research*, April/May 1987, pp. 16–24.

Define the Respondent Group

We would like to interview any and all persons who will play a role in deciding whether the product will be bought and how it might be improved. When the New Zealand Wool Testing Authority came up with a new wool testing service, it had to test the concept with three levels in its channel—brokers who sell the raw wool, scourers who scour the wool and prepare it for shipment, and exporters who sell the wool to manufacturers.[15] A cement company, which created a new concept in cement for use in construction, had to seek advice from brick makers, siding makers, architects, builders, designers, and regulators, among others, in addition to the people who would be buying the buildings. Some industrial products may involve 5–10 different people at each buying point; durable consumer goods usually involve more than one person. Yet that peanut butter mentioned above could probably be tested with just one person in a family setting—the homemaker who does the buying—or could it?

That's why we think about **stakeholders**—any person or organization who has a stake in the proposed product. Our new product wastebaskets are filled with products that made sense to the end user but could not get to them—e.g., when professional sanitary engineers refuse to endorse a new system of water treatment.

Reaching this full set of influencers sounds simple, but is complex and expensive. Some people try to seek out a smaller number of potential buyers who are "lead users," or influencers, or large users.[16] This approach saves some money and gets more expert advice but often fails to reflect key differences (and misunderstandings) in the marketplace. It would seem to be a technique for situations where there is a "right" understanding or perception or preference.[17] Of course, we should always watch out for critics, people who have a reason for opposing the concept. A developer came up with a device that "read" electro-cardiograms and needed the reactions of cardiologists; but the obvious conflict of interest made the interviewing tricky. Compaq (to its regret) interviewed data processing managers (users of mainframes) and asked what they thought about using networks of PCs to replace mainframes!

Some new products people, aware that they will first have to interest the innovators and early adopters in a market, concentrate their concept testing solely on them. If this group is interested, it's a good bet others will be also.

Select Response Situation

There are two issues in the response situation: (1) the mode of reaching the respondent and (2) if personal, whether to approach individually or in a group.

---

[15]Arch G. Woodside, R. Hedley Sanderson, and Roderick J. Brodie, "Testing Acceptance of a New Industrial Service," *Industrial Marketing Management*, 1988, pp. 65–71.

[16]The lead-user concept was discussed in Chapter 5 under concept generation.

[17]This is discussed (and tested) in Jan P. L. Schoormans, Roland J. Ortt, and Cees J. P. M. de Bont, "Enhancing Concept Test Validity by Using Expert Consumers," *Journal of Product Innovation Management*, March 1995, pp. 153–62.

Most concept testing takes place through personal contact—direct interviewing. Survey samples typically run from about 100 to 400 people, though industrial samples are usually much smaller. Personal contact allows the interviewer to answer questions and to probe areas where the respondent is expressing a new idea or is not clear.

Some research suppliers offer a service of interviewing in which the client can submit product concepts on a shared-cost basis. In the Omnibus program at Moskowitz Jacobs, a fully equipped central testing facility conducts periodic waves of interviewing which yield 100 interviews at a cost per concept of around $3,000. Other research firms use pseudo stores in vacant locations at shopping malls. The high costs of personal contact have led developers to try other methods, especially the mail and the telephone, though both media offer problems today. NBC used cable TV. Viewers from 20 cable systems were conscripted, they viewed pilots in their homes, and were interviewed by telephone for their responses. Of course, creative people in the television industry were aghast that programming people would use concept testing, in any form. What is art coming to![18]

The second issue concerns individual versus group. Both are widely used. Groups (usually just called focus groups) are excellent when we want respondents to hear and react to the comments of others and to talk about how it would be used.

Prepare the Interviewing Sequence

Simple interviewing situations state the new product concept and ask about believability, buying intentions, and any other information wanted. The whole interview may take only two or three minutes per product concept if the item is a new packaged good and all we really want is a buying intention answer.

Usually we want more than that. In such cases, we first *explore the respondent's current practice* in the area concerned, asking how people currently try to solve their problems, what competing products they use, and what they think about those products. How willing would they be to change? What specific benefits do they want? What are they spending? Is the product being used as part of a system?

This background information helps us understand and interpret *comments about the new concept*, which are asked for next. The immediate and critical question is, "Does the respondent understand the concept?" Given understanding, we then seek other reactions:

- Uniqueness of the concept.
- Believability of the concept.
- Importance of the problem.
- Their interest in the concept.
- Is it realistic, practical, useful?

[18]Louis Weisberg, "Audience Reaction Steers TV Program Pilots," *Advertising Age*, February 28, 1985, p. 26.

- Does it solve a problem?
- How much they like the concept.
- How likely they would be to buy.
- Their reaction to the price.
- Problems they see in use.

We are especially interested in what changes they would make in the concept, exactly what it would be used for and why, what products or processes would be replaced, and who else would be involved in using the item.

You can see that services offer a problem here. A service offers an image, or a feeling, or a hard-to-measure convenience. This makes it difficult for the respondent to give useful information along the lines just listed.

In all this interviewing, remember we are not taking a poll but, rather, *exploring what people are doing and thinking*. Only a few questions will be in standard form, for tabulation. Each new concept addresses a very specific problem (or at least it should), and we need to know what people think about that problem in the context of the new concept. It doesn't pay to get too formal in the questioning, unless conducting many concept tests where there is a database for comparison.

Conduct Trial Interviewing

As in all research work, it is important to do some trial interviews with people in the target respondent group. Trial interviews are especially needed on concept testing, given the communication problems inherent in new things.

Interview, Tabulate, Analyze

The analysis for standard products is quite brief and may be summed up in one statistic—the top two boxes (or some variation, such as top box plus 30 percent, settled on from experience in an industry). But we usually want much more. Some surprise findings will require further thought and even further interviewing. The analysis stage differs from that in other surveys—it is a group activity, product managers and technical people are involved, it is a creative session, and numbers are not as important as general confirmation of earlier thoughts.

Variations

However good the above procedure is thought to be, there are stalwart objectors. Avon markets 50 new products every 60 days, with a three-month development cycle. Every two weeks they meet with some of their test bank of 150 sales reps. Many ideas are shown to them for their quick reaction, by computer-driven projectors. Their "appeal rating" correlates very well with sales, in some cases more accurately then field consumer concept testing predicted. A garment must be cut to fit a body, and bodies vary greatly.

Lastly, we don't know yet the ultimate value of computer simulations. Really new products, especially technology-based ones, do not concept test well. People cannot fathom what is being offered, and tend to be too cooperative. It is too costly to wait until working models are ready before getting user inputs, so perhaps the virtual reality world will be able to project things people can understand. Right now, the verdict is not in.[19]

Conclusions

The advantages of concept testing and development prior to full screening are many. It can be done quickly and easily, it gives the screeners invaluable information for sorting out less-valuable concepts, proven market research technology exists and is reasonably confidential, we learn a lot about buyer thinking, and segments and positionings can be developed in tandem with the concept. Unfortunately, some developers (especially industrial designers) still refuse to do concept testing. Herman Miller, for example, was unable to market successfully a Hygiene System that incorporated a toilet, sink, and tub. It had not been concept-tested, and after it failed, the designer claimed that industry people still did not understand it.

Nevertheless, concept testing is a bit treacherous—mistakes are easy and can be costly. It is not a tool for amateurs. There have been classic flops, most of which passed concept tests—dry soups, white whiskey, clear soda, and so on. The original chewable antacid tablet floundered because the concept test missed the idea that people then wanted water with antacids. One firm studied executions of a single new product idea by three copywriters and found that the most important determinant of high scores in the concept test was the skill of the copywriter.

People find reacting to entirely new concepts difficult without a learning period, the stimulus of a concept statement is very brief, many situation variables will change by the time the product is marketed, and certain attributes cannot be measured in a concept test—for example, rug texture, shower nozzle impact, and what color will be "in" next season.

Perhaps most troublesome, the technique has just enough slippage in it that persistent product champions often argue successfully against its findings.

Summary

This was the first chapter covering the tools used to evaluate new product proposals. Because evaluation actually begins prior to ideation (i.e., deciding where to seek ideas), we first looked at the product innovation charter. By focusing the

---

[19]For some thoughts on this, and some of the work in process, see Bart Ziegler, "Old Market Research Tricks No Match for New Technology," *The Wall Street Journal*, November 1, 1994, p. B1.

creative activity in certain directions, the charter automatically excludes all other directions and thus, in effect, evaluates them negatively.

Once the strategic direction is clear, most firms undertake a market analysis of the opportunity described by it. The customer should be a major input to any product innovation program, and an excellent time to seek this input is immediately after strategic decisions have been made. Then, as the ideas begin to roll in, an initial response is made—highly judgmental, quick, and designed primarily to clean out the worthless ideas.

Once an idea passes that test, more serious evaluation begins. The tool at this point is concept testing, or concept development, which now has a lengthy history of successful use. The chapter gave the overall procedure for concept testing, including its purposes, options in concept format, respondent selection, and the interviewing procedure.

An immediate benefit of concept testing is that it gives management the information needed to make the judgments required by the scoring models used in the following step—the full screen of the concept, which is the subject of Chapter 10.

Applications

More questions from that interview with the company president.

1. "You know, most of our new products people do a great deal of marketing research—concept testing, attitude surveys, and the like. But let me read something that one automobile designer thought about marketing research." [She then read from a yellowed clipping on her desk.]

   Market research is probably the greatest single deterrent to excellence in modern business. It's a crutch for managers with no vision and no conviction. On the surface, it sounds sensible enough: Find out exactly what the buyers want before you come to a design. But in practice, it's impossible. The public doesn't know what it wants without being shown the choices, and even then, preference is apt to veer off in the direction of Kmart. Market research gives you Malibus with Mercedes grilles, refrigerators in avocado hues, and Big Macs with everything. You do not, however, produce greatness with this technique.[20]

   Perhaps you would comment on that statement.

2. "Last year, a firm in New York, called Telesession Corporation, claimed that it had perfected a system of conference calling where telephones could be used for a focus group. Telesession claims to have used it on specialized groups as well as homemakers—for example, hospital lab directors and electrical engineers. It even has a deal whereby packages are mailed to the persons to be interviewed (after they agree to participate) with instructions not to open the package until told to do so during the conference call session. I'm thinking of three divisions—orthopedic

---

[20]"The Best Car in the World," *Car and Driver*, November 1979, p. 92.

equipment (crutches, suspension systems, etc.), advanced electronic systems for use in assembly line controls, and commercial fax machines. Could they use this system of concept testing effectively?"

3. "A cosmetics competitor is trying to speed up its new product work on lipsticks by a system that uses (1) brainstorming to create ideas (392 in a recent session); (2) evaluation of those ideas by the same group of people, down to only the best 50 ideas; and then (3) focus group sessions for concept-testing those ideas down to the few that should be developed rapidly. Do you see anything wrong with this system?"

4. "I would be curious to test your personal judgment on some new ideas from one of our recent idea sessions. They were all accepted in later concept tests with consumers, and that concerns me. Are we safe to go ahead?

   a. A gasoline-powered pogo stick.

   b. A combination valet stand and electric pants presser.

   c. Transistorized golf balls and an electric finder.

   d. An Indian arm wrestling device so you can arm wrestle with yourself.

   e. An electrically heated bath mat.

   f. Chocolate candy in an edible chocolate box."

CASE: WOLVERINE CAR WASH

In 1968, Jerry Waldrop opened his first car wash, called the Wolverine Car Wash, in Columbus, Ohio. He had never worked for car washes but had run various small businesses as he worked his way through Ohio State University. He was convinced that better ways of running car washes rested primarily on money, which he was fortunate enough to have access to. Given ideas, money, and small-business talent, he was sure he could succeed.

And he did. By 1992, he had four establishments, was one of the leading car wash independents in the Midwest, and was still seeking better ways to do things. In 1984, he had put in a car detailing service ($110 for total cleaning of a car, inside and out, motor, under fenders, everywhere), and it was selling well.

About this time, he participated in a college concept-generating program that the son of his office manager was running in a course he was taking at another university. The subject was "The car wash—how can it be improved?" The experience was interesting—and fun to a guy like Jerry—but now he was giving hard thought to one idea from that session—a *portable car* wash that offered home or office delivery service. The idea itself wasn't new, of course, but several aspects of this particular proposal were.

The idea was this: Many people would get their cars washed more often (and probably waxed, too) if they didn't have to take the time to drive to the wash facility and chance having to wait in line. The answer to these people was a portable car wash. Somehow, a self-

---

Source: This is a realistic, but hypothetical, case situation.

contained car wash unit would be built that could be pulled around town, taken to a home or to a company parking lot on order, hooked up to a source of water (it would do its own immediate heating of the water), and have the vehicle(s) driven through it. Granted the washing would be less thorough than at the central units, but more personal attention would probably offset the facility size. And the service would be of maximum convenience, for which selected individuals would probably pay a good price.

But Jerry really wondered what to do next. He knew the car wash business and the people who bought the service. He had thought favorably about the idea, impossible as it seemed at first, but now figured he had better do something other than rely on gut feelings.

He had heard of concept testing at a recent Chamber of Commerce meeting and thought this might be the time to try it. So, he called the university marketing department, was referred to the placement office, and ended up with two marketing majors (of whom you are one). He asked each of them to prepare a concept testing proposal. The proposal was to contain a statement of the specific concept, the research format(s) of that concept, and the general research methodology.

He told them that if the idea passed the concept test, he planned to have a unit built and put into service on a limited basis in Columbus. He could start it with businesses, or with homes, or in shopping centers, so he hoped the concept test would help on that decision, too. And, what would he have to tell people about the new service? That is, what questions and problems would they have? And...but then he thought he had better let the students get started.

10   THE FULL SCREEN

Setting

As we saw in Chapter 9, business approaches to the prescreening tasks vary considerably. The full screening step also varies, because businesses differ so much in what follows the screening. Some firms need very little technical work to come up with a suitable product. For them, the screen is a minor exercise on the way to a much more important step—field testing of the finished item, product use testing.

For other firms, the technological breakthrough is the whole ball game; their R&D may require millions of dollars and many years. The full screen is the last low-risk evaluation, and managers want it done well.

Consequently, this chapter cannot present what any particular firm should do. That's up to the new products manager. But we can present the range of alternatives and a middle ground that actually fits most firms. It can easily be modified. See Figure 10–1 for how screening relates to concept testing and the protocol step that follows from it.

Unfortunately for you, the step is not glamorous. It isn't discussed weekly in the business press, and, in fact, you may never have heard of a full screen step until you read about it in this book. But business has heard of it, and has been using it for many years. Research on it continues, as we will see later, even in large firms known for their ability to generate successful new products.[1]

Purposes of the Full Screen

Recall where we are in the product innovation process. After the original idea emerged, we put it into concept format and then gave it a brief initial exposure

---

[1]Procter & Gamble is one, as reported in Robert E. Davis, "The Role of Market Research in the Development of New Consumer Products," *Journal of Product Innovation Management*, September 1993, pp. 309–17.

FIGURE 10–1

Flow of New Product Concepts through the Screening/ Protocol Process

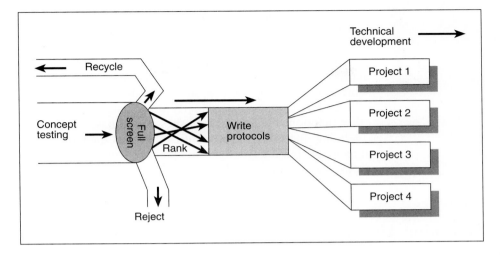

for reaction by key players. Concept testing then enabled us to add the thoughts of potential users to the set of market and other data collected since the time of the product innovation charter. Along the way, we have been compiling the inputs of key functional people in the firm—technical, marketing, financial, operational, and the like.

This work (which is situation-dependent, and may take from a couple days up to several months) culminates in a step called the full screen. It is full in the sense that we now have as much information as we're going to get before undertaking technical work on the product. The following material deals with how that step can be made most worthwhile, and the first issue is, why do we do it? There are several good reasons.

First, we need a screen that helps us decide whether technical resources (R&D, systems design for services, engineering, etc.) should be devoted to the project and, if so, how vigorously. This decision rests on whether we *can* do the job and whether we *want* to do it. "Can do" means feasibility—is technology up to the task, do we have it, and can we afford it? "Want to" means will we get out of the project the profits, market share, or whatever it is we are doing product innovation for? Sometimes these are called **feasibility of technical accomplishment** and **feasibility of commercial accomplishment.**

Second, the screening step helps manage the process—by (1) cycling unacceptable but potentially worthwhile concepts back into concept development where more work may make them acceptable, (2) rank-ordering the good concepts such that we have some options on standby when an ongoing project stalls or is canceled, and (3) recording the appraisals on rejected concepts to prevent "reinventing the wheel" when a similar concept comes up again later. The latter may seem almost trivial to you, but to managers who screen hundreds or even thousands of new product concepts a year it is not trivial. It's a good "corporate memory," too, to help settle arguments later. For example, businesspeople know that "a winning new product finds scores of 'parents' who proposed it, whereas a losing new product is always an orphan." In firms that like to reward creativity, it helps to know who suggested what, and when.

Third, the screening process encourages cross-functional communication. Scoring sessions are peppered with outbursts like "Why in the world did you score that rachet idea so low on such-and-such a factor?" The screening process is a learning process, particularly in making managers more sensitive to how other functions think. And it flushes out all basic disagreements about a project (including the ever-present politics) and sets them up for discussion. These disagreements put the spotlight on "potholes" or hurdles that the concept will face during development, and show where new people may be needed.

Screening Alternatives

There are three schools of thought on how the full screening should be done. Some firms, especially smaller ones and those not doing much new product work, prefer what really is an opinion poll, where one or more people make a judgment on some informal check list.[2] In some of these cases participants may have a printed list of evaluation points as memory joggers, taken from the more formal lists that follow.

Second, there are some packaged goods firms whose development process is really nontechnical—it is limited to me-too products and simple variations on what is already on the market. Knowing they can easily make the item and market it reasonably well, the only issue is whether consumers will like it. Thus, they do a more complete concept test (Chapter 9) and what they call **pre-market testing sales forecasting models,** which we will meet in Chapter 12. They don't have to forecast technical and commercial feasibility. When there are major technical issues (and there more often are, today, as the Procter & Gamble footnote showed), even the packaged goods firms won't depend on concept testing.

So, the third approach is what we will study here. It involves the use of a **scoring model**, which is nothing more than a mechanical arrangement of check-list factors with weights (importance) on them. A scoring model serves the purposes listed above; the other methods do not. This means that without a reasonably formal scoring model system (with inputs from all functions), technical people must do their own screening. Someone has to decide which concepts will get technical development effort and, historically, R&D departments have used what they call **portfolio models** to do the same thing scoring models do.

---

[2]Even some very capable firms feel they can't answer the issues in the more complete scoring models shown later. One unit of AT&T uses "Do customers care, Do we care, Can we do it, and Can we stay ahead if we do?"

The Scoring Model

Scoring models are simple but powerful things. Let's look at them through the eyes of a student who has a decision to make.

Introductory Concept

Assume a student is trying to decide what social activity to undertake this weekend. The student has several options, and more options may appear between now and then.

The student could list criteria on several decisions that are personally important, specifically:

1. It must be fun.
2. It must involve more than just two people.
3. It must be affordable.
4. It must be something I am capable of doing.

These four criteria (here called **factors**) are shown in Figure 10–2. Of course, 20 or 30 factors might be involved in this student's weekend social decisions, but let's stick with the 4. These factors are not absolutes; they can all be scaled—some fun, lots of fun, and so on. Figure 10–2 shows a four-point scale for each factor.

Next, each scale point needs a number so we can rank the options. With that done, the student can proceed to evaluate each option (as indicated in Figure 10–2) and total up the score for each. The final answer is to go boating—even though it isn't quite as much fun—primarily because it can involve lots of people, it is cheap, and the student is a capable rower.

FIGURE 10–2   Scoring Model for Student Activity Decision

Factors	Values			
	4 Points	*3 Points*	*2 Points*	*1 Point*
Degree of fun	Much	Some	Little	None
Number of people	Over 5	4 to 5	2 to 3	Under 2
Affordability	Easily	Probably	Maybe	No
Student's capability	Very	Good	Some	Little
Student's scorings:		*Skiing*	*Boating*	*Hiking*
Fun		4	3	4
People		4	4	2
Affordability		2	4	4
Capability		1	4	3
Totals		11	15	13
Answer: Go boating.				

But, suppose the student protests at this point and says: "There's more to it than that. If I go hiking, I'll get more exercise, but if I go skiing, a certain person is apt to be there." Or the student may argue that affordability is more important than the other factors because without enough money, there is no need to score the other points. Or the student may say, "Having fun is really more important than skill, so let's double the points for fun." And then there are objections: "skiing really is not all that much fun, boating is more expensive than you think," and so on.

A scoring process is what we actually use in making decisions like this, whether we realize it or not. The student's objections contain the basic problems of new product scoring models, and we will see how the criticisms can be handled to fashion a system that works pretty well.

The Procedure

It takes a while to develop a system, but once it is running, the fine-tuning does not require much effort.[3]

What Is Being Evaluated.   In the case of the above student, we chose to base the model on four arbitrarily selected factors. Selecting factors in real life is not that easy, and how we pick them is no accident. *First, if we could, we would use only one* factor. There is one factor that covers both technical and commercial accomplishment, a financial term called **net present value of the discounted stream of earnings from the product concept**, considering all direct and indirect costs and benefits. That mouthful is simply the finance way of saying "the bottom line on an income statement for the product, where we have included all costs (technical, marketing, etc.) and then discounted back the profits into what their value is today." That factor is shown on Level One in the abbreviated graphic of Figure 10–3. If it happens we can make a pretty good estimate of that net present value, no other factors would be needed. But we almost never can; at this early stage all financial estimates are quite shaky.

So, we use **surrogates** (or substitutes) for it. Level Two in Figure 10–3 shows the obvious two: the likelihood of technical accomplishment (meaning whether we can create something that will do what customers want) and the likelihood of commercial accomplishment (meaning, whether we can sell it profitably). There is again nothing left to do. Those two convictions would predict financial success on Level One, and we are finished.

Unfortunately, experience shows we usually can't make these two estimates either. So, we reach for more surrogates, this time at Level Three. To save space,

---

[3]Though quite easy when done in the mode of the scoring model example given later in this chapter, we should note that an immense body of theory lies behind all scoring decisions. For example, our scoring model is technically a linear compensatory model. That model, plus the conjunctive, disjunctive, and lexicographic models, is discussed (and compared in a new product screening exercise) in Kenneth G. Baker and Gerald S. Abaum, "Modeling New Product Screening Decisions," *Journal of Product Innovation Management*, March 1986, pp. 32–39.

FIGURE 10–3

Source of Scoring Model Factors

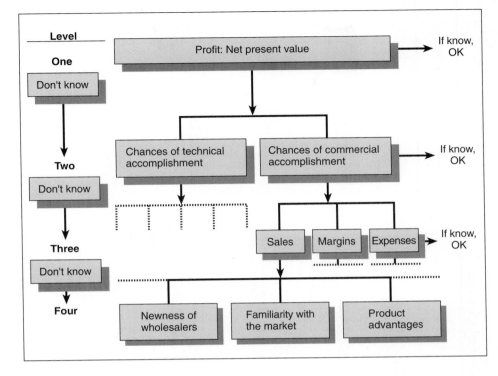

Figure 10–3 shows only the three that produce commercial accomplishment; if we know our sales, our margins on those sales, and our marketing and administrative expenses, we have the commercial half of the answer.

Alas, again we fall short; we don't have a very good fix on those figures either at this early point. Note, however, that the packaged goods firms developing marginally different new products, discussed above, *can* make these estimates and do so in their forecasting model. Most firms have to seek surrogates for the Level Three factors too.

This leads us to Level Four, which is where the action is. Level Four factors have answers, or at least answers we can estimate better than the factors at higher levels. Figure 10–3 lists only three of the many factors at this level.

The reasoning goes like this: If you tell me whether the new product will enter a market with which we already have great familiarity, chances are we will be able to communicate with buyers in that market. This raises the chances for good sales (up to Level Three), and greater sales make for more likely commercial fulfillment (up to Level Two), which, in turn, leads to profit (Level One, we're home). So, the trick in all this is to spot those Level Four factors that contribute to the technical and commercial operations in this firm on this particular product concept. Level Four factors constitute the scoring model shown in Figure 10–4. Some firms include profit, sales, and so on, as factors even though their surrogates should be there already.

FIGURE 10–4 Scoring Model for Full Screen of New Product Concepts

Category	Factor	Scale 1	2	3	4	5	Score	Weight	Weighted score
Technical accomplishment	Technical task difficulty	Very difficult				Easy	4	4	16
	Research skills required		Have none required		Perfect fit		5	3	15
	Development skills required		Have none required		Perfect fit		2	5	10
	Technical equipment/processes		Have none required		Have them				
	Rate of technological change	High/erratic			Stable				
	Design superiority assurance	None			Very high				
	Security of design (patent)	None			Have patent				
	Technical service required		Have none required		Have it all				
	Manufacturing equipment/processes		Have none required		Have them now				
	Vendor cooperation available		None in sight		Current relationship				
	Likelihood of competitive cost		Well above competition		Over 20% less				
	Likelihood of quality product		Below current levels		Leadership				
	Likelihood of speed to market		Two years or more		Under six months				
	Team people available	None right now			All key ones				
	Dollar investments required		Over 20 million		Under 1 million				
	Legal issues	Major ones			None in sight				Total 210
Commercial accomplishment	Market volatility	High/erratic				Very stable	2	3	6
	Probable market share		Fourth at best		Number one		5	5	25
	Probable product life		Less than a year		Over 10 years				
	Similarity to product line		No relationship		Very close				
	Sales force requirements		Have no experience		Very familiar				
	Promotion requirements		Have no experience		Very familiar				
	Target customer	Perfect stranger			Close/current				
	Distributors		No relationship		Current/strong				
	Retailers/dealers	Trivial			Critical				
	Importance of task to user		No relationship		Current/strong				
	Degree of unmet need		None/satisfied		Totally unmet				
	Likelihood of filling need	Very low			Very high				
	Competition to be faced		Tough/aggressive		Weak				
	Field service requirements		No current capability		Ready now				
	Environmental effects		Only negative ones		Only positive ones				
	Global applications		No use outside national		Fits global				
	Market diffusions	No other uses			Many other areas				
	Customer integration	Very unlikely			Customer seeks it				
	Probable profit	Break even at best			ROI>40%				Total 240
									Grand Total 450

Concept: _____
Date of screen: _____
Action: _____

194

You may recall that in Chapter 2 we talked about key concepts that drive product innovation. The factors of any particular scoring model should include all of the success factors for the firm using it.

But, in general, a firm should start with the list of factors in Figure 10–4, scratch out any obviously inapplicable ones, insert any obviously omitted ones, and then use it a few times to see how the scores set with the people involved. Over time the list should be reduced as much as possible, and always kept fluid. Nothing about this system should be set in stone; after all, it is just an aid to decision.[4] The Wilson Sporting Goods case, at the end of this chapter, will show how each situation is somewhat different.

The Scoring. Given a scoring form such as that shown in Figure 10–4, the team members who will be doing the scoring first undergo a familiarization period during which they get acquainted with each proposal (market, concept, concept test results). Then each scorer starts with the first factor (in this case, the difficulty of the technical task) and rates each one by selecting the most appropriate point on the semantic differential scales given in the third column. These scorings are multiplied by the assigned importance weights, and the factor totals are extended. The scorings continue for the other factors, and the ratings are then totaled to get the overall rating for that concept by each individual. Sounds complicated; it isn't.

Various methods are used to combine the individual team member's ratings, an average (mean) being the most common. Some firms use the Olympic method of dropping the highest and lowest ratings before averaging. Some firms have an open discussion after the averages are shown, so individuals can make a case for any view that is at odds with the group. Many firms have found that groupware (e.g., Lotus Notes) aids the process greatly.

Unusual Factors. On some factors, a bad score constitutes a veto. For example, in the case of the student seeking to decide what entertainment to pursue this weekend, a money shortage may block anything costing more than $30. This problem should be faced in the beginning so no time is wasted drumming up options costing more than $30. Industry is the same, and a key role for the product innovation charter is to point out those exclusions. Some call these **culling factors**.[5]

---

[4]For further information, especially from a more corporate management view, see Thomas D. Kuczmarski, *Managing New Products: The Power of Innovation* (Englewood Cliffs, NJ: Prentice Hall Inc., 1992), pp. 135–57. From the consumer products view, see Larry A. Constantineau, "The 20 Toughest Questions for New Product Proposals," *Journal of Product and Brand Management*, no. 1, 1993, pp. 51–54.

[5]See Rodger L. DeRose, "New Products—Sifting through the Haystack," *The Journal of Consumer Marketing*, Summer 1986, pp. 81–84. This article shows some direct connections between product strategy at Johnson Wax and the firm's new product screening; for example, its screening factors include "only safe products," "use existing capabilities," and "reflect the company's position and style."

Another problem occurs when the factor being scored has all-or-nothing, yes-or-no answers, for example, "Will this concept require the establishment of a separate sales force?" This type of factor is handled by using the end points on the semantic differential scale, with no gradations. If possible, such factors should be scaled—for example, "How much additional cost is involved in setting up sales coverage for this concept?" Columns might be "None," "Under $100,000," "$100,000 to $300,000," and so on.

The Scorers or Judges.   Selecting the members of a scoring team is like selecting the members of a new products team. The four major functions (marketing, technical, operations, and finance) are involved, as are new products managers and staff specialists from information technology, distribution, procurement, public relations, human resources, and so on, depending on the firm's procedure for developing new products.

Top business unit managers (presidents, general managers) should stay out of the act, except, of course, in small firms. Such people inhibit the frank discussions needed when assessing the firm's capabilities (e.g., in marketing or manufacturing). Of course, some CEOs are intuitively so good at this task they can't be excluded.[6]

Screening experience is certainly valuable. So is experience in the firm and in the person's specialty. Technical people generally feel more optimistic about probable technical success, and marketers are more pessimistic.

Problems with individuals are more specific. Research indicates that (1) some people are always optimistic, (2) some are sometimes optimistic and sometimes pessimistic, (3) some are "neutrals" who score to the middle of scales, (4) some are far more reliable and accurate than others, (5) some are easily swayed by the group, and (6) some are capable but erratic. Scoring teams need a manager to deal with such problems. Some firms actually weight each evaluator's scores by past accuracy (defined as conformity with the team's scores). Dow Brands uses a computerized groupware approach primarily because they like the scorings to be anonymous.

Weighting.   The most serious criticism of scoring models is their use of weights, because the weightings are necessarily judgmental (an exception from new research will be discussed in a moment). Let's go back to the student seeking a weekend activity. To a money-cautious student, affordability deserves more weight than the other factors. But how much more? Should it be weighted at two and the other factors at one?

Because of weighting's importance, some firms measure its effect using sensitivity testing. Scoring models are actually just mathematical models or

---

[6]One leading packaged goods firm's CEO was so expert at selecting among product manager job applicants that other evaluations were considered unnecessary.

equations, so an analyst can alter the scorings or the weightings to see what difference the alterations make in the final score. Spreadsheet programs handle this easily, and so does most groupware.

Profile Sheet

Figure 10–5 presents an alternative preferred by some firms for its graphic capability. The profile sheet graphically arranges the five-point scorings on the different factors. If a team of judges is used, the profile employs average scores. The approach does indeed draw attention to such patterns as the high scores given near the bottom of the profile (in Figure 10–5) compared to those near the top.

FIGURE 10–5

The Profile of a New Product Proposal

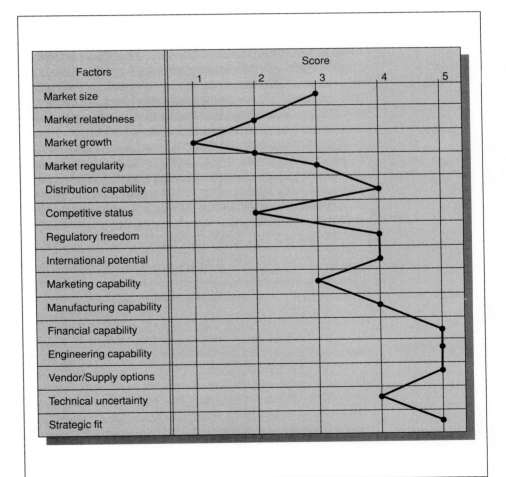

A Research-Based Model

Figure 10–6 shows a major contribution to our collection of scoring models, a study of successful and unsuccessful products.[7] Some 100 Canadian industrial firms cooperated in the study, which correlated success and failure with the characteristics of the project/product *at the time it would have been screened.* Each firm in the study identified a recent success and a recent failure. Managers then cited a total of 80 descriptive characteristics when asked why each product failed (or succeeded). From these, 48 that *would have been known at the time of the screening* (pre-R&D) were selected. For example, a failure is sometimes caused by unexpected competitive entry, but no one could have known this at screening time.

Factor analysis reduced this set of 48 reasons to the 13 underlying factors or dimensions that captured the essence of the 48. Next, the regression coefficients were calculated (correlation between each factor's score and the success or failure of the product), and *8 of the 13 were found to be significant.*

FIGURE 10–6   Research-Based Scoring Model

The Eight Significant Factors	Weight from the Regression Coefficients
Product superiority, quality, uniqueness	1.744
Product is superior.	
Product has unique feature.	
Product is higher quality.	
Product does unique task.	
Product cuts user's costs.	
Product is first of kind.	
(See source for the other 42 variables.)	
Overall product firm/resource compatibility	1.138
Market need, growth, and size	0.801
Economic advantage of product to end user	0.722
Technological resource campatibility	0.342
Product scope (mass rather than narrow specialty)	0.225
Market competitiveness	−0.301
Newness to the firm	−0.354

Note: This table reads as follows: The most important factor in screening industrial products is the degree of product superiority, quality, or uniqueness. This superiority factor is derived from six specific scorings, the first of which is how superior the proposed product is to its probable competitors. If a score for all six variables is determined and then put into a score for the factor as a whole (see source for method), that factor is then given a weight of 1.744. After all eight factors have been scored, the total is determined and compared with other product proposals.

Source: Robert G. Cooper, "Selecting Winning New Product Projects: Using the NewProd System," *Journal of Product Innovation Management*, March 1985, pp. 34–44.

---

[7]Robert G. Cooper, "Selecting Winning New Product Projects: Using the NewProd System," *Journal of Product Innovation Management*, March 1985, pp. 34–44.

The regression coefficients serve as the weights for the eight factors in the model, the two negative weights being for factors that were scaled, with the "bad news" getting a higher score. Figure 10–6 shows the results for the eight factors.

Note that each of the factors is derived from two or more of the 48 original items given by the managers. The first factor—"product superiority, quality, uniqueness"—was derived from six original items, and they are shown just below the heading. This particular factor is very important (1.744 weight) and positive. The figure shows that the typical industrial firm should use eight factors in its scoring model, with the weights indicated. (The original source lists the original items for the seven other factors below the first.)

Even better, of course, if the firm has lots of new product experience, is to go back and develop data on *their own successes and failures,* as was done in this study; then the statistical analysis would yield factors and weights most appropriate for that firm. The service is being sold commercially.[8] There are some concerns that the judgments managers make now are influenced by the known outcomes of the concepts being scored.

Special Aspects

A few other aspects round out our discussion of scoring models. One concerns the product champion (discussed fully in Chapter 12). Champions are sometimes needed to push past normal resistance to change and to see that the concept gets a fair hearing at all turns. They try to give the scorers all favorable information and may argue that standard forms don't fit their special situations.

Some developers are trying to use computer technology with **expert systems** (often called knowledge-based systems). Such systems are essentially scoring models, with the factors developed on the basis of expert experience.[9]

Last, experience shows that managements sometimes misuse scoring models. One consumer products manufacturer threw out a scoring model system because it:

1. Was rejecting products that would help round out the line.
2. Was rejecting products that would help forestall competitive entry into the market.
3. Was rejecting too many products, according to the sales department.

The first two problems arose from either faulty factor selection or faulty factor weighting and were easily solved. The third arose because the cutoff score was set too high. Scoring models require competent management.

---

[8]By The Adept Group, in Jacksonville, Florida. Research on this method continues but the applications are almost always confidential. An exception is in Robert E. Davis, "The Role of Market Research."

[9]For more on this topic in an application to financial services using an algorithm called INNOVATOR, see Sundaresan Ram and Sudha Ram, "Expert Systems: An Emerging Technology for Selecting New Product Winners," *Journal of Product Innovation Management,* June 1989, pp. 89–98.

Summary

If an idea progresses through early concept testing and development to the point where it is a full-blown concept ready for technical workup, it must then be screened. Screening is commonly done with scoring models, whereby the firm's ability to bring off the required development and marketing is estimated. If the concept scores well by whatever criteria the firm uses, it is sent into technical development.

Just prior to that, however, some firms try to spell out a protocol—an agreed set of benefits and other requirements that the technical development and marketing phases must deliver. And once the team feels the product parts of the protocol have been achieved, the concept is in prototype form. It can be taken to the field for further concept testing. The concept test is much more productive when the concept is in prototype form, though it may be more expensive because substantial technical expenditures have already been made. These matters of protocol and prototype testing will be treated in Chapter 11.

Applications

More questions from that interview with the company president.

1. "Our small electrical engines division recently threw out a screening system that was based on a fairly complete scoring model, as they called it. Seems the model kept rejecting too many of their product ideas, some of which looked like sure winners to them—and to me, incidentally. Under their new system, a top-management committee reviews these ideas personally, without all that paperwork, and it looks like things will be better. Do you have any reaction to that?"

2. "Back in late 1981, the Dow Jones people announced that they had to cancel their plans for *Wall Street Journal Magazine.* They had spent over a year in planning, but when they showed prototype copies of the new publication to test readers, the readers were somewhat short on enthusiasm. They wanted more information on personal finance and several other areas that the firm had been planning to handle in their regular publications like the *Journal* and *Barron's.* Couldn't something have been done to find this out earlier and save that year of very expensive planning? They're currently thinking of reactivating this magazine idea for one or more of the strong independent Asian economies, perhaps Singapore and perhaps Taiwan."

3. "Yet, another new service that tries to give consumers information on TV shows and movies is rather widely criticized. A firm named ASI Market Research, Inc., has a service called Preview House. The service hooks up movie theater audiences (which it gets from telephone lists with promises of free movies) with an instantaneous response machine that has dials for

recording likes and dislikes. The firm can test upcoming shows, entire movies (e.g., if they had tested *Heaven's Gate*, a bundle might have been saved), records, and so on. Granted, audiences go especially big for sex, puppies, little children, and so on, but if that's what they like, that's what they want. Mr. Magoo goes especially well. What do you think of a service like this?"

4. "If it happens that one of our divisions absolutely must use a scoring model, as you call it, I strongly prefer the one you said that division of AT&T uses. You know, just get answers to the four questions: 'Do customers care, Do we care, Can we do it, and Can we stay ahead if we do?' What more is relevant? That list covers technical feasibility and commercial feasibility both, doesn't it?"

CASE: WILSON SPORTING GOODS—PART I[10]

In the late 1980s, the Wilson Sporting Goods Division of PepsiCo, Inc., began trying to bring engineering and other technology to the sporting goods business, and continued the effort well into the 90s. Materials-based technologies had already produced easy-to-hit tennis balls and a more responsive softball (which produced games with scores of 50 to 48).

Other firms were also active. Puma produced a running shoe with an electronic device that measured time, distance, and calories expended. AMF had a chemical compound to reduce the shock for tennis rackets.

The reason for Wilson's special interest in technology was its conviction that technology could be used to lure consumers back into the market. Tennis and golf had fallen off rather badly, for example, and many participative sports were suffering in varying degrees. There had been successes, however: better running shoes showed that technology could advance a sport, shoulder pads benefited from space-age technology, baseball centers were now sometimes polyurethane. Computers had already helped tennis rackets, golf ball designs, and more. Of course, there were also failures.

But the present need was for some way to screen through the many ideas that came naturally out of such a campaign. Wilson had the engineers, and the firm knew sports. It had a broad product line, an excellent distribution system, and was one of the leading firms in the athletic goods industry. But money in the industry was short, especially for higher-risk R&D. So, Wilson needed a scoring model to help select the new product ideas most likely to contribute to company profits. They have asked you to develop one.

The firm's considerable experience in new product work enabled it to shoot for a full scoring model (not just a few factors), and it wanted a good weighting system built in. Wilson executives did not indicate whether the firm routinely used concept testing as a prescreening step, but it probably did.

---

[10]Part II is at the end of Chapter 12.
Source: The original thrust for this case came from Hal Lancaster, "For the Poor Athletes Who Blame Their Tools, New Ones Are Coming," *The Wall Street Journal*, May 14, 1985, p. 37. Later additions came from several sources, with the pump glove details from Justin Martin, "What Fits Better than a Glove?" *Across the Board*, September 1992, pp. 41–46.

Unfortunately, the sporting equipment market had hit a rough period in the recession of 1991–92, sales showing annual gains of only 4–5 percent, greater push by consumers to find lower cost equipment, and some shifting of activity to lower cost sports such as camping, soccer, and volleyball. More money was being spent on the clothing worn during sports, and less on equipment.

Too, there had been some efforts where firms in the industry had been less than successful with new-technology equipment, and perhaps their troubles might suggest key factors for your scoring model. Spaulding Sports Worldwide, for example, decided that baseball gloves had remained unchanged for 70 years, and choose to develop an improved product. They knew from their many research studies and focus groups that ballplayers always wanted custom fit, custom fit, and custom fit. So they retained Design Continuum, Inc., a Boston design firm that had developed the Pump sneaker for Reebock International.

A project team was formed, and the work begun. Spaulding chose to shoot for a new glove that would still look, behave, and feel like a ball glove. They went to work on the stretch points (on the back of the glove) and the flex points (in the pocket of the glove). These permitted a tip-to-tip closure around the ball. Material chosen for the stretch points was neophrene-lycra blend (like wet suits), and the flex material was to be nylon.

After searching for all possible ways to help close the glove, designers went back to the same pump idea they had for the sneakers. An air bladder was sewn into the back of the glove, and prototypes built. Tests were conducted on company people and on baseball players in winter leagues. Some 40 prototypes later, they had what they wanted. The ball players said they liked it.

But then Spaulding found that they would have to use five different manufacturers to make the specialized parts of the glove. Leading glove manufacturers all rejected the opportunity of assembling the final item, so the operation was performed in the Philippines. Production product suffered for a while (the first batch squeaked), but eventually good product came off the line. Dubbed AirFlex, it was introduced at a national sporting goods show, where Reebock people saw it, and promptly sued to stop its display there. Though later negotiations permitted Spaulding to continue marketing AirFlex, Reebock soon paired up with Rawlings (the leading glove manufacturer) to produce and sell another version of the pump glove.

Also at the meeting, Spaulding people were surprised to find that a Japanese firm had been marketing a type of pump glove called AirFit. It wasn't close enough to cause a legal problem, but there soon were three suppliers. At that time, it still wasn't clear what would happen, because some managers felt that when children have a chance to use the item, then grow to like it, and then continue its use as they move up to college and professional baseball, "Everybody will want one." In the meantime, retailers' comments were quite critical: "A serious baseball player couldn't care less whether a glove has custom fit," and "I don't remember selling one."

You don't have the information to compose an entirely new scoring model for use on the new product concepts discussed in this case, but you can put together the five most important factors under each of the technical and commercial halves of the model in Figure 10–4. Give them weights. Then apply your model to a new product concept they had recently been toying with—a new set of bowling pins that would exploit metalurgical technology, enliven the game, and attract new attention to it. The pins would be space-age metals. Beyond the task of *developing* a scoring model for Wilson, give some thought to the problems of *implementing* the scoring model system in this firm. Which of the functional groups (departments) would be the biggest problem, that is, which would be least likely to live with the results of a scoring session?

11 FINANCIAL ANALYSIS

Setting

Now that we have finished the full screen, we know the product concept meets our technical capabilities (present or acquirable) and that it meets our manufacturing, financing, and marketing capabilities as well. Too, we know it offers no major legal problems, etc. So, we are ready to charge ahead.

Or are we? Most managers don't think so—they are very interested in the financial side of this proposition. In fact, they have been interested in money from the very start of a project—think back to the product innovation charter where we talked about the size of potential markets and objectives on market shares and profits. And they will still be interested in money when they look back and total up whether the whole project was worthwhile.

Now seems to be a good time to take a closer look at the *managerial* side of financial analysis—how should we manage a new product project such that it achieves reasonable financial goals?[1]

The Real Problems of Financial Analysis

The term *financial analysis* when applied to new products conjures up visions of sales forecasts and profit calculations. By using traditional financial analysis, we can get a good read on the current proposal.

Actually, sales forecasts and financial analysis systems are no problem as such. We have an immense warhead of forecasting methodologies, most based on many

[1]Every segment of new products management activity has depth of specialization, but this book cannot go into the details of any of these topics. It *can* give references to readers who wish to go deeper. Any general financial management book will give a step-by-step method for doing a net present value method of capital budgeting. Several excellent articles are cited in this chapter for mathematical models and for sales forecasting in general.

years of experience. We know, for example, what makes for sales (recall the discussion on awareness, trial, availability, and repeat buying in Chapter 9 and the A-T-A-R model). This model does an excellent job and serves as the basis for some very advanced mathematical systems used by some of the most sophisticated new product marketers in the world. And every firm has people who can make an income-statement-based net present value calculation (using discounted cash flow methods). We have had years of experience with it. The usual approach, step by step, is given in the Bay City case at the end of the chapter, with data for a new product.

The only drawback is that those systems require information—particularly data. A-T-A-R requires a solid estimate of how many people/firms will become aware of our new item, how many of those will opt to try some of the item in one way or another, and so on. Each of these figures is very difficult to estimate. For example:

- Apple did not *know* we would buy millions of its PowerBook.
- Nabisco did not *know* we would storm the dealers for its Snackwell's.
- J&J did not *know* we would consume millions of disposable contact lenses.

Too, the financial model requires product cost, prices, the current value of money, probable taxes on the future income, the amount of further capital investments that will be required between now and when we close the books on the product, and much more.

These will never be certain, even after living out the product's life cycle. Sales will be known, but we might have had a better marketing strategy. Costs are always just estimates. We will never know the true extent to which a new item cannibalized sales from another product. If we had not marketed the new item a competitor probably would have. And on and on.

The fact is, we rely on estimates. Management's task is to make the estimates as solid as we can and then manage around the areas of uncertainty in a way that we don't get hurt too badly.

On minor product improvements we do this pretty well—a new Troy-Bilt lawn mower with a pepped-up engine is not a wild guessing game. On near line extensions, we also do well, but with more misses. Totally new products, using technologies never so applied before, are pure guessing games. For over 30 years business schools used a Polaroid pricing case in which Edwin Land was trying to decide whether people would pay $15, or maybe $25, or (dream on) $50 for his first instant camera! They paid the top price, in huge numbers, making Land a very rich "financial and technical genius."

Recent Experiences

Some more recent managers have done the same. A 1995 *Fortune* article actually was entitled "Ignore Your Customer."[2] Chrysler didn't believe car buyers

---

[2]Justin Martin, "Ignore Your Customer," *Fortune*, May 1, 1995, pp. 121–26.

when they said they saw no value in a minivan. Compaq rejected rejections of the PC network server and made many millions of dollars. Barry Diller didn't believe people who said we didn't need another network (Fox). An air-based system of package movement? VCRs? Fax machines that just sent pieces of paper a bit faster than the mails did? A heart pump? Winners all, and very big ones.

How about when customers themselves tell us to market something new—surely we can trust them. They liked the taste of the New Coke and said they would buy it. They liked the idea of (lower fat) burgers that McDonalds called McLean. They said they liked the idea of a pregnant Arnold Schwarzenegger. And so on. Business closets are full of things customers demanded or said they would buy, but didn't!

Fortune's conclusion was that smart companies are using nontraditional methods to get sales and profit estimates. Steelcase didn't ask business managers what they would like as a special office for teams—they went out and observed teams in action, and returned to the labs to design what *they thought* would be better. Called Personal Harbor, it was. Urban Outfitters does not use focus groups and surveys—they go to stores and hangouts and watch customers in action—what they are wearing and how they wear it. Urban Outfitter's founder said, "We're not after people's statements, we're after their actions."

Could anyone have believed that teenage girls would buy and proudly wear clunky boots with heat-sealed rubber soles? Dr. Martens (Stephan Griggs) did.[3]

The ultimate perhaps in showing how managers do their best to forecast the future, but still hedge a bit, came in 1993. A fire destroyed the Japanese plant of Sumitomo Chemical Company, makers of resins for encapsulating computer chips. It turned out that most of their customers were *not* the JIT (just-in-time) purists they claimed to be. Seems they had "JIC" (just-in-case) supplies stashed away in various warehouses![4]

Summary of the Problems

Target Users Don't Know.   They don't know what the new product will actually be, what it will do for them, what it will cost, and what its drawbacks will be. They haven't had a chance to use it. They don't know what situation they will be in when we get the new item to them. And they're busy!

When Users Might Know, They Often Won't Tell Us.   There are many reasons why intended users keep some information from us or offer outright falsehoods.

---

[3]Richard C. Morais, "What's Up, Doc?" *Forbes*, January 16, 1995, p. 42.

[4]The March 1995 issue of *The PA Perspective*, a newsletter published by Princeton Associates consulting firm, in Buckingham, PA.

Market Research Methods Are Good, but Leave Much to Be Desired. Focus group horror stories abound. Telephone surveys must be concluded in about two minutes. Observation methods are never quite complete. And many studies are poorly executed.

Market Dynamics.   Competitors don't sit still. In fact, they are trying very hard to ruin our data, just as we do to theirs. Resellers, regulators, and market advisers are in a constant flux.

Developers Can Never Know Just What Types of Marketing Support Their New Item Will Have in the Firm—Sales, Service, Etc.   No sales manager can make promises a year ahead about sales time and support, for example.

Biased Internal Attitudes.   Product champions can be very persuasive, as they should be. Politics are always present. Many new products managers won't be ready to show just how good the new item is for some time, so they try to delay official forecasting.

Poor Accounting.   Accounting systems are oriented to the financial reporting task; they are not built to provide data in a format that new products managers could use.

Almost Every New Product Is Being Rushed to Market.   This is not only cycle-time dramatics, but the natural tendency of new products people to get to the market. They often will not stop for field testing of the new item. (Steelcase management, responding to some disappointments, now demands that new office furniture systems be *thoroughly* tested in *end user offices*.)

Almost All Forecasting Methods Are Based on History.   New products don't have any history. Common forecasting methods are extrapolations, and work well on established products. Even forecasting methods that seem free of history (use of leading indicators and causal models) use *relationships* established in the past.[5]

Turns of the Technology Wheel.   We can't be sure how long it will take people to change to our technology. A classic case concerns Kodak's frustrations in trying to estimate whether and when CD technology would replace film in the photographic market.[6]

---

[5]An interesting view on forecasting methods is in Joseph P. Martino, "Technological Forecasting," *The Futurist*, July–August 1993, pp. 13–16. He gives a classification like the one just mentioned, but also talks about genius forecasting, pushing the panic button, window-blind forecasting, and others, down to "No forecast!"

[6]See Joan E. Rigdon, "Kodak Tries to Prepare for Filmless Era Without Inviting Demise of Core Business," *The Wall Street Journal*, April 18, 1991, p. B1.

Actions by Managers to Handle These Problems

Given that we badly need financial analyses and that good analyses are almost impossible to make, what is a manager to do?

Improve the New Product Process Currently in Use

Most of the horror stories given earlier from the trade press are embarrassing to their managers. In most of them a key step was skipped. In an effort to hurry or to capitalize on the conviction of someone working in or around the project, a bad assumption was made. For example, New Coke was heavily taste-tested, but was not *market*-tested—that is, no one was actually asked to buy the product with that new name. Same for the low-fat burger. Chrysler was wiser—it knew that consumers were negative toward the minivan because they couldn't see the value in it until they actually drove it for a while. So they made sure they drove it. Top new product professionals today know good new product process, but many others don't. They lack information and don't realize it. All the standard forms will not make up for omissions of key data pieces.

Set the Forecast Up as a Living Thing—Use the Life Cycle Concept of Financial Analysis

Too many firms use a system that focuses financial analysis at a particular point—perhaps a stage-gate in today's buzz vocabulary. That point is often right where we are in this book, at the time of full screen. The other popular time is later, near where some major financial commitment must be made—e.g., building a plant or releasing an expensive marketing introductory program. Managers talk about a point of no return. It is indeed a stage-gate, a hurdle, and new product managers may spend weeks getting ready for the meeting.

But, both times are exaggerated. Technical work can begin without committing the firm to a huge technical expenditure. Building a plant can often be avoided by contracting out early production, or by building a large pilot system for trial-marketing in a restricted rollout. The marketing budget can be broken up in many ways.

Far better is for managers to see their project as a living thing—a bottom line that is created gradually, over the life of the project, never being completely accurate, even well after the item is launched. (See Figure 11–1.) A product innovation charter is accepted only because the management believes the combined technologies and market opportunities fit well with each other and with the firm. A PIC describes a home field where we can't ever be sure of the final score but where we should be able to win. A concept test result doesn't assure financial success either, but it can say we are one step further along—the intended user agrees there is a need for something like our concept and wants some to actually try out. An early field use test with a prototype also won't assure success, but it can say intended users like what they see. It delivered what they wanted

FIGURE 11–1

*Financial Analysis
as a Living Thing:
The Life Cycle of
Assessment*

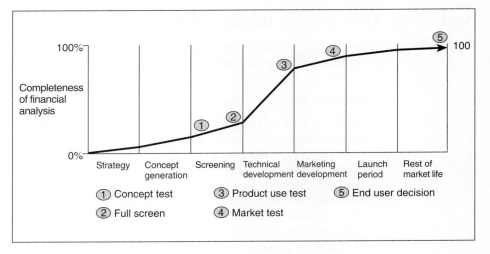

in their trial use of it. An advertising agency or a sales manager cannot guarantee success either, but they have ways of assuring that the new item will be brought to the attention of potential end users and that it will be tried. If it delivers, it will sell, and if manufacturing was able to do what it felt it could, there will be profit in the item. And so on. All phases are but parts of a whole.

A fertility scientist doesn't assure a happy, intelligent child, just a conception. An obstetrician, a pediatrician, parents, teachers. . . many people and processes bring a child to successful maturity. Along the way we don't stop at every step and appraise against *maturity*. The fetus cannot walk. The best we can do is ask whether progress to date is consistent with a successful life cycle.

Financial analysis should be the same—where are we today? Is what we know at this time consistent with profit goals? Is there reason to change our past projections? Some financial analysts now prefer to set up with full financial sheets at the beginning, and then compare progress against those spreadsheets. Many boxes are blank in the beginning, but will be filled in as we go along. But, the profit figures at the bottom of the page are not current forecasts, just current *goals*. As long as current progress is consistent with those goals, we proceed. A successful cola taste-test is not a reliable indicator of consumers' ultimate trial. If we get trial, the taste test says the chances are we will get repeat business.

The life-cycle concept of financial analysis enables us to avoid setting up systems where make-or-break decisions rest on one sales forecast or one cost forecast.

Reduce Dependence on Poor Forecasts

If it is difficult to make sales and profit forecasts, are there ways of avoiding having to make them? Yes, several, and many firms use them, though with caution.

Forecast Only What You Know.   This is an attitude. It says, why try to forecast what people in the marketplace will do if there is no reasonable way we can do so? A blank in a spreadsheet can be filled in with a range of estimates to see where the failure point is. If that is very unlikely, then go ahead.

Approve Situations, Not Numbers.   This a variation on what was mentioned earlier. Analyze to find what the success factors are, and then look to see if the situation offers them. If so, go ahead, knowing that success should come about even though we don't know just how much. An extreme example of this occurred once when a marketing vice president was asked to predict what he would do if he could get a license to use the Coca-Cola trademark on a line of new products. His answer was, right now I don't know, but with that trademark it's only a matter of how much, not whether.

Another way of betting on a situation has a parallel in horse racing; some betters bet on the jockey, not the horse (about whom they may be able to learn very little). Many firms bet on a top-notch scientist, or a top-notch sales force, or a top-notch trademark/reputation.

Another situation variable is *leadership*. Some firms build the *champion system* and give champions lots of rope. They expect champions to force their way past a restrictive financial system. This makes for a strange but very workable practice of evaluating teams and their leaders, rather than the ideas they come up with. You may recall reading in Chapter 4 about the film producer who builds a staff of outstanding creative people and depends on them to work miracles with ordinary scripts. A competitor invests in top scripts instead. But both were avoiding the necessity of relying on complex forecasts and financial analyses.

People who love to fish do this all the time; they spend lots of money to find and reach top trout streams. One manager recently said, "If there is a good trout stream with lots of trout in it and a good angler with good equipment, we don't need an accountant to tell us how many fish we will catch. Whatever happens will be good."

This strategy is not as folksy as it may sound. A firm must know what the success factors are in any situation. One of those two movie producers may be wrong. Notice how the manager included the trout stream, the angler, *and* the good equipment. Campbell Soup for a long time (and perhaps still today) knew that its success on new soups depended on two things—the taste of the soup and the manufacturing cost. Their name and skills could overcome any other limitation, but not a bad taste or a high price. Precise forecasting wasn't necessary under this strategy, but being sure on taste and cost was.

Commit to a Strategy of Low-Cost Development and Marketing.   There are times when a company can do the type of product innovation that some call temporary products. Develop a stream of new items that differ very little from those now on the market, insert them into the market without great fanfare, and watch which ones end users rebuy. Drop those that don't find favor. Japanese makers of electronics goods do this regularly, with Honda introducing several hundred new items in a year; there even are cities in Japan where firms introduce their flood and since consumers know this, marketing costs can be kept low.

Go Ahead with Sound Forecasts but Prepare to Handle the Risks.   This strategy especially appeals to managers who feel business is suffering from "paralysis by analysis." There are lots of ways to put risk back into product innovation while managing it well. One approach is to isolate or neutralize the in-house critics (a strong reason for setting up project matrixes and spinouts). Don't let people who have an inherent conflict of interest with the particular new product affect the financials.

Another approach defers financial analysis until later in the development process. One firm realized it was consistently killing off good new product ideas by demanding precise financial analyses at the time of screening. It didn't have the data. Another strategy is to use market testing rollouts (see Chapter 21). If a financial analysis looks weak but the idea seems sound, try it out on a limited scale to see where the solution might lie. Or, as one president said, give us the volume and we'll find a way to squeeze a good profit out of it. This thinking violates several popular management theories (e.g., empowered teams) but it may be necessary at times.

Managing risk is a major field in itself today, since we know business needs risk as a source of profits. Figure 11–2 shows the risk situation new products managers face in their evaluations—they know their product will bring more risk than the average risk of the firm, but how much? The fact seems to be that firms do not know what their current level of risk really is (the first vertical line) so the risk premium is not very useful in quantitative evaluations. And the "required rate of return" line moving upward across the figure is itself just a conception, not a measurement. It may have many different slopes, giving the product innovation premium many different roles.

Figure 11–3 compounds this problem by showing that the risk of a new product, if put into one figure as demanded in Figure 11–2, is itself just some kind of average. The mean profits expected from the four new products in Figure 11–3 are the same, but the distributions of their possible outcomes vary widely. B and C in particular hide some major risks.

Stop Using One Standard Format for Financial Analysis on New Products. Many firms have such standards, arbitrarily applied to every project. The benefit is that upper management can more quickly get a picture from standard forms. The drawback, of course, is that the picture may be wrong.

Look, for example, at the issue of singles versus home runs, as discussed in Chapter 4 on strategy. Most product innovation (in numbers of items) is strictly singles—product improvements and close line extensions. This innovation is managed deep within the ongoing operation; no empowered teams, no huge technical breakthroughs. The item is often demanded by a key customer or key channel, and the decision to develop it is not based on item profitability at all.

FIGURE 11–2

Calculating the New Product's Required Rate of Return

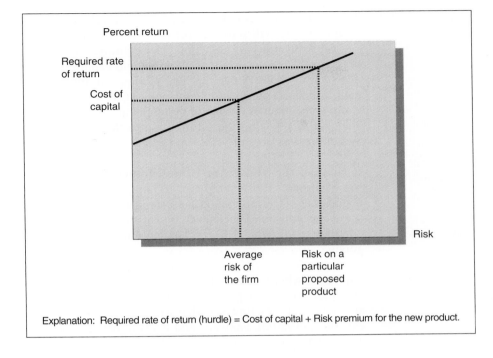

Explanation: Required rate of return (hurdle) = Cost of capital + Risk premium for the new product.

FIGURE 11–3

Risk Curves—Frequency Distributions of Outcomes

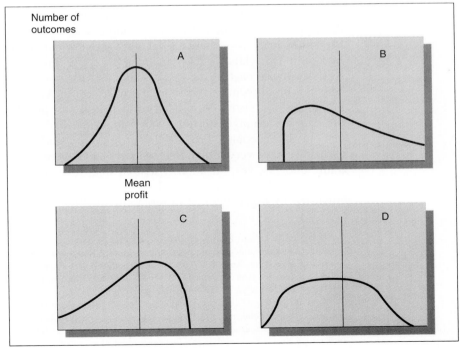

The risks are very small; sometimes the development is in a partnership with a customer who will provide profitable volume.

But home runs are something else entirely. They are a big gamble—big risks, big gains. They need lots of attention and cannot be handled easily with methods such as those in the previous section. So, the approach is to have *two* systems of financial analysis, one for singles and one for home runs. A third alternative is obvious—have no standard system at all, just develop a *financial analysis for each project*, keying the information to those issues where the risks really lie and unknowns prevail.

If None of the Above Are Useful, Improve the Current Financial/Forecasting Methods.   For example, marketing people sometimes make use of mathematical sales forecasting models (more in a moment). These models were developed for use on consumer packaged goods firms over 30 years ago, but improvements continue to this time. Efforts also continue to make them work better on durable goods.[7]

Some firms are beginning to analyze their own past efforts too. More progress will come when firms systematically study their most recent 50 (or 25 or whatever they have) new products, to summarize what financial methods were used, and how well they forecast what were the actual outcomes. This is what we now call success/failure analysis, and leads to best practices. It is rather common in other phases of new product work—for example, recall the screening model work by Cooper in Chapter 10.

There have been some recent improvements in accounting methods, and there probably will be more. For example, some people are now willing to use **threshold** analysis—where a level is set above which we accept and below which we don't. This calls for less precision except in those cases right at the margin. **Activity-based costing**, or ABC, is another fast-moving frontier, though it would help new products managers more if it were seen as ABA—activity-based *accounting*, including revenue flows and some measure of profit contribution. Accounting data are arranged to tell a story about particular programs of activity, not just raw data accounts. Product-line profitability studies are ABA. Unfortunately, to date we have very little ABA for individual new product projects. R&D expenditure budgets, yes, but total costs *and* total revenues, no. We will never know our real profits because of indirect costs and benefits—how much is profit enhanced by higher morale in research units?[8]

---

[7]See Glen L. Urban, John S. Hulland, and Bruce D. Weinberg, "Premarket Forecasting for New Consumer Durable Goods: Modeling Categorization, Elimination, and Consideration Phenomena," *Journal of Marketing*, April 1993, pp. 47–63. Another report shows how past models are combined and rearranged: see Ann Martensen, "A Model for Marketing Planning for New Products," *Marketing and Research Today*, November 1993, pp. 247–67.

[8]A useful review of changes now going on in accounting that should help new products managers can be found in Samuel Rabino and Arnold Wright, "Accelerated Product Introductions and Emerging Managerial Accounting Perspectives: Implications for Marketing Managers in the Technology Sector," *Journal of Product Innovation Management*, March 1993, pp. 126–35.

FIGURE 11–4   Hurdle Rates on Return and Other Measures

		Hurdle Rates		
Product	Strategic Role or Purpose	Sales	Return on Investment	Market Share Increase
A	Combat competitive entry	$3,000,000	10%	0 Points
B	Establish foothold in new market	$2,000,000	17%	15 Points
C	Capitalize on existing markets	$1,000,000	12%	1 Point

Explanation: This array shows that hurdles should reflect a product's purpose, or assignment. For example, combating a competitive entry will require more sales than would establishing a toehold in a new market. Too, we might accept a very low share increase for an item that simply capitalized on our existing market position.

Even the traditional net present value method is being reviewed to see how it can be improved. We see new views of R&D personnel, improvements urged for the centerpiece (cost of capital),[9] and criticisms of the innovation-inhibiting tendency of all NPV calculations.[10]

Lastly, some new products managers make a general plea that all financial analysis should be advisory—not fixed hurdles and mandates but flags that warn of potential problems. Of course, hurdle rates can be *managed* in the sense of their being situational (see Figure 11–4).

Sales Forecasting

Given the previous discussion of general problems in new product forecasting, we should now take a look at the three general approaches used to forecast a new product's sales. They are shown in Figure 11–5. The right-hand column shows the forecasts, or outputs of the forecasting system. The middle column states the key variables determining how much will be sold. These behavior variables include at least awareness, trial, availability, and repeat. (Recall Chapter 8's discussion of the A-T-A-R model.) If potential customers go through the A-T-A-R sequence, sales will follow.

The left-hand column contains the two sets of factors that determine how many potential customers work their way through the A-T-A-R sequence and the speed with which they do so. The factors are used in two ways: (1) We can use the left-hand column to predict the A-T-A-R and then (2) use that to predict sales. Or (3) we can go directly from the left-hand factors to a sales prediction based on opinions, judgments, market shares, and the like.

---

[9]Timothy M. Devinney, "New Products and Financial Risk Changes," *Journal of Product Innovation Management*, September 1992, pp. 222–31.

[10]George T. Haley and Stephan M. Goldberg, "Net Present Value Techniques and Their Effects on New Product Research," *Industrial Marketing Management*, 1995, pp. 177–90.

FIGURE 11–5

*Structure of New
Product Sales
Forecasting
Alternatives*

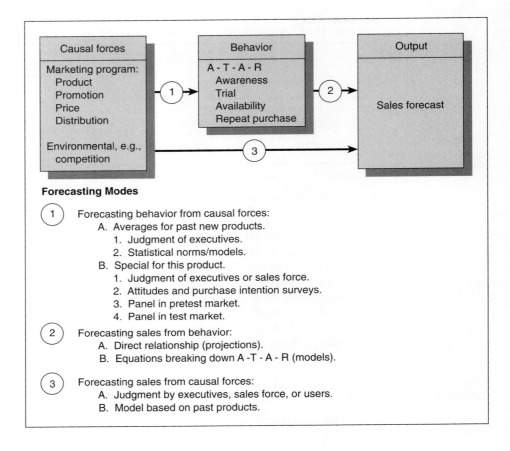

Most of the forecasting modes in Figure 11–5 are self-explanatory, but a few deserve added comment.

Statistical Norms for Behavior from Causal Forces

In the chapters on marketing planning we will talk about how experienced sales managers can usually look at a planned marketing effort and tell us how much distribution we're going to get, how much awareness, and so on. But market research directors also can pull out data from past introductions, showing, for example, that "whenever we market a general usage software item, we get at least 40 percent trial based on our strong market franchise."

Attitudes and Panels

Again, think back to concept testing. The top-two-boxes question comes in here. If 70 percent of the testers said they would definitely or probably purchase the item, this response can be calibrated from experience into a forecast of, say, 50 percent actually doing so. If buyers are asked to rank our new product along with the market leaders, average rankings of product preference can be calculated. The forecasted market shares can be made equal to the percentage preferences ranking. It's shaky but sometimes done.

Models Based on Past Products

The A-T-A-R model (Chapter 8) is very simple. Given the data, it can be used to construct a sales forecast (or a profit forecast). Market research scientists long ago pushed the early, simple models into far more powerful forecasting devices.

Here's how. Each factor in the A-T-A-R model can be taken as a *dependent variable* and a secondary equation constructed for it. For example, trial may result from (1) degree of unmet need in the market, (2) economic well-being of the potential users, (3) their risk-taking attitudes, (4) the intensity with which competitors are expected to attack our new offering, and (5) ease of purchase. Given all those, we can use the equation to calculate a figure for trial.

Then, going one step further, we can put each of the trial *independent* variables as *dependent* variables in their own equations. For *ease of purchase* as a dependent variable, independent variables could include (*a*) product availability in the marketplace, (*b*) the general price level of this product type, and (*c*) the frequency with which the potential user is in the marketplace where such products are sold.

All of this makes for sophisticated models, but these models (given the data) yield good sales forecasts. They are used almost entirely on consumer packaged goods, where firms have lots of new product experience on which to develop the model's parameters and to calibrate the raw percentages they get from consumers. And, they are mainly used early in the process, where real market data are scarce. The chief research tool is simulated test marketing (also called premarket testing), a pseudo sales method of market testing discussed in Chapter 20, but the models can work with data from other sources as well, even assumptions.

Model makers are rapidly accumulating experience and sharpening their models, which are now readily available to consumer packaged goods innovators, and they are quite inexpensive compared to test markets and rollouts and allow diagnostic output as well as sensitivity testing.

Unfortunately, they also require massive amounts of data to work best, are built heavily on assumptions, and are so complex that many managers are wary of them. Having started in the 1950s and 1960s, they often incorporate assumptions that are no longer valid—e.g., reliance on mass advertising and easy-to-get distribution. But they are now a mature industry, a large and profitable one.

It is interesting that the most successful firm by far uses the simplest methodology and requires the least data. BASES II combines a concept test and a product use test. Its staff members calibrate the trial and repeat percentages from their massive files of past studies, and use a set of experience-honed heuristics (rules of thumb) to translate those percentages into market shares.

But, product innovators outside of consumer packaged goods still most often use the simple version of the A-T-A-R model (Chapter 8) if they use any forecasting model at all. Research continues toward improving all of the sales forecasting models.[11]

Summary

This chapter has dealt with the matter of how to make judgments on the financial merits of new products. There are good basic methods for doing financial analysis (net present value calculations using discounted cash flow), and there are excellent methods for doing sales forecasting. Most firms use them daily. However, new products managers know they rarely have the data these sophisticated methods really require. So, they use the methods when they can, but also rely on a series of "risk-reducers"—actions that give them nonquantitative guides to probable financial success. These were discussed. We also looked at steps being taken to increase the quality of the product development process itself, and new methods of accounting.

The method of making financial analyses is given in the Bay City case, which comes after the "Applications" section. The case offers data for a new electronics product and gives the opportunity as well to look at some nondata issues involved in financial analysis.

At this point in the new product development process, we are ready to look into the first of the two major development streams of activity—technical development. We get to marketing development, the other stream going on simultaneously with the technical, in Chapter 17.

Applications

More questions from that interview with the company president.

1. "You're still a student, but when you tell me about all the problems new products managers have putting together financial worksheets you sound like the people we have around here. They complain that the financial analyses we use call for more data than we have. They say the results are unreliable and all that, but what they really want is no financial appraisal at all—just leave them alone and they'll eventually bring back the bacon— big slabs of it. How else can we keep reasonable managerial control over the use of sometimes very great corporate resources?"

---

[11]For a summary of where we stand on these sales forecasting models, see Vijay Mahajan and Jerry Wind, "New Product Models: Practice, Shortcomings and Desired Improvements," *Journal of Product Innovation Management*, June 1992, pp. 128–39.

2. "One thing I know for certain—I don't want any sales managers or technical research people making new product forecasts. I've never seen such lousy forecasting as we get from these people. Sales managers either love a new item so much they think it will outsell everyone, or they think it is a dud and underforecast just as badly. Absolutely no objectivity in them. And the technical people, well, they become so enamored of their inventions that they lose all objectivity too. What I like is forecasting done by independent people—project managers or new products managers in separate departments. Have you run into any good ways of keeping sales managers and technical researchers out of forecasting? You agree that they should be excluded, don't you?"

3. "I was talking just the other day about our most recent acquisition—a chain of four large general hospitals on the West Coast. These are private hospitals, and we fully intend them to be profitable, but it is a service, I guess, and there are some *public* service overtones in the deal, whether we want them there or not. My concern, as we talk about evaluating new products, is how would this new division go about making financial evaluations on new service proposals? The same as our divisions that make goods?"

4. "Actually, I agree with one thing you said a while ago, and that related to the desirability of making financial analyses on a threshold basis. I realize how many unknowns there are in the new products business. As a president, I realize too that many of the financial projections I read are just air. If a new products group can convince me that they can sell *at least* X volume, and at that volume their costs will be Y, *or lower*, then I am inclined to go along with them. But, deep in my heart, I don't like it— those thresholds are just as much subject to manipulation as are the more structured NPV projections."

CASE: BAY CITY ELECTRONICS

Financial analysis of new products at Bay City Electronics had always been rather informal. Bill Roberts, who founded the firm 25 years ago, knew residential electronics because he had worked for almost 7 years for another firm specializing in home security systems. But, he had never been trained in financial analysis. In fact, all he knew was what the bank had asked for every time he went to discuss his line of credit.

Bay City had about 45 full-time employees (plus a seasonal factory workforce) and did in the neighborhood of $18 million in sales. His products all related to home security and were sold by his sales manager, who worked with a group of manufacturers' reps, who in turn called on wholesalers, hardware and department store chains, and other large retailers. He did some consumer advertising, but not much.

Source: This is a realistic, but hypothetical, situation.

Bill was inventive, however, and had built the business primarily by coming up with new techniques. His latest device was a remote-controlled electronic closure for any door in the home. The closure was effected by a special ringing of the telephone: for example, if a user wanted to leave a back door open until 9:00 P.M. it was simple to call the house at 9:00 and wait for 10 rings, after which the electronic device would switch the door to a locked position. A similar call would reopen the door.

The bank liked the idea but wanted Bill to do a better job of financial analysis, so the loan officer asked him to use the forms shown below in the "Bay City Appendix" as Figure 11–6 and Figure 11–7. After some effort, Bill was able to fill out the key data form, Figure 11–6, and his work is reproduced here. To date, Bay City had spent $85,000 in expense money for supplies and labor developing the closure and had invested $15,000 in a machine (asset). If the company decided to go ahead, it would have to invest $50,000 more in a new facility, continue R&D to validate and improve the product, and—if things went according to expectations—invest another $45,000 in year 3 to expand production capability.

He also had to fill out the financial worksheet, Figure 11–7; for this he used a friend of the family who had studied financial analysis in college. The friend had relied on a summary of how to do this, and this summary is attached. He also warned Bill that there were lots of judgment calls in that calculation, "so don't get into an argument with the people at the bank about details."

While waiting for his appointment at the bank, he spent some time just thinking about his situation. Did the numbers look good? Where were the shaky parts that the banker might give him trouble on? Most of all, he was curious about whether a friend of his at the LazyBoy chair firm in Monroe had to do the same thing, and would 3M require the same type of form from his daughter who now worked for them? Frankly, he didn't feel he personally had learned much about his situation from the exercise and was already wondering whether there weren't better ways for him to go about reassuring the bank that their loan was a good proposition.

BAY CITY APPENDIX: FINANCIAL ANALYSIS FOR NEW PRODUCTS

New products financial analysis requires two separate activities: (1) gathering the full set of data and other givens in the situation and (2) using them in calculations to derive whatever final figure is sought. These two tasks are shown in Figures 11–6 (the key data form) and 11–7 (the financial worksheet).

COMPILING THE KEY DATA

Economic conditions.   Most firms have ongoing economic forecasts, but sometimes a team wishes to differ. If so, the difference should be noted here.

The market or category.   The market for the new product is defined carefully, and the growth rate assumption is noted. Also, the current total market unit and dollar volumes are recorded.

Product life.   The number of years used in the economic analysis of new products is usually set by company policy, but any particular project may be an exception.

Pricing.   Start with the end user list price, work back through the various trade discounts to get a factory net, then deduct any planned special discounts and allowances. The average dollars per unit sold is the price used in worksheet calculations.

FIGURE 11–6

Key Data Form for Financial Analysis, Part A

Financial Analysis Proposal: *Bay City Electronics Closure*[*]
Date of this analysis: _____ Previous analysis: _____

1. Economic conditions, if relevant:
   Corporate scenario OK

2. The market (category):
   Stable—5% growth

3. Product life *5* years

4. List price: *$90*
   Distributor discounts: *$36*
   Net to factory: *$54*

   Other discounts:
   Promotion: *$1*
   Quantity: *$1*
   Average dollars per unit sold: *$52*

5. Production costs:
   Explanation of any unique costing procedures being used:
   None. Experience curve effect.

   Applicable rate for indirect manufacturing costs: _____
   20% of direct costs

6. Future expenditures, other capital investments, or extraordinary expenditures:
   Build production facilities: $50,000
   Ongoing R&D: $15,000; $10,000; $15,000; $10,000 for first four years after intro
   Special UL test during the 2nd year will cost $5,000
   Expand facilities in 3rd year for $45,000

7. Working capital: *35* % of sales
   10% inventory; recover 80% in period 5
   15% receivables; all recovered in period 5
   10% cash, all recovered

8. Applicable overheads:
   Corp.: *10* % of sales
   Division: *_* % of sales

9. Net loss on cannibalized sales, if any, expressed as a percent of the new product's sales: *10* %

10. Future costs/revenues of project abandonment, if that were done instead of marketing:
    Abort now would net $3,000 from sale of machine.

11. Tax credits, if any, on new assets or expenditures: *1% of taxes due to state and federal, based on positive environmental effect.*

12. Applicable depreciation rate(s) on depreciable assets: *25% on orig. plant and machines; 33 1/3% on expansion facilities*

13. Federal and state income tax rate applicable: *34* %
    Comments:

14. Applicable cost of capital: *16* %
    ± Premiums or penalties: *high-risk project 8* %
    _____ _ %
    Any change in cost of capital anticipated over life of product? *No*

[*]This key data form is filled in with demonstration data for the Bay City Electronics case.

FIGURE 11–6
(CONCLUDED)

*Key Data Form
for Financial
Analysis, Part B*

15. Basic overall risk curve applicable to the NPV: Standard OK ✓

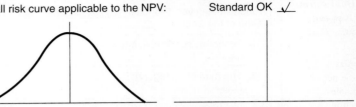

16. Key elements to be given sensitivity
    testing (e.g., sales, price cuts)
    (see below)

17. Sunk costs:
    Expenses to date: *Ignore*
    Capital invested to date: *$15,000*

18. Elements of new product strategy that are especially relevant on this proposal:
    (e.g., diversification mandate or cash risk):
    *Strategy calls for us to strengthen company in diversified markets, which this
    product will do.*

19. Basic sales and cost forecasts:

Year	Unit sales	Direct production cost per unit	Marketing expenses
1	*4,000*	*$16*	*$100,000*
2	*10,000*	*12*	*80,000*
3	*18,000*	*11*	*50,000*
4	*24,000*	*9*	*60,000*
5	*5,000*	*14*	*10,000*

20. Hurdle rates:
    Must have 40% gross margin after production costs.

21. Any mandatory contingencies: *None*

22. Other special assumptions or guidelines:
    *(1) The total $110,000 of facilities and machines will salvage for $10,000 when
        production is finished.*
    (2) The firm has other income to absorb any tax loss on this project.
    (3) Ignore investment tax credit.

    _____

    Sensitivity testing (Calculate the effect on NPV of the following):
    (1) We may have to cut the price to $34 net at start of third year.
    *(2) Our direct manufacturing cost estimate may be overly optimistic. What if we never
        get the cost below the original $16?*
    *(3) Competition may force much higher marketing costs—what if starting in year
        2 the level we have to spend at is just twice what we forecasted above?*
    *(4) How about a worst-case outcome, in which all of the above three contingencies
        are tested at one time?*

FIGURE 11–7   Financial Worksheet, Bay City Electronics

Product Proposal: Electronics Closure   Date:

	0	1	2	3	4	5
			Years on the Market			
Unit sales	0	4,000	10,000	18,000	24,000	5,000
Revenue per unit	0	52	52	52	52	52
Dollar sales	0	208,000	520,000	936,000	1,248,000	260,000
Production costs:						
Direct	0	64,000	120,000	198,000	216,000	70,000
Indirect	0	12,800	24,000	39,600	43,200	14,000
Total	0	76,800	144,000	237,600	259,200	84,000
Gross profit	0	131,200	376,000	648,400	988,800	176,000
Direct marketing costs	0	100,000	80,000	50,000	60,000	10,000
Profit contribution	0	31,200	296,000	648,400	928,800	166,000
Overheads (excluding R&D):						
Division	0	0	0	0	0	0
Corporate	0	20,800	52,000	93,600	124,800	26,000
Total	0	20,800	52,000	93,600	124,800	26,000
Other expenses:						
Depreciation	16,250	16,250	16,250	31,250	15,000	15,000
Cannibalization	0	20,800	52,000	93,600	124,800	26,000
R&D to be incurred	0	15,000	10,000	15,000	10,000	0
Extraordinary expense	0	0	5,000	0	0	0
Project abandonment	3,000	0	0	0	0	0
Total	19,250	52,050	83,250	139,850	149,800	41,000
Overheads and expenses	19,250	72,850	135,250	233,450	274,600	67,000
Income before taxes	(19,250)	(41,650)	160,750	414,950	654,200	99,000
Tax effect:						
Taxes on income	(6,545)	(14,161)	54,655	141,083	222,428	33,660
Tax credits	(65)	(142)	547	1,411	2,224	337
Total effect	(6,480)	(14,019)	54,108	139,672	220,204	33,323
Cash flow:						
Income after taxes	(12,770)	(27,631)	106,642	275,278	433,996	65,677
Depreciation	16,250	16,250	16,250	31,250	15,000	15,000
Production facilities	50,000	0	0	45,000	0	0
Working capital: Cash	0	20,800	31,200	41,600	31,200	(124,800)
Working capital: Inventories	0	20,800	31,200	41,600	31,200	(99,840)
Working capital: Acc. Rec.	0	31,200	46,800	62,400	46,800	(187,200)
Net cash flows	(46,520)	(84,181)	13,692	115,928	339,596	492,517
Discounted flows	(46,250)	(67,888)	8,904	60,803	143,725	168,001
Net present value	$267,025					
Internal rate of return	73.7					
Payback	Nov., Year 3					

Test 1: NPV = $88,885
Test 2: NPV = $149,453
Test 3: NPV = $196,013
All 3: NPV = ($99,699)

Worst case is very undesirable, even here where indirect effects, sunk costs, and salvage were omitted.

Production costs.   Is anything unusual being done on this project? Actual anticipated cost goes directly onto the financial worksheet. Cite factory burden percent rate.*

Future special expenditures.   Typically, these include factory facilities, licensing rights, the one-time introductory marketing cost, up-front payments to suppliers, further R&D on improvements and line extensions, and plant expansions as volume grows. These are all *investment outflows*.

Working capital.   This estimates cash, inventories, and receivables needed to support the sales volumes. How are they to be recovered?

Applicable overheads.   Some firms assign only direct overheads—those caused by the new product (such as an expanded sales force or a new quality function). Other firms believe overheads tend to grow as functions of volume and should be included.

Net loss on cannibalized sales.   These are dollar sales lost as the new product steals sales from current products. This is to be deducted from revenue. Some experts believe if we don't do this a competitor will, so they omit it.

Future costs/revenues of project abandonment.   Along the way, the project may have accumulated facilities, people, patent rights, inventories, and so on. If abandoned now, disposal of these will produce revenue, money that is actually a *cost of abandoning the project*. But, disposing of radioactive chemicals may be expensive, thus a *revenue* of going ahead.

Tax credits.   Federal or state incentives for activity in the public interest.

Applicable depreciation rate.   Policy question, set by management.

Federal and state income tax rate.   Company figure, provided.

Required rate of return.   This one tells us the cash flow discount rate to be used, and can be complex and political. Theoretically, the figure to use is the *weighted average cost of capital*, including the three sources of capital—debt, preferred stock, and retained earnings. Often it is simply the *firm's current borrowing rate*. Maybe the *rate of earnings from current operations*. New products managers want it low; conservative financial people may want it high. The actual rate to be used is often an arbitrary decision.

Whatever the rate, the next step is to decide how the riskiness of this project compares with the rest of the firm's activities. Look at Figure 11–2, which shows that a relationship between risk and rate of return exists for every business, as discussed in the chapter.

Given the current average cost of capital and the level and slope of the line, the manager can mark off the risk of the particular new product, go up to the risk/return line, and then read off the required rate of return. Except in unusual circumstances, that required level will represent a premium over the current cost of capital. The premium is entered in section 14 of the key data form.

Risk curve.   Figure 11–3 shows the typical curve of possible profit outcomes from a given new product project, as discussed in the chapter. In the B pattern, for example, chances are the project will have a lower payout, but a very high payout is also possible. Imitative competition is expected, but if it doesn't come, the profit will be high. This risk pattern information is good to keep in mind when making the financial analysis, though few firms undertake the probability-adjusted risk analysis it permits.

Sensitivity testing.   After an analysis has been completed using original data, the analyst goes back and recalculates the profit using other figures for especially sensitive factors.

---

*For thoughts on use of activity based costing, see Bernard C. Reimann, "Challenging Conventional Wisdom: Corporate Strategies that Work," *Planning Review*, November/December 1991, pp. 36–39.

Elements of strategy.   When evaluating new product proposals, it is important to remember the strategy that prompted them. Less-profitable products may well be warranted under certain strategies.

Basic sales and cost forecasts.   This section gives the primary data inputs. The number of units to be sold, the direct production cost per unit, and the total marketing expenditures.

Hurdle rates.   A company sometimes has hurdle rates on variables other than rate of return.

Mandatory contingencies.   A firm may want one or more contingencies worked into the analysis every time, not left optional.

Other special assumptions or guidelines.   This is the typical miscellaneous section, totally situational.

Beyond the key data form.   **Sunk costs:** Sunk costs should not enter into this analysis. Sunk money is just that—sunk. It stays sunk whether we go ahead at this time or abandon the project. **Salvage:** NPV forms sometimes call for the dollars obtained at the end of the product's life from sale of salvaged equipment. The amounts are usually small, and are best omitted. **Portfolio:** If the new item is playing a special role as part of an overall portfolio of projects, the value of that role should be mentioned. The new project may contain high risk but still be worthwhile to balance a large number of low-risk projects. Or the reverse.

12   PRODUCT PROTOCOL

Setting

When a new products group finishes the full screen and the financial analysis coincident with it, they have reached what many feel is the most critical single step in the new product's life—more critical than the market introduction and more critical than the building of manufacturing capacity. This is the point where very important things *all around the firm* begin to happen.

Review

Granted, some managements still use a relay race system, where one department does its work, passes the product concept to the next department which does its work, then... and so on. The leading product innovators do not—they use some type of *concurrent system,* one in which all of the players begin working, doing as much as they can at any time as the project rolls along. When technical work begins, process engineers are not sitting around waiting for the final prototype to be tossed to them. When process engineers are laying out the manufacturing system, procurement people are not waiting for final word about when certain components are going to be built. And while all of this technical/operations work is continuing, marketing people are not sitting around waiting for a handoff that will trigger their thoughts about advertising and customer technical service.

No, they all begin work at the same time, and in fact many have been watching the concept testing and screening to see how positive the early word is. If a concept looks like a winner, even if financial screening won't take place for a couple months, these down-the-line people are already starting to do what they will *eventually* have to do. Some workers actually may be a year ahead of need, especially if there is some built-in delay in what they do.

For example, while process engineers are waiting for product specs so they can begin their work, packaging people have been thinking about the concept. Many products require packaging—durable, value-producing packaging, or impressive shelf-talking promotion packaging. Packages, in turn, require product names. So purchasing cannot order new packages until brands are settled, and brands cannot be settled until product content is known and marketing strategy is settled. Marketing strategy involves price decisions, which must await costs, which must await final manufacturing systems and component costs, which is where this paragraph started.

What do we do? We do it all, side by side, doing what we can, when we can, making minor commitments at some risk, holding on costly commitments.

Occasionally we do what one firm actually did—produce a product (brand, packaging, advertising, pricing, everything) while still waiting for a chemist to settle on the item's actual formulation. All of these efforts are risky and will never work well without *something that keeps the team together*, something that allows them to make reasonable speculations.

That something currently has no standard form, no accepted name, and no established practice. But most firms are doing part of the task, a few all of it, waiting for the activity to gel.[1] In this book we will call the activity **protocol preparation**, and the output is a **product protocol**. Other names that it goes by are **product requirements**, **product definition**, and **deliverables**. All terms mean the same thing—what the final package of output from the development system will be—what benefits or performance the product will deliver to the customer, and what changes the marketing program will bring in the marketplace.

Use of the term *protocol* follows from its dictionary definition: A signed document containing a record of the points on which agreement has been reached by negotiating parties *(Webster's New World Dictionary)*. The negotiating parties are the functions—marketing, technical, operations, and others. Signed agreement is a bit formal, perhaps, but the financial analysis which triggered this phase depended on certain assumptions—product qualities and costs, certain support facilities, certain patents, and certain marketplace accomplishments. If they are not delivered, all bets with management are off. Since most projects today involve some form of multifunctional team, the whole group is responsible for writing a protocol. Although new products do indeed require trade-offs, they are negotiated in a very positive use of the term.

A word on the matter of negotiations. Negotiations here are not the adversarial activities stereotyped from labor–management struggles. But there are

---

[1]At the 1994 International Conference of the Product Development and Management Association, the following firms, among others, expressed activity in this area: Apple Computer, IBM, Quaker Oats, Compaq Computer, Hewlett-Packard, and PRTM Consulting. In a study on speeding up the new product process, the Number 1 reason for product delays was poor definition of product requirements. See Ashok K. Gupta and David L. Wilemon, "Accelerating the Development of Technology-Based New Products," *California Management Review,* Winter 1990, pp. 24–44.

often technical limitations that may make quick agreement difficult. For example, customers may want a product that "removes all grease in 10 seconds," but technical people say no solvent could do this in a kitchen setting. So, should they begin basic research? Management answers no, but what time frame is possible now? Technical responds that they can't know for sure, but 15 seconds seems to be tops, given today's state of the art. Marketing asks if they know how they will achieve this. No, but it seems to be an achievable goal. This type of discussion may go on for days, as various customer requirements are dealt with.

Too, there are sometimes negotiations between two desirable parts of a protocol—things all functions want, but that conflict. For example, a market situation may be so competitive that real innovativeness is necessary at this time, yet the firm's overall strategy may be to make more incremental advances. It's better to settle this conflict immediately. A recent recap of the famous Chrysler minivan development showed how often Lee Iacocca and others had to fight traditional thinking in the automobile industry to really meet customer needs and desires.[2]

Protocol preparation is the subject of this chapter. In prior chapters of this book you had a chance to see the new product process from an overall perspective—how it goes from strategy through to market success, how the strategy gives the process focus, how concepts are created and gathered, how concepts are then tested and evaluated, and how the evaluation process comes to a temporary conclusion with the full screen and financial analysis.

Purposes of the Protocol

Figure 12–1 shows what happens now. In the middle of the figure lies the augmented product diagram you first saw in Chapter 2 (Figure 2–7)—showing that what the customer actually buys consists of one or more core benefits, a formal product presentation (physical form or service sequence), *and* an augmentation of things from presale technical service to a money-back guarantee. All three of these layers must be designed and executed, and two functional groups play a role in all of them, as shown by the arrows leading into the augmented circles.

Figure 12–1 also shows that the technical departments (with help from manufacturing, quality, procurement, and others) work pretty much as a unit, and marketing (with help from its allies in sales, market research, promotion, channel management, and others) does the same on the right side of the diagram. Both groups keep in close touch each other.

The issue is: *What do these two groups need to do their work?* The answer differs by firm and industry and situation, but whatever it happens to be, it should be consolidated into a protocol statement. The protocol is, in fact, one step in the life cycle of a concept, as you saw in Figure 3–3 of Chapter 3. It is more than the simple statement approved in the screening, and less than what will exist

---

[2]Alex Taylor III, "Iacocca's Minivan," *Fortune*, May 30, 1994, pp. 56–66.

FIGURE 12–1

*The Integrating
and Focusing Role
of Protocol*

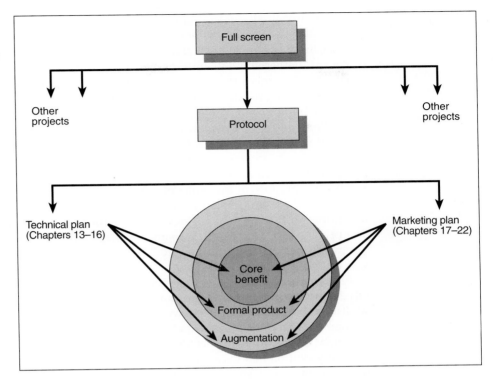

when the first prototype appears. But it is what we need now, what all departments need to begin their work.

   This idea of how others use the protocol is what gave it the name *product
deliverables*—what each department will deliver to the final product that
the customer buys. For a new type of golf footwear, a deliverable from technical might be "can be used in all types of weather and on all turf conditions."
A deliverable from marketing might be personal trial use by at least 80 percent of the golf professionals in Europe, the United States, Australia, and South
Africa. A deliverable from information technology might be "800 number service with less than five minutes waiting time, covering the needs of 80 percent of callers from the United States this year and from the other markets by
end of the second year."

   Not all deliverables are known at this time, of course, but the critical ones
should be. Otherwise, we are not ready for release into a system of parallel (or
concurrent) development. If, on that golf footwear, we don't know the importance of bad weather and turf conditions, the golf pro's influence on affluent
golfers (what we are producing we can see will have to be expensive), the crit-
icalness of trial (key benefits will be hidden), and the certainty of technical questions on a complex product like this, then we haven't done our homework. The

fact is, protocol (like many things in use today) states requirements that force us to do what we should be doing anyway, such as good market research!

In Chapter 4, on the product innovation charter, you read that the PIC is rather like a soft harness on a team of horses. It is not a ball and chain, but it clearly directs and integrates the team. A second general purpose of the protocol statement is the same for the participants in new product development. *It communicates essentials to all of the players, helps lead them into integrated actions, helps direct outcomes that are consistent with the full screen and financials, and gives all players their targets to shoot for.* Some new products people think the mere call for the document leads to early customer contacts that should always be made, but often aren't.

A third purpose of the protocol relates to time through the process, or cycle time. The Coleman Company recently told how they had used a better product definition process to help cut development time on a new home lantern from two years to one. On prior developments, they said, "We were always changing our minds and not getting anywhere." So a definition that "set clear boundaries" was established.[3]

Fourth, if done right, the protocol gives requirements in words that can usually be measured. It thus permits a development process to be *managed*. It tells what is to be done, when and why, the how (if that is required by some power beyond our control), the who, and perhaps most important, the whether. That is, we know at any time whether the requirements have been met; this will automatically caution that we are not ready to market an item if there is still an open requirement, unless specifically waived.

In classic lay language, if you don't know where you're going, any road will get you there. Without protocol and its call for measurements, you've no idea where (or when) you will end up.

Protocol's Specific Contents

You have just read what is in a protocol, in general terms. The details can vary greatly, and will for some time until our practice on this new step tells just how to do it. But we do know that there is a scale of demand or commitment. Not everything that we call for *must* be delivered. Some firms use the terms *musts* and *wants*—that is, some requirements we must have, and some are simply what we *would like* to have if feasible and practical within technology, cost, and time frames.

Others have used such terms as *critical utility factors* (CUFs), which denote the difference between must and want by hard CUFs and soft CUFs.[4] But each firm has its own language for these things. Some have put the musts in a

---

[3]Brian Dumaine, "Earning More Money by Moving Faster," *Fortune*, October 7, 1991, pp. 89–94.

[4]Shad Dowlatshahi, "A Novel Approach to Product Design and Development in a Concurrent Engineering Environment," *Technovation*, no. 3, 1993, pp. 161–76

protocol and the wants or hoped-fors in an attachment (or literally, in one case, on the *backs* of pages!).[5] The following sections list items often found in protocols, and an abbreviated version of a simple protocol is given in Figure 12–2.

Target Market

You read in Chapter 2, on strategy, that most firms *manage* most of their new product projects with PICs, concept testing, screening models, protocols, and so on. Other projects are *wildcatting*—betting on a technology that hasn't yet been shown to work, betting on a new application where some end user will partner with us to see what works, or just betting on a scientist with a good track record to come up with saleable new products. None of these are appropriate for a protocol; we just don't have the knowledge to write one, and its only effect would be to bother the developers, who, actually, will ignore it completely.

In most cases, however, we know the target market very well—first in finding their problems to solve, later in asking if our new product concept meets their need and seems reasonable to them, and still later in screening factors (e.g., do we have a sales force that can reach them or will we have to build a new one?). Target market needs to be spelled out here—specifically. Some firms like to have a primary target market, one or more secondary (smaller) target markets to move to after successful introduction, and at least one fall-back target market if the primary target marget gets blown out of the water by technical failure, regulation, competition, or whatever, during our development.

Product Positioning

This one is trickier, and is still difficult to use in some firms. **Product positioning** is the concept that came out of the advertising world about 30 years ago. Essentially, it says, "Product X is better for your use than other products because..." It announces the item as new and gives the end user a real reason for trying it. In the process, it shows the end user what problem it attacks, and what about it makes it better than whatever they are using now. This concept will be developed more completely when we get to Chapter 17, but for now it is usually enough to state the target market and say why the product is better. Fortunately, this should be easy, because positioning should have been decided in the concept test. That's what a concept test does, assures us that stakeholders will be interested in trying an item and a claim (positioning).

Technical people are often not told what the positioning of a new item will be. It's almost as though we say, develop a new item and do it in a way the customer will like. That's not management; that's abdication. Even in large packaged goods firms today, with their excellent staffs, products a bit off the

---

[5]Puritan-Bennett uses one category of protocol benefits called *excitement needs*, which if filled would happily surprise the end user. See John H. Hauser, "How Puritan-Bennett Used the House of Quality," *Sloan Management Review*, Spring 1993, pp. 61–70.

FIGURE 12–2   **Abbreviated Sample Protocol for a Trash Disposal/ Recycling System for Use in the Home**

1. **Target market:**
   Ultimate: Top 30% of income group. in cities of over 100,000, with upscale lifestyle.
   Intermediate: Stakeholders in building industry for homes over $300,000, especially developers, architects, builders, bankers, and regulators.
2. **Product positioning:**
   A convenient, mess-free method for recyling items in the home.
3. **Product attributes (benefits if possible):**
   • The system must automate trash disposal in a home environment with recycling (separating trash, compacting, placing bags outside, and rebagging the empty bins and notifying user when the bag supply is running out) at a factory cost not to exceed $800.
   • The system must be clean, ventilated, and odor-free. The user will want an easy-to-clean appliance. Rodents, pets, and angry neighbors could become a problem if odors exist.
   • Installation must be simple. Distributors and other installation personnel must have favorable experience in installations.
   • The system must be safe enough for operation by children of school age.
   • The entire working unit must not be larger in cubic feet than twice a 22 cubic foot refreigerator.
4. **Competitive comparison:**
   None: First of a kind.
5. **Augmentation dimensions:**
   Financing arrangeable with us, if necessary. Generous warranty. Competent installation service, and fast/competent post-installation service. Education about recycling and about the product will be difficult and essential.
6. **Timing:**
   Being right overrides getting to market fast. But the window will not be open more than two years.
7. **Marketing requirements:**
   • Marketing announcement must be made at national builders shows and environment/ecology shows.
   • A new channel structure will be needed for the intermediate target market, but it will eventually be collapsed into our regular channel.
   • We will need a small, select sales force for this introduction.
   • To capitalize on announcement value, we need 50 installations during the first four months.
8. **Financial requirements:**
   • Development and intro period losses will not exceed $20,000,000. Break-even is expected by end of second full year on the market.
   • Ultimately, this project must achieve a five-year net present value of zero, based on 35% cost of capital.
9. **Production requirements:**
   • Once we announce, there must be no interruption of supply.
   • Quality standards simply must be met, without exception.
10. **Regulatory requirements:**
    Regulations are from many sources and vary by states and localities. There are various substakeholders here; we need to know them well. A surprise, significant holdup (after launch) cannot be allowed on this development.
11. **Corporate strategy requirements:**
    Corporate strategy is driving this project, and has personal leadership at the corporate general management level. We seek diversification of markets, enhanced reputation for innovativeness, and sustainable margins higher than those in our major markets today.
12. **Potholes:**
    This project has massive pothole potentials, because of its newness. The most worrisome ones are (1) regulatory approval of health issues, (2) accomplishing the $800 cost constraint, and (3) getting fast market approvals for early installations.

beaten track often get neglected; many of these firms' R&D staffs have had to build market research departments to do concept testing on items they are originating. Misunderstandings on positioning have probably been the cause of more technical/marketing fights than anything else.

Product Attributes

As we discussed several times before, product attributes define the product. They are of three types—features, functions, and benefits. Benefits include uses. Protocols can list any of these, and do. "The new bulk laxative will dissolve completely in a four-ounce glass of water in 10 seconds" (Dow-Merrell). This is function—how the item will work, not what it is (feature) or what the benefit is of fast dissolving. Note that by being asked for speed, technical people were allowed to select any chemical they wished (and did, it is now second only to Metamucil in this market). Stride Rite called for a new version of Topsiders by requesting that it "must not slip on polished wood at 30-degree pitch."[6] The protocol could have asked for a "safer" shoe (benefit) but they knew that slipping on a slanting deck was a big safety problem and the specifics helped technical. Benefits are the most desirable form for a protocol to use—better than functions or features.

Functions.   Function attributes sometimes cause confusion. Marketers tend to use them a lot, and they are often called performance specs, or performance parameters, or design parameters. One everyone knows is: "The car must accelerate from 0 to 60 miles per hour in 8 seconds." This requirement does not tell us what features will yield that performance. What it *does* do is answer the question of how the customer achieves the benefits of exciting (or safe) startups.

Some people feel a performance parameter (a function) may come to be expressed as a design parameter. For example, on the matter of the car pickup above, the statement might be "Use the new German 11-Z4 engine." Such a new engine would be a technology but clearly might be a *solution* to a need, not a *description* of it; there are probably many other ways rapid pickup could be achieved. Car platforms are heavily laced with such statements.

Protocols for services are especially likely to be in performance terms, since the production of a service is a performance, not a good. But protocols are also much less necessary on services because of the smaller investment in technical development. These producers can, in many cases, get to prototype very quickly, so that prototype concept testing or even product use testing can easily gain confirmation of customer need fulfillment.

Features.   Features are also a problem. Technical people often come up with features first, based on technologies they have. Some scientist at a firm such as PPG might figure out a way to make a boat deck out of finely ground glass left over from some production operation. The thought is pursued for several months only

---

[6]"Setting the Pace in Shoe Design," *The Wall Street Journal*, August 13, 1987, p. 21.

to be knocked out by a shipbuilders' need for reduced weight. A full protocol state-ment might have avoided that waste of time. In another case, a scientist did in fact figure out a solution to a certain worm infestation in children, only to be told that this infestation occurs only on scattered Pacific islands and could never con-stitute a viable market for a pharmaceutical firm. That's why firms ask scientists to keep others informed, and to seek input about markets being worked on.

The bigger problem with features is that they deprive the firm's most cre-ative and inventive people of the freedom to use their skills. A large computer firm 30 years ago was known for having a strong technical research staff. They originated some useful technology, but the firm never achieved much success in reacting to changing needs in the marketplace. Some insiders said it was the result of a system that had a central engineering staff take each situation and spell out the features and characteristics their research staff were to produce. One such spec sheet ran 13 pages, and the scientist getting it said he felt like a beginning law clerk. He left the firm as soon as he could.

An extreme version of a protocol was reported by a pharmaceutical firm in which a new products manager sent a comprehensive advertising layout to his technical counterpart in R&D with an attached note, "Please prepare an item that will back up this ad." The first reaction was negative, until technical realized they were given carte blanche to do whatever they wanted, so long as the result met the listed claims.[7]

Occasionally, a firm knows from long-time market contact what features are associated with what functions (performance) and benefits. They occasionally will put through a work request that calls for "a new pump with electronic valves that give faster reaction to down-line stoppages and thus prevent blowouts." If the valves are standards, this protocol statement gives feature, function, and benefit.

Detailed Specifications.   On occasions, customers make such decisions and call for products with specific features. This is dangerous. If the customers are qualified and have reason to know better than we do what features will do for them, we better listen. In Chapter 5 we talked about getting finished product con-cepts from lead users (sometimes even a finished prototype).

Another case where features may be needed is where a firm is benchmark-ing competitive products. One strategy is to have the "Best of the Best." Take the best features in the market, all products combined, and assemble them in your new product. This sounds great, but it means our product design is being led by competitors, not end users.[8]

---

[7]One retired scientist creates laughter during his speeches when he refers to such "unalterable laws" as MS = MD. This translates into Monkey See = Monkey Do. "Marketing generally cannot relate to a product or product category that does not already exist." See *Marketing, a Bimonthly Briefing from the Conference Board,* December 1987, p. 4. The scientist, Raymond C. Odiso, presented the total set of "laws" in a Conference Board Research Management Report, according to the cited source.

[8]This is explained very well by Milton D. Rosenau Jr. in "Avoiding Marketing's Best-of-the-Best Specification Trap," *Journal of Product Innovation Management,* December 1992, pp. 300–302.

Still other situations where features will appear in protocols are (1) where regulations stipulate a particular feature (e.g., prescription containers), (2) where end users own major items of equipment that impose limitations (e.g., under-dash space limitations for tape decks), (3) where established practice in a customer industry is too strong for one supplier to change (e.g., for many years software makers had no choice but to put MS-DOS as a feature requirement), and, regrettably, (4) where upper managements have personal preferences.

In general, as a conclusion to this section on attributes, it is still the best policy to write protocols in benefits, using performance if that helps explain and doesn't inhibit too much.

Competitive Comparisons

Benchmarking has been mentioned, but there are many other competitive standards that can be put into a protocol—matching some important policy, the degree of differentiation we have to meet, and many aspects of the marketing plan (e.g., size of sales force, price, distribution availabilities).

Augmentation Dimensions

Just as the product itself was described in attributes above, the augmentation ring of the product can also be cited. Sometimes the product itself may be me-too but with a new level of service, or a better warranty, or better distributor support. Recall that there are three rings in the fully augmented product—ring one (core benefit) is covered in the positioning statement, ring two (the formal product) is covered in the attribute requirements, and ring three (augmentations) is covered here.

Timing

Most new products today must come out faster, but not all do. Some involve major technical breakthroughs that cannot be put on the clock. The distinction needs to be clear to all. And if there is a date to meet, it should be right here.

Marketing Requirements

Only in recent years have marketing requirements been seen as a part of protocol, so there is no widespread agreement on what should be in this section. One of the earliest public mentions of marketing requirements came from Apple Computer, when the firm was receiving the Outstanding Innovation Award from the Product Development and Management Association; they mentioned them, but specified none at the meeting. We hear about virtually every aspect of a marketing plan and its objectives being used by various firms. Here are some of them:

Trade show schedule

Trade channel, new form.

Trade channel, service output.

Sales force, size, training.

Positioning awareness level.

Trial use to be obtained.

Availability level.

Repeat use, satisfaction.

Advertising break date.

Brand awareness.

In what is apparently the only research report covering marketing requirements, the authors found target markets, channels, and price.[9]

Financials

Here we see price level, discounts, sales volume, sales dollars, market share, profits, net present value, and more.

Production

This one is much like marketing requirements, items focusing on what the function will prepare to do, and what that will accomplish—thus, plants to be built, volumes, and quality to be achieved.

Regulatory Requirements

These are highly varied, but managements today understand the need to have advanced agreement on them.

Corporate Strategy Requirements

This area is growing, but most of the key ideas (e.g., core competencies) have already been captured in the product innovation charter, if the firm uses one. Development startup is too late for most strategic items. One angle that does come at this time, however, and one important enough to list as a requirement, is upper management support assurance. It's easy to just assume the team will have such support. And a new products team doesn't in any way

---

[9]Glenn Bacon, Sara Beckman, David Mowery, and Edith Wilson, "Managing Product Definition in High-Technology Industries: A Pilot Study," *California Management Review,* Spring 1994, pp. 32–56. The six firms studied so far were General Electric, General Motors, Hewlett-Packard, IBM, Motorola, and Xerox.

"bring management to the mat." But, managements should get a clear picture of just what is expected of them, as seen by the project people.

Key Potholes

This is no fancy management term. It means just what it means when you're driving down the boulevard on a rainy night. There are potholes in product innovation—things can happen (though they shouldn't) that will bring a new product down. A management that doesn't take a good look ahead deserves to hit one. We don't usually drive into *known* potholes, so listing them here helps.

An Example of Requirements

The 10 items in Hewlett-Packard's product definition were recently given as:[10]

> Understanding user needs.
> Strategic alignment, charter consistency.
> Competitive analysis.
> Product positioning.
> Technical task assessment.
> Priority criteria.
> Regulation compliance.
> Product channel issues.
> Product endorsement by upper managements.
> Total organizational support.

Several of these items use company terminology, but the list indicates a respected leader in product innovation which views the protocol as comprehensive.

Protocol and Quality Function Deployment (QFD)

QFD was invented in the Japanese automobile industry years ago as a tool of project control in an industry with horribly complicated projects. The tool has not achieved its theoretical promise in use, although it has been talked about a great deal. QFD is credited with a major contribution to the U.S. automobile industry's comeback against Japanese competition. But, a higher percentage of firms are finding one part of QFD useful, and that one is the so-called House of Quality. (See Figure 12–3.) The value of the house (or better, matrix) is the way it summarizes multiple product aspects in one place and in relationship to each other.

---

[10]As reported by Shiela Mello, at the 1994 International Conference of the Product Development and Management Association, Boston, MA.

FIGURE 12–3

Partial Protocol, Set Up in House of Quality (QFD) Style

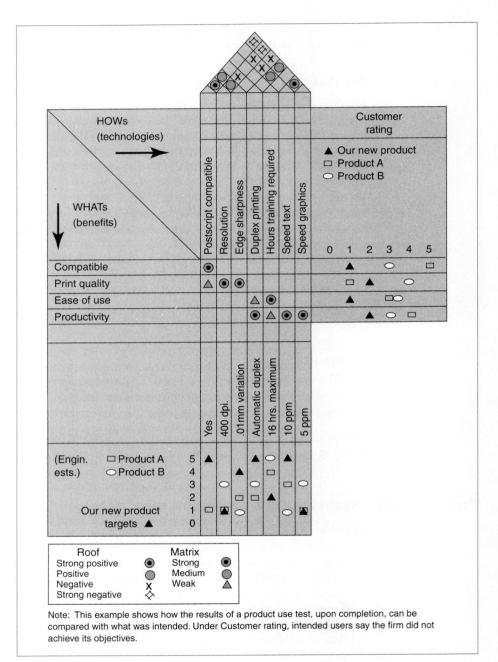

Note: This example shows how the results of a product use test, upon completion, can be compared with what was intended. Under Customer rating, intended users say the firm did not achieve its objectives.

Source: This modified diagram is from Milton D. Rosenau Jr. and John J. Moran, *Managing the Development of New Products* (New York: Van Nostrand Reinhold, 1993), p. 231. Rosenau wrote an earlier book called *Faster New Product Development,* but the new coauthored book includes the acceleration materials.

The left rectangle in the figure is variously called requirements, whats, needs, or benefits. That section is the part of protocol relating to what the end user will get from the product. It is usually filled with benefits, though sometimes (as above) features are so mandatory that they are put there. These are sometimes weighted in a second column. The upper section of the diagram (again in various arrangements) speaks to how those whats will be achieved, usually technologies although sometimes design parameters. In the automobile example earlier of fast pickup speed, a what might be teenage pride among peers, the top section might have the new engine (a technology) or a performance parameter (the 0–60 time) or a design parameter (a major weight switch putting more load at the point of drive-wheel contact). Practice varies such that we can't give instruction here, but there are other sources.[11]

The right side of the House lists what we know about competitive products, The right side also lists (when the data are available) how our end product actually compares to competition, etc. Figure 12–3 identifies each part. We will return to the House of Quality when we get to Chapter 16, "Product Use Testing."

Some Caveats, or Warnings, about the Difficulty of the Protocol Process

If this matter of protocol sounds simple, you have been done a disservice. It is very difficult indeed. For one thing, it is fraught with politics. The departments are all in natural competition for power and budget. Key individuals are as different as night and day, being scientist, marketer, accountant, and factory manager. The situation itself is fluid and changing, seemingly never nailed down. Management senses the importance of the various projects and puts heavy pressure on them. A big winner on the product frontier can make a career, exonerate a general manager's other disappointments, and make for very large bonuses. Of course, a major failure can make a mess of everything close to it.

All of this means people have their own agenda for incorporating into a protocol (or not incorporating into it). Most want the other people nailed down to specific accomplishment requirements (with dollar signs and dates clearly attached) but with no such promises on themselves.

Given that a protocol is needed early on, just prior to starting broadscale work, many people are not yet on the scene. They have more pressing, near-term problems, so they delay the process or weaken it by their absence.

However, beyond the politics and pressures, we also see a hardening of the requirements in a protocol. People think they have been all wise, when developing

---

[11]For an early, general business explanation, see John R. Hauser and Don Clausing, "The House of Quality," *Harvard Business Review*, May–June, 1988, pp. 63–73. For an application see Hauser, "How Puritan-Bennett Used the House of Quality." See also Milton D. Rosenau Jr. and John J. Moran, *Managing the Development of New Products* (New York: Van Nostrand Reinhold, 1993), pp. 225–37.

FIGURE 12–4   **Protocol Accomplishment**

Requirement	Company Call	Customer Call
1. Reduce setup time	OK	OK
2. Lower initial cost	OK	Not needed
3. Easier replacement during manufacturing process	OK	OK
4. Safety in customer's plan	Doubtful	Later
5. Easier federal approval on finished item	?	Not needed
6. Lower cost disposal of trim	Vendor	Later
Date:		

Explanation: A form such as this, listing all protocol requirements, can serve as a good exercise for the team: How are we going to measure each of the requirements? Must we go outside? When do we do all this? Is a judgment call enough or do we need data?

the document, and presume the contents are all set in concrete. But it shouldn't be seen that way. It is an *aid to management*, not a *substitute for thinking*. All protocols have to change, some of them many times. But the burden of proof is on those who want to change a requirement.

Ironically, in some situations the protocol is ignored, so a smart new products team manager will prepare something like the protocol accomplishment form shown in Figure 12–4. It is needed, especially, for product requirements (benefits, etc.) and there should be agreement in advance about who is going to make the call on each. Some can be made by the team, but others must be made by the person the product is being made for.

Along the way, bureaucracy sneaks in. One leading computer firm recently made a presentation on product requirements that must have contained at least 25 acronyms; the "sound" of that presentation was right out of government.

Finally, most of these problems go away if preparation of a protocol is assigned to a multifunctional new products team. Technical doesn't write one, and neither does marketing. Most assuredly, top management does not write one.

Summary

This chapter has dealt with a powerful concept—product protocol. As an agreement among the functions about the required output or deliverables from a specific new product program, it sets the standards for it. The purpose is to communicate the required outputs as product benefits and other dimensions, integrate the team onto the same frequency, make clear the timing importance, and make it easier to manage the process against specific targets.

You saw a simplified version of a typical protocol. At this time we are ready to blow the whistle and charge into the development activity. Action will flow along three lines, the triple process talked about in Chapter 2—product, marketing program, and evaluation. Each line of activity has its own requirements, and they should be reasonably precise if they are to do their job.

Applications

More questions from that interview with the company president:

1. "Let's cut right to the quick on this one. I understand the theory of having benefits rather than features, but to me it is just that, theory. I knew one of the top people at that computer company your book talked about—the one where a corporate new product engineering group spelled out the specifications of each new product before technical work was funded. I heard the same criticism your author did, so I called this woman and asked her about it. She said the facts were right, but the implication was wrong—corporate staff did indeed spell out most of the features, but only to get the project moving. She said if they just gave their research people the benefits or needs of the customer, those dreamers would never reach a prototype. Every item would be a Taj Mahal. You know, I think she had a point. What do you think?"

2. "I really don't think you understand what parallel or concurrent new product development is all about. You said you had studied in your course that all of the functions get involved. No, concurrent development means just that—*technical development phases*—design engineering, etc. They are all doing work very much alike, they work with each other, they can feel how things are going and when they can take a chance and make a premature commitment. Marketing people can't do that. Even production people (process engineering) have trouble on this score."

3. "I've never liked that term *requirements*. It seems negative, like something imposed on a manager or a department. Same with *deliverables*. Yet I sure agree that we should have targets for everyone in a new product operation. Maybe that term, targets, would be better. Do you have a better term in mind?"

4. "Seems one of our senior R&D people went to a new products management conference a while back, and he returned steamed. Called me for a talk right away. Now, you know what a protocol is, and so do I. But he didn't. At the conference a speaker said it was a device whereby the head of a new products team communicated to R&D exactly what was wanted from the technical group. R&D even had to 'sign on the dotted line' swearing that they thought it could be done. He said top management could give directions like that, but no new product team manager could. Said he used to serve on those teams and the managers were just facilitators, not really managers. They didn't have any authority."

And, he threatened to quit if I made him *promise* to deliver anything in particular. He used terms like *stifling*. I wish you had been in here that day. What would you have said to that senior scientist?"

CASE: WILSON SPORTING GOODS—PART II*

Glance back at the Wilson case, given at the end of Chapter 10. Assume that a new products group has proposed applying some new metalurgical technology to bowling pins. Apparently they think there are some space-age metals that simulate wood very well and that would give the pins much more "bounce to the ounce." That is, they will keep the basic weights and shapes, but the materials have more responsiveness, or action. Granted, the bowling game might never be the same again, but it would be a lot more interesting to hit the new pins than current pins.

First, think about whether the protocol idea would fit the situation of these bowling pins. Then, write up five lines of benefits that consumers would probably put stress on if they were interviewed. Decide how you would actually measure whether the benefits were being achieved when the new pins were used in play.

Second, refer to the list of contents in a protocol, and see if there are any other points that could be added to the benefits you just wrote out. There won't be many in a simple situation like this, but there will probably be some. Look especially at the marketing requirements.

---

*See Chapter 10.

The Technical Development Stage of the New Product Process

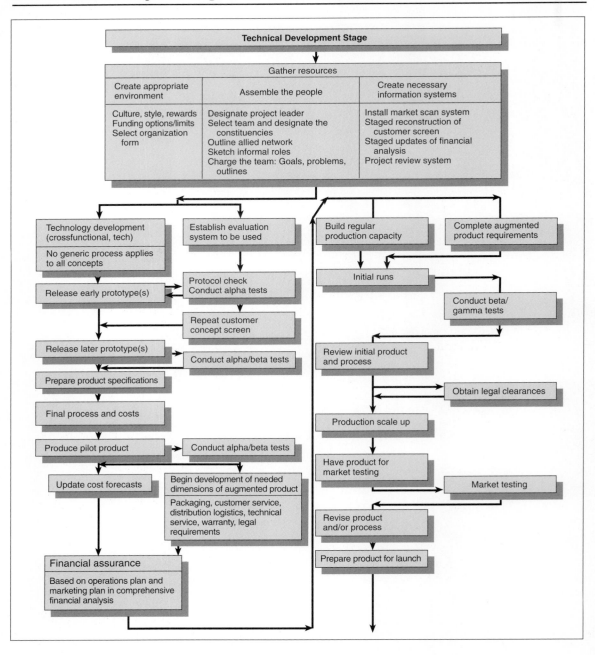

P A R T

IV TECHNICAL DEVELOPMENT

Somewhere during the preceding process of evaluation, a decision was made to develop the concept being considered. The decision may have come quickly (a key customer wanted the item and was ready to help develop it) or slowly, after concept testing and extensive review of capital and operational expenditures required. Management focus now changes from analysis to design.

The next question concerns fulfillment. Can we find ways to produce what was called for in the product protocol? There may be extensive technical search (e.g., for a new pharmaceutical) or none. The key problem may be in industrial design or in the very technical characteristics of a 686 chip. It may consist of nothing more than confirming a recipe that was used to produce new cookies for the concept testing. Or, as in the case of Frito-Lay's O'Gradys, two years of technical developments may be necessary.

This is the key creative stage, and it is totally situation-specific. There is still a strong art form here, even when dealing in scientific areas. Previously pretty much left in the hands of the technical staffs, it now has the attention of managers in all functions. Of all the changes made in the product innovation process the past 10 years, half are certainly packed into this stage.

The next four chapters will deal with this effort. They will show how the technical/design development phase is caught up in the same revolutionary changes affecting all management in the 1990s. They will talk about commitment, direction, product quality, bureaucracy, customer satisfaction, and the managerial requirements of this effort. About structural organizational alternatives on the one hand, and on the very soft human requirements on the other. About the need to do everything faster than we have done before. About how we are asking managers today to do things never required of them in the past—teams, networks, cultural changes. And then about the aspects of the task where we are still quite uncertain, such as how to use the immense capabilities of the industrial and engineering designers, how to gain true functional integration, not interface, and how to make sure our processes fit some newly strong players in the game: services and global markets. Lastly, we will see how companies determine whether their new product does indeed meet the needs of the customer, whose problem started it all.

The sequence of activities (the steps, or stages, or phases) for the technical development work varies between industries, firm size, firm strategy, and many other factors. There literally is no pattern that a manager can (or indeed, should) apply without substantial changes. But, we can see some general outlines, and they are shown in the illustration on page 243.

One reminder is relevant. Occasionally, someone studying product innovation for the first time wonders whether his or her particular interest (say, marketing, or engineering, or design) is being served by discussion about what seem to be the affairs of other departments. Today, there really is no such person as a marketer, or a designer, when it comes to new products. All *must* understand the *total* operation, all must *contribute at many points*, all must see product success as a *team* accomplishment. Marketers must understand the problems of technical people because there are things they can do to help on those problems. Marketing people may be members of a team or leaders of teams. Manufacturing people are present when scientists begin to configure product, so they can speak to its manufacturability—they ask, "What good is a new item if I can't make it?" Technical people are still present during marketing planning, because they may have a better feel for some of the customers' problems and service needs.

13 DEVELOPMENT STRUCTURE

Setting

This chapter will begin our journey through the technical phase by looking at what it takes for managerial success in that effort. Obviously, the firm needs technical capability and resources appropriate to the task. But our interest is on the managerial side—what are the requirements for that? By 1990, managements of firms around the world clearly recognized that their businesses would have to change dramatically. Much of their concern focused on products which were too similar to competition's, were not generating growing markets fast enough, and were offered to the market in ways that left customers thoroughly dissatisfied. Product innovation in America and Europe took too long, far too long. There was much concern over the general level of product quality.

The result is already history—redesigned work, customer involvements, high-performance teams, smashed bureaucracies, and a general new enthusiasm across the board. *Fortune* called it a "Search for the Organization of Tomorrow."[1]

3M was virtually born to free-form innovation. Merck learned how to manage its technical function in ways that unlocked innovativeness. And Rubbermaid, in the ho-hum market of housewares, showed what could be done when top management made a genuine commitment to the needs of its customers and to the design and manufacture of products that worked. Most of these innovative firms turned to teams to overcome what was the entrenched power of departments—called **chimneys** because they think vertically (inward to the function), are very strong, and seem to be tall vertical structures on organization charts. Market information began to reach all who needed it, and technical groups created parallel and concurrent operations that devastate the historical linear movement of projects. One proponent called the new system a "seamless

---

[1]Thomas A. Stewart, *Fortune*, May 12, 1992, pp. 92–97.

enterprise."[2] Incidentally, line managers (e.g., VPs of those chimneys, such as marketing or manfacturing) have not given up easily—a battle rages between teams and functional managers.

Manufacturing and marketing planning are now begun at the start of the project, and technical work is not ended until the product is successful. Within the technical process itself, the whole complex of design-engineering-purchasing-manufacturing has jelled, thanks to computer-aided design and similar tools.

One of the most dramatic aspects of this concurrency is the merging of design into project teams. When Chrysler went to develop the 1993 line of LH cars, management deliberately built a team at the very start. For the first time in its history, designers would no longer just design the new line and "throw it over the wall" to engineering and manufacturing. They were members of a team that would do the designing. The project set new records in development cycle time, beat cost objectives, and met with market approval.[3]

The Players and Some Terms

The technical phase of a new product project involves people, departments, and actions that absolutely defy definition. There is no reason to think that it will ever be otherwise, so we do the best we can.

First, rather fundamental creative technical work is done in different departments depending on the industry involved. Chemical and pharmaceutical industries use the term *Research and Development*, the research part being where a new chemotherapeutic agent is found. Activity may take a few weeks or 10–15 years. Development is the stage when the new chemical is moved through necessary changes to meet market needs on strength, form, delivery system, etc., and then tested. This stage too may last many years. Development (in the sense of R&D, a department with that title) ends with a complete set of specifications for which a manufacturing process will be created. But, manufacturing people also do "development," with a little "d," that carries through to where the product is on the shipping dock ready for sale.

Second, there are industries where design, really industrial design, is the key ingredient—for example, in office furniture, where there are usually no R&D departments, no basic research for new chemicals or materials. Instead, the creation of the new occurs in the minds of designers, and the end point for that work is again a set of specifications for manufacturing people. The manufacturing people still need to create their new process and the item again ends up on the shipping dock ready for sale.

---

[2]Dan Dimancescu, *The Seamless Enterprise: Making Cross Functional Management Work* (New York: Harper Business, 1992).

[3]Information from Glenn Gardner, vice president of the Large Car Platform Engineering Team, in two presentations to the Product Development & Management Association.

In still other industries, there is no new material to be created and no dominant esthetic design function, but still there is creation. For example, new stereo speakers, new foods, new sneakers, and many more—perhaps more than both of the previous categories combined. These firms provide a semantics problem, because they may use R&D, or design, or something else. They may use engineering. Engineering is a science or an applied technology (both are used). The stereo speaker is probably designed primarily by an engineer (if the innovation is technical) or by a design engineer (if styling elements are important) or even by an industrial designer if the innovation is entirely restyling of common technology.

Many people in product innovation are engineers—and they spilt into what are occasionally warring groups: design engineers, functional or form engineers, and process engineers. The first might have designed the speakers for the first stereo systems, the second might have further designed them into actual units of given size, materials, etc., and the third designed a process by which the exact products could be made in quantity. All tasks are critical, all are creative, all have professions for participants to belong to, and generally, all feel they could do the whole task if necessary.

Somewhat the same problems come up when we talk about phases of technical development. What is called development in one industry (or even firm) may be called something else in another industry. A. D. Little, a leading consulting firm specializing in the technical side of product innovation, provided the list of steps or product forms given in the illustration for the introduction to Part IV. The steps are as widely useful as any, but keep in mind that the very next situation we talk about may use different terms, and no reader wants to stop for definitions at each situation.

A few special instances are worth a note. Some firms are trying to use the term *concept development* to cover that technical work (in any industry and done by whatever name) which starts with a verbal statement of the concept and ends with something physical (or a set of tools and work systems in the case of services). *Concept-to-prototype* is a term used sometimes. The phase of work that comes next, converting the first prototype into a manufacturable item, is called *product development*, which as a term violates most of the definitions above!

The services industry is particularly frustrated (and frustrating) in this semantics minefield. Most industry terminology emerged in the era of physical things, so terminology builds on prototype, working model, etc. Much of this doesn't fit service firms at all, although they tend to use established terminology anyway.

Characteristics Required in Today's Technical Development Activity

There are at least five requirements, some more important than others. All have their origin in the key concepts discussed in Chapter 2.

Commitment to Four Principles

We are increasingly convinced that there are several principles which tend to lead us to good process management. They are tough and often sacrificed.

Focus.   In very competitive situations managers often go to focus; that is, they try to zero in on part of the playing field, part of the market, or part of the technology. Narrowing focus yields greater capability and a shared vision, like the power of a laser. However, in a reverse twist, focus also means we try to solve the customer's whole problem, at least as much as we can. Ours is not a point solution. For example, product *disposal* is now getting attention in the design stage, and designers resist the rush-to-completion mentality of cycle time.

End User Drive.   During technical development today, the end user's problems are at the top of every page. Technical development isn't over until the customer agrees that we have solved the problems we began with. For example, U.S. Surgical has grown dramatically by having salespeople who are technically competent to understand surgeons when they tell about the difficulties they have. Too, end user drive says to make a product that is the *right* product, don't just make the *wrong* product *better*. Such firms as Honda, NEC, Sharp, and Sony have become good at what they call **demand articulation**. And, perhaps most important, end user drive means a great deal more than "customer satisfaction." In fact, trends along the latter line have been criticized as counterproductive in the technical development operation.[4]

Productivity.   Everyone seems to agree that we must destroy oppressive bureaucracy in the new products operation. Any organization, however, even on a kids' baseball diamond, needs some bureaucracy, and even venture teams that have been spun out from their firms need a little. It is a glue, and its policies reduce the time spent on routine decisions.

However, don't forget John A. Young. As CEO of Hewlett-Packard, he managed one of the world's most successful innovation factories, but things had started to slow down. Customers commented on how long proposals took. Young discovered that a new product required contacts with *no fewer than 38 committees*. Just for a *new name* on the firm's NewWave Computing software the project manager had to work with nearly 100 people on 9 committees.[5] That is oppressive bureaucracy. H-P's "penchant for egalitarianism and mutual respect had led them into a quagmire of consensus." Today an H-P new products manager may be able to get by with only three committees to worry about.

A consulting firm found much the same set of conditions and analyzed them down to threats like these: unwritten rules of the game, awkward engineering organization, ineffective program management, lack of discipline in work schedules, excessive handoffs, and general lack of sharp performance in every single

---

[4]Irwin Gross, "The Perils of Customer Satisfaction," *Across the Board*, April 1994, pp. 56–57.
[5]Barbara Buell, "Hewlett-Packard Rethinks Itself," *Business Week*, April 1, 1991, pp. 76–79.

aspect of the technical development operation.[6] Most participants are now convinced that they need to measure things better—how long does something take, what does doing that particular step cost? These measurements are called **metrics**, and new products management is increasingly using them.

Several of the most important tools in this chapter are directed to fighting back the natural growth of bureaucracy. It apparently doesn't work to use entrepreneurship (or intrapreneurship). This idea of going outside of, or around, bureaucracy doesn't succeed and doesn't last.[7] CEOs today are apparently convinced that the entire firm must be unshackled.[8] Interestingly, managements are not reaching out for more formality, more system, more standard methods of doing things. Quite the opposite. For example, one management system widely hailed the past 10 years has been that of **stage-gate**, phased reviews where set deliverables are checked by top management. The creator of the term has been studying managements again and now sees a much looser, fluid, more adaptive, and less procedural process being used.[9] Managers are again talking about freedom to fail, having fun, and giving teams some fanfare.

Unfortunately, what may be good for, say, public relations or controllership, may be wrong for new products. When firms optimize each function they usually end up suboptimizing the whole. For example, General Motors for many years has provided two keys with a new car, one for ignition and one for other uses such as doors. This customer inconvenience was defended by data showing it was cheaper to produce steering wheels in one plant and doors in another; keys could not be coordinated across such distances.

The Quadriad of Speed, Quality, Cost, and Value.   It takes all four (explained in Chapter 2), and there is evidence that they often come together. That is, a development system that produces new products fast may, surprisingly, also make them of better quality, at a lower cost, and thus a better value for the customer. This is Nirvana, a fine goal. Of course, these four items sometimes fight with each other. We will deal more specifically with the speed issue in Chapter 14.

A Clear and Accepted Product Innovation Charter

A product innovation charter offers several contributions to the technical development process. One, it provides the focus discussed above. Two, it gives the

---

[6]Michael S. Rosenberg and Bruce McK. Thompson, "Rooting Out the Causes of Inefficient Product Creation," *Prism*, Second Quarter, 1993, pp. 97–111. *Prism* is A. D. Little's external house organ.

[7]James S. Hirsch, "At Giant Kodak, 'Intrapreneurs' Lose Foothold," *The Wall Street Journal*, August 17, 1990, pp. 1B ff.

[8]G. Pascal Zachary, "Opening of 'Windows' Shows How Bill Gates Succeeds in Software," *The Wall Street Journal*, May 21, 1990, p. 1.

[9]Robert G. Cooper, "Third Generation New Product Processes," *Journal of Product Innovation Management*, January 1994, pp. 3–14.

goals and objectives. These help settle lots of questions down the line, resolve priority issues, and keep every eye on what is most important for the group. Three, the PIC helps assure top management support and delegation. We discourage the disruptive surprises that sometimes crop up at just the wrong times. For example, the president almost casually mentions three weeks prior to launch that a new item should be priced at a 15 percent discount from the leading firm.

Some new product professionals insist that it is not natural for CEOs (who average five years in office) to support projects that run longer than that—not if such support reduces short-term sales and profits. One has proposed a split of top executive power—a CEO and an LEO (Long-Term Executive Officer). They would report, in tandem, to the board of directors.[10]

Leadership

Using today's methods of managing the technical development process, the most important decision top management makes on a new product is the selection of the group leader. The second most important decision is to stay out of the way and let the leader lead.

But who is a leader? Or, better, who will develop into a leader? This person has a nonauthoritative position; that is, a leader has no line authority over such co-workers as *peers*, *peers' subordinates*, *temporary employees*, *vendors* (subcontractors, suppliers), *customers*, and *bosses*. The leader leads in a milieu that can change from supportive to hostile overnight, with parameters that are almost completely unknown (e.g., competitive reactions), and with a new and even more inexperienced team of people.

Yet that person can overcome virtually every obstacle. That person alone can enthuse and motivate a group of people to do what seems impossible. Fortunately there is lots of this leadership around, managers with successful track records in this work and many managers who are as yet undiscovered. Unfortunately, it is almost impossible to pick out the undiscovereds. Toyota and Honda prize their new car managers so highly that they have them stay as managers of their cars after launch, through three major upgradings, and then back onto the start of another new car project. They keep them on new product projects, and off of the general track to top executive positions (with their concurrence).[11]

Compounding all of this is the conviction of some firms that a new products project actually needs two leaders, a creative, inspiring type for early on, and a tough disciplinarian for the later stages. Very rarely do we find people who can do both.

---

[10]Thomas D. Kuczmarski, "Key Issues and Challenges for the Coming Decade," *Journal of Product Innovation Management*, January 1994, pp. 73–75.

[11]See Alex Taylor III, "Why Toyota Keeps Getting Better and Better and Better," *Fortune*, November 1990, pp. 66–79.

Culture

Few people disagree with the importance of culture in business. There is even the saying that "Every firm should have a culture, even a bad one." For product improvements and near line extensions, the new products people must take the culture of the ongoing organization. At Heinz, for example, the Big Red brand team (tomato catsup, etc.) will dominate its new products work. But as the task hits more cross-functional conflict, the culture must be more supportive.

Culture is a very soft term, but for new products a good culture brings us:

- *Freedom.* The freedom to roam around the firm, freedom to have extensive interaction across functional lines, freedom to differ with bosses, freedom from punishment for an honest mistake made in the quest for a new method, freedom to participate in a task assignment.
- *Egalitarianism.* As humans, people are essentially equal. Each deserves respect and courtesy.
- *A constructive environment.* A constructive environment in which people are happy, upbeat, positive, encouraged, challenged, rewarded, networked.
- *Absence of hidden agenda.* Open statement of goals and objectives, forthright appraisals.

It is said that styles of management create cultures. But cultures come slowly; management change can come suddenly. Culture may be overemphasized; it only permits action and accomplishment. It does not itself produce any output from the new products system. Still, it is a dedicated topic with managements today, and the team working with no clear culture in place is at risk. So, too, is a team operating with almost exactly the wrong culture, as happened at Lexmark in 1992. That operation, a leveraged buyout by IBM executives, had been steeped in IBM culture, yet when it went outside to get away from that culture, they brought it with them.[12]

Ownership

If a person takes whole (or part) **ownership** in a project, that person has "bought in." There is enthusiasm, commitment, energy, and pride. It is *not* entrepreneurship—white knights do not ride around a firm waving a sword and conjuring up new products. *Groups of skilled specialists* create new products, not individual leaders. Some firms use the term product *champion* to describe those who have taken ownership, but want all members of the team to join in the ownership.

What does it take to have ownership? Three things: Training, empowerment, and motivation. *Training* helps assure that no one will take ownership without

---

[12]Paul B. Carroll, "Culture Shock: Story of an IBM Unit That Split Off Shows Difficulties of Change," *The Wall Street Journal*, June 23, 1992, p. A1.

the skills and knowledge required by the task. *Empowerment* means that a person has been cut loose. It is far more than delegation (which usually has strings attached—budgets, policy, procedures, etc.). It could be stated this way: "You know the nature of this project, you have a statement of mission such as a PIC, you know the firm's general standards, you are smart and trained, and you know how to use corporate staff (legal, etc.). Given all those, we are ready to trust your judgment." *Motivated* means the person has been encouraged to want to succeed, and we will talk about that in a bit more detail later.

Functional people will sometimes not want to take ownership. Power yes, but not ownership. And they often can't, because the conditions above haven't been met. A Citicorp manager once said the bank had to move innovation of retail products to a corporate new products group because the line departments just weren't doing the job. They refused to take ownership (including the responsibility for failure).

A new car owner recently called his dealer about several minor items. The telephone service attendant gave one set of instructions, the check-in manager gave a different set, the body shop corrected them both, and finally the parts manager had yet a different view of what should be done. One customer, but four "dealers." None had taken ownership. They used to say that bad new products were developed by committees. They were right.

The Set of Organizational Structure Options

The five basic options for the structural side of new products organization are shown in Figure 13–1. These options are five segments of a continuum, and although quite different, they do have several things in common.[13]

The first, **functional**, means the work is done by the various departments, with very little project focus. There may be a new products committee or a product planning committee. The work is usually low risk and probably involves the present line of products—improvements, new sizes, and so on. The ongoing departmental people know the market and the business; they can get together and make the necessary decisions easily and effectively. Literally, the functional people working on a project are a group, but they are not a team.

Of course, not much innovation occurs that way. So, we have the other four options—all teams. Three of them (in the middle of Figure 13–1) are matrix variations. If the people on the Optical Scanner project in Figure 13–2 get together to make some decisions, they may be 50/50, or the power may lean toward the head of the functional department, or it may lean toward the project manager. Leaning toward the project is called **projectization**, as defined in Figure 13–1.

---

[13]The five-option set was created by Erik W. Larson and David H. Gobeli. They reported the results of empirical testing in their "Organizing for New Product Projects," *Journal of Product Innovation Management*, September 1988, pp. 180–90. The only change made here is that what the authors called project team is here called venture, to reflect recent preferences.

The **functional matrix** option has a specific team, with people from the various departments (such as manufacturing, R&D, marketing, and finance), but the project is still close to the current business. It requires more focus than routine product improvements, but the departments call the shots. Team members think like functional specialists, and their bosses back in the departments win most of the face-offs.

FIGURE 13–1   Options in New Products Organization

	Options			
Functional With or without committee	Functional matrix	Balanced matrix	Project matrix	Venture Inside Outside

0%_____20%_____40%_____60%_____80%_____100%
Degree of projectization*

*Defined as the extent to which participants in the process see themselves as independent from the project or committed to it. Thus, members of a new product committee are almost totally oriented (loyal) to their functions or departments; spinout (outside) venture members are almost totally committed to the project.

FIGURE 13–2   The Matrix Concept of Business Organization

Program/Project Leader	*Marketing*	*R&D*	*Manufacturing*	*Finance*	*Others*
Boltron project Gary Shilling	Ron Thomas	Fred Mansfield	Jim Swaston	Christi Statler	—
Gates project Beth Politi	Ron Thomas	Dennis Hilger	Mary Morrison	Hartmut Richert	—
Optics program Barb Mertz	Kirk Weirich	Dennis Hilger	Ken Fedor	Heather Dumont	—
Tenson project Andy Anderson	Gideon Feldkamp	Lucy Mazrui	Jim Swaston	Heather Dumont	—
Bell-tron project K. C. Gupta	Loretta Berigan	Sabine Klein	Ken Fodor	Coyne Grady	—
Others					
—	—	—	—	—	—

Explanation: For the Boltron project, Gary Shilling is the leader, also called manager, coordinator, and so on. Ron Thomas is on the team representing marketing, Fred Mansfield for R&D, Jim Swanson for manufacturing, and Christi Statler for finance. Functional people often represent their departments on more than one team—see Dennis Hilger and Heather Dumont. If a project uses a functional format or a venture (see Figure 13–1), there really is no matrix. Otherwise, all people in the functional columns are like Loretta Berigan, who reports to K. C. Gupta for the Bell-tron project and to her department head for the function. When their wishes intersect, she must work her way through the differences to avoid a timely or costly conflict.

The **balanced matrix** option is for situations where both functional and project views are critical—neither ongoing business nor the new product should be the driver. This traditional matrix was for a long time held in disfavor for new products, because either the new product required push or it didn't. Using 50/50 thinking would just make for indecision and delay. Texas Instruments used balanced matrix for many years in its product innovation—and then discarded it for just this reason.[14] But, today's managers have apparently found ways to make it work. See Figure 13–3 for recent data.

The **project matrix** option recognizes the occasional need for stronger project push. Here projectization is high. Team people are project people first and functional people second. A packaging team member will be "carrying the message" to the packaging director. Department heads complain that their people have sold out to the project and are trying to drive the project even against the departments' best interests. And they are.[15] Example: When IBM was trying to relearn how to compete in the personal computer business, it set up a separate company called IBM PC Co. One of the early steps of that division's leadership was to take its executive group to Tokyo in September 1990; there would be no going home until they came up with a plan to break down functional boundaries. The plan was completed December 18![16]

The **venture** option extends projectization to its ultimate. Team members are pulled out of their departments and put to work full-time on the project. The

FIGURE 13–3

Performance Success of the Five Basic New Product Organizational Options

Organizational Option	Percent of Projects		Percent Successful or Marginally So
Functional	13%		63%
Functional matrix	26%		79%
Balanced matrix	16%		88%
Project matrix	29%		92%
Venture	16%		94%
Total	100%		
Total projects: 540			

Source: Erik W. Larson and David H. Gobeli, "Organizing for Product Development Projects," *Journal of Product Innovation Management,* September 1988, pp. 180–90.

[14]Bro Uttal, "Texas Instruments Regroups," *Fortune,* August 9, 1982, pp. 40–45.

[15]Steven C. Wheelwright and Kim B. Clark, "Organizing and Leading 'Heavyweight' Development Teams," *California Management Review,* Spring 1992, pp. 9–28.

[16]Catherine Arnst, "A Freewheeling Youngster Named IBM," *Information Processing,* May 3, 1993, pp. 134–38.

venture may be kept in the regular organization, or it may be spun outside the current division or company—a **spin-out venture**. How far out it goes depends on how critical it is that there be no influence on the team from current departments, policies, and so on. The original IBM PC venture team manufacturing member argued for having outside manufacturers make most of the key pieces in the system. The new product had to be made fast, and the team didn't think IBM's manufacturing department could do it fast enough. They won. Ford sent its "new" Mustang team to a converted furniture warehouse in Allen Park, Michigan, a few miles south of Dearborn.[17] Other firms have sent venture teams to another part of the city or to another part of the firm's building complex.

The venture form also merges into the joint venture (where another *firm* cooperates in the activity). Allied Chemical began using spinouts to develop what it called orphan technologies—R&D developments that didn't fit the business when they appeared and sat around on shelves, sometimes for years. Another spinout was Metaglas Products' work to develop lightweight alloys used in cores for electrical transformers.

Ford used a venture team for its classic Taurus/Sable project, a venture format previously rare in the auto industry.[18] Reports overflowed with such phrases as "stealing a page from the Japanese," "the first step was to throw out Ford's traditional organizational structure," "normally the five-year process is sequential," "Team Taurus took a program management approach," "worked together as a group," and "took final responsibility for the vehicle."

Ventures are not for everyone, partly because the firm may not be able to do what ventures require. For example, one study of ventures found that all but 1 of the 11 successes in the sample sold to established customers, used experienced market research personnel from the parent organization, obtained market-experienced personnel from outside, and based the new product on market need, not technological capability. The 17 losers in the study almost uniformly did not.[19]

Exxon created a series of ventures in the office products area, and they all failed to achieve their objectives. A study of them showed they lacked congruencies between each new venture and its market.[20]

New products organization may involve many other terms and approaches. A few of them are common enough that we should show their relationships to the above classification:

Product Manager.   This common term is applied to people who manage ongoing products.

---

[17]Joseph B. White and Oscar Suris, "How a Skunk Works Kept Mustang Alive—on a Tight Budget," *The Wall Street Journal*, September 21, 1993, p. A1.

[18]For example, see "How Ford Hit the Bull's Eye with Taurus," *Business Week*, June 30, 1986, pp. 69–70.

[19]Eric von Hippel, "Successful and Failing Internal Corporate Ventures: An Empirical Analysis," *Industrial Marketing Management*, 1977, pp. 163–74.

[20]Hollister B. Sykes, "The Anatomy of Corporate Venturing Program: Factors Influencing Success," *Journal of Business Venturing*, Fall 1986, pp. 275–93.

A *new* products manager handles new products and may or may not also be handling ongoing ones.

Task Force and Project Team.   These terms apply to new product teams, and their use is so varied that they are virtually useless. The five terms used for the options (above) are much more descriptive and should replace these older terms.

Another Look at Projectization

Any time two or more people from different departments (functions) of an organization gather to work on a project, issues of priorities are raised. Should they put first priority on the project or on the function they represent? Legislators face this problem daily (well-being of the total society versus well-being of the voters back home). So do student homecoming committees, civic development groups, and many others.

When a sales manager, for example, goes to a new products *committee* meeting, there is little doubt about priorities because committee members are engineers or marketers first and committee members second. The sales manager is "functionalized," not projectized. Committee members want the company to make profit; they are not disloyal. But, they have independent opinions about how any particular new product may contribute to profit. The sales manager may see a new package size as meeting customer demands and adding sales; the engineer may believe production costs will go up more than the sales volume; accounting objects to another line item that may just split customers' current purchases and add to cost; R&D says work on the new package size will pull a key person off a far more important project needed next year.

These are not idle concerns. They are the reality of new product life, and they are legitimate (ignoring the political problems that also arise). Projectization is the way we handle them. If a project is important and faces lots of opposition of the types just mentioned, then we increase the projectization. We go to functional matrix, balanced matrix, or project matrix. If the opposition is very high (e.g., imagine the problems when steel firms first started making plastics products), then we move to the venture.

Summary of Operating Characteristics and Making a Selection

Figure 13–4 summarizes how the five organizational options differ on various dimensions. We choose among them much the same way we buy a refrigerator. We begin with what we want the organization to do and then buy as much organizational power as needed to do the job. The more the power of the team, the more the cost to the firm in terms of personnel, disruption, and so on.

We determine how much team power is needed by study of the situation. The form in Figure 13–5 can be used, and the factors can even be weighted as is done on scoring models (Chapter 10). You can add special factors that fit the situation.

FIGURE 13–4   **Operating Characteristics of the Basic Options (see Figure 13–1)**

	Spectrum of Options				
Operating Characteristics	*Functional*	*Functional Matrix*	*Balanced Matrix*	*Project Matrix*	*Venture*
Decision power of leader	Very little _____ Almost total				
Independence of group from depts.	None _____ Total				
Percent of time spent on one project by member	Very low _____ Total				
Importance of project(s)	Low _____ Critical				
Degree of risk of project(s) to firm	Low _____ High				
Disruptiveness of project(s)	Low _____ High				
Degree of uncertainty in most decisions	Low _____ Very high				
Ability of team to violate company policies	None _____ Almost total				

Interpretation: This array shows how the various options of Figure 13–1 differ on each of several operating characteristics. The three matrix forms are at points between the extremes of functional and venture.

FIGURE 13–5   **Decision Rules for Choosing among the Five Basic Organizational Options**

To aid in the decision as to which of the five basic organizational options (Figure 13–1) to use on a particular project, score the situation on each of the following factors. The more the factor exists (e.g., the more difficult), the more points this project gets.

Score	*Factor*
_____	1. How critical is it, at this time, to have new product revenues?
_____	2. In general, how difficult is it to get to new products through this firm?
_____	3. How important is it that we beat competition to the market on this project?
_____	4. How much personal risk is there for persons working on projects like this?
_____	5. Will the products require new procedures (e.g., methods, or materials) in their manufacture?
_____	6. Will the products require new procedures (e.g., stakeholder sales calls) in their marketing?
_____	7. How high is the dollar contribution expected from products that come from this project?
_____	8. Are there unusual politics surrounding this project?
_____	9. How difficult will it be to acquire needed skills from elsewhere in the firm?
_____	10. Will the products from this project be free of connections with other products in your line?
_____	11. Are you, as a firm, experienced in using the more highly projectized forms of organization?
_____	12. How difficult will technical accomplishment be on this project?

Interpretation: If the total score given to the proposed project is below 30, the functional or functional matrix modes would probably work. From 30 to 40 the project probably requires a balanced matrix. Beyond that the situation probably calls for project matrix or even a venture.

Summary

This chapter has dealt with two powerful background issues that we use to design an organizational arrangement for the technical development phase of product innovation. The first was a set of characteristics that seem to be the outside drivers—the need for a PIC, leadership, culture, empowerment, and so on. Then we looked at the specific structural options an organization designer has to work with. They can meet pretty much all situations given creative and careful implementation. We can now move to the matter of peopling those forms—the team, its leader, its members, and how it functions, in Chapter 14.

Applications

More questions from that interview with the company president:

1. "I'll tell you one thing, we have learned that focus is critical in almost everything we do. Of course, getting people to focus is tough—they continually resist losing options. For example, our purchasing people have made great strides in narrowing down the list of suppliers in each area. But the engineers don't like it. They keep pushing to open up supplier lists, so such-and-such a firm, which they think has some technology they need, can be contacted. What do you think?"

2. "Now, when it comes to customer satisfaction and customer integration, I am a fanatic. You wouldn't believe how much we have learned about our customers' needs from discussion sessions we have with them. But, hold on. To integrate customers into the technical development parts of our new products operation would be very dangerous. A lot of what we do must be secret—we can't patent most of our ideas, and timing is everything. That's why we put so much emphasis on speed of development. But I still get pushed to do more. Help me. Tell me all the things we might do to get integrated customers but at the same time minimize our risks of losing our secrets."

3. "You mentioned culture! Now there's a human relations cult if I ever heard one. Human resource and organization design people are great, and out of their work has come some of the most valuable new business methods of the past 15 years. But, culture isn't one of them. It's vague, never defined, full of soft terms like *happy*, *egalitarian*, and *forthright*. Life just doesn't work this way. Don't misunderstand me, managers must respect their people, and we can't let strong opinions get in the way of our increasing productivity. But good people want honest motivations, not games or manipulations. Yeah, I said manipulation, because that's what the culture thing is. Tell me, what kind of a culture do you like best in the classroom where you are using this book? Is that culture inconsistent with the general ideas of management we have had for years?"

4. "Another term you mentioned was *empowerment*, and I noticed you let out a soft chuckle on that one. I imagine that's because you expect me to be against it. But you're wrong. Humans work best when they feel empowered, given a charge to do something and the power to do it 'their way.' My concern here is that I don't see why this is new. Good managers have always delegated when given people they knew could be depended on to get the job done. What does empowerment give us that delegation doesn't?"

CASE: MARKO PRODUCTS

As a major and profitable division of a large conglomerate for the past seven years, Marko Products was one of those acquisitions that worked out well. It specialized in medical supply products (items bought by physicians for use in their offices, not medical products for the patient).

Marko's president, Bill Wong, was an aggressive executive who tried to keep his firm poised for maximum market impact. He had installed the product manager system three years ago and was pleased that it seemed to be working well. The product managers were in the marketing department, and although they did not have the almost unlimited informal authority of their packaged goods counterparts, they were respected around the firm.

Marko had two manufacturing divisions: one for consumable supplies (such as bandages and rubber gloves) located in a different state, and another for equipment (examining tables, cabinets, ophthalmoscopes, etc.) located at headquarters. All R&D was physically centralized, but the VP for that function had divided her staff into six parts, each dedicated to a particular technology, such as rubber, laminated materials, or electronics.

One sales force sold the entire line, but in the more populated regions, the firm used separate salespeople for supplies and for equipment.

Top-management staff included a long-range planning group, an international marketing division organized by areas of the world, a governmental/public relations department, finance, human resources, and legal. Packaging and quality control were part of the manufacturing staff.

Marko Products' management chased tough goals in profit and market dominance. They planned to hold the Number 1 or 2 spots in each major market or else would pull back promotional and R&D support.

Wong recently held a two-day planning retreat for his management committee (VPs of the major functions), which produced new product innovation charters for each of its businesses. It had been a productive session but not without controversy because most of the managers thought Marko should concentrate on what it did best: manufacture top-quality examining room furniture. They argued that furniture earned most of the profits and that supply was a commodity business that Marko had entered only because it came with the cabinetry business of Mainline Medical (a firm Marko acquired six years ago). Bill Wong was pleased that he had persuaded them to become more aggressive and to set their sights on bigger and better things.

Source: This is a real case slightly camouflaged.

Following are two of the charters:

Medical office equipment, nonscientific: Marko will actively develop any and all new products in what might be called the "furniture" category, for use in doctors' and hospitals' examining and consultation rooms. The items will typically (and desirably) utilize our skills in "metal bending" and our knowledge of examining room procedures. The goals of this activity are (1) to add $70 million profit contribution over the next four years and (2) to ensure that we dominate (actual or close) in each major market we enter.

To do all this, we will rely primarily on our marketing department for input on market needs, supported by input from knowledgeable technical staff who maintain market contacts. Each new product will be unique in at least one critical dimension, and we hope it will make a contribution to examining room procedure. We intend to continue our reputation as the leading light in this industry, and all new items will be of the highest quality ["absolutely no schlock," as Wong put it]. Our major contribution will be in designing products that can be manufactured to the traditionally high standards of our operations group.

Disposables: In recent years, the medical community has turned to disposables to solve many of their operating problems, and Marko wants to take advantage of this trend. Our two small lines of disposable gloves and disposable aprons will be the springboard for this activity. The key to dominance here is predicting what new methodologies the medical personnel will agree to convert to disposability next. We want to develop products that extend disposability and are thus unique. Finding these product concepts will be difficult and will require a combination of office procedure knowledge, attitude study, and technical capability.

Profit goals are unclear for this operation, but we do want the program to get us into at least 10 new lines over the next five years, to dominate at least 8 of those lines (plus gloves and aprons), and to be the firm contacted by persons in medicine who see an opportunity for disposability. Minimum ROAs will be developed as the projects come along.

Some new disposable products will be reasonably nondifferentiated add-ons to capitalize on our position in a given market.

Wong now wondered what organizational structures would be appropriate for each of the PICs. If not possible now, toward which ideal could he work? In addition, he wondered how several terms he had recently heard used on new products would relate to these two areas, whether they would apply to both, etc. The terms were empowerment, culture, and projectization.

14 DEVELOPMENT TEAM MANAGEMENT

Setting

Chapter 14 is the second of a three-chapter set on how the internal technical development process is managed. First, we deal with the team, a form of management now a given in less-routine new product processes. Second, we face probably the most talked-about issue in project management today—speed, or cycle time.

The subject of team management is a difficult one. Team structure and management fills the business literature.[1] We know so much, yet we seem to know so little. There is a growing conviction that most team management is the same as individual management; good business common sense seems to prevent most big problems.

What Is a Team?

It is treacherous to describe, build, and manage teams—because there are teams, and teams, and teams. Drucker focused on the dilemma when he talked about sports teams:[2]

- *Baseball teams:* They are like assembly line "teams." Their work fits together, and all the players are needed, but they generally work as individuals, in their own ways. The double-play combo is a clear exception. Work is generally in a series.
- *Football teams:* These have fixed positions, but they play as a team. Japanese car teams are of this type. Work is parallel, not in series. But one player does not come to the aid of another.

---

[1] See Shona L. Brown and Kathleen M. Eisenhardt, "Product Development: Past Research, Present Findings, and Future Directions," *Academy of Management Review*, no. 2, 1995, pp. 343–78.

[2] Peter F. Drucker, "There's More Than One Kind of Team," *The Wall Street Journal*, February 11, 1992, p. A16.

- *Tennis doubles teams:* The players work with and support each other. The result is important only as the team scores a point or wins a match. Partners are dedicated. Volleyball teams are another example, as is the jazz combo.

Baseball and football managers are quite strong, but there are no tennis doubles managers. Some training people feel that volleyball is the best analogy for today's teams: there are more players, they develop skills at all positions, and the very unique role for the manager is comparable to that of the new product team manager.

The new products team is so far from the traditional and comfortable hierarchical world that there is great learning required, there is a shortage of people who currently know how to play the game, and performance appraisal is tough because only the team's overall performance matters. It offers the greatest risk to upper level managements. Since the team members all have different backgrounds, and play different roles, there is no one to "score" them against.

Building a Team

Most managers and almost all researchers have concluded that new product teams must be created to fit their situations. There is no right method, or correct paradigm, just as there is no right method of concept testing, or spelling out a product innovation charter. Nor are there right people; most team members and team leaders tell of their own personal growth during such assignments. Sales managers and scientists, alike, must become something else, something appropriate to a group task.

The Team Assignment, Mission, and Charter

A clear understanding by everyone involved as to what the team is for, its **mission**, and its **strategy**, is critical. One manufacturer of reasonably technical medical care products wanted only the moderate risks of **innovative imitation**, so R&D was made responsive to the directions of marketing. New projects originated only in marketing, key product attributes were determined before R&D began, and a marketing manager ran each project. Another firm in an allied industry wanted to implement an **aggressive technical innovation** strategy, but two qualified R&D directors came and went before management realized the short-term focus of a dominant marketing department was totally misleading the teams.

Funny things happen when new product teams lack strategy, because they pick up whatever strategy they think is correct, and technical people may feel that team success is measured by technical performance. The customer has a different opinion.

In Chapter 13 we talked about empowerment, but it can become abdication. Managers prefer to talk about **self-directed teams**, meaning that their internal methods of operation are theirs to choose, but within standard over-all restraints of company policy.

Selecting the Leader

Given the overall strategy and the decision on just how much team the firm needs for the job at hand, it is time to select a **leader**. Sometimes, this is auto-matic—for example, when the firm uses a product manager system and the new product concerns an addition to a particular person's product line. Or when, as in the case of 3M, the project originates from a particular person's technology.

Leaders must be *general managers*. They lead without direct authority, and so must win personal support. Various studies show that team leaders must have strong self-confidence (based on knowledge and experience, not just ego), have empathy (be able to look at things from another person's point of view), have a good self-awareness of how others see them, and be expert in personal com-munication. An even more interesting list of factors is shown in Figure 14–1.

But the irony is that they probably have to be strong in one set of direc-tions and strong in opposites too. Tom Peters said a team leader must have a total ego *yet* no ego, be an autocrat *and* a delegator, be a leader *and* a man-ager, tolerate ambiguity *yet* pursue perfection, be good at oral communication *and* at the written form as well, acknowledge complexity *yet* be a KISS (keep it short and simple) fanatic, think big *and* small, and be an action-fanatic *while* building for the future.

FIGURE 14–1   Factors Associated with Project Leadership

1. General management skills.
2. Green thumbs: make little seeds grow into big things.
3. Blank-page vision: lead without a map.
4. One-man band: play all the instruments (at least to some extent).
5. "Miss-a-meal" pains: be hungry, impatient.
6. Christopher Columbus syndrome: explorers who can't sit in port.
7. Night sight: vision improves while others grope in the dark.
8. Lead from the middle: able to work in the trenches and cause change in the whole organization.
9. Velvet hammer: hit without inflicting lasting damage.
10. Stamina: physical and mental.
11. White liar: trick people into doing what they later will be proud they did.
12. Veterinarian: hear the clues, even when the situation is not speaking.
13. Ideaphile: love ideas—anybody's, anytime—store them, talk about them.
14. Biblical: "Let my people go," leave them alone, encourage them, praise little victories.
15. Audacious: think big and bold.
16. Tinker, tailor, try: be able to try, try again.
17. Execution overkill: relentless, meticulous execution, with the job done right.
18. Manners matter: "thank you" and "please," 50 times a day.

Source: Larry Wizenberg, *The New Products Handbook* (Homewood, IL: Irwin Professional Publishing, 1986), pp. 212–15.

Sometimes people wonder about whether the leader should be chosen first, or selected by the team members themselves. The latter is an attractive idea, and is used occasionally, including once in a well-publicized program at Signode Corporation. But, most managements prefer to pick the leader, and then let that leader identify the team players. This increases the likelihood of good team chemistry and commitment, but also assures that a capable leader is leading.

Selecting the Team Members

When selecting the members of a new product team, it is important to remember that each one of them is on the team as the representative of a group of others "back home" in their department. The R&D team member can't do all the technical work and may do none, but does stimulate, direct, and encourage others in R&D to do it. This is usually in the face of competition from other R&D representatives on other teams, who are also trying to win time for *their* projects. The same goes for team members from the other functions. Chrysler wants team members to be change agents. Bausch and Lomb (B&L) wants members to have real functional influence and a broad-business view. B&L believes so strongly in teams that a conference speaker from the firm brought along (and introduced) five core members of his team.

So, we seek people who are knowledgeable in their respective areas, have the respect of their departments, and want to be on the team. If they have to be talked into the job, they will probably not do it well.

Most people in a business are of three types regarding their interrelationships outside their departments. Teams need the **integrators**, who love to relate to people from other departments or other firms. They naturally give, and get, respect. **Receptors** respect others and welcome information from them but do not desire personal relationships. They are good contacts but not particularly good team members. **Isolates** prefer to be left alone. They are deep specialists in their field and really want nothing to do with people from other functions. They are rarely able to play a role in new product team operations.[3]

A good way to think about this is that team members should naturally be **collaborative**, not just **cooperative**. The difference is vital.

How many members should a team have? First, let's distinguish between core team, ad hoc team, and extended team. (See Figure 14–2.) The **core team** is those people who are involved in *managing* functional clusters. Thus, one marketing person may represent, speak for, or help guide 10–12 others in the sales and marketing areas. The core team members are active throughout, and are supported by an **ad hoc group**. Ad hoc members are those from important

---

[3]Another listing focuses on personal skills of people (problem finders versus problem solvers): Mosongo Moukwa, "A Structure to Foster Creativity: An Industrial Experience," *Journal of Creative Behavior*, First Quarter 1995, pp. 54–63.

FIGURE 14–2

*The Team: Core,
Ad Hoc, Extended*

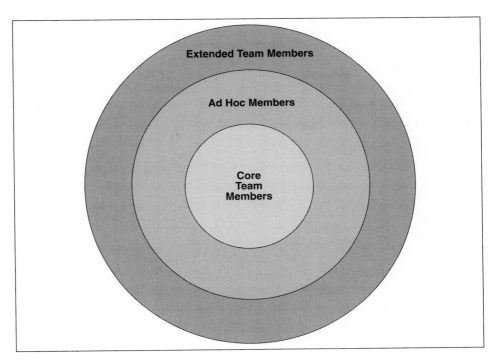

departments (e.g., packaging, legal, logistics) whose importance is brief in time and thus not needed on the core team. **Extended** team members are less critical, may almost seem incidental. They may well be in some other division of the firm, work at corporate staff, or with another firm.

Roles/Participants

People working on new products are sometimes not just functional representatives; they may assume other roles, some well-known and necessary. Figure 14–3 shows the full set and what they do. Although these roles are not always present (e.g., an **inventor** may not be needed), they usually are. Sometimes, who is playing which role isn't clear, and people may actually compete for the role they want.

The most well-known role is that of **product champion** (also called **process champion** or just champion). Projects get hung up at times by movements outside the team, in the supporting infrastructure. People lose interest; political conflicts arise; volume and cost projections turn sour; technical breakthroughs aren't achieved. The product champion's role is to push past these roadblocks, or at least try to. Champions can't win every time, but their task is to see that no project dies without a fight.

FIGURE 14–3   **Roles/Participants in the New Products Management Process**

Participant*	Activity	Participant*	Activity
1. Project manager	Leader Integrator Translator Mediator Judge Arbitrator Coordinator	4. Strategist	Longer range Managerial Entire program
2. Product champion	Supporter Spokesperson Pusher Won't concede	5. Inventor	Creative scientist Basement inventor Idea source
3. Sponsor	Senior manager Supporter Endorses Assuring hearing Mentor	6. Rationalist	Objectivity Reality Reason Financial

*The participant's role may be either formal or informal.

In most cases, the **project manager** plays the champion role. At other times the champion is self-appointed, often a technical person associated with the discovery that started the project. Today, many firms see the *core team* as the champion, since all should have strong concept commitment. Other firms are beginning to think that the champion idea has outlived its usefulness, since political obstacles should be addressed by the firm, not by an individual fighting what in many cases takes on a David/Goliath character.[4]

Generally (and ideally), the champion is expected to be vigorous and enthusiastic but to play within the rules. Champions rarely run roughshod over the rules. For example, a champion in a firm that made infant vitamin products surreptitiously charged a market research survey against the budget of a marketing research director who opposed a project the champion wanted. The survey proved the champion correct, and the product was successful!

The second most important role in Figure 14–3 is that of **sponsor**. This person does not drive anything but is higher up in the firm, is supportive, and lends encouragement and endorsement to the champion. Teams are wise to develop sponsors, whom some call godfathers or mentors. Figure 14–4 tells the story of a product champion, but note that the story was told by a sponsor.

The other roles in Figure 14–3 are indicated by the activities listed for them.

---

[4] Albert L. Page, "Assessing New Product Development Practices and Performance: Establishing Crucial Norms," *Journal of Product Innovation Management*, September 1993, pp. 273–90.

FIGURE 14–4   The Saga of Donald Gorman: Champion

An abbreviated version of a story told by L. J. Thomas, senior vice president, Eastman Kodak Company, in May 1980.

"I will focus attention on a particular Kodak inventor, now retired, who was responsible for available light movies, Donald Gorman—an inventor and researcher of the first order.... He was uncompromising. He had absolutely no regard for anything short of total victory.... He is always looking for a better way.... It was in Gorman's allegiance to the customer, in his quest for picture quality, that the available light movie program began.

"He needed a camera with a rapid pulldown [after the program was well underway]. There was such a camera—the Wittnauer Cine-Twin. Gorman learned that the Kodak patent museum had a Wittnauer in its collection, and he asked that it be sent to the Research Labs. It was sent to him and without the museum's knowledge Gorman dismantled it to look at the shutter. He quickly saw that the mechanism was ideal for his experiments.

"Gorman had really begun to interact with other members of the organization, many of whom were trying to discourage him because he had what they thought was a crazy idea.... At this point in his work, Gorman was badly in need of support from the top. Enter Dr. Chapman, Kodak's chairman of the board and chief executive officer at that time.... On one particular Tuesday morning, Gorman was projecting something from another projector for him on the screen. After that demonstration Chapman said, 'Mr. Gorman, come out from behind that projector and tell me what you are up to these days.' Gorman said, 'Dr. Chapman, I am glad you asked.'

"Of course Gorman hadn't gone through the proper channels because he had gone right to the top. All of us know that this is not always the best way to proceed. One moral here, never underestimate the power of a quiet lunch with the right people.

"Good decisions were Dr. Chapman's great contribution, just as innovation and invention in research were Don Gorman's. The two work together—and both are essential."

P.S. This story also highlights the role of the sponsor.

Source: L. J. Thomas, "Available Light Movies—An Inventor Made It Happen," in *Living Case Histories of Industrial Innovation* (New York: Industrial Research Institute, 1981), pp. 5–9.

Network Building

So far our people focus has been on the team leader and the team members, but sometimes there is no team. In fact, since most new products are improvements or close line extensions, most new products are developed in the functional mode, within the ongoing organization, entirely without a special team. Then, too, the extended team includes people well outside the core and ad hoc team. In all of these cases, the participants who actually do the new product work constitute a network, and a simplified version of one is shown in Figure 14–5.

A **network** consists of nodes, links, and operating relationships. **Nodes** are people important to the project in some way. **Links** are how they are reached and what important ties they have to others in the network. **Operating relationships** are how these people are contacted and motivated to cooperate in the project.

Who are the nodes? This is the toughest part. Any given project may enlist the support of hundreds (or even thousands) of people. Only judgment can decide how many of them should be put into a formal network and managed. One of the problems is that each node is itself usually a center of a satellite network, so that a network is actually a network of networks! Gets complicated fast.

Networks drawn up on paper or computer are not meant to substitute for intensive, walkaround management styles. And they are fluid—changing from time

FIGURE 14–5

Product Innovation Network, Abbreviated Version

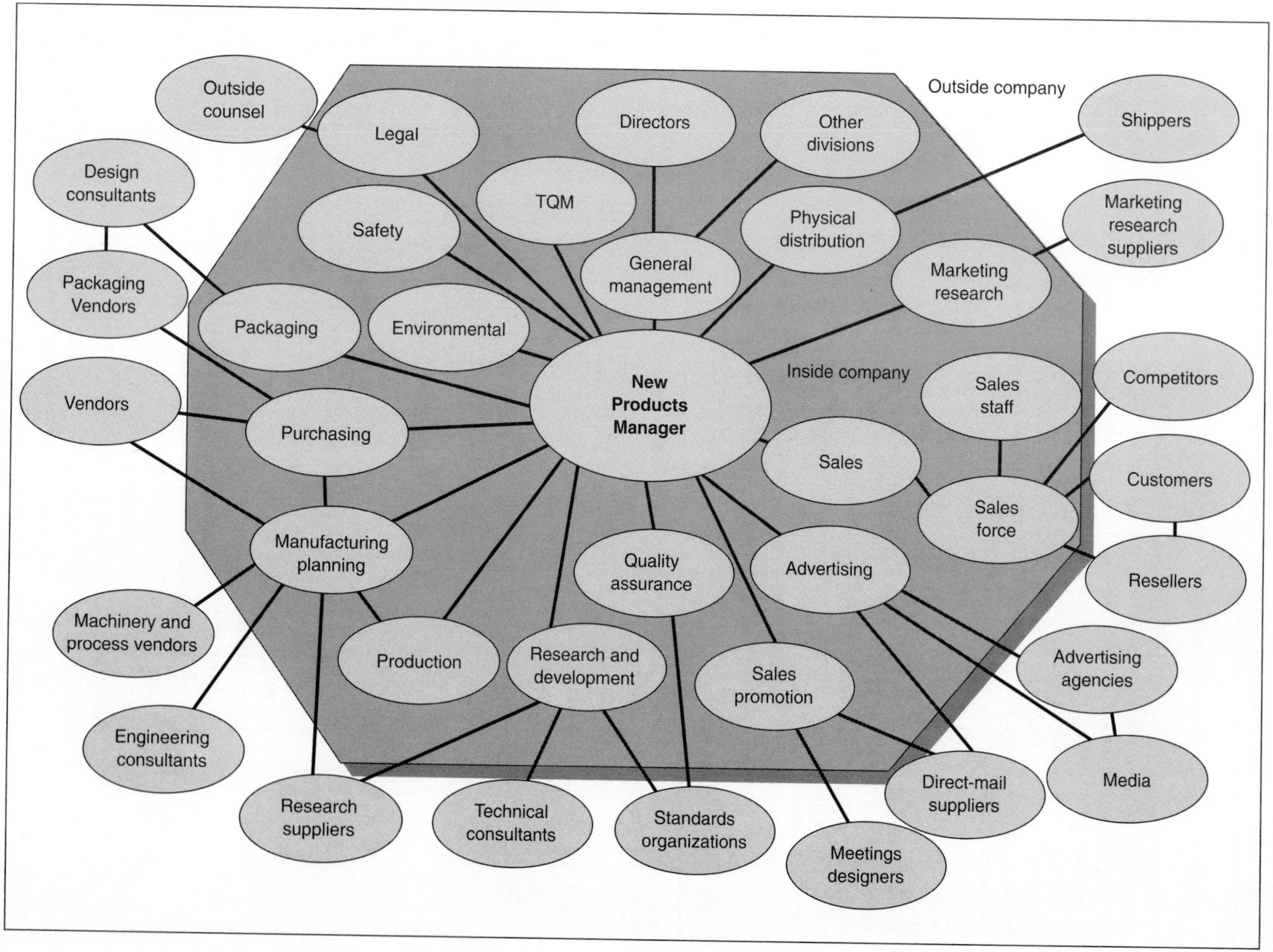

to time in the life of the project, and from project to project as the importance of various functions ebb and flow. For example, the purchasing department was for a long time omitted from networks, or placed way out on the edge. But today's focus on speed, quality, cost, and value has moved purchasing to a front row seat.

Network makers admit it's a lot easier to draw nodes and linkage lines than it is to work them.[5] But there is no choice, and networks are an aid, even if quite informal or even just mental pictures. Perhaps their greatest danger is that they can easily become bureaucracies. One manager, when asked during a training program, refused to draw up the network for a project he was then managing. He said he didn't want to see it all on one sheet and risk being overpowered by its complexity. Also, he didn't want his boss to see the massive indirect costs involved in the activity.

Network people remind us that good project leaders are what network professionals call **fly-eyed**, because fly eyes are actually thousands of eyes able to see many things at once. Leadership is also said to be **polycephalous** (many-headed), because it takes many people to manage a network properly. One head simply cannot do it, with or without fly eyes.

Training the Teams

An appointed team is not yet ready to operate. There must be top management support (discussed later) and, hopefully, a good image around the firm. Other managers sometimes come to doubt or fear a team, and they can isolate or ostracize it.

But the real need at this time is training. It would be nice to say we have a large cadre of experienced new product team members and leaders. We do not. Generally, firms start a team off with an intensive two- or three-day training session for the team members. At Digital Equipment, this pretraining is so critical that teams spend up to a month on it. However, training sessions cannot bring team members up to the needed skill levels unless there is considerable skill to begin with.

An experienced team builder says he finds these mistakes commonly made:[6]

- *Confusing "getting to know one another" with skill building.* Barbecues are great, but they are no substitute for skill training.

- *Offering sensitivity training instead of behavioral skills training.* Focusing on interpersonal issues may cause stress, and loss of self-esteem. Talk about winning the game, and what that takes.

- *Confusing the acquisition of knowledge with the acquisition of skills.* One doesn't learn how to bat a baseball by reading a book, and neither does one learn how to be a good team player that way.

---

[5]An excellent source for network training is Jessica Lipnack and Jeffery Stamps, *The Networking Book: People Connecting with People* (New York: Methuen, 1986).

[6]William C. Byham, "Lessons from the Little Leagues," *Across the Board*, March 1992, pp. 52–53. Byham is the author of a clever explanation of today's team and network management methods: *ZAPP! The Lightning of Empowerment* (Pittsburgh: Development Dimensions International Press, 1989).

- *Trying to get training done fast.* Squeezing the training schedule is penny-wise and pound-foolish.
- *Doing the wrong things at the wrong time.* The team will operate over many months, through various project phases; the team members don't need to be trained at the start in all the skills they will ultimately need.

Team members need to have the skills of interpersonal and interfunctional relationships (for the latter, see Chapter 15). They need to understand all of the players—customers, vendors, resellers, and more. Most people have served on committees, and thus have a warped view of what will be expected of them.

Managing the Team

Managing a team of the type being developed for more important projects in the new products field is extremely difficult. The task embodies all of the ideas from Part IV of the text. A few special thoughts follow.

Ongoing Management of the Team

The most pressing problem on new product teams probably involves giving pep talks. Burn-out is a genuine, and not uncommon, problem.

The innovation-derailing patterns of behavior that new products face are almost unbelievable. One veteran listed three: The "not-invented-here syndrome, the tendency to fight over turf, and the rush to gun down any wild geese who challenge the system."[7] Team and nonteam participants have an unending supply of new ways of resisting change. Here is just one:

> *The ambassador syndrome:* On coming to the conclusion that more entrepreneurship is needed, management creates a team that will force its way past department blockades. But, the departments all appoint ambassadors to the team, not individuals free to bypass department power.

Another aspect of the team management problem may appear trivial—the ability to run *effective meetings.* New product people seem to be in meetings continuously. Some product innovators have caught on to this need and are now studying their own team meetings for ways to speed them up and improve the decisions. (See the Europa International case at the end of Chapter 15 for another possible solution.)

At issue on many teams is the matter of *compensation.* Team leaders and team members are usually paid a straight salary or salary plus bonus. Bonuses are equally split between company performance, individual performance, and project accomplishment. It is rare to have compensation ride on the new product's performance. The reasons for this are strong: employees should be treated

---

[7]Walter Kiechel III, "The Politics of Innovations," *Fortune*, April 11, 1988, pp. 131–32.

equally (fairly), team members do not have the financial risks of an entrepreneur, and it is easier to transfer managers into and out of teams if compensation plans are equal. Still, all agree that finding good people willing to risk career bypass by serving on a new products team and motivating them to give the necessary high level of effort and stress is a legitimate problem.[8] Firms that use equity awards (e.g., stock) tend to be smaller ones in Silicon Valley.

Of course, there are team leaders who very much want the challenge and risks of entrepreneurship. Procter & Gamble, the company that created the brand management system so long ago, changed in 1987 from strong *brand* managers to strong *category* managers, with a true team structure. But they at least partially changed back in 1992, and a reason may have shown up when a former P&G brand manager complained that management could no longer see how good a person he really is. He wanted the opportunity to build his own pedestal.

A classic team in the annals of new products development was that on the Eagle, a new minicomputer at Data General. Its exploits were chronicled in the bestseller, *The Soul of a New Machine*, and followed up five later years later.[9] The team was so motivated in its entrepreneurial form that it decided to develop a *breakthrough* machine on a project that nonteam people had been led to believe was a *me-too* machine. But, loyalty to the *team* was so great that the players could not resume a strong loyalty to the *firm* when the project ended. Nine of the 14 engineers in the book left Data General. The team leader and the three managers who reported to him had also left. Teams, depending on their management, can be extremely powerful, but also extremely dangerous. Of course, they may have returned later, as John Sculley thinks occurred at Apple; though a third, typically, were burned out and left, most returned in a few months to begin work on another new project.

Closing the Team Down

Strong differences of opinion arise regarding when a new product team should be closed down and the product turned over to the regular organization. Some firms *close out early*, well before the item is marketed; they bring in operating people bit by bit. A second practice lets the team *prepare* for the marketing (e.g., write the plan or train the people), but at the last minute, the *regular people launch it*. When this is done, the key team people are usually kept close to the action to help solve problems. A third, and rarer, practice lets the team actually *market the item* and either become the nucleus of its standing management as a new division or turn it over to the regular organization after it has been successfully established.

No matter when the ongoing staff members are to take over, they should be brought into the action in a way that lets them link into the new product organization.

---

[8]Hollister B. Sykes, "The Anatomy of a Corporate Venturing Program: Factors Influencing Success," *Journal of Business Venturing*, 1992, pp. 253–65.

[9]Tracy Kidder, *The Soul of a New Machine* (New York: Avon, 1981). The follow-up analysis was done by William Bulkeley in "Computer Engineers Memorialized in Book Seek New Challenges," *The Wall Street Journal*, September 20, 1985, p. 1.

As one manager put it, "Treat this as a whirling gear being meshed with an idle gear; send a few people into the on-going organization early, to get the idle gear up to a speed where it can accept the rest of the new operation."

The Drive for Speed

Behind many of the things we have talked about so far in Chapters 13–14 is today's most discussed management goal—**speed**, or **accelerated product development** (APD).[10] The firm that gets to market first has a major short-term advantage, and may sustain that advantage for many years if its follow-up development practices are sharp.[11]

But accelerating development takes something from the process. It is poor management to slash time right and left, cut budgets across the board, and demand everyone double efforts and finish faster. Far better is to use such devices as **benchmarking**, where a firm studies other firms who have been successful in speeding up their operations. Kodak used the consulting firm of Arthur D. Little to lead them in just this type of study for speeding up their design, engineering, and product development work.

Key, though, is the fact that the **cycle time metric** commonly used to measure progress means *from idea to the shipping dock.* This assumes there has already been technical accomplishment—the R of R&D has been concluded successfully. Basic research does not respond well to the clock or the calendar. Too, ideation and pretechnical evaluation are concluded. Third, note that getting the item manufactured (on the shipping dock) is the end of the measurement; but *that is not the purpose of the project.* The PIC probably has something in terms of profit, sales, or market share. These are not achieved on the shipping dock, so a better metric would be *from idea to market success.*[12]

The emphasis on speed over the past 5–10 years has prepared us to know when we can safely cut, and when we had better not. Figure 14–6 summarizes the options.[13] Actually, many firms have found most of their speed from a direct attack on lackadaisical attitudes and practices. It is very possible that most actions are perfectly obvious to managers who become convinced their top bosses are serious about speed.[14]

---

[10]Newsworthy yes, but not without some warnings: William Bulkeley, "The Latest Thing at Many Companies Is Speed, Speed, Speed," *The Wall Street Journal*, December 23, 1994, p. A1.

[11]An interesting, but challenging, piece of evidence on this comes from the science of Darwinian evolution. Chris Farrell, "Survival of the Fittest Technologies," *New Scientist*, February 1993, pp. 35–39.

[12]See Bengt Barius, "Simultaneous Marketing: A Holistic Marketing Approach to Shorter Time to Market," *Industrial Marketing Management*, 1994, pp. 145–54.

[13]One of the best case histories of what speed can do are: N. R. Kleinfield, "How 'Strykeforce' Beat the Clock," *New York Times*, March 25, 1990, section 3, p. 1 (a story of a new grinder at Ingersoll-Rand).

[14]A handy metric is one that measures current cycle times. See Abbie Griffin, "Metrics for Measuring Product Development Cycle Time," *Journal of Product Innovation Management*, March 1993, pp. 112–25.

FIGURE 14–6   Set of Techniques for Attaining Speed in a New Product Project

Organization Phase
1. Use projectization—project matrix and venture teams.
2. Use small groups and other techniques to thwart bureaucracy.
3. Empower a team, motivate it (incentives and rewards), and protect it.
4. Destroy turf and territory.
5. Make sure the supporting departments are ready when called on.
6. Clear the tracks in shared departments.

Intensify Resource Commitments
1. Integrate vendors; reduce numbers as necessary.
2. Integrate other technology resources.
3. Integrate resellers; reduce numbers as necessary.
4. Integrate customers; reduce numbers, get them some product fast, even rough.
5. Use simultaneous/parallel/concurrent engineering.

Design for Speed
1. Computer-aided design and other forms of rapid prototyping.
2. Design-aided manufacturing: reduce number of parts, set tolerances with eye on the manufacturing
   process, design modules, one-way assembly.
3. Use common components across families.
4. Make the product easy to test.
5. Design-in the qualities that make for fast trial—relative advantage, etc.

Prepare for Rapid Manufacturing
1. Simplify documentation.
2. Use standardized process plans.
3. Use computer-aided manufacturing.
4. Go to just-in-time delivery of materials and components (flexible manufacturing).
5. Integrate product use testing, and start it early.

Prepare for Rapid Marketing
1. Use rollouts, not test markets.
2. Seed the firm's reputation ahead of marketing.
3. Spend what it takes to get immediate market awareness.
4. Make trial purchasing as easy as possible.
5. Get customer service capability in place ahead of need, and test it.

Source: The above is a composite of techniques from many sources, but particularly useful for further study of this subject were: Rene Cordero, "Managing for Speed to Avoid Product Obsolescence: A Survey of Techniques," *Journal of Product Innovation Management*, December 1991, pp. 283–94; Murray R. Millson, S. P. Ray, and David Wilemon, "A Survey of Major Approaches for Accelerating New Product Development," *Journal of Product Innovation Management*, March 1992, pp. 53–69; Edward F. McDonough III and Gloria Barczak, "Speeding Up New Product Development: The Effects of Leadership Style and Source of Technology," *Journal of Product Innovation Management*, September 1991, pp. 203–11.

Overall Principles and Guidelines

- **Do the job right the first time.** A small amount of time in the early phases can save many times that later, in rework alone. It makes little sense to speed up a poor process.
- **Seek lots of platinum BBs rather than one silver bullet.** Small savings add up.
- **Training of everyone involved.** People who don't know their jobs won't know how to speed things up.
- **Communication.** Huge amounts of delay can be traced to someone, somewhere, waiting for a piece of information. This means we have to set aside 1.5 weeks of production time for an electronic part that is actually produced in 19 minutes.
- **Flexibility.** Look for machines that can do many jobs, people who can switch from one job to another, stand-by vendors, and more. Attitudes too: Mattel's Top Speed toy cars depended on an open-minded designer, so they brought in a new person.
- **Fast decisions.** Managers know that people sometimes get blamed more for things they *do* than for things they *don't do*. Retraining them to make decisions as soon as they reasonably can *and* managing them in such a way that we don't destroy that willingness are musts, and tough.
- **Cutting things wisely.** There is a common bureaucratic practice of meeting a budget cut of 10 percent by cutting all of its components 10 percent. A better method is to take perhaps a 50 percent cut in non-critical steps, and 0 percent in the key ones. It's all risky, but why not take the risk on things that are more forgiving?

Specific Actions in the Various Parts of a Program

We cannot go through all of the actions in Figure 14–6. Many are obvious anyway. But there are a few that deserve comment.

Several of the actions embody resource readiness. A PIC helps assure it by directing us to skills and markets we are good at, and small groups do the same. Integrating our resources with those of others—for example, by strategic research alliances—is especially helpful. Alliances are growing—upstream to vendors, downstream to resellers and customers, and sideways to competitors and other sources of technical and marketing assistance.[15]

Another technique is to avoid "overengineering." A rough prototype may not make developers happy, but perhaps customers can examine and test it in their own minds and facilities. "Clean and neat" doesn't sell anymore; "clean enough for the task at hand" does.

---

[15]A good list of do's and don'ts (on alliances) can be found in Judith C. Giordan, "Forging Sound Strategic Alliances," *Research Technology Management*, March–April 1995, pp. 11–12.

Some people in design, engineering, and manufacturing are surprised to see *marketing people* interested in speed. Speed as a management strategy originated in the early technical phases. But a month saved on the way to a market share goal is a month saved, whether in a design coup or in quicker product trial. The tendency of potential customers to postpone trial is legendary; we all do it. Yet we now know a lot about how to speed up trial, and we will look at the methods in Chapter 18. Also, we are now working with resellers—distributors, retailers, and the like—to get their input and cooperation early, really teaming up with them to do a job we will both benefit from.

All members of the team should know that product adoption doesn't just happen—technologies don't diffuse without a fight. Even the popular xerographic process (and the famous 914 Xerox copier) was delayed by being "ahead of its time." The marketing technique of leasing helped stimulate diffusion, but the market's lack of understanding of the item's full usage potential and lack of digital technology for color copying added at least 10 years to the time-to-market success figure.

Lastly, note the role of the *computer*. . . for CAD and CAM, for design integrated manufacturing, for simulations of all types (including sales forecasting), for communication, for just-in-time systems, and more. Note, too, that JIT systems have to be watched because they tend to bring rigidity—fixed models, fixed recording systems, efficient manufacturing layouts, etc.[16]

Caution: Although there is no question that most firms will benefit as they speed up their development processes, there will also be problems. There are lots of costs involved in speed, costs that are not evident and which can sometimes be disastrous.[17] For example, flexibility today is king of concern in Japanese manufacturing—being able to make scores of new products, usually on the same line. Honda tells of marketing over a hundred new motorcycles in one year. In the meantime, Dell Computers used line simplification, adapting production lines to handle just a *few* configurations, improving product quality and delivery times, and achieving great sales and profit growth on superior customer satisfaction. Massive lines or simple lines? Both can succeed. Another caution is that speed systems operate best in firms that apply the ideas across the board. Trying to have speed on just an occasional project doesn't seem to work.

Finally, managers all hope they don't speed to the point where they have to solve problems like the Ford Mustang team did: a wiggle/shimmy in the new model's prototypes was temporarily solved by redesigning the rear view mirror so it wouldn't wiggle in response and thus tip off the driver to what was happening.

---

[16]Ulli Arnold and Kenneth N. Barnard, "Just-In-Time: Some Marketing Issues Raised by a Popular Concept in Production and Distribution," *Technovation*, August 1989, pp. 401–31.

[17]For the cautionary side, see C. Merle Crawford, "The Hidden Costs of Accelerated Product Development," *Journal of Product Innovation Management*, September 1992, pp. 188–99. Some of the concerns there, especially the incompatibility of technical accomplishment and speed to market, were confirmed in Abdul Ali, Robert Krapfel, Jr., and Douglas LaBahn, "Product Innovativeness and Entry Strategy: Impact on Cycle Time and Break-Even Time," *Journal of Product Innovation Management*, January 1995, pp. 54–69.

Summary

This was the second of a three-chapter set on managing during the technical development phase. It covered issues surrounding the subject of team, especially what a team is and how the various organization options of Chapter 13 yield different types of teams. Then we looked at what is involved in actually setting up a team and managing it through to completion—selecting the leader, selecting the team members, training them, and so forth. Lastly, the chapter dealt with an extremely important issue today—getting bureaucracy out of the new product process and speed into it. This is a complex issue, with many options and some dangers.

As a closing thought, there are two new types of new product teams emerging on the scene. One is a higher-level, multifunctional group (often heads of the key functions) whose task is to *manage the project teams*. As teams proliferate, they need a reporting home of some type. The other emerging team is a group of experienced new products people whose task is to *assist project teams in developing appropriate processes to follow*. The latter may just be a person with the title New Products *Process* Manager. Process is critical, and a firm needs some place to house the organization learning constantly taking place.

Chapter 15 concludes this set by addressing the matter of design, and then pointing out several problems that arise when managing in the way Chapters 13 and 14 have urged.

Applications

More questions from that interview with the company president.

1. "I understand the team leader's job is a lot like the job of a professional quarterback, or at least that's what the head of our sporting goods division recently said. What do you think he had in mind? Surely he didn't think the quarterback is a manager! He must not know those pro football coaches very well. Next thing you know, he'll be telling us college and high school quarterbacks have that type of job too!"

2. "Actually, I'm not convinced that any particular organization formats are better than others. I've run into too many exceptions. For example, that great portable tape player, Walkman by Sony, was conceived and pushed through by Akio Morita, Sony's chairman of the board. He got the idea from seeing a past chairman wearing a headset in the office, and he personally directed the project through its technical phases, even over the opposition of his people in manufacturing and sales. Even gave himself the title of project manager. I'll bet that approach doesn't fit any of your academic formats. And, I'll bet you wouldn't discourage it."

3. "Angela Lopez is head of our division that sells consulting service to smaller colleges of various types, not the big, state universities. You

probably don't even know such consulting exists, but it does, and it is very profitable for us. But, at lunch Tuesday, Angela hit me with two tough questions. Seems she has been reading about this emphasis on speed in developing new products and wondered if it was an opportunity for her training operation. They develop new consulting services regularly. One right now is designed to help smaller colleges train retired people living in the college's area in how they can earn money to supplement their pensions. She said: 'How do I decide whether speed is *desirable* as a new training program? Is speed *feasible* for services?' "

4. "Several of our divisions say they get tremendous help from their vendors when it comes to new product development. But, to tell you the truth, I think they're just lazy. They've got good talent in those divisions, or darn well should have, and all they're doing is letting vendors get a bigger piece of our innovation profits. Most vendors don't pull their share in these funny partnerships. Besides, the initiative should be theirs, not ours; they stand to gain more from so-called integrated operations and alliances than we do."

CASE: THE CYCLOTRON CORPORATION (REVISED)

Shortly after the microwave oven began to sell at levels indicating its successful move from beachhead to growth, the Electronic Kitchens Corporation (EKC) moved aggressively into the next phase of its planned new product work. It had not been first with the microwave, but it had the technology and had entered soon enough to get a respectable position in the new market.

EKC was a wholly owned subsidiary of a large conglomerate; therefore, it had access to large resources and had capitalized on this strength to build a strong capability in all phases of electronics applying to kitchens—residential, commercial, industrial, space, and so on. It had achieved sales of slightly over $700 million with various types of ovens, routine and special freezing appliances, timer-controlled appliances of all types, safety controls for use on its own and other appliances, and the like.

The R&D department was one of the best (if not the best) in the industry, and the new product strategy was to capitalize on that technical strength while staying in the general area of food preparation. The firm intended to be first in each market or a quick second based on technical adaptation. It accepted risks.

However, when a scientist invented what later came to be known around EKC as the black box, it decided to spin out a new organization to handle the product's further development and marketing. The new division was named Cyclotron Corp. and was staffed with about 40 people; much of the EKC corporate resource base (e.g., assembly line structure and worldwide sales force) would be available to Cyclotron until it proved successful.

The black box was an electronic device that apparently created a flow of heat (not microwaves); that is, it sent heat in a circular pattern around whatever happened to be on the shelf

Source: This is a realistic, though technically hypothetical, situation.

of the device. It went fast and, in effect, echoed the winding patterns around cores in golf balls and baseballs. This high-intensity heat cooked much faster (safely and controllably) than traditional gas and electric ranges; it had advantages over convection ovens as well.

Chet Vinton, the scientist in charge of the technical work while it was in R&D (actually some rather basic work, highly creative and innovative) said:

> People will be able to do all of their cooking in this new box, though they may still prefer the slightly better speed of the microwave in some cases. But our device will be better than anything else, plus it will give better browning and heat control and distribution than the microwaves do, and won't have the scare sometimes involved with the microwaves escaping from the cabinet.

He was very anxious to get the concept into development, since he had already given the item two years of time in research. Everyone agreed that this item was unique, and the management committee of the new Cyclotron division was excited. Fortunately, the physical layout of EK gathered resources into essentially contiguous buildings.

Uncertainty about a patent made the firm very secretive about the technical nature of what it planned to call the Cyclotron Kitchen. Chet himself was unhappy that he didn't get the assignment as technical head of the new division, and knew he would have to champion the product vigorously. He had since been given a new research assignment, and was very secretive about the black box technical process until a couple patents came through.

Assume you have just been named general manager of this new "firm." You and your staff will serve as the new product team. You were originally hired into the advertising department and then spent four years in field sales and two years as sales training director. Your direct reports are people who, like you, had been in several positions in their functional groups—R&D, manufacturing, and corporate planning staff (finance management and that of several other departments was to be performed by EKC people, until full-time assignment could be defended).

You naturally are concerned about getting this team under way, and about problems you may have with them. But, as you thought about your task, you wondered about just what personal characteristics helped you to get this job. Was it anything you could now capitalize on, and if so, think through just how you would go about it?

In addition, you remembered a slogan of the EKC chief executive officer: You are only as good as your uncorrected weaknesses let you be. He always stressed the unresolved. Do you have any personal characteristics that might stand in the way of your doing a good job here? What might you do to resolve them?

You also thought about several other items the CEO had mentioned from time to time. One was what he called *sink holes*—things that could go wrong. Not potholes—they are just annoying—sink holes can hold a house. Sink holes can kill a new operation. He had also bragged about how well EKC new products people had cut development and marketing times the past few years. He had joked about how you wouldn't have to worry about bureaucracy in this new assignment because the group was so small. He took pride in being a good leader (actually, you had to admit that marketing people did have good relationships with technical and manufacturing people). One thing he did *not* like, however was the idea of empowerment. Even as a separate division, he had made it clear you reported to him and used the resources he gave you; that conversation made you wonder whether Cyclotron was created to give the intense focus required for unique creation (as you were told) or to separate EKC from any legal problems that might come from the new technology!

15 DESIGN AND SPECIAL MANAGERIAL NEEDS

Setting

Chapter 13 talked about today's management of the technical development task, and offered a set of options for organizational structure. Since most of those options involve a team, Chapter 14 talked about teams, and how they are managed to achieve the speed of development that is essential in so many industries today. Chapter 15 looks at a string of goings-on in this phase from the new role played by the designers to global considerations.

Design

Design as a term has many uses. To the car companies it means the styling department. To a container company it means their customer's packaging people. To a manufacturing department it most likely means the engineers who set final product specifications.

Design can be the basis for a total company strategy, or an afterthought where industrial designers are asked to pretty up a product that is just about ready to be manufactured. Look at the long-term strategies of these two firms (in recent years they have begun to move toward each other):

Herman Miller. From its very beginning the strategy had been to invest in furniture designers who would, in their own ways, create new pieces of furniture to be used in offices. Their new products program was totally driven by this commitment; there was little in the way of effort to study a product on the market and improve it in some way. Their designers worked essentially in the proverbial closed room, where the door opened every few years so a designer could hand to production a new item that was ready for sale. Market research was publicly stated by top management as *not* the basis for new products.[1]

Steelcase.   A much older and larger office furniture manufacturer about 40 miles up the road from Herman Miller, Steelcase was quite different. They were "metal benders"; that is, their strategy was based on their ability to manufacture office furniture that worked, needed almost no repairs, and lasted forever. They followed creative inventions of others. When Herman Miller came out with the office panel system (the Open Office) in 1968, and jumped out to huge sales volumes, Steelcase watched and waited; eventually they entered the market with their high quality product and lower costs and better dealer organization, and captured first place in the market, outselling Herman Miller by almost 2 to 1.

At first glance one might say Herman Miller was design-driven, and Steelcase was manufacturing-driven. In today's language this would be wrong. Industrial designers do lead Herman Miller, but there are other designers—design engineers—who help make Steelcase successful. We'll see in a moment that the terminology situation is not very helpful to textbook writers and to students.[2]

The Impact of Design

In a trend that is growing dramatically, design has widespread impact. For example:

- *On manufacturing,* where it saves time and cost, and enhances quality. No amount of factory automation can make up for poor design. For several classes of goods, up to 80 percent of a product's cost is determined by the time it is designed.

- *On product use.* Well-designed products are easy to use, and easy to explain. No lengthy instruction books are necessary. No magnifying glass is needed to read labels on the product.

- *On service.* Properly designed, products are easy to install, and easy to maintain and repair. Modular construction is more common than people realize, and sure to grow more.

---

[1]Rejection of marketing research as a conduit for customer input to development still lingers today. For the argument that *design* people should provide the user focus, see Bill Stumpf, "Six Enemies of Empowering Design," *Innovation,* Spring 1992, pp. 29–31. Mr. Stumpf is a designer at Herman Miller.

[2]See Michael Evamy, "Call Yourself a Designer?" *Design,* March 1994, pp. 14–16. This article was part of a series on the matter of design definition in this publication. Useful also is Karl T. Ulrich and Steven D. Eppinger, *Product Design and Development* (New York: McGraw-Hill, 1995).

- *On product disposal.* Products are now being designed with disposal in mind, e.g., a technique called **design for disassembly** that permits products to be taken apart for separate recycling of metal, glass, and plastic parts.
- *On living,* well beyond what we think of as designed products—scenes, roads, parks. Most of our surroundings today are simply much more attractive than they used to be, and functional too.

In fact, Figure 15–1 shows the variety of design dimensions, using only the two criteria of "purpose of design" and "item being designed." Design is not just a field in which artists draw pictures of new microwaves. It blends form and function, quality and style, art and engineering. In short, a good design is aesthetically pleasing, easy to make correctly, reliable, easy to use, economical to operate and service, and fits recycling standards. Look at what Black & Decker did with the SnakeLight.

The problem for new product managers is simply that design is too important to be left to designers. Historically, in the era of powerful functional chimneys and slow, linear, stage-based development, industrial designers dominated the action in most firms making tangible products. Today, they have to share this traditional role with several other functions—an example being where NCR Corporation hired packaging engineers and cognitive engineers (psychologically trained) to help design products that complement the way people think and act.

The net result was recently expressed:

> Large multinational companies have begun to "unchain" product designers capable of bridging and building upon the expertise of both marketing and engineering. Working at last as equal members of multidisciplinary teams, under the new kings and queens of the product development process "project," "product," or "programme managers."[3]

FIGURE 15–1   Range of Leading Design Applications

Purpose of Design	*Item Being Designed*
Aesthetics	Goods
Ergonomics	Services
Function	Architecture
Manufacturability	Graphic arts
Servicing	Offices
Disassembly	Packages

Comment: Design is a big term, covering many areas of human activity, especially new products. The new products field contributes to two classes of items, and to all six classes of purpose. Some people hold that even the other four classes of items are really products to the organizations producing them.

---

[3]Christopher Lorenz, "Harnessing Design as a Strategic Resource," *Long Range Planning,* October 1994, pp. 73–83. The author makes it very clear that he considers the industrial designer as the greatest among equals.

Ironically, by "joining the team" and seeming to lose power, design stands on the verge of winning its ultimate position of influence. But it is the new product manager's task to bring this about.

The Players and Their Relationship

Confining ourselves now to the field under study (the development of new goods and services), let's look at the set of people who participate in the product design task.

Direct Participants	**Supportive Participants**
Research & development	Design consultants
Industrial designers and stylists	Marketing personnel
Engineering designers/ product designers	Resellers
	Vendors/suppliers
Manufacturing engineers and system designers	Governments
	Customers
Manufacturing operations	Company attorneys
	Technical service

Figure 15–2 shows one model of how these people participate. The representation is somewhat linear, but with substantial overlapping or parallel effort.

It is easy to see how this model of operations gives people problems, particularly the designers. Industrial designers, trained to develop aesthetics (styling), structural integrity, and function (how the product works), directly overlap with the design engineers, who are technical people who convert styling into product dimensions or specifications. Technical people are not devoid of ideas on styling, and stylists are not devoid of thoughts on how the mechanics can work. This is especially true on common products (like shoes or dinnerware) where all parties have experience.

The other dimension of complexity is added by some of the supportive participants in the preceding list. Suppliers usually know their materials better than their customers do. That's why Black & Decker picked its supplier for the Snake-Lite before its design was finished. Large firms (e.g., Philips), have the funds to establish large central styling centers where styling skills exceed those of the typical plant stylist. Customers almost always have overriding ideas to contribute. Consequently, the styling function is a synthesis of many views beyond those of the direct participants. If we add all of the other company people listed as supportive, we get back to the list of functions usually represented on the teams discussed in Chapter 14.

The result of all this can be chaos, and in general the problems are thought to be at the heart of why some countries' producers are so often beaten out by new products from Japan and Germany. In Japan, for example, product design means more than how a product looks and feels to the user, it often means engineering applications. To one observer, design in Japan "means the

FIGURE 15–2

*Model of the
Product Design
Process*

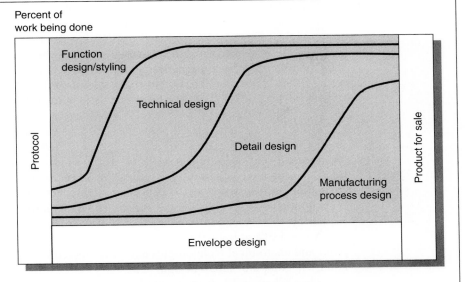

Percent of
work being done

Function
design/styling

Technical design

Detail design

Manufacturing
process design

Protocol

Product for sale

Envelope design

Technical development time scale

The members of a core team all participate in all four stages, but leadership in the first stage is often given to industrial designers, the middle two to engineering design, and the last to process design or manufacturing design. Terms in use vary widely. In chemical and pharmaceutical industries the design and engineering functions are replaced by research and development. And in some firms the term product engineering replaces engineering design; they want to contrast product engineer and process engineer.

For services, the same steps apply, but instead of a "thing" we are developing a service sequence and technical capability. Think of an investment service developed in a financial institution, or a cable TV system, or office design service.

Simultaneous with technical development (on goods *and* services) is the development of the augmented aspects of the product—pre- and postsale service, warranty, image, and so on. This activity, most often led by marketing people, is called *envelope design*, running across the bottom of the figure.

total-enterprise process of determining customer needs and converting them to concepts, detailed designs, process plans, factory design, and delivered products, together with their supporting services."[4] This merges a holistic view of end user needs and a holistic structure to meet those needs. Design is seen as a vertical means of fulfillment, and individual skills are not central.

---

[4]Daniel E. Whitney, "Integrated Design and Manufacturing in Japan," *Prism*, Second Quarter 1993, pp. 75–95.

In the United States and Europe, participants end up playing musical chairs from one project to the next (as roles change). The most critical problem in the model of Figure 15–2 is faced by the design engineer, and we will get to that in a moment. But most discussion centers on the industrial designers (stylists). These people are particularly able to see things, both as they really are and as they might be. They also have strong problem-solving skills and are expert in the media (sketching, drawing, modeling) through which they communicate their ideas.

Events of the past 15–20 years have forced industrial designers to choose among four professional career alternatives: (1) stick to the traditionally sought we-do-it-all role on products with low technology, but back off to just styling on those with new technology; (2) study the necessary new technologies and continue the "full" design role, (3) convert totally to a stylist role (increasingly common among young designers), pairing up with engineering and systems designers; (4) permit themselves to be integrated into company teams.

A good example of the second choice is the designer who picked up computer and anatomical technologies and developed the first fully simulated human hand, via computer-aided design.[5] The Chrysler development of its LH line, discussed in Chapter 13, is an example of the fourth alternative. It probably will be the role in common use, once the dust settles, though many design purists and traditionalists will fight a strong retreat action. Design and marketing operate in drastically different cultures, and cultural gaps are hard to erase.

Current Situation Is in a State of Flux

Most of the problems surrounding design concern concurrency—overlapping the steps in technical development. Designers of award-winning products have summed up what excellence requires of design:[6]

- Design from the outside in, customer's use being central.
- Partner deeply—with all relevant units of the firm.
- Partner widely—with all stakeholders involved.
- Define product up front—protocol and firm prototype—prior to ordering tooling and manufacturing.
- Get physical fast—prototype as fast as you can.
- Design for manufacturability—it's as important as ergonomics and aesthetics.
- Surprise the user—build something in that the user doesn't expect, deliver more than promised.

---

[5]Mike Jones, "Gripping Stuff," *Design*, July 1989, pp. 487–88.

[6]According to a writer who studied winners of the 1993 Annual Industrial Design Excellence awards: see Bruce Nussbaum, *Business Week*, June 7, 1993, pp. 54–57.

Produceability Engineer.   But if there is no easy solution, firms cast about for other alternatives. One being tried today is the produceability engineer. This is an independent third party who understands both design and production, and who can work in the design studios to see that production requirements are met by design decisions. Because the person is a third party, turf battles are partially avoided. But it is not a satisfactory solution—today we know that adding another person rarely is. Effort continues.[7]

Benchmarking.   Another trend is to use benchmarking. This practice of identifying the practices of successful firms has proven very successful but may not be good news to the designers. The benchmarks are sometimes laid down as product requirements, thus again restricting design freedom.

Vendor Integration.   Another part of the model that is in flux is that of the vendor/supplier. Partnering upstream is not uncommon today, though there are security risks, patent uncertainties, cooperation that cannot be mandated in an emergency, and the like. But most companies tell us they are doing it, using the following tools in a style called **integrated:** marketing, in reverse, searching technologies demanding that suppliers value engineer their product, getting source guarantees, putting supplier people on the new product teams, analyzing cost inputs, making contingency plans, making colocations, rotating employees, and demanding that suppliers make a profit even if they have to tell them how to do it. It is in any vendor's best interest to be offering something an end user genuinely needs, so both parties gain from integrated activities.[8]

Computer-Based Design Technology.   Another development is helping to bring people together and at the same time show the importance of all players. That is the *technology of the acronyms*: CAD (computer-aided design), CAM (computer-aided manufacturing), CAE (computer-aided engineering), DFM (design-for-manufacturing, sometimes called DFA, design-for-assembly), and variations.

These technologies offer lots of advantages—people have to work together to understand and use them, they force the integration of all needs into one analytical set, they are fast, and they do more than the human can do alone even if there were ample time. They also help improve the images of team players who may lack status. For example, manufacturing used to have to take a backseat to design and marketing. It was uncommon in many firms for the factory people even to be invited to meetings; they were expected to take what came from design and make it, somehow. In most firms that time is gone, and it should be in all firms.

---

[7]See Gerda Smets and Kees Overbeeke, "Industrial Design Engineering and the Theory of Direct Perception," *Design Studies*, April 1994, pp. 175–84, for ideas on how users deal with the expressiveness of products, and the impact of that on industrial design activities.

[8]The good and the bad of this partnership are shown in Fred R. Bleakley, "Some Companies Let Suppliers Work On Site and Even Place Orders," *The Wall Street Journal*, January 13, 1995, p. A1.

One innovation in this area is getting the most attention. It is DFA, a complex and expensive program that takes whatever the designer has designed and tells how it fits with the manufacturing facility. There are now several versions, but the first one came from Boothroyd & Dewhurst, a Rhode Island software firm. Because the manufacturing conditions and information about the particular assembly operation (whether furniture, cars on an assembly line, or whatever) have been programmed in, the DFA program can react to any design proposal with information about its time and cost result. It also points out the major design elements contributing to slow time or high cost, so the designer can work directly on them.

Unfortunately, the designer does not have comparable software that would be called DFM (design-for-marketing). Unless the protocol is very clear and accepted, or unless marketing or customer people are present during the design process, developers may be acting favorably to factory time/cost but unfavorably to customer value and usefulness.

Other examples of current progress are (1) stereolithography and (2) MCAE (mechanical computer-aided engineering). Stereolithography is software that in just one to three days can convert a container of liquid into a hard plastic prototype. The process, which used to take a modeler several weeks, sends "hardening" beams of electrons into the container causing the liquid to solidify in tiny bits at a time, yielding very precise models.

MCAE permits engineers to test before they build, with all criteria being considered. It's a type of simulation that plays what-if games with a design.

Special Managerial Needs during Technical Development

There are several unique managerial difficulties in product innovation today. Each one has a record of being troublesome to new products managers.

Top Management Attention

Probably the most common lament of product innovators is about their top management—the CEO of a nondivisionalized firm or the general manager of an SBU, plus their executive (or management) committees. New products people claim that only top managements have the power to make decisions essential to their projects. But, in all fairness, top management support is needed for the overall new products *program*—they don't have time to be champions for *individual projects* except rare, crucial ones. New products managers make their own way through the daily jungle of functional conflicts.

Specifically, how can top management help? They should be smart, experienced general managers, for starters. They should know how to make timely decisions, and realize the unique and extraordinary need of the new products staff for strategic direction, clear objectives and goals, and a responsiveness to policy and organizational troubles as they arise. They should spot the key checkpoints to watch, and they should know the subtle difference between taking an *interest* and *interference on details.*

The top manager should support—nay, demand—a product innovation charter. They should supply a sponsor if one does not arise, and they should very clearly and emphatically make it known that functional interface friction (see below) is a sign of managerial failure. Add, too, a longer-term financial view and a managerial style that supports risk taking and good communication. As many managers say, they should **walk the talk**, or, do as you say you're going to do!

Unfortunately, some top managements suddenly get interested in a new product when its introductory expenses begin showing up on the quarterly financial plan; inquiry after inquiry leads to change after change, and by the time the item finally gets to market it is indeed a poor product. Conversely, financial crunch time sometimes leads to top management oversupport, stemming from a desire to get the promised revenues into the books as soon as possible, or to take some personal glory from the team's accomplishment.

These are some of the worst things a new products manager can hear: "If I can help you in any way, let me know," "Find some new products I will like," and "If anyone gives you a hard time tell me." A moment's thought will show that these are essentially worthless.

Top management's interest and support should be clearly *signaled*—by open statements of confidence, by appointments of people who clearly are comers in a firm, by a stream of little things like dropping in at the laboratory or a focus group once in a while.

New products people live in daily fear that some functional head (e.g., VP marketing, VP R&D, or some powerful corporate staffer) will become negative and fail to support people from that function who work on a new products team. Functional heads are often career competitive, and the risk of new products can be damaging.

Even worse, top managements are dependent on strong functional heads for success in the *ongoing* operation. A president cannot just order a VP of engineering to move the best engineers onto a particular new product project, not if that VP claims the best people are needed to support an ailing multimillion dollar product which supplies the profits that pay for the new product work! A consultant who works a lot with top managements says the "barons" of the functions may hold more power than the CEO, especially when they ask directly: "What is more important—the current budget and forecast or that new product?" There is a harsh trap in that question, one that weak or inexperienced top managements are reluctant to deal with. Quantum Corporation is said to have addressed this problem by stating clearly that the path to the CEO's office leads through management in the new product area.

Functional Interface Management

Product innovation involves three key functions: sales/marketing, R&D/design/engineering, and manufacturing/operations. Try as we may, there will probably always be friction at the interfaces between such different groups of people, yet these key functions *must* cooperate often and effectively.

Most of the time, people on these interfaces get along pretty well, and some very well. But, as Figure 15–3 reveals, problems can exist. When they do, the entire project is threatened.

Different Interfaces.   Interfaces exist at three organization levels: (1) department heads, (2) core team members, and (3) operating people within each department. Department heads get along the best, usually because they have learned the value of repressing counterproductive differences. Core team members are often chosen for their ability to work across functions, so problems are minimized there. But when a third-level scientist must deal with a third-level marketer, sparks may fly. The errant behavior takes place out of sight from the brass and near-brass, and is almost childlike. It is often deliberately hidden.

The interfaces also vary by time, some continuing and others just flaring up in a crisis. The continuing ones are the most damaging, but the flare-ups are the most frustrating.

FIGURE 15–3

Incidence and Consequence of Interface Problems

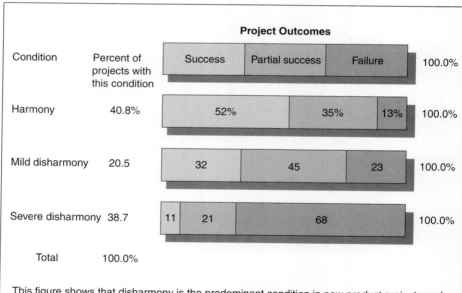

This figure shows that disharmony is the predominant condition in new product projects and that the degree of harmony correlates with the success of a project. However, we don't know whether disharmony causes a project to fail, or the problems a project is having causes disharmony among the group.

Source: William E. Souder, *Managing New Product Innovations* (Lexington, MA: Lexington Books, 1987), pp. 168–70.

Why the Friction?   Scores of differences between the three functional sets of people have been identified by research studies over the years.[9] Some go deep into the psyche of stereotypes, and most new products people can identify with this complaint: "Those marketers can't get through the day without a two-hour lunch at the most expensive restaurant in the area." And this one: "Ever try to get a scientist to say clearly yes or no, or to give a date?" Or, "Why don't manufacturing people ever admit they goofed up?" These are wildly unfair generalizations, but they have a basis in daily life. The people do differ on their general time frame, for one thing, and on their measure of success, for another.

These personal differences are exaggerated by separation. Research long ago showed that communication goes down with the square of the distance between two people.[10] Yet, corporate size has led us to build huge research centers hundreds of miles from the offices of marketers and the production lines of manufacturing people. Problems caused by these separations have led today's managers to welcome **digital colocation**, using the resources of communications technology (e.g., Lotus Notes).

Sometimes interface problems are caused by ineptness in upper management. The head of R&D in one firm gave such a lashing to a staff scientist for telling marketing some bad news about a product test that the individual wouldn't even talk to marketing for over a year. Neither did the other scientists. Their stock answer was "Call the boss and ask him."

A manufacturing manager recently tried an amusing challenge to show marketers how they overlook their own functional myopia. He listed 10 of the general pressures being put onto the manufacturing function in business—to gain flexibility, cut costs, increase quality, etc. He then applied them instead to marketing, as shown in Figure 15–4. If you lean toward marketing, is your reaction to these demands at all influenced by that interest?

Managing the Interfaces.   Most interface management is straightforward, and any experienced manager knows a score of things to do. For others, Figure 15–5 shows the highlights of the research findings. The essence lies in three statements:

- Top managers get the interfaces they deserve, because they can eliminate most of the problems any time they choose to do so.
- Interface management primarily takes time, not skills. One new product manager said he solved his team's problems by giving at least 40 percent of his time to seeing that all key players spent a lot of time with each other, on and off the job.

---

[9]See Richard D. Hise, Larry O'Neal, A. Parasuraman, and James U. McNeal, "Marketing/R&D Interaction in New Product Development: Implications for New Product Success Rates," *Journal of Product Innovation Management*, June 1990, pp. 142–55.

[10]First reported by Jack Andrew Morton, *Organizing for Innovation: A Systems Approach to Technical Management* (New York: McGraw-Hill, 1971); confirmed by T. J. Allen, *Managing the Flow of Technology* (Cambridge, MA: MIT Press, 1977).

FIGURE 15–4   **A Test of Interface Sensitivity**
The Pressure on the Manufacturing Function Today, as Applied to the Function of Marketing

---

This is a chance for persons professionally interested in marketing to sense their reaction to urgings (demands) if put on them by people working in manufacturing. All of the actions are felt to be appropriate (even badly needed) in the area of manufacturing, but they have not been demanded of marketing until now. Are they appropriate?

1. **Use computer-integrated marketing.** Customer sales, logistics, costs—all into one computer system, accessible.
2. **Wage a war on waste.** Throw out bad coupons, wrong media, and old campaigns.
3. **Demand top-quality, standardized training for marketers.** All of them, but especially sales reps.
4. **Form more marketing partnerships.** Up and down the channel, with any group that influences our customers.
5. **Reevaluate accounts and prune those that are not profitable.** Use much more selective marketing.
6. **Put better marketing teamwork into place.** Arrange marketing people into teams, with customer focus, not geographical assignments as now.
7. **Adopt gain-sharing systems.** Let teams share bonuses, based on customer satisfaction surveys.
8. **Lower your unit costs.** Make a real attack on inefficiency, based on tight measurements of productivity and using innovative technologies.
9. **Focus your marketing programs.** Have fewer but better promotional campaigns, at the world-class level.
10. **Achieve a total quality orientation.** Develop new measures for all marketing actions that impact service quality, with full commitments to them.

Source: Allan J. Magrath, "What Marketing Can Learn from Manufacturing," *Across the Board*, April 1990, pp. 37–42.

- Participants who continue to be a problem should be taken out of new product team situations; they get some perverse satisfaction out of reactions to their behavior.

Services

Before we leave the topic of managing during technical development, let's take a look at a product group that might not seem to have technical development—services. Service firms do not have the customary R&D departments, engineering design, product design, manufacturing engineering, and so on. Or do they?

Services and goods are often arrayed on a scale of (1) pure service, (2) primarily service and partly a good, (3) primarily a good and partly service, and (4) pure good. Examples, in order, are counseling, an insurance policy, an automobile, and a candy bar. Only in the first category does the product provider have nothing tangible to do R&D/engineering on, and there are very few of them. (You might argue that the consultant was the result of technical accomplishment by finishing a college degree!)

Second, even on pure and "heavily" service products, there are tangible support items (such as ads, warranties, policies, instructions). They need design and they need production. The fact that this task may be given to an advertising agency doesn't avoid the point, because design and production of electronic brake controls can be contracted out too.

FIGURE 15–5

Clues to Good Policy in Interface Management

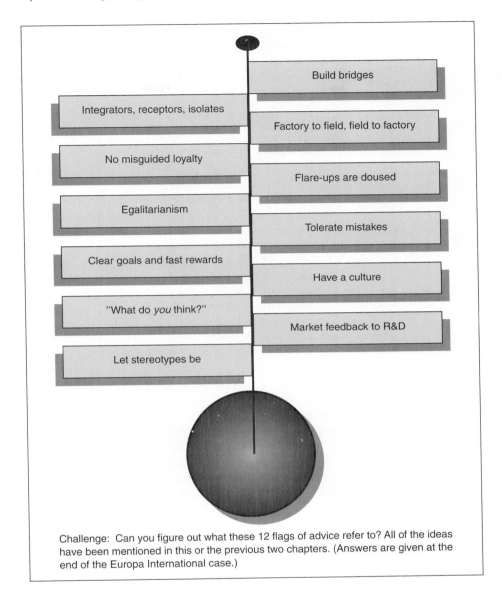

Build bridges

Integrators, receptors, isolates

Factory to field, field to factory

No misguided loyalty

Flare-ups are doused

Egalitarianism

Tolerate mistakes

Clear goals and fast rewards

Have a culture

"What do *you* think?"

Market feedback to R&D

Let stereotypes be

Challenge: Can you figure out what these 12 flags of advice refer to? All of the ideas have been mentioned in this or the previous two chapters. (Answers are given at the end of the Europa International case.)

Because of these facts, the creation of service products tends to mirror the systems used on goods. The tools all fit (e.g., the product innovation charter, problem-based ideation, trade-off analysis, screening, protocol, prototype). Their purpose in each case is virtually identical, and services have frequently been cited as examples in this book.

The ideas behind these tools also fit: organizational structure options, empowerment, speed, the role for top management, culture, and interface relations.

The San Diego Zoo, for example, did a complete reorganization in which functional departments were made invisible to displays such as Tiger River. Each display area is run by "a team . . . led by a keeper . . . isn't hooked up to the zoo's mainframe . . . members are jointly responsible for the display. . . hard to tell who comes from which department. . . . "[11] Sound like the teams we have been talking about?

Of course, these concepts must be applied creatively, but still the parallels are there. Services firms, for instance, seem to have little in the way of R&D, but someone must design new systems for the performance of services. This function is apt to be almost anywhere in the firm, with rarely a services design department. Perhaps there should be.

Iterations are less expensive in the development of services (no tangible good to change), so they are more frequent; most development runs rather fast to prototype because there is less cost to do so. Functional interface frictions are about the same, only the players are often different. For example, bank marketers don't have manufacturing engineers to disagree with, but they do have very strong branches, where many of the services are produced. Marketers probably play a greater role in product innovation on services, but service firms seem less likely to have strong strategies for this work; consequently, their influence is mainly on product modifications, not new-to-the-world products.

One difference between services and goods is often claimed: that there is no inventory of services, since they are produced at the point of consumption. Technically yes, but new products people see a connection—in the service business we inventory service *capability*. Take the example of McDonalds—they sell parking convenience as a service, but that convenience was actually created when the parking lot was built.

Even the consultant mentioned above as an example of a pure service knows enough to drive the right make of car (expensive or cheap) when calling on a client, carry the right business case, and display the right clothing. All have an impact on how well the intangible service recommendations will be accepted and used. And such supportive goods are clearly a part of the new product creation task.[12]

Global Considerations

Very few product innovators today think nationally. In almost every case, they see foreign markets as viable options and organize accordingly. Structurally, global product innovation can be handled in several ways:

---

[11]Thomas A. Stewart, "The Search for the Organization of Tomorrow," *Fortune*, May 18, 1990, pp. 92–98. For new services in the Hyatt hotels see Joseph Weber, "Farewell, Fast Track," *Business Week*, December 10, 1990, pp. 192–200.

[12]A rare study on *industrial* services is Ulrike de Brentani, "New Industrial Service Development: Scenarios for Success and Failure," *Journal of Business Research*, 1995, pp. 93–103.

1. Make no special arrangements. Export what is developed for the home market. On the one hand this is called the **export approach**, yet when market conditions around the world are substantially the same, then this approach of one product for all countries is called **global strategy**.

2. Keep structure the same, but develop versions of the new item to meet the needs of viable foreign markets. For example, if Philips comes up with a new razor for the European market, smaller, heavier, or safer versions may be developed for sale in Africa, the Pacific Rim, and other markets. This approach is usually thought of as a variation of the export approach or called **international strategy**.

3. Use the facilities of the home firm, but have separate projects directed by managers in each viable foreign area. These foreign managers learn of available technologies in the home firm, study their local markets to see how each might apply, and then set up projects to develop what is needed there. This is often called a **multinational strategy**. Nestlé prefers this method, and calls it on-the-ground development, but the degree of on-the-ground varies from country to country.[13]

4. Assign the basic responsibility for product innovation to each foreign business large enough to have the resources for it. This usually means some local R&D, local manufacturing, and almost totally local marketing. The manager of each foreign business is a general manager and develops strategies and organizations according to technology and market opportunities. The people working in, say, Spain are free to "buy" service from the headquarters firm in Switzerland *if they wish to do so*. Operational cultures and policies will vary greatly from country to country. This strategy has no common name, but **local drive** would fit.

5. The last alternative is a mix of the above, variously called **matrix**, **country of excellence**, and other names. Essentially, the firm wants to be a major player in all viable markets of the world, but wants to develop strategies appropriate to each of those markets. It is often done by world region, continent, or other larger geographical division. NEC, Philips, P&G, L. M. Ericsson, Matsushita, ITT, and Lever are firms using such strategy. The term *matrix* gives the idea, whereby there may be exporting from one country to another, an international approach on another line where central technical facilities are necessary to innovation, multinational on yet another line or division, and in others a system where for each region the firm selects a country that has had success on the line and gives them the line responsibility to extend that success to other countries in their area however they think best.

---

[13]Carla Rapoport, "Nestlé's Brand Building Machine," *Fortune*, September 1994, pp. 147–56.

Within each of these strategies the actual new products practices do not vary much, nor should they. A recent study comparing new product practices in U.K. and U.S. firms found few differences, so few in fact that the article had to be refocused to other matters.[14] There are problems in making adjustments to meet the varying level of resources in different countries (e.g., industrial design resources in Continental Europe and the United States are much greater than in the United Kingdom) and in keeping some degree of control over such powerful programs that are scattered all over the globe. The operation may involve technical creation in Germany, production in Brazil, financing from London, and marketing in Canada, all the while being directed from an electronic management center in Chicago. The consequence of all this is the demise of what used to be called national designs.[15]

Summary

In the overall sequence being followed in this book, we have now completed enough technical work (or systems design for services) to have some kind of prototype. It is not ready to market until the end users who asked for it tell us we have something useful. This they will (hopefully) do in some form of product use testing. For example, a firm may just ask customers to look at an item and guess whether it would do the job for them. Or, proxy opinions may be collected from resellers or end users' consultants. Or a tough, full-scale test of the item in use may be conducted. The entire matter of customer reactions will be taken up in Chapter 16.

Applications

More questions from that interview with the company president:

1. "About this matter of design, I am stumped. I agree design is critical today, and I always support it. But, you've got to admit that it costs money, and often conflicts with function; for example, a beautifully styled computer mouse may hinder ergonomic activity. As a general executive matter, how do you suggest we evaluate these trade-offs? How can we find where to stop styling and let the engineers rule?"

2. "A minute ago you showed me a figure that had a bunch of words like *bridges* and *egalitarianism* on it. I know they are supposed to help reduce interface friction, but it seems to me they apply mainly to manufactured

---

[14]F. Axel Johne and Patricia A. Snelson, "Product Development Approaches in Established Firms," *Industrial Marketing Management*, 1989, pp. 113–24. Agreement comes from Timothy M. Devinney of the University of New South Wales in a personal perspective in "Significant Issues for the Future of Product Innovation," *Journal of Product Innovation Management*, January 1995, pp. 71–75.

[15]Marilyn Stern, "Is National Design Dead?" *Across the Board*, September 1993, pp. 32–37.

goods. Confidentially, one of our divisions is about to begin work on a private electronic communications system for use between parts of large firms—it would replace much of a firm's commercial telephone service, current fax systems, and more. Don't know what it would look like, but it will be a beauty if we can pull it off. Question, can you take that list and give me an example of each of those points, applied to the people working on this new service?"

3. "We have a 'Gap' type clothing operation that is now large enough to make its first attack on worldwide markets, and for now it is committed to what it calls, if I remember it correctly, product line extension and adaptation from the United States to selected other countries. But, there is some question about how to organize this activity. Management plans to make the decisions on adaptation in their St. Louis headquarters, and at least for now they will sell through importers or agents in other countries, occasionally through the marketing department of one of our other clothing divisions. What thoughts would you have about assigning this responsibility? That is, should it be given to the design department in the United States division, to the product managers in the marketing department, or to a separate group set up just to handle this global-to-be operation?"

4. "I had to laugh when you mentioned the importance of top management. I've been president of two different divisions and now president of the corporation for several years. I've heard that line—just give us your support and we can get that new item to market quickly. Sure they can—and fall flat on their faces too. They do bad enough without our help; can you imagine what disasters would happen if I started telling people, 'I sure do like Joe Higgins; I'll support him all the way!' Listen, right now our Mountain States banking division has a team of people working on debit cards—they think there is a way to sell these cards and make a profit, even if they wipe out half of our credit card interest income. What would you have that division president do if he were asked to give 'top-management support' to that project? I think the idea is that debit cards would be tied to long-term borrowing contracts and home mortgages, or something like that."

CASE: EUROPA INTERNATIONAL

Gunter Schmidt, director of new businesses for the Europa International hotel chain (head-quartered in Frankfort, and similar to several other large, full-line chains such as Marriott and Hilton), had just finished reading an interesting report from *Fortune* magazine about a

---

Source: The technology of this case is real; the case setting is realistic but hypothetical.

new type of software.* It was then available from four American firms: Ventana, IBM, Lotus, and Collaborative Technologies (though IBM later bought up Lotus). It was called **groupware**. The fee for licensing varied from $25,000 to $50,000. Created originally for meetings, it was now getting wider application as a tool for almost any problem analysis and solution. On the marketing side, it could replace focus groups for people with keyboard competence.

The essence was that 5 to 15 people could be gathered on a network, either in one room, or in rooms scattered around the country or the world (users didn't care whether the other end of the network was in Boston or Bangkok), and then proceed to discuss an issue by using their keyboards only. There was no open discussion in the room, anyone could write at any time without interrupting others, and any statements could be read by all. Questions could be asked and answered, ideas could be pooled and then systematically evaluated by some scoring system. A common arrangement was for people to sit in a horseshoe. Some of the systems were so complex that they required a facilitator to be present; others were not.

The article told how some firms were citing productivity increases from using the software. IBM had cut meeting times by 56 percent and Boeing saved $6,700 per meeting. Boeing also cut 90 percent of the time it usually took to develop a standardized control system for use on machine tools. These were the first solid evidence of productivity gains from using computers, historically void of actual dollar and time savings. Other advantages were that the impersonal mode brought forth many ideas and comments that otherwise would have been repressed (politics), people can read faster than they can listen, ideas on the screen got credibility regardless of their source (this "democratization of data" was a great benefit for women and minorities), and the customary bazooka effect of "You've got to be kidding" was almost eliminated.

Groupware was very consistent with the rush to team operations in the early 1990s. Several of the firms using the system talked about cutting out levels of management. And people leaving a groupware meeting seemed to have bought in better; they personally participated in the decisions reached. There was clearly more loyalty to the meeting results.

However, it was not all rosy. Beyond the expense of the system and its operation, there was little gain for meetings that were informational—either from one speaker or for periodic status reports. Attention wandered some if participants were at isolated sites, and users noted that managements could submarine the whole thing. For example, higher level managers tended to visit the meeting room and walk around, looking at the individual screens. They also sometimes spoke out in an obvious request for support on actions they were urging. They also had later access to every comment through the electronic files. And some executives resented the ability of individuals using the system to reach connections with others on their views, not previously known. Hierarchy was clearly being threatened.

Overall, the reactions to date had been so enthusiastic that Schmidt thought he had better give it some consideration. He particularly noted that users included service organizations (a hotel, an accounting firm, a bank and a power company) and that several of them had mentioned their global operations. Among the applications mentioned, he was especially interested in the ones involving product planning meetings, developing marketing strategies, overall strategic planning, and even the selection of a name for a new service.

How could Europa International use groupware? Where would it seem to fit in the overall new products process, and where not? The chain had recently been putting new projects

---

*The article mentioned was David Kirkpatrick, "Here Comes the Payoff from PCs," *Fortune*, March 22, 1992, pp. 93–102.

on a team basis, and had been trying to install new (empowerment-type) cultures in operations around the world. Yet their operations were widely scattered, they had language differences, each hotel was permitted considerable flexibility in its strategy and operations, many of their middle and upper-middle managers were not frequent computer users, and he thought some cultures would resist having managers actually sitting at a computer like a clerk. He also knew that several of the firms in the article were frequent experimenters with new technologies and what he called fads, so he discounted most of the results they claimed.

Answers to Figure 15–5:

1. Build human and operational bridges between sides of key interfaces.
2. Put integrators and receptors into team work. Leave isolates alone.
3. Use job rotation between functions, especially between marketing and technical.
4. Watch for subordinates who think you *want* them to fight for your function.
5. Move quickly to resolve disputes; don't let anything fester.
6. Treat others (and expect to be treated) as equals. Ranks rankle.
7. Understand that functions you secretly resent will make honest mistakes too.
8. Avoid vague rules. Let everyone know how the game will be played, in advance.
9. Study up on culture, and structure the right one for your situation. Hold to it.
10. Ask for opinions across the functional interfaces. Respect capabilities of all.
11. See that technical people have a chance to know well what the customer needs/wants.
12. People *are* different. Let them be, and learn to be comfortable with the differences.

16   PRODUCT USE TESTING

Setting

The first output of technical development is a prototype, which is checked against the protocol statement that guided its development and perhaps sent to the marketplace for a confirmatory concept test. The methodology for that is essentially the same as the original concept test except now we have a more tangible expression of the idea. Usually the end user is not satisfied that the prototype would work, so more development work is done. The cycle continues until the firm has a good approximation of what will be the eventual product—a prototype that stakeholders like.

At this time, most firms like to make up a quantity of prototypes (whether on the bench or in some pilot production setup). And for the first time they can give the end user a product concept that is in a *form for extended use*. No more guessing. The task is to devise a method for testing the end users' experience with the new item, and we call the activity **product use testing**, or **field testing**, or **user testing**. Sometimes it is called **market acceptance testing**, though this term may also mean *market* testing, as in Chapters 20 and 21. Product use testing (PUT) is the topic of this chapter.

The importance of product use testing shows up in several of the key concepts discussed in Chapter 2 as driving the whole new product process—*the unique superior product*, the *repeat buying percentage* in the A-T-A-R paradigm, and the *requirements in the protocol*. A product that does not meet end user needs fails on one of the three key causes of failure.

One other reminder: this chapter applies equally to services and to goods. A recent article in *The Wall Street Journal* lamented the confusion in airports. A key cause is poor signage, which never gets pretesting for clarity.[1]

---

[1]Bridget O'Brian, "Signs and Blunders: Airport Travelers Share Graphic Tales," *The Wall Street Journal*, March 28, 1995, p. A1.

What Is Product Use Testing?

Use testing means use under normal operating conditions. Consumers put a tire on a car and drive it, technicians put notebook computers in the hands of warehouse personnel, a bank installs a new check-cashing service at three branch points, and so on. The product will probably not be perfect at this time, for more reasons than poor design. An example of *manufacturing* difficulties came from Weyerhaeuser. Their new UltraSofts disposable diapers (from a pilot plant setup) worked well, very well, and sold at a discount price. However, the pilot plant, where there were fires and other breakdowns, was a poor predictor of full-scale production lines. And suppliers refused to sign long-term contracts on the key diaper liner.[2]

Testing should continue until the team is satisfied that the new product does indeed solve the problem or fill the need that was expressed in the original protocol. Sometimes this can take quite a while, as shown in a Gillette deodorant. (See Figure 16–1.)

Is Product Use Testing *Really* Necessary?

Here is a composite statement of what we commonly hear at product use testing time:

We've been working on this thing for months (or years), and we've spent a ton of money on it. Experts were called as needed. Market research showed that end users would want a product like this. Why dally around any longer? Top management is leaning on us for the revenues we promised, and we continue to hear that a key competitor is working on something similar. Look, we're now in an up mode; stopping to test suggests to management that we don't have faith in what we've been doing. Besides, customers can't just take the new item and try it fairly; they have to learn how to use it, then work it into their system, listen to our ads (or reps) advising them what to do and how good the results are. (Norelco tells all razor purchasers to try their method for 30 days before drawing any conclusions about how it works!) Worst of all, a competitor can get his hands on our creation and beat us to the market! No, it's just not worth the time and money to do extended use testing.

Now, sometimes that statement is a fact, not an argument. For example, the first fax machine probably could not be use tested by end users—there was no network of others with whom to communicate! Same for the picture-telephone. Same for the first color TV when there were no programs being broadcast in color. How could one have use-tested the Internet? Hopefully, it won't be as bad a situation as that in a well-known cartoon, where one lab scientist holds up a flask and says to another scientist,"It may well bring about immortality, but it will take forever to test it."

---

[2]Alecia Swasy, "Diaper's Failure Shows How Poor Plans, Unexpected Woes Can Kill New Products," *The Wall Street Journal*, October 9, 1990, p. B1.

FIGURE 16–1   The Product-Testing System Used for Gillette's Dry Idea Deodorant

---

1. Technical lab work in 1975 suggested available technologies to achieve a drier deodorant.
2. A 2,000-person concept study (cost: $175,000) determined that "Yes, roll-ons are good, but they go on wet and make you wait to get dressed." A concept was at hand.
3. Laboratory project assigned to scientist: find a replacement for water as the medium for the aluminum-zirconium salts that did the work.
4. A prototype using silicone was developed, and it wasn't wet or sticky. But it did dissolve the ball of the applicator (In-house lab test.)
5. Next prototype was tested by volunteers from the local South Boston area. It was oily. (Outside research firm employed to test college students in the area. Gillette often used in-house tests of employees too.)
6. By late 1976, a later prototype tested well on women recruited to sweat for hours in a 100-degree "hot room." (Test of market users in the Boston area who served on a regular panel.) Unfortunately, though it worked well, it eventually turned into a rock-hard gel.
7. By early 1977, another prototype had passed the "hot room" tests and was then sent to company-owned medical evaluation laboratories in Rockville, Maryland. (In-house test on rabbits and rats.) It passed the test.
8. Packaging was being developed and tested by in-house package design engineers. Early packages leaked.
9. However, the package dispensed a product that test subjects felt was too dry going on! (Test of market users.)
10. They then returned to a conventional roll-on bottle, added a special leak-proof gasket, and enlarged the ball so the antiperspirant could be applied in quantities large enough to be felt. Another test of market users confirmed that people did indeed feel drier. This conclusion, when put with the earlier data that the product did have a good antiperspirant effect, was enough to go to market.

Note: This procedure used several different types of tests, with different objectives and formats, and with reiterations. The product was cycled until successful.

Source: Neil Ulman, "Sweating It Out," *The Wall Street Journal*, November 17, 1978, p. 1; and "For Some Concerns the Smell of Success Isn't Exactly Sweet," *The Wall Street Journal*, December 28, 1977, p. 1.

Are These Arguments Correct?

These arguments are persuasive, especially when put forth by the person on the top floor who has funded the work to date. But, except for very rare cases such as with the fax machine, they are incorrect. What we have is an unknown, with lots yet to be learned. The user whose problem started the project still hasn't told us that our product *solves* that problem.

Even more, the risks and costs of use testing are usually small compared to the loss of the earnings flow from a successful product. See Figure 16–2. About the only argument that really carries weight is the competitive one, and then only when our new product can be copied and marketed quickly. Many food products are like this, as are other items where no technical accomplishment is involved. If use testing clearly makes us second (or even third) into the market, most firms will opt for immediate marketing—without use testing. And, of course, they expect to fail often. Food products suffer an 80–90 percent failure rate, based on the minor improvements they offer, the small retail availability such products can get, and the fickleness of consumers who apparently cannot predict their behavior in a concept test.

Even in those industries, however, there should be more serious consideration of the counter arguments *for* use testing. Here they are.

FIGURE 16–2

Variable Gains and Losses from Program of Product Use Testing

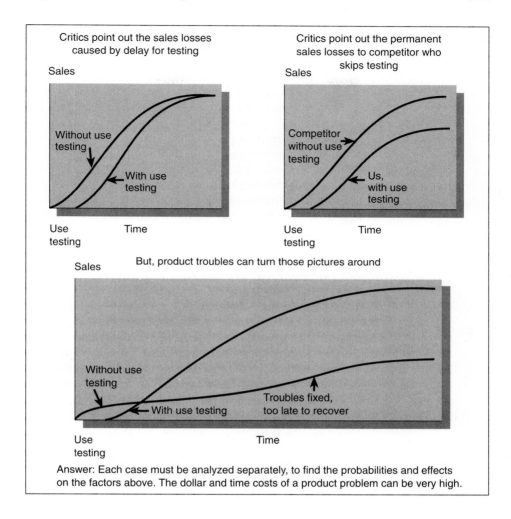

Critics point out the sales losses caused by delay for testing

Sales

Without use testing

With use testing

Use testing   Time

Critics point out the permanent sales losses to competitor who skips testing

Sales

Competitor without use testing

Us, with use testing

Use testing   Time

But, product troubles can turn those pictures around

Sales

Without use testing

With use testing

Troubles fixed, too late to recover

Use testing   Time

Answer: Each case must be analyzed separately, to find the probabilities and effects on the factors above. The dollar and time costs of a product problem can be very high.

Regarding Competitors' Reaction.   A firm developing new items is well advised to build its innovation on a technology base where it has some insulation from competitive copying (see the strategy discussions in Chapter 4). Second, competitors today are finding that copying someone else has small gains—others will copy *them*, price competition will take the profits away, the imitator usually copies the innovator's mistakes too, and the competitors we must worry about most are themselves involved in technology-based developments that cannot be thrown over on short notice.

Let's look at the case of Amdahl and IBM. In 1982, Amdahl was an established and successful maker of mainframe computers—big ones. But that year it rolled out a new line and "offered a convincing demonstration of how to do everything wrong.... When [the machines] did arrive, they were infested with so many bugs that Amdahl field engineers had to scurry about doing retrofits. . . . Predictably, the results were devastating. . . . Share slumped to around 12 percent, from 17 percent."

Three years later, Amdahl announced its next generation of computers. It took the time to "do the job right," even though IBM got the jump on it. "By insisting on exhaustive, pre-rollout testing, President Lewis made sure the machines worked." The result was spectacular, with sales of 250 machines costing between $3 million and $9 million apiece. The following year, share was back up to 15 percent and climbing.[3]

Two years later, IBM itself marketed the AS/400 minicomputer (called the most successful product launch in IBM history). By the introduction date, potential buyers had field-use-tested 1,700 of the computers! A year later, they had bought 25,000 of them. Maybe these two firms know something about competitive advantage and copying.

Customer Needs Are Complex Sets.   In almost every industry, there is no one, simple, end user need. Any new item foists onto the end user a learning curve, there are trade-offs, and there is "baggage"—things that came with the new item that often surprise even the developer. For example, consider the case of GTE Airfone, the firm that developed and marketed a technology to permit telephone calls to go from ground to seated individuals on airborne planes. What seemed like a natural is going very slowly—turns out that many fliers don't want to be disturbed during their rare quiet times. And nearby passengers don't think much of the idea either. Apple, for another example, was in a hurry to market the original Newton. When intended users heard about the new communicator, they raved, and many bought. But then they found that using it was not quite as simple as they had thought, habits had to be broken, frustrations abounded. Apple has spent years changing and improving the product, still without the success it originally intended. All because they didn't want to stop for a full use-test of the product the first time. End use is indeed complex, and there is no way it can be simulated in laboratories, where use is isolated from user mistakes, competitive trashing of the concept, and objections by those in the user firm or family whose work or life is disrupted by the change.

End users also often have trouble communicating their wants and their satisfactions, short of having the finished item. For example, two firms (Mars and Hershey) marketed food items with new synthetic fats (from NutraSweet and Procter & Gamble, respectively). Both cases faltered on a surprise difficulty: just what do consumers really want in a dessert or a candy bar? Is sweetness an index of enjoyment, does the term *fat substitute* destroy expectations of pleasant taste, and so on. One firm went national and the other into an expensive test market before these obstacles became clear.[4]

---

[3]Marc Beauchamp, "Learning from Disaster," *Forbes*, October 19, 1987, p. 96.

[4]For Mars, see Gabriella Stern, "Attempt to Cut Candy Calories Sours for P&G," *The Wall Street Journal*, August 25, 1993, p. A1. For Hershey, see "Simple Pleasures," *Across the Board*, May 1994, p. 39.

Can We Deliver a Total Quality Product?   Recall the idea of the augmented product—where there is a core benefit, then a formal product, and then the many augmentations of service, warranty, image, financing, and so on. The new product process tends to focus on the core benefit and the formal product, and even that may have implementation problems (see Weyerhaeuser, above). But firms often just assume they will be able to deliver the outer ring of augmented product quality—the sales force will be able to explain the new item well, early product breakdowns will not chase other potential buyers away, the finance division will approve generous financing arrangements, the advertising effectively answers competitors' claims, and warehouse personnel won't make a simple mistake and destroy half the product. These things happen, and often. Horror stories abound:

Black & Decker once pulled thousands of flashlights off store shelves and stopped shipment on a new line of smoke detectors that carried the Ultralife [battery] after Kodak discovered an unexpected buildup of material that affected its shelf life. The discovery was made during marketing, not during use testing.

General Electric took a $450 million pretax charge for a new refrigerator compressor, which was never field-tested because the firm was sure it would work. The impossible happened.[5]

P&G was well into test markets with two new Party Cakes before finding that pans used to bake the character cakes either charred or smoked while in the oven. The products had to be pulled from the shelves, and customers given refunds.

Wolverine World Wide marketed a new running shoe, only to find that "20% of runners stressed a seam in the gel pouch inside the heel, rupturing it over time. The cost: a one-year delay and $5 million."[6]

Coca-Cola marketed a new soda machine called Breakmate, a microwave-oven-size soda fountain for the home, the office, and on picnics. (Their haste was partly based on belief that PepsiCo would soon market its own soda fountain, but PepsiCo did a use test as part of a test market and dropped the idea.) Coca-Cola ended up unable to build the proper distributor service capability, the product when used in the South attracted ants and roaches "from a hundred miles away," and some of the drip trays grew so much mold they looked "like a science project." It was a very expensive failure, even in executive pride and reputation.[7]

To bypass product use testing is a gamble that should be considered only when there is just cause. The burden of proof is on whoever argues for skipping it. Intel seemed to have a very good reason to cut short its testing of their highly

---

[5]For the full story on this disappointment, see Thomas F. O'Boyle, "GE Refrigerator Woes Illustrate Hazards in Changing a Product," *The Wall Street Journal*, May 7, 1990, p. 1.

[6]Rita Koselka, "The Dog That Survived," *Forbes*, November 9, 1992, pp. 82–83.

[7]See John R. Emshwiller and Michael J. McCarthy, "Coke's Soda Fountain for Offices Fizzles, Dashing High Hopes," *The Wall Street Journal*, June 14, 1993, p. A1.

publicized Pentium chip, and perhaps they did—the problems that appeared occurred only rarely (one needed 9th decimal calculation for one glitch to appear). But some managers' arguments are weaker. Like this one: "We don't like to do in-home use testing of our (paper) products, so we take care to make them right the first time!"

Knowledge Gained from Product Use Testing

Figure 16–3 shows the key pieces of knowledge that use tests provide.

Preuse Sense Reactions.   Almost every product gives the user a chance to react to immediate sensations of color, speed, durability, mechanical suitability, and so on. Initial reactions are important, especially on service products. For example, managers at Saturn feel the most important single reaction of a potential new car buyer is the impression upon first entering a dealership. In the marketing of the first Saturn, managers designed dealerships for a good impression and measured to see they got it.

Early Use Experiences.   This is the "does it work" knowledge. Key specifics are such things as ease of use, surface variables, can they manage it, are there still bugs, and is there any evidence of what the item will eventually do.

FIGURE 16–3

*Set of New
Knowledge from
Product Use Tests*

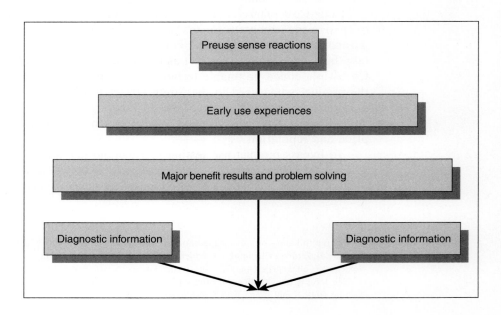

Major Benefits Results.   This is the ultimate test against the protocol, meaning physical features, perceptual features, functional modes, and perceived benefits, including solving whatever problems led to development of the item in the first place. In some industries this latter point is a special problem. Computer hardware and software firms, for example, are under great competitive pressure and prefer to run what they call **beta tests**. These are use tests, at selected customer sites, but they are short-term. They are designed to tell the manufacturers one thing: does this product work, free of bugs? In fact, some have their people competing to see who can find the most bugs in a new item—better now than later.[8] Their beta tests are not designed to tell them about meeting customer needs and solving problems—such testing takes longer than the few weeks usually allowed on computer products. (Of course, more time is allowed if there are bugs and other problems, such as with what industry observers call **vaporware**.)

Unfortunately, these beta tests are conducted under such time pressures that managers tend to ignore danger signals. What might become a classic was NCR's development of its Warehouse Manager computer package. In hurrying this product to market, the firm committed several mistakes:

- Concluded the beta tests before there was time for key bugs to show up. The program actually sabotaged customers' accounting and cost systems.

- Neglected to test thoroughly a part of their package that they licensed from another firm—Taylor Management.

- Continued selling and installing the $180,000 program after hearing of horrendous problems with it. Several big installations were made even after NCR ordered a halt to further sales.

- Promised "single source solution" to technical problems when in fact they depended on Taylor to handle problems on their part of the package.

- Took the stance with individual customers that the product worked well so the problems must be caused by the customer.

Note that inadequate use testing can lead to far more problems than product adjustments. NCR's difficulties brought numerous suits; these hassles multiplied the cost of adequate product testing many times.[9]

---

[8]Douglas W. Clark, "Bugs Are Good: A Problem-Oriented Approach to the Management of Design Engineering," *Research Technology Management*, May–June 1990, pp. 23–27.

[9]Mile Geyelin, "How an NCR System for Inventory Turned into a Virtual Saboteur," *The Wall Street Journal*, August 8, 1994, p. A1.

Some of these beta testers are now edging into the other knowledge domains in this list, so one might call their newer tests **gamma tests** (third in the flow of alpha, beta, and gamma).[10]

Diagnostic Information.   This is an important section, not the miscellaneous one it may appear. New products managers are looking for how items are used, and what mistakes are made. Use tests often suggest ways to improve performance or to reduce cost. General Foods carried to the very last test the issue of the relative proportions of instant coffee and roasted grains for Mello Roast; it needed the best trade-off between the lower cost of the grains and the effect on flavor. New product developers also seek specific pieces of information needed to back up their claims. Marketers want confirmation of target markets and product positionings. Product integrity is also on trial during a use test, since only the users' perceptions tell us whether the parts tie together into a meaningful whole, and whether product fits application. Lastly, developers are watching for any other red flag, a signal that users had some problems understanding the new item, or were slow to accept the results they got, and so on.

Testing Dimensions

Any product use test, whether one of several or alone, whether industrial or consumer, whether for Egypt or Alabama, should be crafted carefully. This means making at least 13 decisions (special cases may call for others).

A. *Testing Dimensions concerning What We Need to Learn*

1. An Open Set.   What we need to learn is totally situation-specific; nevertheless, the objectives should be specific and should include the requirements spelled out in the protocol. (See Chapter 12.) Some managers like to do what is often called a Potential Problem Analysis at this point.

B. *Testing Dimensions concerning Contacting Test Groups*

2. User Groups.   Some use testing is done with *lab personnel* at the plants where the products are first produced. Alexander Graham Bell became the first telephone user when he called his assistant.

Experts are the second testing group (e.g., the cooking staff in a test kitchen). Car companies have styling professionals; wine companies have tasters. Experts will give more careful consideration than will typical users and probably will express reactions more accurately. They will not be interested in the same things that interest customers, however.

---

[10]Beta testing is a large and complex subject. One very helpful study is Robert J. Dolan and John M. Matthews, "Maximizing the Utility of Consumer Product Testing: Beta Test Design and Management," *Journal of Product Innovation Management*, September 1993, pp. 318–30.

The third test group option, *employees*, is widely utilized though often criticized. Company loyalties and pressures and employees' lifestyles and customs may distort opinions and attitudes. Obvious problems of possible bias can be overcome to some extent by concealing product identities and by carefully training and motivating the employee panel.

Stakeholders are the next choice, and the set includes customers and noncustomers, users and nonusers, resellers, end user advisers (such as architects), users of competitive products, repair organizations, and technical support specialists whose reactions to new products have been sought.

Market researchers doing the use testing are very careful to pick the right number of stakeholders. Sample size may vary from three to six on experts, 30 or more for employees and from 20 to several thousand for end users. A joint operation between Whittle Communications and Philips Electronics bet $70 million on a use test for a medical news service via TV; it involved 6,000 physicians.[11] Windows 95 was apparently tested at thousands of sites.

As usual, sample size is primarily a function of what is being tested. Any sample should be representative of the entire population for which the product is targeted and the results should be accurate (have **validity**) and be reproducible (have **reliability**). A hair products firm marketed a new hair tonic for men, after use testing, and it flopped primarily because it was tested in humid areas of the country. In drier areas, the product evaporated too quickly to do the user any good.

3. Mode of Contact.   There are three pairs of options here. First is *mail* versus *personal*. The mail method is more limited than personal contact in type of product and depth of questioning, but it is more flexible, faster, and cheaper. Burlington Industries used the telephone to ask people to serve on special one-time mail panels that evaluated new fabrics. Business-to-business firms often insist on personal contact, since they need a closeness far beyond that on most consumer products.

Second, there is a choice between *individual* contact and *group* contact. Most firms prefer individual contact, especially at this critical point in the development cycle, but it may be cheaper to deal with groups. (The traditional focus group is not a place for *use* testing.)

Third, the individual mode of contact brings up the question of *location*. Should the test be conducted at the *point of use* (home, office, or factory), or should it be conducted at a *central location* (test kitchen, shopping center, theater, or van)? The point-of-use location is more realistic and permits more variables to operate. But it offers poor experimental control and permits easy misuse. In contrast, the central location offers very complete facilities (such as kitchens, two-way mirrors, eating areas, pseudo stores), good experimental control, speed, and lower

---

[11]Patrick M. Reilly, "Whittle, Philips Plan Interactive M.D. TV," *The Wall Street Journal*, June 26, 1992, p. B1.

cost. The central-location approach is winning out, but industrial firms will almost certainly stay with on-site studies. Sometimes one can be creative—TV networks test new pilot programs in Las Vegas, not at all representative of U.S. cities, but oddly, a place where a wide range of people have time and desire to look at pilots, between runs at the machines and tables.

4. Identity Disclosure.   A key issue concerns how much the user should be told about the brand or maker identity of the product. Some testers prefer open disclosure, while others (the majority) prefer to keep it secret. It may be that the brand cannot be hidden—as with many cars, some shoes, and many business products. Persons have perceptions about various firms and brands. Knowing a new item's brand introduces **halo-image effects**, maybe distorting user reactions. It helps to think about what is being tested. Developers may need a competitive comparison (only blind tests can determine this), or they may want to know if users *perceive* the new item to be better (honest perception requires brands).

A good compromise is to do both, first a blind test, followed by a branded test. This covers most of the issues. Service products can rarely be tested blind.

5. Degree of Explanation about Usage.   Some people conduct use tests with virtually *no comment* other than the obvious "Try this." But such tests run the risk of missing some of the specific testing needs. A second degree of explanation, called *commercial*, includes just the information the customer will get when actually buying the product later. The third level is *full explanation*. It may be necessary to include a great deal of information just to ensure the product gets used properly. Rolm gave Nissan's employees 90 days of training in the use test for its CallPath system. Some people do one round of testing with full explanation, followed by a brief round at the commercial level.

C. Testing Dimensions concerning Product Usage

6. Degree of Control over Use.   Most new medicines can be tested legally only under the control of physicians. This *total control* is essential when accurate data are required and when patient safety is a concern. Many industrial products also require total control to avoid dangerous misuse.

But most testers want users to experiment, to be free to make some mistakes, and to engage in behavior representative of what will happen later when the product is marketed. For example, a new blend of coffee may be tested under conditions of perfect water, perfect measuring, and perfect perking, but it should also be tested in the kitchen the way coffee preparers will do it—right or wrong.

So two modes of looser control—*supervised* and *unsupervised*—have developed. If a conveyor belt manufacturer wants to test a new type of belting material, company technical and sales personnel (maybe even their vendor's people) will be at the user's plant when the material is installed (supervised mode). After early runs indicate there are no mistakes, the belting people go back home, and the material is left to run in an unsupervised mode for the full testing period (though developer personnel are never very far away).

Services are almost always under some supervision because they cannot be "taken home" to use. Olga restaurants test new menus in a few locations (supervised mode) and then roll them out if everything works well.

7. *Singularity.*   The product may be tested in many combinations, but three ways are standard (see Figure 16–4):

- In a *monadic* test, where the respondent tests a single product for a period of time. Services usually must be monadic, though there are exceptions.
- In a *sequential monadic*, where there are back-to-back monadic tests with the same respondent.
  It is sometimes called a *staggered paired comparison*.
- In a *paired comparison*, where use of the test product is interspersed with that of a competitive product.

More sophisticated experimental designs exist, but they are only used in special situations. The monadic test is the simplest; it represents normal usage of products. But it is less sensitive in results. The usual *side-by-side*, or simultaneous form of paired comparison, is the most unrealistic test, but it is by far the most sensitive. A *sequential monadic* is probably the ideal combination, though it takes longer. In the staggered format, a user may try out a toothbrush for one week, then change to another for the second week, then go back to the first one.

FIGURE 16–4   Variations in Singularity as Applied to a New Toothbrush

Type	*Products*	*Instructions*
Monadic	The new product alone.	Try this new toothbrush, and tell me how you like it.
Paired comparison*	The new product and another toothbrush—(1) the market leader or (2) one known to be the best or (3) the leader in the segment selected for the new product or (4) the one currently used by the testee.	Try these, and tell me how you like them, which you prefer, etc.
Triangular*	The new product and two of the others. A variation is to use two variants of the new product and one of the others.	Same as on paired comparison.

*These multiple-product techniques can employ either of two product use approaches:

Side-by-side: Please brush your teeth with this toothbrush, and then brush again with the other one. Then give me your reactions.

Staggered (often called a sequential monadic): Please use this toothbrush for a week, and then switch to the other for a week. Then give me your reactions.

Even monadic tests usually involve a silent competitor—the product being used before the new one appeared. When an established category (such as photocopiers) is involved, then it is almost a must to test a new product against the category leader. But in the absence of an established category, as was the case with the first fax machine, what does the developer do? The first fax should have been tested against photocopying, overnight delivery, and/or the messenger service. If there is no direct predecessor, product developers usually just run a monadic test and then ask the user to compare the new product with whatever procedure was being followed before.

8. Duration of Use.   Some use tests require a *single* product experience (this may be all that is needed for a taste test), some require use over *short periods* of up to a week, and some require use over *extended periods* of up to six months. The longer period is needed if substantial learning is required (a shift in a paradigm) or if initial bias must be overcome. A longer period is also needed if the product faces a full range of variations in use (e.g., entertaining in the home, carelessness in the office, or high-pressure overtime in the plant). Again, researchers opt more often to use several modes. The initial, quick test predicts the early reactions of those people we call "innovators." Failure here, even if perceptions are unjustified, will often doom a good product. On the other hand, favorable initial impressions must be sustained well past the novelty stage. Many products have flared briefly before sputtering to an early death.

Tests over a month long are rare on consumer products and difficult to defend to management. But if a new piece of business equipment will be positioned on its cost-cutting advantage, the use test had better run long enough for the user to see a significant cost reduction. Incidentally, those long tests of paint panels in the fields along highways are lab tests, not use tests. There is no testing of user carelessness in application, thick versus thin paint coatings, and the many other variations one gets in a true home use test. Apple gets closer when they test PowerBooks with common indignities such as spilled soda, and simulated bouncing in a car trunk. But again, this is not true use testing, where customers are far more inventive of destructive ways.

D. *Testing Dimensions concerning the Product Itself*

9. Source of Product.   Generally speaking, three different sources of the product are employed in a use test—*batch*, *pilot plant*, and *final production*. If the firm will employ just one type of use testing, then the final production material is far and away the best. Batch product should be used alone only if the production process is prohibitively expensive.

As with many other phases of product development, the decision on source of product is a trade-off between the cost and value of information. Being penny-wise at this point has proven over and over to be pound-foolish.

Often overlooked is the product left in the hands of users at the end of the test. In most cases, the product should be collected and examined for clues about user problems and actions during the test. If a patent application will follow soon, it is very important to pick up *all* of the product; otherwise, developers risk losing the originality requirement of the patenting process.

10. Product Form.   One view favors testing the *best single product* the organization has developed. The opposing view favors building *variants* into the test situation—colors, speeds, sizes, and so on. The latter approach is more educational but also much more costly. Services are almost always tested in multiple variations, given that it is usually easy to make the changes.

The decision rests on several factors, the first being how likely the lead variant is to fail. No one wants to elaborately test one form of the product and then have that form fail.

Further, what effect will added variants have on users' understanding of the test? The more they test, the more they understand, and the more they can tell us. For example, a maker of aseptic packaging for fruit juices realized the juice and the package were both new to consumers, so the firm tested orange juice in the new package first and subsequently tested the new apple and cranberry juices. (Incidentally, the firm shipped the orange juice to its European factory for packaging so that it would spend the same time in the box as did the apple and cranberry juices.)

E. Testing Dimensions concerning Measurement and Analysis

11. Mode of Recording Reaction.   Essentially, three options are available, as demonstrated by Figure 16–5. First, a five- or seven-point verbal rating scale is generally used to record basic *like/dislike* data. Second, the respondent is usually asked to compare the new product with another product, say, the leader or the one currently being used, or both; this is a *preference score*, which can be obtained several ways. Third, for diagnostic reasons, testers usually want *descriptive information* about the product that covers any and all important attributes. Examples include taste, color, disposability, and speed. A semantic differential scale is the most common here. This is where we gather all of the other information called for in the objectives.

A research firm was involved in studying opportunities for a new sausage and had previously asked consumers to rate the sausage products then available on a variety of attributes, including greasiness and saltiness. The results showed strong aversions to both of those attributes, which were associated with low overall scores for product quality.

The researchers presumed from this response that the ideal sausage would have low levels of greasiness and saltiness, and several test products were developed accordingly. Needless to say, use testing proved just the opposite—the two top sausages in the test ranked first and second in saltiness, and they were among the greasiest. Some of the least-greasy test products had some of the lowest overall scores. We have come to expect the unexpected, and plan for it.

Marketing research has spawned a large group of exotic research methodologies found to be useful occasionally in new product testing. For example, brain

FIGURE 16–5

*Data Formats for
Product Use Tests
(samples selected
from the many
available)*

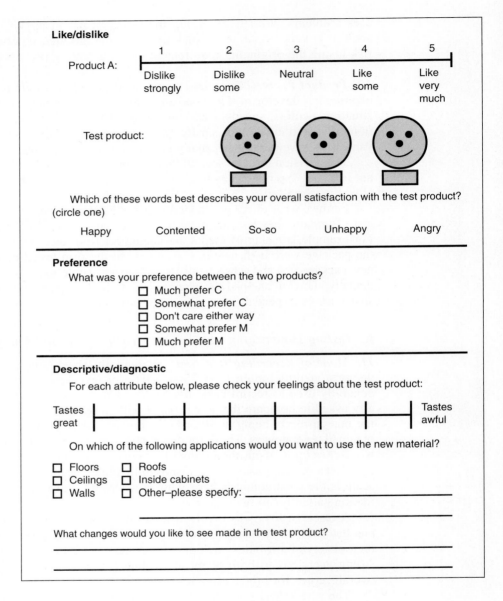

wave measurements help disclose users' inner thoughts, especially if they have a strong emotional reaction to the product being tested. Voice pitch analysis has been used to overcome product testers' efforts to be "helpful" and avoid hurting the tester's feelings. Galvanic skin response has been tried too.

One additional piece of information is very important at this point—intent to purchase. Recall that near the end of the concept test, we asked respondents how likely they thought they would be to try the product if it became available on the market (the top-two-boxes question). We have now asked them how well they liked the product and whether it was preferred to their currently used product. So again, we ask the buying intention question, this time as a measure of use test results, still not a predictor of actual trial rates.

In many *business* product use tests, the market research flavor of this section is missing. They want all relevant information, and get it by close personal investigations and observations. Users may find applications the developers didn't even think of. There are few formal questionnaires in evidence.[12]

12. *Source of Norms.* Testers have long realized that they want *comparative* figures, not just *absolutes*. That is, if 65 percent of the users liked a product, how does that percentage compare with previous tests of somewhat similar items? If previous winners all scored over 70 percent on the "like" question, then our 65 percent isn't very impressive.

The 70 percent figure is a **norm**. Where we get norms and how we use them is often a serious question. The major source is obvious—the library of past experiences, thoroughly studied and averaged. The files of marketing research supplier firms are also helpful, but norms pulled from the air at committee meetings are virtually worthless.

13. *Research Service.* The first option is between personnel *within* the company and personnel *outside* the company; the firm may or may not have the necessary personnel skilled in information technology analytical capability.

Second, the *functions* (marketing, technical), historically, have jockeyed for control. Today, however, we have the development team be responsible—the same team that handled the prototype concept testing. If vendor personnel are members of such teams, then they too participate.

Special Problems

Some special ideas holding the attention of veteran new products people run through all product use testing situations.

Don't Change the Data Just because They Came Out Wrong. One firm discovered a user problem in a use test but the president said, "They're just going to have to live with it." Unfortunately, the use test did not ask whether users were *willing* to live with it. They weren't, and the product failed. In many tests technical and marketing people warn of user problems only to be told that they are being negative. (Kill the messenger?)

---

[12]A review of some practice along these lines is Aimee L. Stern, "Testing Goes Industrial," *Sales and Marketing Management*, March 1991, pp. 30–38.

Be Alert to Strange Conditions.   One industrial firm noticed that several electrical measuring instruments showed signs of tampering after a field test. On examination, they found users were making a particular change to aid the product's function; after a few telephone calls, they had an improved product design ready to go out for more testing.

What If We Have to Go Ahead without Good Use Testing?   Try to work some use testing into the early marketing stages (e.g., in the rollout method discussed in Chapter 21) and try to have some alternatives ready to switch to as a hedge against negative outcomes.

Summary

Chapter 16 has dealt with the issues of whether a product solves customer problems, how it compares to other products in this regard, and what else can be learned about it at this stage. Getting this type of information would seem critical, but strong pressures are exerted to skip product use testing. We talked about the arguments for skipping and showed why they should be followed only when overpowering.

That paved the way for discussion of the 13 dimensions of product use tests, ranging from "What we want to learn from the test" to "Who should conduct it?" Each dimension has several options, and selecting from among them usually follows an analysis of the situation.

At the end of the testing, the product may have to be routed back into technical work to resolve problems, or it may be dropped. Otherwise, we now proceed to commercialization and the preparation of finished product, which, of course, is just a later version of the concept going into the greatest use test of all: marketing. Marketing is the topic of Chapters 17–19.

Applications

More questions from that interview with the company president.

1. "That story in your book about NCR and the inventory management system is awesome. It seems to say that NCR was never interested in finding out whether their new product actually met customer needs or not! Guess they were under terrible pressure—maybe on cash flow, competitors, or something. Looking through your list of 13 decisions, where did they actually fall down—was it just on duration?"

2. "I think some research suppliers oversell a bit—they want us to do too much market research. For example, one of the biggest firms published data on a 'blind' versus 'identified' product test. Here are the results:

Branded		*Unbranded*	
Prefer A	55.5%	Prefer A	45.6%
Prefer B	44.5	Prefer B	54.4
Prefer A	68.0	Prefer A	60.7
Prefer C	32.0	Prefer C	39.3
		Prefer B	64.4
		Prefer C	35.6

I'm told the differences were highly significant statistically. The research firm concluded that there was no choice *between* blind and identified but that both should be used in just about every case where there was any reason to even suspect an effect of branding. Do you agree?"

3. "We recently acquired a small toy company, and I'm scheduled to meet with their management next week. I know they really don't do much use testing—I think someone told me they have a bunch of kids come to their plant and play with proposed toys. Must work for them, we paid a huge multiple for their stock. What should I tell them, or be looking for, relative to your list of 13 decisions?"

4. "Our pharmaceutical division, of course, develops new pharmaceutical products for use by doctors and hospitals. The technical research department does all the testing (they have different names for the various tests). The last phase is clinical testing, where the drugs are given to humans in a manner that will substantiate claims made to the Food and Drug Administration. The clinical tests are conducted by M.D.'s in the clinical research section, which is in our R&D department along with all the other technical people. Now it seems to me those clinical tests are designed to satisfy more people than just the FDA—physicians, pharmacists, nurses, and so on. But M.D.'s in clinical testing are not too high on marketing research-type thinking, so it dawned on me that I should see that at least one thoroughly trained marketing research person was assigned to clinical research—to help me make sure the clinicals have maximum impact later in marketing. Do you agree?"

CASE: MOUNTAIN DEW SPORT

In 1989, PepsiCo was about ready to enter the isotonic beverage market. Product had been decided upon, financing was approved, marketing strategy was decided, and the firm planned to market test its new product in Eau Clair, Wisconsin, a BehaviorScan market of Information Resources Inc. The brand chosen was Mountain Dew Sport. At issue now was whether the product was indeed right for this market. Decisions had to be made on how to conduct product use tests. To date, employees using the company fitness center had been given samples of

Source: This case is prepared from many public information sources.

Mountain Dew Sport to drink and had given their opinions. But the firm also wanted reactions from their intended market users, so a full product testing plan needed to be decided.

The isotonic market came into being in 1965 when Dr. Robert Cade, a nephrologist for the University of Florida football team, invented a beverage he used for "optimal" fluid replacement to provide energy for the football players and to stabilize their blood sugar levels. He took the name Gatorade from the team's nickname.

Years later he sold his product to Stokely-Van Camp, which was then acquired by Quaker Oats Company. Quaker added national distribution and aggressive marketing effort; the result was a $500 million business, indicating sustained consumer demand for the product and a tremendous opportunity for other beverage firms.

PepsiCo had developed an internal strategy that called for creation of new products in beverage categories outside of its traditional carbonated soft drink business. It was stipulated that any such product should utilize the firm's existing bottling and distribution network.

The development of the product had been largely a matter of formulation and brand development, since the Gatorade business had been established many years before. For formulation, PepsiCo studied Gatorade and then made certain modifications to yield a product they thought would be more appealing. The new item would come in both bottles and cans, the glass bottle had a larger opening (for quicker drinking), and there were slightly different levels of carbonation, sweetness, sodium, and mineral nutrient contents.

The firm apparently felt that the strength of the market made concept testing unnecessary, so the only prescreening was done with Pepsi-Cola marketing managers and senior executives. Emphasis was put on branding, packaging, and labeling issues, more than product formula.

Meanwhile, in the marketplace, there had been double-digit growth in Gatorade, and usage was spreading from teams to individuals, many of whom were working out alone. Distribution was primarily through the grocery trade, but PepsiCo would bring distribution also to convenience stores, petroleum stores, and the thousands of vending machines scattered at public parks, school athletic fields, and so on.

There were a few small competitors—Snapple Natural Beverage Company, Sports Beverage Inc., and PowerBurst Corporation—but Quaker controlled 90 percent of the market. Quaker was large, of course, with revenue of $5 billion, but PepsiCo was a $15 billion company. The typical buyer of Gatorade was an 18–34-year-old athletic male, concerned with replenishing his body fluids and minerals after a strenuous workout. Users were in all income and demographic categories. Drinks were generally bought and consumed on a single bottle basis, not six-packs.

Information about Mountain Dew Sport indicated that it would replenish fluids and key nutrients, have a formulation of carbonation, sodium, and sweetness that would interact well with body chemistry, be appealing in color and taste, packaged to speed up individual usage, priced at competitive levels, and in packaging that was recyclable.

The strategy called for hitting a slightly different user segment. In an effort to broaden the market for its product, PepsiCo expanded the targeting of isotonics to include all "sweaty" occasions. This included tennis and golf players, persons mowing the lawn, construction workers, and anyone else working up a sweat on the job.

Mountain Dew Sport seemed to be positioned as a quick, thirst-quenching beverage for all sweaty occasions, designed to replace lost fluids and nutrients through a sweeter, better-tasting formula, with just a touch of carbonation (which Gatorade did not have).

Given the highly competitive nature of the market, it was important that the new drink be marketed quickly. Plans were made to roll out from the BehaviorScan market test as soon as things looked OK there.

But, at the moment, the issue of use testing was on the table.

Twin Streams—The Simultaneous Evolution of the Product and Its Marketing Plan

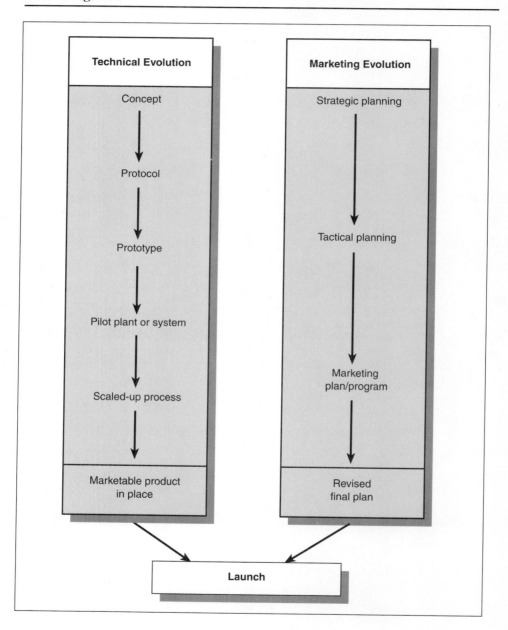

V   MARKETING

For the full length of the technical development process (which runs through the market launch), a parallel activity continues on the so-called business side of the firm, particularly marketing. The intensity is less early on, and there may be long periods of almost total inactivity as technical work gets hung up somewhere. However, a launch marketing plan gradually begins to take shape right alongside the gradually evolving technical form. This parallel activity has been called the Twin Streams, and is shown on the opposite page. It is a portion of the Triple Streams driving concept you met in Chapter 2.

Somewhere in that process, management becomes convinced that the new product should be marketed. This starts what is usually called the **commercialization stage**. The term comes from "commercializing" a technical invention, and it overlaps Part IV, "Technical Development," and Part V, "Marketing." All of the functions (engineering, production, marketing, etc.) are working before and after the commercialization decision. The change is often triggered by a commitment to produce the new item, and to risk the high costs of building a plant. During commercialization, marketing activity picks up intensity.

But remember that marketing actually begins near the start of the project. The product innovation charter calls for a market focus—usually a particular use or user that will eventually become our target market. After concept generation, concept testing uses a concept statement that soon will turn into our product positioning statement. But marketing activities cool for a while after that until technical can come up with a prototype that seems to show it meets the protocol statement of requirements (see Chapter 12). Of course, this sketch of the development/marketing period does not match most service products—on them, there is far less technical development work, and the whole thing telescopes dramatically.

The next five chapters deal with marketing activity both before and during the commercialization period. Launch-planning decisions use all of the previous activity, and a great deal of new thinking and testing, to build eventually toward launch capability. Launch planning has one phase where all of the previous work is organized, a second phase—called strategic launch planning—where the strategic decisions of marketing are made, a third phase where the tactical matters are decided, and a fourth stage where the strategic and tactical decisions are tested in the marketplace. These topics are the subject of Chapters 17, 18, 19, 20, and 21. A fifth stage (Chapter 22) is added to Part V because its planning is done at the same time and it concerns the postannouncement period: **launch control**, or managing the new product to success.

A final launch-plan is built from *five sets of decisions*, made somewhat in sequence. (See Figure V–1.) They are as follows. First, any new products team must accept some givens. That is, the firm has an established operation—one or more sales forces, a financial situation, and so on. Teams can skirt some of these limitations, but not all of them. So the first "decisions" are not really decisions in the voluntary sense; they are called **strategic givens**.

Second, there is another set of conditions that *are* decisions, but they have been put into place early on and won't be changed (without a fight) when launch planning starts. Specifically, the PIC probably called for a form of leadership (first-to-market, follower, etc.) and that has been achieved. For another, the firm may have a strong commitment to speed, in which case leisurely test markets are probably out of the question. Because these issues often appear in the PIC, they are called **guideline decisions**.

Third, the marketing planners will make a set of **strategic decisions** on matters where there are options; these are difficult and often critical. Some constitute a set called **strategic platform strategies** because they set the stage for action, and others constitute a set of **strategic driving decisions**; the latter drive the tactics.

Fourth, many **tactical decisions** must be made, though in this book we will have to concentrate on the most important of these.

FIGURE V–1

The Five Decision Sets That Lead to a Marketing Plan

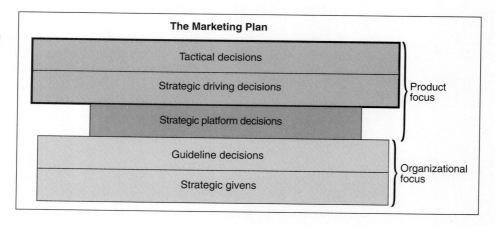

Chapter 17 deals with the strategic givens and guideline decisions, Chapter 18 with the two types of strategic decisions, and Chapter 19 with the tactics. Be warned, of course, that terms in the new products field are flexible, and one person's tactic is another person's strategy and still another person's given.

During commercialization, people are *buying* machinery rather than *estimating its cost*, finalizing sales call schedules, registering brands, locking in R&D specifications, and spending money. There are more and more people involved, with coordination meetings, massive information accumulation, greatly elevated risks and tempers, euphorias and disappointments, security problems, politics, and a far-too-attentive top management. Costs run higher than anticipated, market test results are unclear, competitors begin to hear of the development and do unexpected things, and some packaging machinery is a couple months late, making premature the announcement of the firm's ability to make delivery to customers. Near-panic has set in, and it will not cease for some time.

Closing out Part V is a chapter on public policy issues. These are with us throughout the process, but they come to the fore at time of launch and thereafter.

One caution is appropriate: Chapters 17–19 cover an activity that many people do not understand. They *think* they do, and some of them are actually in marketing departments. Our problem is not that people draw a blank—blanks are easy to fill in. Instead, we suffer from the existence of many myths—conditions *people think exist but do not*. Figure V–2 lists 11 of these myths. I encourage you to keep these in mind, and perhaps refer to them from time to time. As you read the next three chapters, see if you can find what makes each one a myth. Check your answers with those at the end of the Chapter 19 case.

FIGURE V–2   Some Common Myths about Marketing Planning for New Products

---

Here are some statements that we often hear around people who have not done much new product marketing. All are myths, as explained at different places in Chapters 17–19. See if you can figure out the reasons on your own, and then check your answers with those at the end of Chapter 19.

1. Marketing people make the decisions that constitute a marketing plan.
2. The technical work is essentially complete when the new item hits the shipping dock. Marketing people take over.
3. It's important that marketing people be required to use strategy-tactics paradigms. Clear thinking helps rein in their excess exuberance and excitement.
4. The marketer's task is to persuade the end user to use our new product.
5. The more sales potential there is in a market segment, the better that segment is as a target candidate.
6. The PIC guides the development stage and the marketing plan guides the marketing stage.
7. The pioneer wins control of a new market.
8. A new product's goals are of two general types: sales (dollars or shares) and profits (dollars or ROIs).
9. People generally are pretty smart buyers—they will not be influenced by meaningless package designs.
10. A launch is no game—when we say go, that's it, sink or swim, and it had better be swim.
11. As with Broadway shows, opening night is the culmination of everything we have been working for.

---

17 THE TASK OF STRATEGIC LAUNCH PLANNING

Setting

Given the conditions just described in the introduction to Part V (and you should go back to read it if you missed it), it is necessary to draw together all of the thinking that has preceded commercialization. We look at what has to be done, and try to organize the activity. Focus is on those things that will best guide our strategists in their work.

Nature of the Launch Plan Development Process

The first question is obvious—who will do this planning work? The answer varies from firm to firm, but practice is now closing in on using pretty much the same team that has been active in the technical work. The composition of a new products team will change over the life of the project, but the core set of functions remains—technical, manufacturing, marketing, and finance. This core team will finalize all marketing decisions, including target market, positioning, key prices, etc. But most of the analytical work and creative design of marketing actions will be done by a cluster of marketing managers—from advertising agency, to marketing researcher, to product manager, to sales manager, and so on.

If there is a team czar (otherwise known as a leader, manager, or facilitator), the first leader was probably technical, though not with service products. Many new product teams (e.g., 3M and Honda) are managed first by engineers and scientists, and Honda lets that person continue through launch and into on-going operations. Others prefer to change at the point of commercialization and put a marketing person in charge. Consumer packaged goods firms, historically, gave team leadership to marketing brand managers at the very beginning, but Nabisco is leading a change to partnership between technical and marketing from the start through to launch.

The important thing is to have heavy marketing input, primarily because marketing will guide the implementation of the plan. The launch plan itself may be called a business plan, but more commonly it is the marketing plan or marketing program. In today's business, the marketing plan is recognized as a plan for the full business activity of launch; that's why full-function teams are essential. But this is not the place to discuss plans. Instead, Appendix D contains an outline of a marketing plan and a discussion of some aspects of it.

A second issue about the nature of launch planning is that it is not at all the neat, sequenced set of decisions implied by this and the following two chapters. It might be nice if one group made big, strategic decisions, and another group then made mid-sized, somewhat-strategic decisions. . . down to the nitty-gritty tactical decisions such as how big a booth the new item warrants at the introductory trade show. It won't happen this way, and it shouldn't. The quality of one tactical advertising decision may make or break the new product. Anyway, the sequenced process would never end in time for the item to go to market, not with any product uniqueness anyway.

Likewise, you may see the process as going from general management, to product line management, to product managers, or from general management to functional managers. Today, and in the leading firms for many years, it doesn't work that way. There is continuous up and down—in fact, new product planners complain constantly about the interference from top management, especially at the very point of announcement. And there is continuous interplay between functions. That's why we have multidisciplinary teams.

Relationships Marketing

Another key player during launch is the end user. Or, more correctly, the full set of stakeholders in the marketplace who will determine whether the new product gets a fair trial. You may recall that we have talked about the fact that end user involvement is desirable throughout the new product process. These users and other stakeholders should also participate in launch planning, and to help assure this, many firms have adopted **relationships marketing**.

The marketing plan should create in the marketplace the same tight cooperation that technical people have used during development. But this is apt to be tough for a new product, especially when the chosen market segment has had no previous connection with the firm. So such relationships must be built, through advertising and selling, yes, but also through service, through involving them in the selling process, and though considering their reaction to everything we do—pricing, packaging, branding: the full set. This means **bonding**, it means asking their reaction to what we plan to do (if time and competitive conditions permit), and it means following their early use of the product through to satisfaction with it.

This is sometimes called **interactive marketing**, and firms are finding surprising ways of doing it. For example, a study of how banks market new trust services showed clients react positively to being asked to play a role as co-producer. They *want* to participate, and they expect to be asked to help determine the exact new service they will buy.[1]

The Strategic Givens

See the Part V opening illustration for clarification on how strategic givens relate to the other decisions needed in the launch planning activity. Since these tend to "come with the territory" when a project is undertaken, we tend to forget them and their importance. They cover the full range of the organization's operations, and are often "set in concrete" without our knowing it. They form that awful "resistance to change" which new products people frequently lament about. In fact, they are such a problem that top managements often set up venture groups or skunkworks, organizational forms supposedly immune from the restrictions that are endemic to the firm.

Some of the most common examples of problems we have with these givens are indicated in the following examples. Scott Paper company was the proud owner of a huge, efficient paper production facility. Though nowhere in writing, it turned out that no new product project (at that time) had a chance if it did not require use of that facility. Sybron Corporation had a division in the dental furniture business; the division desperately needed new cash flow, and they had a new (and unique, superior) chair ready to go. But the corporation had a mandatory 50 percent gross margin requirement that the division product planners were sure would be waived when management saw the new chair. It wasn't, even when the gross margin came in at 47 percent. The division collapsed.

Sometimes the given comes from an individual—a strong member of upper management whose personal druthers become corporate law. A firm in the ethical drug products field had a sales manager totally committed to an indirect channel of drug outlet distribution. Ostensibly this practice fit the firm and the industry, but a new products team came up with a nutritional product that also showed potential in the grocery products channel. The team was hoping for dual-channel distribution, but had to sacrifice several millions of dollars in their product plan in the name of the $30 million protected by the wholesaler-only channel policy. Only after two years of frustration was the policy waived—the new product produced more revenue than the rest of the firm combined!

Other examples of these operational understandings show up in relations with regulatory authorities, in ethical postures, in advertising policies, in centralized (or decentralized) manufacturing facilities, in geographical preferences,

---

[1]Karen Karu File, Benn B. Judd, and Russ Alan Prince, "Interactive Marketing: The Influence of Participation on Positive Word-of-Mouth and Referrals," *The Journal of Services Marketing*, Fall 1992, pp. 5–14. Two overall looks at relationships and interactive marketing are: Martin Everett, "It's No Fluke," *Sales & Marketing Management*, April 1994, pp. 47–52; and Dean Tjosvold and Choy Wong, "Working with Customers: Cooperation and Competition in Relational Marketing," *Journal of Marketing Management*, 1994, pp. 297–310.

in pricing policies, and in almost every phase of the entire operation. One often forgotten is the firm's posture toward brand names. Many firms today realize that their brand names are among the biggest assets they have. This is **brand equity**, or the asset value of brands. If this is how the firm sees brand names, much more effort must be put into handling line extensions and new brands that compete with present brands.

If these restrictions are really important and recognized in advance, they are put into the PIC guidelines (see the guideline decisions below). But some items here called givens are far more subtle, perhaps not even recognized as firm, perhaps being held to for reasons that new products people don't even know about. Many are pure and simple habit, convenient and comfortable routines.

The point is, they need to be identified and studied. If the launch team wants to challenge such restrictions, fine, but they should do so early and should be prepared to lose. Ultimately, as company organizations are now changing, most of these restrictions will yield. They are silo or chimney holdings, and the horizontal management philosophy of today is designed to bypass just such restrictions.

The Guideline Decisions

Some of the conditions identified above as givens are not that subtle. They are matters where a clear decision needs to be made. Such decisions serve across the entire strategic launch operation—they form a base for all strategic decisions. Their value is that they are made first, as early in the planning as possible. They are so powerful and influential that reversing one can cause havoc all across the planning team. They have often been thought of as the type of decision made at corporate level by a strategic market planning group.

Seven of the more common ones will be discussed here.

Market Concentration

Here there are five alternatives: Total market, market segment, microsegmentation/niche, multiple segments (one item for each), and mass customization. **Total market** is infrequently chosen by firms developing new products today. There are too many competitors focusing on segments of the market, and nothing will appeal to all customers.

Segmentation and **microsegmentation/niche** are variations that are the most popular. The only difference between them is the relative size of the segment that a new products manager selects to focus on.

Multiple segments is an advanced form of micro in that the firm tries to have a line of products, with one item for each segment. This is a policy question at the corporate strategic level and will affect all new product programs.

Mass customization is micro carried to the extreme. It is a policy that prepares the firm to offer individualized new products to any person/firm in the market at the time of purchase. It usually involves modularization, as in the case of the Korean bicycle manufacturer who asks retail buyers to fill out a request form for the set of features they want; that particular combination of bicycle parts is assembled and delivered to the store within 10 days. Motel operators such as Marriott Courtyard offer regular customers a chance to put their room requirements into the computer—a room of the desired type is set aside for each registered guest prior to the day of arrival.

To show the importance of the difference here, mass customization actually forces the development of product **process capability** at the time of purchase, not actual new products. It's more of a service.

Leadership Posture

To new products people, there are four leadership posture choices: market leader, market follower, market challenger, or nicher. A **market leader** doesn't have to be a pioneer, but develops an innovation that will propel the firm into leadership shortly. The **market follower** (1) may plan to improve on the pioneer's product very rapidly (called quick second) or more slowly or (2) may slash production costs and go for the price buyers. A **market challenger** is usually new in a market and will aggressively challenge for a leadership (or major share) position. The new product will be unique. A **nicher** is none of these things, or all of them—the firm is simply focusing on a small piece of the market and may have a specially designed product or simply one positioned for that segment. See Figure 17–1 for a picture of these strategies competing. Which of the four types is missing and how do you know?

Product/Market Matrix

This is the traditional strategic market planning matrix discussed in Chapter 4 on product innovation charters. The options are to have a **product improvement** (for the current product to current customers), a **market penetration** (an improved product that will take added share in the current market), a **new market development** (where we want new customers and/or uses for our current product), or a **diversification** (a new product going into markets we are not now in.)

Strategic Integration

Sometimes a launch plan does not truly stand alone. It may have specific goals set for it, but the firm wants something else from it. Specifically, does the new product's launch **stand alone,** or is it to lead to **something else such as a bridge** to another market. Not only do the goals change—many other dimensions do also. For years Japanese TV manufacturers entered European markets not with the intention to maximize profits, but to gain the manufacturing volume that would lower unit costs. The lower costs then permitted them to enter the U.S. TV market with a low-price policy.

FIGURE 17–1

*Several Styles
of Running.
Who wins?*

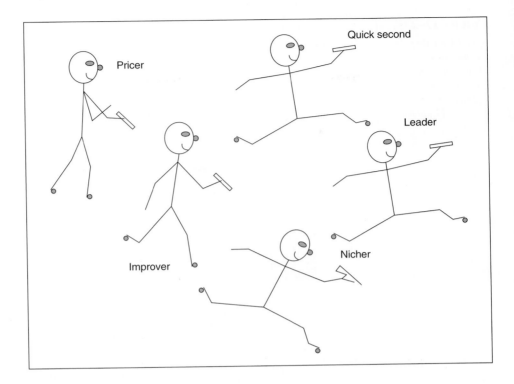

Speed of Market Entry

Speed is such a popular management tool today that everyone assumes the development phase is being pushed as fast as can be. Naturally, there are exceptions, such as new-to-the-world technologies; in those cases everything must await the hoped-for technical breakthrough. But generally, the word is rush, rush. The marketing phase can be speeded up too. (See Figure 17–2.) Therefore, the launch plan should have a speed guideline decision, from among these four options: **No emphasis** on speed, prelaunch **speed to launch date**, postlaunch **speed to success**, or **pre-** and **postlaunch speed**.

Production Requirements

Few things are as disappointing as to see a company parking lot piled high with unshipped boxes of a new product. But one of them is to see a production department shut down for want of product parts while the accounting department holds millions of dollars in unfilled orders.

   Underforecasting can be very costly, partly from lost sales when customers switch, but partly also from the very expensive catch-up production that will follow. Throughout much of 1995 Apple was unable to fill some of the orders for its PowerBook, a profit-eating situation that threatened the job of its CEO.

FIGURE 17–2

Speed Can Be Gained in Marketing Too (When the Goal Is Success, Not Just the Launch).

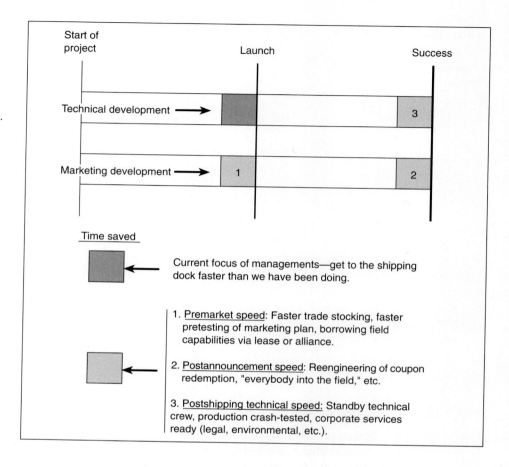

Furthermore, the nature of the buying process may require that customers never be without access to product (e.g., in a hospital system that converts to the new item). Because of variations like this, it is a good idea to get a guideline decision between **production available to all at the very start**, or **no interruptions of supply once established**, or **normal supply requirements.** Trade-off between these options should not be placed on the shoulders of production department planners.

Goods/Service Mix

New products once were classified as products or services. A product was tangible, a service was not. Of course, they never were all one or the other, but today we see new items being so clearly combinations of goods and services that we now classify them as **primarily a good, primarily a service**, or **half and half**. Occasionally there is a product that is **almost totally tangible** or **almost totally**

intangible. The distinction may appear obvious to you, but it isn't all that obvious to managers involved in the activity. Biased perspectives abound!

Goals

The product innovation charter gives a basic set of goals that have been leading the team to this point. They were dollar and nondollar, and that set may still be complete. But, usually much has been learned in the development process, competitive conditions have changed, and management needs have changed. Therefore, early in the launch-planning process, the goals should be revisited and updated.

Unfortunately, business firms use a complex set of measures as goals, and research to date has not been able to find a recommended set.[2] The most used set of measures for individual products is as follows (from lists numbering in the hundreds):

Customer Acceptance Measures
- Customer acceptance (use)
- Customer satisfaction
- Revenue (dollar sales)
- Market share
- Unit volume

Financial Performance
- Time to break even
- Margins
- Profitability (IRR, ROI)

Product Level Performance
- Product cost
- Time to launch
- Product performance
- Quality guidelines

Other
- Nonfinancial measures peculiar to the new product being launched. Example: competitive effect, image change, and morale change.

Regardless of how measures are expressed, there should be absolutely no doubt in the minds of any launch planners about what the launch is to produce or achieve.

The Strategic Core of the Launch

Many people (from members of the board of directors, to agency copywriters, to distribution directors) will be asking one question that must be answered: What, in a nutshell, is the core strategy of this launch? They don't want details, but they must in one way or another integrate their thinking with that of others.

The **core strategy statement** ideally identifies the intended customer segment (target market), positioning (how our item is better than others being used),

---

[2]Abbie Griffin and Albert L. Page, "An Interim Report on Measuring Product Development Success and Failure," *Journal of Product Innovation Management*, September 1993, pp. 291–308.

and what particular mix of marketing tools will be used to carry the message. As example is:

> The new PC computer repair service will be marketed to *large organizations with multiple locations*, for whom our *100 percent global* availability will be stressed. We will primarily use a *personal selling approach* to reach, and serve, these customers, backed up by *publicity* and some *announcement advertising in general business magazines.*

Such core strategy statements are sometimes heard on elevators when a president asks a new product manager the strategic plan for a new item. Unless the building is very tall, that product manager must get to the core fast.

Here is another example: "We've got a product that works, but customers won't easily believe it. Such items have failed in the past. So the key to our success is getting them to try it, to see for themselves whether it works. No advertising or sales call can do that, so we are relying on a mailing of free product to every class A customer."

Another example: "This market is a zoo. Noise dominates. There is no way we could afford to take this slightly better product through that noise, so we have focused in on a small market segment of people who use another product of ours. We will work with them until we have the success that can be moved out to other customers."

Another example: "Our strategy, short and simple, is price. We have the lowest cost of all players, and we are hitting the big users with deals they cannot refuse. We will have this chance for only about four months, so we are hitting with all of the promotion our budget allows."

Another example: "In a nutshell, we must become teachers. Our new product is a breakthrough, but it is complex. Either we can explain what it is and how it works, or we're dead. We're not sure we can do that, so we're going to roll it out to our best customers first and stay with them until we find out how."

Gillette sold razors in order to get us to buy his blades. Anheuser-Busch sold Eagle snacks to keep their key beer distributors happier with the account. Hallmark marketed a line of small gifts so their small gift shop owners could build up profits, and thus stay in business. 3M found that Post-it notes had to be seen to be appreciated, so they sampled it widely, in places that would give great visibility.

If the team cannot spell out one of these core launch strategy statements, then chances are they are not ready to prepare the plan.

Mini-Plans

A new product is not marketed just to end users. From the beginning of the project the team has been aware of a set of stakeholders out there, people whose attitudes or practices contribute to product adoption by the end user. This set includes resellers of all types, advisers of all types (medical, architectural, consultants, and many more), service firms (product evaluation, installations, training, maintenance, financing), regulators, and many more. Within the family, we know that food products may have a specifier, a buyer, a preparer, a user, a disposer, and

FIGURE 17–3

A Marketing Plan Has Many Mini-Plans

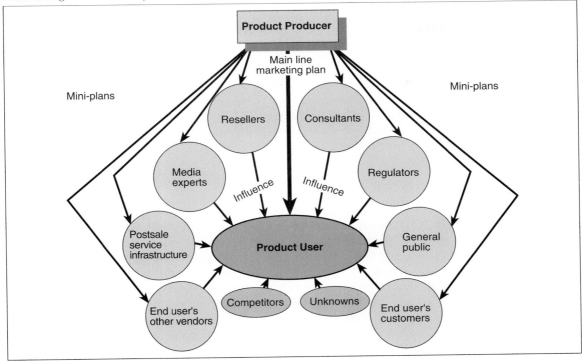

more. These are not all the same person. Even within the family we have advisers and commenters. Outside the family we have co-workers, etc., etc.

The launch team will need to develop several key **mini-marketing plans**—plans designed to bring a key adviser or distributor on board. (See Figure 17–3.) This is always complex, but think of the telecommunications field today, or worse perhaps, think of writing a launch plan for a new computer operating system designed to displace part of the worldwide Windows 95 market. How many mini-plans would be necessary?

Marshalling Internal Support

One set of mini-plans involves groups within the firm, and the act of creating them and implementing them is called **internal marketing**. Under normal circumstances, particularly if there is a multifunctional team guided by a product innovation charter, getting support "around the firm" is possible. But other departments have their own agenda. So an internal marketing program is advisable. It starts with a scan of the full internal support system, with a candid look at every person or group whose work is critical to success. Are they currently capable? Can they be made capable? Where are the turf restraints and the bureaucratic bulwarks?[3]

Technical

The team doing the marketing is well prepared to work on technical product verification (support of claims), technical information for labels, packages, package inserts, selling literature, and training of key personnel. Problems, if there are any, probably relate to shortage of key people who are busy on other projects. Technical people should be asked to prepare answers for questions that will flow from expected competitive responses.

Manufacturing

Work here has also been underway for some time, depending on when a firm makes its commercialization decision. The manufacturing process may be finished and in place, or still unfolding. Marketers are interested in products that meet technical claims, that meet quality standards, and that are ready when shipment is to begin.

But they are also looking ahead: for possible cost reductions, for example, for scheduled improvements and line extensions, and for information in response to questions from the field. Perhaps most important, arrangements should be made on what will be done if something goes haywire about the product itself or if the production line breaks down. A New England firm making a multilayered industrial fabric blanket found that the blankets tended to come apart after being used for several months. They shouldn't have—they were well tested. But when they did split, experienced production people had a standby procedure ready to start up; one of them said, "On a new technical item like that, we just assume something will go wrong." Marketing people are very anxious that this attitude be present in their launch too.

Packaging

Many goods require little packaging, and most services have none. But packaging is apt to be very important, especially when the new item will be distributed through self-service environments, when the product category is already established so the new item will have to force its way in, and when many strongly entrenched competitors sit next to one another on store shelves.

---

[3]For more on this subject see Walter E. Greene, Gary D. Walls, and Larry J. Schrest, "Internal Marketing: The Key to External Marketing Success," *The Journal of Services Marketing* 8, no. 4 (1994), pp. 5–13.

Decisions about packaging are often made at the highest levels in the firm. More money is spent on packaging food and beverage products than on advertising them.

What Is Packaging?   Three "containers" are usually included in the term packaging, and some variations exist on those. **Primary packaging** is the material that first envelopes the product and holds it, perhaps a bottle for pills or a polyethylene bag for a computer CPU.

Secondary packaging is outside of a primary package. It may gather a group of primary packages and holds them for transportation or display, or it may be a cardboard box that holds the pill bottle.

Tertiary packaging is the bulk packaging that holds secondary packages for shipment—the large cardboard box or the pallet, for example.

The Various Roles of Packaging.   The various roles for packaging are easy to see. The major ones are **containment** (hold for transporting), **protection** (from the elements and the careless), **safety** (from causing injury), **display** (to attract attention and **inform** and **persuade**). All are important to a new products manager, sometimes enough so that there are legal problems; packaging design is a part of logo and trademark, where rights can be valuable.

But there are other roles. For example, **assisting the user** in some way— with instructions (pharmaceuticals or food) and with a use function (beer cans and deodorant dispensers). At other times packages are designed to permit reusability, meet ecological demands on biodegradability, carry warnings, and meet other legal requirements. They may aid disposability.

The Packaging Decision.   Packaging is part of the new product manager's network. But it is so multifunctional it tends to have its own subnetwork (see Figure 17–4). It centers on a person most often called the director of packaging. The packaging decision may take months; it is a key target in most accelerated development programs.

Each company tends to develop a somewhat unique approach to packaging, but there are common steps. First, a packaging person is put on a new products team. Field trips are mandatory, as is access to the various market studies that have been made. A unique packaging approach for Pfeiffer's salad dressing was found when a packaging staffer visited supermarkets and noted that salad dressings were displayed by type rather than by brand; most competitive bottles were shaped like whisk brooms with flatiron heads.

The process for package development resembles that for the product itself. Tests include dummy packages, in-store displays, color tests, visual tests, psychographic tests, physical tests, distribution tests, warehouse legibility, and even some in-store selling tests. For example, 96 women out of 100 chose a pink cosmetic package over an otherwise identical yellow one. In another case, a cosmetic firm tripled sales when it changed from a blue package to a yellow package. Almost without exception, people will buy food products with circles on them

FIGURE 17–4

*Packaging
Network*

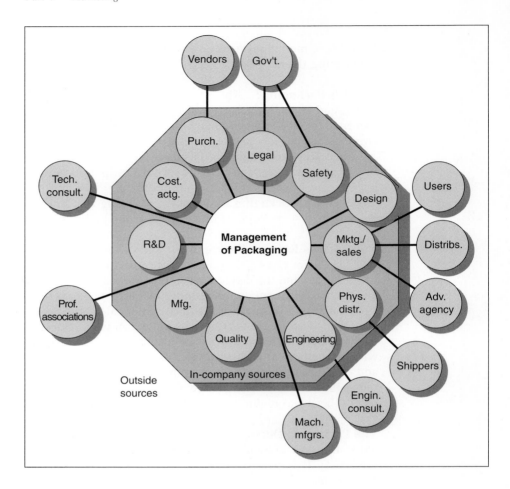

over similar products with triangles on them. They will also say the circle products taste better or work better, even when contents are identical. Packaging can be very powerful.

Human Resources

For the typical new product launch, key personnel are scattered all over, from technical to sales. They are selected, assigned, trained, and motivated in the routine ways of a firm. But when it comes to commercialization, it behooves a new products manager to scan the internal horizon. Not every position will be filled with capable people. Not all of these are well trained. And since most of them have conflicting tasks and leaders, the new products manager has to put on the champion hat. Good contacts with the human resources department are invaluable in this work.

Others

The legal department must respond to the law. Safety directors do the same, as do the environmental staff except that they also have political and pressure groups. Physical distribution people deal with government regulations, union regulations, fixed tariffs, and more.

Mistakes

The last act of preparation for making the required strategic decisions is a reminder that some new products managers often talk about. It concerns mistakes, and their desire not to make them. This is not the evasive action of a weak new product manager. Rather, as one put it, "We have a tough job, so at least I don't want to shoot myself in the foot!"

Summary

Chapter 17, the first of a three-chapter launch planning set, covered that mix of things required for strategic decisions in the launch plan. It discussed the nature of the launch planning process and the role of relationships marketing and the people who will do the work.

But, most important, the chapter dealt with a set of strategic givens—restraints imposed on the planning team by the on-going company operation. It also explained a set of guideline decisions that needed to be identified. Many of these came in the guidelines section of the PIC but others will be made now.

Later the chapter dealt with the need to have a clear core strategy statement—sometimes called strategy in a nutshell. It covers the key to successful launch. Next came mini-marketing plans, partial plans for addressing all those people (inside the firm and outside of it) whose cooperation and assistance are necessary in the launch. When they concern in-house departments such as manufacturing, technical, and environmental affairs, such plans are called internal marketing.

Given all this, planners are now ready to put shape into their marketing plan by making two sets of strategic decisions. These are given in Chapter 18.

Applications

More questions from that interview with the company president.

1. "I read a while back about a cocktail party in Detroit where someone casually mentioned that a particular photographer (known to be a Ford favorite) was in Paris. This intrigued a Chrysler executive standing nearby

because he wondered why Ford would send a top photographer to Paris. A wire to Chrysler's Paris office yielded the answer—Ford was photographing new models at the foot of the Eiffel Tower. The word was that Hong Kong was next on the schedule. Chrysler correctly concluded that Ford was planning to introduce the models under an international theme. Consequently, Chrysler quickly developed a campaign showing Chrysler models at American landmarks—places Chrysler believed the American auto buyer could identify with more quickly. Chrysler was right and got a big jump on Ford that year. To me, that's smart thinking.

"I heard about another company that rented a large training room in a Chicago hotel for a routine sales meeting. The room had been rented the day before to a direct competitor, one of whose salespeople had left behind a notebook containing details on a completely new product. These slips do happen. What would you do if you were the head of marketing for that competitor and found out that one of your salespeople had left that notebook behind? You're about four weeks from advertising break, and the product is a new concept in sun glasses (the lens material is finely ground quartz crystals, not glass or plastic)."

2. "I like the way you keep referring to yourself as a new products person, not a marketer. Our marketers sometimes have trouble winning the confidence of other managers. I am thinking particularly of the troubles they have getting support of financial people and legal people for their new product programs. It seems to me sometimes they focus too much on their sales plans, their advertising, and their trade shows. Finance and legal aren't shown what *they* can do to help a launch. Oh, I know about general job lists, and how a budget is due at a given time, and how legal approval of advertising is scheduled. But I mean really help, play a positive role, be a member of the team, and so on. What could you suggest?"

3. "Packaging must be terribly important today on lots of products. We spend a fortune on it. I read recently about a detergent packaging gimmick—an 'overcap.' It goes onto a bottle, over the regular cap. It can be torn away and sent in for a refund. Less likely to be cheated on than a coupon. Now that's creative. Are you creative? Could you come up with some ideas like that? We think there is a big packaging opportunity to differentiate our nonalcoholic beer. New products people on that line would sure appreciate some packaging ideas they have never heard of. Good ones, that is, not just a bunch of foolishness."

4. "Those guideline decisions you showed me are a good idea—folks around here tend to forget what they previously agreed to. Still, I wondered if they would apply to services. Confidentially, we are currently planning a new business in Singapore. It seems our production people were spending lots of time learning about the Pacific Rim, where parts and component production could be farmed out. So we took a couple of experienced people and gave them a charter to develop a new business selling their

market knowledge to other purchasing and manufacturing people reaching into Asia for the first time. Could you tell me which of those guideline decisions would fit this project and what sample answers might be?"

CASE: BARSTOW CHEMICAL COMPANY (REVISED)

It had been evident for some time that any firm heavily committed to chemicals was going to have to do something to escape the brutal price competition so prevalent on commodity-type chemicals. So, Frieda Fletcher, general manager of Barstow Chemical Company's Specialty Chemicals Division, had asked her staff to suggest ways their resources could be used to come up with new product concepts that they could develop and with some modest help be able to market.

Barstow's home office was in Stamford, Connecticut, but Fletcher's group had been moved to Pittsburgh to "get away from the heavy chemicals mentality," as the chairman had put it. The move seemed to work because the Specialty Chemicals group now had four major projects under way: two in chemicals that could be sold to the automotive industry for undercar finishing, a fabric strengthener they weren't sure of a use for yet, and a shampoo.

The shampoo had been an accidental spin-off of the undercar treatment project. A chemist was working on chemicals that resisted cleansers of the type used in car washes and by car owners. He tried to find the strongest cleansers he could and even made up some new ones just to be sure the protectants really worked.

The surprise came when he tried a relatively simple concoction that cleaned everything he had been testing yet seemed very soft on the materials and on the hands of workers. (The firm would not comment on the chemicals used in the new concoction.)

At the moment, Specialty Chemicals had a prototype product and had tested it with all ages, sexes, and social classes of people. It worked about the same with all of them: not better than present shampoos, unfortunately, because all of the shampoos tested were about the same (except for smell, thickness, and so on), but certainly as well. It was also safe and had passed several government tests. So far, it had no added conditioners.

The problem, of course, was how to sell it. The firm considered (and rejected) selling the formula to another firm already in the shampoo business; they wanted to market it themselves, as part of the overall corporate strategy to diversity, as described above. General manager Fletcher was well aware that they were inexperienced in consumer marketing. So she wanted to put down some ideas that would serve to help guide the sales and marketing people as they put together a marketing plan for the shampoo. They all knew about target markets and product positioning statements (ideas that they used on industrial chemicals as well). But before getting into those matters, she thought, perhaps those guideline decisions in Chapter 17 might be what she wanted.

The company actually didn't know too much about the shampoo market and would be undertaking market research soon. But in the meantime, Fletcher was fortunate that one of her new products managers (Jose Jimenez) had formerly worked in a shampoo company, so she asked him to use his personal experience in the shampoo market to come up with

---

Source: The situation of this case has been camouflaged, including the name and location.

decisions on each one of the guideline issues. The new shampoo, as stated, worked about the same as the current market leaders, but it did have two noteworthy features. One, the formula was usually in a very thick gel and, in fact, could be as thick as Vaseline. Two, its natural aroma was quite pleasant and fresh, much like almonds. Fletcher said it would take some effort to get the chemical firm's management to approve specific targets and positionings (without wanting to play a role in deciding them), so she wanted to get them thinking along more strategic lines soon. The new products would be something they had never done before, but with the one experienced marketer on board and the firm's general experience in marketing, she felt sure they would understand the guideline issues and could react understandably to whatever decisions they made on them at this time. Then, later, they could move on through the specifics of target, positioning, branding, and matters like that.

Fletcher felt that to break into the shampoo business might require some "off the beaten track" marketing, and hoped her staff was up to the task. She asked you to help Jose on that guidelines assignment.

18 STRATEGIC ACTION DIMENSIONS

Setting

With the givens and the guidelines agreed to, the team can now narrow toward the marketing plan by making strategic *platform* decisions that set overall tones and directions, strategic *action* decisions that define who we are going to sell to and how, and *tactical* decisions by which we implement the strategic driving decisions. Platform decisions often get overlooked, for example, on the level of aggressiveness. If it is decided to be very aggressive (a platform decision), the target market (a driving decision) must be rather broad, and the introductory advertising plan (a tactical decision) will probably call for mass media and a strong attention-getting campaign.

The first two of these sets are covered here in Chapter 18; the tactical set comes in Chapter 19.

Strategic Platform Decisions

Each launch planning team will want to make up its own list of platform decisions, because they vary significantly from industry to industry, goods to services, industrial to packaged goods. But some of the more common ones are the following.

Permanence

On **permanence**, there are three options. The first is the usual one—we are **in to stay**, and no thought is given to getting out. The second is **in to stay if we meet our goals**. This cautions against alliances that would make escape difficult; it is especially useful when a firm is using the new product to enter another sphere of activity. Such a market development project can be

339

tentative—probe an area, try hard to make it a winner, but pull out if competitive capability is inadequate.

The third option is **temporary**. This may sound strange—spending months or years developing a new item only to limit its life to a few months or at most a couple of years. But this temporary option is used a lot. Baskin-Robbins, for example, has a basic cadre of flavors but runs others in and out to give variety. Sometimes temporary products catch on and become permanent. Many tactical decisions change if the plan is temporary—using contract manufacturing rather than building new plant, and "borrowing" a sales force from agents or other manufacturers.

Aggressiveness

Aggressiveness refers to an attitude as much as to dollars. An **aggressive entry** seeks lots of attention early on, so most of the promotional dollars are spent early, and most of the resources go to getting early trial. In contrast, some firms will **slink into the market cautiously**. They are uncertain about something important—maybe product performance, maybe competitive reaction, maybe sales force capability to deal with a new type of market. This is not a negative posture, just one where being aggressive has a risk the firm wants to avoid. For example, some firms like to enter a new market cautiously so as not to alarm the leaders in that market.

Third, the aggressiveness can be **balanced**. This simply means the firm is not trying to be pugnacious or slinking. The average of all new product introductions in a given industry would be balanced, but this does not mean normal; for some firms, aggressive *is* normal.

Sometimes this is a good place to raise the issue of marketing costs as an **investment**. Much of the marketing budget for a new product will pay off over many years; it is not an expense in the sense of an annual advertising budget. If the spending strategy is too stingy, try thinking about it as an investment.

Type of Demand Sought

This may have been settled earlier, but if not, the decision should be made now. Does the firm want to capture **selective demand** by taking market share from competition, or does it want to expand the total market by building **primary demand** for the category. The difference is critical to most of the strategic actions, including the market segment being targeted. Fortunately, selective versus primary tends to come up at the very start, when selecting end users' problems.

Competitive Advantage—Product versus Price

Another decision that tends to come up early concerns the basic offer we make to the marketplace: Will our product lower end user costs by virtue of its **price**? Or will our product offer new benefits by virtue of its **differentiation**? Today managers often expect to have new products that offer benefits by virtue of differentiation *and* that can be sold at a price below leading competition. So there is a middle choice on this option too: **both.**

Product Line Replacement

Most new products relate to existing products in the company's line: How should we manage the replacement of the existing by the new? Some firms, perhaps without realizing it, follow the strategy of let nature handle the switch. But recent research shows several distinct strategic options.[1] Several of them are as follows:

- **Butt-on:** The existing one is simply dropped when the new one is announced. Example: Ford's marketing of Mondero and dropping of Sierra.
- **Low-season switch:** Using butt-on, but arranging the switch at a low point between seasons. Tour companies use this switch when they develop their new catalogs.
- **High-season switch:** Using butt-on, but arranging the new item at the top of a season. Example: Polaroid used this strategy often, putting new replacement items out during the Christmas season.
- **Roll-in, roll-out:** This is another butt-on, but arranging it by a sequence of market segments. Mercedes introduced its C series country by country.
- **Down-grading:** Keeping the earlier product alongside the new, but with decreased support. Example: The 386 chip stayed alongside the 486.
- **Splitting channels:** Putting the new item in a different channel or diverting the existing product into another channel. Example: Old electronic products often end up in discounter channels.

The important point is, have *some* replacement strategy decision. And have it early enough in launch planning that the total market offer (including augmentation such as service, warranty, and brand image) can be built to suit the strategy.

Competitive Relationship

Occasionally a product innovation charter will have a statement something like this: "The product(s) that will come from this program will not be aimed at XYZ Company, nor threaten a piece of business that is important to that firm."

---

[1]John Saunders and David Jobber, "Product Replacement: Strategies for Simultaneous Product Deletion and Launch," *Journal of Product Innovation Management*, November 1994, pp. 433–50.

Colgate once had such a statement relative to Procter & Gamble, but abandoned it in the 1980s. Other firms do just the opposite, shooting their new item directly *at* a specific competitor.

The practices lead to a three-option set: **make no reference to specific competitors**, **aim directly at a specific competitor**, and **avoid a specific competitor**. Unintentionally trying to do two or three of those mires the tactical managers in a frustrating set of conflicts.

Scope of Market Entry

This issue relates to a firm's desire to do market testing. Some introduce their new items into part of a market, watch what happens, and then roll them on out to the entire market as they overcome any problems. This will be discussed more in Chapter 21. But even in a rollout, there is still the option of trying to **roll out very rapidly** (barely holding up long enough to find crisis problems) or **roll out deliberately, as performance warrants**. And, of course, it appears most firms **go to the total market at the beginning**.

Image

The issue here is: Will the new product need **an entirely new image**, **a major change in an existing image**, **a tweaking of an existing image**, or **no change whatsoever in an image**? For example, the butt-on strategy of market replacement will destroy the prior brand if necessary to properly position the new. But the side-by-side strategy needs a continuing positive image in the item being upgraded. Images are strong and long-lasting, so changing them should be undertaken lightly. Yet, an image can also be distorted by an almost trivial mistake in an ad or a label. And setting out to establish a new image can be frightfully expensive.

Strategic Driving Decisions

In the above analyses leading to *givens*, *guideline decisions*, and *strategic platform decisions*, one could conclude that we must be about finished. Most of the thinking in those sets is unpleasant, because we are deliberately focusing effort or attention on single options from sets. Do this, rather than that and that.

The flip side is that once these higher-order decisions are made, the rest are easier. So we now turn our attention to strategic *driving* decisions, those that you may think of as the *real* marketing planning decisions: target market, product positioning statement, creating value for the chosen target, and branding.

The Target Market Decision

Competition today forces the overwhelming majority of companies to market new items to specific target groups. Markets are so complex that one product cannot come close to meeting all needs and desires.

Alternative Ways to Segment a Market

What ways do new product marketers use to target a specific market segment? Thousands of them.

End use. Athletic shoes are specific for various types of athletic activity. Plastics are sold for hundreds of different applications. CD buyers have different time frames in mind. To test your own end use orientation, try listing the many different shirts/blouses/pants/slacks/suits/dresses you have had in your possession—say, starting with designer blouse, dress blouse, and so on. Men, start with T-shirt, golf shirt, dress shirt, and so on. Notice how often the type of garment is defined by the activity it is worn for. Clothing manufacturers design for use, though not only for use.

Geographic. Convertibles are not marketed aggressively in Norway, and Golden's fried pork skins are made for the South.

Demographic. Bran cereals are often targeted to the mature segment, Grey Poupon for the upscale, and Right Guard for males (originally).

Behavioral. Xerox's Notes was developed for people who needed to communicate in groups across great distances, and Kevlar bulletproof jackets are for people exposed to guns.

Psychographic. Many products are targeted to lifestyles—tax shelters, clothing, cars.

The PIC usually makes quite clear what market group the new project will focus on, and the target market may be clear from the *original concept generation*. For instance, a sales rep notifies management that *offices with southern exposure* are having problems with the new personal computer screens, and a new monitor evolves.

Second, the firm's *method of operation* may constrain the choice. If a firm's sales force calls on hospital accounting departments, its new line of tabular records will probably be so targeted. Third, a focus may come from *concept testing* or *product use testing*.

A twist of great interest to new products people is called **benefit segmentation**, or a variant of it. Via concept testing (and other research), you have found people who see a real benefit in a proposal. What better market target segment than that group, whether old, female, exhibitionist, unemployed, or whatever?

Another current twist in target market selection is the trend toward smallness. Retail scanners and sales information systems yield the databases that display very small targets (neighborhoods or industrial subsets) with unique purchase patterns. Direct marketers have always used tighter segments than have mass media marketers, stemming from their databases. They talk about **database marketing** and **database product innovation**, and speculate that within 10 years it will dominate. These clusters have been labeled **micromarkets.**[2]

David Olson, new product researcher at the Leo Burnett advertising agency, uses scanner data to cluster food buyers into six groups:

Loyalists, who buy one brand at all times, like it, and don't use deals.

Rotators, who have a two- or three-product set, move around in that set, and don't use deals.

Deal-selectives, rotators whose movement is determined by presence of deals. Price-driven, who buy all major brands, always on deals.

Store brand buyers, who do as their name implies.

Light users, who buy too little for a pattern to show. Light users comprise the biggest group in most categories.

The ultimate smallness, of course, is **mass customization**, where the individual is the target. Business-to-business firms have often used mass customization in dealing with their major clients or customers, but without naming it. A recent sale of locomotives by General Electric to CSX (for the latter's Chesapeake & Ohio railroad) was billed by one observer as a "Jack Welch [GE]—John Snow [CSX] deal."[3]

And then there are the many very creative methods. Parametric Technology Corporation recently pointed to **switchables**, firms with short design cycles. Another firm went after the **high-profit customer** (note: not the high-*volume* customer). Still another targeted on **share-determiners**, firms who will determine the shape of an industry and are sure to grow.[4]

As we approach the marketing date, intense pressure builds up in the organization to add just a few more buyer groups, a few more store types, a few more uses or applications, because "The product is good for them too, isn't it?" We call this the *broaden the market* fallacy. The new item cannot be good for lots of different groups, unless it is so general it doesn't have any zing for any of them. And targeting to diverse groups can cause *conflict and dissonance in the promotion*. Does a fourth grader want a peanut butter sandwich like the one shown being eaten by a senior citizen?

Changing the target can also be disaster if promotion materials are all prepared, trade show schedules are fixed, packaging, pricing, and branding are

---

[2]For the essence of this subject, see "Database Marketing," *Business Week*, September 5, 1994, pp. 56–62. An example: Blockbuster keeps records on 36 million households; it can recommend movies based on past rentals, and modify other aspects of its service for tiny clusters of buying families.

[3]See William M. Carley, "GE May Be Pulling Ahead of GM in Locomotive Race," *The Wall Street Journal*, December 23, 1993, p. B4.

[4]Adrian J. Slywotzky and Benson P. Shapiro, "Leveraging to Beat the Odds: The New Marketing Mind-Set," *Harvard Business Review*, September–October 1993, pp. 97–107.

difficult to change on short notice, and the concept test and the product use test were conducted with the original target group. With a quick switch, we fly blind.

Lastly, keep in mind that whatever we do, the end users may disagree. In a classic rebellion a few years ago sports utility vehicles were adopted by boomers for regular use. They were tired of minivans (or outgrew them) and it didn't matter what the car companies *told* us these vehicles were targeted for (or that the government said they were trucks). Some firms capitalize on this end user penchant by just launching the product and following up to see who the buyers are. They then focus their promotions accordingly. It is strictly a wildcat operation—no charter, no concept testing, no use testing, etc.

Targeting May Also Use Diffusion of Innovation

New products are innovations, and we call the spreading of their usage **diffusion of innovation**. The original adoption and diffusion of the microwave oven was very slow, but it has been quite rapid for the cellular phone. For a cancer cure, it would be almost instantaneous.

Two things increase the speed of an innovation's adoption—*the nature of the innovation itself* and the extent to which *early users encourage others to follow*. Let's take the innovation first. Over the years, research has derived five factors for measuring how "adoptable" a new product is.[5] Here they are:

> The **relative advantage** of the new product. How superior is the innovation to the product or other problem-solving methods it was designed to compete against?
>
> **Compatibility.** Does it fit with current product usage and end user activity? We say it is a **continuous** innovation if little change is required, a **discontinuous** innovation if much is. Incompatibility produces learning requirements, and these must be overcome.
>
> **Complexity.** Will frustration or confusion arise in understanding the innovation's basic idea?
>
> **Divisibility** (also called **trialability**). How easily can trial portions of the product be purchased and used? Foods and beverages are quite divisible, but new homes and word processing systems are much less so.
>
> **Communicability** (also called **observability**). How likely is the product to appear in public places where it is easily seen and studied by potential users? It is high on new cars, low on items of personal hygiene.

An innovation can be scored on these five factors, using primarily personal judgment plus the findings from market testing during earlier phases of the development. Launch plans can then be laid accordingly.

---

[5]The classic source on this subject is Everett M. Rogers, *Diffusion on Innovations* (New York: Free Press, 1962). Many researchers have contributed to this list of factors.

Next is the degree to which early users actively or passively encourage others to adopt a new product; if they do, its spread will be rapid. So, targeting interest has focused on the **innovators** (the first 5 to 10 percent of those who adopt the product) and on the **early adopters** (the next 10 to 15 percent of adopters). The theory of innovation diffusion states that if we could just market our new product to those innovators and early adopters, we could then sit back and let them spread the word to the others.

Other categories of adopters include the **early majority** (perhaps the next 30 percent), the **late majority** (perhaps another 30 percent), and the **laggards** (the remaining 20 percent).

The obvious question is, "Can we identify the innovators and early adopters in advance?" Not always, but the following five traits have often emerged from the studies. They apply to business firms as well as to individuals.[6]

1. *Venturesomeness*—the willingness and desire to be daring in trying the new and different; "sticks his neck out"; "deviates from the group social norms."

2. *Social integration*—frequent and extensive contact with others in one's "area," whether work, neighborhood, or social life; a strong industrial counterpart.

3. *Cosmopolitanism*—point of view extending beyond the immediate neighborhood or community; interest in world affairs, travel, reading.

4. *Social mobility*—upward movement on the social scale; successful young executive or professional types.

5. *Privilegedness*—usually defined as being better off financially than others in the group. Thus the privileged person has less to lose if the innovation fails and costs money. This trait tends to reflect *attitude* toward money as much as possession of money.

Early users do come, typically, from the innovator group, but it is difficult to predict which ones. In the industrial setting, it's thought that early *business* adopters tend to be the largest firms in the industry, those who stand to make the greatest profit from the innovation, spend more on R&D, and have presidents who are younger and better educated. In general, the business adoption process goes slower, and the counterparts of opinion leaders are harder to find.[7]

Launch planners have some flexibility here—they don't have to select just one market segment to target to. Some start first with innovators, then roll off to early adopters shortly after launch, then gradually add the early majority and so on through the set.

---

[6]For example, see Stéphane Gauvin and Rajiv K. Sinha, "Innovativeness in Industrial Organizations: A Two-Stage Model of Adoption," *International Journal of Research in Marketing*, no. 10, 1993, pp. 165–83.

[7]Ralph L. Day and Paul A. Herbig, "How the Diffusion of Industrial Innovations Is Different from New Retail Products," *Industrial Marketing Management*, August 1990, pp. 261–66.

However it comes about, the target decision essentially measures (1) how much *potential* is in each target market option, (2) how well our new product *meets the needs* of people in each of those markets, and (3) how prepared we are to compete in each—that is, our *capacity to compete* there.

Product Positioning

A **product positioning statement** is created by completing this sentence: Buyers in the target market should buy our product rather than others being offered and used because

Positioning originated in advertising, with the buyer's mind as a memory bank with slots, or positions, for each competing alternative, ranked by sales volume like rungs on a ladder. Product innovators could: (1) Try to outperform the top firm and take over the top rung, (2) position relative to the top firm and fight for a better lower rung (Avis' classic slogan, "We try harder"), (3) reposition the leader or any occupant of a desired position by a really dramatic event (Royal Doulton attacked Lenox's higher position by using ads that said: "Royal Doulton—the china of Stoke-on-Trent, England, versus Lenox, the china of Pomona, New Jersey"), or (4) differentiate the product from those already on the ladder and thus break the one ladder into two or more ladders, one for each segment.

Positioning is now seen as an ingredient of *total* strategy, not just an advertising ploy. Product, brand, price, promotion, and distribution must all be consistent with the product positioning statement.

New products managers have a big advantage on positioning—*the end user's memory slate is clean;* potential buyers have no previous positioning in mind for a new item. Now is the best chance ever to effect a particular positioning for their item.

Alternatives in Positioning

The alternatives used today in positioning fall into two broad categories. The first is to position to an **attribute** (a feature, a function, or a benefit). Attributes are the traditional positioning devices and are most popular. Thus, a dog food may be positioned by a **feature** as "the one with as much protein as 10 pounds of sirloin." **Function** is more difficult and rarely used, but an example is the shampoo that "coats your hair with a thin layer of protein." (You are not told how this is done or what the benefit is.) The **benefits** used in positioning can be **direct** (such as "saves you money") or **follow-on** (such as "improves your sex life," an indirect result of the cleaner teeth or cleaner breath given by this toothpaste).

Feature-function-benefit work as a triad, and they are sometimes used that way. For example, a new Drano product was headlined with just three words: THICKER, STRONGER, FASTER. These happen to be feature, function, benefit. But trying to use all three can be confusing, and target buyers won't spend much time on clarification.

The second alternative in positioning is to use **surrogates** (or metaphors). For example, "Use our dietary product *because it was created by a leading health expert.*" This says the product differs because of its designer. Specific reasons *why* the product is better are not given; the listener or viewer has to provide those. If the surrogate is good, the listener will bring favorable attributes to the product. See Figure 18–1 for the various positioning alternatives, their definition, and examples of each, from a diverse collection of goods and services, as well as business and consumer products.[8]

FIGURE 18–1   Surrogate Positioning—Definition of Alternatives, with Examples

Listed below are the type of surrogates currently being used. No doubt there are many others awaiting discovery. For each, the definition is given, followed by one or more examples. The surrogates are listed in order of popularity in use. The claim in each case would be that "Our product is better than, or different than, the others because...."

Nonpareil:...because the product has no equal; it is the best (the Jaguar car and Nissan's 300ZX, the "convertible of convertibles").

Parentage:...because of where it comes from, who makes it, who sells it, who performs it, and so on. The three ways of parentage positioning are *brand* (Le Temps Chanel timepieces), *company* ("Everything we know about peanut butter is now available in jars" for Reese's peanut butter, "No one potpourries like Glade" for the new Peachpourri, and new "Adventures in Wonderland" TV show that has no features in its advertising but clearly comes from Disney), and *person* (the RL 2000 chair, designed by Ralph Lauren, *Dazzle*, a new book by Judith Krantz).

Manufacture:...because of how the product was made. This includes *process* (Hunt's tomatoes are left longer on the vine), *ingredients* (Fruit of the Loom panties of pure cotton), and *design* (Audi's engineering).

Target:...because the product was made especially for people or firms like you. Four ways are *end use* (Vector tire designed especially for use on wet roads), *demographic* (several airlines have service specially designed for the business traveler), *psychographic* (Michelob Light for "the people who want it all"), and *behavioral* (Hagar's Gallery line for men who work out a lot, "fit for the fit").

Rank:...because it is the best-selling product (Hertz and Blue Cross/Blue Shield); not very useful on a new item unless also positioned under parent brand.

Endorsement:...because people you respect say it is good. May be *expert* (the many doctors who prescribed DuoFilm wart remover when it was prescription-only) or a person to be *emulated* (NEC cellular phone keys were designed for Mickey Spillane).

Experience:...because its long or frequent use attests to its desirable attributes. Modes are *other market* (Nuprin's extensive use in the prescription market), *bandwagon* (Stuart Hall's Executive line of business accessories are "the tools business professionals rely on"), and *time* (Bell's Yellow Pages). The latter two of these are also of limited use on new products.

Competitor:...because it is just (or almost) like another product that you know and like (new RPS air service, just like the leading competitor except cheaper).

Predecessor:...because it is comparable (in some way) to an earlier product you liked (Hershey's new Solitaires addition to the Golden line).

---

[8]Evidence that the current concept of positioning can be applied to services as well as to goods is found in Christopher J. Easingwood and Vijay Mahajan, "Positioning of Financial Services for Competitive Advantage," *Journal of Product Innovation Management*, September 1989, pp. 207–19.

The Decision Process

How one gets to a new product's positioning is somewhat systematic and somewhat artistic. Unless there was a mistake somewhere, the benefit we have been developing should be unique (since it came out as a solution to the problem we decided to solve). If the development team took some approach other than user benefit as a base for the new item (e.g., technology.driven, or from one of the attribute analysis techniques such as morphological matrix) we should look at competitive positionings, at how users *perceive* their positionings, and then hunt for worthwhile gaps. The analytical technique for this is the gap (or map) analysis discussed in Chapter 7.

The Taylor Wine Company once identified a small group of heavy wine users and asked them what brands of wine they preferred; surprisingly, none of the wines the heavy users bought was being positioned on its great taste. Taylor did so position a wine of theirs, and succeeded immediately.

If there is no longer an open feature-function-benefit positioning that users want, developers can try to *build* preference for some unique attribute their product has, or they can turn to surrogates.

This is where the art begins. Study of the list of alternatives in Figure 18–1 should reveal some good possibilities. These can then be copy tested with the target market to see if they communicate ideas we want the buyers to have. For example, in the early 90s the Skil Corporation, makers of the very successful circular hand saw, developed a line of benchtop tools such as a table saw. The new tools' features and benefits were not particularly unique, so the announcement headline said, "Besides evaluating its features, one should also consider its *ancestry*." And, "Over *six decades ago* Skil introduced the world's first circular saw...Today we are continuing the Skilsaw *tradition*...lives up to its *namesake*...member of our new *family*...long-standing *reputation* for quality." This is surrogate positioning.

Creating Unique Value for the Chosen Target

Once a market segment has been targeted and a positioning statement created for it, we have a chance to cycle back to the product itself and see if we can enhance its value to the chosen market. After all, the role of a new product is usually to build gross margin dollars, dollars that come primarily from the values it has over its price.

Figure 18–2 shows how the buyer actually receives a bundle of things a product consists of. Here it is viewed as a package, bought and taken home, but the augmentation idea is the same as on the bull's eye figure used earlier. Even though most efforts during the technical phase are focused on the core benefit, we try during later stages to add benefit in other ways—packaging, warranty, presale service, brand, and so on.

Most firms now try to "freeze specs" late in development, and schedule others for soon after launch, to sustain value in the product. As the first product is

FIGURE 18–2

*Purchase
Configuration—
What the Buyer
Actually Buys*

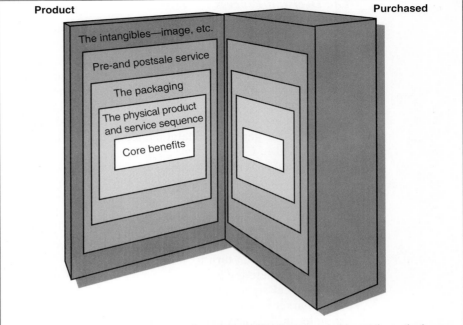

Explanation: One or more core benefits are wanted by the buyer; but to get them, the buyer must also take delivery on the physical product or service sequence, its packaging, its attendant service, and all intangibles that go with the brand and firm making/selling it. These other purchase "layers" may enhance the total value or detract from it, but they each offer opportunity for differentiation or for the core benefit to be destroyed or overpowered if not handled correctly by the new product manager.

coming down the pike, the first couple of line extensions should be in development. Then, after launch, when competitors are casting around for ways to come out with catch-up versions, we market them first.[9]

Securing a Good Brand

Every new product must be identified, and the accurate term for what identifies products is **trademark**. Under U.S. federal law, a trademark is usually a word or a symbol. That symbol may be a number (how many of the following prod-

---

[9]For more on this defensive use of line extensions and product improvements, see C. Merle Crawford, "How Product Innovators Can Foreclose the Options of Adaptive Followers," *Journal of Consumer Marketing*, Fall 1988, pp. 17–24.

ucts can you identify? 6, 21, 45, 57, 66, 76, 380, and 5000)[10] or a design (e.g., the stylized lettering in GE, the golden arches of McDonald's, or the paint firm's Dutch boy). The law doesn't care how unusual the trademark is and just requires it to identify and differentiate the item using it.

Most businesspeople and their customers use the term *brand* instead of *trademark*. This book uses *brand* when talking about marketing strategy and *trademark* when talking about the legal aspects. Technically speaking, services have **service marks**, not trademarks, and businesses have **trade names**, not trademarks).[11]

Trademark Registration

Another definition, however, is very important: **registration**. Historically, and still today in most countries, the *first user* of a trademark had exclusive rights. But in the United States you can ask that your trademark be registered. If you can get it registered, you can keep that trademark forever, even if another firm later displays proof of prior use. See Figure 18–3 for the process.

What happens if, shortly after launch, other manufacturers begin encroaching on our mark? We move aggressively to stop them. Alladin began putting on its labels "Alladin thermos bottle." Do you know what thermos bottles are? If you do, as most people do, then the term no longer just describes one maker's brand of vacuum bottles. Alladin was sued by the firm that owned the thermos mark, and Alladin won; the original owner had not been protecting it. *Thermos* became a generic. Any company can use it. Over the years, so did aspirin, cellophane, brassiere, dry ice, shredded wheat, trampoline, yo-yo, linoleum, cube steak, RIP, corn flakes, kerosene, high octane, raisin bran, lanolin, nylon, mimeograph, and scores more: billions of dollars in value lost. But today, makers of in-line skates know that Rollerblades is aggressively protected. The same goes for Mattel's Frisbee.

Even lawyers chuckled recently when two trademark searching firms hit the headlines. One of them claimed a competitor had misused its trademark! And don't forget to seek protection for the new brand in all countries where it might be marketed. Most critical is a watchful eye on promotion materials. To squeeze advertising copy and give it more zip, product managers will occasionally use their mark possessively (Boppo's great taste), or as a verb (Boppo your letters). This type of use assumes customers think of Boppo as a generic, and if the owner of the brand feels this way, then others can too.

---

[10]If you want to guess their identities, they are, in order, a car, a restaurant, an ale, a line of condiments, a gasoline, another gasoline, a car, and a car. Numbers and letters should be used with care: see Teresa M. Pavia and Janeen Arnold Costa, "The Winning Number: Consumer Perceptions of Alpha-Numeric Brand Names," *Journal of Marketing*, July 1993, pp. 85–98.

[11]Leonard L. Berry, Edwin E. Lefkowith, and Terry Clark, "In Services, What's in a Name?" *Harvard Business Review*, September–October 1988, pp. 28–30.

FIGURE 18–3   Registration of Trademarks by the United States Patent and Trademark Office

Here are three conditions set forth by the U.S. Patent and Trademark Office for the giving of REGISTRATION. There are a couple of others, but these are the ones that concern new products managers.

First, the trademark cannot be *too descriptive* of a product type.
A court once found the brand Light too descriptive when used as the brand of a cigarette. The judges felt that Light identified all cigarettes with the lighter taste of a low-tar cigarette, not just the one firm's brand. Similarly, Overnight Delivery Service would not be acceptable as a competitor to Federal Express.

Second, the proposed trademark should not be *confusingly similar* to the marks of other products.
This is the toughest requirement, given the huge number of goods and services on the market today, and the 127,000 U.S. trademark applications in 1991 alone. Here is an example of the problem. Quality Inns International, a nationwide motel chain, decided to develop a new economy hotel chain. Quality Inns wanted to name the new chain McSleep, capitalizing on the Scottish fame for wise spending. Reaction was prompt—McDonald's lawyer said its use of the mark would not be tolerated. McDonald's felt that the "Mc" (called a *formative*) would lead people to believe the motel chain was part of the McDonald's Corporation—using its good name and reputation to help Quality Inns. As a further confusion, McDonald's was at that time building a chain of truckstop-style operations called McStop, which offered gasoline, fast food, and lodging at one site.
A federal district judge ruled for McDonald's, and Quality Inns switched the new chain's name to Sleep Inns. The judge punned that his ruling was a McPinion. McDonald's also blocked a New York store from using McBagel.
Not funny to Mead Data Central was a court decision to allow Toyota to market a Lexus car against Mead Data's mark of Lexis for its legal-information network. The data firm then launched a sweepstakes in which the prize was an Infiniti (a Lexus competitor)!

Third, the trademark should not be *immoral or misleading*.
It should not disparage people or institutions, and it probably should not be the name of a person.

Marketers, of course, are not lawyers. Trademark decisions should only be made in conjunction with an attorney.

What Is a Good Brand Name?

Getting a good brand is not easy, because most good combinations of letters have already been taken. But, if Xerox can work out OK, and Clabber Girl too, then there is hope for all. Experts have given us criteria to follow. Let's look at them.

What Is the Brand's Role or Purpose?   If a brand is purely for identification, then an arbitrary combination of letters will work well. This combination is called a **neologism**, and examples include Kodak, Exxon, Weejuns, and Nerf. But if the brand is to help position the product (useful when the seller lacks advertising dollars), then we want to use letters that already have meaning, such as CareFree, DieHard, Holiday Inn, Rely, and Kno-draft air-conditioning units.

Will This Product Be a Bridgehead to a Line of Products?   If so, the name should not limit the firm, as Liquid Plumr tended to do. Can you accept *Liquid Plumr crystals*? What started as Western Hotels had to change to Western International and, finally, to Westin.

Do You Expect a Long-Term Position in the Market?   If so, a more general and less dramatic name is preferable; but if you're only going to be around temporarily, something like Screaming Yellow Zonkers snacks can (and did) work.

How Good Is Your Budget?   If you don't have the funds to put meaning into a meaningless combination of letters, better avoid that type of brand.

Have You Remembered the Physical and Sensory Qualities of the Brand?   Specifically, the brand name should be easy to pronounce, easy to spell, and easy to remember. Some believe Honda was careless when it chose Acura; phonetically, the spelling should have been *Accura*, and Americans would have had little trouble, but Acura works much better on an international scale. And, before we get too critical about pronunciation, we should remember Grey Poupon and Häagen-Dazs!

Is the Message Clear and Relevant?   Product characteristics should come forth clearly. For example, the meaning of *Isovis* motor oil to the engineers who named it probably was "equal or constant viscosity," but to the average consumer, it was just a mix of letters. New products people are too close to their developments; their brand proposals should get careful buyer testing. A real misfire was La Choy's Fresh and Lite line of low-fat frozen Chinese entrees—critics thought it might be a feminine hygiene product, or perhaps a beer.[12]

Does the Brand Insult or Irritate Any Particular Market Group?   For example, women told Bic that Fannyhose was objectionable, so the firm switched to Pantyhose. And the French firm that marketed a drink under the name of Pschitt certainly thwarted the brand's extension to the United Kingdom and the United States.[13]

Beyond these general principles, there is no end to the specific advice given by branding experts. See Figure 18–4 for some of their suggestions. The branding decision is often very important; it can be botched or brilliant.[14] This is made

---

[12]"Flops," *Business Week*, August 16, 1993, p. 76.

[13]For more, see Gael M. McDonald and C. J. Roberts, "The Brand-Naming Enigma in the Asia Pacific Context," *European Journal of Marketing*, no. 8, 1990, pp. 6–19.

[14]Lest we think that branding is mainly a tool of consumer product marketers, see David Shipley and Paul Howard, "Brand-Naming Industrial Products," *Industrial Marketing Management*, 1993, pp. 59–66.

FIGURE 18–4   **Collection of Practitioners' Suggestions about Branding**

1. Use digitals for modernity.
2. Family brands are quick, cheap, and void of surprises.
3. Use "stop" letters (called *plosives*): B, C, D, G, K, P, and T.
4. Use geographical connotations: Rebel Yell, and Evening in Paris.
5. Do something ridiculous: P. Lorillard had Whatchamacallits cigarettes.
6. Embellish an ordinary word: the vine leaf intertwined in "o" of Taylor Wines.
7. Put one odd letter in the name: Citibank, Toys 'R' Us.
8. Borrow clout: General Mills' Lancia pizza mix picked up the sports car image.
9. Use the word *The* in the brand for dignity: The Glenlivit.
10. Use personalities: Reggie Jackson candy bars.
11. Use an attention grabber: My Sin cologne.
12. Reinforce a low-price strategy with a name like Klassy Kut Klothes.
13. Play with the letters: *Serutan* is *Natures* spelled backward.
14. Add a symbol to reinforce the brand: Travelers' red umbrella, the rock of Prudential.

clear in what will probably become a classic case—the Saturn brand General Motors created for a new smaller car. They worked from early in the life of the project to build a brand along with the new car—and succeeded.[15]

The Process of Selecting a Brand

Given an overall marketing strategy and the role that brand will play, the best thing probably is to have some discussions (1) with intended users (to learn how they talk about things in this area of use) and (2) with phonetic experts, who know a great deal about such things as word structures. This is the stage where P&G caught Dreck (Yiddish and German definitions included garbage and body waste), so it was changed to Dreft. When down to less than 10 candidates, get a legal check on their availability, and negotiate over the remaining 2 or 3. It's good to keep two or three brands alive and approved, just in case an unexpected problem pops up.

Figure 18–5 tells a story about brand selection in the crazy real world; some managers find it too close to the truth to be funny.

Summary

In Chapter 18, we have extended our look at the launch-planning process by going into the platform decisions and the driving decisions. Both sets have a strong effect on the strategies chosen. The chapter also looked at three of the biggest

[15]David A. Aaker, "Building a Brand: The Saturn Story," *California Management Review*, Winter 1994, pp. 114–33.

areas of decision—target market or segment, positioning of the new item for that segment, and choosing a good brand name. We can now turn to those many things that make up the tactics portion of the marketing plan, but there is far too little space for an in-depth study in the many areas of operational marketing. We will look at those issues which give new products managers the most difficulty.

FIGURE 18–5   How To Develop, Market, and Identify a New Product: Horror Story or Unfortunate Reality?

1. Sales, research, and advertising meet to discuss new product's designation (generic) and trademark.
2. Research proposes "methyladenaliumenfluoropolydia."
3. Ad manager struck speechless. Points out pronunciation difficulty and suggest "liquid rock."
4. All present compromise. Settle on generic of "fabric."
5. Computer gives them 117,973 choices for a trademark.
6. Group pares choices down to 15. Computer's feelings hurt.
7. Group overrules using company's founder's name spelled backwards.
8. Compromise again. Decide on "DIGIR," which is *rigid* spelled backward.
9. Sales manager vetoes: was in North Africa in '72. Claims it is Arabic word for unauthorized pilgrimage to Mecca and therefore unsuitable. Suggests "diccalf," which is *flaccid* spelled backward. Overruled.
10. Group then selects "ZONKO" because it doesn't mean anything spelled any which way.
11. Legal vetoes. Discovers it is obscene word in Slobbovia.
12. Legal throws out five others. Already registered.
13. Bucked to higher authority. VP sales OKs (1) "ZIZ-BOOM," (2) "BIZ-ZOOM," and (3) "ZOOM-BIZ."
14. Company ships to Washington product bearing all three trademarks.
15. Proof of shipment to Patent Office with application for trademark.
16. Patent Office advises number one already registered; application rejected.
17. Patent Office advises number two too descriptive; application rejected.
18. Patent Office advises number three too similar to latest NASA rocket; application rejected.
19. Patent Office reverses itself. Approves number two choice, "BIZ-ZOOM;" company rejoices.
20. Advertising and public relations form their battalions and launch massive promotional attacks for "BIZ-ZOOM" fabric.
21. Orders for "BIZ-ZOOM" roll in. Sales manager measured for white hat and halo. SM smirks smugly.
22. Black hat appears. Millions using "BIZ-ZOOM" as a generic term for fabric. Competitor has registered "BUZ-ZAM." If customers ask for "BIZ-ZOOM," they get "BUZ-ZAM." "BIZ-ZOOM" now completely generic; "BUZ-ZAM" isn't.
23. B.I.G. Daddi, company president, starts asking embarrassing questions like, "Why wasn't trademark protected all along the line?"
24. Horse gone, company now locks barn door. Sends hundreds of letters to writers, editors, and retail advertisers asking them PLEASE to capitalize the trademark and use quotes and proper generic with it.
25. Company goes through travail of educating and orienting all employees to assure proper use of trademark.
26. Company goes to court. Litigates with trademark pirates. Contributes substantially to support of judges, bailiffs, and lawyers.
27. Massive advertising campaign instituted to instruct trade on proper use of trademark. Costs quite a bit and erodes budget more than somewhat.
28. Snoqualmie Indian in Pacific Northwest named Bizzoom sues company for using his name without permission.

Source: Unknown.

Applications

More questions from that interview with the company president.

1. "My daughter is a newly appointed assistant professor at a school in North Carolina, and she recently was joking about how similar the development of courses is to the development of new products. In fact, she said courses have to be planned for and their marketing has to be just right. Even to using positioning as a concept. I wonder if you could take a new college course, tentatively titled Using the Internet for Business, and show me how you could position that course, using each of the various methods for positioning a new product."

2. "One of our divisions recently came up with a new way of testing new brand names (at least it was new to us). They had a new financial information database service that they were getting ready to market. So they narrowed the list of possible service marks down to five and then went to an American Banking Association meeting to ask attendees what type of product (in their case, a service) each of those brands signified. As each of those bankers guessed various product types, the company learned what the brand was saying—what message was being conveyed. You see any dangers in that?"

3. "We're in the furniture business, and I'll bet you have used some of our stuff if you spent any time in your college dorms. But, I'll tell you something, there's not much profit in that business—too many competitors, too much standardization in products. You know, buying on bids from purchasing department product spec sheets. I was aware of what you said a while ago about core benefits, and creating product value *around* that core, like in service, image, warranty, etc. But, I'm not sure we could use that approach. Given that, physically, our desks and beds have to meet specs, how might we create value around *that*, to help us defend slightly higher prices?"

4. "One of our divisions has made a mint on video games—those used in game centers, at home, and anywhere else younger people gather. But they fell on hard times—let their line grow beards. Kids turned them off. So we had to overhaul the operation, bring in a couple of top people from Hollywood, and get new items onto the market. We now have two great new concepts—I can't tell you what they are, but believe me, they use technologies never in video games before. But, I know those folks are better at electronics than marketing. I want to help them use *diffusion of innovation* ideas to reach just the right kids for this new stuff—it's going to take them longer to learn and longer to play, there will be international team competition from the very start, and a lot of other things. Knowing how kids emulate each other, there must be some role for diffusion of innovation."

CASE: CHILLED FOODS

In the first half of 1989, the American food industry was working feverishly to capitalize on a new technology and what it felt was a new consumer interest—chilled or refrigerated foods. The products were shipped and stored at retail under refrigerated conditions, not frozen. These prepackaged foods were ready to be taken home and heated or lightly cooked. The industry activities were varied. For example:

Marks & Spencer. A British firm based in London, Marks & Spencer was a large retailer, selling food under its St. Michael private label. Arrangements were being made to introduce chilled products under this label into the United States through a regional chain of super-markets it had acquired. The firm had been a pioneer in prepackaged, refrigerated food and in the United Kingdom marketed a line of "yuppydom" foods, such as Salmon en Croute with cream sauce at $5.34 for two servings. Its reputation was for top-quality products, with a short, integrated farm-to-store distribution system.

Campbell. After first trying to market its Fresh Chef line of refrigerated sauces, soups, and salads in 1987 (later withdrawn), Campbell was in 1989 test marketing Fresh Kitchen refrigerated sauces, entrees, and desserts.

Philip Morris. A 1986 effort by its General Foods division to market a Culinova line of fresh entrees failed due to problems in distributing these chilled products. But in 1989, the new Kraft General Foods division was test marketing Chillery entrees, salads, pasta, and desserts.

Nestlé. Nestlé's Carnation division was already national with a Contadina Fresh line of sauces and pastas, which are less temperature sensitive than entrees. In addition, another division (Nestlé Enterprises) was test marketing the FreshNes line of entrees and salads in Columbus and Cleveland.

The issues faced by these firms (and, according to industry insiders, by several others in early stages of planning) were (1) how to get the products delivered to the stores and maintained conveniently in those stores until sold, (2) deciding just where in the midscale/upscale range these products would end up, (3) finding the product lines (such as entrees or salads) where the sales volume would be the best, and (4) making sure the new technology could work its way into a market already overloaded with deli offerings, precooked meals, and other similar products. Less-critical matters were how best to assure the buyer that the items had not spoiled, how spicy should these products be, and how to price them.

And, in the meantime, branding problems arose. Should these new items be tied to the strong family brands that these firms all had? If so, what secondary branding should distinguish them? In secondary branding or nonfamily branding, what image should be projected by the brand? That is, how upscale? How could the essence of chilled foods best be communicated? Or should the brand even try in a situation such as this?

Please give them whatever help you can on these issues, particularly those on branding. The questions seem to go beyond branding to include positioning, packaging, etc.

Source: Some of the information in this case came from Barbara Toman, "Will U.S. Warm to Refrigerated Dishes?" *The Wall Street Journal*, August 18, 1989, p. B1.

19   CREATIVE IMPLEMENTATION OF THE STRATEGIC PLAN

Setting

Chapter 18 set up the strategic platform decisions and the strategic driving decisions: target market(s), product positioning statement, and branding. Now we can move into the tactics area and look at some of the *special tools and concepts developed to help us in this area*. Obviously, this is not a chapter on how to advertise and sell new products. That's a topic for several whole books.

The Launch Cycle

First, let's correct an impression many people have. They see the launch as a matter of announcing to the world the good news about our great new product. What actually takes place is a **launch cycle**. The launch cycle is a subset of the product life cycle (PLC). See Figure 19–1. It consists of preparations during the prelaunch period, the announcement, the beachhead phase, and then the early growth stage that links the launch cycle back to the PLC.

Preparation is when we build our ability to compete. This means the training of sales and other promotional people, building service capability, putting out **preannouncements** if they are in order, and arranging for stocking of the product at the reseller level. Only on very rare dramatic occasions is there one day when the announcement takes place. The car companies once keyed their announcements (with appropriate on-camera unveilings) to a date in the fall. But such drama does not play well today. In the first place, it is almost impossible to keep a secret.

Instead, we see a *sequence* of announcements, often geared to keeping competitors guessing and to keeping competitors' customers from stocking up just prior to our being available. One sequence goes like this: (1) product testing, beta testers sign confidentiality forms; (2) anticipation—position releases telling about the problem being solved; (3) influentials—press kits for editors,

FIGURE 19–1

The Launch Cycle

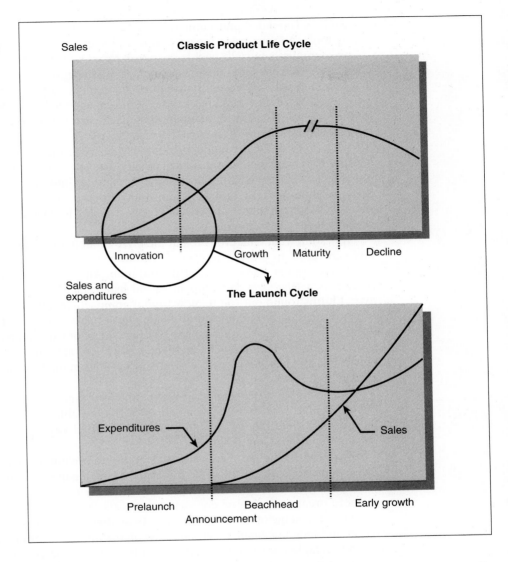

industry researchers, and some customers; (4) broadcast PR—full press releases, product for reviews; (5) promo pieces—the start of advertising. Stages 2 and 3 are used for preannouncements, usually subtle **signaling,** sometimes orchestrated through planned leaks by selected individuals and sometimes just allowed to happen. The intent is to hype interest in the upcoming product and to motivate buyers to hold up long-term competitive orders until the new item is revealed. Of course, in many markets, there is almost no attempt to keep secrets. For example, the whole world knew Microsoft Corporation was announcing their new Windows 95 on August 24, 1995.

Signals (intended and unintended) can be given by use of any of the marketing tools. A lower price is easy to hint at. Others are current advertising, trade shows, comments by salespeople, a speech by a CEO at a security analysts' luncheon in New York City, tips from vendors of packaging or production machinery, stocking calls made on distributors or retailers, appointment of new sales representatives with certain industry experience, and on and on. Some are so subtle they are missed. But in the main, they can be very effective, so much so that they constitute a field of unfair advertising law.[1]

The flip side of preannouncements is the harm that can be done by competitors who hear about our product. When it became known that Ford was introducing a new minivan called Windstar, Chrysler put into operation an aggressive price promotion. This brought them many buyers who otherwise might have awaited Windstar, but it also tweaked interest in Chrysler's own new minivan scheduled for the following year.

It is somewhat dangerous to cut the price of an item *being replaced*, because this can result in current buyers all deciding to await the new; this makes it tough to clear out trade stocks of the old item. An early successful British computer maker (the Osborn Company) went bankrupt when this happened. However, Philips found out (on its new digital compact cassette machine) that if the price of the replaced item is cut too much, customers will clean out retail inventories *before the new product arrives.*[2] The president of Compaq recently remarked at an international conference that there really is no "announcement" any more—new items are just developed and moved into the market, usually on a limited market area basis.

Occasionally a firm can use preannouncment signaling to keep the finance markets happy, but there is a danger of not being able to fulfill the signal. In the software field this has resulted in what is called **vaporware**—signaled but not delivered until much later, if ever.

Firms with smaller shares are more likely to preannounce, large firms will avoid preannouncing if they fear government criticism of monopoly, there will be less preannouncing in industries that are very competitive, and there will be more preannouncing where switching costs are high.[3]

The third stage of the launch cycle—**beachhead**—is not as obvious as preparation and announcement. The name denotes a military landing on enemy soil, a good metaphor for many launches. Another expression is get the ball rolling, and marketers talk of priming the pump, getting a fire started, getting off the

---

[1]Oliver P. Heil and Arlen W. Langvardt, "The Interface Between Competitive Market Signaling and Antitrust Law," *Journal of Marketing,* July 1994, pp. 81–96. A broader view of the tool is in Oliver P. Heil and Rockney G. Walters, "Explaining Competitive Reactions to New Products: An Empirical Signaling Study," *Journal of Product Innovation Management,* January 1993, pp. 53–65.

[2]Kyle Pope, "Philips Tries, Tries Again with Its DCC," *The Wall Street Journal,* October 3, 1994, p. B1.

[3]Jehoshua Eliasberg and Thomas S. Robertson, "New Product Preannouncing Behavior: A Market Signaling Study," *Journal of Marketing Research,* August 1988, pp. 282–92.

ground. In each situation, a standstill is followed by movement in a manner similar to that of a kite pulled into the wind, a descending bobsled, or a military invasion force expanding from a small strip of shoreline.

Announcement kicks off the beachhead phase. And as in the military, communication systems fail, unexpected problems arise, supplies become scarce, and general confusion may reign. As the months go by, a subtle change in emphasis occurs as initial announcement gives way to "reason why" and then to the rationale of trial and the reinforcement of successful experience.

The key decision in the beachhead phase is to end it—inertia has been overcome, the product has started to move. This decision triggers a series of actions. Improvements and flankers will now be brought along as scheduled, new budgets will be approved and released, and temporary marketing arrangements will be made permanent (such as a temporary sales force, an advertising agency, or a direct-mail arrangement).

One new products manager said he knew this decision had been made when the firm's president stopped calling him every couple of days for the "latest news."

Communicating the Story to Prospective Buyers

Now let's go back to the launch planning effort, where it is now time to prepare the advertising, train sales people, and so on. For this we need to review the prevailing marketing mix. Look at Figure 19–2. It shows that the manufacturer (or creator of a service) can allocate its limited funds in five different ways—from spending to improve the product or add line extensions to it (that will make the item more attractive to buyers) to having a retailer use in-store promotion for the new item.

Developers have been following a mix from the very beginning—where decisions were made on R&D budgets. Pharmaceutical firms put the bulk of their money into technical research (product), White Consolidated (white goods) puts it into manufacturing process development (product), and Avon and Mary Kay into personal selling (promotion).

The Communications Plan

Communications is the term most widely used to cover all of the information and attitude effort we put into changing how the end user sees our situation. It involves everything from technical product data to strong persuasion. The communications **requirements** are the specifics that *must* be communicated in our plan. They have been with us almost since the beginning of this project—for example, when we focused in on skiers because we were sure our new plastics technology could deal more effectively with the need for skis to both slide and hold. A communications requirement might be to *remind skiers about their problems with sticking skis, tell them we have a solution, what it is, how they can get it, and so on.* This comes from the PIC, from concept testing, and especially

FIGURE 19–2

*The Basic
Marketing Mix*

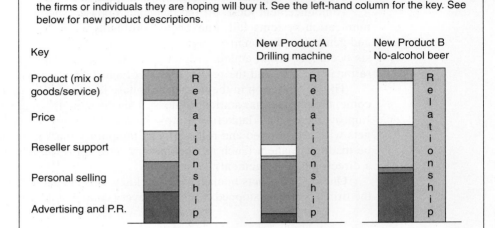

Demand for a new product comes about because of a combination of five stimulants put on top of a standing relationship (image, feeling, franchise) between the firm introducing it and the firms or individuals they are hoping will buy it. See the left-hand column for the key. See below for new product descriptions.

Key

Product (mix of goods/service)

Price

Reseller support

Personal selling

Advertising and P.R.

New Product A
Drilling machine

New Product B
No-alcohol beer

Laser drilling machine: High-tech, breakthrough, sold direct to heavy industry, from leading maker.
No-alcohol beer: Me-too product, hitting the price buyer, sold through restaurants and stores, from Miller's.

What would the two columns look like if Product A was a low-cost import, me-too, sold by distributors, for an unknown maker, and the no-alcohol beer was a technical breakthrough?

from the product protocol statement (where marketing requirements were listed alongside technical requirements). It can be quite short or long, but is a powerful tool in all that follows. It should be based on a solid understanding of the end user's attitudes and behavior.

The communications task is performed with a **communications mix** (or **promotion mix**). But this is complex—there are four mixes—one for communications to the reseller by us, a second for communications to the end user by the reseller, a third for communications to the end user by us, and a fourth for the total communication effort by our team to the end user. See Figure 19–3 for the four mixes of promotional activities, and think about the difficulty of orchestrating four different promotional mixes as a group effort, with one clear message to the end user! Service firms appreciate a simplification of their task because there is usually no reseller. Direct-selling manufacturers also benefit this way.

The task here is to make the best choices—a mix from each set, imaginatively implemented. New products people, in particular, have wide freedom— a clean sheet of paper. There are some restrictions, from the givens in ongoing company operation and from the resellers, who will listen to us but in the end set their own mixes. But still there is always room for creativity.

FIGURE 19–3

A Tricky Complex of Promotional Mixes Support the Overall Marketing Mix

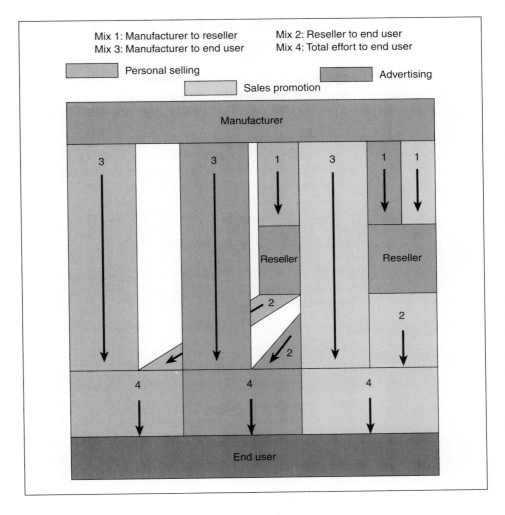

The Copy Strategy Statement

Given the requirements that communications tools are to deliver, let's look at a device used to direct the advertising and most of the sales promotion. Its name varies a lot in practice, but **copy strategy statement** is a common one. It can be used to convey to every advertising and promotion creative person the following items (among many others):

The market segment being targeted.
The product positioning statement.
The communications mix and the pieces covered by this statement.
The major copy points to be communicated.

These claims are usually product attributes, including features, functions, and benefits as well as uses, but they can be almost anything important to that end user making a favorable decision. Here are some examples:

Windows 95 has been tested by over 2,000 firms, in 10 countries.

The provider of this insurance policy is the largest in the world.

Black Pearls perfume was designed by Elizabeth Taylor personally.

This cellular phone has no geographical limitation.

Dockers are available at Penny's.

Future neurosurgeons benefit from the hand-and-eye skills of computer games like this one.

There is no limit. But there must be focus on any one list. Communication capabilities today are under great pressure—humans are exposed to millions of messages and thousands of firms. It's fully OK to list lots of points in a selling piece or an ad, but only a few of them should be on the requirements list. Only a few *must* be accomplished at this time. Incidentally, the copy strategy statement should be written by the team, not by the persons who will create the pieces for it.

Personal Selling

The salesperson is the workhorse of most new product introductions. Even on packaged goods, personal selling is clearly essential—not very often today can we *pull* a product into good retail availability just by virtue of ads on the product story. So sales operations are changing. One observer commented recently:

We don't need people saying "Nothing happens until somebody sells something." This notion was born when Willie Lomans ruled the day. The idea of getting the troops hyped, fired, and revved up, won't do the job today. The change has nothing to do with selling; it has everything to do with buying. Today, successful selling strategies must be built around strong relationships, trust, confidence, and—most important—the salesperson's expertise.[4]

So personal selling operations require the exact things a new product has the least to offer. The new products manager has to work hard to provide them. Fortunately, being professionals, salespeople know (or learn fast) what will sell, and are anxious to have new products *if* they are based on meeting customer needs.

One issue that is sometimes difficult to decide is, how early should we involve salespeople? An industrial firm developing new metal-grinding machinery will have downstream customer coupling, and by the time the project is

---

[4]John R. Graham, "What We Don't Need Can't Help Us Anyway," *Marketing News*, June 22, 1992, p. 4.

ready for marketing, the sales department has been involved for a long time. Advertising people have not been. For a new canned soup, advertising people (including advertising agency personnel) are involved early on, but the sales department usually is not. For services, the new product developer is apt to *be* in the sales department.

Some managers want to keep salespeople away from product development ("No need for them to know," "We must continue selling today's products today"). Some firms find the answer in having sales *managers* involved. A common tactic is to have small groups of district or regional sales managers rotating on advisory teams.

A much more difficult question comes up when the new product needs a *new* sales force—for markets not covered now. Hopefully less-disruptive adjustments can be made. Sometimes it is possible to add *some* of the uncovered customers, or hire a small group of specialists to hit the major pockets of new customers.

How to Motivate Sales People.   A new product is an intrusion. It takes time. It disrupts schedules. It involves change and risk. Salespeople are known for wanting new items to sell, but there are still negatives. Salespeople are not usually given reduced territories when asked to sell a new product. (Note, advertising agencies often work on commissions or percentages.) So, it is important (1) to *investigate* in advance any possible reasons why salespeople might object to the new product, (2) to give them all the *training* and *materials* they need to be effective, and (3) to make sure the product is *available,* in their territories, when they start writing orders for it.

The key is to do our job such that they can do their job. That means to have a product that customers will understand and want to try, and to train the sales force to understand and communicate the story. This training should use the latest technologies. SmithKline Beecham, when introducing a new feline vaccine, prepared an interesting "game show for its sales meeting. It was loaded with 'neato' video graphics, computer animation, music, and sound effects." At the end of the meeting, there was a round of written questions on product knowledge, the winners of which got to compete for cash prizes. The competition involved regional teams of six members, and all audience members bet on which team they thought would win. Questions were "very difficult" and the contestants spent a lot of time preparing.[5]

The Client-Building Team.   Over the last few years, under the prodding of very large buyers, business firms are reluctantly turning to a new mode of customer contact. Rather than have product-line-based sales forces, they are going to *customer-based* sales forces. Each rep sells a longer line, but brings to the customer a team of company people who can address customer problems. The new

---

[5]Cyndee Miller, "Training Pays Off—in Cash," *Marketing News,* July 22, 1991, p. 23.

approach builds good relationships, though tough to sell at first. Wal-Mart had to force the system upon its suppliers, but the firm is now P&G's biggest single customer. A customer-based sales organization requires less of the hard-sell pushing that product-based sales forces can provide.[6]

Price

Price is one of the key tools in a marketing mix, but, oddly enough, it rarely has a strategy or a pricing plan of its own like advertising and selling do. The reason is that price is the other side of the value coin, and value is what this entire operation is about. Price decisions are never made alone, so you have been reading about price actions numerous times in Chapters 17–19. You will note shortly that price is often used temporarily to overcome a trial barrier. We almost never see a pricing manager, or a pricing department. But one thing is true, for every dollar cut from a price, that leaves one less dollar to spend on some other marketing activity. It is sometimes said that a price cut is an admission that a firm can't find any other way to help the buyer. And one other thing, when we work for a year or two building a new product based on solving an important customer need or problem, top management wonders why it cannot carry a premium price.

Alliances

Technical departments have, in recent years, come to realize that they needn't have every possible technical capability required on a new product project. Instead, they form strategic alliances with universities, government units, private research centers, and even competitors to access what they need. Marketing people have been doing this for many years, and still do. In fact, the trade channel itself is a strategic alliance. Independent firms sign a franchise agreement wherein each side promises to do certain things, the result of which is to accomplish a task. Manufacturers don't *have* to use retailers—Avon dropped theirs many years ago.

Advertising is another area for alliances—long-standing agreements are signed with advertising agencies. Service organizations are often brought into a franchise situation. Ditto for warehousing companies, for competitors (to gain sales forces that can reach markets where it is more profitable to use an established organization than to do the whole thing ourselves) and exhibit firms (for trade shows).

It has been said that, today, one can alliance with someone, somewhere, for every task that needs to be done.

---

[6]For more on this swing in sales force thinking, see Patricia Sellers, "How to Remake Your Sales Force," *Fortune,* May 4, 1992, pp. 96–103; and Joseph Conlin, "Teaming Up," *Sales and Marketing Management,* October 1993, pp. 98–104.

A-T-A-R Requirements

In Chapter 8, you met the A-T-A-R model. It displayed the four key steps that an end user must move through if there is to be satisfied adoption of a new product—Awareness, Trial, Availability, and Repeat Use. They make a good framework for deciding just what marketing activities will be undertaken.

Awareness

Awareness is the necessary first step toward adoption (though there are rare cases where a product can be consumed in ignorance or a hurry, with awareness following that trial). Awareness means different things on different products, but is needed on all.

Measuring Awareness

Let's look at three quite different new products. First is a *candy bar.* To a lover of candy bars, the mere mention of a new bar is enough to trigger interest and probably trial purchase. Second is a new *word processing software package* being considered by a leading author of novels. Mere mention is not enough; there must be considerable information because of the inconvenience of trial and the cost of the package. Third is a new *method of cleaning up black water in municipal water-treatment systems,* and the target is civil engineers specializing in recommending municipal water treatment systems. There is so much at stake in their first trial recommendation that they may compile information over several years before making it.

All three people "heard of" their new items on a single day, and in a single message. They may even have heard the positioning and understood it. But one is minutes away from trial and the others months or years away. We don't want awareness for its own sake, we want it because it leads to trial. To measure it, we need to define it. For example, "Have you heard of a new candy bar made from burnt raisins and ground barley?" Some element of the positioning must be present, else there is no reason to try it.

Some business marketers measure it by whether people send in an inquiry for more information. Philips once apparently didn't think about awareness of *what*—it used some very unique MTV-style three-minute commercials about DCC, but forgot to tell what the acronym stood for.

Methods for Getting Awareness

People working in every industry have a good understanding of how to get awareness of a new product in their industry. The ideal probably is a mix: an announcement ad or sales call, then favorable mention by a friend, then seeing the item in use, then a reminder of some type, then getting some professional endorsement in a news account or column, then a reminder of some sort, and then an opportunity to buy it (which stimulates consideration of all the information previously gathered).

Providing all these stimuli is apt to be expensive; the less the product has going for it the more we have to spend on it. And there is never enough money to "do the job right."

Fortunately, the marketplace can help us on awareness and trial if we are following the process of this book. That's because we made sure there was a problem and then worked until we had a good *solution*. If the activity (bowling, eating, machining, surgery, whatever) is important to the customer, so much the better. *An interested, dissatisfied customer, for whom we have good news, needs little more than announcement to get awareness.* It helps even more if the situation is newsworthy (sports, politics, financial markets, health, etc.) and if the product is one that customers see in use frequently (car, TV set, clothing, and the like).

Availability/Reseller Stocking

Services are usually sold direct, and so are many goods. But most goods use resellers, such as distributors and retail dealers. They help us push the product down the channel, but only rarely does a new product offer them really new business without any major effort and cost. For example, Abbott's of New England nearly went broke trying to get its new chowder products into supermarkets. So, it persuaded some of the stores' deli counters to offer single portions of hot chowder. The products were soon in 20 percent of U.S. supermarkets.

Most resellers do a large volume of business in a rather standardized way, with a small margin. Many have constraints on what they can and cannot do— franchise agreements, long-time personal relationships with sales representatives, channel leadership roles, and selling and service systems of their own. They are not at all anxious to make changes in their systems.

Therefore, their thinking should be represented in the product development process—well up the development line, when product attributes are still being worked on. Otherwise, it is usually sufficient to have the resellers' views represented by experienced salespeople—sales managers and what are sometimes called trade relations directors.

We start with a statement of what the reseller's role will be. This role normally includes, for stocking distributors, (1) prestocking activities such as training and installation of equipment, (2) stocking of the new item, (3) preparation for promotion, including training salespeople and service people, and (4) actually doing the promotion, whether just listing the item in a catalog, adding the item to selling schedules, or working with individual buyers to determine their needs and convert interest into sales.

Somewhere along the line we have to know that resellers *can* do what we want and need, and that they *will* do it. Assuming they "can do," the "will do" is a matter of motivation, and for this we arrange a program of encouragement,

---

FIGURE 19–4   Alternative Tools and Devices for Motivating Distributors

A. **Increase the distributor's unit volume.**
   1. Have an outstanding product.
   2. Use pull techniques—advertising, trade and consumer shows, public relations, missionary selling.
   3. Give the distributor a type of monopoly—exclusivity or selectivity.
   4. Run "where available" ads.
   5. Offer merchandising assistance—dollars, training, displays, points of purchase, co-op advertising, in-store demonstrations, store "events," and repair and service clinics.
B. **Increase the distributor's unit margin.**
   1. Raise the basic percentage margin.
   2. Offer special discounts—e.g., for promotion or service.
   3. Offer allowances and special payments.
   4. Offer to *prepay* allowances to save interest.
C. **Reduce the distributor's costs of doing business.**
   1. Provide managerial training.
   2. Provide dollars for training.
   3. Improve the returned-goods policy.
   4. Improve the service policy.
   5. Drop-ship delivery to distributor's customers.
   6. Preprice the merchandise.
   7. Tray pack the merchandise or otherwise aid in repackaging it.
D. **Change the distributor's attitude toward the line.**
   1. By encouragement—management negotiation, sales calls, direct mail, advertising.
   2. By discouragements—threats to cut back some of the above benefits or legal action.
   3. Rap sessions—talk groups, focus groups, councils.
   4. Better product instruction sessions—better visuals, better instructions.

---

based on items from the list in Figure 19–4. Without any question, proof that the new item will sell is the best motivation. But channel firms can be tough if they feel mistreated.[7] Elizabeth Arden Division of Unilever had to cancel a planned introduction of a new Elizabeth Taylor fragrance called Black Pearls because the firm slashed monies for department store salespeople. The stores refused to stock it, forcing Arden to plan distribution through mass merchandisers, but the whole deal was ultimately canceled, even though Black Pearl advertising had started running. The division looked to lose millions of dollars, and its president resigned by mutual consent. Moral: Don't deal carelessly with a necessary team player.

Central Computer Products, Filmore, California, knew it might have problems of awareness and channel stocking, so it offered a $69.95 accounting software package for free (actually, just a $6.95 shipping and handling charge).

---

[7]For more see Elizabeth J. Wilson and Arch G. Woodside, "Marketing New Products with Distributors," *Industrial Marketing Management,* February 1992, pp. 15–21. For how 3M choose the best channel for a new industrial product, see V. Kasturi, Melvyn A. J. Menezes, and E. P. Maier, "Channel Selection for New Industrial Products: A Framework, Method, and Application," *Journal of Marketing,* July 1991, pp. 69–82.

The widely publicized maneuver created favorable word-of-mouth, and the firm leapfrogged over a retail trade already crowded with such packages. Over a million orders came in.[8]

One trade channel where the players seem to have run out of creativity is that of food products. Large retailers now often "sell" their scarce space, charging manufacturers sizeable **slotting allowances**—so much per store for minimum shelf positions. Again, however, a really new item for which there is consumer demand will face less resistance.

Trial

Getting awareness is often difficult, but usually possible. The same goes for availability and some reseller promotion. Trial is another matter. Trial is the stumbling point for most products that fail, and it is the cause of winning products not winning a great deal more.

What We Mean by Trial

Trial of a new product is *limited usage,* hopefully under normal usage conditions, that will permit the customer to verify claims and learn the advantages and disadvantages of the good or service. Trial is on a scale from a taste test of a new cheese in a supermarket to a three-year experiment by a major company on a new telecommunications system. There must be learning, relative to the adoption decision; thus, the cheese taste may be a full trial if taste by the tester is the only issue. But if the rest of the family has a say, or if the package may or may not keep the cheese fresh, or if the product tends to turn grey while sitting on a table or in a sandwich, then the taste test was not a trial.

Trial may be **personal, vicarious,** or **virtual.** It's tough to "try" a burial service. Elevators and plant location services are also difficult, though visiting the site of a previous buyer simulates trial. This is partly a vicarious experience. Virtual trial can be achieved by various electronic setups, and even a pseudo-virtual experience via video.

A key requirement is that a trial must have some cost associated with it. The more important the trial, the more the cost, or there is not enough motivation for the necessary learning to take place. The cheese taste test, just mentioned, had very little cost (a few seconds of time, possible embarrassment in the store if the taste is awful), so the customer would consider little more than the taste, and perhaps color, aroma, and texture.

That is usually not enough *for the next step in the process*—the acceptance of the item, its adoption into a usage system, or its repeat purchase. The cheese taster probably would want to buy a small package and take it home for the *real* trial.

---

[8]"Business Bulletin," *The Wall Street Journal,* August 19, 1993, p. A1.

Barriers to Trial

Resistance to trial takes the form of barriers. **Barriers to trial** cause customers to delay or even permanently postpone trial. They must be anticipated and overcome. Here are what we consider to be the major barriers to trial:[9]

Lack of Interest in the Claim.   They don't see the advantages to them, they don't have the problem, they are too busy for this minor issue, etc. Body deodorants were shunned by men for years because they "didn't need them." Later, the market delayed adoption of the microwave oven (an item that for several years was called the "most expensive coffee-warmer in town"). Another base for lack of interest is a strong negative belief, such as on the topless swim suit for women, the birth control pill, and porno videos.

Lack of Belief in the Claim.   It may be that the positioning statement doesn't offer enough proof, or that the customer simply doesn't feel the product can do what the claim says. No-suds detergents were perhaps the classic here—without suds, how could the detergent clean?

Rejection of Something Negative about the Product.   Every product has disadvantages; one of them may be strong enough to kill trial. This happens with cancer chemotherapy occasionally; patients fear the dreadful downside effects. Another negative of new products is a *change in role;* many professional people refuse to sit at a computer keyboard.

Complacency.   Regardless of what the product has and doesn't have to offer, there will be many people who just don't get around to trying it. Most potential customers have busy lives, and lots to think about other than trying a new item.

Competitive Ties.   Most potential customers are now buying something that we are hoping to replace. Makers of those other products have been busy building strong relationships with their customers, perhaps even tying them into long-term service contracts, warehouse-loading discounts, and just strong personal friendships. The loyalists mentioned as a market segment in Chapter 18 are very slow on trial. On the other hand, there are other segments of people (innovators and early adopters) who just routinely try anything that comes out, especially if there is an introductory deal on it.

Doubts that Trial Will Tell Them What They Really Would Like To Know. For example, how will flower show judges score the metallic shine on a new strain of roses?

---

[9]Some of these came from S. Ram and Jagdish N. Sheth, "Consumer Resistance to Innovations: The Marketing Problem and It's Solutions," *Journal of Consumer Marketing,* Spring 1989, pp. 5–14.

Lack of a Usage Opportunity.   Not every product is used daily or even weekly. Lots of potential triers may be waiting for an opportunity, delayed sometimes by poor weather conditions or a blip in the economy.

Cost of Purchase and Use.   Prospective users may lack the funds to try the product ever, and they may lack the funds to try it just now. Either way, for any but low-priced items, cost can be a major deterrent.

Routines, Automatic Buying, and Consuming Systems.   A producer of word processing software recently offered to accept any *competitive* package for the low upgrade price on its latest version. Many of the products we buy (and especially those that business buys) are tied up in usage routines that people don't like to break. Some people have even admitted they try to avoid *hearing* of new items in routine categories!

Risk of Rejection, Failure.   Lots of people (those in business too) don't relish the personal risk of an unsuccessful trial of a new item, especially if that usage had to be sold to a supervisor or spouse. Not any more perhaps, but for years it was known that purchasing agents could buy a new IBM product with no fear of criticism if it didn't work out; not so the other brands.

How to Overcome Those Barriers

We hear of these barriers early—for example, in concept testing and product use testing, as well as from experience in the industry. Our problem is finding the time and money to address them all. Figure 19–5 shows techniques that are used.

Note how many ways the barrier solution uses *price*—free goods, couponing, a signing bonus, deferred payment, refunding cost of competitor's stocks, entering with a penetration (low) price, discounts, rebates, free service, free replacement offer, cooperative advertising, direct cash payment for trying, and others. In most cases, the buyer is deferring trial because of anticipating loss of something—loss of time, loss of money, loss of prestige, etc. The most obvious answer is to pay the buyer for such loss.

This emphasis on price has led sellers to adopt complex discount schedules (it's easier later to drop a discount than to raise the list price). Using discounts also fits with the most popular of the new product price strategies:[10]

> *Premium or skim*—a price clearly above the market, but appropriate to a differentiated product, nonthreatening to competition, and with room for some price manipulations.
>
> *Meet the market*—though there may be no *one* market price, this strategy says pick a price that takes price out of the play as much as possible.

---

[10]For an actual case, with data and a "solution" as between skim, meet, and penetrate, see Arch G. Woodside, "Pricing an Industrial Technological Innovation: A Case Study," *Industrial Marketing Management,* 1995, pp. 145–50.

FIGURE 19–5   **Methods for Overcoming the Barriers to Trial**

Here are methods suggested for overcoming the major cases of barriers to trial.

Lack of interest in the claim—education in promotion materials, forced vicarious trials.

Lack of belief in the claim—evidence, compiled and clearly presented, plus free goods to reduce the cost of learning for themselves, plus endorsements.

Rejection of something negative about the product—same as with lack of interest, plus development effort to overcome the negative, plus careful targeting to avoid these people, plus a direct attack on the objection using humorous self-kidding promotions that make the objection less serious.

Complacency—couponing and other action-stimulating devices, plus free goods if necessary, plus endorsements of urgency.

Competitive ties—a "signing" bonus to cover the costs of changing suppliers, plus strong arguments directed specifically against the competitor's product, plus prearrangements to defer premature commitments to competitors.

Doubts that trial will tell them what they really would like to know—offer endorsement or names of their acquaintances who made the trial and got the right information, plus defer payment for the trial period.

Lack of a usage opportunity—create a usage situation, usually by paying for it. If user just bought a year's supply, offer to refund the costs of one year's storage. Preannouncements will perhaps make them defer a rare usage opportunity (keeping the "window" open for a short while).

Cost—using penetration pricing strategy will help, though that approach is expensive. Temporary pricing reductions such as from discounts and rebates, plus try to cut the customer's total outlay that includes use of the product, servicing the product, and replacing the product, plus reduce up-front cost, plus take whatever dollars you think you may have to give them in discounts and see if you can buy something with that money they would like better (e.g., training of their personnel, insuring against rejects, cooperative advertising).

Routines—send in a service team to help work out the arrangements, plus stress one big advantage that would make some inconvenience worthwhile, plus provide simple non-routine-busting usage opportunities, such as with demo disks for software, plus restress the benefits of our routine over the one they are now using, plus offer special inducements to persons who are "routine gatekeepers."

Risk of rejection—use endorsements to put the user in with a fine group of others who tried the product, plus use a brand name that gives rationale for trial, plus offer them a specific cash payment if the trial doesn't work out well for them.

Penetration—a low price is used to buy a piece of the market. The low price will be met perhaps, but in the meantime share is gained. But such a strategy is probably a cop-out if the product is unique and superior. Dangers: tough to raise later after share is achieved, and if met immediately, just wastes the opportunity and at a lower price.

A cautious premium price seems to achieve the benefit both ways—brings some of the product's value to our bottom line and gives marketers freedom to meet special opportunities, yet doesn't price us out of the market.

Repeat Purchase

If our target market buyers do a serious trial on our new item, and *if* we had previously been assured from the product use test that people would like it, repeat buying is virtually assured. There are competitive actions to repel and counter. There is the continuing problem of complacency, especially in markets where our item's benefits are not crucial to anything. There is the careless new product manager who fails to keep a ready supply available for the buyer who wants to repeat. And, as always, we need to be sure customers are satisfied with their total relationships with our firm, well beyond the product itself.

Usually we have actions in the marketing program to encourage further usage—for instance, new uses for the item and ready availability of additional product as well as of continued service.

Summary

Chapter 19 was the third of a three-chapter set on the subject of marketing planning. It dealt with what some call the tactical portion of the planning task. We looked at the launch cycle, the communication program, and the requirements of success: awareness, trial, availability, and repeat purchase (A-T-A-R). Each is very difficult to attain given the on-going nature of life and business out there in the market and the actions of other players such as competitors. Since a marketing launch entails hundreds or even thousands of actions, we focused on those that seem most critical and most difficult in practice, relative to new products.

Once the full marketing launch plan has been worked out, many firms like to devise some way to hold a dress rehearsal—just to see if there are any glitches. After all, millions of dollars may be spent in the next few months. So, in Chapters 20 and 21, we will look at what is called market testing. It is the third of a testing triad—with concept testing (Chapter 9) and product use testing (Chapter 16).

Applications

More questions from that interview with the company president.

1. "You frighten me when you mention alliances in the marketing launch. Hardly a week goes by but what some scientist says we simply must join an alliance. Don't scientists ever work alone any more? Anyway, even though we need alliances on the technical side, that's no reason for them on the marketing side. I don't think I recall hearing about alliances over there—you mention ad agencies? And resellers? No, those are just contracts for service, and in almost every case those are pseudocontracts—they can be broken if it's important. Why does your text call them alliances?"

2. "I am a member of a committee in our Booksellers Association. We have a medium-sized chain in that business—not a Barnes & Noble or a Borders, but we do pretty well. Our committee has worked up a new service to 'sell' to our franchised retail outlets—they don't have to take every new service the trade association works up, but we have a good one—it relates to helping them avoid getting caught by one of these professors who writes a book and then goes around the country buying large quantities from several stores (at massive discounts), just to win a spot on the *New York Times* best-seller list.

Most of those books end up back on the market again, at great discounts, taking good customers from us. We are getting a group of industry experts to report any suspicious activity they spot, or even hear about. We will evaluate and verify, and then will fax each outlet the particulars. Question: We've picked an ad agency to prepare mailings to the stores, asking them to join up. Cost is only $50/month per store. Can you do what you talked about, that is, write out a Copy Strategy Statement for me to give the agency?"

3. "Incidentally, some of the folks in the software division have come up with an idea for a new service. Seems as though they found that computer people around the world have real trouble learning about new software—not its existence and its general claims (that's in all the magazines and direct mail they get, in their own languages even). No, what we're going to sell is reports of all favorable and unfavorable comments that appear in the press, anywhere in the world, about all new software. The customer can access this information, online, with reports classified by type and by brand of software, and in six languages. They think software users, particularly those out of the mainstream of personal business contacts, will like it. But, and this is a problem they worry about, the whole field of software is full of announcements, news, people yelling. How in the world can they break through all that noise to get prospects informed of this new service (I guess you'd say aware) to where they can *make a decision to try it?* (They have a trial package, by the way: five-day, 20 inquiries, for a very small fee.)"

4. "Sampling is another tool we like—you know, like that trial package I just mentioned. Samples are really effective in getting trial among the people who are somewhat inclined toward a new product in the first place. But several of our divisions can't use samples per se because of the nature of their products. Could you tell me what might be a substitute for samples in the marketing of a new type of each of the following?

   a. Retirement condos.

   b. Coffins.

   c. Milling machines.

   d. Diamond rings.

   e. Replacement tires."

CASE: SPIRALURGY FURNITURE INC.

The following is a story of something that will happen somewhere around 1998–2000. It can't happen now because the metallurgy is not yet available. But a development group in a university town we can call Sands, located in northern California, knows what they want to do: make lowcost, functional furniture for selected markets. When available (from the space program) the metal will permit making chairs, beds, desks, and wardrobes (portable closets) in a spiral-extruding process. Extrusions are usually straight or flexible, but this metal has a molecular, built-in desire to spiral, and that spiraling can be controlled. It can be tiny, for a table leg, larger for a chair leg, and larger still for a desk top. It can be pressed while at very high temperatures during the extrusion process to make sheets of material that would be used for seats and assembled as sides and bottoms of the storage unit. Some degrees of flexibility can be introduced by addition of several chemicals, so they visualize flexible chairs, lamp fixtures, and more. The material is one of the toughest materials ever seen—even saws won't cut it unless equipped with a diamond edge (and that edge doesn't last very long). Assembly is easy, using the natural (though taut) spiraling effect of the material.

The advantages are several. Though utilitarian, the metal itself is a rather attractive off-white color, and unless pressed, the surfaces are attractive rounded spirals of different diameters. The material sets in such a way that it is virtually indestructible, even in student housing (a target the developers are currently working, given their location and positions as professors in the engineering school). Of course, it is peculiar too. Some people will absolutely hate it because the metal has a tendency to spring back against any attempt to bend it. In development work at a laboratory near Sacramento, one of the developers lost part of an ear while trying to bend a leg to fit under a computer storage drawer. Landlords and women may object to buying it because subsequent roomers may not like that feature, or other features that may appear later in the development. Retailers will find it easy to sell, but the low price will make margins (in dollars) well below those in current furniture, even the "synthetic oak" at mass outlets.

Lots is yet unknown about the material—for example, its ability to hold paint and what type of paint, and whether the material tends to return to a more natural state over time (it hasn't so far, in four years of use). Though immune from damage by liquids normal in a residence, there are certain acids that will etch the surface.

It would seem this proposal might serve to apply the A-T-A-R concepts in Chapter 19. If the developers do indeed get an expected venture capital investment by a large manufacturer of lower-cost office furniture, and if they market a line of furniture for school markets (college, at first, and K–12 a few years later), what problems can you see them having on awareness, trial, availability, and repeat? Assume for now that the furniture does perform well. How should they plan on getting the attention of students and renters? And how should you bring them to where they might be willing to try the product? How might availability be achieved in your area? Are there natural outlets for products like these? If so, how might we approach them? How could the developers be sure they can expect a good rate of repurchase (given that some of the market's largest buyers will be buying for multiple students)?

Answers to the issues in Figure V–3:

1. *Teams* make these decisions, not one functional group.
2. Marketing people have been in all along. And there should be no "taking over" because technical people should stay.
3. These paradigms *aid thinking*. Exuberance and excitement we have, but they don't replace thinking.
4. Not *marketing*'s—the *entire firm*'s. Every part of the firm has contributed to what we offer the end user. Hopefully, the end user has a problem and will welcome the product.

5. A good target market has several dimensions, not just sales potential. A large piece of a favorable segment may be much more profitable.
6. The PIC guides *all* stages—it is a strategic plan for the entire operation through to whatever its goals call for.
7. Data don't support this. Quite often, a follower comes up with the winning design.
8. Goals may be expressed in customer satisfaction terms too, but there are usually other goals unique to the situation—e.g., build a bridge to new market dominance.
9. Perhaps if really meaningless, but they should be meaning*ful,* helpful in telling the product story.
10. The launch is *managed*—if we start to sink, let's hope there is a large dipper handy. (See Chapter 22.)
11. Opening night is the first salvo in a drive to achieve the project goals—success. A successful opening night brings little profit, but a long run brings a big one.

20 MARKET TESTING

Pseudo Sale

Setting

At this time, glance back at the illustration in the introduction to Part V. It shows the twin streams process, and where we are at this time. We have a physical product or the complete specifications for a new service. Early concept testing showed a need, and the use test indicated the emerging product met that need, without serious drawbacks. And we have a marketing plan.

Now what do we do? Market the item quickly, before competition finds out what we are up to? Or find a way to check out what we have done, to see if it really looks like we will be successful, before spending what usually is a lot of money on the launch? The option open to us is called **market testing**. Chapter 20 gives the overall picture for market testing and introduces the first of the three methods—pseudo sale. Chapter 21 discusses the other two general methods of market testing.

Where We Are Today

Over the years, one *type* of market testing has been the most common one and the one people talk about—test marketing. Many people mistakenly think *market testing* means *test marketing*, but actually, there are several other methods. Test marketing is now a minor player, having suffered a major loss of ground to newer, faster, and cheaper techniques.

The basic idea of **market testing** is to test the combined package of product *and* its marketing plan. So, what better method than that of science—finding a representative piece of the market, and trying it out there? Marketers implemented the entire plan in a couple of cities or metropolitan areas, kept a couple other identical areas as a control, and then projected the test results to the total market. Naturally, they called it **test marketing**.

Of course, the marketplace made a poor test tube. As we will see later, the test marketing approach, using those matched cities, always had drawbacks. By 1970, managers didn't want to wait around the 3–12 months that test marketing took. Competitive pressures piled up, managers were no longer so sure whether a test market was really successful, newer options became available, and managers grew smarter—they now had a better feel for just the one or two things they needed to know.

Fortunately, technologies came along that helped fuel the development of other market testing methods—mathematical models for forecasting sales with much less than complete market data, store-loading systems where it was no longer necessary to go to the trouble of "selling in" the inventory, scanner systems of retail store checkouts that compiled product data not even dreamed of in the good old days of test marketing, and communications systems that permitted a form of trial marketing over areas far greater than test market cities and from which one could quickly roll on into the total market as soon as assurances appeared.

The consequence is a variety of market research methods that, used alone and in various combinations, will meet the needs of any new products manager. But before getting into those methods, let's take a good look at the manager's situation.

We Are in a Very Competitive World

Several times in this book we have faced the effects of management's desire for speed—faster cycle time. Sometimes it appears we simply must get the new product to the market in a timely manner or it will no longer be competitive. This means we take risks, the biggest one being the management style of concurrent development or parallel processing. We skip steps not absolutely essential and start the next step before the earlier one is completely done.

The Engineers Have Developed Ways to Test the Components of a Product at the Time They Are Made

In the building of an automobile there was once a time (again more apocryphal than true to life) where the firm rushed to make the component parts (frames, engines, etc.), pulled them together at an assembly operation, assembled them, and then had a worker with a large rubber mallet standing at the end of the line to pound out any misfits. Today, the very principle of quality is that we *build quality in.* Testing for quality is essentially unnecessary as we go "upstream" in the process, build each piece properly and make sure it is right. *Then* we assemble them.

On the marketing side we are now doing the same thing. An ad is a component; so is a selling visual, a service contract, a trained sales rep, a price, a package, and so on. There are literally hundreds of *things* that marketing requires. These things we call **marketing plan components,** and we are encouraged to test them upstream too, not at the end, all together.

They only need further testing if their purchase and use by the customer puts demands on them in **synergy** with other components or with variables in the marketplace. At market testing time we test synergies, not components.

Market Testing Is Not Solely in the Province of the Market Research Department

Market researchers play the lead role in market testing, just as design engineers do in the design of parts. But we have been knocking down the functional chimneys or silos. (See Chapters 13–15.) We have teams leading projects, and sometimes they can get the information they need using methods you might not even recognize as market research. For instance, let's imagine that a new product manager meets with the manufacturing member of a team and an engineer from the one and only customer likely to be interested in a product now under development (say, a big original equipment manufacturer like Whirlpool). The question is, given a price that has been decided, how many of the new items would the customer want for a first run (the item has been previously tested in a product use test with that customer). A figure is worked out, and our people plan our production accordingly.

Was that a market test? Yes. With that customer, everything was in place—our product was ready to sell and our marketing program (including price) was ready. A solid demand estimate was arrived it. Launch followed.

At the other extreme of complexity, on a consumer packaged good being rolled out in the mid-Atlantic region for a month or so before being rolled on into New York and New England, the entire firm is involved. Market research people are gathering some of the information; other managers are gathering other information—e.g., product cost, incidence of product complaints, competitors' reactions, legal hits, ability of vendors to meet their time and quality requirements, ability of shipping to get product to distributors in the required condition, and so on. Reacting to all that information is a *team* problem—facts are not handled in isolation. The leader of a new products team is a manager. The market test of a highly advertised food product or shampoo is a huge responsibility, and puts heavy pressure on market research people. Still, it is the *firm's new products team* doing the testing.

The Market Testing Decision

The full set of market testing technique options will come later; first we need to get a feeling for the decision to test or not to test.

When Is the Decision Made?

The decision of whether and how to test can be made at many different times. Figure 20–1 shows the trade-offs. On the one hand, the longer we wait, the more we will know about our product and its marketing program; that makes testing more useful and more reliable. But the longer we wait to do the test, the higher the costs, the later the entry, the more damage competitors can do, and so on. The solution, of course, is to begin the testing as soon as a technique can be found that will tell us *what we need to know*. Some consumer products market testing actually begins before the product is even firmed up—it works with a concept statement! Other market testing, such as that with the appliance manufacturer above, cannot be done until we have everything in place ready to go.

Is This an Easy Decision to Make?

The really tough thing about market testing is that upper management tends to lean heavily toward doing none of it. They doubt the fancy statistics, they don't like the costs, the team is already behind schedule, and they certainly dislike tipping their hand to competition. They would prefer a secret development, hitting the market as a complete surprise to competitors. Who wouldn't?

Internal decision makers, however, often have doubts—nagging, frustrating, dangerous doubts. Any time we make something new, we cannot really be sure about *anything*. Stop to think about this—with a few rare exceptions, everything we think we know about the new product and its marketing is *not a fact*—it is an opinion, a guess, a judgment, a hope, a dream, an order (from above). The full scenario of the new item's marketing will be played out on a playing field where all too many people still have to react to something. Even they cannot be sure of their reaction, especially when we aren't completely sure what our offer will be, and we sure cannot anticipate what competition will tell buyers about it.

FIGURE 20–1

Decision Matrix on When to Market Test

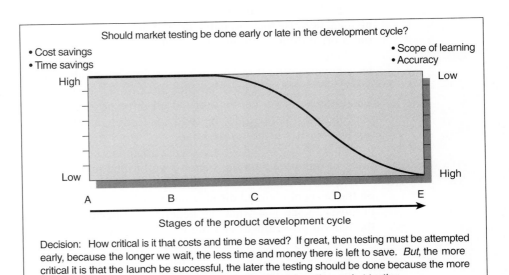

Should market testing be done early or late in the development cycle?

• Cost savings   • Time savings   • Scope of learning   • Accuracy

High   Low

Low   High

A   B   C   D   E

Stages of the product development cycle

Decision: How critical is it that costs and time be saved? If great, then testing must be attempted early, because the longer we wait, the less time and money there is left to save. *But*, the more critical it is that the launch be successful, the later the testing should be done because the more we know about the final product, the more we can learn from the market testing.

It takes a strong manager to say at this point, "I know we have spent a fortune, and we are running late, but I am not convinced we have made the right decisions. I want to take a couple of months (or more) to be sure." What kind of confidence does that inspire in the typical top management?

The fact seems to be this: if a firm (or an industry) believes in market testing and practices it regularly, the decision *not* to do it in any particular case has the burden of proof. Asking for a market test is not a confession of failure on the team's part. This is also true in the sciences and many other fields. Major parts of the entertainment field market test almost every time (staging a trial performance of a new musical in Boston, for example).

The basic *value* of market testing is unquestionable. But we have a warehouse of examples where firms skipped it and were successful. Unfortunately, we have another warehouse full of failures that probably could have been avoided with a market test. IBM marketed the original PC without a market test; but the PC came from a crash 12-month program that had immense risks in it from the start, and billions of market-share dollars were at stake in a very temporary market window of opportunity. These were good reasons for skipping a test. Unfortunately, IBM did not have those good reasons for the IBM Jr., nor did RCA when it marketed the first SelectaVision videodisc player, nor did scores of others.

One of these others was a General Electric division, Fleet Services. Fleet Services developed a service called Car-Pro, a call-in service where a car owner with problems could talk with professional mechanics, and get an objective view to offset suggestions received locally. When the service was marketed, it failed, as it turned out primarily because people wouldn't pay the $49 fee. Although the firm said they had test-marketed the service prior to launch, apparently whatever testing they did missed the price issue.[1] A market test tests the *entire* marketing plan, including price. It's altogether too easy for people to say they like an idea, because they probably do, but that answer is no purchase-predictor without a price dimension on the concept.

Figure 20–2 shows how market testing relates to other testing—the three major tests covering the three major causes for new product failure—CT for "lack of need," PUT for "product does not meet need," and MT for "marketed poorly." Many times a firm is in a hurry at all three of those stages, so it first skips the concept test, then it skips the field use testing, and then, if it also skips the market testing, it will be flying blind.

Interestingly, what we are saying about market testing (as with almost everything in this book) applies equally well to the public sector. Recently, a professor/consultant in California argued that the state had rejected "school choice" on the basis of claimed disadvantages, whereas it should have market-tested the proposal to see just what the benefits and disadvantages really are.[2] Actually, the federal government is a big user of market testing.

---

[1]"Car-Pro," *Across the Board*, March 1994, p. 37.

[2]"Big Unknowns Defeated School Choice," Robert A. Grayson, in "Letters to the Editor," *The Wall Street Journal*, November 29, 1993, p. A11.

FIGURE 20–2

*How Market
Testing Relates
to the Other
Testing Steps*

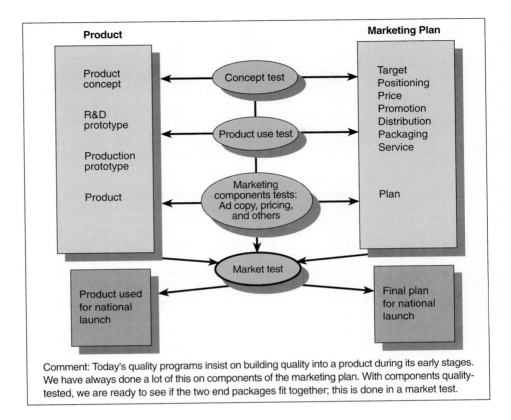

Comment: Today's quality programs insist on building quality into a product during its early stages. We have always done a lot of this on components of the marketing plan. With components quality-tested, we are ready to see if the two end packages fit together; this is done in a market test.

See Figure 20–3 for some classic examples, and we will talk about others as we work our way through Chapters 20 and 21.[3]

The Two Key Values We Get from Market Testing

First, planners need *solid forecasts of dollar and unit sales volume*—not the general market figures or ranges of possible shares that guided earlier planning decisions. Second, the planners need *diagnostic information* to help them revise and refine anything about the launch that seems to require it—product, marketing effort, you name it. There are usually controversies that must be resolved within the team. Examples of diagnostic information abound. Here are a few:

1. Cadbury tested a new fresh cream dessert in a tetra package. Retailers claimed that the package wouldn't stack, so it had to be changed.

---

[3]A version of the decision process managers go through was given as a case study in Steven H. Star and Glen L. Urban, "The Case of the Test Market Toss-Up," *Harvard Business Review*, September–October 1988, pp. 10–16.

FIGURE 20–3   Classics Cases of Firms that Wish They Had Not Skipped Market Testing
---

New Coke: The Coca-Cola Company had perhaps the most famous example of a thoroughly tested product marketed without a market test. Allegedly, some 200,000 people overwhelmingly preferred the New Coke. But when offered the chance to buy it, in the total milieu of a market full of publicity, they refused. Coke had to bring back the old formula, branded Coke Classic, and it is still the leading seller.[*]

TV-Cable Week: Staffers who developed Time Inc.'s competitor to *TV Guide* "repeatedly called for a small-scale market test and were repeatedly turned down." The $100 million investment lasted six months.[†]

Treesweet Low-Calorie Orange Juice: "Clinton E. Owens thought he had all the fixins for success in the juice business...industry veteran...innovative product...jazzy package...eye-catching ads..." A year later, after "betting the farm" without market testing, the product had failed, the juice lines were on the block, and Chapter 11 "was a possibility."[‡]

Toppels: In a 1986 article about companies getting on the fast track, "Frito-Lay skipped test marketing for its new Toppels cheese snack so competitors wouldn't have time to study the ingredients and copy them.[§] 'We felt very strongly we had a winner and didn't want to tip our hand.'" But in 1989, after noting several failures in new snack products, "The debacle convinced Frito-Lay that true market testing is a necessity, even for a market leader."[ǁ]

Sources:

[*]The New Coke story is told in many places, one good summary being "Coca-Cola's Big Fizzle," *Time*, July 22, 1985, pp. 48–52.

[†]"Time Inc.'s $47 Million Belly Flop," *Business Week*, February 17, 1986, pp. 14–15.

[‡]"A Juice Maker Squeezes Itself Dry," *Business Week*, August 10, 1987, p. 42.

[§]Ronald Alsop, "Companies Get on Fast Trick to Roll Out Hot New Brands," *The Wall Street Journal*, July 10, 1986, p. 23.

[ǁ]"Marketers Blunder their Way through the 'Herb Decade,'" *Advertising Age*, February 13, 1989, p. 3.

2. A camouflage cosmetic worked well at concealing scars, as planned, but a much greater market opened up when women decided to use it for concealing minor blemishes.

3. An industrial firm developed a very complex new technology, gave it thorough technical testing, and went into a regional market test. Only then did the firm discover that the new system could be blocked by a group of consulting engineers who had not been included in the marketing plan.

The Decision Factors for Deciding Whether to Market Test

Each new product project has a unique situation, but here are the most common important factors considered in the market test decision.

Any Special Twists on the Launch.   Did the original charter dictate a tight time schedule? There may be special considerations such as the need for new volume to help sell off an operation or need to assist a new CEO to get off to a quick start. Does the charter limit the funds for the project such that it *must* be rolled out, growing to each new stage as profits come in from earlier stages? Is this launch part of a far bigger launch program, e.g., where the firm is trying to gain new industry experience in one world market to permit a critical expansion into another world market?

What Information Is Needed.   We look first to see if this is one of those situations where huge sums of money have been spent and where careers have been staked yet no one knows what will really happen out there when the item becomes available. Conditions permitting, there is a strong argument for thorough market testing. This is partly to avoid a huge loss from market rejection, but also to protect against being surprised by too *much* volume. Nabisco launched Ritz Bitz directly to the national market, and immediately found demand outstripping their bakeries' output capacity. As a consequence, they now try to use the rollout market testing process discussed in Chapter 21.[4] Still, when the firm knew (from consumer reactions) that they had a big winner with SnackWell's, they went national and were many months working their way out of back-orders.

One experienced Procter & Gamble market researcher said he considers skipping the market test if the following conditions exist:

1. Capital investments are small and forecasts are conservative.
2. The use tests went well and consumer interest is high.
3. The company knows the business well and has been successful there.
4. Advertising is ready and successfully tested; sales promotion plan does not depend on perfect execution.[5]

The second type of information need is more *operational*. It is for learning, learning *how* to do something that the launch requires. Remember, a launch involves the whole ball of wax, all functions, manufacturing, selling, servicing, financing, dealing with vendors and resellers, etc. Specifically, the more common needs are:

Manufacturing—besides the volume estimates, we also need the experience of running the system at a low level before turning it to full speed. New product annals are full of sad stories along this line, a recent one being the case of Weyerhaeuser marketing a new concept in disposable diapers (UltraSofts). The manufacturing process called for spraying a liquid onto material, and when they set up a line to serve a market test in western New York state, the liquid got hot and caught on fire. The process was essentially defective, and although the firm regretted the failure of the item (it took off very well), they were glad they were

---

[4]Patricia Sellers, "How to Remake Your Sales Force," *Fortune*, May 4, 1992, pp. 97–103. Punned Nabisco Biscuit president and CEO Ellen Marram: We roll out gradually "so that once appetites are whetted, customers are not left chomping at the bit."

[5]Robert E. Davis, "The Role of Market Research in the Development of New Consumer Products," *Journal of Product Innovation Management*, September 1993, pp. 309–17.

only at test production levels. Earlier, pilot production for prototype material had worked perfectly.

Vendors—can they actually do what they have promised? In the diaper case just mentioned, a key vendor was unable to solve a problem that might have permitted the product to continue.

Resellers—again, can they do what there is reason to think they should be able to? Will there be special demands that we don't know about?

A *servicing infrastructure*—partly ours and partly that of others in the general market picture. To say one can service a product is, unfortunately, sometimes far from a guarantee.

Customers—will they buy, stock, and use the item as expected? Does acceptance of this item require a significant change in purchasing habits or product usage? And is there reason to think we might not be able to bring such a change about? Will there be special service requirements, special return privileges, unexpected demands for training personnel, and so on?

Skipped component testing—did we have to accept, say, an ad campaign or a new free-goods program because of time pressures? Did we skip the product use test? If so, one can be built into the first few weeks or months of a market test.

Cannibalization—most new products threaten to take at least part of their volume from other products the firm has on the market. This is a very difficult forecast to make; many new items have been marketed, sold well, and then discovered to contribute nothing but costs to the firm's treasury.

Conditions that reduce the need for information—the above factors argue *for* information, but today's managers anticipate this problem by building in customer involvement. Firms that involve customers from the very beginning (even to having customer engineers work on their new product teams) get early answers to lots of questions. Some firms approach this level of involvement by having customers pay for the material used in product use testing—e.g., Owens-Corning wanted highway maintenance departments to take a new crack filling product seriously, so they charged for what was used in the use test. Far better learning took place. Too, some firms have programs in total quality management that force some of the learning needed for items noted earlier in this list.

We must remember that the people making the final "market testing versus full launch" decision are not working in the dark. In most cases they have done this many times before and usually have years of experience in the particular business at hand. When the operations manager at Bell Atlantic decides to offer licensed repair services a contract on a new cellular phone installation, this decision is not a guess.

Costs.   Market test costs are of three types: (1) direct costs of the test—fees to market research firms, (2) costs of the launch itself (for production, selling, etc.), and (3) lost revenue that a national launch would have brought. Sometimes the costs of launching are so great that firms don't even consider market testing. For example, in the automobile industry their big cost is getting finished product; once they have cars, there is little inclination to market them in a limited geographical area, or so they have felt. Lately, some Japanese firms have begun rolling some new cars through the West Coast first, as a market test.

Nature of the Marketplace.   If competitors can take retaliatory action that will hurt us, chances are the testing will be quick if it happens at all. Most new products have some protection just by being first in the customers' minds, but few have the ability to keep a market for themselves.

Another marketplace characteristic is that customers may literally demand the new item. New pharmaceuticals, for example, are rarely market tested upon getting Food & Drug Administration permission for marketing. (One can imagine the public outrage if a confirmed remedy for AIDS was put into a six-month test market in Phoenix and Des Moines.)

The marketplace may not be good for market testing. For example, most markets outside the United States and Europe are still very weak on scanner technology and other capabilities for testing. And many products (almost all consumer items not sold through food stores and drugstores) lack sales audits at the retail level even in the United States. Scanners will soon be changing this.

Capability of the Various Testing Methodologies.   The trick is to find a method that fits management needs or that can be modified to do so. As you read through the following discussions on the methods available, keep in mind the requirements from the above discussion. Be a shopper, touring a store of market testing methods. The methods are all good and are proven in practice, often over many years. But do they fit the situation at hand?

Methods of Market Testing

The ingenuity of marketers is legendary. They have developed a seemingly endless array of market testing methods for new products. One firm uses a very large company cafeteria. Another uses small foreign divisions. Still another uses the facilities of a chain of radio stations owned by a sister subsidiary. But the methods tend to fall into one of three general categories (see Figure 20–4).[6]

---

[6]At the time of this writing, the market research industry serving consumer packaged goods firms is continuing its history of rapid technology change and corporate ownership change. Language is changing too, so authors must chase new definitions. People are experimenting with the Internet, virtual realities, and more. For example, one firm tried offering a computer disk method of having consumers shop at a dummy store. We cannot forecast where they will end up. Your professor may have more up-to-date information when you read this, but we suspect the uncertainty in packaged goods will remain for a long time.

FIGURE 20–4

*Methods of
Market Testing
Where Used*

	Product Categories Where Useful				
	Industrial		Consumer		
	Goods	Services	Packaged	Durables	Services
Pseudo sale					
Speculative sale	■	■		■	■
Simulated test marketing			■		■
Controlled sale					
Informal selling	■	■			■
Direct marketing	■				
Minimarketing	■				■
Full sale					
Test marketing	■	■	■	■	■
Rollout					
By application	■	■			
By influence	■			■	■
By geography	■			■	
By trade channel	■		■		■

Pseudo Sale

This approach asks potential buyers to do something (such as say they would buy *if* the product were actually available, or pick the item off the shelf of a *make-believe store*). The action is distinct and identifiable, and much of the marketing strategy is utilized in the presentation; but the key factor here is *little pain for the buyer*—no spending, no major risk. It is, as the name says, a **pseudo sale.** It can be done early on.

Controlled Sale

Here the buyer must make a purchase. The sale may be quite formal or informal, but it is conducted under *controlled conditions*. The method is still research because the product has not been released for regular sale. Some key variable (often distribution) is not opened up but is contrived. Controlled sale is more vigorous than the pseudo sale, however, and much more revealing.

Full Sale

In a **full sale**, firm has decided to fully market the product (not so in the above methods). But it wants to do so on a limited basis first to see if everything is working right. Barring some catastrophe, the product will go to full national launch.

Pseudo Sale Methods

Product innovators use two approaches to get potential users to make some expression or commitment resembling a sale without actually laying out money. The **speculative sale** method asks them if they would buy it, and the **simulated test market** (STM) method creates a false buying situation and observes what they do.

Speculative Sale

This is a technique used primarily by firms in business-to-business markets and consumer durables. It sounds very similar to the technique used in concept and product use tests, differing as follows:

> In the *concept test* we give the new item's positioning claim, and perhaps something about its form or manufacture. Then we ask, "How likely would you be to buy a product like this, if we made it?"
>
> In *product use testing*, we give customers some of the product, have them use it in some normal way, and then ask the same question, "How likely would you be to buy a product like this, if we made it?"
>
> In the *pseudo sale method called "speculative"* we go to the customer, give the full pitch on the product in a version close to ultimate marketing, answer questions, negotiate prices, and lead up to the closing question, "If we make this product available as I have described it, would you buy it?"

Typically, this testing is done by regular sales people using selling materials that are developed and ready to go. They make pseudo sales calls—presenting the new product as though it were available for purchase. The difference this time is that the product is real, as are price (with a full array of appropriate discounts), delivery schedules, selling presentation, and so on. The target customer is real, and the positioning is clear. The buyer has little to do except make a decision. That decision may be just to ask for some samples to try, but that's OK. Trial is industry's way of making the first purchase and is really what we are trying to measure at this time.

Although the tool is used for industrial products, typically, because sale of most industrial products fits the method so well, it can also be used for certain consumer products. Rubbermaid is an example. Rubbermaid sells its products essentially by a push strategy, with some image advertising to consumers, but product presentation is confined to store counters. This setting can be duplicated easily, so Rubbermaid uses the speculative method in a setting that looks much like a focus group concept test (except for using finished product with information on usage, pricing, and so on). The consumer faces a situation much like that in a store and can easily speculate on whether a purchase would be made.

Situations where the speculative method fits include:

1. Where industrial firms have very close downstream relationships with key buyers.
2. Where new product work is technical, entrenched within a firm's expertise, and only little reaction is needed from the marketplace.
3. Where the adventure has very little risk, and thus a costlier method is not defendable.
4. Where the item is new (say, a new material or a completely new product type) and key diagnostics are needed. For example, what set of alternatives does the potential buyer see, or what possible applications come to mind first.

There is no advertising in a speculative sale market test, and the ways of using it are many. For example, some people reject the idea of making a presentation to a buyer and then admitting there is actually no product available to buy. In such cases, they simply tell buyers that "we are getting ready to market a new product, and I want to know if you might be interested."

Simulated Test Market

Packaged goods firms do a great deal of product development, yet the speculative sale method, above, wouldn't work for them. They too wanted a method that was cheaper, more confidential, and faster than the controlled sale and full sale methods that follow. They found it in the A-T-A-R model discussed in Chapter 8.

The method was a spinout from concept testing and comes very early in the development process. For being early, it is sometimes called **pre-market testing**—testing that is done prior to getting ready to market—but *simulated test marketing* is the more common term today. Most usage is well ahead of the time other market testing can be used.[7] The name *simulated test market* came to be used because mathematical formulas are used to simulate the marketplace and at the time we were still calling all market testing test markets.

---

[7]Don't confuse these STM models with other models, such as TRACKER, that are used for interpreting early results in test marketing cities. Marketing scientists have models to cover almost every step in the new product development and marketing process, but here we can cover only the usage leaders.

The central idea is to get estimates of *trial purchasing* and *repeat purchasing*. *Awareness* comes from the advertising agency's component testing, and the firm's managers supply the other factors of *market units*, *availability*, *prices*, and *costs* that are required to turn A-T-A-R into a sales forecast.

Basic Procedure.   Here is the basic procedure used in a simulated test market, with modifications from one market research supplier to another:

1. Respondents are usually gathered in a **mall intercept**—they are approached as they walk through the mall and invited to participate in a marketing study. At least one major supplier selects and invites respondents by telephone. Respondents are qualified both by observation before interviewing (estimates of age, sex, income, family status, etc.) and by questioning (such as product category usage) during a brief interview in the mall corridor. It is important at this point to eliminate persons for whom security would be a problem (e.g., employees of other manufacturers). If the respondent qualifies (fits the criteria for sample selection), he or she is invited to step into a nearby research facility (usually one of the empty mall store areas, though occasionally a permanent facility built in one of those areas).

2. In the facility, the procedure varies depending on the client and what is being tested, but generally the respondents will be given a self-administered questionnaire asking for their attitudes and practices in one or more product categories. Then comes either individual or small-group exposure to advertising stimuli. The advertisements are sometimes couched in a television presentation (e.g., a TV pilot program that is itself being tested) or just any TV show that hides the key stimulus. The ads may be presented without pretense of a television show, or they may be in what appears to be a magazine or on separate tear sheets. Several ads are presented so the respondent isn't sure what is being tested. One of the ads, of course, is for the new product being market tested. It gives the full story, including claims and price.

3. The respondent is then taken into another room, usually what appears to be a very small convenience store with shelves of products. The test manager gives the respondent some play money (one supplier uses cash), not usually enough to make a purchase but enough to make such a purchase less painful. A respondent so inclined can walk right out without making a purchase, even with actual cash.

4. Hopefully, the respondent entering the "store" will now purchase the new product advertised in the first room—this yields the key variable *trial*. The leading seller of STM services does not use a pseudo store. Instead, it asks respondents the standard buying intention question we used in Chapter 16 on product use testing and then simply *gives* trial product to those who express buying interest.

5. Most of the participants are then free to go. Perhaps 10 percent are taken into another room where a focus group of 8 to 10 is held. Another 10 percent may be asked to fill out another self-administered questionnaire covering postexposure attitudes, planned product usage, and the like. If our product was purchased, we will be contacting the respondent later, but if it was not, we want to find out why. Nonbuyers are often given trial (forcing) packages of the product as they leave.

6. Some time later (time varies with the product category involved), the respondent is contacted by telephone. The call may be identified with the mall experience or it may be camouflaged. Information is sought about such things as product usage, reactions, and future intentions. Many diagnostics are obtained at this time, such as who in the family used the product, how it was used, and products it was used with.

7. At the end of the call, the respondent may be offered a chance to "buy" more of the product. This is the first step in a **sales wave**. Product is delivered to the respondent's home by mail or another delivery system, and the call is later repeated, new information gathered, and another sale opportunity offered. Note that we have used the sales wave to give us the fourth key variable in the A-T-A-R model—*repeat*.

These pretests usually involve 300 to 600 people, require 8 to 14 weeks, and cost from $50,000 to $300,000, depending on the number of sales waves. The service is offered in various forms and is being improved continuously. Recently, for example, BASES Group began stopping people as they *entered supermarkets*, gave them the pitch, asked them questions, gave them a coupon, and then followed up with the store later to see how many actually bought the item which was then available in the store. There are many STM services offered for sale, and the leading ones (with their suppliers) are:

- BASES, by BASES Group, Covington, Kentucky.
- MACRO ASSESSOR, by The M/A/R/C Group, Irving, Texas.
- ESP, by NPD Group, Port Washington, New York.
- LITMUS, by Shulman, Ronca, and Bucuvalas, New York City.[8]

Output.   Consumers give their opinions on the product, they buy or ask for some, they react to it, and so on. But the key purpose is to estimate how well the product will sell, so the various services offer trial rate, repeat rate, market share estimates, and volume estimates. The latter comes when they combine trial-and-repeat rates with the client's assumptions on awareness, retail availability, competitive actions, and the like.

A key aspect of the method is its mathematical simulation. If (the client doesn't like the sales forecast from a study, variations are easily tested. For example, the model can be asked what amount of trial would be necessary to get to the desired market share. In turn, the cost of getting that trial (e.g., by doubling the number of coupons currently planned for the introductory period or by lowering the price for a while) can be evaluated.

---

[8]An excellent contrast and evaluation of these modeling operations can be found in Allan D. Shocker and William G. Hall, "Pretest Market Models: A Critical Evaluation," *Journal of Product Innovation Management*, September 1986, pp. 86–107. Unfortunately, these operations, their methods, and their supplier firms change often, so such listings as these in Chapter 20 will always be out of date. Example: Chicago-based Information Resources Inc. (IRI) sold its popular ASSESSOR STM to Texas-based M/A/R/C Inc., which sued IRI because soon after selling the model it teamed up with the largest STM supplier and seemed to violate its "no competition" clause in the original sale contract. See Howard Schlossberg, "Potential Legal Snag Clouds Test Marketing Pact," *Marketing News*, October 29, 1990, p. 8.

There are two variations on the above procedure, and the difference comes in how the data are analyzed. The current leading provider of the service (BASES Group) takes fairly simple approaches to the calculations. They gather the raw trial-and-repeat data from the test, *calibrate it using the vast data from their past studies (*called *heuristics)*, and put it through their version of the A-T-A-R model to come out with market share or actual sales. The other leading suppliers use mathematical models, not heuristics, to derive their forecasts. Their approach demands that more information be supplied by the client, but is more useful in running simulations. We saw these mathematical models in discussing financial analysis in Chapter 11. The heuristics method far outsells the mathematical equations method, but both are highly viable and highly acclaimed. Over time they are tending to come closer together.

Criticism.   The STM technique has its critics. All major packaged goods firms use one or more of the methods, but we don't know how often, or with what confidence. Mathematical complexity is a problem. Simulated market testing has a sense of magic, a mumbo jumbo sometimes encouraged by the sellers of the services. Second, everything in the system is slightly false: the mall intercept creates false conditions at the start, then the stimuli are unrealistically administered, the "store" is obviously fake, and much attention is focused on the behavior of the consumers being tested. Third, the calculations require a set of givens from the client before the formulas can be run (on the percent of stores that will stock the item, for example, or on the advertising budget, on how good the advertising will be, and on competitive reaction). Most of these numbers are assumptions.

Complexity, unreality, and assumptions constitute quite a charge and explain much distrust. Further, the method is not felt to be applicable to products that are totally new to the market—the first TV dinner, for example—because no category data exist in the data bank, or that are highly seasonal (test it and then wait a year?), or that are sold by personal selling or point-of-purchase promotion (rather than mass advertising), or that require significant presale service.

However, the firms supplying the service simply ask, what other method comes close at such an early date? Besides, their sales forecasts are often accurate, although it is felt that perhaps as much as a half of all such tested products that go on into some later form of market testing are unsuccessful there.[9] So, usage and controversy continue.[10]

---

[9]Bruce D. Weinberg, *Roles for Research and Models in Improving New Product Development* (Cambridge, MA: Marketing Science Institute, 1990), p. 8.

[10]The BASES Group recently repeated a long-time claim: "We get within 20% of actual sales 80% of the time," in Christopher Power, "Will It Sell in Podunk? Hard to Say," *Business Week,* August 10, 1992, p. 47. But in most cases these percentages are after the fact. After a tested product is marketed, the many assumptions about stocking and advertising effectiveness are replaced by actual data, and then the original forecast is recalculated. This helps a great deal, but providers of the service say it would be even more unfair to compare market shares calculated early with what eventually happens under totally different circumstances. Keep in mind that STMs are run early, sometimes even before technical work, if prototypes can be used or if verbal statements about the product can communicate its claims.

Leading packaged goods firms have often leapt from the results of a STM directly into national launch. They get to the market fast without the costs of a controlled sale test or a full sale test. We will come back to this issue near the end of the next chapter.

Summary

Chapter 20 was the first half of a two-chapter set on market testing. First we saw where and how market testing sits in the overall new products process. Then we looked at the market testing decision itself, when it is made and how one goes about making it.

That gave the platform for us to look at the various market testing methods that have been invented. After looking at the three basic types, we took up the first of these—the pseudo sale—which comes in the two formats: the speculative sale and simulated test marketing. Chapter 21 will take up the other two methods. Keep in mind that we primarily want good forecasts of sales volumes and good ideas on how to fine-tune the overall launch plan.

Applications

More questions from that interview with the company president.

1. "You know, we recently had a soft drink product (an exotic berry seltzer line) go through one of those simulated test markets, and it was a disaster. The new products people forgot completely about the possibility that the customers who bought the product in the shopping center pseudo stores might not actually get around to trying it. But it happened. Based on in-store purchases, everything was OK, but a good percentage of the purchasers changed their minds later, and, if they used the product at all, it was a limited trial by just one person. Solution, of course: A sales wave test added to the end of the store test. But that increases the cost considerably. Could you tell me when we should use the added sales wave and when we shouldn't?"

2. "I really was confused by something a corporate market researcher said in a seminar we held last week. It concerned our industrial tubing division, which sells extruded aluminum tubing of various smaller sizes for encasing wiring in commercial buildings. She was recommending that they market test their new items by going out to the customers and making what she called fakes—pretending to sell something they wouldn't have yet. This was so silly. Surely you don't agree with her, do you? Besides, it sound dishonest to deceive potential buyers that way."

3. "One of our better divisions is in the publishing business. Among their products is a line of posters sold through college campus outlets. I was

chatting with them recently about market testing, and they said they don't do any of it on posters! Would you like to guess what they said were the reasons for this policy?"

4. "That same division also handles small furniture and other equipment for children. One of their items at the moment is in the shape of a child's car seat—typical format, full support all around, straps, the works. But the catch is that this car seat is made of reinforced nylon and is inflatable. It deflates slowly, for storage and carrying. Pumping is powered by the cigarette lighter. So far the reactions have been enthusiastic, but the developers know they're going to have troubles with the legal and regulatory people. Does this matter of market testing relate to the inflatable car seat situation at all?"

CASE: SimTest Division, Electronic Measurements, Inc.

Bill Bergen, executive vice president and chief operating officer of Electronic Measurements, Inc. (a large marketing research firm), was on his way back from lunch in the cafeteria when he almost bumped into Ann Toliver. Ann, head of the SimTest Division's new customer department, seemed preoccupied. She invited Bill to stop for a chat, and he found out why. A member of Ann's staff (Chez Tronwath) was preparing for a presentation to the marketing group at a client—Midwest Condiments—and Ann had been helping him.

Midwest was a small-to-medium-sized regional producer of a line of catsups, mustards, and other condiments. It had begun in 1974 with a tasty pickle relish and had added other items over the years since then. The company had been advertising from the beginning and held good share in its markets. But early this year, it had been acquired by a big food company—MasterFoods—and was now getting ready to move out nationally. Midwest had been told to sharpen its market research practice and to adopt better ways of market testing its new products. Two MasterFoods brand managers were made available for advice on how to plan better market research, and word had gone out to Electronic Measurements and some other firms that Midwest would be interested in learning what they had to offer.

As it happens, they had a lot to offer, and Ann Toliver was preparing a proposal for a simulated test market. Ann and Chez had been out to see Midwest the day before and had learned that a new line of sandwich spices was on its way to market. Apparently, the new line would be marketed in special shakers, so when making a sandwich, the consumer could sprinkle one or more types of spices onto the filling. Ann and Chez couldn't learn the content of the spice bottles, but apparently the combinations were unique and original.

The issue was, should Midwest use Electronic's simulated test market service in market testing the new spice line? The product had passed concept tests and had done well in a limited home placement use test involving employees. The testers didn't think the product was the best they had ever heard of, but it did make sandwiches more interesting, was easy to use, and had created lots of talk in the households where used. The price was reasonable. The spice line would be targeted to busy people who ate lots of sandwiches but were bored with them. Positioning was straight to the fun and excitement of more interesting sandwiches.

Source: This hypothetical case is based on realistic business circumstances.

So far, no one had actually been asked to buy the product. The advertising agency had developed copy for local TV and in-store display use, tasting samples would be made available in most stores, price would be a bit upscale (Grey Poupon?), and the bottles and labels were clearly of upscale design.

Midwest was concerned about two things: (1) Would people take the product seriously enough to actually buy some and try it? and (2) Would they continue using it after the novelty had worn off? (The product use tests had lasted two months, but each bottle lasted longer than that, so few users had run out during the test.)

Ann and Chez had just finished putting together their presentation to Midwest, and Ann asked Bill if he would like to see it. Bill said he would, and a time was set for the following morning.

And then an odd thing happened. On his way on down the hall, he passed the office of CEO Edie Hopkins. Edie had developed the SimTest Division and done so well at it she got the nod to replace Electronic's founder when he took early retirement. She said she had made a visit to MasterFoods earlier in the week and was amazed to find that the MF sales force had absorbed the Midwest Condiment sales force. The condiment line would be sold along with the rest of the MasterFoods items. This surprised her because she had heard stories about the Midwest Condiment sales vice president, now just a regional sales manager for MasterFoods. Apparently, he had fantastic rapport with regional food chain buyers, built on his uncanny ability to predict winners and losers in the food business. People said he had never stocked the trade with a loser, either at Midwest or at another food company where he began his career. Edie knew no sales manager had product authority at MasterFoods (except for local, so-called micromarketing promotions). She wondered how he would handle the sell-in of new items he didn't think would be successful.

The SimTest Division of Electronic Measurements offered a market modeling service based on consumer reactions to advertising and product display in one of the firm's four mall test centers. The test centers were much like several other research firms' centers. Consumers were found by mall intercepts or solicited by phone and invited to the center, screened for market fit, interviewed about product awareness and usage, invited to screen a proposed new TV sitcom, exposed to several TV ads (including the test product), invited to shop the firm's pseudo stores, given the test product if they didn't buy it in the "store," and followed up later to see if they had used it and whether they wanted more.

Electronic had been at this for about nine years, so it had a solid database and had finetuned its sales forecasting models to make accurate forecasts of new product sales and market shares. The models did require some assumptions, and Bill was worried that Midwest might not be sophisticated enough to make them. For example, SimTest needed to know what percent of stores would stock the product, what type of awareness the planned advertising and in-store displays would generate, and what were viewed as competitive products, if any.

Bill saw this as an opportunity; he and Edie could sharpen their client presentations and, at the same time, learn a few things about their staffs. He proposed that they role-play Midwest management the following day, and the SimTest group (Ann and Chez) would make a presentation *to them*. The presentation would aggressively argue that the new spice line should be market tested via the SimTest service.

All the players (including Chez, who would actually make the presentation) knew this was no easy sell. MasterFoods brand people had been using simulated test marketing for several years and were generally satisfied with it. But Midwest had never used it. Word was that if Midwest did anything at all, it merely put out a new item in a limited area near the plant and watched what happened. Losers were quickly "deep-sixed," as a Midwest product manager put it.

The SimTest Ann and Chez were thinking of would cost about $195,000 and take three months.

21 MARKET TESTING CONTINUED

Controlled Sale and Full Sale

Controlled Sale Methods

The two pseudo sale methods of market testing discussed in Chapter 20 are unrealistic. They are useful as an early test and occasionally reliable as a final measure when the only issues involve how the customers react to the concept in a commercial setting. Users can argue, for example, that the STM fits well with how we actually buy food products—we see a commercial and then later meet the item on a store shelf. We buy or we don't buy. (See Figure 21–1 for information about all three categories of market test methods.)

Historically, however, we have relied on other market testing methods that introduce the matter of cash—real purchasing under some competitive environment. Marketers have sought market testing methods with a strong dose of reality but which also "control" away one or more dimensions of the situation. Launching new products usually requires *distribution*, or *sell-in*. Marketers have always wished for a market testing method that *assumes* distribution, or gets it automatically without having to spend time and money to get it. This wishing has resulted in the **controlled sale** market testing methods.

Informal Selling

Much industrial selling is based on clearly identifiable product features. Product developers want potential buyers to see the product and hear the story, to make a trial purchase (or accept the offer of free trial supply), and to actually use the product. Repeat sales should follow unless product use testing was poorly done. Personal selling is the primary promotional tool, and there is little need to assess advertising.

So, the obvious approach is to train a few salespeople, give them the product and the selling materials, and have them begin making calls. This informal selling method can even be handled at trade shows, either at the regular booths or in special facilities nearby. An example came from a 3M division that was in

FIGURE 21–1

A-T-A-R and the Market Testing Methods

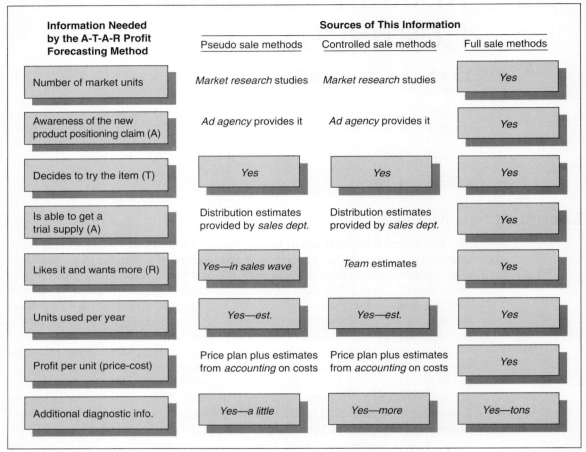

Information Needed by the A-T-A-R Profit Forecasting Method	Sources of This Information		
	Pseudo sale methods	Controlled sale methods	Full sale methods
Number of market units	*Market research* studies	*Market research* studies	Yes
Awareness of the new product positioning claim (A)	*Ad agency* provides it	*Ad agency* provides it	Yes
Decides to try the item (T)	Yes	Yes	Yes
Is able to get a trial supply (A)	Distribution estimates provided by *sales dept.*	Distribution estimates provided by *sales dept.*	Yes
Likes it and wants more (R)	Yes—in sales wave	*Team* estimates	Yes
Units used per year	Yes—est.	Yes—est.	Yes
Profit per unit (price-cost)	Price plan plus estimates from *accounting* on costs	Price plan plus estimates from *accounting* on costs	Yes
Additional diagnostic info.	Yes—a little	Yes—more	Yes—tons

a crash program to market a new optical fiber splice; for market testing the item, the team manager found a trade show running just three months prior to launch date, where almost every potential buyer of the item would be present. As a footnote on this successful test, the night before the show opened it was necessary for the team to find why some fibers were slipping out of the splices; for this, they used a toy microscope purchased at a nearby mall.[1] New product marketers have to be quick on their feet.

The presentations in the **informal selling** method are for real, and cash sales take place. Often, enough time remains between the order and the expected date of shipment that production can be arranged after sufficient orders are obtained.

---

[1]Steve Blount, "It's Just a Matter of Time," *Sales and Marketing Management,* March 1992, pp. 32–43.

Informal selling differs from the speculative sale method discussed in Chapter 20. There we asked people if they *would* buy; here we ask them *to* buy. And, just as Rubbermaid was mentioned as a consumer products firm using speculative selling, we find consumer firms using informal selling. All products sold primarily by salespeople directly to end users can use it (most controlled sale methods avoid the retailer/distributor stocking problem). So can services of most types.

Direct Marketing

Another simple method of controlled sale is by **direct marketing**. Though usage of the term direct marketing varies, here it includes the sale of a (primarily) consumer product by the maker directly to the consuming unit by means of the mail, telephone, TV, fax, or computer network. As examples, L. L. Bean and Lands' End are large direct marketers. They can easily test a new service of some type or a new product or product line simply by listing it in *some* of their catalogs and counting the orders. The advantages are several:

- More secrecy than by any other controlled sale method.
- The feedback is almost instant.
- Positioning and image development are easier because more information can be sent and more variations can be tested easily.
- It is cheaper than the other techniques.
- The technique matches today's growing technologies of credit card financing, telephone ordering, and database compilation.

Minimarkets

Whereas the informal selling and direct marketing methods essentially avoid distributors and retailers/dealers, a third method involves outlets on a very limited basis. The new products manager first selects one or several outlets where sale of the new product would be desirable. In no way a representative sample, these are more likely to be bigger outlets where cooperation can be obtained. Instead of using whole cities (as in test marketing), we use each store as a mini-city or **minimarket,** thus the name.

Black & Decker, for example, could contact a couple of "big barn" outlets and make arrangements to display and sell a new version of its SnakeLight. It could not use local TV or newspaper advertising because the item is available in only one or two outlets, but the stores could list the item in *their* advertising, there could be shelf display and product demonstrations, and sales clerks could offer typical service. Some method (such as offering a rebate or a mail-in premium) could get the names of purchasers for follow-up contact by market research people.

The minimarket situation is more realistic, actual buying situations are created, great flexibility is allowed in changing price and other variables, somewhat more confidentiality is possible than with test marketing, and it is cheaper. Of course, it is still somewhat contrived, in that the ability to get distribution is not tested—minimarket testing is still controlled sale. Too, store personnel may "overattend" the product, that is, pay too much attention to it and give it assistance the item will not get when fully marketed. And, of course, sales cannot be projected to any national figure.

Several market research firms offer this service to manufacturers, using stores with which they have previously set up relationships and also using their fleet of vans to rapidly get product out to more than just a few stores. At least one of the firms has special new product racks in supermarkets, where the new items are displayed.

Note this method is not very scientific; it is used to catch the first flavor of actual sale and/or to work on special problems the developers are having (such as brand confusion, price, package instructions, product misuse, or different positionings). It tells us the trial, and gives some feeling about repeat.

One variation on minimarkets has gotten lots of attention in the consumer packaged goods field, though its method has not been applied to other consumer goods and services or business products. Called BehaviorScan, it was developed by IRI, the same firm previously active in simulated test marketing. The technology came about when retail store checkout scanners became available. IRI uses eight cities of around 100,000 people (e.g., Marion, Indiana and Visalia, California). In each city, it contacts all of the retail outlets for grocery store products, and asks them to install scanner systems if they don't already have them, at IRI expense. In return the retailers agree to share the scanner data with IRI, and to cooperate in a few other activities. Acceptance of this offer has been outstanding. Next, IRI sets up two panels of 1,000 families each in each city. Participants agree (1) to have electronic technology installed on cable-based television sets, (2) to report their exposure to print media, (3) to make all of their purchases of grocery store products in the BehaviorScan stores, and (4) to use a special plastic card identifying their family. The families get various incentives (such as lottery participation) to get their initial and sustained cooperation.

The key parts of this system are (1) cable TV interrupt privileges, (2) a full record of what other media (such as magazines) go into each household, (3) family-by-family purchasing, and (4) a complete record of 95 percent of all store sales of tested items from the checkout scanners. Immediate stocking/distribution in almost every store is assured by the research firm (this too is a controlled sale method). IRI knows almost every stimulus that hits each individual family, and it knows almost every change that takes place in each family's purchase habits.

For example, assume Kraft wants to market test a new version of cheddar cheese, called Cajun. It contracts with IRI to buy the cheese category in one or more of the eight cities. It then places Cajun in a city and starts local promotion. Another of the cities can be used temporarily as a control. Kraft gets the right to put its commercials (via cable interrupt) into whichever of the homes (e.g., younger families) it chooses. Kraft knows whether the families watched TV at the times of the commercials, whether they bought any of the Cajun, whether they bought it again, and so on.

The two panels in each city allow Kraft to use two different positionings in its TV advertising, one positioning for each of the panels. And so on, and so on. The variations and controls stretch the imagination. Kraft can find out how many of the upscale homes who watched the initial commercial bought some of the product within the next two days. And what they bought on their prior purchase, what they paid, what else they bought at the time, and the like.

Scanner Market Testing

There are many variations on minimarket testing, all designed to meet special situations and needs. One of them came out of the same firm that developed the BehaviorScan minimarket service.

Once BehaviorScan was established, clients began asking the firm for more scanner data (fast and detailed in contrast to traditional market audit data that were slow and with less detail). They wanted to keep the BehaviorScan laboratories, but they also wanted data on large areas, preferably the entire country. So IRI developed what became known as InfoScan, a system of auditing sales out of outlets selling grocery store products. These audits were done in stores with scanner systems, and the data were reported for major metropolitan markets—first a few, and now over a hundred. In fact, the coverage is so good that the InfoScan total market service is bought now as a national system. However, it is bought for single markets as well, and here is the variance that complicates where we put it in the Chapters 20–21 listing.

IRI has such good contacts with the stores it uses that, for a price, they can assure stocking of a new product. Without this assurance, the sell-in is left to whatever the firm can do. So, InfoScan data can be used in a *minimarket test*— say, buying market stocking in Indianapolis and Denver and measuring sales of the new item there. Most minimarket test methods (see above) are in a small subset of stores and thus do not allow advertising in the areas leading media— all local media are available in an InfoScan market. Or InfoScan data can be used in a test market where they introduce the new item by *natural sell-in,* regular calls on retailers and wholesalers in, say, Nashville and Albuquerque. If they want to, they can buy store data for two other cities, say Rochester and Kansas City, where they do *not* sell the new product, for comparison with the two where it is being sold. The city pairs are not as carefully selected and matched as they are in traditional test marketing. Third, InfoScan data can be used where a firm starts selling a new product in major markets of the west, moves it out to nearby markets in the mountain states, and so on across the country. In a moment, we will see that this is a *rollout* market test.

InfoScan thus is a *method of market test design and data gathering.* By itself, it is not a method of market testing, but supports most of them. To help in this, IRI has also developed household panels in all of their markets, so clients can follow individual family purchases, taking on some aspects of their own BehaviorScan laboratory system. Some consumer firms' managers call InfoScan a *live* test market to distinguish it from the simulated test marketing models, and others call it an *in-market* test to distinguish it from the smaller city "laboratories" of the BehaviorScan electronic testing service.[2] In the meantime, the great majority of business firms (all of those outside packaged goods) have no such system available.

The excitement of the InfoScan service is the flexibility to do many different things in many different markets with allied coordinated services and, most of all, in rich detail in days, not months. The A. C. Nielson Company responded by altering its traditional every-60-days store audit system to take on more of the InfoScan character, but as of this writing, IRI has passed Nielsen (now located in a huge conglomerate headquartered in Switzerland) in market share.

Full Sale Methods

In full sale market testing *all* variables are *go,* including competition and the trade. They test the realities of national introduction. First will come test marketing and then the fastest growing method of all, rollout.

Test Marketing

Test marketing refers to that type of market testing in which a presumably representative piece of the total market is chosen for a dress rehearsal. Typically, these market pieces have been cities, or more properly the metropolitan markets built around cities. They are what we bring to mind when we hear that a new product is "being tested" in Evansville, Atlanta, Boise, or Portland.

What happens, typically, is that a firm first picks, say, two cities to sell the new product into, and two cities very similar to the first where the product is *not* sold. All four are watched closely, stocking of the new product is audited, sales are audited—either by the InfoScan system we were just talking about or by one of the traditional methods of collecting store purchase data and store inventories from which sales can be calculated. What they had plus what they bought less what they have left over on the auditor's next call equals what they must have sold (ignoring what walked out).

This auditing service can be bought from the traditional leader, A. C. Nielsen, or from one of many regional and local market research firms that offer auditing capability.

The *purpose* of most test marketing today has changed. Whereas the early purpose was to predict profits and thus help decide *whether* to go national, firms today use it more to fine-tune their plans and learn *how best* to do so. Test marketing is too expensive to be used as a final exam.

---

[2]IRI goes much further in designing variations on the basic service. For example, besides the controlled *market* testing just described, they also offer controlled *store* testing where activities in one chain are studied.

This is a critical distinction, as shown by the market testing traditionally used for Broadway plays and musicals. Some of them *have* to play Detroit or Boston to prove their worth, but these are shoestring operations destined for an off-Broadway location. Big-time shows spend the real money getting *to* Detroit, where they fine-tune the operation, confirm volume and cost forecasts, and so on. A major production that fails in Detroit is a rarity.

Pros and Cons.   In contrast to other test methods, test marketing is intended to offer typical market conditions, thereby allowing the best sales forecast and the best evaluation of alternative marketing strategies. It reduces the risk of a total or major flop.

The test market offers the most abundant *supply of information* (such as sales, usage, prices, reseller reactions and support, publicity, and competitive reactions) and many less important but occasionally valuable by-products. For example, a smaller firm can use successful test market results to help *convince national distributors* to chance stocking the item.

The test market also permits *verifying production.* ITT Continental Baking had to withdraw its Continental Kitchens line of prepared entrees from a test market because suppliers of the retort pouch couldn't maintain deliveries. Nabisco had trouble with Legendary Pastries when a seemingly harmless ingredient in the canned topping mix caused the product to explode on kitchen shelves. Both firms saved great sums of money by opting for a test market.

Other firms have been surprised by the effects of *humidity* or *temperature, abuse* by distribution personnel, *ingenious undesirable uses* of the product, and *general misunderstanding* by company or distributive personnel.

Of course, the method is *expensive:* direct costs easily run $300,000 to $500,000 per city; many indirect costs (for preparing product, special training, etc.) must be considered as well.

These costs are often acceptable if the data are accurate, thus allowing the test markets to be projected to a national sales figure. But researchers have known for a long time that *test market results are not really projectable.* We cannot control all *environmental factors,* company people tend to *overwork* a test program, dealers may *overattend or underattend,* and the constant temptation exists to *sweeten the trade package* unrealistically in fear that inadequate distribution will kill the entire test.

In addition, there is the question of *time.* A good test may take a year or more, which gives competition full view of the test firm's strategy, time to prepare a reaction, and even the chance to leapfrog directly to national marketing on a similar item. Kellogg watched the early results of General Foods' Toast-Ems in test market and then went national ahead of General Foods to grab the major market share with Pop Tarts. Procter & Gamble, "once the archetypal cautious player [has] become a much speedier player."[3] Several years ago their

[3]Christopher Power, "Will It Sell in Podunk? Hard to Say," *Business Week,* August 10, 1992, p. 46.

Duncan Hines frosting was leapfrogged by General Mills' Betty Crocker brand. General Mills' vice chairman Arthur Schulze once said that if someone else gets there first, you just have another me-too product.

Too, *competitors can mess up a test market city,* with a flood of coupons and other devices to falsely decrease the test product's sales. The general manager of General Foods' beverage division recently told of test market "informants who live in the town and pay off the supermarket managers to be allowed to hang around. You see these mysterious characters watching how fast the Mighty Dog is moving and in what sizes." Other test market participants tell of bulk new product purchases by competitive salespeople to falsely increase sales reports.[4] Quaker used heavy coupons and ads to thwart Pepsi when it test marketed Mountain Dew Sport drink in Minneapolis.

Finally, there is an inevitable temptation to *rationalize away a test market difficulty* by citing what the now-known trouble was and how the firm "can take care of it on national launch."

The Test Parameters.   A large body of test market literature is available, and most of the leading market research consulting firms stand ready to design tests appropriate to any situation, so no depth of detail is needed here. The most common questions are, "Where should we test?" and "How long should the test run?"

Picking Test Markets.   Each experienced test marketer has an ideal structure of cities or areas. Ad agencies keep lists. Picking two or three to use is not simple, but the most common factors are:

1. *Demographics*—population, income, employment, and so on.
2. *Distribution*—the structure of retail and wholesale firms, including any difficulties of getting in.
3. *Competition*—you need enough, but not too much.
4. *Media*—newspapers, radio, and TV covering just that market, not a huge surrounding area.
5. *Category activity*—no strong regional, ethnic, or economic peculiarities in product consumption.

Test areas need to be stand-alone, where there will not be a lot of sales leakage into other areas, and yet be representative of the nation or a big piece of it.

Duration of Test.   There is no one answer to the question of how long a test market should last, as was made clear by one marketing vice president who said he needed 24–36 months for a new plant care item but only 6–9 months for a candy snack. See Figure 21–2 for some data on purchase cycles; the wide variations are just one factor in the duration decision.

---

[4]This technique is still being used, this time in the book industry, where some authors have made purchases in those stores whose sales are being audited for inclusion in national bestseller lists. Most firms have urged salespeople to recruit neighbors to make purchases and spur stocking by stores.

FIGURE 21–2   Purchase Cycles on Selected Product Categories

	Purchase Frequency (weeks)	Average Four-Week Penetration (percent)		Average Purchase Frequency (weeks)	Four-Week Penetration (percent)
Air fresheners	6	12.3%	Fruit drinks	4	27.8%
Baking supplies:			Presweetened		
Brown sugar	17	13.6	powdered drinks	8	13.2
Cake mixes	10	29.6	Laundry care:		
Chewable vitamins	26	0.8	Heavy-duty		
Cleaners:			detergents	5	50.4
All-purpose	35	3.4	Soil and stain		
cleaners			removers	25	4.7
Window cleaners	27	7.1	Liquid bleach	6	18.3
Rug cleaners	52	2.4	Margarine	3	71.7
Bathroom			Milk additives	9	11.8
cleaners	25	4.2	Mouthwash	13	9.7
Coffee	3	53.1	Pet food:		
Frozen foods:			Cat (total)	2	14.1
Frozen entrees	6	19.5	Dog (dry)	4	23.2
Frozen pizza	8	21.1	Dog (total)	2	41.8
Furniture polish	27	7.0	Raisins	18	8.3
Hair care:			Salad dressings	6	32.9
Hair color	12	4.7	Salad toppings	8	1.2
Shampoo	8	23.4	Snacks	3	17.7
Juices/drinks:			Steak sauce	23	5.4
Fruit juices	3	33.6	Toothpaste	9	33.1

Note: The first column is the average time between purchases of the category cited, by the households in the ADTEL panel. The sound column is the percentage of panel households that make at least one purchase in a four-week period. Both figures contribute to the decision on test market duration.

Source: ADTEL, Inc.

The Rollout

Test marketing is not dead, but marketers now prefer a market testing method called **rollout**. It gives the dress rehearsal value of a test market but avoids many of its problems. It is sometimes called tiered marketing or limited marketing.

Assume a major insurance company develops a new policy giving better protection at lower rates for people who exercise regularly. Management decides to market test the new service by first putting it out for sale in California, an area presumably prime for such a policy. Its independent agents do their job, the policy sells well, so the company offers it to the rest of its West Coast agents. Again, it sells well, and the **geographical** extension continues. One 3M division markets items in Argentina before rolling them out to the countries in Europe. Colgate follows a "lead country" strategy, and recently marketed Palmolive

Optims shampoo in the Philippines, Australia, Mexico, and Hong Kong before rolling into Europe, Asia, and other world markets.[5]

The starting areas are *not representative areas* but, rather, areas where the company thinks it has the right people and perhaps the right markets to get the thing going. Some firms want the area to be difficult, not easy. For example, Miles Laboratories was marketing diabetes self-testing glaucometers and realized that two of its sales divisions would have to cooperate; the Diagnostic salespeople knew the technology, and the Consumer Healthcare salespeople knew the retail druggists. They picked New York City, saying, "Because of the complexity of the market, if we could be successful in New York City, we could roll it out to other parts of the country with reasonable assurance of success."[6]

Second, there was no doubt about what the company was doing: *it was launching the new product.* So was General Mills when it launched MultiGrain Cheerios in 25 percent of the country and rolled out over the next year. See Figure 21–3 for the decision on when to roll out and how far to increase the roll-out before switching to a full national launch.

Let's take another example. Assume an industrial adhesives firm develops a new adhesive that works on many **applications,** including fastening bricks to steel plates, fastening insulation siding to the two-by-four studs in a house, and fastening shingles onto plywood roofing sheets. It has been field tested in all three applications and has been tested in informal selling to roofing firms in one use (shingles), where it received a good response. Should the firm offer it for all three applications at once? Arguments against this include (1) the adhesive has not been market tested in the first two applications, (2) such action would strain resources, (3) multiple uses might confuse customers, all of whom are in the construction field and will hear of all three selling efforts, and (4) the new products manager wants to have some successful experience to talk about when entering the brick and siding fields, because they are highly competitive.

Answer: Market the new adhesive in the shingles business first, gain experience, build up some cash flow, and establish credibility. Then, gradually begin selling it to the siding firms and make whatever changes are indicated. Still later, roll it on into the brick field.

A third example of rollout would be the same adhesives firm if there were only one major application and the product (1) was only marginally better and (2) required lots of training for the distributors' reps. The adhesives firm could choose to begin selling the adhesive through one of its best (and friendliest) distributors, a firm willing to go along on the new item. When that went well, it

---

[5]U.S. multinationals have been urged to use Russia as a geographical rollout area. It offers a large market, with much less world-class competition, allowing the test company to gain experience and volume. Russian leaders have adopted policies on re-exporting, etc., to aid such tests. See James L. Hecht, "Let Russia Be Your Product Testing Lab," *The Wall Street Journal,* August 24, 1992, p. A8.

[6]Leslie Brennan, "Meeting the Test," *Sales and Marketing Management,* March 1990, p. 60.

FIGURE 21–3

*The Pattern
of Information
Gained at
Various Stages of
a Rollout*

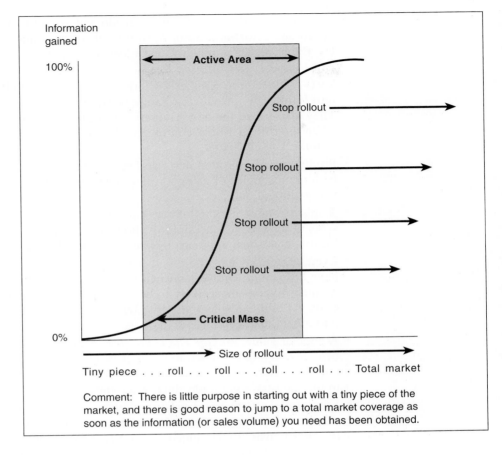

Comment: There is little purpose in starting out with a tiny piece of the market, and there is good reason to jump to a total market coverage as soon as the information (or sales volume) you need has been obtained.

could gradually roll it out to other distributors with whom it had increasingly less **influence,** using prior successes to persuade them.

A fourth example can be found in the magazine publishing field, where new magazines are often offered first through the newsstand **channel,** and then, if they sell well, they are offered in direct mail promotion for mail subscribers.[7]

Other Forms That Rollout Takes.   Those examples catch the four leading forms taken by rollouts—geography, application, influence, and trade channel. Here are some other rollout situations:

---

[7]Patrick M. Reilly, "Publishers Turn Page on Hype, Taking Subdued Approach to Magazine Rollouts," *The Wall Street Journal,* January 8, 1991, p. B1.

- Sega wanted to get a jump on Nintendo and Sony for shelf space ahead of fall and Christmas. So in April it used selected stores of Toys "R" Us, Babbage, Software City, and Electronic Boutique to sell some new items into.[8]
- P&G responded to Kimberly-Clark's move of their Pull-Up diapers into Europe by introducing Pampers Trainers into Ireland and Holland. They also rolled the new Trainers into Canada, but refused to state when the rollout would continue throughout Europe or from Canada into the United States.
- Prodigy was first rolled into San Diego, and Discover card into Atlanta; both are examples of using a rollout when the nature of a service is still being worked out.
- Tom's of Maine uses rollouts to enter markets one at a time, without the costs of advertising and slotting allowances. They use radio with a localized personal approach. Strategy is "model for growth."
- Even large firms must do this if they are entering a market where they have little clout. United launched its shuttle service by targeting on frequent flyers—most likely to be interested and reachable at lower costs via billboards near airports. With volume here, they too moved into other "markets."
- A popular game, *Magic: The Gathering,* could easily be copied, so the firm developing it wanted to sneak in without too much attention or too much evidence of success. They rolled out for almost a year, leading up to the industry's big trade show when they went national.
- Sometimes a firm has a product whose acceptance requires a change in market thinking, but where concept tests are not reliable. In 1995 PepsiCo introduced Pepsi XL, a 70-calorie version, in five major Florida markets (with InfoScan major-market data service). The rollout had to first demonstrate that a mid-diet segment actually existed.[9]
- We will long remember one of the most ballyhooed introductions of all time—that of Windows 95, in August of 1995. But Microsoft had been running beta-site tests for over two years, adding new applications and users every month, to a total of over 2,000. This was a rollout, and August 1995 was not a single, total-market introduction.

Contrasts with Test Marketing.   A rollout has many advantages. The biggest are that it gives management most of the knowledge learned from a test market, it has an escape clause without losing the full budget if things bomb, and

---

[8]Jim Carlton, "Sega Leaps Ahead by Shipping New Player Early," *The Wall Street Journal,* May 11, 1995, p. B1.

[9]Laurie Grossman, "Pepsi Plans a Test of 70-Calorie Cola for Young Adults," *The Wall Street Journal,* March 29, 1995, p. B4.

yet we are well on our way to national availability as early rollout results start coming in. This is important in the competitive battle, because test marketing gives the competition time to launch their products while we are still in test market or getting geared up to go national.

Does this sound like the best of all worlds? What's the catch? In many situations, there isn't any catch, and the technique is justifiably growing rapidly. Other firms may find rollouts to be just as big a risk as full launch. Here is why:

1. Their biggest investment may be in a new production facility, and to roll out requires the full plant at the start.

2. They may be in an industry where competitors can move very fast (e.g., because no patent or new facilities are required), so a slow marketing gives them as much chance to leapfrog as would test marketing.

3. Available distributors are powerful, and none are willing to trust them.

4. They need the free national publicity that only a full national launch can get them; rollouts tend not to be newsworthy.

What does a firm do? The answer is to go through the same decision process given in Chapter 20. Many of the answers depend on conditions at the moment—maybe a firm doesn't want any unfavorable publicity, maybe it wants fast cash in an acquisitions battle, maybe top management is new and wants a couple of successes before the first loss, and so on. There are no recipes here.

Wrap-Up on Market Testing Methodologies

Each of the 10 methods in the three categories of Figure 21–4 can be used alone, and many firms use the one they think is best in terms of cost and what they can learn. However, some firms want a system of two or more techniques.

Such firms usually begin with a pseudo sale method—the speculative format if they are industrial or in a business where personal selling is the major marketing thrust, or a form of STM if they are in consumer packaged goods. Pseudo sale is cheap and quick. Learning is limited, but it is a good leg up on the problem. It often doesn't hold up the process.

The firm then turns to one of the controlled sale methods, especially informal selling for industrial firms or minimarkets for consumer firms. If the second test will be the last, firms tend to slide directly into a full sale method. Thus, an industrial firm might use a speculative sale followed by an applications rollout. A packaged goods firm might start with an STM followed by a geographical rollout, or an STM followed by a minimarket and then full launch.

Figure 21–4 gives some opinions on the popularity of the various methods and some thinking about what may happen in the future.

FIGURE 21–4

*The Past and
Future for Market
Testing Methods*

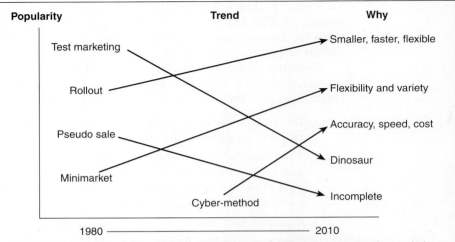

Comment: Given that we could never agree on how to measure a technique's popularity (whether by number of users, dollars spent, value to user, etc.) and lacking valid research reports, this figure is meant to be a representation of change. Our needs have changed, and will change more. There will be new technologies too, especially something here called Cyber-method. Built on electronic networks, data is fed from InfoScan-type store setups. Measurements will be built to answer just the one or two key questions an organization has, with exquisite degree of detail, and (maybe later) a virtual market that models reality down to households and individual business firms.

Summary

Chapters 20 and 21 have covered the market testing phase of the overall evaluation task that involves putting product together with marketing plan. The techniques of market testing vary from the simplistic (and quite unreliable) one of making a sales presentation about the new product to potential buyers and then asking them if they would buy it if available, to a rollout.

The appropriate market testing methodology for any particular new product cannot be stipulated here. Some new product innovation is of such low risk that no market testing can be defended. The toughest issue of all is probably that of technology-based firms that develop what they feel the customer needs and *will* want. However, customers don't *know* they want these new items until they have had a long chance to see them and think about them. Examples are many, ranging from the bathtub to the microwave oven. As a result, technical innovators sometimes distrust any kind of intermediate testing.

The bottom line seems to be that we now have a set of methods to meet the needs of almost any developer, and total use is growing. The biggest addition has been the rollout, where the product is being marketed; there in no "interruption just to test some more." Many firms will deny using market testing, but be active users of rollout.

When entering any controlled sale or full sale market test, and at the national launch, many firms have adopted some of the thinking of space launches—using a launch control system to prepare them for unexpected, but possible, traumatic events. This is the topic of Chapter 22.

Applications

More questions from that interview with the company president.

1. "I am personally familiar with the United Airlines shuttle situation you mentioned, but I didn't know they rolled it out first to us frequent flyer types. That was very clever. Yet, what happens when they grab a foothold with the FFs and want to move to another group of flyers—do they have to change their advertising copy, all of their posters and signs in the shuttle area, etc.? They all point clearly to frequent flyers.

2. "I get a kick out of how scientific market researchers can become, with their careful samples, balanced quotas, etc. But at a conference in California recently, a speaker was telling how Honda market tested over 250 models of motorcycles in one Japanese city, in one year! Says they do it all the time. And there's a city in Japan where all the electronics firms test their TVs, compact disk players, etc. They introduce hundreds of models too. The electronic stores there look like supermarkets, with over a thousand items to choose from. How in the world could you defend that?"

3. "Several of our divisions have lately been using this so-called minimarket testing method. We had some shaving products use BehaviorScan, and a new upscale bandage line used a somewhat similar service from A. C. Nielson. But I am increasingly concerned about the panel members in those test cities. My concern is not that the people become accustomed to the testing or that they overreact to stimuli. These are valid concerns, but there's not much I can do about them. I am concerned, however, that our people do not *know the effect* of these things on the data we get. How would the results of our tests be affected if people like the testing too much? Or if they tend to become professional test participants and begin thinking like judges?"

4. "About 10 years ago I was in the food specialties business, and I can recall a New Cookery line marketed by Nestlé; it was greatly talked about at the time. Well, the line didn't work out in test market quite as well as expected. In fact, it was soon withdrawn with no plans announced for the future. Seems as though retailers complained the products in the new line were often priced higher than competitive products. Some said the items lacked a clear-cut reason for being because although advertised as low-calorie, the catsup product, for example, was only marginally lower in calories than Heinz and Del Monte catsups. Other comments were that 'people here aren't thinking much about diet and health when they're

shopping' and 'the concept was too esoteric and incomprehensible to the ordinary consumer.' Now, maybe the line was just a few years ahead of its time, but it came from a fine firm, and the advertising was by one of the biggest and most successful advertising agencies. Just how could such a disappointment have come about?"

CASE: SQUARE D REMOTE LAMP DIMMER (REVISED)

In the late 1980s, the Consumer Products Division of the Square D Company had completed technical development of a new product designed for the home: a remote dimmer to use on table lamps. It used a fairly new technology for its time, but of course would now be well out of date. The product would soon join other consumer division products (particularly door chimes, weatherproof wiring devices, circuit breakers, and smoke detectors) for sale to the retail market.

The idea for the product had come originally from Ron Rogers, national sales manager of the division, and was based on his previous experience with motor speed controls and his having read a report on dimmer technology. The development had taken 14 months and cost less than $20,000. The product used a radio frequency that did not interfere with radios, TVs, or other household items. Its signal could penetrate house walls, with a 30-foot range. The remote unit had an on/off control as well as brightness-level control over lamp wattage. At the time of launch the unit would work only on upright lamps, but eventually they thought they could make the dimmer technology work for wall lamps and even ceiling lighting.

Ron decided that the U.S. market (the product's major potential at that time) consisted of 75 million households with an average of eight table lamps in each. That would indicate a potential sales volume of 75 to 600 million units. There was no direct competitor to the new dimmer, although wall-switch dimmers had been available for many years. It was not known whether there would be any patent protection, but the likelihood was not strong.

The product was primarily designed for use by a person returning home after dark. After entering the garage, a click on the Square D Dimmer would turn on one or more lamps inside the house or apartment, so that the person never had to enter a totally dark area. It would also appeal to handicapped persons, who would use it from bed and going from room to room. As a third use, parents could use it to turn off or on a lamp in a child's room without disturbing sleep. And there were many more possible users, such as one to turn on a lamp in the basement or on an outdoor porch if a strange sound occurred.

The unit would come with four possible channels, A to D. Thus, the user might buy one unit with the A channel to turn on a lamp in the kitchen or entry hallway, and a B channel unit for use inside the house to turn on lamps in some other room.

The lamp dimmer retail package consisted of two pieces heat-sealed inside a display hanger. The first piece was a small space-capsule-shaped control that screwed into the lamp; the bulb was then screwed into the unit so that the control piece was between the bulb and the lamp socket. The second product piece was the remote control, which was much like a small TV remote control unit. The product was priced to retail for $33.50, with better than average trade margins because retailers would be doing most of the promotion.

Source: This case was compiled from information provided by the firm..

Square D was a large and prosperous firm in the industrial equipment arena, although the Consumer Products Division was much younger. The lamp dimmer product had not been use-tested in the home, although some engineers and company managers had used it in their homes. The principal market study to date was a survey of manufacturers' reps, who endorsed the concept. This division sold through a national force of reps who called on such retail organizations as hardware stores, mass merchandisers, and department stores. Most marketing strategy was push oriented with a minimum of consumer advertising. They thought retailers would be willing to stock the item, put up in-store displays that encouraged potential buyers to pick up a unit and use it on a small lamp incorporated into the displays. They also hoped some retailers would give it some space in their weekly advertising if they allocated them an additional $2 promotional discount per unit bought. Granted, the technology was not exciting, and there were many more-advanced electrical adjustment products on the market. But none of them did what this product would do, and none of them could offer something similar at the low price.

The issue for you is, how would you have recommended to Mr. Rogers that the product be market tested? Or would you have recommended no market testing? Please state your recommendation with supporting logic.

22   LAUNCH CONTROL

Setting

Once the new product is ready to market, the long trek through the development process may appear to be ended. The people involved in the program are happy, satisfied, and anxious for a well-earned rest.

Nevertheless, the group was charged with launching a *winning* product. Just as managerial control over the *development process* was needed (checking actual progress against the plan and making adjustments where it appeared there would be trouble meeting the schedule), control over the *marketing of the new product* is needed. Launch control lasts until the new product has finished its assault on given objectives, which may take as long as six months to a year for an industrial good and commercial services or as little as a few weeks for some consumer packaged goods.

What We Mean by Launch Control

Comparing a NASA space capsule to a youngster's slingshot will explain the subject of this chapter. After firing at a crow in the upper branches of a tree, the youngster quickly panics and runs if the rock sails well over the crow and heads directly for the kitchen window in the neighbor's house. That's when the youngster would rather be in the NASA control headquarters in Houston, Texas, because NASA scientists launch *guided* space capsules, not *unguided* slingshot rocks. NASA would have anticipated that an in-flight directional problem *might* occur and thus would simply make an in-flight correction allowing the space capsule to continue its *controlled* flight. Not having in-flight corrective powers, the youngster simply runs.

This analogy isn't as farfetched as it may sound. It offers the new products manager a choice—NASA or a run for cover. Good tracking systems make successful launching of new products more likely. The manager who has to run for cover simply wasn't a manager.[1]

Unfortunately, only a minority of firms systematically apply managerial control to new product launches. Historically, the day of launch was thought to seal the fate of a new product. Prior to launch, management could pour overtime dollars into a project that was behind schedule, but there was no counterpart of overtime on the launch side.

That view is being rejected. If troubles are anticipated properly and if contingency plans are thought out at least informally, then there is indeed time and opportunity to correct marketing troubles early—perhaps early enough to achieve original goals.

Apparently, most managements today are at least receptive to the concept of a guided launch; a few use such a system, some are experimenting with parts of systems, and the rest are watching what the others are doing.

The Launch Control System

A launch control system contains the following steps:

1. Spot Potential Problems.   The first step in getting ready to play NASA on a new product launch is to identify all potential weak spots or potential troubles. These problems occur either in the firm's actions (such as poor advertising or poor manufacturing) or in the outside environment (such as competitive retaliation). As one manager said, "I look for things that will really hurt us if they happen, or don't happen."

2. Select Those to Control.   Each potential problem is analyzed to determine its **expected impact**. Expected impact means we multiply the damage the event would cause by the likelihood of the event happening. The impact is used to rank the problems and to select those that will be controlled and those that won't.

3. Develop Contingency Plans for the Control of Problems.   Contingency plans are what, if anything, will be done if the difficulties actually occur. The degree of completeness in this planning varies, but the best contingency plans are ready for *immediate* action. For example, "We will up commission on the new item from 7 percent to 10 percent, by fax, to all sales reps" is a contingency plan. It's ready to be put to work immediately. "We will undertake the development of a new sales compensation plan" is no contingency plan.

4. Design the Tracking System.   As with NASA, the **tracking system** must send back usable data fast. We must have some experience so we can evaluate the data (Is our slow-down in technical service typical on big electronic devices like ours, or do we have a problem building?). There should be *trigger points* (e.g., trial by 15 percent of our customers called on, by the end of the first month).

---

[1]People marketing new products are not the only ones using NASA-type systems today. Manufacturing quality control managers have the same difficulties in anticipating problems that might endanger product quality, watching to see if these problems are coming up, and being ready to do something if they do.

These points (unmet) trigger the contingency plan. Without them, we just end up arguing. Remember, money to execute a contingency plan has to come from somewhere (someone else's budget), and thus every plan faces opposition from people who want to delay implementing it.

If a problem cannot be tracked, no matter how important its impact may be, then we don't have it under control. For example, a competitor's decision to cut price by 35 percent is an act; it cannot be tracked like dealer stocking percentages can be. But we *can* have a contingency plan ready if it happens. This situation is not ideal, because managerial control tries to anticipate a problem before it gets here; then we implement the remedial action in time to soften the negative effects. (See Figure 22–1.)

FIGURE 22–1

Graphic Application of the General Tracking Concept (with remedial action)

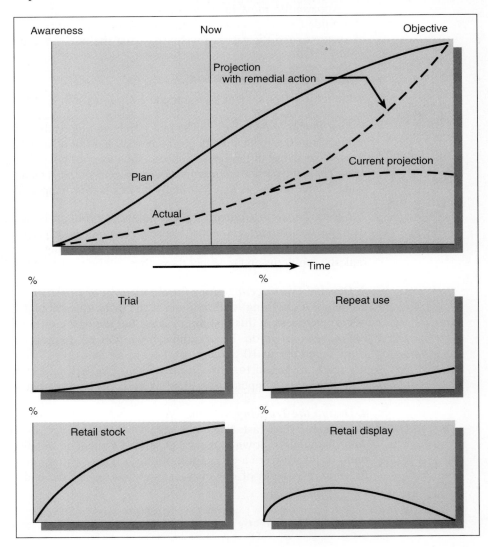

On the following pages, we will look in depth at each of these four steps in a launch control system.

Step One: Spot Potential Problems

Four techniques are used to develop the list of potential problems. First is the *situation analysis* made for the marketing planning step. For example, government lawyers may recently have criticized an ingredient used in the product. Or buyers may have indicated a high level of satisfaction with present products on the market, suggesting trouble in getting them to try our new one. The *problems* section in the marketing plan will have summarized most of the potential troubles from the situation analysis.

A second technique is to *role-play what competitors will do* after they have heard of the new product. Vigorous devil's advocate sessions can turn up scary options that competitors may exercise—they usually have more options than we think of at first glance.[2]

Third, *we look back over all of the data* accumulated in the new product's "file." Start with the original concept test reports, then the screening forms, the early Alpha testing, the rest of the use tests (especially the longer-term ones with potential customers), and records of all internal discussions. These sources contain lots of potential troubles, some of which we had to ignore in our efforts to move the item along.

For example, a food product had done well in all studies to date except when the project leader ran a simulated test market (see Chapter 20). The sales forecast from the research firm came out very low. Study of the data indicated that consumers interviewed by the research firm had given a "trial" forecast of 5 percent, whereas the agency and the developer had been anticipating a trial of 15 percent. The difference was highly significant because success depended on which estimate was right. The developers believed *they* were right, so they stopped the STM tests and introduced the product. However, they made *trial* the top-priority item on the problem list. Shortly after introduction, surveys showed that 15 percent was the better estimate, and the contingency plan was happily discarded. But they were ready if action had been warranted.[3]

Fourth, it is helpful to start with a satisfied customer or industrial user and work back from that satisfaction to determine the **hierarchy of effects** necessary to produce it. On consumer packaged goods, this hierarchy is the same one used earlier in the A-T-A-R model. Figure 22–2 shows that model when applied to the marketing of three ethical pharmaceutical and nutritional specialty items.

---

[2]Some ways of anticipating competitive actions are given in Carolyn M. Vella and John J. McGonagle, Jr., "Shadowing Markets: A New Competitive Intelligence Technique," *Planning Review*, September–October 1987, pp. 36–38.

[3]From the files of David Olson, vice president for new product research at Chicago advertising agency Leo Burnett.

Note each product had a different problem and required different remedial action (contingency plan). All three items were marketed by one firm in one year.[4]

The hierarchy of effects will vary in other situations. Thus, for example, the satisfaction point for an industrial drill may be "known, provable, substantially

FIGURE 22–2

A-T-A-R Launch Control Patterns (actual) for Three Pharmaceutical/ Nutritional Products

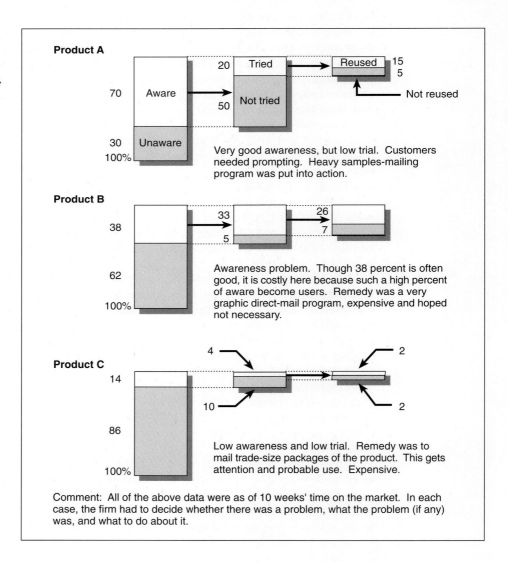

Product A

70 Aware
20 Tried → Reused 15 / 5
50 Not tried   Not reused
30 Unaware
100%

Very good awareness, but low trial. Customers needed prompting. Heavy samples-mailing program was put into action.

Product B

38
33 / 5
26 / 7
62
100%

Awareness problem. Though 38 percent is often good, it is costly here because such a high percent of aware become users. Remedy was a very graphic direct-mail program, expensive and hoped not necessary.

Product C

14
4 / 10
2 / 2
86
100%

Low awareness and low trial. Remedy was to mail trade-size packages of the product. This gets attention and probable use. Expensive.

Comment: All of the above data were as of 10 weeks' time on the market. In each case, the firm had to decide whether there was a problem, what the problem (if any) was, and what to do about it.

[4]Even in established markets (such as consumer packaged goods), the common measures vary. For example, a study in the United Kingdom cited three measures: number of first-time triers, their rates of repeat buying, and how their buying related to other brands in the market. See Dee M. Wellan and A.S.C. Ehrenberg, "A Successful New Brand: Shield," *Journal of the Market Research Society*, January 1988, pp. 35–44.

lower output cost." But reaching that point requires the customer to measure actual costs. It also requires the customer to have data on what the drills cost previously. These are like rungs on a ladder—the customer cannot get to the top (satisfaction) without having stepped on the rungs of "know previous costs" and "know actual costs of the new drill." Both are potential problems, given that most firms do not have such sophisticated cost systems.

Later in this chapter (in Figure 22–6) you will see a sample launch control plan for a new industrial multimeter. There the five key potential problems were: salespeople will fail to call as requested, salespeople will fail to understand the product, potential customers do not order a trial instrument, buyers do not place quantity orders after the trial, and a competitor markets a similar item. All were potential "killers," and one of them did strike.

For another contrast, let's look at a new service. *Peapod* is an online grocery shopping service used via computer from the home. Introduced into the Chicago area in 1990, Peapod was concerned about the common claim that consumers would not pay extra for the convenience of shopping online. In their case, conventional wisdom was wrong; in fact, consumers were willing to pay a $29.95 start-up fee, $4.95 monthly service fee, plus $6.95 and 5 percent of their grocery total per order! But the firm was ready.[5]

Another example concerned a consumer durable product—this time a combination of the sturdy mountain bike and the thin-framed nimbler racing bike. But Huffy, the maker, failed to anticipate one potential problem that became a $5 million mistake. Huffy chose to distribute the new bike through their regular channels (mass merchandisers and chain specialty shops like Toys "R" Us). Unfortunately, the special hybrid bikes needed individual sales attention at the point of sale; such knowledgeable salespeople only work at bike specialty shops. A launch control system might have discovered this soon enough to permit necessary changes.[6]

Yet another example concerns the product you have met twice before in this book—the digital compact cassette machine (DCC) marketed by Philips Electronics. Their original launch of this product met with the following problems, all of which could have been anticipated and managed:

- Advertising: Missed on the matter of product understanding—example: the ads used the acronym DCC without defining it.
- Resellers: Sent it out to all dealers, but in the relaunch marketed only to those dealers who supported the concept and were willing to invest their money in the educational effort it required.
- Price: Early models didn't sell, so they cut the price to move them out of the stores before the replacements arrived. Not being sure how much of a cut this would require, they cut too much—shelves were bare before the new ones came in, and dealers started sending back their stock of tapes.

[5]Susan Chandler, "The Grocery Cart in Your PC," *Business Week*, September 11, 1995, pp. 63–64.
[6]"Flops," *Business Week*, August 16, 1993, pp. 76–82.

- Consumer attitudes: Consumers love CD-ROMS, but they do not believe that tape can be as good. True or not, this belief was a potential disaster, and it worked against them.[7]

All of this is not to say the companies were wrong—all new products are a gamble, and we never have enough time and money to do the job right. But the problems represent what we are looking for when we do our launch control—knowing what bad might happen, we can at least be on the lookout for it, and hopefully have something in place ready to go if it does happen.

Oddly, one problem usually overlooked is that of being *too* successful. It's kind of a happy hurt, but it can be expensive and should be anticipated if there is any particular reason to think it might happen.[8]

Before leaving the matter of potential killer problems, don't forget that the firm has yet to prove it can do what it proposes to do—that is, produce and distribute a product that does what we claim it will. So launch control plans also contain problem items such as:

- Vendors fail to deliver the new fillibrator parts in the volume promised.
- The new conveyor lines will be stretched to their limit. The stress limits provided by suppliers may be in error, and/or our manufacturing workforce may misuse the technology.
- Samples of the new product are critical in this introduction, yet we have not proven our ability to package the small units needed.

These too are potential problems. Any one of them can cause the new item to fail, so we must manage our way through them. Incidentally, this reinforces a key issue in new products management today: The development does not end when the item arrives at the shipping dock. It ends when enough good-quality product has performed satisfactorily in the hands of the end user. The full team manages the launch control operation.

Last, note that one item has not been mentioned—actual sales. We do not control sales and do not have tracking lines and contingency plans for low sales. It might seem we should, and most control plans put together by novices include sales. But stop and think: If the sales line is falling short of the forecast, what contingency plan should be ordered into action? Unless you know what is *causing* poor sales, you don't know what solution to use.

Instead, we use the above efforts to list the main reasons why sales *may* be low and then track *those reasons*. If we have anticipated properly, tracked properly, and instituted remedies properly, then sales will follow. Otherwise, when sales lag we will have to stop, undertake research to find out what is happening, plan a remedial action, prepare for it, and then implement it. By then, it's

---

[7]Kyle Pope, "Philips Tries, Tries Again with Its DCC," *The Wall Street Journal*, October 3, 1994, p. B1.

[8]Joshua Hyatt gives examples of this problem, including one successful firm that barely avoided bankruptcy from a too successful launch, in "Too Hot to Handle," *Inc.*, March 1987, pp. 52–58.

far too late. Contingency planning is a hedge bet; it is a gamble, like insurance. Most contingency planning is a waste, and we hope it all will be.

Step Two: Select the Control Events

No one can managerially control the scores of potential problems that come from the analysis in step one. So, the planner's judgment must cut the list down to a number the firm can handle. (See Figure 22–3 for a graphic representation of what follows.) Some people say never more than six, but a new televised shaving product would surely warrant more contingency planning than the launch of a new line of jigsaw blades.

The judgment used to reduce the list of problems is usually based on the potential damage and the likelihood of occurrence. Figure 22–4 shows how the two factors combine to produce nine different categories, of four types. Those with little harm and little probability can safely be ignored. Others farther down the diagram cannot be. At the bottom/right are problems that should be taken care of now; they shouldn't have gotten this far. In between are problems handled as suggested by the patterns on the boxes. How they are handled is very situational, depending on time pressure, money for contingencies, the firm's maturity in launch control, and the managers' personal preferences.

FIGURE 22–3

Decision Model for Building Launch Control Plan

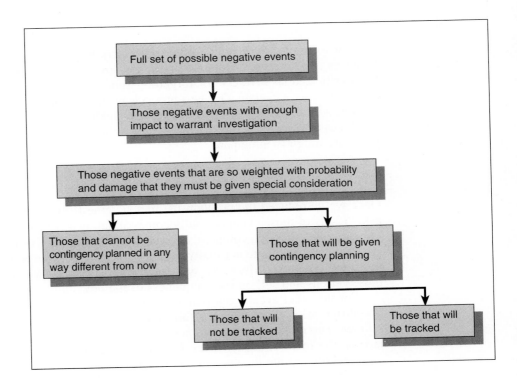

FIGURE 22–4

*Expected Effects
Matrix for
Selection of
Control Events*

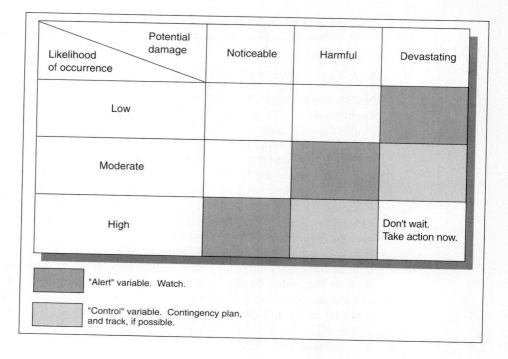

Likelihood of occurrence \ Potential damage	Noticeable	Harmful	Devastating
Low			
Moderate			
High			Don't wait. Take action now.

"Alert" variable. Watch.

"Control" variable. Contingency plan, and track, if possible.

For example, most new product managers have been burned on previous launches and so have developed biases toward certain events. They may have been criticized so severely for forgetting something on a previous launch that they never forget it again. One new products manager recommended that the problems be sorted into two piles—potholes and sinkholes. Potholes are harmful, but sinkholes are disaster. Potholes rarely hurt us because we anticipate them; sinkholes are tough to anticipate.

Step Three: Develop Contingency Plans

Once we've reduced the problem list to a size the firm can handle, we have to ask: "If any of those events actually comes about, is there anything we can do?" For example, although competitive price cuts and competitive product imitation are on many lists, there is usually little the firm can do. The competitor is going to try to hold most of its share, and the developer is usually better off to ignore those actions and sell on the uniqueness of the new item.

For the other events, our planned reaction depends on the event. Let's take two different types: a company failure and a negative buyer action (consumer failure). The most common company failure is inadequate distribution, particularly at the retail or dealer level. Correcting the problem usually just depends on how high a price the company is willing to pay.

Retailers sell the one thing they have—shelf space exposure to store traffic. Shelf space goes to the highest bidder, so if a new product comes up short, the remedy is to raise the bid—special promotions, more pull advertising, a better margin, and so on (see Chapter 19). These were rejected options when the marketing program was put together, so contingency planners usually have lots of alternatives from which to choose.

A consumer failure is handled the same way. To get awareness, the marketers' program called for particular actions (sales calls, advertising, etc.). If it turns out that awareness is low, we usually do more of the same action—increase sales calls or whatever. If people are not actually trying the new item, we have ways of encouraging trial (such as mailing samples or trade packages as in Figure 22–2, or giving out coupons).

Many product developers have marveled at how easy good contingency thinking is while preparing to launch, compared to doing it under the panic conditions of a beachhead disaster.

Step Four: Design the Tracking System

We now have a set of negative outcomes for most of which we have standby contingency plans ready to go. The next step is developing a system that will tell us when to implement any of those contingency plans. The answer lies in the concept of tracking.

Tracking.   The tracking concept in marketing has been around for a long time but probably got its greatest boost when Russia launched the Sputnik satellite. This launch led to the absorption of the rocketry lexicon into all leading languages. Though we had guided missiles for some time before that, they lacked the drama of a launch into outer space, especially with the spectacle of television.

The concept of tracking as applied to projectiles launched into space fits the new product launch well. There is a blast-off, a breakout of the projectile into an orbit or trajectory of its own, possible modification on that trajectory during flight, and so on. The launch controller (whose title originated in the concept of managerial control) is responsible for tracking the projectile against its planned trajectory and for making whatever corrections are necessary to ensure that it goes where it is supposed to go.

Applying this tracking concept to new products was as natural as could be. Earlier, Figure 22–1 showed the graphic application of the basic concept to a new product.

Three essentials are involved: first is the ability to lay the *planned trajectory*. What is the expected path? What is reasonable, given the competitive situation, the product's features, and the planned marketing efforts? Although it is easy to conjecture about such matters, setting useful trajectory paths requires a base of research that many firms do not have when they launch a new product.

The new product research department at Leo Burnett Company, a large advertising agency, studied all of the new product launches that the agency had

FIGURE 22–5

Advertising Weight versus Awareness Created for Selected Products

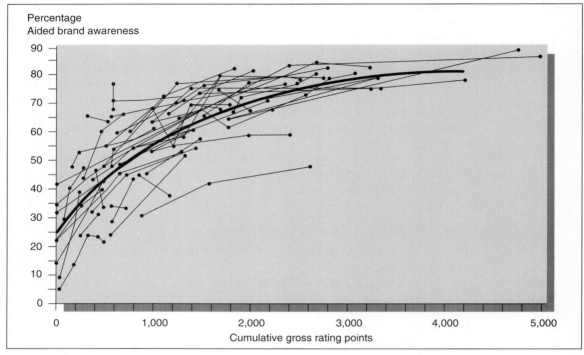

Source: David Olson, unpublished working paper, Leo Burnett Company.

participated in and plotted the actual awareness tracks and trial tracks.[9] From these scatter diagrams, the director of research computed generalized paths that could be applied to future new product situations (see Figure 22–5). A firm that lacks experience can sometimes acquire the data it needs from such outside sources as advertising agencies, marketing research firms, trade media, or industry pools.[10] Such ready-made options are important in these days of global marketing; fortunately, there is an increase of market research data and service organizations with international operations.

Second, there must be an *inflow of actual data* indicating progress against the plan. This means quick and continuing marketing research geared to measure the variables being tracked.

Third, we have to *project the probable outcome* against the plan. Unless the outcome can be forecasted, we have little basis for triggering remedial action until the outcome is at hand.

---

[9]David Olson, "Anticipating New Product Problems—A Planning Discipline," unpublished working paper.

[10]A source that may help some readers is Christopher J. Easingwood, "Early Product Life-Cycle Forms for Infrequently Purchased Major Products," *International Journal of Research in Marketing*, no. 1, 1987, pp. 3–9.

The key is speed—learning fast that a problem is coming about, early enough to do something that prevents it or solves it.

Selecting the Actual Tracking Variables.   Now we hit perhaps the toughest part of launch control. How will we actually measure whether one of our key problems is coming about?

If the problem is some specific step of action or mind, like awareness, then the answer is clear—find out how many people are aware of the new item. Trial is easy; repeat purchase is easy. What about trade support? Many new product marketers fear they will not get the push they need. But does trade support mean stocking the product? Displaying the product? Advertising the product locally? Giving presale service? Gearing up to give postsale service? The launch planner has to decide.

We need relevant, measurable, and predictable tracking variables. A variable is *relevant* if it identifies the problem, *measurable* if we can get a statistic showing it is or isn't, and *predictable* if we know the path that the statistic should follow across the page.

Look back to Figure 22–1. The top graph displays awareness: "Have you heard of . . . ?" It is a percentage of all people in the target market. The track line, labeled *plan*, shows what we *expect* to happen. The broken line shows what we find *is* happening, and what we fear *will* happen if we do nothing. The tracking variable is relevant, measurable, predictable.

But let's look at dealer support. At the bottom of Figure 22–1 is a track of retail stocking, the percentage of target dealers who have stocked the item so far. This too is relevant, measurable, and predictable (based on our past experience). But what about shelf space? The height of the stocking, the number of facings, and the department in which it occurs are all aspects of shelf space. They differ in relevance, they are all tough to measure without actually calling on stores and looking at the shelves, and we are apt to lack the experience we need to predict them. Figure 22–1 also shows retail display, but such a track is mainly a guess.

Additionally, watch out for situations where even a fairly obvious variable may be tricky to define. Take awareness (perhaps the most common variable tracked), for example. In Chapter 19 we talked about the marketing program to achieve awareness, and how it can be the ability to recognize the brand name or knowledge of the product's positioning or the ability to recall the brand. Awareness is a state that leads to trial, and that varies across product classes.

There is no way to settle this argument, so most firms just arbitrarily pick a reasonably good definition that they can measure and they use it every time.

Many developers shun launch control because of problems in finding good tracking variables. If they can't easily measure the emergence of a problem early on, the whole idea of controlling the way to success makes a lot less sense.

Selecting the Trigger Points.   Given that we have found useful variables for warning that a problem is coming about, the last step is deciding in advance how bad it has to be before turning the contingency plan loose. Say, for example, we have a low budget situation and are worried that customers may not hear of our new item—low awareness. If our objective for three months out is 40 percent of customers aware, and tracking shows we actually have only 35 percent, should we release the standby direct-mail program?

This is not an easy decision to make under beachhead conditions, for political reasons as well as for time constraints. Throwing the switch for direct mail admits that the original advertising has failed. This admission is not popular, and arguments will be made that the advertising is working as planned and the awareness will soon increase.

To avoid these no-win situations, agree in advance what the trigger level will be and put the triggering decision in the hands of a person with no vested interest. With this step, the tracking plan is complete. With diligent implementation, the launch will probably be "controlled to success."

Nontrackable Problems.   What do we do when we have a problem that worries us but cannot be tracked because we can't find a variable for it, or because we don't have a track that the variable should follow, or because there is nothing we can do if the problem is found to be coming about? The answer is, very little.

Typically, management watches sales, and if they are falling below the forecast, someone is asked to find out why. This means interviewing salespeople, customers, distributors, and so on. It's a difficult inquiry because things are changing so fast and because most participants have vested interests—they may not reveal the true problem even if they know it.

When the cause is found, a remedy is devised. If it's not a fast-moving market, time may be available to get the new product back into a good sales pattern. If it's too late, the new item is dumped or milked for a while. The loss may be very little if the costs of launch were low, as they often are for small firms, for line extensions, and for products that were never expected to amount to much.

A Sample Launch Control Plan

Figure 22–6 shows a sample launch control plan. In it are samples of real-life problems, specific variables that were selected to track them, trigger points, and the standby contingency plans ready to go into effect. Note particularly that this was not a large firm, it had no market research department, and it was not then sophisticated in how to launch new products. Still, the plan covers the main bases, permits launch control to be in the hands of available managers, and provides effective action if any of the possible problems come about.

Larger firms with big budgets will have more sophisticated plans, but in principle they will be exactly the same—problem, tracking variable, trigger point, and remedial plan ready to go. Very small firms may have the energy to deal with only a couple of problems; the manager may use what we call **eyeball control** to move around the market and find if they are coming about, and then have in mind what will be done if they are.

But whether in the mind, in the format of Figure 22–6, or in a sophisticated formal plan, the essentials are the same.

FIGURE 22–6   Sample Launch Control Plan

Setting: This launch control plan is for a small or medium-sized industrial firm that is marketing a unique electrical measuring instrument. The device must be sold to the general-purpose (i.e., factory) market, whereas past company products have been sold primarily to the scientific R&D market. The firm has about 60 salespeople, but its resources are not large. No syndicated (e.g., audit firm) services are available in this market.

Only a few parts of the marketing plan are presented here, but the control plan does contain the total set of control problems, a plan to measure those that could be measured, and what the firm planned to do if each problem actually occurred.

Potential Problem	Tracking	Contingency Plan
1. Salespeople fail to contact general-purpose market at prescribed rate.	Track weekly call reports. The plan calls for at least 10 general-purpose calls per week per rep.	If activity falls below this level for three weeks running, a remedial program of one-day district sales meetings will be held.
2. Salespeople may fail to understand how the new feature of the product relates to product usage in the general-purpose market.	Tracking will be done by having sales manager call one rep each day. Entire sales force will be covered in two months.	Clarification will be given to individual reps on the spot, but if first 10 calls suggest a widespread problem, special teleconference calls will be arranged to repeat the story to the whole sales force.
3. Potential customers are not making trial purchases of the product.	Tracking by instituting a series of 10 follow-up telephone calls a week to prospects who have received sales presentations. There must be 25 percent agreement on product's main feature and trial orders from 30 percent of those prospects who agree on the feature.	Remedial plan provides for special follow-up telephone sales calls to all prospects by reps, offering a 50 percent discount on all first-time purchases.
4. Buyers make trial purchase but do not place quantity reorders.	Track another series of telephone survey calls, this time to those who placed an initial order. Sales forecast based on 50 percent of trial buyers reordering at least 10 more units within six months.	No remedial plan for now. If customer does not rebuy, there is some problem in product use. Since product is clearly better, we must know the nature of the misuse. Field calls on key accounts will be used to determine that problem, and appropriate action will follow.
5. Chief competitor may have the same new feature (for which we have no patent) ready to go and markets it.	This situation is essentially untrackable. Inquiry among our suppliers and media will help us learn quicker.	Remedial plan is to pull out all stops on promotion for 60 days. A make-or-break program. Full field selling on new item only, plus a 50 percent first-order discount and two special mailings. The other trackings listed above will be monitored even more closely.

Objections to Launch Control

Every manager has heard of contingency planning and uses a lot of it. But on new products? Here they often draw the line. Some say it takes too much time and costs too much, because of the market research and the unused contingency marketing materials. Life insurance is wasteful too, if you don't die!

But their occasional concern that "we can't forecast what all of our troubles may be" is a stronger issue. New products are risky, and we are trying to change buyers' behavior. Competitors are never idle. Proponents readily admit these things, but they answer that it is also costly to turn on a dime, crisis management can be frightful, and we should strive harder to do our jobs right the first time. A crisis seldom offers the time required to develop sound plans.

A trickier objection is that contingency planning can destroy morale, having people stop right in the midst of launch planning to talk about what can go wrong. This relates to management style and is strictly a personal preference. Same thing when they don't want new product managers doing "escape clause" thinking. Or having to lay out plans for cutting budgets in case of sales disappointments. This can actually upset a team that has been working cohesively for some time, because the cutbacks will not fall evenly.

No Launch Control on Temporary Products

Some products live unintentionally short lives. Occasionally, however, products are marketed that the managers know from the start will be on the market only a short time. Such products include fad products, temporary fillers of a hole in a product line, products keyed to a market participant's special needs, and *occasional* products. One producer of occasional products is Baskin-Robbins, which has a standing set of flavors always available and another stable of flavors that move into and out of the line.

Temporary products have much less need for launch control, mainly because there is nothing that can be done—everything is committed. Advertising and personal selling monies are needed to load up distributor/retailers (no out-of-stocks can be allowed, because they represent permanently lost sales) and to build immediate sales. Sales promotion works only on awareness and trial. There are no follow-on products scheduled, production is contracted out if possible, inventories are moved out, and production runs are matched to the reorder rate. No long-term service facilities are built, prices are held steady (or at the most, reduced), and most effort after announcement is put into market intelligence needed to know when sales are leveling and heading down. By the time any launch problems are identified, the time to solve them is past.

Product Failure

Despite everyone's best efforts, products do sometimes fail or appear to be failing. When this happens, the firm first thinks of how additional money can best be spent, and strategy is reviewed. Of course, time permitting, the product can be changed or standby add-ons can be sent to market while longer-term changes are being made. If the market situation is particularly difficult and solutions lie only in longer-time product changes, it may be necessary to pull the product temporarily or, at least, to stop all promotion and hold the market in a freeze until the problem solution has been found. If things in the development area don't move along successfully, it is usually necessary to abandon the product which means to abandon the market opportunity. Most firms have many new product options and like to get their losers out of sight and out of mind. The politics are bad, people are scurrying to escape the sinking ship, critics are reminding everyone how they predicted this trouble, and so on. Of course, if new plants were built, if major promotional programs were undertaken, or if in any other way major financial commitments were made, then there will be efforts to hold on. At least until there has been time to put through a "relaunch."

If abandonment is necessary, the manager's job is not finished. A lot of people need to be notified (including customers, governments, distributors, and trade groups). If persons or firms have become dependent on the product, it may be necessary to have a gradual stock-reduction program, to stockpile parts, and to offer a period of repair service.

Summary

This chapter brings us to the point where we introduce the product. We have the product, we have the marketing program for it, and we are prepared to control its way to success.

The requirements of launch control are a plan, measurement of progress in the market, analysis of events to determine if prearranged contingency actions should be put into play, and continuing study to ensure that any problem becomes known as soon as possible so action can be taken to avert or at least ameliorate it.

Launch control and tracking are especially tough because most of the activity is out in the marketplace, variables will change, and measurements are difficult and expensive (not like walking through the factory in the eyeball control method). However, the methodology is available, and when the situation warrants this effort, a new products manager can certainly gain from it.

We can now turn our attention to a topic ever-present in new product work. Are there public policy issues involved in the new product's manufacture, distribution, use, or disposal? Are there ethical issues involved? What the developer thinks is, of course, not the point. What does the *public* think? What do *government people* think? This issue is the subject of Chapter 23.

Applications

More questions from that interview with the company president.

1. "Thanks for telling me about that launch control idea you were studying. But look, I'm a bit mixed up on one thing. You mentioned (1) critical events, (2) control events, and (3) tracking variables. You say you have to list all three things? Isn't one event likely to be on all three lists? For example, take awareness of the new product's key determinant attribute. Not getting it is a critical event, selecting it for control makes it a control event, and tracking it makes it a tracking variable. Right? Help!"

2. "I've had occasion several times over the past year to see a new product land in trouble—great expectations and terrible sales. And the saddest part is that so many people try so hard to deny the inevitable—the product has bombed, and the quicker one gets away from it the better. Otherwise, it's just sending good money after bad. In fact, I'm going to make a speech to that effect at our next general executive meeting, and you could do me a favor. Would you please develop a list of all possible reasons why someone might want to string a loser along? That would help me be sure I've answered all of the objections before I give the speech."

3. "Don't get me wrong—I believe in contingency planning and in what you call launch control. If you have anticipated a problem and have an action planned in case it comes up, I'll buy going ahead, at least for now. But a lot of companies don't necessarily agree with me. I recall one time when one of the big electronics firms was in quite a dispute with its dealers over whether a new device they had launched would catch on. It might have been RCA and that Selectravision compact disk they developed. Anyhow, the dealers said no way. The company insisted it just takes longer on innovations like theirs. They wouldn't have had that argument if they had done their contingency planning, right? They would have had standby plans ready to go. Tell me, if a new product team neglects to do contingency planning and then hits trouble, what can they do then to get a handle on the problem as soon as possible? (Preferably before someone like me tells them to pull the plug.)"

4. "If I remember right, the whole idea of launch control depends partially on having a track or plan that each variable should follow if everything is going OK. I believe you showed me some figures with those plan lines on them. But it seems to me those plan lines are just pure conjecture, at least in the case of really new products. For example, one time I was reading about Arco Solar Inc. (a division of Atlantic Richfield). It had a solar-powered plate that could be set on a car's dashboard and feed power to the car's battery. That power was to make up for the natural self-discharge of a battery, the drain from electric clocks, and so on. Now, how in the world would they know what the normal path of awareness or trial would be? Are they unable to use launch control? Lots of our divisions are developing really new things like that."

CASE: INTERFOODS, INC.
Valley Butter

Interfoods, Inc., was a large international food company headquartered in Paris whose Colombian subsidiary was about to introduce a new butter product called Valley Butter. There were doubts about this introduction, so the product manager, Carlos Minago, wanted to be sure the launch went well.

Interfoods began its Colombian operation by acquiring a Bogotá firm that had, among other products, a line of nonbutter products. These included a *nonrefrigerated* margarine called Planet, which sold nationally with around 80 percent of that market, and a *refrigerated* margarine called Dairy Planet, which was distributed only in the major cities (because of the need for refrigeration) and had a 90 percent market share. Planet made little money and was no longer being actively promoted. Dairy Planet was very profitable. The total spread market was about $4 million at the factory and at this time was divided 50 percent to butter, 30 percent to refrigerated margarine, and 20 percent to nonrefrigerated.

Moreover, that 50 percent share for butter had been achieved within the past three years, and almost all went to the Ahoy brand. Butter had previously been a very expensive import, but the Ahoy firm produced it locally and was rapidly gaining sales from Dairy Planet. Its price was now only about 30 cents against Dairy Planet's price of 19 cents.

The Valley Butter project had been under way for about a year and a half, although corporate management in Paris wasn't enthusiastic about it. They wanted the market to stay with margarines, where Interfoods dominated, and they didn't really think the Colombian Interfoods people knew much about butter.

General knowledge was that taste was the big thing in butter and that taste had been winning Dairy Planet customers to Ahoy. So, Valley Butter was supposed to taste better than Ahoy—and it did (though it took six versions; the previous five had flopped when tasted by employees). The most recent in-home, blind, paired-comparison use test showed Valley was preferred by a statistically significant 55 percent to 45 percent. To get this preference, the cost was unfortunately increased to the point that Valley would not be as profitable as new brands were supposed to be.

No test market would be undertaken because the butter market was essentially the three cities of Bogotá, Medellin, and Cali. Colombia as yet had no research firms offering simulated test markets or scanner market testing. The strategy was to use fairly heavy advertising backed by four consumer promotions (two pricepacks deals and two premium offers printed on the wrappers) to force trial. The advertising would be a three-month saturation drive on TV stations and in movie houses, plus radio and newspapers. The total budget for Valley advertising would be more than Ahoy had been spending but less than the firm would normally spend because of the higher product cost and the firm's basic desire for the market to stay with margarines.

The sales forecast called for a 10 percent market share after one year, but management made it plain they expected much more than that soon thereafter or it wasn't worth the effort. The target consumers were the top economic class—about 10 percent of all people in the leading cities.

Source: The situation of this case has been camouflaged.

The product was positioned as the "better-tasting butter," and the copy strategy was simply to communicate the positioning. *Valley* was chosen as the name because it connoted delicious-tasting butter and an image of quality. It came from a list prepared by the ad agency and was selected by consumers as easily remembered and pronounced and connoting a high-quality butter. The packaging would also be expensive (foil wrapper versus Ahoy's plastic wrap). A consumer packaging test confirmed that the package communicated a quality image. The price was to be the same as Ahoy's. Colombian Interfoods had a national sales force of about 55 people, but Valley would be handled only by the special 10-person sales force created just to sell Dairy Planet in the major cities. The sell-in by this smaller group would begin about two weeks ahead of advertising break.

It was company policy to have launch control plans, so Carlos now had the job of preparing a list of potential problems, narrowing them down to the ones he had to do something about, and then planning how he would track them and what he would do if any of them occurred.

23   Public Policy Issues

Setting

Along the way through the past 22 chapters, we have been dealing with the various problems of developing and launching a new product. But to simplify things, we have deferred until now some major questions of public policy. They concern the relationship between the firm (people, product, whatever) and the citizenry. In every country on earth, there are ways in which the new product function is limited or directed. And usually for very good reason. So managers need to understand the rules, and they need to understand the edges of the law where issues are usually under movement or unclear.

Chapter 23 gives the life cycle of a public concern, discusses the attitudes of business regarding product innovation and public policy, and deals with the most critical of the concerns—product liability. It then goes into the other concerns, such as environment, and some related managerial issues.

Bigger Picture: A Cycle of Concerns

All public pressure situations go through a life cycle of the following phases (see Figure 23–1).

Phase I: Stirring

Individuals begin to sound off long before enough people have been injured or irritated to cause a general reaction. Letters to company presidents, complaints in newspaper articles, letters to political representatives, and tentative expressions of concern by knowledgeable authorities are typical of phase I. Most people ignore these periods, but they are easy to identify, looking back. Consequently, the stirring phase may last a long time—decades, in fact.

FIGURE 23–1

*Life Cycle of a
Public Concern*

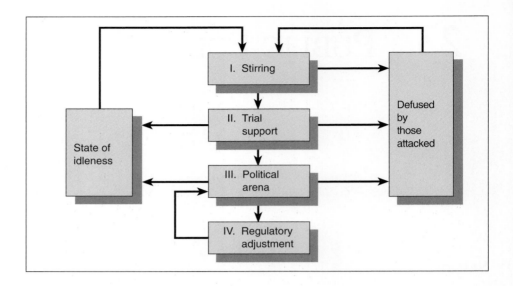

The problem for new products managers is that they don't know what will happen. Flare up, or die away?

Phase II: Trial Support

As the stirrings over an issue increase, a champion may decide to take it on as a cause. Such champions used to be individuals, and were often unknown, as Ralph Nader was when he tackled auto safety. Today, cause support tends to come from organizations, whose leaders are attempting to marry the basic unrest in a situation with a desire for contribution and publicity. The key question to them usually is, "How widespread is the unpublicized unrest?" Or, "How dramatic can the headlines be made?" This may sound crass, but remember, there are scores of budding issues at any time, and an organization may lose its power if it squanders its scarce resources on issues that die out.

In any event, phase II is a period when the would-be leader and the muted cause are on the stump, seeking a political base. If achieved, the action moves to phase III unless the industry being attacked can defuse the situation or the cause fails to capture broad support.

Phase III: The Political Arena

By the time an issue has acquired a political base among the voting public, the opportunity for defusing has usually passed. Now, companies must gird up for political battle in state and/or federal legislatures or in the various regulatory arenas. The issue is the content of new laws or regulations, and companies usually recognize the widespread consumer demands and are only trying to achieve the least costly and least restrictive mode of meeting them. Occasionally, companies fight vigorously against settlement. The cereal industry did and won on several dimensions. However, the political base is usually all the cause leader needs to force some modification in a practice, one severe enough to require legislation or a court ruling.

Phase IV: Regulatory Adjustment

New regulatory legislation is rarely precise, and this imprecision leads to a period of jockeying by the adversaries over its interpretation. The Consumer Product Safety (CPS) Act, for example, directed the CPS Commission to order the seizure of any *imminently hazardous consumer products*—four terms each impossible to define. Imprecision may well be a necessary or even wise approach in regulation. The phase often lasts for years, and sometimes general shifts in a country's political thinking cause various issues to move into or out of the idle state, a point dramatically underscored by the sharp decline in product-related political controversies in the Reagan and Bush administrations.

Business Attitudes toward Product Issues

Business firms deal with public policy issues on a much broader base than just new products. So they have reached a structure of beliefs on this matter of interface between business and society. Most of those beliefs support product innovation, and society agrees. Granted, there are some issues that we haven't yet figured out. For example, how do we pay the costs of product misuse where the consumer was unable to read and understand labels? What is the responsibility of a food company whose customers want great taste but whose government wants quality nutrition? In general, most of the headlines today are for old problems—our concerns are "at the margin," that is, dealing in areas of temporary uncertainty and change.

For example, people in the mid-90s are honestly confused on how we address the problem of pornography on Internet. Ten years from now we will have decided.

The new product that causes unexpected concern on the public policy front is probably the result of careless management. Note, *unexpected*. A lot of our problems we expect, and in most cases have methods to avoid them or hedge bets or prepare to deal with them. Of course, no manager can walk through the minefield shown in Figure 23–2 without occasionally tripping up.

Current Problem Areas

New products managers face many specific problem areas (product liability, environmental concerns, and many more) as they attempt to deal with social and legal pressures—product liability is the most complex and at the moment the most frustrating, partly because of the seriousness of the potential suits and the costs of error.

FIGURE 23–2

*The "Battle" as
Viewed by a New
Products Manager*

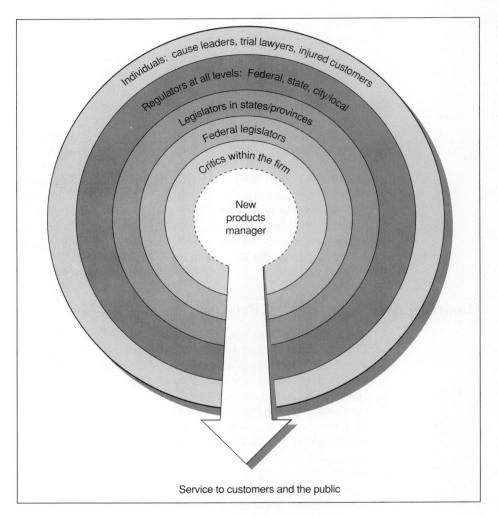

Service to customers and the public

These issues are worldwide, though our discussion will mainly use American examples. Members of the European Economic Community are still wrestling with the product liability question because of their 1985 commitment to strict liability; although going slower than it was supposed to, the directive will apparently be implemented. Germany is a world leader in environment. At the same time, however, many nations in the world have yet to face even the product liability issue.

Product Liability

The scenario here is simple: You buy a product and are injured. The injury may have come when you carried the product home, when you opened it, when you stored it, when you used it, when you tried to repair it, or when you disposed of it. If you were injured and if you think the maker or the reseller of the product did (or didn't do) something that caused the injury, then you have a product liability claim. If guilty, the accused party is liable for the cost and the pain of the injury, plus punitive (punishing) damages as well.

Historically, product liability applied to goods, not services, and there have been many lost attempts to extend the law to cover services specifically. Yet, services are products (both in fact and as we use the terms in this book); they are sold and bought in good faith, injuries do occur, and some redress should be possible. For example, an engineering consulting firm gave an opinion that a building was in good shape; the buyer later found this was untrue when an injury took place. Negligence on services can (and often does) produce a product liability case.

How important is product liability? Most suits are settled out of court so we don't have good dollar data. Many billions of dollars are at stake, though suits are not as common as the press on asbestos, breast implants, and cars make it appear. We know how to manage in this area, and new products managers heed their lawyers.[1]

Typology of Injury Sources

Here is a list of the ways we get into trouble, and most of them are double trouble on new products.

1. Many products have **inherent risks**. For example, blood transfusion carries the risk of hepatitis infection, and dynamite will explode. Because the risk in these products cannot be avoided, we get more understanding in the courts.

2. **Design defects** can cause the manufacture of an unsafe product in three different ways. First, the design may create a **dangerous condition**, say, a steam vaporizer whose center of gravity is so high that the unit is likely to spill. Second, an essential **safety device** may be absent. For example, a hair dryer may lack an overheat cutoff switch. Third, the design may call for **inadequate materials**, which perform their function at first but may eventually deteriorate and become dangerous.

3. **Defects in manufacture** have perhaps always been a new products problem. Inadequate quality techniques may result in defective units even if the product is well designed. Poorly welded ladders are an example.

4. The manufacturer may produce an acceptable product but **fail to provide adequate instructions for use or warnings against particular uses**. If used improperly, the power mower is a potentially dangerous device. The instructions should tell the user how to use it *and* how not to use it. But courts are much

---

[1]Two authors who have tried to straighten out the misunderstandings are Gregory B. Rogers, "Factors Contributing to Compensatory Damage Awards in Product Liability Cases Involving Personal Injury," *Journal of Products Liability*, 1991, pp. 19–29; and Frances E. Zollers, "Labels, Tables, and Fables: A User's Guide to Product Liability Studies," *Journal of Products Liability*, 1991, pp. 1–17.

more interested in how strong the warnings are against misuse (even unforeseeable misuse). Thus, Sears and several other suppliers recently had to pay $4.8 million to a Corpus Christi, Texas, man who was burned when fumes from a barbecue grill being used *indoors* exploded. A half-dozen warnings were in the literature, but the plaintiff's attorney charged that the warnings should have been written in larger letters.[2]

What constitutes adequate warning will never be known for sure, but here is what courts have used in recent years: The warning should be placed conspicuously on the product, it should be where the user most likely can be expected to see it, it should communicate the level of danger, it should instruct the user in how to avoid the potential hazard, sellers should not engage in marketing activities that vitiate an otherwise adequate warning, and it should not be accompanied by statements that the product is safe. The user should be told what may happen if the warning is ignored. Too, makers must be prepared to prove that the user *got* the warning, not just that the maker *posted* it.[3]

5. Finally, dangers sometimes appear **after use**, and the manufacturer's liability may continue into this period. For example, manufacturers of spray cans have to urge that the discards not be burned in fireplaces.

Caution

We must approach the product liability matter cautiously because of the tendency of the press to distort problems. For example, it was widely publicized recently that an overweight physician with a heart condition had bought a Sears mower, suffered a heart attack while starting the mower, and was awarded $1.8 million. In fact, court records showed that the mower mechanism *was defective* and required *an abnormally large number of pulls*. The doctor, incidentally, *did not have a heart condition*.

A U.S. representative railed in a House speech about the number of boxes of cookies the Girl Scouts must sell just to pay their liability premiums. But the Girl Scouts of America denied they have a product liability problem, let alone frivolous lawsuits.[4]

Casual readers of the press rarely have enough information to reach a good judgment, though they do form opinions.

The Four Legal Bases for Product Liability

The four main routes to liability for a product manufacturer are shown in Figure 23–3. All cases require a basis for the claim, and the manufacturer has to

---

[2]Leo Smith, "Trial Lawyers Face a New Charge," *Fortune*, August 26, 1991, pp. 85–89.

[3]For the thoughts of a lawyer talking to marketing people, see Howard J. Newman, "Warnings about Product Dangers," *Marketing Management*, no. 4, 1993, pp. 62–64.

[4]Richard B. Schmitt, "Truth Is First Casualty of Tort-Reform Debate," *The Wall Street Journal*, March 7, 1995, p. B1.

have done something—at the very minimum, make, sell, or lease the product to someone.[5]

Negligence. In the 1980s, under common law, injury claimants had to prove that (1) the manufacturer was **negligent** in operations, let the product become defective and thus injurious, and (2) there was direct sale from the manufacturer to the injured user (**privity**). Perhaps a wagon maker was careless and failed to attach a wheel securely to the axle. The wheel came off, the driver was injured, and negligence was easy to establish. The wagon maker failed to exercise "ordinary" care (the care that a reasonable person would use). The mistake could be made by salespeople, advertising, labeling, retailers, and wholesalers, because one aspect of negligence is **failure to warn**.

In 1916 a court ruled that a defectively manufactured product was *inherently* dangerous; it didn't have to be sold direct. By 1966, every state had accepted this line of reasoning, and lack of privity as a defense against negligence was useless.

Warranty. It was still difficult to prove negligence. Thus warranty, a development of the first half of this century, is relevant. **Warranty** is a promise, and

FIGURE 23–3   Forms and Sources of Product Liability

A manufacturer or reseller may be found guilty of product liability via these four routes:

	Negligence	*Warranty*	*Strict Liability*	*Misrepresentation*
Source	Common law, 1800s; Once required privity, but dropped in 1960.	Uniform Commercial Code; Enhanced by Magnuson/Moss Act.	Court decisions, 1960s.	Common law.
Conditions	Defective product by design or manufacture, and with failure to warn.	Defective product: Implied warranty of merchantability or of fitness for particular purpose. Express warranty: Untrue claim.	Defective product: No requirement for negligence or privity, and no disclaimer is allowed. Reasonably foreseeable.	Untrue claim or misrepresentation that led to injury. User relied on it. No need for defective product.
Defense	Not negligence; product not defective.	Not implied by common usage; Not actually stated; Normal puffery.	Buyer knew, so assumed risk. Unforeseeable misuse. Product not defective.	Was truthful. Normal puffery. Buyer should have known better.

---

[5]A good general source on the following issues is George D. Cameron, *Business Law: Legal Environment, Transactions, and Regulation* (Plano, TX: Business Publications, 1989).

if a promise can be proved and is not fulfilled, the seller can be charged with breach of warranty, whether negligent or not. A careful manufacturer of a new product may still be found guilty of causing injury.

Warranty is express or implied. An **express** warranty is any statement of fact made by the manufacturer about a product, whether made by salespeople, retailers, or others. The major issue with express warranty is the degree of puffing a court will allow.

Implied warranty arises when a maker offers a product for a given use. An implied **warranty of fitness for a particular purpose** is part of the sales contract and means the product is of average quality and can be used for the purposes for which such products are customarily used. The buyer is justified to depend on the seller being right—an expert who knows how people customarily use the item.

But there was constant court bickering over who said what to whom and whether the distributor could have known as much as the maker. Our society is too complex for law that confuses more than clarifies, so we next saw the development of the strict liability concept.

Strict Liability.   Under the concept of **strict liability**, the seller of an item has the responsibility for *not putting a defective product on the market*. If the product is defective, the manufacturer can be sued by any injured party even if that party was only a bystander. *There need be no negligence; there need be no direct sale; no statement by the seller will relieve the liability.*

However, the manufacturer may be able to use three key defenses. The first is **assumption of risk**. If the user of the product learns of the defect and continues to use it regardless of the danger, a suit may not be sustained.

Second, the manufacturer has the defense of **unforeseeable misuse**, meaning the injury occurred because the user misused the product in a way that the seller could not reasonably have anticipated. Managers of new products may lack the expected experience, yet courts expect them to be completely market-wise.

Third, the defense may be that the product, though causing injury, is **not defective**. For example, a man hit his eye on the pointed top of a small ventilation window on the side of his car. Though he leaned over and accidentally bumped the window, the jury held that this injury did not mean the window was defective. Presumably, the plaintiff should have been more careful.

Misrepresentation.   Actually, a product itself doesn't have to be defective (as it does in the three other situations above) so long as an injury took place when the product was used on misrepresentation (intentional or not) by the seller. These cases are rare, but an example was the helmet manufacturer who made a helmet for motorcyclists and showed a motorcyclist wearing one in a picture on the carton. An experienced police officer bought one for use while riding on duty, but the helmet was not made to be used as a safety helmet. The court ruled there had been misrepresentation.

Other Legislation

Many industries have had unique problems leading to specialized legislation. The Food and Drug Administration, for example, was created in 1906. There are restrictions on alcoholic beverages, automobiles, scientific instruments, metals, and scores more. Attention frequently goes to the Consumer Product Safety Act and its Consumer Product Safety Commission (CPSC). Although the commission's direct impact has been much less than anticipated, the indirect impact has been substantial. It has power to set standards for products, order the recall of products, issue public warnings about possible problem products, stop the marketing of new products, ban present or proposed products, and levy substantial civil and criminal penalties. Manufacturers have made many changes to avoid trouble with the law.

Attempts at Standardization and Clarification

Manufacturers have had special troubles dealing with the varying laws of 50 states, and object to cases where a user changes safety equipment on a machine and then sues when injured, or when a machine was built before better technology was discovered yet they are responsible by today's standards. Their biggest complaint concerns the discouragement of innovation. High-technology firms are reluctant to develop new products if there are major risks of trouble. Pharmaceutical companies call it "drug lag." New medical devices have almost ceased to come out.[6] Evidence is piling up on this point.[7]

Many in government agree with these concerns, and attempts have been made to pass federal legislation to settle them. Opposition by consumer and trial lawyer groups have beaten these proposals back every year.[8] There is some progress in particular product areas, such as general aviation, where some of the above issues have been taken care of selectively.[9]

Other Areas of Public Policy Debate on New Products

This is a huge topic, and in a book like this we can only scan the issues, point out why they are important, and cite some sources for readers who would like to investigate one or another of them.

---

[6]Laura Jereski, "Block that Innovation," *Forbes*, January 18, 1993, p. 48.

[7]See Paul A. Herbig and James E. Golden, "Innovation and Product Liability," *Industrial Marketing Management*, 1994, pp. 245–55. Also, W. Kip Viscusi and Michael J. Moore, "Product Liability, Research and Development, and Innovation," *Journal of Political Economy*, 1993, pp. 161–84.

[8]"Snatching Defeat from the Jaws of Victory," *Business Week*, August 1, 1994, pp. 76–77.

[9]Howard Banks, "Cleared for Takeoff," *Forbes*, September 12, 1994, pp. 116–22.

Environmental Needs

People sensitive to loss of quality environment are striving for change and are getting it. Business sometimes leads the way, but twists and bends in the road often frustrate the task of developing new products.

A new product is said to hurt the environment (1) if its raw materials are scarce or hard to get to, (2) if its design or manufacture causes pollution or excess power usage, (3) if its use causes pollution, as on cars and insecticides, and (4) if any disposal problem cannot be handled by recycling.

The Managerial Dilemma

The above concerns are justified. The dilemma seems to deal with the problems of reconciling trade-offs between cost and efficiency in the firm and between price and environmental benefits to society. And there is much we do not know—even about the environmental effects of our new products. Social costs and social benefits are not easily measured. Even environmental firms have found the swamp here—such as when Greenpeace badly overstated the damage done by destruction of oil drilling platforms in the North Sea. Interestingly, we are finding we don't even know what happens in landfills—new anthropological studies show that material in dumps reacts differently than we thought.

Improvements are many, involving action on all of the needed areas. Honeywell asks buyers of its home smoke alarms to return them to the factory for disposal. Some firms have begun market testing in Germany and Scandinavian countries to pass what is felt to be the world's toughest greenness test.[10] Rubbermaid, with its acclaimed Sidekick school lunch bucket, is developing new items aimed squarely at these needs.[11] Cars pollute less, recycled paper is appearing in packaging, and on and on. Of course, there are occasional bloopers—P&G was congratulated for its ecology-friendly Ariel Ultra detergent in Europe, but was blindsided when critics found they had used animal testing in its development.

There are many times, even today, when the cost-benefit analyses come out wrong, but a strong need for environmental protection is here to stay. This focuses us on: protocol (to get the real needs), design (to creatively solve problems), and

---

[10]Though maybe not a precursor for the test of the world, the situation in Germany is worthy of study. New laws implemented in the middle 1990s sharply changed the new products picture. For example, some product packages (including foam packing and aspirin boxes) must either be returned by retailers to the manufacturers who used them or be returned by consumers to retailers who will shunt them to recyclers who will then bill manufacturers for the costs. See Philip White, "Waste Not," *International Design*, May–June 1992, pp. 67–69.

[11]See Zachary Schiller, "At Rubbermaid, Little Things Mean a Lot," *Business Week*, November 11, 1991, pp. 27–30.

FIGURE 23–4

*Public Policy
Problems and the
New Product
Process: How
Our System
Relates to
Environment
as an Example*

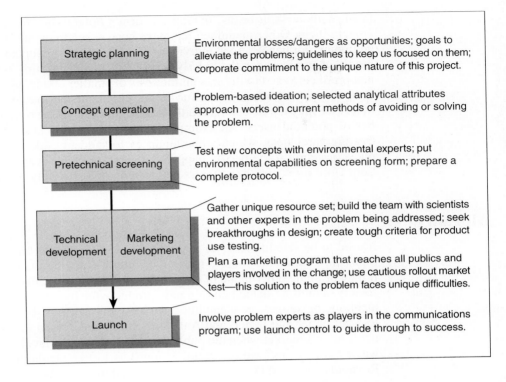

testing (to learn the effects of our creations).[12] We are even learning better ways
to do green marketing.[13] See Figure 23–4 for how the overall new product system contributes to public policy problems just as it does to other problems.

Worthy Products

The makers of Folgers, Maxwell House, and Nescafé were under strong pressure from a consumer group in 1991 to stop buying coffee beans from El Sal-
vador. P&G decided to offer a new blend of coffee, under the Maryland Club

---

[12]It is no longer enough to slap green colors on packages, with pictures of ferns and waterfalls.
See Michael Evamy, "Eco-Friendly, But Fern-Free," *Design,* November 1990, pp. 30–32; and
Vasanthakumar N. Bhat, "Green Marketing Begins with Green Design," *Journal of Business and
Industrial Marketing,* no. 4, 1993, pp. 26–31.

[13]Joel J. Davis, "Federal and State Regulation of Environmental Marketing: A Manager's Guide,"
SAM Advanced Management Journal, Summer 1994, pp. 36–44; and Maxine S. Lans, "New Laws
on Green Marketing Are Popping Up All the Time," *Marketing News* (a publication of the American
Marketing Association), February 15, 1993, pp. 22–24.

label, without such beans, though the firm's Folgers brand would continue to contain them. Other manufacturers have been asked to create special exercising equipment for handicapped individuals, better foods for people who need to diet, modified products for the elderly (e.g., with bigger printing on washer dials), and products keyed to the special interests of smaller ethnic groups. The Orphan Drug Act provides federal aid for the development and marketing of drugs that otherwise may not be commercially feasible because of the relatively small number of potential users. An example resulting from this law is a new drug for treating narcolepsy, which is the tendency to suddenly fall asleep regardless of place or action if the person happens to laugh or enjoy even a small bit of elation. Until now, 40,000 sufferers had to remain completely emotionless.[14]

Morality

It used to be satellite receiver makers who were criticized for bringing pornography into our living rooms. Today it is Internet, and by the time you read this it may be some other mode of communication. Here, morality concerns whether society should be denied certain new products for its own good. We have new alcoholic beverages, new gambling devices, and new sex devices. Radar-detectors get better and better, and Anheuser-Busch was forced to withdraw a product from test market when the public complained that the level of alcohol in what was a "kid's drink" would "train" youngsters to like alcoholic beverages. R. J. Reynolds marketed Dakota cigarettes, targeted to 18- to 24-year-old women with a high school education or less. Dual-drive VCRs permit (encourage?) illegal taping from rental videotapes. New telephone technology permits us to learn who is calling us before we pick up the phone.

Product innovators know what is going on and carefully position their products as they wish. Society stops them when they are wrong. They rarely walk into a surprise, and no one expects a weakening on this point. But it is difficult to predict the outcome of any particular controversy, something product developers must try to do, in advance.

Monopoly

The charge of monopoly is occasionally applied to new products. Some economists believe market dominance constitutes monopoly and outstanding new products can lead to (or protect already achieved) market dominance.

---

[14]An odd case arose in 1987 when Genentech complained to the FDA that profits from its human growth hormone orphan drug were being threatened by an Eli Lilly product. A supposedly unprofitable orphan drug was so profitable that the company sought protection against Lilly. See "Genentech's Custody over an Orphan Drug," *Business Week*, March 23, 1987, p. 39. By 1989 the issue involved several products and led to an article entitled "These 'Orphans' Don't Need Nurturing Any More," by John Carey and Joan O'C. Hamilton, *Business Week*, July 2, 1990, p. 38.

Apart from fringe exceptions, the free market forces have almost always prevailed. Bell and Howell once claimed that Kodak secretly developed some film products and introduced them before Bell and Howell had a chance to retool its own cameras and projectors to use the film. Bell and Howell lost. But recently, in the United States, things have turned. Right now we cannot predict where they will go.

In 1993 Xerox was found guilty of antitrust by refusing to sell some copier parts to independent operators selling and servicing high-volume copiers and printers. They paid a $225 million settlement.[15] In 1994, a vigorous Justice Department challenged a patent licensing agreement of a type that had been approved for years. Bayer had to license an insecticide licensed from a European firm for exclusive sale in the United States.[16] Amgen, IBM, Hewlett-Packard, and Digital Equipment are among the many firms now involved with suits over alliances or consortiums.[17]

Personal Ethics

Some criticisms are difficult to fit into the above categories. People who react to them more often call them matters of **personal ethics**, not economics or business management. They are issues where people pretty much reach individual decisions, rather than seek court decisions. Here is a set of them—not complete, but in sufficient variety to let you see the problem product innovators face. As with all personal ethics situations, they are not just in the marketplace—they are in the labs, factories, and offices too. As Pogo said, We have met the enemy and he is us.

To get the full effect of this problem, read the following ethics situations. Would you, or would you not, support continuing each of the 13 practices? How would you handle them if they came up in *your* new products organization? That is, what would you do *managerially*, not individually? Try to find a person who will make an individual set of answers for comparison with your answers—both sets having been made privately first. Note that personal ethics situations exclude the clearly illegal—e.g., scientists have been known to steal company secrets and sell them to competitors, but such cases are not issues in ethics.

1. Ideation or concept generation often leads us to explore the minds of customers, to find something they want or will want when they hear about it. Your firm uses *intrusive techniques*, such as unannounced observation and psychological projective techniques. A customer recently said it is unethical to trick people into telling you what they want.

[15]Milo Geyelin, "Xerox Agrees to Vouchers in Settlement," *The Wall Street Journal*, December 8, 1993, p. B8.
[16]Brigid McMenamin, "Eroding Patent Rights," *Forbes*, October 24, 1994, p. 92.
[17]See Andrew Pollack, "Antitrust Actions on the Rise," *The New York Times*, Sunday, November 10, 1991, sec. 3, p. 12.

2. One of your divisions has a *purely imitative product innovation charter*. Is it ethical to help a firm market something that is not new in any way?

3. Your market research director uses focus groups for concept testing, and lets company people *secretly sit behind the mirrors* as your customers react to the new concepts. They often joke about customers' product usage practices.

4. You introduce a temporary product that will be replaced when a better one in development is ready a year from now. You are told *not to let distributors or your sales force know* it is only temporary.

5. You work for a management training firm and are about to market a new seminar service for banks. Your firm, for a fee, will run seminars during which you will train bank personnel in investment counseling. But there is no product use test on the seminar, and *you don't know that the bank people will really learn how to counsel*.

6. You work for a detergents company and recently learned that over the years thousands of rodents have been force-fed each new product, including versions in development. Each *force-feeding goes on until half of the rodents die* (the so-called LD50 test).

7. You are currently working on a patented item that schools will use for map displays. It is so good that virtually every K–12 school will buy several of them. You come across the cost figures and calculate that the *gross margin will run about 80 percent*. A co-worker comments that the price could be cut in half and the company margin would still be a healthy 60 percent.

8. You work for a leading software firm which introduces new versions of its word processing system with many *unannounced features*. That is, there are things the system can do but users are not told about them. The firm then markets a line of instructional books that include these features; competitive instruction firms, not knowing of the features, thus have books that are much less helpful to the users. (Of course, there is the other side of the coin—perhaps it is not ethical for an independent author to profit from an instruction book to be used by purchasers of Word Perfect. Should only Word Perfect get that market?)

9. You work for a database service that recently began collecting patient records from physicians and now offers a new service of *information for pharmaceutical firms*. The records sometimes contain names, and often include age, sex, etc., of the patients. Information includes nature of illnesses and treatments.

10. The Food and Drug Administration has charged that your new Freshland spaghetti sauce is processed and sold nonrefrigerated; it therefore *cannot be called "fresh"* as it is, in its brand name. Your firm counters that it is fresher than the leading competitor's and, besides, lots of products are advertised as being fresh when they really aren't, according to the arbitrary FDA definition.

11. A set of "educational" game cards, made by your firm and not really very educational, are known to be bought by less-intelligent parents for their children. There are several far better sets of such cards on the market.

12. Your firm's new product strategy is to stir up the waters—marketing a long line of similar products to confuse customers and keep them from being able to "buy intelligently."

13. You have a line of party products that seem to be in sync with many younger people, but are sexually oriented. You market them through mass outlets, not adult stores, and although some retailers won't stock the items, many will. Sales have been outstanding.

The Underlying Residual Issues

A few really tough issues thread their way through the public policy issues discussed in this chapter. They are such that we will never be free of problems. One of them is: *What are reasonable goals for action here?* A risk-free existence is totally unreasonable. Zero-defect quality control is a goal in many firms. But, with the complexity in most of today's consumer products, nothing short of government decree would stop consumers from making errors—and then only because they would not be making any decisions at all.

Besides, even if we could hope to reach a 99.99 percent level of risk reduction, that would still leave 2,400 people on the wrong side of the statistic in the U.S. alone. Worldwide, it would be perhaps 50,000.[18]

Another one is the *trade-off problem*. Even when a particular situation seems to have a clear-cut guiding principle, we often find a contrary principle of equal merit. Which of two worthy options should be accepted? The discoverer of DDT won a Nobel prize because the material would markedly enhance world crop productivity and thus reduce world starvation. Yet the discovery was ultimately banned in large areas because it produced undesirable effects.

A third is, *Where should the costs fall?* In many of the controversies that affect new products, the argument is not so much, *What should be done?* as, *Who should pay for it?* Because (1) no production system can ever make products perfectly and (2) no consumer group will ever use products with perfect wisdom, there will always be injuries and waste. Who should pay? Governments are already under pressure for tax reduction. Insurance companies know the negative reactions to inflated rates. So, the no-fault approach is becoming popular—what manufacturers call the *total*-fault approach. The manufacturer assumes all responsibility and is expected to pass along the costs somehow.

What Are New Products Managers Doing about All This?

At the start of this chapter, we said that managements today generally have the public policy problem in hand. They have learned how to run the new product process to minimize the problems. The previous sections showed many ways in which actions are being taken. Here are a few more that are quite general.

---

[18]Many areas of controversy are discussed in Warren T. Brookes, "The Wasteful Pursuit of Zero Risk," *Forbes*, April 30, 1990, pp. 161–72.

Strategy and Policy

More top managers are personally involved today. They want safe and useful products, because they sell better. For example, at a firm making v-style accordion gates for children, the CEO rejected a proposal, and said the team could do better—they soon designed something better *and* less expensive. Second, product innovation charters set the standards in guidelines, and they also point out opportunities in regulations.

Control Systems

Managements today demand tough standards, rigorous auditing at all points, good record keeping, and training of new product employees. Disaster plans help. When Campbell's routine checking program disclosed a can containing botulin, the company immediately stopped shipments from the plant involved, canvassed 102,000 food outlets in a 16-state area, and inspected 65 million cans. A new manufacturing process was abandoned, two dozen spoiled cans were discarded, and the firm was back on top of the situation. Pfizer found a potentially flawed heart valve and had to contact 55,000 people with the implant. They had the records to do so.

Product Testing

Firms learn how customers will use products; and if that use looks like it will cause problems, then action is taken now, not after injuries mount. Then they add stress testing to catch misuse and overuse. They use common sense: Anybody could have seen that the all-terrain vehicles would be a problem, and they were.

Marketing

They prepare adequate warnings. The Manville Corporation was defending against asbestos-death lawsuits as early as 1929. The firm's chief physician allegedly urged caution labels in 1953, but they didn't go on until 1964 and even then apparently did not indicate the gravity of the risk. Bankruptcy was ultimately necessary to survive.

Firms today manage the marketing and distribution process with the same vigor they use to manage design and manufacturing. If a product is unsafe in lay people's hands and must go through professional channels, it is plainly labeled with an explanation why.[19]

---

[19]For another good general source of preventative actions, see Marisa Manley, "Product Liability: You're More Exposed than You Think," *Harvard Business Review*, September–October 1987, pp. 28–41. This article cites the case of a hair bleach product from Curtis that was so marketed and labeled. When an injured customer sued, the court ruled she was responsible by buying the item at a beauty show, mixing the two products, and ignoring the labels.

Market Testing

Market tests, combining product and promotion, can spot miscommunications. Distributors may not understand promotions, discounts, instructions, or service. People who shouldn't buy an item may be doing so.

Education

Managements now consider themselves in the education business, first with *company personnel* (through ombudsmen, consumer affairs officers, scientific advisory panels, etc.) and second with the *consumer* (through labels, warranties, how-to sheets, and more instructional advertising).

External Affairs

Most industries now aggressively greet every legislative thrust on new products, and vigorous public affairs programs are standard fare. Industries work together more and even include consumer units on their task forces. Going almost unnoticed are routine announcements such as this newswire release on July 19, 1991, by P&G:

> The Procter & Gamble Company is voluntarily withdrawing Duncan Hines Pantastic Party Cakes...from a limited test area.... Five consumers have reported charring or smoking of the baking pan included in the party cake kit. Peter Morris, Vice President–Product Research, said, "Based on extensive product testing, we have found no safety problems. But rather than run any risk, we think it's in the best interest of our consumers to voluntarily withdraw this product from its limited test area until we can further investigate these few incidents."

Summary

This concludes our trip through a troublesome dimension of the new products process. The pressures are very real, and the difficulties are at times almost overwhelming. Some unresolved issue have no answers, and new variations in the general problem areas will continue to unfold.

New products managers, however, are finding they can manage under these circumstances if they do their homework well. Avoiding needless troubles requires that they understand the process, stay close to their legal departments, get management's support at critical times, and follow up marketing with more aggressive launch control than ever before used in American industry. All temptations are to do just the opposite because time can be the Achilles' heel of new products management, as we have seen more than once.

Although we have covered the major areas of product policy concerns in the new products field, you should know that there are far more problems and issues buried in the labs, plants, and offices of today's new products manager. Every industry has scores of them. As a final example, think of the problems scientists in the pharmaceutical industry have when they go to do field testing on an experimental drug known to be dangerous. With whom must they work? Whose approvals are necessary? What controls should they have to use on the actions and record keeping of physicians and hospital personnel? And how far and hard should they search for side effects—to the third generation? Does it matter if the medicine being tested came from a rare frog on the endangered species list? Does it matter if the drug (assuming it is successful) will cost over $4,000 a month for 10 months of treatment, and have a lifetime dosage level of $1,000 a month?[20]

The point here is this: Thousands of people deal with these troublesome issues every day—they know the problems and they have worked out balance between need to know and need to move ahead. They manage, risks and all.

Applications

More questions from that interview with the company president.

1. "The worst thing about product liability is what they call strict liability. Now, I know it's hard to prove negligence against a typical large corporation of today, but that's no reason to go to the other extreme and say a company is guilty when there is no evidence it did anything wrong. We market thousands of products involving thousands of people. Strange things are going to happen. Employees are not robots—they make human errors. You've probably already made a mistake or two today, yet if you were in a business, you could be sued, found guilty, and then hit with a punitive damages ruling like a common criminal. That's just not fair."

2. "We're currently about to market a new type of hair dryer. It's not a blower in the usual sense—there are no wires that get hot. Instead, we have combined two chemicals that tend to heat up if they are charged with an electrical current. The air is directed through the wire mesh container in which these chemicals are kept (they're solids, not liquids), and whenever there is electricity, there is heated air. If you feel you understand the moral and legal issues of product liability, would you please tell me what you think we should have done, and what we should do in the future, to conform with what the public generally expects of us and with what the law requires of us? We still have several months before we market the new dryer, but the product specifications are frozen and the item is currently about to be started through production."

3. "Two other firms I know about were less fortunate. Morton-Norwich Products introduced Encare, a vaginal suppository contraceptive, and American Home Products came out with a similar product called Semicid

---

[20]For an interesting summary of the problems, see George Anders, "Testing a New Drug Entails Daunting Costs and Clashing Interests," *The Wall Street Journal*, January 7, 1994, p. A1.

at about the same time. Both advertised that the products were safer than IUDs and that, unlike the 'pill,' they had no hormonal side effects. They called the items a safe, medically tested, positive method of birth control, which they are. But the Federal Trade Commission has ruled that the firms cannot claim a comparative advantage over other methods unless they also state that the new product is not as *effective* as the others. The FTC says the only novel aspect of the new products is the suppository form, and that has very little advantage to the consumer. Both firms now have to distribute a new pamphlet telling the advantages and disadvantages of all forms of birth control. All of this may be well and good—I don't know—but the aspect that bothers me is that the two firms were ruled responsible for telling consumers the *good* things about their competitors, not just the bad. Why do you suppose the FTC ruled the way it did? And is this a forecast of what we are all going to face? Since when am I responsible for helping potential customers choose a competitor's product?"

4. "When you first told me about those, what do you call them, public policy issues, I was thinking about our health industry group. It is rapidly developing a line of health maintenance organizations (HMOs) by acquisition, primarily, and several by invitation of leading hospitals. They will all be in the service business and not-for-profit operations (they have other advantages for us), so it is pleasing to think that at least this part of our corporate family won't raise public policy issue problems. That's right, isn't it?"

CASE: ONLINE SERVICE PROVIDERS TASK FORCE

The online service firm, by 1996, had become an established part of life in the computer age. Such firms offered the leading sources of access to Internet as well as access to a wide range of services within their own systems. The three leaders were CompuServe (the oldest and largest), America Online (the soon-to-be largest), and Prodigy. They offered an online computer-based service to homes and businesses that worked this way: A person slipped a personal diskette into a PC (previously hooked up with a modem to the telephone line) and typed in an entry message, first into the service itself and then, if desired, on into Internet, and eventually to other types of networking. Offerings included stockbroker services, business information, electronic encyclopedia, travel reservations and tickets, news, classified ads, magazine subscriptions, merchandise, trip routing, service listings (e.g., restaurants), and much, much more. For many subscribers (who paid a monthly charge and a per-hour charge) the leading value of the service was the chance to send messages to their friends also on the service. This e-mail activity was very inexpensive and trained subscribers in the skills they would soon need when on Internet.

From a central menu, the user selected categories and then went into subcategories, detailed information, action options (buying), and so on. The systems were user friendly

---

Source: This case was developed from a large variety of public sources, especially David Kirkpatrick, "Online Services," *Fortune*, May 1, 1995, pp. 86–96. The 1996 task force meeting was perhaps an imaginative invention, but betting is that it did take place.

from the beginning and used simple English commands. Originally, users had substantial costs for a new PC and for a modem, but these had pretty much become commonplace.

Over the past 10 years there had been shifting in market share, but all three leaders were large and (in CompuServe's case) financially successful. America Online was the most aggressive and led in developing new subscribers. Even their name fit in well with what became the major part of their business and the basis for the industry's current problem—access to Internet.

There were various ways to reach the Internet, and aggressive access providers existed in every area of the United States and around the world. Before 1993, there had been virtually no mention of public policy issues on these services. There was no stirring. There were no suits for injurious service or for damaging the environment or for providing unworthy products, etc. No politician had adopted their videotex service as a crusade cause. Occasionally there were brushes with legal aspects—a New York state court had already ruled that Prodigy could be held liable for slanderous and libelous comments made on Internet through its connection, and CompuServe occasionally censored users' e-mail.

However, as more people used online services Internet cyberspace became contaminated. Internet was a network that was open to people anywhere in the world who had the necessary software for connecting into it. Once in, they has access to an unbelievably large set of information on what they called the World Wide Web. Anybody could (at a fairly high cost) set up their own Website (page) on Internet. Messaging, bulletin boards, merchandise being sold, even advertising being displayed to users of Internet. Services and information offered for sale used passwords.

What happened, however, could probably have been anticipated. Pornography entered, including pictures, stories, e-mail messages, chat groups, the works—what precipitated the problem in this case were the child porn arrests in September 1995. A large group of people had been using Internet to transmit photos that constituted child porn. They were arrested and charged. There was apparently no question they were acting illegally.

But for the managers of the online services, there were two problems. First, what could or should they do to prevent illegal activities? American Online was directly concerned as the access provider in the porn cases, but the other two leaders knew they could be next. Second, for the longer term, what other types of trouble might they get into? Not from the illegal types (they would have to be handled some way or another) but rather from the ethical or social responsibility type.

Although online was a service, not a good, and product liability had traditionally applied to goods, the providers knew they were just a court decision away from being involved. Already legal people were referring to the "permanent *injury* to young minds from the pornography." And already people concerned about the pornography problem were blaming the access providers. The First Amendment (free speech) was being seen as in need of compromise with other freedoms.

Too, industry must recognize the possibility that their new position of power might start people thinking about new definitions for environmental pollution, worthy products, personal ethics—the full set.

So, as they had done in 1995 to deal with the criminal case, they formed a task force of managers from the three firms to deal with the broader social responsibility question. Other online services might or might not participate: General Electric's Genie, News Corp.'s Delphi Internet, Apple Computer's eWorld, and Microsoft's Network. So too might sellers of the software for direct access to Internet.

You work for one of the three firms calling the meeting and have been asked to go to the first task force meeting with a statement—what problems the industry might face, what the rationale would be, what defense you would have, and for the most likely ones, what you should do to reduce your chances of ending up in court again.

BIBLIOGRAPHY

This bibliography displays (1) general books on the product innovation subject in recent years, both business- and college-oriented, and (2) selected other publications frequently sought for their reference value or some unique contribution. Books and articles on specialized aspects of new products management are given as footnotes throughout the text.

Betts, Jim. *The Million-Dollar Idea.* Point Pleasant, NJ: Point Publishing, 1985.
   (A collection of some of the most helpful ideas from past issues of *The New Product Development Newsletter.*)

Boothroyd, Geoffrey; Peter Dewhurst; and Winston Knight. *Product Design for Manufacturing.* New York: Marcel Dekker, 1994. (By some of the pioneers in this field.)

Booz Allen & Hamilton. *New Products Management for the 1980s.* Chicago: 1982.
   (A survey of industry practice, dated now but often referred to.)

Choffray, Jean-Marie, and Gary L. Lilien. *Market Planning for New Industrial Products.*
   New York: John Wiley, 1980. (Focuses principally on advanced techniques of management science as applied in the industrial field.)

Clark, Kim B., and Steven C. Wheelwright. *Managing New Product and Process Development.* New York: Free Press, 1992. (A Harvard case book.)

Cooper, Robert G. *Winning at New Products: Accelerating the Process from Idea to Launch.* 2nd ed. Reading, MA: Addison-Wesley Publishing, 1993. (A business-oriented book based on recent research findings.)

Deschamps, Jean-Philippe, and P. Ranganath Nayak. *Product Juggernauts: How Companies Mobilize to Generate a Stream of Market Winners.* Boston: Harvard Business School Press, 1995. (Stories of successful companies.)

Dolan, Robert J. *Managing the New Product Development Process.* Reading, MA: Addison-Wesley Publishing, 1993. (A Harvard case book, emphasis on marketing science.)

Gruenwald, George. *New Product Development.* 2nd ed. Chicago: NTC Publishing Group, 1992. (A business-oriented book especially for consumer packaged goods.)

Guile, Bruce R., and James Brian Quinn. *Managing Innovation.* Washington, DC: National Academy Press, 1981. (Collection of seven stories of successful product innovation in eight industries, from a parts catalog to a bridge construction service.)

Hisrich, Robert D., and Michael P. Peters. *Marketing Decisions for New and Mature Products.* 2nd ed. New York: Macmillan, 1991. (A college text.)

Hooley, Graham J., and John Saunders. *Competitive Positioning: The Key to Marketing Strategy.* Englewood Cliffs, NJ: Prentice Hall, 1993. (A business-oriented book.)

Hopkins, David S. *The Marketing Plan.* New York: The Conference Board, 1981. (Basic compilation of marketing plans in survey of members.)

Katzenbach, Jon R., and Douglas K. Smith. *The Wisdom of Teams: Creating the High-Performance Organization.* Boston: Harvard Business School Press, 1993. (A business-oriented book that presents the idea of teams in a construct of horizontal management.)

Kidder, Tracy. *The Soul of a New Machine.* New York: Avon Books, 1981. (A classic story of a new products team as they developed a new minicomputer for Data General.)

Kinnear, Thomas C., and James R. Taylor. *Marketing Research.* 4th ed. New York: McGraw-Hill, 1991. (A basic college text on the subject.)

Kotler, Philip. *Marketing Management: Analysis, Planning, and Control.* 7th ed. Englewood Cliffs, NJ: Prentice Hall, 1991. (A general marketing management text.)

Kuczmarski, Thomas D. *Managing New Products.* 2nd ed. Englewood Cliffs, NJ: Prentice Hall, 1992. (A business-oriented book that emphasizes the management consultant's view of strategy and organization.)

McGrath, Michael E. *Product Strategy for High-Technology Companies*. Burr Ridge, IL: Irwin Professional Publishing, 1995. (How to achieve growth, competitive advantage, and increased profits; a consultant's experienced view of the matter, primarily from the top-management perspective.)

McQuarrie, Edward. *Customer Visits: Building a Better Market Focus*. Thousand Oaks, CA: Sage Publications, 1993. (A business-oriented book.)

Meltzer, Robert J. *Biomedical and Clinical Instrumentation*. Buffalo Grove, IL: Interpharm Press, 1993. (Fast tracking from concept through production in a regulated environment.)

Moore, William L., and Edgar A. Pessemier. *Product Planning and Management: Designing and Delivering Value*. New York: McGraw-Hill, 1993. (Broad scope with special attention to systems that use management science and especially computer modeling.)

Moskowitz, Howard R. *Food Concepts and Products: Just in Time Development*. Trumbell, CT: Food & Nutrition Press, 1994. (A business book.)

Nystrom, Harry. *Technological and Market Innovation*. Chichester, England: John Wiley & Sons, 1990. (A report of research conducted primarily on industrial firms in Sweden.)

Osborn, Alex F. *Applied Imagination*. 3rd ed. New York: Charles Scribner's Sons, 1963. (The basic brainstorming work.)

Pinchot, Gifford, III. *Intrapreneuring*. New York: Harper & Row, 1985. (By the creator of the intrapreneuring concept.)

Pine, B. Joseph. *Mass Customization: The New Frontier in Business Competition*. Boston: Harvard Business School Press, 1992. (The story as told by the person credited with creating the concept.)

Rosenau, Milton D., Jr. *Faster New Product Development*. New York: AMACOM, 1990. (A business-oriented book focused as indicated by its title.)

———, and John J. Moran. *Managing the Development of New Products*. New York: Van Nostrand Reinhold, 1993. (A business-oriented presentation, stressing the technical phases known as development.)

Schnaars, Steve P. *Managing Imitation Strategies*. New York: Free Press, 1994. (How later entrants seize markets from the pioneers; 28 case histories, plus patterns from them.)

Slade, Bernard N. *Compressing the Product Development Cycle Time: From Research to Market Place*. New York: AMACOM, 1993. (How to achieve a faster movement through the technical phases.)

Smith, P. G., and Donald G. Reinersten. *Developing Products in Half the Time*. New York: Van Nostrand Reinhold, 1991. (One of the original sources on this subject. Business book.)

Souder, William E. *Managing New Product Innovations*. Lexington, MA: Lexington Books, 1987. (Compilation of the author's research findings from 10 years of studies, mainly industrial.)

Thomas, Robert J. *New Product Development: Managing and Forecasting for Strategic Success*. New York: John Wiley & Sons, 1993. (For the business practitioner, with special emphasis on forecasting.)

Twiss, Brian C. *Managing Technological Innovation*. 3rd ed. New York: Longman, 1986. (A U.K. technical perspective.)

Ulrich, Karl T., and Steven D. Eppinger. *Product Design and Development*. New York: McGraw-Hill, 1995. (A view of the new product process through the eyes of design—broader than some in this area.)

Urban, Glen, and John R. Hauser. *Design and Marketing of New Products*. 2nd ed. Englewood Cliffs, NJ: Prentice Hall, 1993. (An updated and expanded version of their original book, which first made heavy use of mathematical modeling for sales forecasting and other purposes.)

Utterback, James M. *Mastering the Dynamics of Innovation*. Boston: Harvard Business School Press, 1994. (How companies can seize opportunities in the face of technical change.)

von Hippel, Eric. *The Source of Innovation*. New York: Oxford University Press, 1988. (The basic source of the lead user concept and its use.)

Walsh, Vivien; Robin Roy; Margaret Bruce; and Stephen Potter. *Winning by Design*. Oxford, United Kingdom, 1992. (The product creation story from the vantage point of designers.)

Wheelwright, Steven C., and Kim B. Clark. *Revolutionizing Product Development*. New York: Free Press, 1992. (A business-oriented book.)

Wizenberg, Larry, ed. *The New Products Handbook*. Burr Ridge, IL: Irwin Professional Publishing, 1987. (A business-oriented book.)

Zangwill, Willard I. *Lightening Strategies for Innovation: How the World's Best Firms Create New Products*. New York: Lexington Books, 1993. (A business-oriented presentation of the book's title.)

SOURCES OF IDEAS ALREADY GENERATED

New product ideas come from many places, some of which are peculiar to particular firms or industries. Here are the more broadly used sources.

Employees

Many types of employees can be sources of new product concepts. Salespeople are an obvious group, but so are technical groups, manufacturing, customer service, packaging employees, and, in the case of general consumer products, any employee who uses the products. Manufacturing and engineering personnel are frequently part-time inventors who should be encouraged to submit their ideas. These people need to know that their ideas are wanted, and special mechanisms (and even cultures) must usually be constructed to gather those ideas.

Employee suggestion systems are not dependable ways to turn up ideas, and special idea contests have an equally disappointing record. Toyota ran an Idea Olympics for some time and in one year produced 1,300 employee-inventor entries. The firm did not comment on the quality of the ideas.

The most helpful suggestions come from employees whose work brings them in contact with customer problems. For example, a drill manufacturer's service department found that many drills were burning out because customers were using them as electric screwdrivers. Adding a clutch mechanism to the drill created a new product. Complaint-handling departments also become familiar with consumers' use of products. Salespeople know when a large order is lost because the firm's product is not quite what the customer wanted.

Dun & Bradstreet had a fine new products track record and reported that most of its new product ideas came from field personnel. Eligible D&B employees could receive $5,000 for suggesting an idea that went national. Some firms have used an "idea miner"—an employee whose job is to scout around among other employees, encouraging and collecting their ideas.

Customers

The greatest source of new product ideas is the customer or user of the firm's products or services, although their ideas are usually only for product improvement or nearby line extensions. Some people believe the majority of all new products in certain industries originate with users. Because some specialized user groups are personally involved with devices, new product people occasionally delegate new product concept development to them. Similarly, most auto parts and components manufacturers look to their giant OEM buyers for new product initiatives. On the other hand, one firm solicited 2,800 ideas from customers and was not able to use a single one.

The most popular ways to gather consumer ideas are surveys, continuing panels, special focus groups, and the mail. Some firms get so many suggestions in the mail that they do not read them. Industrial firms usually take the more initiative approach of using personal contacts by salespeople or technical staffs, especially lead users.

Resellers

Brokers, manufacturers' reps, industrial distributors, large jobbers, and large retail firms may be quite worthwhile. In fact, some mass merchandisers have their own new products departments and invite manufacturers to bid on specifications. Many industrial representatives are skilled enough to be special advisers to their clients, and selling agents in the toy industry not only advise but actually take on the new products function if the manufacturer wishes.

One chemical distributor suggested using a low-cost polyethylene bag to line steel drums to prevent corrosion, and a millwork producer learned about a new competitive entry from a dealer and then suggested how the new item could be improved. Both suggestions were successfully implemented. Kroger once told manufacturers that its customers want more easy-to-cook, single-portion frozen dinners, and another chain suggested a low-calorie enchilada.

Suppliers/Vendors

Most manufacturers of plastic housewares are small and thus look to the large plastics firms for advice. Virtually all producers of steel, aluminum, chemicals, metals, paper, and glass have technical customer service departments. One of their functions is to suggest new products made of the firm's basic material.

Competitors

New product idea generators are interested in competitors' activities, and competitors' new products may be an indirect source for a leapfrog or add-on new product; but competitors (as with government-mandated cross-licensing of ideas) are rarely sources of new product ideas except in industries where benchmarking has been accepted as a strategy. The first firms bringing a new product to a particular market segment (such as the smaller city banks) do use their innovative competitors as sources, but this is effective only when market segments are insulated. At Ford Motor Company, once the engineers get their hands on a new competitive product, it is systematically torn down into its 30,000 parts. All are cataloged and then mounted on panels so others can examine them.

The Invention Industry

Every industrialized country has an "industry" consisting of a nucleus of inventors surrounded by firms and organizations that help them capitalize on their inventions. Though tending to lose out to corporate research centers, individual inventors still submit almost a fourth of all patent applications. The auxiliary or supportive group includes:

Venture capital firms	Banks
Inventors' schools	Inventors' councils
Attorneys	Small Business Administration
Trademark and patent offices	Technology expositions
Consultants on new business	Patent shows
Patent brokers and others	Inventor newsletters
Inventor assistance firms	State entrepreneurial aid programs
Individual investors	University innovation centers

Currently, both the inventor and the potential manufacturer are frustrated by the communications, legal, and funding problems existing in this supportive network. Fortunately, this highly fragmented new industry is in the process of shaking down and should soon settle on several dominant organizational formats with which manufacturers can deal.

One example of this emerging format was InstanTechEx, a service provided by Dr. Dvorkovitz & Associates. Dvorkovitz sponsored an annual international technology exchange exposition where hundreds of firms and scores of governments displayed technological advancements that they wanted to sell. The show was a supermarket of technology and an emerging format for standardizing the new invention industry.

Other new organizations are merging the financial, legal, and managerial consulting assistance that inventors usually require, either as venture firms that actually take over and develop the idea or as facilitator firms that reach out to established manufacturers. In the meantime, some firms have what they call "inventors' farm systems" to get both quantity and variety of invention input. NordicTrack makes inventors their primary source of new products, and cultivates that group with almost as much marketing effort as used on their customers.

Miscellaneous

Among the many other sources of outside new product ideas are the following:

1. Consultants. Most management consulting firms do new products work, and some specialize in it—for example, McKinsey, A. D. Little, Mercer, and PRTM. Some consulting firms are devoted exclusively to new products work and include idea generation as one of their services. Unfortunately, the stigma of being outsiders is strong in the new products field, as exemplified by the not-invented-here syndrome. Companies report very favorable experiences but also many horror stories. One alternative is to bring industry experts to discussion sessions with company personnel. General Mills has used a newspaper food editor, a trade journal editor, an advertising copywriter, a restaurateur, a division manager of a food chain, and four company junior executives.

2. Advertising agencies. This source of new product ideas is badly underrated. Most agencies have the creative talent and the product/market experience to generate new product concepts. Some agencies have full-blown new products departments, and some take their concepts all the way to market, including premarket tests and rollouts. Consumer product agencies do more new products work than industrial agencies do, although the West Coast agencies specializing in the computer industry render a wide range of services because their clients are often small.

3. Marketing research firms. Normally, marketing research firms get involved in the idea-generating process by assisting a client with need assessment. They often stumble across an opportunity that they pass along to a client. Some of the bigger marketing research firms also serve as management consultants.

4. Retired product specialists. Industrial new products people, particularly those with technical strength, often retire from their firms and become part-time consultants to other firms. One company actually tracks the retirements of all qualified specialists in its industry. Conflict-of-interest problems may arise, and divulging competitive secrets is ethically questionable, but most arrangements work around these problems easily.

5. Industrial designers. Industrial design firms sometimes function as part of a team implementing a new product decision that has already been made. However, many industrial designers are extremely creative. Industrial design firms and individual industrial designers are increasingly capitalizing on their own new product strengths. Industrial design departments of universities are sometimes assigned by government and other service organizations to do original new products work.

6. Other manufacturers. Most firms have potentially worthwhile new product ideas that they do not want because these ideas conflict with the firm's strategy. These ideas are usually allowed to remain idle. However, one such firm, General Electric, created the concept of a Business Opportunities Program in which it offered its spare technologies for sale. Sometimes, the offering was just an idea, but at other times, prototypes and even molds, dies, and finished goods inventories were offered, depending on how far GE had taken an idea before deciding not to develop it further. In later years, GE expanded this service by listing the technologies of others in its monthly editions of *Selected Business Ventures* and in annual compilations in its *New Product New Business Digest.*

7. Universities. Professors and students occasionally offer new product ideas, especially in schools of engineering, the sciences, and business. Dentists, physicians, and pharmacists are scientific groups that play a major role in new products work.

8. Research laboratories. Most of the world's leading countries now have at least one major research laboratory that will do new products work on contract from manufacturers and that occasionally comes up with interesting new product ideas. The Battelle Memorial Institute in Columbus, Ohio, received millions of dollars for its role in getting xerography off the ground. Other leading research laboratories are the Illinois Institute of Technology, the Stanford Research Institute, and Great Britain's National Engineering Laboratory.

9. Governments. The Patent Office of the U.S. government offers several services designed to help manufacturers find worthwhile new product ideas. The *Official Gazette* provides a weekly listing of (1) all new patents issued, (2) condensed descriptions of the patented items, and (3) which patents are for sale or license. Patent Office reports and services also make known what government patents and foreign patents are available.

The military services have a want list of products that they would like to buy, the Department of Agriculture will help manufacturers with new products, and state governments have programs to aid industries.

One by-product of today's regulation of business is increased assistance from regulators for solving such problems as unsafe products and unsafe working conditions. For example, the Occupational Safety and Health Act stimulated several companies to develop first-aid kits.

10. Printed sources. The hundreds of technical and scientific journals, trade journals, newsletters, and monographs are occasionally sources of ideas for new products. Most of the ideas indirectly result from accounts of new products activity. Some publications are more direct sources of new product ideas—for example, *Newsweek*'s annual *New Products and Processes, New Technology (London)*, the *Soviet Technology Bulletin*, and such compilations as *New Product News.* Though not new product ideas directly, there are now at least two online computer databases of actual new products marketed: *Thomas New Industrial Products* and *Predicasts, New Product Announcements.*

11. International. Minnetonka executives got the idea for pump toothpaste while browsing in a West German supermarket. Powdered Tide was developed by scientists in Cincinnati, but Liquid Tide used a formula for surfactants from Japan and a mineral salts antagonist from Belgium. Unfortunately, few firms have systematic programs to find ideas from other countries. Some establish foreign offices to monitor various technologies, others ask their advertising agencies' foreign offices to gather ideas, and still others subscribe to one or more reporting services.

12. Internet. At this time we can only guess what will happen, but some Web sites already are getting into new product ideas, and various bulletin boards post suggestions for product change.

Managing These Idea Sources

These sources of ideas do not function without special effort. For example, salespeople must be trained how to find users with good ideas and how to coax the ideas from them. International markets must be covered on the spot by trained people. Studying the competition must be systematic to catch every change in competitors' products. Each special source is also a potential source for the competition, and the firm that utilizes these sources most appropriately will acquire the best ideas.

OTHER TECHNIQUES OF CONCEPT GENERATION

Chapters 6 and 7 presented the leading ideation techniques with the best track records and the greatest chance of producing valuable new product concepts. Perhaps hundreds of other techniques are available, some of which are proprietary (confidential to the consulting firm that originated each), and some of which are techniques given here but with different names.

Forty-five of the other techniques have been selected for brief review here. They are probably not necessary, but different individuals have found them useful. Perhaps you will too.

Techniques to Aid Problem Analysis

Composite listing of needs fulfilled. By simply listing the many needs met by currently available products, there is a good chance some otherwise overlooked needs will come to mind. This mechanical process is successful only if the listing is pushed to one's mental limits.

Market segmentation analysis. By using one segmentation dimension on top of another, an analyst can develop a hierarchy of smaller and smaller market segments. For example, bar soap segmentation could use sex, age, body part cleaned, ethnic groups, and geographic location. All possible combinations of these would yield thousands of groups—for example, elderly Jewish women washing their faces in New York City. Each combination is potentially a group whose needs are peculiar and currently unmet. (Psychographic and behavioral segments are especially useful today.)

Dreams. This approach analyzes the dreams of people who have the problem(s) under study. Dreams offer a greater range of insights, equitably involve other persons in the problem situation, and offer paranormal aspects of the dream itself. Various famous people, one of whom was Robert Louis Stevenson, have attributed part of their creativity to dreams.

Techniques to Aid Scenario Analysis

There are many techniques for finding meaningful seed trends (trends that could be extended). Some are discussed in Chapter 6, and here are nine more.

Trend people. Many believe certain people have a predictive sense and should be watched. *Women's Wear Daily* is one publication that uses this method, and the people it watches are well known to regular readers.

Trend areas. Major changes in American life and practice traditionally begin on the West Coast and gradually make their way east. Although television and other mass media have reduced the time lag, some firms station personnel in California just to be closer to the changes going on there.

Hot products. The automobile, television, and the computer have had a dramatic effect on lifestyles in this century. Others that may do so include fiber optics, biogenetic engineering, condominiums, VCRs, the compact disk, and Internet. One way to gather meaningful seed trends is to study such products and their effects. But watch out for false prophets, such as the CB radio of the 1970s.

Newspapers. Some persons like to read leading newspapers, particularly *The New York Times*, cover to cover and make note of every trend, activity, or idea that might occasion a significant scenario change.

Hypothetical. A few persons believe one should use just any seed trend to create arbitrary scenarios. The more hypothetical, the better, because the exercise is to stimulate creativity.

Technological changeover. This approach predicts when one technology will substitute for another and seeks the implications of the substitution for all products and systems involving either the new or the old. Doing this involves time series analysis, graphic analysis, and forecasts by technical people.

Technical innovation follow-on. This procedure analyzes the implications for technical breakthroughs across a broad spectrum of technology, not just the immediate technology in which the breakthrough came. For example, a breakthrough in solar heating could be analyzed for effect in plumbing, clothing, furniture, or even entertainment.

Technological monitoring. Some scientists keep journals of technological progress. Every meaningful event is carefully logged, and from time to time the journals are studied for meaningful trends. The technique helps guarantee the analysis of one event in the context of other events.

Cross-impact analysis. First, list all possible changes that may occur over the next 20 years in a given area of activity (say, transportation). Then, apply these changes to other areas of activity, much as is done in technical innovation follow-on, above. The difference is that this method is not restricted to forecastable breakthroughs.

Techniques to Enhance Group Creativity

Phillips 66 Groups. To increase participation, Dr. J. Donald Phillips broke Osborn's 12-person groups into subgroups of 6 members each, sending the subgroups to break-off rooms for six minutes each, rearranging the subgroups, sending the new subgroups off for another six minutes, and so on. Rearrangement was Phillips's key to eliminating the problem of dominant or conflicting personalities. The Phillips 66 groups are sometimes called buzz groups, free association groups, and discussion 66 groups.

Brainstorming circle. This approach forces the conversational sequence around a circle, and each person expands or modifies the idea expressed by the prior person in the circle. The brainstorming circle is more orderly and forces all persons to participate equally.

Reverse brainstorming. This approach concentrates on a product's weaknesses or problems rather than on solutions or improvements. The discussion attempts to ferret out every criticism of, say, a vacuum cleaner. Later, attempts are made to eliminate the weaknesses or solve the problems.

Tear-down. The rule of suspended judgment is reversed in this approach. Instead of avoiding criticism, tear-down requires it, and participants must find something wrong with the previous idea to get a talking turn.

And also. In this approach, each speaking participant enlarges or extends the previous idea. No lateral moves are permitted unless the chain runs dry. The approach has been called idea building and modification.

Synectics. In its pure form, synectics does not differ much from brainstorming. Synectics provides more structure and direction by having the participants think along the lines of certain operational mechanisms—usually analogy and metaphors. The system has a forced sequence through these mechanisms and other steps—viewpoint, forced fit, and so on. However, in recent years the two individuals involved in creating this approach have led their respective creativity firms into use of many ideation techniques. Analogy prevails as a critical feature, but the term *synectics* has come to mean two businesses running creativity seminars.

Gordon method. Prior to developing synectics, W. J. J. Gordon used groups that were not told what the problem was. In this method, if a discussion is to develop new ideas for recording musical performances, the group is encouraged to discuss opera. Eventually, the leader turns the discussion toward the problem but still without divulging it.

Delphi. Although occasionally touted for ideation, Delphi is really a method of organizing a forecasting survey. Panels of experts are compiled, they are sent a questionnaire calling for forecasts within a given area of activity (e.g., hospitals or data processing), the questionnaires are tabulated and summarized, the results are returned to the panel for their reaction and alteration, new summaries are prepared, the results are sent out again, and so on. The iterations continue until conformity is reached or until impasse is obvious. The method is essentially a cop-out because the individuals still must use some method to make their own forecasts. But in certain situations it has been deemed effective, and it can be used quite easily in modified format. It is especially desirable where the industry itself is new, and there are no historical data to aid forecasters.[1]

Think tanks. This too is more a matter of organizing people than a mechanism of stimulating creativity. Think tanks are centers of intensive scientific research. Xerox, for example, maintains a center in Palo Alto at which, among other things, scientists are working on artificial intelligence. What they are studying today may be meaningful 5 to 20 years from now. The key to success here is the environment, which is thought to be stimulating to creativity. If the people in a think tank are charged with converting their outlandish ideation into useful products for marketing, the term *skunk works* is often applied.

Techniques of the Analytical Attribute Approach

Benefit analysis. All of the benefits that customers or users receive from the product under study are listed, in the hope of discovering an unrealized benefit or unexpectedly absent benefit.

Use analysis. Listing the many ways buyers make use of a given product is also sometimes revealing. Some firms, 3M among others, have spent large sums asking consumers to tell them of new uses. Johnson Wax got into the car-polishing business when it found that its floor wax was being used on cars. One must contact users, however—not just list the uses already known to the company.

Function analysis. Between feature and use is an activity called function. Thus, for shampoos, we know the chemicals and product features present, and we may know the full reasons for using shampoos. But it is also creative to list all possible ways that shampoos function—scraping, dissolving, depositing, evaporating, and so on.

Attribute extension. Also called parameter analysis, this technique begins with any attribute that has changed recently and then extends that change. Thus, for example, bicycle seats have gotten smaller and smaller. Extending that idea, one might imagine a bicycle with no seat at all; what would such a bicycle look like, and what would it be used for?

Relative brand profile. Every brand name is flexible or elastic, meaning it can be stretched to cover different product types. People can understand a Minute Maid jelly or Minute Maid soup. But people also tell us that they cannot accept other stretchings—such as Minute Maid meats. Various market research techniques can be used to make these measurements, and any stretch that makes sense to the buyer is a potential new product. Incidentally, this thinking applies to goods and services, industrial as well as consumer.

Pseudo product test. By using what psychologists call a projective technique, one can ask consumers to evaluate what is presented to them as a proposed product but is actually an unidentified product currently on the market. Typically, they will find unique characteristics matching the needs they have. These attributes can then be the base for a new product.

---

[1]A good summary on this point and other aspects of Delphi is Vincent-Wayne Mitchell, "Using Delphi to Forecast in New Technology Industries," *Marketing Intelligence* (U.K.), 1992, no. 2, pp. 4–9.

Systems analysis. This is a technique for studying complete systems of activity rather than products. Standard Brands once studied food preparation systems that involved margarine. It noted that virtually every one included an instruction to "melt the butter or margarine, stir in flour," and so on. From that came a stick-form sauce base called Smooth & Easy.

Unique properties. This technique is primarily valuable in technological fields. The analyst seeks unique properties of any product or material currently on the market. To aid in this, one usually begins by listing all common properties because the unique ones quickly pop out.

Hierarchical design. An organization chart design is formed, with product usage at the top and material types fanning out below. One such design began with deodorants, followed at the second level by roll-on, stick, and aerosol. The brands were listed under roll-ons. Under each brand could be package size or target market segment. Another design had light construction at the top, followed by wood, steel, and concrete. Wood was broken into metal roof, tar or shingle roof, and so on. The technique is mainly a way of forcing one to see all aspects of a situation, which is the essence of the analytical attribute approach.

Weaknesses. All weaknesses of a product or product line (the company's own and those of the competition) are identified. This primarily defensive technique identifies line extensions and flanker products. Every resolvable weakness offers a new product concept.

Achilles' heel. Some analysts prefer to prune the list of weaknesses to one or two that are so serious a competitor might capitalize on.

Theoretical limits test. Both opportunities and threats can be visualized by pushing a known apparatus or device to its theoretical limits. The technique works especially well on a reasonably new technology that appears to have exhausted its usefulness.

Techniques to Enhance Lateral Search

One school of thought holds that all nearby creativity produces only insignificant line extensions and modifications. These people have only disdain for matrixes, analogy, and attribute analysis. They insist the mind must be pushed beyond where it wants to go, in a lateral search. This approach was not mentioned in Chapter 7, but here are some techniques they recommend.

Free association. This approach begins when the ideator writes down one aspect of the product situation being studied—a product attribute, a use, or a user. The trick then is to let the mind roam wildly while jotting down every idea that comes out. The process is repeated for other aspects of the product situation. The associations are usually quite direct in the early stages when creativity is being stimulated; but with time, they become much less related and much more valuable as insights.

Stereotype activity. Here one asks, "How would _____ do it?" The blank is filled in with a stereotype. Particular individuals can also be used, and the question can be reversed to ask what the stereotype would *not* do. Thus, a bicycle manufacturer might ask, "What type of bicycle would a senator ride? Loudspeaker on it? Pedal both ways?"

Cross-field compilation. As scientific disciplines have become increasingly blurred, a creative technique has been developed to bridge the between-field barriers. If a firm works primarily in the chemical area, its product developers may systematically scan developments in, say, physics or biology. Scientists in those fields may not know that some of their ideas have applications in chemistry.

Key-word monitoring. Closely allied to the big-winner approach is the task of monitoring newspapers and magazines and tallying the number of times key words appear. One firm used this approach to spot increasing use of the zodiac, and it promptly marketed a series of successful products featuring the zodiac symbols. Some take this approach with electronic databases and call it database tracking.

Use of the ridiculous. Just to show that anything can be done, some ideators deliberately try to force themselves to use ridiculous approaches. In one session, participants were asked to write out the most preposterous methods of joining two wires together. One answer was "Hold them with your teeth," and another was "Use chewing gum." Those present were astounded to realize they had just reinvented alligator clips, and they promptly gave serious consideration to the chewing gum. It turns out that some ingredients in chewing gum may sometime be marketed for use in wiring!

Study of other people's failures. Any product that has failed offers a chance for the next trier to spot its problem. Robert McNath runs a firm called Marketing Intelligence Service Ltd. in Naples, New York, where he displays over 10,000 actual failed products in a barn-like store. The failures apparently stimulate creativity.

Lateral thinking—avoidance. Some people have stressed the use of avoidance techniques to keep an idea from dominating thinking as it has in the past.

Keep asking, "Is there another way of looking at this?"

Keep asking, "Why?"

Deliberately rotate attention to a phase or aspect of the problem other than the logical one.

Find an entry point into the problem other than the one habitually used.

List all possible alternatives to every aspect of the analysis.

Deliberately seek out nonstandard concepts other than those inherent to the problem.

Try "unconcepting" or "disconcepting," or try dropping a concept. Fractionalize concepts and other aspects of the problem.

Bridge two or more concepts to form still other concepts.

Other people call the approach disparate thinking, zigzag, and divergent thinking. This method was claimed to have partially solved a long-standing problem of light bulb theft in the Boston subway—light bulbs were made to screw in counterclockwise.

Forced relationships. The two-dimensional matrix and the morphological matrix are based on relevant product or market characteristics. Sometimes, however, interesting viewpoints are achieved by forcing relationships between normally unrelated (or even opposed) things. The forced relationships technique has spawned many preferences; the most quoted is the catalog method. In this method, a catalog, journal, or magazine is selected, and then a relationship is forced between everything in it and something else (perhaps a product or a consumer group). Some suggest using the table of contents in magazines or the Yellow Pages in telephone directories. Other names for the forced relationships approach are pick-a-noun and random walk.

Creative stimuli. The idea subject is specified first—the problem, the product, and so on. Then the tangible goal is stipulated—the desired result or what the specified idea should accomplish. Last, a long list of words, names, and phrases is studied for ideas that accomplish the tangible goal. These are proven stimulants (why, we don't know). Some of them are:

Guest stars	Charity	Family	Photography
Alphabet	Education	Timeliness	Interview
Truth	His and hers	Videotape	Testimonials
Outer space	Style	World	Decorate
Chart	Nation	Birth	Showmanship

Gauge scale	Weather	Ethnic	Floor, wall
Zipper	Habit, fad	Push button	Participation
Fantasy	Transportation	Snob appeal	Music
Folklore	Symbolism	Romance	Direct mail
Subconscious	Calendar	Parody	Seasons
Hobbies	Rhinestones	Graphics	Strawberry
Holidays	Curiosity	Sketch	Telephone

For a complete set of the stimuli words and phrases, see Donald Cantin, *Turn Your Ideas into Money* (New York: Hawthorn Books, 1972). A much newer version that combines stimulating terms with variations on the checklist is the product improvement checklist (PICL) by Arthur VanGundy. It is available from New Product Development Newsletter, P.O. Box 1309, Point Pleasant, NJ 08742.

Big winner. Many successful firms, teams, or individuals in sports, politics, television, and so on, are uniquely in tune with the thinking of society. Studying these big winners may lead to principles that can be generalized to new products. As of 1995, for example, something might be found by studying the San Francisco 49ers, sports utility vehicles, cellular phones, World Wide Web, Barry Bonds, large-screen TVs, Steven Spielberg, and Patty Sheehan. One consulting firm compiled a list of the 20 all-time best-selling packaged goods; from this list, the firm generalized principles to transfer to clients' new products.

Competitive analysis. Many firms claim that by studying the strategic plans and actions of competitors, they can detect new product approaches, especially defensive ones. For this purpose they watch competitive announcements, surveys, financial reports, trade show exhibits, detailed analyses of their products, and other such techniques. Life-cycle models help a firm estimate when competitors will take over any of its markets and thus stimulate new products to defensively cannibalize sales.

Technological mapping. This is a form of relevance-tree forecasting in which the competitive capability of each competitor is predicted. It lays the groundwork for decisions to push or play down certain technologies in the home firm. Strategic analysis permits direct forecasting of probable future changes in competitors' technological commitments by studying mergers, acquisitions, sell-offs, patent applications, patent sales, and so on. A keen analyst can predict major market swings and thus suggest new product opportunities (or lack of opportunities) for the firm.

SMALL'S IDEATION STIMULATOR CHECKLIST

1. Can the dimensions be changed?

Larger	Economy-size packages, photo enlargements, puffed cereals
Smaller	U.S. paper money, hearing aids, tabloid newspaper, pocket flashlight, microfilm
Longer	King-size cigarettes, typewriter carriage for bookkeeping
Shorter	Men's shorts, women's panties
Thicker	Rug pads, heavy edge on drinking glasses, glass bricks
Thinner	Nylon hose, seersucker suits, wristwatches
Deeper	Deeper pockets in work clothes and army uniforms, grooved battery plates
Shallow	Wading pools, children's drinking fountain
Stand vertically	Skyscrapers (to increase floor space on expensive land), upright piano
Place horizontally	Ranch-style homes (to avoid stair climbing)
Make slanted or parallel	Reading stands, car mirror, eyeglasses frames
Stratify	Plywood, storage pallets, layer cake
Invert (reverse)	Reversible coats, soft shoes to be worn on either foot, inverted ink and glue stands
Crosswise (bias, counter)	Bias brassieres and slips, pinking shears
Coverage	Mechanical artificial hands, ice tongs
Encircle	Spring cake form, knitted coasters to slip on bottoms of highball glasses, Life-Savers
Intervene	Buffers used in drug products to temper a harsh active ingredient
Delineate	Contour lathe, Scotchlite reflective sheeting
Border	Mats for pictures, movable office partitions, room separators

2. Can the quantity be changed?

More	Extra-pants suits; three stockings—a pair with a spare
Less	Variety of 1-ounce boxes of cereals, ginger ale splits
Change proportions	Nested chairs or dishes, hot-cold water faucets
Fractionate	Separate packings of crackers inside single box, 16-mm movie film usable as two 8-mm films, faucet spray
Join something	Trailer, hose couplings
Add something to it	Cigarette filter tip
Combine with something else	Amphibious auto, outboard motors, roadable airplanes
Complete	Freezer unit added to refrigerator, Bendix washer and dryer single unit

3. Can the order be changed?

Arrangement	Car steering wheels left-handed in United States, right-handed in England; Dewey decimal system of filing
Precedence	Rear-drive automobiles

Source: From Marvin Small, *How to Make More Money* (New York: Pocket Books, 1959). © Copyright 1953, 1981, Marvin Small. Reprinted by permission of Pocket Books, a Simon & Schuster division of Gulf & Western Corporation.

Beginning	Self-starter, red tab to open cigarette package, red string to open Band-Aids
Assembly or disassembly	Prefabricated articles, knockdown boat kits
Focus	Kellogg packages—name placed in left corner instead of center; Hathaway shirt ads—men with eye patch

4. Can the time element be changed?

Faster	Quick-drying ink, dictating machine, intercom system
Slower	High-tenacity yarns for longer-life tires, 33⅓-rpm long-playing records
Longer	Jiffy insulated bags for ice cream, wood preservative
Shorter	Pressure cooker, one minute X-ray machine
Chronological	Defrosting devices, radio clocks
Perpetuated	Photographs, metal plating, permanent magnets
Synchronized	Uniform vacation periods, group travel tours
Anticipated	Thermostat, freezer food-buying plan
Renewed	Self-charging battery, self-winding watches
Recurrence	Switch clocks for lights and electrical appliances
Alternated	Cam drive, electric current

5. Can the cause or effect be changed?

Stimulated	Generator
Energized	Magneto, power steering
Strengthened	AC-DC transformer, Simonize car coating
Louder	Volume control, acoustical aids
Softer	Sound insulator, rubber heels
Altered	Antifreeze chemicals, meat tenderizer
Destroyed	Tree spraying, breath and perspiration deodorants
Influenced	Legislation to permit sale of colored oleo, wetting agent catalyst
Counteracted	Circuit breaker, air-conditioning, filters

6. Can there be a change in character?

Stronger	Dirt-resistant paint
Weaker	Pepsi-Cola made less sweet, children's aspirin
Altered	Aged or blended whiskey, transit-mixed cement
Converted	Convertiplanes (for vertical or horizontal flights)
Substituted	Low-calorie salad dressing (made without oils)
Interchanged	Interchangeable parts, all-size socks
Stabilized	Sperry gyroscope, waterproof plastic bandage
Reversed	Two-way locomotives
Resilient	Form-rubber upholstery, cork floors
Uniformity	Standards in foods, drugs, fuels, liquor
Cheaper	Coach air travel, paper cups
More expensive	Cigarettes in cardboard or metal boxes, deluxe editions of books
Add color	Color television, colored plastics
Change color	Variously colored toothbrush handles, automobiles, electric light bulbs

7. Can the form be changed?

Animated	Moving staircases, package conveyors
Stilled	Air brakes
Speeded	Meet-slicing machine
Slowed	Shock absorbers, gravel driveway
Directed	Flowmeters
Deviated	Traffic islands
Attracted	Magnetic devices
Repelled	Electrically charged fencing
Admitted	Turnstiles
Barred	Gate, fence
Lifted	Forklift truck
Lowered	Ship locks
Rotated	Waring blender, boring machine
Oscillated	Electric fan
Agitated	Electric scalp stimulator

8. Can the state or condition be changed?

Hotter	Electric hot plate, washed coal
Colder	Freezer, thermos jug, water cooler
Harden	Bouillon cubes, cream shampoo (instead of liquid)
Soften	Krilium soil conditioner, water softeners
Open or closed	Visible record equipment, electronically operated doors
Performed	Prefabricated housing, prepared Tom Collins mixer
Disposable	Bottle caps, Chux disposable diapers, Kleenex tissues
Incorporated	Counting register on printing press, cash registers
Parted	Caterpillar tractors, split-level highways
Solidified	Bakelite and other plastics, citrus concentrates
Liquefied	Chemical plant foods
Vaporized	Nasal medication vaporizers
Pulverized	Powdered eggs, lawn mower attachment to powder leaves, disposal garbage pulverizer
Abraded	Snow tires or chains
Lubricated	Self-lubricating equipment
Wetter	Hydraulic brakes
Drier	De-Moist for cellars, tobacco curing
Insulated	Fiberglas, Dr. Scholl's foot appliances (insulate feet against pressures)
Effervesced	Alka-Seltzer
Coagulated	Jell-O and Junket desserts
Elasticized	Latex girdles, bubble gum, belts
Resistant	Rubber footwear
Lighter	Aluminum luggage, automatic electric blanket
Heavier	Can opener with weighted stand

9. Can the use be adapted to a new market?

Men	Colognes, lotions
Women	Colored-tip cigarettes
Children	Junior-size tools, cowboy clothes
Old	Walking stick chairs
Handicapped	Chair lifts
Foreign	*Reader's Digest* foreign editions

THE MARKETING PLAN

Basic marketing management books have rather complete descriptions of the marketing planning process. This appendix will not duplicate that material, but will focus on the actual form of the marketing plan itself, that is, the *plan*, not so much the *planning*, which is covered in Chapters 17–19.

No two firms use quite the same format of marketing plan, but Figure D–1 gives a marketing plan outline based on the best information we have. The plan generally follows these guidelines:[1]

Summarize the analysis done for this plan.

Give overall strategic thinking.

Give the tactical actions, including those for departments other than marketing.

Make sure everyone knows the financial situation and how the plan will be measured and evaluated.

The outline should communicate the plans to everyone involved, have built-in control mechanisms, and serve as a permanent record.

Contents

Certain sections of the marketing plan deserve additional comment. But remember: If the new product is a line extension, many of the early sections of the plan are unnecessary because the information is not new. You will recall that as part of the early evaluation process it is wise to thoroughly study (or restudy) the industry in which concept are going to be generated. The list of information gathered for this is shown in Figure D–2.

Consumers/Users/Buyers. This section addresses the key element in the product's rationale. Data are given on the various buyer categories, the extent to which buying differs from using, the existence of influencers, and the specific process by which users acquire the merchandise. This includes buying motives, brands considered, information sought, product preferences, images, and unmet needs. It also covers how products are actually used and by whom.

This section will help anyone who reads the plan to understand the decisions described later—for example, on targeting, positioning, and push-pull strategy. It also summarizes the general equilibrium of the market and highlights any instabilities that can be capitalized.

Competition. All plan readers must be told about the competitive situation because many of them are not in a position to have regular contact with it. Specific company and brand names should be listed, and a detailed comparative description given for each. All of our differences should be clear. If the product manager doesn't know the determinant attributes in this market or how the new product compares on those attributes with products already out there, the firm isn't ready to market the new item.

The competitors' overall business and marketing strategies are also needed, especially those which appear to be effective. This includes positioning, pricing, claims, and distribution.

Exogenous Factors and Change. Markets are not static, and everyone involved needs to be apprised of likely changes. No surprises should appear, and none will if the planner has been

---

[1] A still-excellent source of guidance for writing new-product marketing plans is David S. Hopkins, *The Marketing Plan*, Report no. 801 (New York: The Conference Board, 1981).

careful. Some often overlooked changes are government regulations, competitive product improvements, direct selling (skipping a distributive level), price breaks, new competition based on new technologies, and future changes in how this type of product is bought and/or used.

FIGURE D–1   Outline of Marketing Plan for a New Product, to Be Adapted to Fit Individual Firms

---

I. Introduction. This section briefly describes the product, tells who prepared the plan, and its timing.

II. Situation analysis.
  A. Market description.
    1. Consumers, users, and other market participants.
    2. Buying processes pertinent to this plan.
    3. Direct and indirect competitors.
    4. Current competitive strategies.
    5. Market shares on sales, profits, and budgets.
    6. Available distribution structure, plus attitudes and practices.
    7. Key environmental or exogenous factors.
  B. Full description of new product, including all pertinent test data and comparisons with competition.

III. Summary of opportunities and problems.
  A. Key exploitable market opportunities.
  B. Key problems that should be addressed by this plan.

IV. Strategy.
  A. Overall guiding statement, including key actions and their quantitative and qualitative objectives.
  B. Market targets/segments, with positioning for each.
  C. Overall marketing efforts
    1. General role for product, including planned changes.
    2. General role for advertising, including copy platforms.
    3. General role for personal selling.
    4. General role for such other tools as sampling and trade shows. Copy platforms for any creative units.
    5. General role for distributors (wholesale, retail).
    6. Price policy, including discounts and planned changes.
    7. Any special roles for nonmarketing departments.

V. Economic summary.
  A. Sales forecasts in dollars and units.
  B. Expenses budgets by category of activity.
  C. Contribution to profit, with pro forma income statement.
  D. Risk statement: major problems, with cash flows.
  E. Future capital expenditures, with cash flows.

VI. Tactical plans. This section is situational to the firm. It includes each tool, what will be done with it, objectives, people responsible, schedule, creative units needed, etc.

VII. Control
  A. Key control objectives for reporting purposes.
  B. Key internal or external contingencies to watch.
  C. Information generation schedule.

VIII. Summary of major support activities needed, including data processing, warehousing, technical service, R&D, finance, personnel, public relations.

IX. Chronological schedule of activities.

FIGURE D–2   Basic Market Description

Market Size
Definition: By nature of product, by supplier, by user.
Sales: Dollars, units, by total and subgroups.
Trends: Growth total and rate by subgroups.
Key segments: Demographic, attitude, behavior.
Special aspects where appropriate: Cyclicality, seasonality, erratic fluctuations.
International variations and trends.

Distribution Structure Available
Retailers: Types, shares, demands, activities, current margins and profits, trends and
    forecasts, attitudes.
Wholesalers: Distributors, jobbers, agents, types used, functions performed, policies, compensation,
    attitudes, trends, variances, by segments.
Bargaining power and channel control.
Degree of, and trends in, vertical integration. Variations by geographic area.
Use of multiple or dual channels.

Competition
Current brands.
Manufacturer source for each.
Sizes, forms, materials, etc. All variations, temporary and permanent. Quality levels.
Prices: Final discounts, special, changes.
Market shares: Dollars, units, by segments, using various definitions of *market*.
Changes: Trends of entries and exits, reaction times.
Profits being achieved: sales, costs, ROIs, paybacks, trends.
Promotional practices: Types, dollars, effectiveness.
Manufacturing and procuring practices.
Financial strengths.
Special vulnerabilities, instabilities.
Possible new entrants, current R&D activities, skills, track records.
Full description of derived demand aspects.
Industry life cycle analyzed by segments.

Special Aspects
Government and regulatory restrictions, especially trends and expectations.
Third-party influences: Scientists, institution, research centers, associations, standards, pressure groups.
Effects of inflation, labor rates, union activity.
Upstream participants: Supplier manufacturers, importers, technology control.
General social attitudes and trends.
Industry productivity and efficiency in use of personnel and other resources.
Trends in industry costs: Materials, labor, transportation.

Product Description.   In some cases, a product can be described in a few sentences; in others, readers of the plan almost need a seminar. Product complexity cannot be allowed to destroy understanding. The plan should guide other people in doing their parts in the overall marketing effort, so they need to know just how good this new product really is. The plan should summarize the key findings of concept testing and product use testing. It should include product strengths and weaknesses, perceptual problems, unusual uses of the product, physical characteristics, costs, and restrictions applied to any applications.

Objectives.   A statement of what is expected from marketing this new product should be included near the start of the strategy section. But let's differentiate between objective and goal. A *goal* is a long-term direction of movement (sometimes not easily quantified) used for guidance, not internal control. For example, "It is our goal to become a leader in the snacks market." An *objective* is an intermediate point on the road toward attainment of a goal. For example, "It is our objective to capture a 15 percent share of the snacks market during our first year on the market." Objectives should be clearly and precisely stated in fairness to the new products manager. A narrative at this point in the plan will help clarify objectives.

Restraints.   Every new product marketing effort has some built-in restraints that should be made clear. Here are some examples from previous marketing plans:

> The new product will be marketed in accordance with the division's customary reliance on its industrial distribution system.

> The sales force is currently questioning the ability of the new products department to come up with winners. Because the morale of the sales force is quite important to this division, actions will be taken to ensure the success of this particular product.

> The strategy will not introduce potential problems of interpretation by the Federal Trade Commission, nor will it conflict with outstanding consent decrees.

Such restraints as these can have obvious effects on a marketing plan; if they are not stated, readers may not understand why certain actions are being taken

Management of the Task

Putting together a marketing plan is a complex process, filled with grand strategic decisions interspersed with trivia. Experienced new product marketers never underestimate the contribution of the many nonmarketing departments in the firm, but novice new products people often do. For this reason, the new products team should be doing the marketing planning right along with the product development. As team members help construct the plan itself, they will have suggestions to make. Each function involved in the new product's marketing has ideas about what that function should do; they differ from what other people think that function should do. All are experienced people, and we have worked with them for some time. We would like to just ask each of them what they want to do and then put their requests into a package and call it a marketing plan. Some plans are actually developed that way.

Such plans don't work very well, however, unless we have a new product that essentially sells itself, or unless the new item is a simple line extension, marketed totally as a new member in a line of products. The product line marketing plan captures the new item and tells what will be done.

In rare instances our new item doesn't have to be marketed at all in the usual sense. For example, we may be making it in response to a military order, where the sale was made at the time our bid was accepted. Or we may be developing an item for a major producer of complex products (such as automobiles); in such a case, the producer essentially told us what to make, and all we have to do is deliver it and stand by to service it.

But these are exceptions; in most cases, the new item needs its own strategy, at least in concept. Otherwise, the various players will never come together to make up a team.

Let's distinguish between planning and a plan. *Planning yields a strategy; the plan states the strategy, adds the tactical details, and directs the implementation.* New products can use both, but the strategy is critical. Once the new products manager begins to concentrate on the plan, with its many budgets, dates, and other details, no strategy in the world can keep the players motivated, integrated, and effective.

Some new products managers orchestrate the team by dint of personal leadership. These people may miss dates and budgets but market a successful product. In some situations, a product marketed well over budget—but on time—makes more money than a product marketed within budget but three months late.

This line of thinking does not apply to established products, which need annual or quarterly marketing plans. They already have the infrastructure, the stature, the support base within the firm, and the experienced players that the new product lacks.

So, as you go through the actual marketing planning process, keep in mind that we are looking at things that really make a difference. That's all that most new product managers have the time to seriously think about.

One other thought: Top-management approval is needed on marketing plans. "Whoever pays the fiddler calls the tune," so new products managers must deal with the frustrations caused by highly participative top managements.

The Strategic Components

Chapters 17–19 explain the components of marketing strategy for a new product and the general approach to how they are derived. This section of a marketing plan simply summarizes them and explains the background thinking on any issue known to be controversial in the firm. The target markets are explained first, followed by the product positioning statement (several versions of the item are being positioned differently for different target groups). After that the marketing plan becomes very situational, reflecting company practice and personal interests. Marketing mixes differ so in nature, complexity, and implementation that it does little good to outline a method for telling people about them.

It is typical that firms state their general mix strategy—what is the lead horse and how the other tools support that one. All people who will be implementing the plan should understand how the product, the price, the promotion, and the distribution partner up, and what their individual roles are. If they work well together, it is like any other team situation—good synergy can double the power.

Details and Implementation

What follows the general statement about strategic components is the full listing of what each tool will be doing, when, managed by whom, etc.: media schedules, sales staffing and calling schedules, all of the printed materials needed, sales meetings, and (in some cases) the hundreds of things that must be done to implement the launch. This section of marketing plans tends to give marketing planning a bad name. To many people, the plan document (actually a very large book in many cases) is the purpose of planning, yet huge planning documents quickly become file documents under the relentless pressures of change. Better to have a smaller overall plan and a set of tool documents prepared and implemented by the various departments in the firm.

GLOSSARY

abandonment   The discontinuance of a marketed product. Also called product deletion or product elimination. Abandonment may occur at any time from shortly after launch (a new product failure) to many years later.

acquisition   The purchase by one organization, of people, technology (process, facility, or material), product rights (trademarks), or entire businesses from other organizations. Acquisition is a method of expanding one's product offering by means other than internal development.

activity based accounting   Process of developing costs and revenues (and thus profit contributions) for separate activities, in this case new products projects.

adaptive product   Also called adapted product, this market entry acquires its uniqueness by variation on another, more pioneering product. The degree of adaptation is more than trivial (to avoid being an emulative or me-too product).

adopter categories   Persons or firms that adopt an innovation are often classified into five groups according to the sequence of their adoption of it: (1) innovators (the first 2 to 5 percent), (2) early adopters (the next 10 to 15 percent), early majority (the next 35 percent), late majority (the next 35 percent), and laggards (the final 5 to 10 percent). The numbers are percentages of the total number of actual adopters, not of the total number of persons or firms in the marketplace. There is wide disagreement on the exact percentage in each category.

adoption of innovation   The process by which an innovation spreads throughout a population. It consists of adopter categories (innovators, early adopters, etc.) and a specific process of adoption by each adopter.

alliance   (See *strategic alliance*.)

alpha test   The testing of a new product in-house, not with potential users (beta test). The testing may be in a laboratory setting or (as in the case of glues or computers) in some part of the developing firm's regular operations.

analytical attribute approach   A class of concept-generating techniques not based on the problem find/solve route. The techniques are many, usually logical, and tend to make variations in products currently on the market. Attribute analysis and relationships analysis are two categories of this approach.

announcement   Second stage of the product launch cycle.

applications engineering   A strategy of applying one's technical skills to new areas. Adhesives manufacturers have often followed such a strategy.

A-T-A-R (awareness-trial-availability-repeat)   A paradigm consisting of four key steps by the intended user; the steps take the person or firm from a state of ignorance about a new product to the point of product adoption. (See *awareness, trial, availability* and *repeat.*)

attribute   (See *product attributes.*)

attribute analysis   A bundle of idea-generating techniques built on the concept that any product improvement is a change in the attributes of its predecessor. Also a term used to mean the same as analytical attribute approach.

augmented product   The view of a product that includes not only its core benefit and its physical or service-procedure being but adds other sources of benefits, such as service, warranty, and image. The augmented aspects are added by action of the seller, such as with company reputation.

availability   A measure of the extent to which target customers can get a new product if they wish to do so. Often stated as a percentage of outlets where the product is stocked or percentage of total market volume done in the stores where stocked (called share of all-commodity-volume).

awareness   A measure of the percentage of target customers who are aware of the new product's existence. Awareness is variously defined, including recall of brand, recognition of brand, recall of key features or positioning, etc.

balanced matrix   An organization option that uses matrix in approximately balanced proportions between the project and the departments.

basic market description   Market research done before or immediately after selecting an arena for product innovation charter focus. Prepares the firm to innovate in that area.

beachhead   The third phase of the launch cycle. It comes immediately after announcement, is quite frenetic, and ceases when the product is withdrawn or moves into the fourth (growth) stage.

benchmarking   A process of studying successful competitors (or organizations in general) and selecting the best of their actions or standards. In the new product program, it means finding the best process methods and the best process times and setting out to achieve them in the firm doing the benchmarking.

benefit   A product attribute expressed in terms of what the user gets from the product, rather than its physical characteristics (features). Benefits are often paired with specific features, but they need not be. They are perceived, not necessarily real.

best practices   Set of practices in the new products field that correlate with successful product introductions. Obtained by benchmarking or survey.

beta test   The type of product use testing that follows alpha testing and takes place on the premises of intended market users. The procedure may concentrate only on whether the product performs as expected or on whether the performance meets the needs of the user, as perceived by that user, in which case it is called a gamma test.

blind test   The type of product use testing in which the identity of the new item's producer is kept secret. Unbranded, in contrast to a branded test.

brainstorming   A group method of problem solving used in product concept generation. It is sometimes thought to be an open, free-wheeling idea session, but more correctly, it is a specific procedure developed by Alex Osborn, with precise rules of session conduct. Has many modifications in format of use, each variation with its own name.

brand   A name, term, design, symbol, or any other feature that identifies one seller's good or service as distinct from those of other sellers. The legal term for brand is trademark. A brand may identify one item, a family of items, or all items of that seller. If used for the firm as a whole, the preferred term is trade name. (See *trademark, family brand*, and *individual brand*.)

brand equity   The dollar value of a brand. High brand equity suggests opportunity for line extensions that capitalize on the brand strength.

brand extension   A product line extension marketed under the same general brand as a previous item or items. To distinguish the brand extension from the other item(s) under the primary brand, one can either add a secondary brand identification or add a generic. A brand extension is usually aimed at another segment of the general market for the overall brand. (See *family brand* and *individual brand*.)

brand generic   The second half of a product's identifying title. Brand is the first half and identifies one seller's version, while the generic is the second half and identifies the general class of item. Example: Jell-O (brand) gelatin dessert (generic). Not to be confused with generic brands (such as on some low-price items in supermarkets) where there is no individual brand (see *generic brands*).

brand image   The perception of a brand in the minds of persons. The image is a mirror reflection (though perhaps inaccurate) of the brand personality or product being. It is what people believe about a brand—their thoughts, feelings, expectations.

brand name   That part of a brand that can be spoken: letters, numbers, or words. The term *trademark* covers all forms of brand (name, mark, etc.), but brand name is the form most often meant when trademark is used. (See *brand* and *trademark*.)

brand personality   The psychological nature of a particular brand, as intended by its sellers, though persons in the marketplace may see the brand otherwise (called brand image). These two perspectives compare to the personalities of individual humans: what we intend or desire, and what others see or believe.

brand positioning   (See *product positioning*.)

branding, family   (See *family brand*.)

branding, individual   Using separate brands for each product, without a family brand to tie them to other brands of that firm. (See *family brand*.)

business analysis   A term of many meanings, and in marketing is usually associated in some way with the evaluation of new product proposals. In format, it may consist of a five-year, discounted cash flow, net present value type of financial analysis, or it may be a more comprehensive analysis of the entire situation surrounding the proposed product. Chronologically, it may come early in the development process (when it is used to decide whether expensive R&D should be undertaken) and/or late in the product development cycle when the commercialization decision is being made.

checklist   A memory-jogger list of items, used to remind an analyst to think of all relevant aspects. It finds frequent use as a tool of creativity in concept generation and as a factor consideration list in concept screening.

codevelopment   (See *alliances*.)

commercialization   A stage (usually the last) in the development cycle for a new product. Commonly thought to begin when the product is introduced into the marketplace, but actually starts when a management commits to marketing the item. (See *new product development*.)

component testing   The testing of various parts of the marketing program, separately. Market testing tests them in unison, but during the development process each item in the marketing mix may be put through separate testing. Copy testing is the most common form of component testing.

concept   (See *product concept.*)

concept generation   The act by which new concepts, or ideas, are created. Also the definition of the second phase of the overall product innovation process, during which the concepts are created. Sometimes called idea generation or ideation.

concept statement   A verbal and/or pictorial statement of a concept (for a product or for advertising) that is prepared for presentation to potential buyers or users to get their reaction prior to its being implemented. Product concepts are followed by prototypes, advertising concepts by one of several forms of semifinished production.

concept statement, commercialized   A term used in distinguishing two types of product concept statements. A commercialized product concept statement is prepared in an advertising format, as a persuasive statement. A noncommercialized product concept statement is prepared in neutral, nonpersuasive format.

concept testing and development   The process in which a concept statement is presented to potential buyers or users for their reactions. These reactions permit the developer to estimate the sales value of the concept (whether product or advertising) and to make changes in it so as to enhance its sales value.

concurrent engineering   A term applied to the development process when the steps overlap, rather than take place in a sequential, linear fashion. Step two (e.g., motor placement) begins well before step one (motor size requirement) is finished; in fact, step three (motor soundproofing) and step four (motor housing) may also begin before step one is finished. The overlapped process gets quite confusing and rather risky given that earlier outcomes may not be what was expected. The method is at the heart of accelerated product development.

contingency plan   The action, ready in standby, that will be taken if a given state of affairs comes about during the new product launch. Usually tied to one or more triggers in the launch control process.

control   Usually called managerial control. Refers to practices that result in a project or other activity that achieves its objectives. Guided missiles are "controlled." Midterm correction and contingency planning are characteristics of managerial control.

controlled sale   A category of market testing techniques in which the ability of the firm to obtain distribution is not tested. Distribution is forced (e.g., by giving the outlets free product).

core product   The central benefit or purpose for which a consumer buys a product. Varies from purchaser to purchaser. The core product or core benefit may come either from the physical good or service performance, or from the augmented dimensions of the product. (See *augmented product.*)

coupling   The joining of efforts between the firm innovating on new products and other firms or persons. Coupling can be upstream (with vendors), downstream (with customers), or sideways (with competitors).

creative stimuli   A method of ideation whereby one thinks of a problem or a product and then studies a set of words or phrases that research has shown to be stimulating.

critical path scheduling   A technique of project control, now usually incorporated in various software programs. The technique puts all important steps of a given new product project into a sequential network.

cross-functional   (See *multifunctional.*)

cumulative cost curve   The shape of a line that depicts a firm's cumulative costs of developing and marketing a new product. It is plotted against the cumulative time, so it runs from zero (start of project) to 100 percent of time (launch). The curve necessarily runs from lower left to upper right.

customer service   Identifiable, but essentially intangible, activities offered by a seller in conjunction with a product, such as delivery and repair. Not to be confused with intangible products (services), types of products for which the activity is the primary purpose of a sale. The sale of service products may be accompanied by the provision of customer services.

cycle time   The time of development. From when an idea is in hand until it is "on the shipping dock."

decay curve   The curve representing death of concepts during the development stage. Begins on the left with 100 percent of concepts and ends up on the right with the percent actually marketed successfully. Usually declines rapidly. Also called the mortality curve.

decline stage of the product life cycle   The fourth stage of a product life cycle, in which sales of the product fall off from their levels during the maturity (third) stage.

deliverability   The extent to which an organization is viewed as being capable of actually delivering to the customer and adequately servicing a particular new product concept. The measure is an attribute of the concept, much as manufacturability is. (See *manufacturability.*)

demand-pulled innovation   Innovation caused or at least stimulated by the needs, wants, or desires of customers. Contrasts with supply-pushed innovation. Other terms for these two ideas are market- or customer-driven innovation and technology-driven innovation.

design   A term of many meanings. In product innovation, it usually means the activity of going from the product concept to a finished physical item—technical development phase. The four parts of this design phase are functional/styling design (traditionally called industrial design), technical design, detail design, and manufacturing process design. In Europe, design is sometimes used to encompass the entire product innovation process. (See *engineering design, manufacturing design.*)

determinant attribute   An attribute of a product category that (1) distinguishes such products from each other and (2) is important to buyers.

determinant gap map   A two-dimensional map that uses two determinant attributes to plot all brands in a product category. The plotting is done by an experienced analyst, not by the consumers themselves (perceptual map).

diagnostic information   Information obtained from any of the evaluative steps of a product's development that goes beyond the current evaluation to give guidance to later steps. A product use test, for example, rates the product's usefulness but also gives suggestions on packaging, positioning, pricing, etc.

diffusion of innovation   The process by which the use of an innovation is spread within a market group, over time, and over various categories of adopters. (See *adopter categories.*)

dimensional analysis   An analytical attribute approach technique whereby new concepts are generated from an exhaustive listing of the dimensions of products in a given category.

disciplines panel   A variation of brainstorming in which each participant represents a scientific discipline relevant to the problem under study. Typical panels have psychologists, chemists, engineers, lawyers, and others.

diversification   The act of adding diverse product(s) to a line to move the seller into new markets. The degree of diversification can vary greatly.

DPI   Initials stand for development process improvement.

dual drive   The strategic combination of technology and market as sources for product innovation. Contrasts with market drive and technology drive. Innovations are based on at least one specific technical strength of the firm and at least one specific market opportunity.

early adopters   The second identifiable subgroup within a population that begins use of an innovation. They follow innovators and precede the early majority. (See *adopter categories* and *product adoption process.*)

early majority   The third identifiable subgroup within a population that adopts an innovation. Preceded by early adopters and innovators. The early majority like to await the outcome of product trial by the two earlier groups. (See *adopter categories* and *product adoption process.*)

empowerment   The act of giving whatever power it takes to enable a manager (such as a project manager) to get a job done. A way of overcoming a nonauthority situation. Risky in that it causes frictions in other established line situations.

emulative product   A new product that imitates another product already on the market. Is somewhat different from previous products (not a pure me-too), but the difference is not substantial or significant. (See *adaptive product* and *innovative imitation.*)

engineering design   An activity in the product creation process where a good is configured. Specific form is decided. The activity is sometimes seen as a late step in the R&D process and sometimes as an early step in the manufacturing process. The design engineering department takes the lead in the technical design phase and in the detail design phase of the overall design process. (See *design.*)

entry evaluation   The first evaluation done after a concept emerges. It may be by the person creating it, but usually involves others in the immediate vicinity. Judgmental, experience-based, not with creation of new data or opinions.

evaluation   A set of activities scattered through the third, fourth, and fifth stages of the overall product innovation process. These activities measure the evolving worth of the new product being developed. Includes such steps as concept testing, product use testing, and market testing.

evolving product   Like a butterfly, a new product does not just emerge. It begins as a concept (or even just an opportunity), then goes through various stages, such as protocol, prototype, pilot plant product, and marketed product.

expected effects matrix   A matrix of two dimensions: damage and probability. Used to classify negative events that might take place during the launch of a new item. A high score on both dimensions increases the need for action.

express warranty   Spoken or written promises made by the seller of a product about what will be done if the product proves to be defective in manufacture or performance. Contrasts with promises that are only implied by common knowledge of the product or by customary practices in a trade. (See *implied warranty.*)

facilitator   A person on a team (or assigned to it) whose task is to enhance the group's productivity and output. A type of leadership consistent with today's reduced reliance on hierarchies.

failure rate   The percentage of a firm's marketed new products that fail to achieve the objectives set for them. Should not be confused with the decay or mortality rate. The term *failure* *rate* should only be used on products that go to the full intended market target, not a trial or rollout subset. (See *decay curve*.)

family brand   A brand used on two or more individual products. The product group may or may not be all of that firm's product line. The individual members of the family also carry individual brands to differentiate them from other family members. In rare cases, family brands have other family brands as members, each of which have individual brands. Automobiles fit the latter situation, as with Oldsmobile (family), Cutlass (family), Ciera (individual). (See *branding, individual*.)

family packaging   Using one design or other key packaging element to integrate the packaging of two or more individual items. The packages clearly belong to one set, but there are usually some individualizations, especially in brand name.

feature   A product attribute that is an identifiable characteristic. Is usually physical (on goods) or a sequence step (on services). Contrasts with other types of attributes (e.g., benefit).

field testing   A term sometimes used to describe product use testing. The word field separates this type of testing from in-house, laboratory-type testing.

first-to-market   The first product that creates a new product category or a substantial subdivision of one. Distinguishes the pioneering product from those that follow.

focus group   A market research technique where 10 to 12 market participants are gathered in one room for discussion under the leadership of a trained focus group leader. Discussion focuses on a problem, a product, or an activity. The group often meets in special facilities for observation and videotaping.

forced relationships   A concept generation technique whereby creativity is stimulated when two or more separate things are brought together. The items are unrelated, and the mere combining of them shows new and unexpected patterns.

franchise extension   New product that capitalizes on a firm's market strength. A franchise is a strength of relationship with customers and may be based on a brand, a sales force relationship, a favorable trade relationship, etc. The new item is often not unique but sells based on the favorable franchise.

full sale   A class of market testing techniques where the marketing is complete and in the mode that would be used under total launch. No limitations on distribution, advertising, and so on, unless planned in launch.

full screen   A screening stage where all preliminary work is finished, a scoring model is usually used, and a favorable assessment is followed by a preliminary business analysis that releases the concept to development.

functional matrix   An organization option in which the matrix leans toward the functions. Participants have dual reporting relationships, but the functional reporting is intended to dominate thinking and action.

fuzzy front end   That period preceding start of technical development. Includes strategic deliberations, concept generation, and, especially, early evaluation when the concept is being evaluated before being accepted. The concept is fuzzy, not the methods.

gamma test   A type of product use test wherein the developers measure the extent to which the item meets the needs of the target customer, solves the problem(s) targeted during the development, and leaves the customer satisfied.

gap analysis   A category of techniques based on the idea that if one can position all of a market's products onto one two-dimensional chart, they will not be spread around like butter on bread. Rather, they will clump in some places and be void in others. Any void (gap) thus offers an opportunity for a new product. The charting uses X and Y axes and plots against such attributes as price, strength, speed, and ease of use.

generic brands   Products named only by their generic class (such as drip-grind coffee and barber shop). Other products have both an individual brand and a generic (Maxwell House drip-grind coffee, Maurice's barber shop).

generic terms, as brand names   (See *brand generic.*)

goods   Products that have tangible form, in contrast to services, which are intangible. (See *services.*)

groupware   Software that allows groups of people to hold team meetings online in computer networks. Leader in the market is Lotus Works.

growth stage of product life cycle   The second stage of the product life cycle, during which sales are increasing at an increasing rate, profits are increasing, and competitors enter the market. Product differentiation takes place, and price competition begins.

heuristic   A rule of thumb, from trial-and-error experience, used to guide decisions when algorithms are unavailable. Commonly used in the new products field because solid experience data are rarely available.

home run   In new product work refers to a major project, big in risk or dollar value. Contrasts with singles, which are improvements and near line extensions.

hurdle rate   Any criterion or test figure that a new product must meet or exceed as it goes through development.

idea generation   (See *concept generation.*)

identity disclosure   The issue of whether to release to the user the name of the firm making the product being tested.

imitative innovation   A strategy of copying the creativity of others, but modifying each copy enough to give it some originality and, hopefully, market value. The improvement is not enough to call it an adaptive strategy. (See *adaptive product.*)

implied warranty   A warranty (promise of performance) extended to the customer but unstated. It usually is assumed from common practice in the trade or suggested by statements made about the product by the seller.

incremental innovation   A strategy of producing a stream of new products, each of which is an improvement on earlier models. Mostly singles (see *home run*).

individual brand   The brand identity given to an individual product, as separate from other products in the market and from other items in the product's own line. A trademark.

industrial design   (See *design.*)

informal selling   A type of market test in which one or a few salespeople make calls on intended market users and full presentations are made. There is actual request for the order. However, product has not been released to the full sales force.

information technology   The full set of people, hardware, and software by which information is processed today. Acronym is IT.

initial reaction   (See *entry evaluation.*)

innovation   (1) The act of creating a new product or process; includes invention as well as the work required to bring an idea or concept into final form. (2) A particular new product or process.

An innovation may have various degrees of newness, from very little to highly discontinuous, but must include at least some degree of newness to the market, not just to the firm.

innovativeness   (1) When applied to the seller, it is the degree to which the firm has the capability, and follows the practice, of being innovative. (2) When applied to a buyer, it is the extent to which that person or firm is willing to accept the risks of early purchase on an innovation.

innovators   Firms or persons that are innovative. The term is often applied to those (1) who are the first to create a new type of product or (2) who are the first to adopt a new product introduced to the marketplace. Innovators are often thought to be opinion leaders. (See *adopter categories* and *product adoption process.*)

interface   The points where different functions in a firm come together during the product innovation process. Usually applies to pairings of the major players: design, R&D, engineering, operations (especially manufacturing), and marketing.

intrapreneurship   The practice of entrepreneurship within a large firm. Intrapreneurship is a style of management to be independent, risk taking, innovative, daring, and typical of the style used in successful start-up firms.

introductory stage of product life cycle   The first stage of the product life cycle. The new product is introduced to the market, sales are slow, promotion is usually heavy, costs are accumulated, and expectation is focused on determining when and if the product will soon enter the second (growth) stage of the cycle.

invention   A new device, process, and so on, that has been created. Can be in either physical or conceptual form. Preexisting knowledge is combined in a new way to yield something that did not heretofore exist. Not to be confused with a product innovation, which is an invention that has been converted by further management and process development into a marketable product.

inventive creativity   The creativity required for product innovation. Is thought to combine artistic creativity and engineering creativity, either of which alone can be very strong but not productive of new product ideas.

itemized response   A unique process whereby one person hearing another person's new product idea is to (1) give a full statement of support by citing several advantages to the idea and (2) express any problems or concerns in positive (what's the best way to solve this) form.

Kaizen   Japanese term describing a process of continuous improvement.

laggards   The fifth, and last, group of users to adopt an innovation. (See *adopter categories* and *product adoption process.*)

late majority   The fourth group of users to adopt an innovation. (See *adopter categories* and *product adoption process.*)

lateral search   A term usually applied to ideation techniques that force the ideator to stretch mentally out of normal channels. The mind assumes unique positions of viewing people or happenings.

launch   A term signifying the marketing of a new product. Can be either in a full-sale form of market testing or to the full market being addressed.

launch control   The process by which a management plans for and supervises the introduction of a new product; the product's progress is monitored against preestablished norms, variances are detected, and corrections made such that the original goals set for the product are achieved.

launch cycle   The subphases of the innovation stage of a traditional product life cycle. The big step of innovation is broken into preparation (for marketing), announcement, beachhead, and early growth.

lead user   Those people or firms who most need the innovation being worked on and who will most likely participate in the innovation process. The idea itself often originates with a lead user and may even appear in prototype form in the lead user's firm.

learning requirements   Various types of learning that new products often require from their purchasers. Without that learning, the purchase, trial use, or satisfaction will be threatened.

leveraged creativity   Working a lesser creativity off the major creativity of others. A strategy of pioneering whereby the innovations are technically new and unique but considerably less significant than the original.

licensing   A strategy or practice of leasing or renting one's technology to others. Can go sideways (competitors), upstream (vendors), or downstream (customers, resellers). A way one firm gains the right to use the creations of another. May be exclusive or nonexclusive.

line extension   A new product marketed by an organization that already has at least one other product being sold in that product/market area. Line extensions are usually new flavors, sizes, models, applications, strengths, and so on.

manufacturability   The extent to which a new product concept or prototype is figured to be capable of effective and efficient manufacturing by available resources. Asked at time of pre-R&D screening, and again prior to authorizing production. Is answered today by computer-aided manufacturing software. Also called producibility.

manufacturing design   The process of determining the manufacturing process that will be used to make a new product. A process design activity. (See *design*.)

market acceptance testing   Usually applies to product use testing, though occasionally also includes that product testing done as part of a market test.

market development   A new sales volume opportunity that, strictly speaking, does not involve product innovation. Current products are taken to new customers or users. Market development often does involve some product modifications, however, and may sometimes approach diversification in nature.

market-driven   A strategy whereby a firm lets the marketplace direct its product innovation. Consumer product firms tend to be the primary users of this strategy.

market rollout   (See *rollout*.)

market testing   The phase of new product development when the new item and its marketing plan are tested together. Prior testing, if any, involved separate components. A market test simulates the eventual marketing of the product and takes many different forms, only one of which bears the name *test market*.

matrix organization   A method of arranging teams or groups of people representing various functions of a firm. Each member of the group reports both to the head of the group (say, a program manager or project director) and to the head of the function where housed (say, the vice president of manufacturing).

maturity stage of product life cycle   The third stage of the product life cycle, when initial rapid growth is over and when sales level off (though there may be intermittent surges and declines over the years before final decline sets in).

metric   A quantitative measurement. In new products we deal with many qualitative measurements, but current trend is to find metrics. Benchmarking is heavily metric-oriented.

minimarket test   A type of controlled-sale market testing whereby the outlets used are a small, nonrepresentative sampling of the market. Product is usually placed into the outlets (not sold), and promotion is much less than planned ultimately. Primarily tests just the customer's willingness to spend some money for a product trial.

mission statement   A part of corporate or division strategy. It describes the essential character of the business and is a necessary input to new product strategy.

mode of reaction   Describes how product testees give their reaction to a product use test. Options include like/dislike, preference, and descriptive/diagnostic information.

monadic test   A product use testing format where only the new item is tested. Contrasts with the paired-comparison method.

morphological analysis   An analytical attribute approach ideation method. Is based on relationships and includes using a multiple set of product forms, attributes, uses, users, and so on in matrix format.

multifunctional   Often called multidisciplinary and cross-functional. Refers to persons or operations involving a multiple set of functions or departments. Product innovation necessarily is multifunctional.

negligence   A source of product liability, more common many years ago. If negligence occurs in the design or manufacture of a product, the manufacturer is liable for the injuries that result.

network   The informal mix of people, departments, or firms necessary to implement a product innovation project. Goes well beyond the persons assigned to the team and includes everyone whose work contributes significantly to the project. A network is established and managed by the project manager. As a verb, networking describes the informal activities of a new products manager to relate personally with all of the players on the project.

new product   A term of many opinions and practices, but most generally defined as a product (good or service) new to the firm marketing it. Excludes products that are only changed in promotion, though some persons like to think of a repositioned product (such as new use) as a new product.

new product development   (1) The overall process of strategy, organization, concept generation, product and marketing plan creation and evaluation, and commercialization of a new product. (2) Sometimes restricted in meaning to that part of the process done by technical (R&D and manufacturing) departments. (3) Sometimes used to denote the person or persons engaged in the new product creation task. New product development concerns activity within an organization, in contrast to the acquisition of finished new products from outside.

new product failure   A new product that does not meet the objectives of its developers. Depending on what those objectives are, a profitable new product can be a failure, and an unprofitable new product can be a success.

new product strategy   Strategy that guides a product innovation program. Is unique to new products and is a spin-off from overall corporate or division strategy.

new products management   Similar to product innovation management and refers to the overall management of a new product project or a total product innovation program.

new products manager   A product manager with a new products assignment. May direct a single project team, or several teams, or an entire product innovation program. Is nonfunctional, or general management in perspective, regardless of department housed in.

nonauthority   Describes a situation where a manager has responsibility for a given outcome, but lacks line authority to command the tasks. Typical of almost all new products management.

operations   A term that includes manufacturing but is usually broadened to include procurement, physical distribution, and, for services, management of the offices or other areas where the services are provided. Supply management.

organization learning   Contrasts with individual learning. Means that organizations improve their new product process by studying past projects. The knowledge stays with the organization, but only if it is sought out.

ownership   The acceptance by a manager of personal responsibility for a given task or outcome. Usually involves nonauthority.

package   The container used to protect, promote, transport, and/or identify a product. May be primary (contains the product), secondary (contains one or more primary packages), or tertiary (contains one or more secondary packages).

paired-comparison   A mode of product use testing where the new product is paired with (usually) the category leader, and direct comparisons are made. Contrasts with monadic testing.

parallel development   Another term for concurrent engineering.

partnering   (See *alliances.*)

patent   The legal right of exclusive use and licensing granted by a government to the person who invents something. An invention is patentable if it is a useful, novel, and nonobvious process, machine, manufacture, or composition of matter.

payback   The date when a new product has recovered its costs of development and marketing. In years, the time needed to reach payback.

perceptual gap   A gap that appears on a mapping of products where the positions of the products are determined by user opinions, not necessarily fact.

phased review   Times during a process where people stop to check progress. Usually asked for by upper managements. May be very formal, informal, or even done only by the team evaluating its own progress.

PIC   Letters stand for product innovation charter.

pilot plant   A trial manufacturing facility where the new process of production is tried out and revised. Small-scale model. Systems can also be tried out in pilot operations.

pioneering innovativeness   A strategy of trying to be the first to market new types of products. The highest order of innovativeness (others are adapting and imitating), it is often based on technical breakthroughs.

pioneering stage   A nonspecific period early in the life cycle of a new type of product, during which the pioneers are trying to build primary demand for the product type more than secondary demand for their particular brands.

pipeline rationalization   Efforts to keep a rational set of new product projects in the pipeline of development.

platform   Term applied to a set of new product projects, especially where more than one project pursues a broad strategy. In the automobile industry, a platform is often a basic body configuration—e.g., the LH platform of Chrysler. But platforms can be brands, packages, customer groups, and so on, based on something in common that gives each project strength.

portfolio   A set of things. Most often applied to that group of projects currently active in a research laboratory but may apply to all new projects under way.

positioning   (See *product positioning.*)

postmortem   A term in rapidly declining use that refers to meetings held after a new product project has concluded—either in success of failure. The meeting is to facilitate organization learning. But the term originated in efforts to pin the blame of a failure, and still suggests that purpose.

precedence   In product innovation, this term refers to the order of market entry. A product is first to market, second, and so on.

preference map   A map used for evaluating an opportunity first discovered on determinant gap maps or perceptual gap maps. It shows preferences customers have for the various attributes being mapped. Perceptual gaps often coincide with areas of no preference.

prelaunch   The first stage of the launch cycle. Involves getting ready to launch the product, including getting distribution and building necessary field service capability.

preliminary market analysis   A type of market research that follows ideation and entry evaluation. Often used to gain greater knowledge of a particular market prior to setting up a concept test plan.

premarket testing   (See *simulated test market*.)

prescreening   Those evaluation steps that follow ideation and precede the full screen. Involves entry evaluation, preliminary market analysis, and concept testing and development.

problem analysis   A part of the problem-based method of concept generation. Relates to finding the problems and involves study of users to learn their dissatisfactions and unmet needs.

problem identification   The first stage of the problem analysis method of ideation. Involves finding, describing, and analyzing the problem(s) of targeted market participants.

process manager   Person charged with building a successful new product process or processes. Assists all project managers in setting up the best process for their projects.

producibility   (See *manufacturability*.)

product   (1) A bundle of attributes (features, functions, benefits, and uses) capable of exchange or use; usually a mix of tangible and intangible forms. Thus, a product may be an idea, a service, a physical entity (a good), or any combination of the three. It exists for the purpose of exchange in the satisfaction of individual and organizational objectives. (2) Occasional usage today implies a definition of product as that bundle of attributes where the exchange or use primarily concerns the physical or tangible form; in contrast to a service, where the seller, buyer, or user is primarily interested in the intangible. Though to speak of "products and services" is convenient, it leaves us without a term to apply to the set of the two combined. The term for tangible products is *goods* and it should be used with services to make the tangible/intangible pair, as subsets of the term product. (See *services*.)

product adaptation   The strategy of developing new products by modifying or improving on the product innovations of others. Contrasts with the strategies of pioneering and imitation. (See *adaptive products*.)

product adoption process   The sequence of stages that individuals and firms go through in the process of accepting new products. The stages vary greatly in usage but tend to include (1) becoming aware of the new product, (2) seeking information about it, (3) developing favorable attitudes toward it, (4) trying it out in some direct or indirect way, (5) finding satisfaction in the trial, and (6) adopting the product into a standing usage or repurchase pattern.

product attributes   The characteristics by which products are identified and differentiated. Usually comprises features, functions (uses), and benefits.

product champion   A person who takes an inordinate interest in seeing that a particular process or product is fully developed and marketed. The role varies from situations calling for little more than stimulating awareness of the item to extreme cases where the champion tries to force the item past the strongly entrenched internal resistance of company policy or that of objecting parties.

product class   The group of products that are homogeneous or generally considered substitutes for each other. The class is considered narrow or broad depending on how substitutable the various products are. For example, a narrow product class of breakfast meats might be bacon, ham, and sausage. A broad class would include all other meat and meat substitutes even occasionally sold for breakfast use.

product concept   A verbal or pictorial version of a proposed new product. Consists of (1) one or more benefits it will yield, (2) its general form, and (3) the technology used to achieve the form. A new product idea becomes a concept when it has at least one benefit and either the form or the technology. Further work in the development process gradually clarifies and confirms those two and adds the third. A concept becomes a product when it is sold successfully in the marketplace; prior to that, it is still undergoing development, even if marketed.

product definition   (See *product protocol.*)

product deletion   (See *abandonment.*)

product development   (See *new product development.*)

product form   The physical shape or nature of a good or the sequential steps in a service. Form is provided by one or more technologies and yields benefits to the user; for example, many technologies go to make a front-wheel-drive form of an automobile. Differences in form of service separate discount and full-service stockbrokers.

product hierarchy   An organizational-chart type of array of the products offered in a given market, breaking first into class, then form, then variations on form, then brand. There are various options within these product hierarchy dimensions, so the array can be designed to fit the needs of the analyst. The hierarchy concept fits services as well as goods.

product idea   (See *product concept.*)

product innovation   (See *innovation.*)

product innovation charter   The summary statement of strategy that will guide a department or project team in their efforts to generate new product volume. Specifies the arena within which the people will operate, their goals and objectives, and the general approaches they will use. May apply to a single project or to a program of projects.

product innovation gap   The difference between a firm's projected sales/profit goals and what its current product line is expected to produce. The gap must be filled by some form of product innovation or acquisition.

product introduction   The first stage of the product life cycle, during which the new item is announced to the market and offered for sale. (See *product life cycle.*)

product liability   The obligation a seller incurs regarding the safety of a product. The liability may be implied by custom or common practice in the field, stated in the warranty, or decreed by law. If injury occurs, various defenses are prescribed by law and judicial precedent. Sellers are expected to offer adequate instructions and warnings about a product's use.

product life cycle (from biology)   The four stages that a new product is thought to go through from birth to death: introduction, growth, maturity, and decline. Controversy surrounds whether products do indeed go through such cycles in any systematic, predictable way. The product life-cycle concept is primarily applicable to product forms, less to product classes, and very poorly to individual brands.

product line   A group of products marketed by an organization to one general market. The products have some characteristics, customers, and/or uses in common and may also share technologies, distribution channels, prices, services, and so on.

product manager   Within an organization, a person assigned responsibility for overseeing all of the various functional activities (such as manufacturing, pricing, and research) that concern a particular product. Actual responsibility varies widely, but the common feature is a narrow, product focus on the part of the manager. In some industries, the term *brand manager* is used in place of product manager.

product/market matrix   A two-by-two matrix in which the column designations are current products and new products, and the row designations are current markets and new markets. The matrix thus defines four types of new product opportunities ranging from the upper-left quadrant of improved versions of "current products to current users" to the lower-right quadrant of "diversification."

product planning   A term of many meanings but generally used to designate a staff position charged with part or all of the task of managing product innovation within an organization. In some firms, it also includes acquisition of products or processes.

product positioning   (1) How consumers, users, buyers, and others view competitive brands or types of products. As determined by market research techniques, the various products are plotted onto maps, using product attributes as dimensions. (2) For new products, product positioning means how the innovator firm decides to compare the new item to its predecessors. For the new item, the mental slates of persons in the marketplace are blank; this is the only chance the innovator will have to make a desired impression.

product requirements   (See *product protocol*.)

product use test   One of several key evaluation steps in the product development process. Involves giving some of the new product to persons or firms in the intended target market and asking them to use it for a time and report their reactions to it. The purposes of a product use test are to (1) see if the item developed by the organization has the attributes prescribed for it, (2) learn whether it satisfies the market needs identified during the ideation process, and (3) disclose information about how and by whom the item is used.

profile sheet   A form that displays the characteristics of a proposed product at the time of screening. Scores are plotted on a diagram for easier analysis.

project   A unit of activity in the product development process that usually deals with creating and marketing one new product. A project involves a multifunctional group of people and may often be part of a larger unit of work, a program, which delivers a stream of new products, one from each project.

projectization   The degree to which a group of people working on new product projects feel committed to the project as against being loyal to the departments where they work. On major innovations, a high degree of projectization is often essential to break through barriers.

project matrix   An organization option in which the matrix leans toward the project. Participants have dual reporting relationships, but the project is intended to dominate their thinking and action.

protocol   A statement of two dimensions: (1) the technical requirements or attributes (mainly benefits, but also features when required) that a new product should have and (2) the marketing requirements—target market, positioning, price, resistance to be overcome, A-T-A-R, and others. A protocol is prepared after the full screen and just prior to assigning the project to technical departments for development effort and to marketing for plan development. The statement is agreed to by all parties, thus the term *protocol*.

prototype   The first physical form or service description of a new product, still in rough or tentative mode. With complex products, there may be component prototypes as well as one finished prototype. For services, the prototype is simply the first full description of how the service will work.

prototype concept test   A concept test done after technical work has produced a prototype. The prototype clarifies many aspects of the concept and leads to more reliable concept test reactions. May precede technical work if the prototypes are inexpensive to prepare (such as food products).

pseudo sale   A category of market testing methods wherein the customer does various things to indicate reaction to the product and to its marketing strategy but does not actually spend money.

quality function deployment   Often stated as QFD. A system of project management developed for use in very complex situations such as automobiles. Especially useful to new products is the first part— the House of Quality—a careful statement of customer needs and wants for the item being developed, followed by stipulation of technologies that will be used to achieve each of those characteristics.

rapid prototyping   (1) Describes the general process strategy of attempting to get a concept into prototype as soon as possible, even if still very rough. (2) Software for producing prototypes by stereolithography rather than by hand molding and shaping methods.

relationships analysis   A category of analytical attribute methods of ideation in which the essential element is bringing together things not normally so considered. Two-dimensional matrixes are the simplest, but morphological matrixes are more productive.

relevance tree   A form of dynamic-leap scenario whereby we first set the goal or desirable end point somewhere in the future, and then work back to the present by describing the intermediate steps that must be taken if we are to go from here to there. The near-term steps show us where to start work.

repeat use   A stage in the basic A-T-A-R model where persons who have tried the product make a decision to like it, use it again, or adopt it in their practice set. Contrasts with rejection of further use.

repositioning   Changing the product positioning, either on failure of the original positioning or to react to changes in the marketplace.

required rate of return   A financial hurdle that is a firm's cost of capital adjusted for the risk of the project. Most new product projects have more risk than ongoing operations, so most required rates are well above costs of capital.

research and development   The function of working through various sciences and technologies to design new products. This usually involves some basic research for creating new technologies and some applied research for converting those basic discoveries (and others) into specific new products.

risk curve   Used to put probabilities onto the net present value output of a financial analysis. Is an array of outcomes, either in normal distribution or in some variance from it.

risk matrix   A matrix of the risks at any particular point in a new product's evaluation process. It shows the risk of rejecting a product idea that would ultimately succeed and the risk of going ahead with a project that would ultimately fail.

risk premium   The amount by which cost of capital is raised to reflect added risks of any particular new product proposal. Such addition yields the required rate of return.

roadblock   A hindrance to creativity. May be personal (a negative person), procedural (many approvals), environmental (distractive), and so on.

rollout   A category of market testing methods that are full sale, but go beyond standard test marketing. Sometimes called tiered marketing. Commitment has been made to full-scale marketing, but the marketing is tentative, a rolling accumulation of geographic areas, or specific firms (such as lead users), or specific applications.

scenario   Technically, scenario is an unfolding picture of the future. In new products work, it more customarily refers to pictures of some future time and place related to a firm's area of interest. The future scenario may be created by extending current trends (the dictionary form) or by leaping into the future and using other methods of deciding what will exist.

scenario analysis   Scenarios are used to study how firms and individuals will be living at some future time; from that, one can determine what problems they will have that they cannot tell us about now.

scoring model   A weighted-factor checklist used to screen new product proposals. Factors are scored, and the scorings are weighted and then totaled to yield a judgment on the concept.

screening of ideas   Evaluation steps prior to R&D and systems design in the product development process. They involve use of scoring models, checklists, or personal judgments and are based on information from experience and various market research studies (including concept testing).

seed trends   Current trends used to spot possible scenarios.

sensitivity testing   The practice of changing one or more of the factors in a financial analysis. The analyses are usually put up on spreadsheets, and what-if questions can be asked by making such changes. Settles issues on how sensitive the model is to errors in the forecast.

serendipity   The ability to gain knowledge from accidental events. Many famous new products have been discovered accidentally, but many potential discoveries were overlooked because the observer was not serendipitous (having a prepared mind).

service   (See *customer service.*)

service mark   A trademark for a service.

services   (1) Products, such as a bank loan or home security, that are intangible or at least substantially so. If totally intangible, they are exchanged directly from producer to user, cannot be transported or stored, and are almost instantly perishable. They come into existence at the same time they are bought and consumed. They involve customer participation in some important way, cannot be sold in the sense of ownership transfer, and have no title. Most products are partly tangible and partly intangible, and the dominant form is used to classify them as either goods or services (all are products). (2) Customer services. (See *customer service.*)

silo   Also chimney. Term applied to a department or function within a business. Inner-focusing, builds barriers to resist encroachments on its power.

simulated test market   A form of market testing, often going by its initials STM, in which consumers are exposed to new products and to their claims in a staged advertising and purchase situation. Output of the test is an early forecast of sales and/or market share, based on mathematical forecasting models, management assumptions, and input of specific measurements from the simulation.

simulation, financial   Tests run on an income statement for new product, measuring the effects of change in any item—e.g., a price increase, an advertising budget cut.

simultaneous engineering   Another term for concurrent engineering.

singularity   The number of other products against which a new item will be tested. If one, singularity is monadic. If two, the singularity is paired comparison.

speculative sale   A type of pseudo sale market test. Consists of a sales call (usually in commercial or industrial markets) where the full presentation is followed by a "Would you buy?" question rather than a "Will you buy?" request for the order.

spinout   A form of new product team organization in which the team is broken out from the ongoing organization. It is the ultimate in projectization and used only in cases where the project will have major barriers to overcome.

sponsor   An informal role or participant. Is usually a higher-ranking person in a firm not personally involved in the project (compared to a champion) but ready to extend a helping hand if needed.

stage gate   Point where one phase or stage of new product activity is finished and another begins. Usually accompanied by phased reviews.

stakeholder   Anyone who stands to gain or lose from the marketing of a new product. Customers, consumers, their advisers, resellers, etc. The broader, the better, today.

state of the art   A term describing the current outer limit of any developing technology. It is as far as we have gone at the present time. The state-of-the-art limit will move out over time.

STM   Letters stand for simulated test market.

strategic alliances   Agreements between different firms, universities, research organizations, and/or governments to merge efforts in a program of activity. Highly varied formats are used. In new products, they usually involve sharing technologies (e.g., IBM and Apple or IBM and Microsoft). Sometimes they are joint efforts to develop new technology that all members of the alliance can use.

strict liability   An extreme variant of product liability (in common practice today) in which the producer is held responsible for not putting a defective product on the market. Under strict liability, there need be no negligence, sale no longer has to be direct from producer to user (privity of contract), and no disclaimer statement relieves the producer of this responsibility.

success factor   A descriptor or activity that will have significant effect on the new product's outcome. Unique superior product is thought to be the highest success factor. Factors that separate winners from losers.

sunk costs   Costs that represent expenses already incurred in the development of a new product. Have been written off, involve no capital asset, and no anticipated salvage value. For purposes of net present value, sunk costs are ignored. After the project is over, an overall recap will include all costs, whenever spent.

supply-pushed innovation   (See *technology-driven.*)

surrogate positioning   Product positioning that eschews product features and benefits, turning instead to 1 of perhaps 8 or 10 substitutes, or surrogates. The two most popular surrogates are nonpareil (our product is simply the best available, no features or benefits cited) and parentage (our product is good because it was designed by the designers or producers of product X).

surrogate question   Any question to which the answer can yield an answer to another question that cannot be answered at this time, if ever. For example, if the key question is, "What retaliation will our chief competitor offer to our new product?" a surrogate question that can be answered would be, "What retaliation did that competitor offer to its most recent serious competitive threat?"

target market   The group of potential customers selected for marketing. A market segment. Combines with positioning and marketing mix to yield marketing strategy.

tastemakers   Those who are the first to adopt product innovations are sometimes called tastemakers, recognizing their influence on followers.

team   That group of persons who serve as on-site managers for a new products project or program. Each team member represents a function, department, or specialty, and together they form the management for that product. Team members may be full-time or part-time, and persons may move on and off a team depending on the continuing need for their specialty.

team leader   A job title that, though generic, is given to the person who is leading the new product team. Also called group leader, project manager, new product manager, program manager, venture manager, and other names.

technology   Essentially, the power to do work. Technologies are one of two bases for product innovation (market strength is the other). Technologies take many forms, the most common being a process, a material, a piece of equipment, a special knowledge, a person, or a science. They may also be a building, a manufacturing facility or know-how, or even something outside technical departments, such as a distributor's bottling and delivery system, a brand manager system, or an order-filling system.

technology-driven   A new products strategy or operation based on the strength of a technology. Technology yields new products, which are then offered to the market. Market-driven is the alternative form of thrust. Dual drive uses both at the same time and is the preferred form today.

test marketing   One form of full sale market testing. Usually involves actually marketing a new product in one or several cities. The effort is totally representative of what the firm intends to do later on national marketing (or rollout). Various aspects of the marketing plan may be tested (such as advertising expenditure levels or, less often, product form variants) by using several pairs of cities. Output is a mix of learning, especially a sales and profit forecast. The term test marketing is sometimes stretched to other forms of market testing, particularly the electronic versions and simulated test markets, but the term is best confined to the full sale activity.

top-two-boxes   In concept and product use testing, it is common to ask the question, "How likely would you be to buy this product?" The answer set is, traditionally, Definitely would buy, Probably would buy, May or may not buy, Probably would not buy, and Definitely would not buy. Listed with boxes in front of each choice, the analyst is looking for the percentage of people who checked either of the top two boxes. The statistic is a common measurement of overall acceptance.

total quality management   Known as TQM. Usually an overall program designed to produce high-quality goods and services. Often firmwide or divisionwide. Built on idea that one must control the quality of inputs and actions in order to achieve quality result (the new product).

tracking   The act of checking on the progress of important aspects or issues in the marketing of a new product. May be comprehensive or casual.

tracking variable   A specific variable used to track a specific phenomenon. Distribution can be tracked, for example, by measuring the "percentage of outlets that have stocked at least one package."

trademark   A legal term meaning the same as brand. A trademark identifies one seller's product and thus differentiates it from products of other sellers. If registered, the trademark obtains additional protection, mainly exclusive use, but special efforts are necessary to keep the registration.

trade name   A trademark used to identify an organization rather than a product or product line.

trade secret   In contrast to getting a patent on an invention, the inventor or firm can simply attempt to keep secret the new aspect of the product. The Coca-Cola formula is a famous trade secret.

trade-off analysis   A type of study that measures users' utility scales for various attributes of a given product category. Given the determinant attributes, and the utility scale for each, one can assemble the perfect product, putting in an optimized set of attributes that yields in total the greatest value to the marketplace. Originally (and still often) called conjoint analysis.

trial   The second part of the A-T-A-R model. Defined in some way to indicate target customers who have heard of the product and like enough about its story to warrant a serious trial of it. The trial must involve some cost or outlay of effort on buyer's part or else does not assure us of genuine interest.

triple streams process   Adds the evaluation stream of activity down the middle of the twin streams of product and marketing plan.

twin streams of innovation activity   The innovation process is building a product and also a marketing plan. The two processes go on simultaneously and, in fact, the marketing plan may originate first if the firm's strategy is to develop new products for specific target markets.

two-dimensional matrix   A simple form of relationships analysis using only two dimensions. Contrasts with the morphological matrix of several dimensions.

universal product code   An identification system involving a series of different-width vertical lines used to identify individual products sold at retail. The code is standardized and can be used on any product (or its package) that has physical form.

use testing   (See *product use testing*.)

value added   A measure of the contribution to a product's worth by any organization that handles it on its way to the ultimate user. Value added is measured by subtracting the cost of a purchased product (or the cost of ingredients from which it was made) from the price that the organization got for it. For resellers, this means the firm's gross margin; for manufacturing firms, it means the contribution over cost of ingredients. Presumably, whatever work that firm did is reflected in the higher price someone is willing to pay for the product, hence that firm's value added.

venture   An option of organization. The team is fully projectized and has left the matrix mode. People are usually working full time on the project. Venture may be internal, spun out, or joint with another firm. Used when the project must be free of substantial restraints within the current organization.

waiver   The release signed by an inventor who wishes to get consideration of a nonpatented idea or product.

warranty   A statement or promise made to the customer that a product being offered for sale is fit for the purpose being claimed. The promise concerns primarily what the seller will do if the product performs below expectations or turns out to be defective in some way. The promise (warranty) may be full (complete protection) or limited (some corrective steps), under terms of the Magnuson-Moss Act of 1975.

GUIDELINES FOR EVALUATING A NEW PRODUCT PROGRAM

This is a rather unique checklist. It is made for use by anyone evaluating the new products program of some organization—an internal review, a consultant, whatever. It presumes the organization uses all of the recommended methods, and it would be nice if the world worked this way. But product innovation managers face many problems—people, resources, competition, etc. They make many compromises, so if you use this guidelines form to evaluate a program, think of the gaps as suggestions or possible considerations. Most people who have tried the form find that they have to say no (or a very qualified yes) to a third or more of the items.

The form is especially good at covering important activities that are especially difficult or of recent development.

The list of guidelines is constructed for use in all types of firms and will have some points that don't apply to any one situation. Too, we must always deal with the problem of unique definitions. The closest thing we have to an authority for terminology in product innovation is the glossary in Appendix E of this book. The terminology used here matches that glossary, but occasionally a second statement has been added for clarity.

If the form is being used within an organization, a good approach is for two or more people with experience in the firm's new products activity to go through the list separately, checking each item individually, as they know it. Then the scorings can be discussed in a joint session to bring out differences, which in turn can be discussed for clarification and possible remedial action.

Yes	Maybe Some	No	
——	——	——	1. The senior managers of this firm or division (general manager plus top key functional heads) are committed to innovation in general. They want innovation in all phases of the operation, including that of product line.
——	——	——	2. This management attitude toward innovation has been clearly and unequivocally communicated throughout the organization.
——	——	——	3. Senior managements, both at corporate and at division, have gone through a planning exercise that established the overall goals for the product innovation function in each division.
——	——	——	4. Outside directors know the future role for product innovation and support actions to achieve it.
——	——	——	5. We have an innovation reward system. It includes insulation against punishment for failure, and there is evidence for all to see.
——	——	——	6. The firm's or division's top executive has assessed the ability and inclination of each senior functional manager to generate innovation, particularly product innovation. This assessment has included input from persons reporting to those senior managers.
——	——	——	7. General managers have learned the art of delegating full authority on new product projects while still sharing fully in the responsibility for them. (This managerial approach is unique to the product innovation function.)
——	——	——	8. New product project responsibility is nonfunctional. That is, project leaders report in such a way that they are free of functional constraints and biases. Specifically, responsibility for new products is no longer housed in R&D.
——	——	——	9. Senior management attempts to assess the productivity of the new products program. Standards of measurement have been established and communicated.
——	——	——	10. If senior management is dissatisfied with the overall product innovation program, specific causes have been determined and remedial plans put into place. Continuing dissatisfaction is not acceptable.

Yes	Maybe	No
	Some	

_____ _____ _____ 11. The firm's failure rate on marketed new products is somewhere between 10 percent and 20 percent. Less than that suggests no commitment to innovation, and more than that suggests an inadequately managed program.

_____ _____ _____ 12. Senior management has studied the industry's new product situation and has shared ideas with other industry leaders. Work is under way to find industrywide solutions to obstacles hindering product innovation in this industry.

_____ _____ _____ 13. Specific people in each division have been charged with opportunity identification—the creative assessment of technologies and markets available to the division.

_____ _____ _____ 14. Senior management is aware of the fundamental conflict between process innovation and product innovation. Efforts are taken to keep either from dominating the other and to see that decisions at the interface are made at general-management levels.

_____ _____ _____ 15. The firm has an overall process for developing new products, and its phases are known to participants.

_____ _____ _____ 16. Product innovators on each project know their group's focus (arena of operation or turf).

_____ _____ _____ 17. They also know the general goal and specific objectives of their project.

_____ _____ _____ 18. Each project group is making use of both market drive and technology drive. That is, they are working to resolve one or more specific problems in a selected marketplace, and they are bringing to that solution one or more technologies at which the firm is very good.

_____ _____ _____ 19. There are no hidden agendas on our new product projects.

_____ _____ _____ 20. All people playing major roles in new product groups are rewarded in some way that reflects the *group's* accomplishment of assigned goals/objectives.

_____ _____ _____ 21. For every new products project, it is clear who is the one person heading up that project and responsible for its success.

_____ _____ _____ 22. Every project is assigned one of three projectization levels—functional matrix, balanced matrix, or project matrix. We try to avoid the purely functional approach, and we use a venture (spinout) only when absolutely necessary. Players understand projectization.

_____ _____ _____ 23. We recognize the values of design. To the extent appropriate, we actively integrate both industrial (esthetic/functional) designers and engineering (technical/functional) designers as key team players.

_____ _____ _____ 24. Our technical/marketing/manufacturing people are close together physically. Preferably, they are no farther than a five-minute walk apart.

_____ _____ _____ 25. We use the concept of the rugby scrum rather than that of the relay team's handoff. All functions are represented at all phase points in the project including project specification and postlaunch.

_____ _____ _____ 26. Managers of new products projects understand that they are really nontitled general managers and that they should manage their team of people as a general manager would. They also understand what a network is and how one should be built and managed.

_____ _____ _____ 27. We actively use upstream and downstream coupling by building in roles for suppliers and other vendors as well as direct involvement of potential customer personnel. These people are almost like members of the team.

_____ _____ _____ 28. We have an overall concept evaluation system in place and use it to carve out a special system for each project.

_____ _____ _____ 29. A basic market or technology study is made of each strategic arena before ideation begins, and that study is updated as needed during the project's life.

Yes	*Maybe*	*No*	
	Some		

_____ _____ _____ 30. We believe in building the marketing plan right alongside the building of the product. It is a twin streams, or coincident, operation.

_____ _____ _____ 31. We accept the idea that new products come into existence only after they have been successfully established in the marketplace. Even after they go to market, they are still only concepts (being modified as necessary) until they meet the objectives set for them.

_____ _____ _____ 32. We have proactive concept generation. That is, we don't just wait for new ideas to come in from the field, the lab, etc.

_____ _____ _____ 33. Our technical people are familiar with what customers think about products now on the market, what they use, and how.

_____ _____ _____ 34. To the extent possible, our new concepts begin their lives stemming directly from solutions to proven problems/needs of the intended customers.

_____ _____ _____ 35. We use a quantitative scoring model for screening concepts prior to any substantial development expenditures.

_____ _____ _____ 36. After screening, we make sure that technical people have a statement of the product requirements (product attributes in benefit format and any other deliverables). The marketing people also receive a statement of marketing requirements (what the marketing program is to accomplish—market penetration, speed, etc.). The product requirements speak to what the product should *do for the customer*. Both sets of requirements combine into a product protocol statement.

_____ _____ _____ 37. We do user-based product use testing on every item we develop, whether a good or a service. At least part of the testing is with typical potential users who are not our friends.

_____ _____ _____ 38. We believe product use testing should measure whether the product actually works as we had hoped, *and also* whether it solves the problem we started with and is satisfactory overall to the customer. That is, if we have been using beta testing, we want to do gamma testing too.

_____ _____ _____ 39. Our marketing program also is tested by exposure to the intended consumers of the new product. The testing method used is situational, but at the very least a rollout is employed.

_____ _____ _____ 40. Our marketing efforts recognize that getting trial use is the most critical (and difficult) of the several steps to sales success.

_____ _____ _____ 41. When marketing a new item, we have identified each potential problem that would be very damaging and that has a reasonable probability of coming about. We have agreed in advance what we would do about each, if it occurs.

_____ _____ _____ 42. We use postlaunch tracking systems for guiding the product to success. That is, we have set up measuring systems to track each critical problem and give us early warning. We have also agreed in advance about what will constitute evidence that each problem is actually coming about.

_____ _____ _____ 43. Marketing strategy is built around the accomplishments of awareness, trial, availability, and repeat use (satisfaction.) The plan clearly shows how each will be achieved.

_____ _____ _____ 44. Marketing plans for new products are distributed in draft form to all persons who are key to the launch process, certainly to the basic functions of technical, production, and finance.

_____ _____ _____ 45. Unless the new item is itself a line extension, we have at least the next two line extensions to it already on their way down the pike. Each follow-on item is intended to foreclose an option our adaptor competitors would find lucrative.

Yes   Maybe   No
　　　　Some

___ ___ ___ 46. All financial evaluations are much more than net present value calculations. In fact, we try to use a sales or profit threshold test rather than a specific dollar test.

___ ___ ___ 47. We try to anticipate ways in which customers will misuse a new product, we develop legally sufficient warnings for those misuses, and we keep records relevant to all aspects of product liability.

___ ___ ___ 48. Attention is given to any potential conflicts between the ethics of an operation and the ethics of the people working on it. Attempts are made to resolve these.